NAFSA'S GUIDE TO
EDUCATION ABROAD
FOR ADVISERS AND ADMINISTRATORS

EDITED BY

JOSEPH L. BROCKINGTON | WILLIAM W. HOFFA | PATRICIA C. MARTIN

THIRD EDITION

NAFSA is an association of individuals worldwide advancing international education and exchange. NAFSA serves its members, their institutions and organizations, and others engaged in international education and exchange and global workforce development. NAFSA sets and upholds standards of good practice; provides training, professional development, and networking opportunities; and advocates for international education.

NAFSA: Association of International Educators, Washington, DC
© 1993, 1997, 2005 by NAFSA: Association of International Educators
All rights reserved. Published 2005.
First edition published 1993. Second edition published 1997. Third edition published 2005.

Portions of Part II, Chapter 3 contributed by Pamela Houston and Michele Scheibe contain works previously published by Mobility International USA. Reprinted with permission of Mobility International USA.

Printed in the United States of America

International Standard Book Number: 0-912207-89-2

Library of Congress Cataloging-in-Publication Data

NAFSA's guide to education abroad for advisers and administrators / edited by Joseph L. Brockington,
　William Hoffa, and Patricia C. Martin.—3rd ed.
　p. cm.
Includes bibliographical references and index.
ISBN 0-912207-89-2
　1. Foreign study—Hanbooks, manuals, etc. 2. American students—Travel—Handbooks, manuals, etc.
3. College students—Travel—Handbooks, manuals, etc. 4. Faculty advisors—Handbooks, manuals, etc.
5. College adminiatrators—Handbooks, manuals, etc.
1.Title: Education abroad, II. Hoffa, William. III. Pearson, John, 1948- IV. NAFSA: Association of International Educators (Wahington, D.C.)

LB2376.N26 2005
370.116—dc 22　　　　　　　　　　　　　　　　　　　　　　　　　　　　　　　　　　2005049127

Contents

Introduction vii

Special Note xiii

Publisher's Acknowledgements xv

Part I: Education Abroad as a Component of U.S. Higher Education
Edited by William Hoffa

1   Education Abroad at the Beginning of the Twenty-first Century 5
    Jane Edwards, William Hoffa, Nancy Kanach

2   The Profession of Education Abroad 25
    Susan Thompson, Randall Martin

3   Data Collection, Demographics, and the Research Agenda 45
    Kathleen Sideli. Additional contributor, Kim Kreutzer

4   Education Abroad in the Campus Context 61
    Maryélise S. Lamet, Mel Bolen

5   Faculty Roles 71
    JoAnn Wallace, Shannon Cates, Tom Ricks, Roy Robinson

6   Credit and Grades 93
    William Cressey, Sara Dumont

7   Financial Aid and Funding Study Abroad 107
    Brad Lauman, Nancy Stubbs, Charles Gliozzo, Elizabeth Lee

8   Technology and Education Abroad 129
    Lisa Donetelli, Katharine Yngve, Mona Miller, Jim Ellis

9   Education Abroad and Community Colleges 151
    Rosalind Latiner Raby, Geremie Sawadogo

Part II: Campus Advising
Edited by Patricia C. Martin

1   Advising Principles and Strategies 173
    Lynn C. Anderson, Christina S. Murray

2   Integrating Intercultural Learning into Education Abroad Programming 193
    Joseph G. Hoff, Barbara Kappler

3   Reaching Underrepresented Constituencies 207
    Carol J. Lebold, Amy Henry, Pamela Houston, Marilyn Jackson, Michele Scheibe, Scott Van Der Meid

4   Whole-World Study 239
    James L. Buschman, Rebecca Hovey, Gurudharm Singh Khalsa, Rosa Marina de Brito Meyer, Michael Monahan, Joan Raducha

5	Health Issues and Advising Responsibilities	261
	Joan Elias Gore, Judith Green	
6	Advising Students on Safety and Security Issues	279
	Patricia C. Martin	
7	Predeparture Orientation and Reentry Programming	293
	Stacey Woody Thebodo, Linda E. Marx	
8	Work Abroad and International Careers	313
	William Nolting, Martha Johnson, Cheryl Matherly	

Part III: Program Development, Campus Management, Marketing, and Evaluation
Edited by Joseph L. Brockington

1	Program Designs and Strategies	345
	Stephen Johnson, Nana Rinehart, Leo Van Cleve	
2	Short-Term Programs Abroad	373
	Sarah E. Spencer, Tina Murray, Kathy Tuma	
3	Planning, Budgeting, and Implementation	389
	Susan Holme Brick, Lisa Chieffo, Tom Roberts, Michael Steinberg	
4	Marketing, Promotion, and Publicity	417
	My Yarabinec, Leo Van Cleve, Andrea Walgren	
5	Program Assessment and Evaluation	445
	Stacia Zukroff, Stephen Ferst, Jennifer Hirsch, Carla Slawson, Margaret Wiedenhoeft	
6	Maximizing Safety and Security and Minimizing Risk in Education Abroad Programs	479
	Barbara Lindeman, Natalie Mello, Joseph L. Brockington, Margit Johnson, Les McCabe	
7	Legal Issues and Education Abroad	511
	Gary Rhodes, Robert Aalberts, William Hoye, Joseph L. Brockington	

Part IV: Overseas Program Direction
Edited by William Hoffa

1	The Program Director and the Program	539
	Skye Stephenson	
2	The Overseas Program Cycle and Critical Components	553
	Skye Stephenson, Anthony Ogden, Karen Rodriguez, Melissa Smith-Simonet	
3	Managing Students and Issues On-Site	573
	Skye Stephenson, Mary Lou Forward	

Contributors 587

References 597

Index 613

NAFSA's Principles for U.S. Study Abroad 631

Other Titles from NAFSA Publications 635

Introduction to the Third Edition

This third edition of NAFSA's venerable *Guide to Education Abroad for Advisers and Administrators* (the *Guide*) is published at a time when there is record interest and participation in education abroad programs by U.S. undergraduates and also a time when there seems to be even more turmoil and uncertainly in world affairs than ever. Eight eventful years have passed since the publication of the second edition. Momentous geo-political events in the world have shaped new realities for higher education, certainly including education abroad. Because this volume has earned a reputation as a repository of seasoned wisdom, best practices, and sound pragmatic guidance, it was clear that a new edition, reflecting these changes in the world and in the field would be needed. The current edition attempts to build on the solid foundation of past publications concerning the work done by members of NAFSA's Section on U.S. Students Abroad (SECUSSA). Because the professional wisdom of experienced advisors and administrators has grown exponentially during these recent years, this book is lengthier and fuller than ever before.

As this volume goes to press, the measures and initiatives called for in the NAFSA Strategic Task Force Report on Education Abroad *Securing America's Future: Global Education for a Global Age* are beginning to be translated from lofty goals and aspirations into policy formulations and recommendations. As the report points out, the "challenges of this new millennium are unquestionably global in nature" and thus, "international knowledge and skills are imperative for the future security and competitiveness of United States." With its call for a national effort to affect the wide-reaching and comprehensive changes needed to provide this type of education to the nation's undergraduates, the report sets forth five action items:

- The federal government must acknowledge international education as a national priority and provide the necessary legislative and regulatory framework and especially the appropriate resources.

Introduction

- The states must make international education an integral part of the strategic planning for enhancing state economic development and competitiveness.

- Colleges and universities must implement strategies that encourage study abroad in all areas and programs of the institution.

- The private sector must encourage and assist educational institutions in producing a globally competent workforce within the United States.

- Professional licensing and accrediting agencies must build global competence into the standards and measures of accreditation.

Following on the late Senator Paul Simon's vision of a "Lincoln Fellowship" program that would provide stipends for 500,000 U.S. undergraduate students to study abroad, there is now a federal Lincoln Commission charged with expanding upon the Simon proposal. As Carl Herrin writes in the Winter 2004 issue of *International Educator*, "It is incumbent for international educators to reach out to decision makers and gate-keepers in higher education—peers and colleagues—in order to advance education abroad opportunities. The responsibility to do so is, in a sense, a professional obligation to educate and advocate."

In these early years of the twenty-first century, two trends stemming from the 1990s continue to shape the landscape of U.S. higher education. Following a decade-long push by the regional accrediting agencies, most, if not all, U.S. colleges and universities are now actively engaged in a wide variety of assessment activities, to demonstrate the efficacy of their educational programs and the extent to which students are meeting institutional learning goals. Education abroad will need to develop its own "culture of assessment" in order to continue to be a part of this most important academic conversation. In *Rockin' In Red Square*, editors Walter Grünzweig and Nana Rinehart and their contributors address the need to "pause and reflect" on "fundamental questions about the basic philosophy informing our work and the paradigm shifts occurring around us" (p. 5). The value of international education is implied and yet little is known about the outcomes of various experiences and whether the types of programs that are designed for students lead to the goal of a "modified, widened, adjusted" (p. 21) lens through which each individual sees a culture. In this edition of the *Guide* we point to some promising steps to define and assess learning outcomes in education abroad, moving beyond satisfaction surveys to a more purposeful approach to kinds of learning we want our students to achieve.

Secondly, there is a generational transition in both the professorate and higher education administration. Senior faculty and education abroad administrators who were hired in the 1960s are retiring and it is not unusual for more than half of the faculty on a campus to have been hired within the past five years. The 2002–2003 "Pathways to the Profession" survey of SECUSSAns showed more than 60 percent of respondents with fewer than twelve years of service in the profession, 22 percent with fewer than three years. Combined with the increasing participation rates for all education abroad programs, the departure of the profession's most seasoned advisers and venerable sages of

Introduction

education abroad means, not only that those in the middle must be ready to assume these vacant leadership positions and provide more opportunities to more students, but that they will have to do so while simultaneously hiring and training new colleagues.

As a profession we must think about what significant expansion of international education activities would mean. There are some locations abroad that already are "saturated" in terms of the number of U.S. students in residence. If our colleges and universities do not offer appropriate language and area studies courses, how will we prepare students and encourage them to study in what are currently less-traditional locations for education abroad programs? Campuses must be prepared to address changing health, safety, or security environments and must employ advisers and administrators with appropriate training and experience. Education abroad must also address the evolving demographics of the U.S. undergraduate population and their needs and interests. With an eye to the future of the profession, NAFSA, the Forum on Education Abroad, AIEA and other interested organizations have agreed to begin a series of discussions and perhaps some workshops dedicated to producing a set of commonly agreed upon terms and definitions. When this process is completed, not only will we be better able to simply talk about what it is we do, we will also be better able to assess what has been learned and done. We have taken some pains to be sure that we are defining our terms as we go.

Increasingly our colleges and universities are stressing the importance of "comprehensive internationalization" or as Jane Knight (1994) has put it, the "process of integrating an international and intercultural dimension into the teaching, research and service functions of the institution." The *Securing America's Future: Global Education for a Global Age* task force report also notes, that "by itself, study abroad will not ensure that our citizens will become internationally literate." The report points out that the education abroad experience for the typical U.S. undergraduate can and perhaps should be part of a larger program of international education. Moreover, considered in the context of the entire undergraduate experience, there is increasing appreciation of the application of experiential learning theory to education abroad, with particular attention to preparatory activities prior to departure and reflective activities after the return home.

In the context of institutional internationalization as well as in keeping with the recommendations of the strategic task force, the next few years must see a broadening of the scope of the conversation on education abroad beyond the campus international office to include the various academic departments and programs and also the professional schools of the university. Education abroad professionals will need to develop new strategies to connect faculty delivering the curricula abroad with the faculty at home. New connections and working arrangements will also be needed among the various administrative offices of the university, to ensure that there is a good academic match between the student and the program abroad. It is also clear that education abroad is not just an experience for undergraduates. Increasingly graduate programs are suggesting, even requiring an international experience. Moreover, we dare not

Introduction

neglect the faculty, as both the guardians of the curriculum and our allies in this common endeavor. Without having recent and regular experiences abroad themselves, the faculty will not be in a position to adequately advise students or help them integrate their experience into their degree studies. Moreover, as there is more variation in the background and interest of participants, there will need to be more options available. Thus, we affirm our use of "education abroad" as the collective term that will describe a wide range of activities, programs, and experiences abroad, some for credit, others not, which ideally will contribute to the development of increased global competence of U.S. students.

The assessment of the changing landscape of U.S. higher education must also take note that increasingly students are opting to spend their first two years at community colleges and then transfer to a university for the remainder of their studies. A recent Community College Survey of Student Engagement (CCSSE 2004) indicates that some 25 percent of students enrolling in the nation's community colleges transfer to a four-year college or university. More than 75 percent of those will complete the degree. The transfer rates from Community Colleges have great significance for education abroad. Not only will there be a need to have a variety of education abroad programs available to this largely "nontraditional" college student cohort, there will also be issues of articulation and transfer of credit from abroad between the two- and the four-year schools. Increasingly education abroad opportunities are being designed for students who attend community colleges. Since more than half of all American students enrolled in postsecondary education attend community colleges, the greater goal of significantly increasing the number of students who participant in an education abroad experience must include these currently underserved populations.

Even before the publication of first edition of the *Guide*, NAFSA had released *The SECUSSA Sourcebook: A Guide for Advisors of U.S. Students Planning an Overseas Experience* (1975), followed by *Study Abroad: A Handbook for Advisers and Administrators* in 1979. During the 1980s, the growth and change in study abroad of previous decades continued unabated. Simultaneous with the multiplication opportunities abroad, on-campus student advising and program administration continued to evolve into a complex and demanding undertaking eventually giving rise to the need for professional education abroad administrators. As institutions began to support education abroad in some form, something like a basic and comprehensive 'text' was needed.

The first edition of *NAFSA's Guide to Education Abroad for Advisers and Administrators* (1993) provided a broad perspective on most important issues and practices that made up the field of education abroad in the early 1990s. The *Guide* offered a paradigm shift away from a focus on 'study' abroad only and back to a broader focus on 'education' abroad, affirming our profession provides support for students a broad range of overseas educational opportunities, academic *and* experiential. The term education abroad also expresses the belief that colleges and universities have an obligation to be proactive in their support of this wide range of activities. The appearance of a second edition of the *Guide* only four years later in 1997, demonstrated that the first edition had met its aims and pleased its readers. Its greatly augmented

Introduction

bulk, moreover, reflected the rapid evolution of developments in the field over only a few short years.

The intended audience of the third edition of the *Guide* continues to be (1) newcomers in search of an inclusive, introductory overview of the variety of professional thought and practice on advising and programming; (2) mid-level professionals whose institutional responsibilities have shifted or expanded; and (3) seasoned practitioners in need of new information, points of comparative reference, or an expanded perspective. Today, the challenges to international educators continue to be much the same as in the 1990s and earlier: how to build on past advances in programs and programming, to acquire and then contribute to the knowledge base needed for professional education abroad administration, to provide advocacy from the campus to the national level, and through our professional activities work to excite the same passion for international education that led us into the field.

In assembling the topics, chapters, and sections of this edition, we have sought to provide the profession with a range of best practices for how to provide an educational experience for the individual student in an ever unpredictable world. To meet these related, but also divergent, needs, this edition of the *Guide* has been reorganized and expanded. Each of the three previous sections of the *Guide* has been reworked and additional chapters added such as: integrating intercultural learning into education abroad programming, short-term programs, and a community colleges chapter, while others have been reworked and reorganized. In addition, we have added an entirely new section (Part IV, Overseas Program Direction) that deals with issues related to on-the-ground implementation of the program abroad. Each of the "parts" of the *Guide* features an introduction by the editor for that part.

Part I of this third edition of the *Guide* again emphasizes the central fact that, while education abroad for students by definition takes place in countries around the world, it begins and ends as very much a U.S. campus activity. Understanding and respecting the national and the institutional contexts of education abroad advising and programming remains an imperative for practitioners. The chapters in Part II discuss advising skills, principles of intercultural communication, the changing nature of the students that we serve on our campuses, expanding the locations and types of options offered (including resources on work abroad), preparing students for the abroad experience, and assisting them upon their return. Part III concerns itself with the pragmatic details of program design and administration from a U.S. standpoint, as well as issues of health and safety, crisis response and the U.S. legal context of education abroad. Complementing the content and perspectives of the earlier sections, Part IV looks at education abroad advising and programming from the perspective of the overseas program director.

In their review of the second edition of the *Guide* (1998), R. Michael Paige and Barbara Kappler (1998) asked how well it conceptualized the field, balanced theory and practice, integrated the research literature, set forth the "best practices" and standards of professional excellence in the various domains of education abroad, and met the needs of different audiences: newcomers, mid-level professionals, and senior professionals. We decided to incorporate these standards into the charge to contributors. Additionally the contributors were asked to incorporate ethical considerations, to take

Introduction

overseas perspectives into account, and to consider the needs of different audiences with a view toward varying professional roles and the many institutional types: U.S.-based and foreign-based, public and private, large and small. They were also asked to be mindful of how their topic related to the work of other organizations and were asked to discuss the history of their topic, along with current trends and future needs.

These goals were laid out with an eye toward making this as comprehensive a text as possible for the education abroad field. The *Guide* is used as a text in some graduate programs that are aimed toward training the next generation of education abroad professionals. It is also used in NAFSA's training for education abroad professionals. Through NAFSA, workshops have been offered on most of the topics covered by the *Guide* and it is our hope that this edition will serve as a resource in that regard.

As editors, we have had the great privilege of working with the many contributors to this edition to assemble what we hope will truly be *the Guide* to education abroad. We thank all who contributed to and supported this edition and wish everyone associated with the project of education abroad all the best as we work toward greater international and intercultural understanding.

The editors would also like to give special thanks to the following individuals whose support and guidance were instrumental in making this edition possible:

- Bill Nolting who as SECUSSA chair, guided the selection of the editorial team

- Susa Thompson, who as chair of the Committee on Communication and Information guided the process of approval and support of this project through NAFSA's administration and worked with the editors to produce the final publication

- John Pearson and Marv Slind, former editors of the *Guide*, for their empathy and wisdom.

Many thanks to our work colleagues and our families for their understanding and support throughout this proces.

Joseph L. Brockington
William W. Hoffa
Patricia C. Martin

Special Note

This publication contains the critical body of professional practice guidance for education abroad. Much of this practice has developed and evolved over the past 30 years or more, and a significant portion of it has been created and expanded by professionals who have volunteered their expertise and experience through the professional section on study abroad within NAFSA: Association of International Educators. Through 2004, that professional section has been known by an acronym, SECUSSA (Section on U.S. Students Abroad). As this publication is going to press, NAFSA has restructured, including replacing the section previously known as SECUSSA with a knowledge community known as Education Abroad.

Because this volume has been produced during this period of structural transition for NAFSA, some adjustments have been made in the text to reflect the changeover. Where the discussion is about contemporary professional practice and the responsibilities of the current and future leaders of education abroad within NAFSA, we have updated our publication's references with this new nomenclature to best reflect the resources on study abroad provided by NAFSA now and in the future. Where the discussion is, however, about historical positions and practices—either still timely or as a way of describing changing expectations and requirements—we have maintained the references to SECUSSA. While we have made a good faith effort to update this publication to reflect this distinction throughout, it is possible that we have not updated every reference. We apologize for any of these acts of omission.

—*Carl Herrin, Chair, NAFSA Education Abroad Knowledge Community*

Publisher's Acknowledgments

"If I have seen further it is by standing on ye shoulders of Giants." —Isaac Newton

This third edition of *NAFSA's Guide to Education Abroad for Advisers and Administrators* is a significant contribution to the field. The work of many individuals has gone into this volume and we would like to especially acknowledge the Herculean efforts of the editors: Joe Brockington, Bill Hoffa, and Pat Martin.

Throughout the process of developing this edition of the *Guide*, Joe, Bill, and Pat have made repeated mention of the outstanding work produced by their colleagues who contributed their efforts to the writing of individual chapters. The success of this project can be attributed to all of these dedicated education abroad professionals. However, at every step along the way the editors and contributors have made special note of the fact that they could not possibly have made this volume what it is without having the outstanding chapters of the first and second editions of the *Guide* to build upon.

There was a universal desire among those who worked on this third edition to include a special thank you to all of those who painstakingly built the foundation upon which this edition rests.

Below is a list of those contributors and editors whose work appeared in the previous editions.

SECOND EDITION (1997)

Editors: William Hoffa and John Pearson

PART ONE: Education Abroad and American Higher Education

Chapter 1. Being an Education-Abroad Professional
David Larsen and Susan Ansara

Chapter 2. The Education-Abroad Office in Its Campus Context
Paul Primak and Paul DeYoung

Chapter 3. Faculty Roles
Bill Barnhart, Paula Spier, and Tom Ricks

Publisher's Acknowledgments

Chapter 4. Academic Credit
Steve Cooper and Kathleen Sideli

Chapter 5. Financial Aid
Nancy Stubbs

Chapter 6. The Office Library and Other Resources
Larry Laffrey, Richard Warzecha, and Margaret Warpeha

Chapter 7. Computerizing Operations
Ruth M. Sylte and James L. Buschman

Chapter 8. Promotion and Publicity
My Yarabinec and Harlan Henson

PART TWO: Advising

Chapter 9. The Current Demographics of Education Abroad
Maria Krane and Beatrice Beach Szekley

Chapter 10. Advising Principles and Strategies
Cynthia Felbeck Chalou, Barbara Lanz, and Kathi Lutfi

Chapter 11. Promoting Student Diversity
Margery A. Ganz and Valerie M. Eastman

Chapter 12. Promoting Whole World Study and Work Abroad
Michael D. Monahan and Joan A. Raducha

Chapter 13: Health and Safety Issues
Deborah C. and Herrin Mickey Hanzel Slind

Chapter 14. Predeparture Orientation and Postarrival Reentry
Rebecca Sibley, Hellen Stellmacher, and Ellen Summerfield

PART THREE: Program Development and Evaluation

Chapter 15. Program Planning, Budgeting, and Implementation
Jack Henderson, Tom Roberts, Paula Spier, and Henry Weaver

Chapter 16. Program Designs and Strategies
Cheryl Lochner-Wright, Joseph Navari, and Heidi Soneson

Chapter 17. Work Abroad and International Careers
Jane Cary and Bill Nolting

Chapter 18. Program Evaluation
Patricia Martin and Ron Pirog

Chapter 19. Legal Issues
Robert Aalberts and Gary Rhodes

FIRST EDITION (1993)

Editors: William Hoffa, John Pearson, and Marvin Slind

PART ONE: Education Abroad and American Higher Education

Chapter 1. Being a Professional in the Field of Education Abroad
Archer Brown and David Larsen

Chapter 2. The Education Abroad Office in Its Campus Context
Paul DeYoung and Paul Primak

Chapter 3. Academic Credit
Eleanor Krawatschke and Kathleen Sideli

Chapter 4. Financial Aid
Nancy Stubbs

Chapter 5. The Office Library and Resource Materials
Catherine Gamon and Heidi Soneson

Chapter 6. Computerizing Operations
James Gehlhar and Kathleen Sideli

Chapter 7. Promotion and Publicity
My Yarabinec

PART TWO: Advising

Chapter 8. The Demographics of Education Abroad
Stephen Cooper and Mary Anne Grant

Chapter 9. Advising Principles and Strategies
Cynthia Felbeck Chalou and Janeen Felsing

Chapter 10. Promoting Student Diversity
Margery A. Ganz, Jack Osborn, and Paul Primak

Chapter 11. Health and Safety Issues
Joan Elias Gore

Chapter 12. Predeparture Orientation and Reentry
Ellen Summerfield

PART THREE: Program Development and Evaluation

Chapter 13. Program Planning, Budgeting, and Implementation
Jack Henderson, Tom Roberts, Paula Spier, and Henry Weaver

Chapter 14. Program Designs and Strategies
Joseph Navari and Heidi Soneson

Chapter 15. Work Abroad and International Careers
William Nolting

Chapter 16. Program Evaluation
Michael Laubscher and Ronald Pirog

Part I
Education Abroad as a Component of U.S. Higher Education

I-1
Education Abroad at the Beginning of the Twenty-first Century
Jane Edwards, William Hoffa, Nancy Kanach

I-2
The Profession of Education Abroad
Susan Thompson, Randall Martin

I-3
Data Collection, Demographics, and the Research Agenda
Kathleen Sideli, Kim Kreutzer

I-4
Education Abroad in the Campus Context
Maryélise S. Lamet, Mell Bolen

I-5
Faculty Roles
JoAnn Wallace, Shannon Cates, Tom Ricks, Roy Robinson

I-6
Credit and Grades
William Cressey, Sara Dumont

I-7
Financial Aid and Funding Education Abroad
Brad Lauman, Nancy Stubbs, Charles Gliozzo, Elizabeth Lee

I-8
Technology and Education Abroad
Lisa Donatelli, Katherine Yngve, Mona Miller, Jim Ellis

I-9
Education Abroad and Community Colleges
Rosalind Latiner Raby, Geremie Sawadogo

Introduction
William Hoffa

The first section of this revised edition of *NAFSA's Guide to Education Abroad* emphasizes the central fact that, although education abroad for students by definition takes place in countries around the world, it begins and ends as very much a U.S. campus-based activity. Understanding and respecting the national and the institutional contexts of education abroad advising and programming is thus an imperative for practitioners.

Chapter 1, "Education Abroad at the Beginning of the Twenty-First Century," offers a broad overview of the historical evolution of U.S. education abroad and the overlapping national and institutional goals it aspires to at the beginning of the current century. Chapter 2, "The Profession of Education Abroad," discusses the professional qualifications, opportunities, and responsibilities of those working in this field. Chapter 3, "Data Collection, Demographics, and the Research Agenda," indicates the many reasons why more and better ongoing data collection and research are needed to validate the value of the educational experiences the field promotes.

Chapters 4 through 7, "Education Abroad in the Campus Context," "Faculty Roles," "Credit and Grades," and "Financial Aid and Funding Education Abroad," each stress the importance of articulating overseas learning with the missions, structures, academic policies, and funding of U.S. colleges and universities. The many ways in which education abroad advising and programming are influenced by the new information technologies available to students and institutions are discussed in Chapter 8, "Technology and Education Abroad." Chapter 9, "Education Abroad and Community Colleges," dispels some of the myths about education abroad advising and programming at two-year institutions and describes the similarities and differences between two- and four-year institutions.

CHAPTER 1

Education Abroad at the Beginning of the Twenty-first Century

Contributors: Jane Edwards, William Hoffa, Nancy Kanach

U.S. Education Abroad from the End of World War I to the End of the Cold War

Professionals working in education abroad will be better advocates, and indeed develop a more satisfying relationship to the enterprise, when armed with an understanding of how study, work, service, and travel abroad fit within the conceptual framework of higher education in the United States. This chapter therefore concerns itself with the context, historical and institutional, in which work in the field of education abroad takes place, rather than the pragmatics of the field. We briefly review the history and underlying agendas of U.S. education abroad so that we can consider how national, institutional, and personal interests are addressed.

Historical Precedents

Until relatively recently, discussions of U.S. education abroad focused almost exclusively on 'study' abroad, defined as academic study in another country for credit toward a U.S. degree. Increasingly, of course, education abroad has come to mean a broader range of activities, including work, internships, field work, and service, all of which serve to prepare students for life and careers in an increasingly interdependent world. U.S. education abroad at the beginning of the twenty-first century is indebted to, and yet stands in contrast with, a number of historical precedents which combine individual travel and learning on foreign soil. As long as scholarship has been valued, there has been movement—throughout the ancient world, across North Africa and around the Mediterranean, and throughout Europe to the universities that served, at different moments in time, as intellectual centers, such as Krakow, Bologna, Paris, Edinburgh, Salamanca, Oxford, and Vienna. In the sense that students set out on travels abroad to learn what cannot be learned at home, today's students, much like the scholars of the Middle Ages, escape the intellectual and geographical restrictions of their home environments and enhance their learning.

But education abroad has come to mean more than the acquisition of academic knowledge.

Part I: Education Abroad as a Component of U.S. Higher Education

Though this broader perspective seems to be an innovation, it also has various historical roots. The most prominent of these is the tradition of the "Grand Tour," popular in the seventeenth and eighteenth centuries among families of privilege. The stated purpose was to introduce young members of the elite to the important cultural and historical sites of Europe and to make international social and political connections. To be sure, some of this was self-serving; but ideally, as these young aristocrats pursued social, diplomatic, and pragmatic ends, they explored the customs and achievements of other cultures, which gave them a wider perspective on their own world and their place in it. In much the same way, it is critical today that students, especially those who aspire to leadership roles in a wide range of fields, be alert to customs and values outside their own local experiences.

Americans first went abroad starting in colonial times, when young men who wished to pursue professional education sought places in German, Scottish, or English universities. Such study abroad was necessary in order to go beyond the limitations of the colonial college educational offerings. Of course, study abroad today is really a different phenomenon: it is about the incorporation of an international experience within the context of a U.S. education, rather than about seeking to complete a credentialed course of study that derives from and serves the needs of another society. It is surely significant that such an experience is now considered a good thing by more than 70 percent of the public (regardless of education level), and a desirable experience by 48 percent of students entering college (Hayward and Siaya 2001).

Programming Between World War I and World War II

The pioneering forays in U.S. education abroad date from the 1920s, when a small number of Junior Year Abroad (JYA) programs began sending students to Europe. These credit-bearing ventures joined the already established faculty-led study tours, which had been developed as noncredit options for cultural enrichment but were beginning to be offered for academic credit.

The University of Delaware (then Delaware College) sponsored the very first JYA program in Paris in 1923. Not atypically, the program was established by a faculty member as a result of his own experiences in France. The Delaware JYA program enrolled eight students, all male, but not all students from Delaware College. Several other JYA programs followed, each with an emphasis on language study and cultural immersion (including a home-stay) and each with a faculty director. Other than the Delaware program, the programs were all sponsored by small, private, liberal arts women's colleges (Marymount, 1924; Smith, 1925; Rosary College, 1925), and thus they mainly enrolled female students. Thereafter, these and other institutions that wanted their students to be part of JYA started to collaborate and to seek coordinating mechanisms to share information and pool resources. The Institute of International Education (IIE), set up the Committee on the Junior Year Abroad in 1927 to help facilitate enrollment, maintain standards, and raise scholarship monies (Bowman 1987).

About the same time, another program model was launched—literally. In 1926, the first of several World University shipboard cruises took 504 students (from a host of different colleges and universities) and 35 accompanying teaching faculty members on a seven-and-a-half month world-issues voyage around the world. The group visited a large number of countries, preparing for each port of call with readings, lectures, and discussions. There were six other "floating campus" voyages between 1926 and 1936. This was very much a group program, organized to attract students from a wide variety of U.S. colleges. Its focus was comparative and contemporary, and it consciously traded depth of cultural immersion for breadth, concluding that it was important for students to experience many cultures and to be able to compare and contrast them for a global vision.

As different as these two contrasting program models were—providing the polarities of immersion within a foreign system and the export of a U.S. model, which may be said to define current activity—both were academic and institutional undertakings. Whatever learning took place outside of the classroom was valued only inasmuch as it reinforced classroom instruction and thus qualified a student for academic credit. Whereas the JYA programs were primarily designed for language majors, the multicountry, faculty-led programs appealed to students of history and politics heading for careers in various international fields. The home college of the student, in each instance, made its own institutional decisions as to whether and how much academic credit could be earned.

The beginnings of education abroad in the 1920s, with contrasting emphases, were soon contained by the geo-political situation in Europe and the Great Depression of the 1930s. With the commencement of World War II, all study abroad activity ceased until 1945. It was only after World War II that study abroad programming resumed, and this time with much greater energy. The immediate postwar decades saw the rise of a vigorous student travel movement, with more and more U.S. students heading overseas in the summer for inexpensive tourism, work, and volunteer service. And although these were, for the most part, college-aged students, their time abroad was not necessarily undertaken for academic purposes.

Programming After World War II

After the war, the new leadership position of the United States demanded a more informed awareness of other nations and cultures on the part of everyone, but especially of young people who would be future leaders.

The Fulbright Program, founded in 1946 and perhaps the single most influential initiative of its kind ever undertaken, was one of the first postwar federal programs aimed at a new kind of informed U.S. involvement in world affairs. Senator J. William Fulbright, a former Rhodes Scholar, placed much faith in firsthand encounters with the people and customs of other countries as one way to advance international cooperation between the United States and other countries. Fulbright's idealism permeated the field of international education in general and education abroad in particular, for much of the remainder of the century. Although the Fulbright program was set up for scholars, graduate students, and recent college graduates, its influence certainly was felt in undergraduate education as well. Returning Fulbright faculty were often outspoken proponents of study abroad programming, whereas visiting Fulbright lecturers opened foreign vistas to U.S. students. More than anything else, given the reciprocity at the center of the Fulbright program, it contributed greatly to the idea of international educational exchange.

The twin emphases of education abroad during this period—students earning academic credit from their own institution and, through their presence abroad, simultaneously helping to build peace and understanding between the United States and the people of other nations—were seen as separate but not conflicting education abroad goals throughout the Cold War. More than balancing the outflow of students was the inflow of an increasing number of international students coming to U.S. campuses to seek degrees. Education abroad was therefore seen as a component of the larger realm generally referred to as international educational exchange, as well as of campus internationalization.

By the end of the 1950s, the basic institutional framework for study abroad for the rest of the century was in place. Not only were U.S. institutions sending students to enroll (with or without supervision) in foreign institutions and programs, but two other models had emerged: the branch campus model, when in 1958 Stanford opened its first site near Stuttgart, and the work-study model, when Antioch College created a program in France that combined study with periods of work, as was done on Antioch's home campus. These models have been altered and expanded in many ways, but are recognizable in the models of study abroad used today.

During the 1970s and 1980s the number and types of programs greatly proliferated, as more and more campuses became active in advising students on overseas opportunities and in setting up and running their own programs. With this growth came a plethora of program designs, as each college or program provider set up programs that served its constituency. What this diversification has meant is that education abroad has become increasingly difficult to think of as a single activity. The term education abroad (even study abroad) now refers to a variety of program types that differ by mission, duration, degree of cultural integration, size, location, and many other variables.

Thanks to the diversification of programming, participation levels in study abroad grew steadily. Yet, even with more than a doubling of the overall numbers of students between 1991–1992 and 2001–2002—from 71,154 to 160,920 students, an increase of 126 percent—only about 4 to 5 percent of all U.S. undergraduates now study abroad as part of their degree studies. In all but several hundred of the 3,400 accredited U.S. campuses, study abroad remains largely a peripheral activity. Further, the majority of those students electing study abroad now do so on short-term programs of less than an academic semester, while the percentage of those spending an academic year in another country has declined to 8 percent (Institute of International Education, 2003). In short, the traditional program models that featured overseas sojourns of at least an academic semester of cultural immersion no longer describe the activity that most students abroad now experience.

Education Abroad and Campus Internationalization

Education abroad has always been conceptualized on the strategic level as one element in the internationalization of campuses and curricula. This

Chapter 1: Education Abroad at the Beginning of the Twenty-first Century

has resulted in processes that have depended on considerable cooperation among institutions, and national organizations have existed to support the discussion and development of campus internationalization campaigns. The Institute of International Education (IIE), the first of the coordinating organizations, was founded as early as 1919. After World War II, IIE was joined by an organization specifically geared towards study abroad, the Council on Student Travel (now the Council on International Educational Exchange [CIEE]). CIEE, which had been running shipboard orientation programs of considerable sophistication since the late 1940s, developed a variety of mechanisms over the subsequent decades to support and foster study abroad nationwide. During the 1970s and 1980s, CIEE developed the model of consortial management of accredited study abroad programs, ran conferences to give opportunities for discussion and collaboration, and offered models in student preparation, program evaluation, and the expansion of study abroad opportunities beyond Europe (Council in International Educational Exchange 2002, 8-15). NAFSA's professional Section on U.S. Students Abroad (SECUSSA, now known as the NAFSA Education Abroad Knowledge Community) was founded in 1971, following a vigorous debate over whether the focus would be on academic programs or, more generally, students abroad, regardless of whether they were studying, working, or traveling. The broader definition prevailed.

Gilbert Merkx suggests that there have been two waves of internationalization in higher education, the first lasting until the mid 1980s, and the second gathering strength from then until the present. The first wave, he argues, was constituency driven from within the institution; the second is motivated primarily by external factors (Merkx 2003).

During the first of these waves, motivations and needs varied enormously according to the nature of the institution, but the growth of scholarly activity during this period and the rapid development in modes of communication and transportation that allowed U.S. citizens to be both better informed about the state of the world and more easily able to reach that world, combined to foster an atmosphere congenial to education abroad. Merkx points out that at certain types of educational institutions—especially liberal arts colleges—study abroad programming and advising was at the heart of campus internationalization. At the beginning of the twenty-first century, many such institutions were able to claim that between 30 percent and 60 percent of graduating seniors have studied abroad for credit, and a few institutions can claim that most of their graduates have had such an experience.

At other institutions, principally large research institutions, internationalization took on one or more different features, including

- the enrollment of large percentages of international students;

- the use of faculty expertise and federal financial support to assist in international development projects around the world; and

- the development and strengthening of academic area studies programs (in many instances financed by Title VI funding, and aimed more at scholars and graduate students than undergraduates).

At such institutions, a commitment to study abroad advising and programming usually appeared

Part I: Education Abroad as a Component of U.S. Higher Education

later and had to compete for campus recognition and support with other kinds of international educational programming (Merkx 2003).

Despite efforts of colleges and universities in the 1980s to provide overseas experiences for students, the number of participants remained small. Study abroad continued to be associated with elite, liberal arts institutions and served mainly those students in the humanities and social sciences. By 1980 the total number of study abroad students was still only 30,615, out of a total student population of 12.4 million, heavily concentrated in elite institutions (Briggs and Burn 1985). The principal concerns in the 1980s in fact prefigured those we have today: how to increase participation and the diversity of those who participate; how to assess and maintain the quality of students' experiences abroad; how to finance study abroad; how to move academic components of time abroad from the margins of the degree program to the center; and how to best prepare students to fully participate in the experience and integrate it with what they do on the home campus.

The second wave of internationalization is driven primarily by external factors. The salient features of the second wave are that it is driven by diverse and diffuse influences that affect many colleges and universities similarly, with many of the driving forces coming from outside academia; inside the campus, nontraditional constituencies are involved, such as the professional schools and the trustees; the new internationalization involves broad and intangible goals that are institution-wide rather than mission specific; central administrations are involved; and administrative concern is now focused on coordination and integration of previously disparate units (Merkx 2003).

To understand the current climate, it is necessary to consider the external pressures that now motivate institutional policy decisions.

The Contemporary Context of Education Abroad

Internationalization of Higher Education as a Response to Globalization

By the end of the 1980s, it became clear that the world was undergoing a series of seismic shifts, usually summed up in the term globalization—something we sense to be upon us but have not yet fully defined or comprehended. Among the several major developments that signaled the need for profound readjustments were

- the end of the Cold War and the bipolar geo-politics that characterized it;

- the leap forward in communications and technology, which allowed ideas, goods, people, capital, and especially ideas to move rapidly across borders and around the world; and

- the realization that all national economies were now part of a global marketplace.

In response to these global changes, institutions of higher education everywhere began to review systematically their academic programs with an eye to producing responsible citizens and leaders for the twenty-first century. The pressures from globalization on the power and authority of nation-states meant that many areas of political and social life that were the subjects of traditional educational programs had now acquired new and unexpected aspects. Issues surrounding the environment, health, and security, among many others, now had to be considered in a much broader perspective than in the past.

Colleges and universities have been seeking ways to organize and deliver an education that responds to and elucidates global concerns, but yet also addresses local ones. There are debates on how best to do this, but even defining the terms of the debate can be challenging. The meaning of the terms globalization and internationalization, as well as the relationship of one to the other, are still subject to various interpretations. Some writers on this topic believe globalization is the next logical stage of internationalization; others use the terms interchangeably; and still others view them as distinct but related concepts (for a summary of the debates surrounding these and related terms, see de Wit 2002). For the purposes of this discussion, we will employ the useful definition devised by Jane Knight: "Internationalization of higher education is one of the ways that a country responds to the impact of globalization yet, at the same time respects the individuality of the nation" (quoted in de Wit 2002). Internationalization in higher education assumes national entities and begins with difference, whereas globalization, when it appears in the field of education, has a homogenizing tendency and ignores borders (de Wit 2002).

Such definitions of course can serve only as signposts, abstract notions that require practical follow through. In fact, many universities have developed a multipronged approach to campus internationalization, including the infusion of international perspectives into the traditional curricula, the upgrading and expansion of language and international studies, the development of new interdisciplinary fields, the creation of high-quality opportunities for study and internships abroad, the recruitment of an international student body, and the development of international linkages in education and research. Some universities have embarked on joint degrees with overseas partners. All these efforts should enable U.S. colleges and universities to provide their graduates with the tools to effectively address critical global issues in the future.

Education Abroad and National Policy

In the late 1980s, a number of experienced international educators and other concerned citizens in the United States began to register alarm at what they saw as the lack of preparation among U.S. undergraduates for entering and competing successfully in an increasingly interdependent and the ever-more-globalized world economy and political order. At the time, a host of national manifestos, reports, and other studies on the state of international education documented this concern.

Of these calls for action, CIEE's *Educating for Global Competence* (1988) became best known (at least within the international education field) for its strong suggestion that the rationale for education abroad must shift, emphasizing the need to prepare students to compete successfully in the world economy. Previous rationales for international education—broadly, achieving peace and understanding through intercultural cultural learning, and, more narrowly, meeting U.S. campus academic goals—gave way to national imperatives. Given the expansion of strategic goals, the CIEE report called for increased financial support for

Part I: Education Abroad as a Component of U.S. Higher Education

overseas programming from educational institutions, from the federal government, and from corporate America, which would benefit from a more globally competent workforce. Over the next decade, task force reports, conference proceedings, and editorials proliferated calling for increased emphasis on the national need for more effective internationalization strategies.

In 2000, NAFSA, working with the Alliance for International Education and Cultural Exchange, helped to lobby the Clinton administration to adopt, finally, a national policy on international education. It was argued that U.S. citizens needed to develop international awareness and cross-cultural understanding in order to provide effective leadership, economic competitiveness, and national security for the next century. In an April 2000 executive memorandum, President Clinton proclaimed a federal international education policy.

The policy enunciated the need to encourage more students from abroad to study in the United States; to promote more study abroad by U.S. students; to support student, teacher, and citizen exchanges; to encourage programs that build international partnerships; to expand opportunities for foreign language learning and in-depth knowledge of other cultures by U.S. students; to prepare and support teachers in their efforts to interpret other cultures; and to advance new technologies that aid the spread of knowledge throughout the world (White House Office of the Press Secretary, April 19, 2000). With the end of the Clinton presidency and then the terrorist attacks of September 11, 2001, this initiative has not been implemented. But the events of September 11 have to a large degree focused national attention more urgently on the need to link global competence with national security.

Another product of this new sense of urgency was the national conference on *Study and Learning Abroad*, convened by Michigan State University and cosponsored by nine of the major national organizations in higher education, including IIE and NAFSA. This meeting, conceived in optimism about the future of international education in a globally interdependent world, took place six weeks after the terrorist attacks of September 11. Nonetheless, an action agenda was established on the assumption, embraced by the field, that we should redouble our efforts to ensure that U.S. students in the twenty-first century are fully prepared to encounter the world in all its complexity (Hudzick, Ingraham, and Peterson 2003). The report of this conference was widely circulated and has been influential in the formation of institutional policy. Other conferences, such as that hosted by Duke University on *Global Challenges and U.S. Higher Education* in January 2003, set out to evaluate current and future national needs for international and foreign language competence and featured leaders from a number of constituencies.

Two years after President Clinton's memorandum, the American Council on Education published its report, *Beyond September 11: A Comprehensive National Policy on International Education*. This report lays out three policy objectives: to produce experts with knowledge to address national needs, to strengthen the nation's ability to solve global problems, and to develop a globally competent citizenry and workforce. In assessing the nation's needs, the report pointed out that "fewer than 1 percent of American graduate students are studying languages deemed by the federal government to be critical to national security" (ACE 2002, 11). Indeed, a report from the United States General Accounting Office in January 2002 highlighted the need for more personnel with foreign language proficiency. More than 70 federal agencies have need for foreign language specialists, especially those with high-level skills, which are usually attainable *only after an in-country field experience* (United States General Accounting Office 2002). The report further states:

- Diplomatic and intelligence officials have stated that lack of staff with foreign language skills has weakened the fight against international terrorism and drug trafficking and resulted in less effective representation of U.S. interests overseas (United States General Accounting Office 2002, 2).

The need to bring educational practice in line with national concerns has once again become a priority for government and for the higher education sector.

NAFSA responded to the same crisis in 2002 by appointing a Strategic Task Force, with wide representation across the spectrum of higher education, government, business, and industry, to reformulate what needs to be done. The task force's report, *Securing America's Future: Global Education for a Global Age* (2003), suggests that internationalizing the education of U.S. students is a crucial national response both to globalization and to the threat of terrorism. Reviewing recent calls to action, the report called for a more forceful national commitment to international education in the interest of national security.

The report repeats most of the recommendations and goals of previous reports, enlarging them in some instances by, for example, urging "20 percent of American students receiving college degree [to] have studied abroad for credit by 2010 and 50 percent by 2040" (NAFSA 2003, 2). It highlights the best practices of a selected number of colleges and universities, to demonstrate what can be done to more fully integrate education abroad into the U.S. education curriculum. What especially characterizes the 2003 NAFSA report, however, is its identification of the present as "a Sputnik moment" and its endorsement of the late Senator Paul Simon's call for a federally funded and federally run Abraham Lincoln Study Abroad Fellowship Program, which would provide financial support to college students enrolling in overseas programs primarily in developing countries.

This call for funding to support international education that shores up national security recalls earlier programs, in particular the David L. Boren National Security Education Act of 1991 (National Security Education Program), which supports area and language study abroad in certain critical areas of the world. Both the proposed Lincoln fellowship and NSEP represent targeted opportunities to address national security issues, in contrast to the earlier Fulbright program, which embodied a more idealistic vision of mutual exchange in the interest of world peace. NSEP is not an exchange, and NSEP scholarship recipients incur a service requirement to work in the Department of Defense, Department of Homeland Security, or State or Intelligence communities. In this way the program can guarantee that NSEP participants will help to alleviate the lack of area specialists in government (Dubois 1995).

Part I: Education Abroad as a Component of U.S. Higher Education

There is effectively a consensus across political lines in the post–September 11 world that it is in the interest of all sectors of society that higher education provide greater access to international experiences. These experiences will not only play an important role in building expertise, but also further the national interest in building a more peaceful and secure world that will permit all nations to thrive.

The Impact of Globalization on Education Abroad

Most institutions of higher education have taken a look at their mission statements, retooling them to envision a broader-than-national perspective in order to encompass a sympathetic understanding of other cultures. Further, they have asked themselves whether they are international universities or national universities with international outreach and perspectives, and—what is most relevant to this discussion—how an institution's study abroad program should be tailored to meet the demands of the new global environment.

Globalization has had many effects on the current shape of study abroad and is influencing its directions for the future. Already we see that students who study abroad are likely to experience a different journey than their counterparts of 40 years ago in terms of both intellectual attitudes and programs of study. One significant change is the appearance of programs in new fields, especially in business and technology. These fields of study were hardly visible in the study abroad arena until recently, but they are now perceived as critical for individuals intent on participating in the new global economy. This situation contrasts sharply with the early years of study abroad, when study abroad was inextricably linked to language learning and the humanities, and, by extension, with cultural rather than career-oriented goals and with the feminine perspective. In 1988, the Advisory Council for International Educational Exchange, in one of its agenda reports that periodically take the temperature of the field, stated:

> Students who study abroad are from a narrow spectrum of the total population. They are predominately white females from highly educated professional families, majoring in the social sciences or humanities. They are high achievers and risk takers. Many have had earlier overseas travel or international experience. Whether by their own choice or lack of encouragement to do so, there are fewer men, members of minority groups, students from non-professional and less-educated families, or science, education and business majors among undergraduates who study abroad (8).

It is only at the beginning of this new century, with the impact of globalization and the development of new programs in professional and vocational areas, that we are beginning to see how this demographic can and must change.

The traditional study abroad experience in the humanities and social sciences has been transformed by the onset of globalization in other ways as well. Nowhere is this more clear than in Europe, which continues to attract the largest percentage of U.S. study abroad participants—62.6 percent in 2001–2002 (Institute of International Education, 2004). U.S. students studying in France, for example, will find themselves a part of a wider system of student exchange. They will be exposed to students from France, of course, but also to students from other areas of Europe and beyond and from different cultural, religious, and racial backgrounds. Also, French students are themselves likely to have studied abroad and may have a more global outlook as a result.

The development of international exchange within Europe provides an interesting counterpart to the U.S. experience. With the development of the European Union as a transnational and regional paradigm has come the need for a multilingual, mutually tolerant, highly educated workforce, whose education at all levels would be radically enhanced by the incorporation of periods of study abroad. To accomplish this, it was imperative to develop mechanisms for recognizing and classifying the educational credentials of a dozen very disparate systems of higher education. As recently as the late 1970s, it was extraordinarily difficult to manage study abroad within Europe, since credit simply did not transfer. All that has changed, and there is a sophisticated research journal, the *Journal of Studies in International Education*, exploring this process and documenting trends and outcomes of the considerable mobility that has developed within Europe in recent years, most recently as a result of the protocol known as the Declaration of Bologna (Haug and Kirstein 2001).

While the European Union is perhaps the most well-developed example of regional educational cooperation, reflecting economic and political alignments, there is another example closer to home. The Program for North American Mobility in Higher Education, run by the governments of the United States, Canada, and Mexico, was established to promote a North American dimension to education and training in a wide range of academic and professional disciplines. Since 1995, 30 consortia have been funded involving approximately 200 institutions of higher education and related nonprofit organizations (United States Department of Education 2004).

Still another development in study abroad that is a direct result of globalization is the growth in courses and programs taught in English in non-Anglophone countries. As the *lingua franca* of international business, finance, and the internet, English has been the language of instruction in programs offered by a host of institutions in the non-English-speaking world. Initiatives at institutions such as Waseda University in Japan, Ewha University in Korea, Universidad Adolfo Ibañez in Chile (to name only three among many), where the strategy is to offer substantial numbers of courses in a variety of disciplines through the medium of English, offer great potential for students from other societies to become both linguistically and culturally competent. Such developments, however, make it very tempting for U.S. students to continue to overlook advanced language training. It is quite rare for U.S. institutions to insist on the development of language skills within professional programs, though in some elite international business programs in the United States, it has been recognized that foreign language training is an important component of the program. In some institutions, students are required to spend a semester abroad in a non-English-speaking country. Of course, all students at top business schools in non-English-speaking countries must learn English as a second language to compete in the global economy. Unless more effective strategies are developed to ensure that U.S. students learn

Part I: Education Abroad as a Component of U.S. Higher Education

languages other than English, they will be working at a disadvantage. Language is the key to other cultures and other modes of thought. Without knowing another language, much of the context of international business and politics is lost and, with it, important unspoken assumptions are lost, too.

Courses taught abroad in English are offered not only to equip students to function in a common language, but also to accommodate the monolingual U.S. student market or to attract students to countries in which the national language is less commonly studied. Attracting fee-paying study abroad students and developing placements for local students in other countries are powerful incentives for offering courses taught in English. Also, many U.S. institutions gauge the success of their efforts at internationalization by the number of students sent abroad, regardless of the length of the program and the language in which the program is offered. Students from other countries are more likely to be expected to take regular courses in the national language of the host country than are U.S. students who participate in study abroad. This can be attributed to the emphasis in U.S. international education on "global and intercultural awareness in response to cultural parochialism, while in Europe the accent is more on the extension and diversification of academic performance" (de Wit 2002, 222). European students are less likely to undertake language and culture programs and more likely to pursue studies in their discipline, or to take intensive language programs with specific targeted outcomes.

Increasing efforts have been made in recent years to send U.S. students to destinations in the developing world and to blend service with learning abroad. There are interesting challenges associated with this relatively new direction, but as a means to ensure that students develop some sense of the obligations of those who are privileged to receive advanced education, and of the developed countries in a globalized world, this is surely a promising trend.

Often, the less traditional destinations invite less traditionally structured study abroad experiences. Students are especially drawn to these areas to do field work or to participate in community service opportunities that bring them in contact with the daily concerns and expectations of the local population. Many study abroad experts find that the traditional program of university studies does not always offer the richest learning experience in these geographical areas, and thus innovative program models are developed using local resources and addressing local challenges. Models are explored in a special issue of the journal *Frontiers* (Winter 2002) dedicated to experiential education.

One of the most challenging aspects of the work of educational abroad professionals during the coming years may be defining education abroad in coherent institutional terms and demonstrating its integration into the larger mission and goals of the academic community (not to mention national goals). Education abroad is not just a matter between faculty, students, and international education administrators, rubber-stamped by the upper echelons of the administration and rhetorically supported by the occasional ex–Peace Corps senator. In fact, thinking about education abroad should always be part of institutional strategic planning. Every aspect of an educational institution needs to be taken into account before embarking on any major innovation.

Institutions support education abroad despite the fact that it is often very costly in proximate budget terms. They do this because, regardless of the particular attitudes on any given campus, the rhetoric of higher education presently mandates a response to globalization. The trustees, the president, and the chief financial officer all have a stake in meeting the expectations of students, parents, donors, funding agencies, and in some cases, the legislature. Some students' choice of institution will be affected by the education abroad programs offered, and thus the dean of admissions will be interested. Parents must endorse education abroad if they are expected to pay for it. Alumni and other donors will have views on the matter. Funding agencies, and indeed accreditation agencies, may ask pertinent questions about institutional responses to globalization. But there is always likely to be a gap between what institutions say they are doing and what they actually do, or can afford to do. Jack Van de Water quotes Charles Ping as saying "commitment to an international agenda is defined as the point of intersection between institutional rhetoric and the institutional budget" (1997, 12). Each campus must struggle with how to define and support its specific internationalization goals.

Education Abroad As Preparation for the Globalized World of Work

More than a decade ago, a report on the attitudes of higher education and U.S. corporations found that job candidates from U.S. colleges and universities, although highly educated in their fields, were "at a serious competitive disadvantage in the global labor market," compared with students from other countries—especially those who have studied in the United States (College Placement Council Foundation/RAND Corporation Report 1994, 80). Although some industry recruiters rate language competency or cross-cultural skills quite low on the list of qualifications for entry-level positions, nonetheless, the flexibility, self-confidence, and perspective that U.S. students bring back from a sojourn abroad are valued by most employers, some of whom recognize that living and learning in a foreign culture can play a unique role in an individual's education and personal development. Most researchers have found that in the upper echelons of management, corporate or otherwise, a well-developed international perspective and cross-cultural skills are considered critical, but recruiters often seem oblivious to this.

A similar study just completed, which was sponsored by Australian Education International (formerly known as the Australian Education Office), the British Council, the German Academic Exchange Service (DAAD), and IIE, investigated the impact of study abroad on a student's chances for employment. The results were remarkably the same as the report a decade ago. It concludes: "Currently, very few employers specifically recruit candidates with an overseas experience, unless they require either cross-cultural skills or a job specifically requires it" (Thompson 2004, 2). Again, most employers looked first and foremost for particular personal characteristics that are, in fact, very often found in students who have had significant overseas experience. The challenge then is to alert employers to the link between those desirable interpersonal skills and the overseas experience.

Language issues are also of some importance in respect to employment. Michael Young, writing about global competence in the legal profession

Part I: Education Abroad as a Component of U.S. Higher Education

makes a number of points relevant to this discussion. In a number of fields, including law, where precision of language plays a central role, professionals with some language facility will function more effectively, even when international negotiations are conducted in English. Young remarks that legal language must be mutually understood and attorneys with language facility—even in one foreign language—are much better prepared "to understand...the dangers inherent in working through a translator and the possible points of misunderstanding that might arise because of different usage of apparently similar terms. Knowledge of a foreign language can help one to understand the legal mind of another culture and how cultural differences can affect an argument" (Young 1988, 111).

It is true, however, that even if U.S. students are abroad for a semester or year of fully integrated living and learning, and even if they acquire more developed linguistic and cross-cultural skills than their stay-at-home counterparts, they are still at a competitive disadvantage compared with foreign students who spend three to five years in the United States earning an academic degree, who have excellent linguistic skills, who understand telecommunications technology, and who are most likely to have majored in business, management, economics, science, or one of the applied technologies. To narrow this gap, more and more U.S. students are now seeking active engagement in an overseas workplace environment, either as part of their academic program, or apart from it. This quest for useful, career-related, globally informed experience represents a significant development in the field of education abroad, and a departure from traditional goals. In light of a new awareness on U.S. campuses that the careers students seek are likely to have an international component, it follows that students will wish to demonstrate to employers that they are worldly and trained, as well as well-educated. Given the presence of this consumer interest, some institutions have necessarily adapted their education abroad programming to meet these interests, whereas others have begun new programming that addresses it directly. In addition, institutions have accepted the responsibility of bringing their students' attention to many types of overseas programs, not all of which carry academic credit, that provide opportunities for hands-on learning.

There remains, of course, much confusion over what precise skills and attitudes students need in order to be considered globally competent. In the introduction to *Educational Exchange and Global Competence* (1994), Richard Lambert presents a synthesis of what the many contributors to this volume say. He defines global competence as a mix of

- internationally oriented substantive knowledge,
- empathy with and appreciation of other cultures,
- foreign language proficiency, and
- a practical ability to function in other cultures.

These are qualities that most colleges and universities should aspire to give their graduates and which employers in both the public and private sectors are coming to recognize as essential to successful careers in contemporary America. Although colleges and universities are finding many ways to foster these attributes, education abroad has become a mainstay of many of their efforts.

Increasingly, therefore, U.S. students, their institutions, and potential employers see education abroad as a means of gaining practical experience useful in the job market.

Internships as a Component of an Academic Program

Internships, service learning, field experiences, and apprenticeships increasingly are proposed not just as useful learning experiences but also as ways to earn academic credit abroad. The field of education abroad programming, responding to this perceived need, therefore includes an ever-growing number of credit-bearing academic programs with practical training components, usually in the form of unpaid workplace internships. In such programs, students take academic courses to provide a background for their work. They receive credit not for the work *per se* as much as for their studied reflections on the experience of being in the workplace. Other academic programs assist students in securing an internship, but do not offer academic credit for this activity, which is considered extracurricular.

Maintaining the academic quality of credit-bearing programs while seeking means to expand students' cultural experiences outside the conventional classroom represents a major challenge. The dramatic growth in campus and employer interest in paid or unpaid internships may be influenced by the practice in Europe of building an internship experience into a degree program, especially in the engineering and science fields. While many U.S. faculty members remain dubious about the academic value of nonclassroom learning taking place abroad (or, for that matter, at home), some will pay lip-service to the personal growth aspects of the experience. Those teaching in institutions with a strong preprofessional curriculum accept that such pragmatic workplace opportunities supplement classroom studies both on campus and abroad, and prepare students for employment in a way that study programs seldom can. Increasingly, as student expectations rise, institutions are under pressure to identify internship options; and organizations and institutions abroad, some in countries where there is no cultural precedent for this kind of activity, also find themselves pressured to adjust to U.S. expectations.

Work Abroad and Other Programming

It is clear to many students and campuses today that the marriage of academic study and workplace experience may do justice to neither, and that what students especially need are stand-alone workplace and practical training experiences. In such programs, students may be freer to apply the specialized knowledge they have acquired in the classroom in a foreign culture, where coming to terms with different norms, styles, and attitudes can be challenging. As is the case with study abroad programs, work abroad offers different levels of language and cultural immersion.

Overall numbers for stand-alone work abroad, internships, service learning, and similar not-for-credit programs were estimated in 2004 by William Nolting to approach 35,000, about one-quarter of the total number of students studying abroad for credit (see the University of Michigan International Center Web site). This estimate is based on a survey of the largest 26 organizations sponsoring paid work, plus current students in another 51 volunteer service organizations. This number represents

Part I: Education Abroad as a Component of U.S. Higher Education

undergraduates only, and does not include work abroad after graduation in many capacities related generally to education: Peace Corps volunteers, missionaries, Fulbright-funded teaching assistants, and all sorts of other program participants. (See Part II, Chapter 8, "Work Abroad and International Careers.") If this kind of experience contributes to the global competence of young people, then the overall picture may be of a less parochial educational system than at first appears.

The question that arises may be whether U.S. campuses, as academic institutions, have any responsibility to support not-for-credit education abroad programming. In response, one can point to many examples of domestic not-for-credit activities supported by virtually all U.S. colleges and universities. These include the career planning office, the office that helps students into volunteer service, student organizations, most performance arts for nonmajors such as choirs, orchestras and bands, theater, co-op programs, athletic teams, and much more. We leave out a substantial part of the education abroad picture if we exclude participants in formally organized, not-for-credit education abroad programs, and deny our students and alumni these options, essential for their career development, if we do not provide advising on such options in our offices.

In spite of considerable increased attention to all kinds of work, internship, service, and field experiences in recent years, the majority of U.S. campus study abroad offices are not yet prepared to give much informed counsel on noncredit international educational activities. Nor is this something other offices on campus necessarily think they should be doing; even fewer keep track of how many students participate in such non-credit-bearing activities. Furthermore, while information on a host of career enhancement opportunities may be known to campus career services offices, relations between international and career offices are frequently undeveloped. At the beginning of the twenty-first century, with abundant evidence suggesting that the campus divide between academic study and other forms of education abroad programming is counterproductive and hurts students, the challenge to leaders in the field is to reduce this gap on every campus. How to manage this without additional resources, and without sacrificing the quality of services related to academic activities abroad, is often a significant challenge.

Education Abroad and the Personal Development of Individual Students

Student participation in an education abroad program—whatever its duration, degree of cultural integration, curriculum, location, and so on—has been historically seen by U.S. colleges and universities as primarily an academic experience, but increasingly it is recognized as a tool for personal development. When students return from overseas and are asked to assess their learning, it is highly likely that they will want to talk about what happened to them, personally. They often tend to see their classroom education as a pragmatic means to the end of earning credit for the experience, and classes are expected to be (and often are) less demanding or engaging than what the students were used to at home. It is worth noting, however, that undergraduates who encounter a foreign pedagogy in a direct enrollment situation often characterize

Chapter 1: Education Abroad at the Beginning of the Twenty-first Century

their abroad experience as more intellectually demanding and more like graduate school than their home experience. Some students have their first experience of independent research abroad, and for many students the experience of learning how to study, and indeed how to learn, in a different environment is as stimulating as it is exhausting.

Their greatest enthusiasm is saved, nonetheless, for matters far more individual: how much they learned about themselves, their capacities, their limits; how much they learned about the strength of their 'American-ness' and how this affected other people; and how much they learned to respect and enjoy the culture or country they had begun to know. Many students will talk about their experience as having been one of the best, if not the best, thing they have ever done. Faculty members, even those dubious about the academic rigor of study abroad, often remark on how changed and improved in attitude, maturity, alertness, and work habits are students who have studied abroad. It is indeed this individual maturation that students, parents, and many educators secretly value most. Few would deny that developmental change is one of the most remarkable and important aspects of the education abroad experience.

Better understanding of the impact of education abroad on the individual student's attitude, values, and personal behavior, especially longitudinally, is something that the field is now beginning to investigate systematically. Although there is already a fairly substantial literature base on this particular aspect of education abroad, much more research is needed. Research projects in this area are fraught with difficulty, as it is often hard to hold a number of slippery variables constant, and above all to determine what the relationship between the experience abroad and change really is. Most studies involve student self-assessment. In spite of the work of Milton Bennett (1986) and others in the field, tools for assessing change that do not involve self-reporting remain inadequate. Current increased emphasis on the importance of research may remedy this.

One of the most thorough treatments of this subject can be found in Kauffmann, Martin, and Weaver's book, *Students Abroad: Strangers at Home*. It focuses on developmental changes within the individual student participant as the result of a meaningful overseas living and learning experience. The authors examine extant research on the effects of study abroad, and identify areas in which study abroad is felt to have an impact: intellectual development, language learning, international perspectives, and personal maturation. It also offers a theoretical framework for understanding the process through which students experience personal growth. These and other findings provide evidence that elements in program design can make a significant difference in the outcomes of a program. This is a conclusion that cannot be repeated too frequently. As we become more sophisticated in program design and implementation, professionals in the field will need to do a better job of monitoring outcomes to be sure that we can be held accountable, something which is increasingly likely to be required in this as in other sectors of higher education.

In any case, students overwhelmingly agree that education abroad has positive nonacademic benefits. (Students are not best placed to judge the academic effects.) In a recent major study of the long-term impact of study abroad, students strongly agree that study abroad

- enabled them to learn something new about themselves,
- made them more comfortable interacting with people from different cultural backgrounds, and
- helped them understand their own cultural values and biases. (Akande and Slawson 2000)

It is significant that two of these three variables are related to the students' understanding of themselves as individuals and within their own culture. The U.S. ethos is one in which ethnorelativism can be hard-won, since the power of U.S. mainstream culture cannot be overestimated, and this is not a geography or culture in which comparisons with other societies are regularly or analytically offered. Thus it may be that before students can become fully engaged with other cultures they must do the work of attaining a degree of cultural self-knowledge.

If this is the case, then education abroad is doubly important for young U.S. students in the age of globalization, since to thrive in the global society they will surely be in need of the perspective and adaptability to which this work is the precursor. The work that is done to create opportunities abroad that include carefully calibrated components to assist in students' personal development—whether this be in the form of journal keeping, discovery activities, values clarification exercises, mini-courses that develop ethnographic skills or analytical techniques—must be central to education abroad if we are to fulfill our own agenda. If we return to Lambert's concept of global competence, then we are indeed asking a great deal of education abroad and its home campus components. We ask that students develop new skill sets, some of which are dependent on the students' new abilities to observe, empathize, and function within a different set of cultural parameters.

Finally, as professionals in education abroad, it is, above all, our responsibility to use our professional knowledge to serve students, as individuals. Whatever national needs exist, whatever future employers require, whatever education abroad programming our own institution provides and supports, these other dimensions of education abroad provide, albeit necessarily, only a context for what we do for individual students. One of the truisms of education abroad is that no two students ever have precisely the same experience abroad. This is evident not only to us, but also to the students. On the other hand, this individual variation exists within the parameters of what is made possible by education abroad advising and programming.

Summary

Education abroad has come a long way from its origins in the independent questing of the wandering scholar and cultural tourism for the elite classes. At the start of the twenty-first century, the lofty motivation for educational exchange offered by Senator Fulbright has frequently been replaced by specific aims, especially those concerned with economic issues of global competitiveness and with national priorities. Activity now encompasses programs that demonstrate an extraordinary range of curricula, pedagogical methodologies, durations, and locations. Heightened security concerns arising

Chapter 1: Education Abroad at the Beginning of the Twenty-first Century

in the aftermath of September 11 continue to be a concern, as countries (and the United States especially) realize the value of learning about countries and cultures that once seemed too remote to worry about. The new challenges facing international educators around the world stem from the accelerating globalization of worldwide economic, intellectual, and cultural institutions. Knowledge of particular countries and cultures, and communicative competence in other languages, must be supplemented by an awareness of emerging global dynamics and realities.

The vigorous discussion on the national level about how best to achieve the goals and desired outcomes of education abroad in all forms is ongoing, and there is no easy resolution in sight. Against this clear national consensus about the need to better prepare students for the global realities they will face, there is institutional and national reluctance to invest the requisite resources. Within institutions of higher education and on the national front, new strategies and opportunities need to be developed to overcome these obstacles. Professionals in the field of education abroad need, more than ever, to work collaboratively and creatively to exploit what is surely a moment of exceptional opportunity.

Chapter 2

The Profession of Education Abroad

Contributors: Susan Thompson, Randall Martin

As with any career, the key to professional success lies not just with knowledge and skills, but also with individual depth, strength of commitment, and belief in the mission behind the work. The profession of education abroad shares many features with other professions. The challenges are great, but the knowledge that international experience changes lives, creates opportunities, and plays an essential role in the globalization of U.S. higher education provides practitioners with rich and rewarding careers. International educators must be global citizens in both heart and mind. They have the opportunity to meet people from every corner of the world and to create their own global network. Moreover, since the field continues to grow, international educators are inevitably involved in its evolution through concerted thought, continued training, service, mentoring newcomers, and active involvement in the field's many professional organizations.

Education Abroad as a Profession

Although education abroad practitioners serve those who employ them—usually colleges and universities, but also agencies and organizations—they are also called on to uphold and promote professional ideals. Professions achieve and maintain their integrity through offering specialized training and certification, establishing and enforcing performance standards, censuring those practitioners who depart from accepted practices, defining criteria for advancement and promotion, and providing awards and honors for those who exemplify the highest standards and best practices. Broadly speaking, these defining criteria apply fully to physicians, lawyers, engineers, architects, and numerous other long-established professions. The profession of the international educator (and, more specifically for the purposes of this book, education abroad advising and program administration) shares many, but not all, of the characteristics of other professions.

Part I: Education Abroad as a Component of U.S. Higher Education

Education abroad advisers and administrators have evolved and expanded a knowledge base, clarified standards of professional practice, and developed a pedagogical theory that applies to students living and learning in a culture they do not call home. Carefully defined standards of professional conduct have been developed and disseminated, and a growing corpus of essential resources exists. Through organizations like NAFSA: Association of International Educators, the Association of International Education Administrators (AIEA), the Council on International Educational Exchange (CIEE), the Institute of International Education (IIE), the Forum on Education Abroad, the European Association of International Education (EAIE), and other associations and organizations, the field of education abroad provides training for newcomers, guidance for experienced practitioners, networking opportunities and organized meetings, workshops, conferences, publications, and communications networks. This sharing of information, standards, and seasoned perspectives fosters a professional consensus and a sense of community.

As a result, institutions of higher education and colleagues around the world are increasingly calling on the expertise of international educators who actively participate in professional organizations to help them work with their students, faculty, and other administrators to accomplish newly defined goals for international and intercultural learning. The European Union has been exemplary in its leadership in the field of student mobility. In many countries, professional associations—such as the British University Transatlantic Exchange Association (BUTEX), the Canadian Bureau for International Education (CBIE), and numerous other organizations—provide training, publications, conferences, and other venues for professional development.

It has been the case until recently that individuals generally have entered the education abroad field by first securing a position, and then developing the specific professional skills needed in their work, through on-the-job training and from helpful colleagues in professional associations and organizations. In other words, unlike what is true for the other aforementioned professions, there has been no single career preparation path for education abroad professionals. Now, however, numerous degree programs in international education exist.

The best known of these is the School for International Training master's program in international education, as well as a similar program offered by Lesley University. In addition to these programs aimed specifically at students entering the field of international education, numerous U.S. universities (e.g., University of the Pacific, University of Minnesota, University of Massachusetts, Boston College, State University of New York [SUNY] Buffalo, George Washington University, Harvard University, Columbia University) also offer academic master's degrees of value to those seeking to become education abroad professionals. Elsewhere around the world, programs exist for undergraduate and graduate degrees and certificates with a focus on international education, international development, and intercultural education and training.

A 2002–2003 survey titled "Pathways to the Profession," sponsored by NAFSA's Education Abroad Knowledge Community—then known as the Section on U.S. Students Abroad (SECUSSA)—provides insight into the academic and professional background of international educators, as well as the reasons for interest in the field and the challenges faced by the respondents. The survey was prepared and evaluated by Joseph Brockington. This survey provides data on a wide range of information and is a valuable resource for all education abroad professionals. The conference presentation from 2003 and summary results for the survey are available on the Education Abroad Knowledge Community Web site.

A host of backgrounds and experiences in areas as diverse as teaching and scholarship, international travel and study, student development/student services, and education administration have generally been regarded as relevant to the work of education abroad. Although each individual may have areas of special strength and expertise either by virtue of background, specific training, or personal predilection, no one is an expert in all the essential areas of this diverse and demanding field. Moreover, the field is constantly expanding.

Whatever background and experience one brings to this profession, there remains the practical necessity to learn as much as possible from field colleagues. Practices that might be regarded as piracy in the corporate world are encouraged in education abroad. An insight, a procedure, an information resource, an approach to a particular program developed and implemented successfully at one institution is more often than not generously shared with others. The general assumption is that when there is innovation, others in the field will hear about it and ask questions. Education abroad advising and administration occur in an arena where questions are, or should, always be answered with a view to contributing to the development of other professionals and promoting belief in the value of education abroad. The willingness to share resources is evident in the expansive and detailed resources available on the Education Abroad Knowledge Community Web site and through other professional resources.

In 1993 the SECUSSA National Team identified four distinct job categories within the field: (1) on-campus adviser; (2) on-campus program administrator; (3) university or agency program representative; and (4) overseas program director. It was further noted that many professionals in education abroad begin in one of these positions and then move to another. Especially at smaller institutions, practitioners are often asked to manage more than one of these professional roles simultaneously. Therefore, the broadest kind of training and a great deal of flexibility are always professional assets.

In general, education abroad professionals remain in their careers because the work is diverse and engaging, and the field is dedicated to what they see as important principles and needs in higher education. The leaders in this field are extraordinarily willing and able to act as role models and mentors to newcomers. Most of the veteran professionals in the field regard mentoring as an extremely important responsibility. As an example, SECUSSA's Lily Von Klemperer Award, bestowed each year on an education abroad professional, honors Liliy Von Klemperer, who devoted so much of her career to mentoring and encouraging newcomers in the field.

Professional Roles

The fundamental skills required to be an effective education abroad professional include imagination, empathy, sensitivity, enthusiasm, and patience. Equally important is the ability to create, develop, present, and manage a budget, and to communicate

Part I: Education Abroad as a Component of U.S. Higher Education

with one's institutional colleagues to gain support for international education. The real challenge for every practitioner, at all levels of experience, is to build a professional knowledge base on the foundation of this personal conviction and integrity, so as to serve the interests and personal needs of students, faculty, staff, organizations, and institutions. Some of the roles an education abroad professional performs are described below.

Advocate/Facilitator

As an advocate for and facilitator of study abroad, the education abroad professional is likely to be the primary on-campus promoter of study, work, and travel abroad, actively pursuing and publicizing overseas opportunities and maintaining as high a profile as possible within the institution. The advocate/facilitator must create a campus environment where opportunities for international experience are viewed as feasible, desirable, and relevant in the context of undergraduate and graduate education. In addition to local advocacy, the education abroad professional should make use of initiatives sponsored by NAFSA and other professional associations, designed to make political leaders aware of the goals and priorities of international education. Political advocacy is an empowering and essential part of the process of advancing the role of international initiatives in higher education.

Liaison/Broker

The education abroad professional will regularly and frequently be called on to be an information link among students, faculty, the administration, the admissions and records office, and other campus entities working to initiate and maintain orderly academic and institutional or organizational procedures. Unless the campus is unusually coherent and well organized (and the students extraordinarily conscientious), the professional, as liaison, has to do an enormous amount of informed and active coordination to facilitate international education. An array of diplomatic skills are required.

Educator/Consultant

The primary work of the education abroad professional is to help each student become better informed, determine personal priorities, consider all options, make choices, develop a set of realistic expectations, and proceed through the steps and obstacles of institutional structures. The education abroad professional has a global outlook and pedagogical expertise, and shares these with colleagues on the faculty and in the administration. As educator/consultant, the professional is expected to know more about the particular educational benefits of living and learning abroad than most others in administrative or teaching positions in higher education. Because these are complex insights, the education abroad professional is thrust into the role of educating faculty, staff, students, and administrators. This role requires the professional to have the courage to act in support of his or her convictions and the experience and determination to work with others to increase high-quality opportunities for students, faculty, and staff.

Economic Manager

The organizations or institutions that offer education abroad must be economically responsible and also recognize the complex and detailed requirements necessary to create high-quality programs. The education abroad professional will be required to know about budget development, fiscal reporting, and financial management.

Legal Issues Adviser

U.S. and foreign laws and a variety of national and local practices concerning banking and currency exchange, taxes, employment practices, leases and purchases (of everything from services to real estate), and risk management apply in differing ways to the activities of professionals in this field. In order to be an effective manager and a responsible adviser to his or her employer, the education abroad professional must learn at least which questions to ask about the programs he or she is involved with, and how to interpret the answers to those questions. (See Part III, Chapter 7, "Legal Issues and Education Abroad.")

A great deal of skill and knowledge is required to perform all these roles successfully. Being in this field is seldom dull, and the variety of tasks and challenges can be truly exhilarating.

Professional Ethics

The field of international education has developed (and continues to evolve) its own distinct professionalism, including the creation of codes of behavior for individuals and institutions. Education abroad professionals who are members of NAFSA, as a condition of membership, are expected to know, respect, and abide by NAFSA's formal *Code of Professional Ethics*. The introduction to this document (1989, revised 2001) states the following:

> Members of NAFSA: Association of International Educators are dedicated to providing high-quality education and services to participants in international educational exchange. NAFSA members represent a wide variety of institutions, disciplines, and services. This Code of Ethics that proposes to set standards for the professional preparation and conduct of all NAFSA members must accommodate that diversity as well as emphasize common ethical practices. The Code sets forth rules for ethical conduct applicable to all NAFSA members. It does not provide a set of rules that prescribe how members should act in all situations. Specific applications of the Code must take into account the context in which it is being considered. In addition to this Code, NAFSA has also enacted guidelines for specific areas of professional practice not applicable to all members. These guidelines are set forth in the *Principles for International Educational Exchange*. Individuals should recognize that professional practices in more than one area could apply to them.

The NAFSA *Code of Ethics* presents an overview of ideal conduct for individuals working in international education.

As with any code of behavior, conflicts and tensions may arise as practitioners struggle to meet the outlined goals. Few have the time, energy, expertise, or absolute virtue to live up to these laudable standards on every occasion and in every circumstance. The expectations of an individual educator's own institution may only compound the challenge by asking professionals to act in a way that conflicts with the broader vision of this professional

Part I: Education Abroad as a Component of U.S. Higher Education

standard. It may be difficult to find a path between perfect loyalty to the institution that pays one's salary and an unflinching allegiance to a loftily defined (but abstract) code of conduct. Nevertheless, these standards represent the collective wisdom of professionals in the field, and they are meant to encourage international educators as they grow in their professions.

The NAFSA Committee on Ethical Practice provides direction and resources on best practices. NAFSA's *Code of Ethics* is an essential document for all professionals in international education, and can be reviewed on the NAFSA Web site. The Education Abroad Knowledge Community Web site includes sample ethical case studies.

Opportunities for Professional Development

A significant portion of the knowledge required in the field of education abroad advising and administration can be obtained through working with colleagues, individual study, and professional organizations. However, numerous undergraduate, graduate, and certificate programs are available to prepare full- and part-time students to be education abroad advisers or program administrators. Individuals interested in the profession should seek information from guidance sources and from mentors in the field. In addition to these formal programs, there are a number of short-term, formal learning experiences that can contribute to one's knowledge and skills. It is important to remember that the education abroad field requires a wide range of skills. In addition to cross-cultural, intercultural, or travel-specific training, programs focused on developing managerial skills, personnel

---

Professional Responsibilities Under NAFSA's *Code of Ethics*

- Maintain high standards of professional conduct.
- Follow ethical practices outlined in the Code of Ethics. Strive to follow the ethical practices outlined in the Principles for International Educational Exchange.
- Balance the wants, needs, and requirements of program participants, institutional policies, laws, and sponsors. Members' ultimate concern must be the long-term well-being of international educational exchange programs and participants.
- Resist pressures (personal, social, organizational, financial, and political) to use their influence inappropriately and refuse to allow self aggrandizement or personal gain to influence their professional judgments.
- Seek appropriate guidance and direction when faced with ethical dilemmas.
- Make every effort to ensure that their services are offered only to individuals and organizations with a legitimate claim on these services.

In Their Professional Preparation and Development, Members Shall:

- Accurately represent their areas of competence, education, training, and experience.
- Recognize the limits of their expertise and confine themselves to performing duties for which they are properly educated, trained, and qualified, making referrals when situations are outside their area of competence.
- Be informed of current developments in their fields, and ensure their continuing development and competence.
- Stay abreast of laws and regulations that affect their clients.

Continued...

Chapter 2: The Profession of Education Abroad

development, the many issues related to risk management, legal issues, planning and supervision, will be of particular benefit.

Varied training opportunities through numerous professional organizations continue to evolve and expand. Workshops, conferences, seminars, and publications all provide professional development and opportunities to meet with and learn from other international educators. The reference section of this book provides contact information. Professionals should strive to participate in education and training programs, and also recognize the importance of sharing their expertise with others.

NAFSA Professional Development Programs

NAFSA members and staff have continuously worked to strengthen the professional development opportunities offered to international educators. Professional development is one of the major NAFSA priorities. NAFSA is committed to help members achieve needed skills, increase expertise, and gain practical experience in international education through a carefully coordinated series of program activities. The Professional Development Program offers a wide range of workshops taught by members of the NAFSA Trainer Corps and other recognized leaders in international education. NAFSA training programs also include Country/Culture Workshops, the Academy for International Education, the Washington Symposium, and Management Development Programs.

Professional Development Programs (PDPs) and Professional Practice Workshops (PPWs) range in duration from four to twelve hours. Virtual workshops are also offered. NAFSA has published a "Statement of Professional Competencies for International Educators" and developed a

- Stay knowledgeable about world events that impact international educational program participants.
- Stay knowledgeable about differences in cultural and value orientations.
- Actively uphold NAFSA's *Code of Ethics* when practices that contravene it become evident.

In Relationships with Students, Scholars, and Others Members Shall:

- Understand and protect the civil and human rights of all individuals.
- Not discriminate with regard to race, color, national origin, ethnicity, sex, religion, sexual orientation, marital status, age, political opinion, immigration status, or disability.
- Recognize their own cultural and value orientations and be aware of how those orientations affect their interactions with people from other cultures.
- Demonstrate awareness of, sensitivity to, and respect for other educational systems, values, beliefs, and cultures.
- Not exploit, threaten, coerce, or sexually harass others.
- Not use one's position to proselytize.
- Refrain from invoking governmental or institutional regulations in order to intimidate participants in matters not related to their status.
- Maintain the confidentiality, integrity, and security of participants' records and of all communications with program participants. Members shall secure permission of the individuals before sharing information with others inside or outside the organization, unless disclosure is authorized by law or institutional policy or is mandated by previous arrangement.

Continued...

Part I: Education Abroad as a Component of U.S. Higher Education

systematic training program. Instructors in the PDPs and PPWs include at least one member of the NAFSA Trainer Corps, a group of trained leaders who have the content knowledge to teach the workshops and have also participated in a workshop on training techniques, adult learning styles, and teaching skills. The NAFSA Trainer Corps includes a group of workshop "deans" who typically have been involved in the development of the workshop curriculum and serve as the program coordinators, along with the chairs of the workshops and members of NAFSA staff.

NAFSA also works with grants and sponsored projects to offer special programs to professionals in education abroad. An example of this type of programming is the Country/Culture Workshop series sponsored by the Bureau of Educational and Cultural Affairs (ECA) of the U.S. Department of State. Country/Culture Workshops are designed to help professionals understand the characteristics of other cultures in the context of social, historical, and political trends, as well as to provide practical cross-cultural training.

NAFSA's Academy for International Education is a twenty-month-long program which includes topics on education abroad advising, international student advising, admissions, development and management of education abroad programs, community programming, and English as a second language (ESL) administration. The program was first offered at NAFSA regional conferences in 2003. NAFSA members and nonmembers have access to professional development programs that offer high-quality training at the local, regional, and national levels. The NAFSA Web site provides updated information regarding current training programs and schedules.

- Inform participants of their rights and responsibilities in the context of the institution and the community.
- Respond to inquiries fairly, equitably, and professionally.
- Provide accurate, complete, current, and unbiased information.
- Refrain from becoming involved in personal relationships with students and scholars when such relationships might result in either the appearance or the fact of undue influence being exercised on the making of professional judgments.
- Accept only gifts that are of nominal value and that do not seem intended to influence professional decisions, while remaining sensitive to the varying significance and implications of gifts in different cultures.
- Identify and provide appropriate referrals for students or scholars who experience unusual levels of emotional difficulty.
- Provide information, orientation, and support services needed to facilitate participants' adaptation to a new educational and cultural environment.

In Professional Relationships, Members Shall:

- Show respect for the diversity of viewpoints among colleagues, just as they show respect for the diversity of viewpoints among their clients.
- Refrain from unjustified or unseemly criticism of fellow members, other programs, and other organizations.
- Use their office, title, and professional associations only for the conduct of official business.
- Uphold agreements when participating in joint activities and give due credit to collaborators for their contributions.
- Carry out, in a timely and professional manner, any NAFSA responsibilities they agree to accept.

Continued...

Mid-Career Education Abroad Professionals

An important group of educators held their first meeting in 2003 at the NAFSA national annual conference. This group is self-identified as mid-career professionals, primarily with five to fifteen years experience in the field. The group is interested in expanding their opportunities for professional development, data collection, research skills, issues related to best practices, and other topics that impact their ability to be successful in their positions and also advance within the field. The Mid-Career Professionals group is also interested in advocacy, training, and the opportunity to identify both peers and mentors. The NAFSA Web site will provide information about the ongoing work of this group and future meeting plans.

Active Membership in Professional Organizations

A number of professional organizations serve individuals and institutions involved in education abroad. Active membership in such organizations is essential for professional development. Unlike scholarly associations that gather primarily to share the results of research activities, the meetings and publications of these organizations are more often dedicated to networking, sharing ideas, and acquiring new skills. Most of these organizations offer ample development and leadership opportunities.

NAFSA: Association of International Educators

NAFSA remains the U.S.-based umbrella professional association for all persons working in the field of international education and exchange. In

---

In Administering Programs, Members Shall:

- Clearly and accurately represent the identity of the organization and the goals, capabilities, and costs of programs.
- Recruit individuals, paid and unpaid, who are qualified to offer the instruction or services promised, train and supervise them respon-sibly, and ensure by means of regular evaluation that they are performing acceptably and that the overall program is meeting its professed goals.
- Encourage and support participation in professional development activities.
- Strive to establish standards, activities, instruction, and fee struc-tures that are appropriate and responsive to participant needs.
- Provide appropriate orientation, materials, and on-going guidance for participants.
- Provide appropriate opportunities for students and scholars to observe and to join in mutual inquiry into cultural differenc
- Take appropriate steps to enhance the safety and security of partic-ipants.
- Strive to ensure that the practices of those with whom one con-tracts do conform with NAFSA's Code of Ethics and the Principles for International Educational Exchange.

In Making Public Statements, Members Shall:

- Clearly distinguish, in both written and oral public statements, between their personal opinions and those opinions representing NAFSA, their own institutions, or other organizations.
- Provide accurate, complete, current, and unbiased information.

Original text approved by the NAFSA Board of Directors on May 28, 1989. Revisions approved by the NAFSA Board of Directors in October 1992, and September 2000. Additional text changes adopted on March 13, 2002, and March 9, 2003.

Part I: Education Abroad as a Component of U.S. Higher Education

addition to providing workshops and training programs, NAFSA also publishes newsletters, *International Educator* magazine, and numerous books and other publications. NAFSA sponsors regional conferences each fall and also holds an annual national conference in the spring that attracts several thousand participants from around the world. Participation in NAFSA activities also has the benefit of bringing education abroad professionals into contact with the full spectrum of international educational exchange. Newcomers benefit from participation in workshops and sessions, and from informational meetings and events. A special session for newcomers to NAFSA is offered each year at the annual conference. Experienced professionals can benefit from submitting proposals to present a session on their areas of interest and expertise. Mentor programs are sponsored by some of the regions within NAFSA. Experienced NAFSA members can apply for acceptance to the Trainer Corps. By sharing expertise with other international educators, professionals develop a network and support system, which is essential to a practitioner's continued growth and success. Volunteering at conferences, serving on NAFSA committees and teams, and other service commitments are educational and professional development opportunities.

NAFSA's Education Abroad Knowledge Community (formerly known as SECUSSA), founded in 1971, is the newest of NAFSA's professional divisions. Within NAFSA, the Education Abroad Knowledge Community promotes all forms of education abroad, including formal study, work, travel, and volunteerism, and sponsors workshops, sessions, discussion groups, and social activities at NAFSA's annual conference and at all NAFSA regional conferences. NAFSA's national and regional conferences generally offer basic training for newcomers. Many NAFSA publications derive from the professional needs and interests of Education Abroad Knowledge Community members. In addition to this publication, the Education Abroad Knowledge Community has produced a comprehensive bibliography on education abroad that can be viewed on the Education Abroad Knowledge Community Web site. The Education Abroad Knowledge Community also sponsors SECUSS-L, an e-mail discussion list open to members and nonmembers. Anyone who looks closely at the three decades of Education Abroad history within NAFSA will be struck by the constant growth in its agenda and number of members; the ongoing energy, innovation, and professionalism of the section; and the variety of issues and goals addressed by these professional. These themes are exemplified in the Education Abroad Knowledge Community's professional development offerings, professional standards, publications, advocacy and data collection, networking and communication venues, membership and diversity, and intra- and interassociational linkages. (See the Education Abroad Knowledge Community Web site for an overview of 30 years of Education Abroad Knowledge Community history.)

Institute of International Education (IIE)

IIE provides extensive resources for international educators, including a listing of education abroad programs published in *Academic Year Abroad*. IIE also conducts an annual census of study abroad activity, the results of which appear in *Open Doors*, which also includes a survey of international students and scholars on U.S. campuses. IIE is an independent nonprofit organization, and it administers the U.S. Student Fulbright Scholarship program, the Benjamin Gilman Scholarship, and the Freeman-Asia Scholarship.

In addition, IIE administers exchange visitor programs, works to internationalize institutions of higher education around the world, supports sustainable development training programs, and assists governments, organizations, foundations, and corporations in their efforts to expand global networks and cooperative projects. The Council for International Exchange of Scholars is a division of IIE and it supports the Fulbright Scholar Program, Occasional Lecturer Program, Scholar in Residence Program, Fulbright International Educational Administrators Seminars Program, and other opportunities for educators to gain international experience.

The Association of International Education Administrators (AIEA)

AIEA was formed in 1982 to provide a forum for Chief International Education Administrators to meet and discuss the broad issues of international education on their campuses and throughout U.S. higher education. AIEA sponsors an annual conference and publishes a scholarly journal, *Journal of Studies in International Education*, and other timely publications. AIEA also offers workshops and seminars, most notably, the seminars on Current Issues in Campus Administration of International Education (Ghost Ranch). AIEA identifies four specific objectives for itself: "provide an effective voice on significant issues within international education at all levels, improve and promote international education programming and administration within institutions of higher education, establish and maintain a professional network among international education institutions' leaders, cooperate in appropriate ways with other national and international groups having similar interests." AIEA also has committees that address specific topics, such as the Public Policy Committee and the Committee on Campus Administration and Programs (CAPS).

Council on International Educational Exchange (CIEE)

Several hundred colleges and universities are institutional members of CIEE. CIEE has a long history of leadership in education abroad. CIEE's mission is "to help people gain understanding, acquire knowledge, and develop skills for living in a globally interdependent and culturally diverse world." CIEE holds an annual conference with sessions, workshops, and discussion groups devoted to a wide array of topics. CIEE administers consortial study abroad programs around the world. CIEE also offers overseas development seminars for faculty, produces publications, and administers programs for working, teaching, and volunteering abroad.

The Forum on Education Abroad

The Forum, an institutional and individual membership organization, was formed in 2001 by recognized leaders in the field of education abroad. Working in conjunction with NAFSA and SECUSSA and other organizations, the Forum seeks to promote high-quality and effective education abroad

Part I: Education Abroad as a Component of U.S. Higher Education

programming through advocating standards of good practice, promoting excellence in curricular development and academic design, encouraging outcomes assessment and other research, facilitating data collection, and advocating education abroad at all levels. The Forum works via the promotion of an ongoing dialogue within the field, articulating research needs and sponsoring applied research, hosting conferences, and producing publications. The Forum seeks to address a broad range of issues that pertain exclusively to the field of education abroad. Membership in the Forum has grown steadily since its founding.

The Alliance for International Educational and Cultural Exchange

The Alliance provides publications, resources, and advocacy for international education. It represents approximately seventy nongovernmental organizations that conduct a wide range of exchange programs. NAFSA is a founding member of the Alliance, and the two organizations work cooperatively on numerous advocacy and governmental policy issues.

Phi Beta Delta

Phi Beta Delta is an honor society for campus staff, faculty, and students. It recognizes scholarly activity in international education.

The Canadian Bureau of International Education (CBIE)

CBIE is the only national organization in Canada exclusively dedicated to international education and the free movement of ideas and learners across national boundaries. CBIE represents the full spectrum of Canadian education. Its membership is composed of colleges, universities, schools and school boards, organizations, and individuals. CBIE's activities comprise advocacy, research and information services, training programs, scholarship management, professional development for international educators, and a host of other services for members and learners. CBIE hosts an annual conference with networking and professional development opportunities, and presentations on current research and trends.

The Association of Universities and Colleges in Canada (AUCC)

This organization represents ninety-three public and private not-for-profit universities and university-degree-level colleges across Canada. Membership in AUCC is de facto accreditation within the Canadian system. AUCC offers an annual conference, publications, and resources and strong advocacy in the Canadian context.

British Columbia Centre for International Education (BCCIE)

The mission of BCCIE is to strengthen the internationalization of the public postsecondary system to respond to international realities and to contribute to British Columbia's future prosperity. BCCIE envisions an integrated and collaborative education system in which an international perspective is infused into the functions and culture of all institutions in British Columbia. The membership of BCCIE includes all twenty-seven public postsecondary institutions. BCCIE works closely with its membership to ensure that its programs and services are relevant, responsive, and effective. BCCIE offers an annual fall or summer retreat which is considered to be one of the stronger international education professional development activities in Canada. It also produces a broad range of publications.

Asociación Mexicana para la Educación Internacional (AMPEI)

AMPEI is the Mexican counterpart to NAFSA and CBIE. The organization offers unparalleled networking opportunities within Mexico, and its annual conference typically offers many bilingual sessions and can appeal to professionals from around the world.

The Consortium for North American Higher Education Collaboration (CONAHEC)

CONAHEC advises and connects institutions interested in establishing or strengthening academic collaborative programs in the North American region. CONAHEC programs include a North American student exchange program, conferences, support for comparative research on education policy issues, and professional development opportunities for campus administrators and faculty.

The European Association for International Education (EAIE)

EAIE is a nonprofit organization that aims to stimulate and facilitate the internationalization of higher education in Europe and around the world, and to meet the professional needs of individuals active in international education. It has a diverse membership of international education professionals ranging from rectors to professors to international exchange coordinators. EAIE has an impressive array of publications and hosts an annual conference and a series of professionally delivered training programs for international educators at every career level.

The British Universities Transatlantic Exchange Association (BUTEX)

BUTEX promotes mobility among universities and colleges in the United Kingdom and those in North America. It represents more than eighty higher education institutions in the United Kingdom with active transatlantic links and interests, most of which have a variety of individual exchange arrangements with North American universities and colleges. BUTEX includes in its brief the promotion of the United Kingdom's higher education in North America and the regular exchange of information among its members on current international education issues. BUTEX hosts a conference every other year in the United Kingdom.

American Councils for International Education

American Councils is an international nonprofit organization that promotes development and exchange between the United States and Eastern Europe and Eurasia. American Councils was founded in 1974 as the American Council of Teachers of Russian (ACTR). In 1998, based on the organization's development and expanded activities, the ACTR board created a new organizational structure, which includes both the American Council for Collaboration in Education and Language Study

(ACCELS) and ACTR as divisions of American Councils.

Additional Professional Development Resources

The following associations may also be useful for country- or region-specific networking or professional development opportunities.

Association of International Education, Japan (AIEJ)

AIEJ helps promote international exchanges and friendship between Japan and other countries through a wide variety of services.

The British Council

The British Council works to connect people worldwide with learning opportunities and creative ideas from the United Kingdom, and supports the creation of relationships between U.K. institutions and institutions in other countries. The British Council offers training sessions, unique programming, and support for linkage building.

The Chinese Education Association for International Exchange

The Chinese Education Association for International Exchange is China's national nongovernmental organization for conducting international educational exchange, developing exchanges and cooperation between the Chinese educational community and other parts of the world, and promoting the advancement of education, culture, science, and technology.

Edufrance

Edufrance has offices in many countries and offers detailed information on higher education in France, advice on programs and institutions appropriate for students' background and goals, and other services including linkage building.

Australian Education International

Australian Education International is a nonprofit organization with a mission to develop and enhance bilateral relationships between Australia and the United States and Canada. The office was established in 1992 and has offices in Washington DC and Los Angeles. Literature about and assistance with study in Australia is provided by AEO.

Australia Education International (IDP)

IDP has the mission of helping make the teaching, consultancy, and research services of Australian education and training institutions available to overseas countries, institutions, and individuals. IDP pursues its mission by acting as a liaison or manager of the delivery of services provided by Australian education institutions. IDP has a broad network of offices around the world.

The International Centre at Queen's University

The International Centre at Queen's University publishes a newsletter and offers an International Educators Training Program (IETP), with special reference to risk and responsibility in study abroad. The organization is engaged in professional development and is working towards the certification of international education professionals in the Canadian context.

University Mobility in Asia and the Pacific (UMAP)

UMAP is a program aimed at increasing university mobility in the Asia-Pacific region. The general objective of UMAP is to achieve a better understanding of the cultural, economic, and social systems of the Asia-Pacific region within the countries and territories of that region, by fostering extended and enhanced cooperation among higher education institutions, by increasing mobility of higher education students and staff, and by improving the quality of higher education.

Numerous other professional organizations around the world serve the needs of professionals in education abroad. These include The Netherlands Organization for International Cooperation in Higher Education (NUFFIC), which provides access to excellent reference information about institutions in the Netherlands and produces high-quality publications.

The American Association of Collegiate Registrars and Admission Officers (AACRAO)

AACRAO sponsors an annual conference that includes sessions of relevance to international educators. AACRAO has a committee on study abroad that organizes sessions at the annual conference. AACRAO also publishes information on educational systems around the world.

This chapter does not attempt to provide information on all of the organizations that support education abroad professionals, but it demonstrates that the resources available are extensive and continually expanding. Professionals associated with organizations that support education abroad that are not included in this chapter are encouraged to provide information to NAFSA for potential inclusion in its Web-based resources. Additional organizational contact information is provided in the Web resources for this book.

In addition to those publications offered by or through some of the organizations listed herein, there are numerous other publications and journals that offer leading research and articles on issues of international education. These include the *Comparative Education Review, Journal of Studies in International Education, Current Issues in Comparative Education, Frontiers: The Interdisciplinary Journal of Study Abroad,* and *Current Issues in Education.*

Many education abroad professionals have found that they have benefited by keeping their individual memberships current in groups that reflect their own particular background, interest, or avocation. These include the Fulbright Alumni Association; the International Society for Intercultural Education, Training, and Research (SIETAR); and other associations related to the teaching of foreign language, area studies, student personnel administration, and specific academic disciplines, among other categories.

Education abroad staff working on college and university campuses may also have access to the higher education groups to which their institutions belong. These groups include the American Council on Education, American Association of State Colleges and Universities, Association of American Colleges, National Association of State Universities and Land Grant Colleges, and other professional associations. All of these include in their research, publications, and conference activities a component on international education that in most cases explicitly encompasses education abroad.

Almost every organization involved in international education has a regular schedule of regional, national, and international meetings and conferences. Attendance at these meetings is important for the new professional, and participation in the program is essential for those who are more experienced. Meetings and conferences present opportunities to share ideas and points of view, to discuss approaches and practices, to learn about new developments and proposals, and when appropriate, to raise questions about and voice concerns regarding standards and practices. The forums presented by professional organizations are the best, most consistently available, and most visible means for exploring new ideas, meeting innovators and experts in the field, and sharing one's own expertise and successes with others at different professional levels.

Professional Development Abroad

Overseas travel for the education abroad professional is essential. One must be as familiar as possible with foreign countries and cultures in order to advise, inform, and design and implement useful, high-quality experiences abroad. Many professionals have lived overseas or have traveled extensively in other parts of the world. Most have participated in a foreign study experience or have become knowledgeable about systems of higher education in other countries. All support the value of participatory learning in another culture—not merely learning about the people and the culture, but learning how people in other cultures learn.

Overseas Familiarization Tours

A number of sponsored activities abroad enroll students on a national or international basis. Many of the program providers have independent boards of advisers, and periodically offer opportunities to campus advisers to visit overseas program sites to acquaint the advisers with their programs. Arcadia University, Butler University, CIEE, the University Studies Abroad Consortium, the American Institute for Foreign Study (AIFS), Denmark's International Study Program (DiS), InterStudy, and the Australian Education Office are among those that organize program site visits.

Leading a Program

Some professionals in education abroad are able to find employment leading short-term programs or serving as resident directors of study abroad programs. These opportunities abound at the postsecondary education level, and may also be available at the secondary school level.

Individual Travel Abroad

There are a number of interesting alternatives to being a tourist abroad, even with limited time constraints. There are hundreds of affordable options for special-interest or adult education travel. Some programs focus on specific interests (archaeology, bird-watching, women's issues), others on methods of travel (trekking, caravans, river boats), and still others on exotic areas of the world. No single source of information describes all these opportunities, but a good guide that focuses on educational work, study, and travel abroad with particular reference to adult participation is published in *Transitions Abroad*. Literally hundreds of voluntary service projects are conducted annually in all parts of the world.

Announcements of overseas seminars and workshops, as well as current application information about the specific programs mentioned in this chapter, are usually published in NAFSA's periodical publications and in other professional associations' newsletters, Web sites, and journals.

The travel, study, and work opportunities noted in this chapter are by no means inclusive, but they do suggest the variety of ways one can continue to learn through an overseas experience. The Baden-Württemberg Seminar, Fulbright programs for administrators in international education, and numerous other opportunities are available.

NAFSA Strategic Task Force on Education Abroad

In 2003, a report titled *Securing America's Future: Global Education for a Global Age* was developed and distributed by NAFSA. The task force was led by two honorary co-chairs, the late Senator Paul Simon, former U.S. senator, and the Honorable Richard W. Riley, former U.S. secretary of education. Carl Herrin, a well-known member of the education abroad profession, served as the chair and leader of the group. The nineteen-member group consisted of professionals in international education as well as leaders from higher education, foundations, and corporations. This diverse group created a consensus document that focuses on a "national liability" created by the U.S. students' lack of knowledge of foreign cultures and languages, and recommends that education abroad become "an integral part of college students' education."

The report is directed principally at the president of the United States and Congress, state governors and legislatures, college and university leaders, businesses, accrediting agencies, and state certification and licensing bodies. Though the task force was planned before the attacks of September 11, 2001, the report came at an extremely important moment in U.S. history. Whereas the European Union and other multinational organizations have long supported programs for student mobility, the United States has not been equally responsive to national initiatives that give broad support for education abroad. The report provides recommendations for expanding funding for education abroad, including a major proposal from Senator Simon for a new federal scholarship program. The report encourages U.S. students to study abroad in areas that are currently considered "non-traditional", i.e. outside Western Europe, and to expand the economic, ethnic, and overall diversity in student participants. The report also addresses the need to "promote the integration of study abroad into the higher education curriculum, and increase opportunities for international internships and service learning." The full text of *Securing America's Future: Global Education for a Global Age* is available on the NAFSA Web site.

Publishing Opportunities

Publishing is one of the best ways for education abroad professionals to share knowledge and expertise with others in the field. The number of publishing opportunities in the education abroad field is growing. NAFSA encourages the submission of articles for its flagship periodical, *International Educator* magazine, and other publications. NAFSA also supports and encourages proposals for longer publications such as pamphlets, booklets, and books. The publication proposal procedure is available on the NAFSA Web site. NAFSA offers a wide range of important resources for professionals in education abroad. Some recent titles include *The Guide to Successful Short-Term Programs Abroad, Crisis Management in a Cross-Cultural Setting, Abroad By Design,* and *Study Abroad: A Parent's Guide.* NAFSA's Committee on Communication and Information (COMINFO) reviews publication proposals and works with NAFSA staff to continue to expand the body of information available in the field.

Frontiers: The Interdisciplinary Journal of Study Abroad publishes high-quality research, essays, book reviews, and other thought-provoking work. *Frontiers* began publication in 1995, and is dedicated to the academic and theoretical aspects of education abroad. *The Journal of Studies in International Education* is sponsored by the Association for Studies in International Education (ASIE), an interorganizational body whose mission is to support serious research related to international education and academic mobility. *The Journal of Studies in International Education* is published quarterly.

Most of the major international education organizations publish newsletters and other literature with a variety of emphases and audiences. There is a constant need for good writers with fresh ideas. Most national conferences provide opportunities to submit juried papers, acceptance of which may include publication as well as presentation. These papers require careful research, considerable planning, and thoughtful writing and rewriting. Newsletters, on the other hand, may accept brief, timely articles or reports on current developments, and unsolicited submissions are often welcome. The rapid development of electronic publishing is also creating opportunities for education abroad professionals to gain publishing experience.

Building Specific Skills

Education abroad careers require a wide variety of skills ranging from accounting and fiscal management practices to publication layout and design, personnel administration, international travel and tour planning, academic and student counseling, and computer literacy. Many education abroad professionals work on college or university campuses and have access to classes and training programs in related skills (e.g., management, computer technology, accounting and finance, graphic design, professional writing). In many cases, tuition is free. Classes can be taken to fill self-identified professional development needs or to complement or supplement work already completed. The training programs offered by NAFSA, EAIE, and other professional organizations are excellent formats for learning skills specific to education abroad. Cross-cultural communication training and foreign language study are also essential skills for international educators. International educators must also have an understanding of crisis management procedures and legal issues related to programs abroad.

Whether you are employed by an academic institution or not, there is ample access in most parts

Chapter 2: The Profession of Education Abroad

of the country to training opportunities. Community groups and service clubs frequently organize training seminars and management courses, as do various industries, management consulting and training firms, and groups with a specific training focus (e.g., Toastmasters International).

Skill-building can be self-taught as well. The opportunity to research and write grant proposals and to administer a grant award on behalf of a sponsoring organization or community group is also a professional development activity. NAFSA makes a number of awards each year in support of local and national program proposals that contribute to the educational exchange process, including, for example, the preparation and orientation and reentry of American students studying abroad.

Another area in which ongoing training, either formal or self-taught, is absolutely essential is computer applications. Beyond basic data manipulation, word processing, and spreadsheet skills, professionals must understand the uses and implications of e-mail, Web sites, and other rapidly emerging technologies.

Another way to build skills is through internships, which can take a number of different forms. Some are institutionalized and others are developed individually to meet personal and professional needs. An idea growing in popularity in recent years is that of administrative exchanges or internships. In this type of internship, an individual works in an education abroad office or overseas program to perform a specific job for a limited period of time. The individual is expected to contribute his or her professional skills and, at the same time, to learn about the new situation and to carry that information back to the home institution. Administrative exchanges or internship possibilities present rich learning opportunities for all of the parties involved.

Recent efforts to increase the level of professionalism within the ranks of international education, and especially education abroad, are resulting in opportunities for administrative staff sabbaticals, leave programs, and other accommodations. These new opportunities will provide time for employees to pursue studies or experiences that will equip them with the knowledge and skills necessary for professional growth. It is important for professionals to share information about the benefits of these programs and to encourage institutions to support interprogram internships as a development activity that will attract and help to retain the best-qualified individuals.

SUMMARY

Whether you are new to the education abroad field, have newly expanded responsibilities, or are an experienced professional simply committed to lifelong learning, you should recognize that you are involved in a dynamic and especially demanding field. Your own knowledge, skills, and talents will be tested every day. Being a professional means working to assimilate and embody the best that others have said and done, as well as following your own best instincts while remaining aware of the special needs of your own institution or organization. There are many established networks for training and professional discourse. Taking advantage of these opportunities will make your work easier and more enjoyable, and will better prepare you to contribute to the growth and development of our professional field.

Part I: Education Abroad as a Component of U.S. Higher Education

As the late Senator Paul Simon said in his introductory remarks to the 2003 report from the Strategic Task Force on Education Abroad, "A nation cannot drift into greatness. We must dream and be willing to make small sacrifices to achieve those dreams." Just as a nation cannot "drift into greatness" neither can professionals or organizations involved in education abroad. Individuals must make sacrifices. Institutions and organizations cannot enhance the role of education abroad in post secondary education without vision, commitment, and planning. The experience of education abroad is a defining moment for most students. The impact of international education on our interdependent world is immeasurable. Many goals have already been achieved, but many more challenges face professionals in education abroad. The leaders of the future will have to accept these challenges and aspire to levels of service that help to create the global community that is our common goal.

CHAPTER 3

Data Collection, Demographics, and the Research Agenda

Contributors: Kathleen Sideli, Kim Kreutzer

Most information sources about education abroad attempt to quantify the experience. Yet each time a figure is included, be it the number of students, programs, or institutions involved, many professionals in the field of international education tend to distrust the data. This collective doubt has arisen because, despite earlier attempts to quantify the education abroad experience, intensive efforts toward accurate data collection in the field have emerged as a critical goal only in the last decade. For most of its history, the education abroad field has struggled not only to develop accurate record-keeping processes but also to justify why these efforts are imperative. It is essential that practitioners in the field come to terms with why it is the profession's responsibility to engage in accurate data collection and other related research. The rationale for this responsibility can be grouped under three categories: academic integrity, responsibility and liability, and advocacy. Only when the education abroad profession has embraced this rationale can it move on to overcoming the challenges involved with creating systems to track students and evaluate their progress.

WHY ACCURATE DATA COLLECTION IS IMPERATIVE

Academic Integrity

One of the primary reasons to track student mobility across the spectrum of programs that students access is to get a handle on the quality of those programs and the achievements of the students. To this end, data should be collected on all students, no matter what type of program they have chosen. Among those that should be included are students participating in faculty-led programs offered by their own institution, even if the programs are offered and administered by a unit outside of the international education office. It is not uncommon for faculty-led programs to operate without close oversight by a central administrative unit or a campus-wide faculty committee. In such cases it may not be possible to guarantee for the campus community that these academic options abroad are of high quality. Current practice in the field is to encourage close cooperation between international education offices and faculty who run independent programs, particularly short-term ones. (See Part III, Chapter 2, "Short-Term Programs Abroad.") Since education abroad is very much a component of student degree studies, it is incumbent on education abroad professionals to work with both faculty and administrative colleagues on campus to build and maintain a range of academic program models and best practices. Creating systems to track student mobility invariably leads to closer oversight of the quality of such programs.

It is also important to track students who select external options available through third-party providers, other U.S. institutions, or directly through international institutions, even if these options do not fall under the purview of the international education unit. Although international education offices may not have immediate responsibility for all external programs (the type of programs that fall under the rubric of 'external' is different from campus to campus), it behooves each campus to learn about the overseas programs selected by its students. This is essential since the students will invariably arrange for credit, most likely through a transfer process, through some campus unit. If the central education abroad unit does not track student mobility on such programs, the academic experiences of those students may fall outside any vetting process, thus jeopardizing quality-control standards over the credits they are earning.

The importance of assessing the various types of learning outcomes that result from the education abroad experience will be reviewed later in this chapter. What is increasingly clear is that it is the responsibility of professionals in the field to quantify for many constituencies the actual results of studying abroad. Although there have been numerous outcome assessment studies, there is a clear need to conduct more of these serious research projects across a wider range of students and programs. Without this research, it will be extremely difficult to effectively promote the effects of the education abroad experience. A recent electronic sampling of large sending institutions showed that fewer than half of those surveyed were conducting any outcomes assessment, although 95 percent were evaluating student satisfaction with study abroad programs (Sideli et al. 2001).

Responsibility and Liability

Given the recent focus on safety and security issues related to students going abroad, two critical reasons for tracking the mobility of all participating students, regardless of program sponsor, are the students' security and the institution's liability. One of the anecdotes circulating about this matter concerns a college president. After a high-profile incident abroad through which a number of U.S. students were impacted, this president was supposedly quoted as saying that he wanted immediate confirmation from his campus officials regarding whether the institution had any students participating in a particular program at the time of the incident. When he learned that the campus had not established any system for knowing the answer to his question, he ordered one devised immediately, so that the next time he asked, he would get a reliable response.

Nevertheless, the claim is often made that campus administrators do not comprehend why it is important for education abroad offices to know where students choose to go, particularly when students use an external provider or independently enroll in an institution overseas. When a crisis erupts somewhere, be it a natural disaster, a widespread health scare, a terrorist activity, or a national skirmish, education abroad professionals should be properly positioned to reach out to the students. Ultimately, these students fall under the school's purview, even if they are temporarily receiving services from another institution or organization. The home campus policies govern what will happen with the academic credits the students earn, whether they can use their financial aid abroad, and how they can enroll in classes upon their return. If a tragedy strikes, the home campus will have to go into action to deal with the problem. Being prepared for such eventualities, therefore, falls within the scope of responsibilities rightly placed on education abroad practitioners.

Once a system for tracking students during their time abroad is devised, information and instructions should be circulated to the students to ensure appropriate follow-through regarding the transfer of credit, financial aid guidelines, registration issues, and other essential program information. With the now-pervasive use of e-mail, maintaining contact with students while they're abroad and sharing concerns and advice regarding their safety and security, particularly during tense moments, should be achievable. Even before September 11, 2001, such good practices were being encouraged. In the aftermath of the attack, such practices should be universally applied.

By devising student-tracking mechanisms, education abroad professionals will also find that they will be better positioned to orient and prepare faculty directors who lead independent programs. Although some faculty who are experienced at taking students abroad might bristle at a study abroad professional who requests that there be safety and security measures in place before a program is considered viable, others will welcome their expertise and assistance. It may be easier to get faculty engaged with the education abroad office if safety and security are used as hooks to initiate communication. From there, the education abroad office can branch out into other issues, including academic quality, program evaluation, etc. It is in everyone's best interests, particularly the students', for a centralized unit on campus to track the movements of all students and all programs. It is not enough merely to hope that you will never have to cope with a tragedy. If and when a crisis arises, you need to be prepared and knowledgeable about students' whereabouts, well before the phone rings.

Advocacy

Another rationale for collecting complete data on study abroad students is to be able to engage in strong advocacy efforts at all levels—institutional, state, and national. Without knowing who and where the students are and what they are engaged in, education abroad offices cannot expect others to meet the office's needs and requests.

At the institutional or organizational level, education abroad professionals can only engage in constructive and cooperative efforts if they share accurate and timely information. It is hard to imagine good working relationships with campus units without keeping a range of offices apprised about the flow of students, including the registrar, bursar, dean of students, health center, office of residence life, academic departments, and schools or colleges. Such cooperation can result in the type of strategic planning that is necessary for the viability of the institution as well as the programs themselves. Data can also demonstrate the accomplishments of students and programs, perhaps by stressing related recruitment and retention issues. Precision with regard to the accuracy of figures can also make a big difference for budget-setting and other fiscal decisions, including the distribution of financial aid.

On another pragmatic level, collecting data regarding student interest and program choices can guide future program development and planning. With the appropriate information, new programming can be encouraged in under-represented areas and program partnerships or consortium relationships can be established in places highly sought after by students. Also, by carefully tracking student flow, particularly with regard to one's own institutional infrastructure, one can justify expansion of staffing, physical space, or technology needs. Coincidentally, the enhancement of technology contributes to better data collection (Van Der Meid 2002).

When educators approach decision makers about facilitating international experiences, they increasingly want concrete data to prove that such experiences benefit their constituencies. Until sufficient studies are compiled that confirm the impact of the education abroad experience on institutions and the students and their subsequent careers, education abroad professionals should be prepared for their requests for assistance and funding to be met with skepticism and hesitation by federal and state governments, as well as philanthropic foundations and private corporations. Although many organizations and government agencies have been supportive of efforts to make financial aid and scholarships more widely available to more students, they have also been dismayed that the field cannot provide data showing that the education abroad experience is safe and productive on many levels.

Although lawmakers have a justifiable need to see more concrete data regarding the successes of the education abroad experience, education abroad professionals should not discount another important constituency—the wider community. The national media do not always have a balanced view of the need for overseas living and learning as an adjunct to domestic study. Journalists often sensationalize incidents and present their readers with an inaccurate picture of the student experience abroad as something dangerous and risky at worst and as superficially luxurious at best. Education abroad professionals need to improve the way they present what they know to be the case: that students can be affected in profound ways by the experience of spending time in a country they do not call home, and that this experience is likely to influence their career choices and their own legacies to society. Families may intuit that studying or interning abroad increases their child's chances of achieving a better job, but they also fret that their son or daughter is taking unnecessary risks or wasting time on too many extracurricular activities. Education abroad professionals need to make the case for the value of international study to the media, but also to the nation at large, if education abroad is to become a respected and understood component of U.S. higher education.

It is clear that educators must have data to make the case for academic integrity, safety and liability, and advocacy, and that the data be inclusive, accurate, and substantive. The desire for better data is not a recent development in the field. What is recent is the renewed fervor with which international educators are approaching data collection. Today, global issues grip the world more than ever before, given recent international developments that point to a need for more, not less, personal interaction on a global level. To justify the forays of U.S. students into other countries, for short or long periods of time, educators need to know how many students are involved, what they are studying, where they are studying, and most importantly, how the experience affects them. So, what do education abroad professionals know about students who study abroad, and when did the collection of such information begin?

History of Data Collection in Education Abroad

The field is greatly indebted to the Institute for International Education (IIE) for tirelessly seeking out methods to collect data on U.S. students abroad. These data-collection efforts date back to 1949, when IIE published its first national census of international education activity, *Education for One World*. In 1954, the census was renamed *Open Doors*, "to suggest the need for both host and home nations and institutions to offer hospitality and support to foreign students if international education is to work," according to William Hoffa (Hoffa 1999). However, from the beginning, the funding for the work done by IIE stemmed from a source—the U.S. Office of Education—predominantly interested in international student and scholar activity. Thus, from the very beginning, comprehensive data on the overseas activity of U.S. students studying or working abroad has proven to be quite elusive, due in part also to the complex nature of education abroad activity.

During the first phase of data collection, from 1949 to 1973, IIE pursued the numbers of U.S. students abroad by asking overseas universities and sponsors of special "courses" abroad to report on the number of U.S. students enrolled in their institutions or programs. IIE was well aware that this approach could not accurately net total numbers but it seemed, at the time, to be the best methodology. The 1958 edition of *Open Doors* reported that activity for 1956–1957 included 12,845 students in 358 institutions in 52 countries (58 percent in Europe, 20 percent in Latin America, 13 percent in Canada).

IIE's frustration with its overseas informants appears frequently in the explanatory text of *Open Doors* throughout the 1960s, and its tendency to include or exclude summer study abroad veered back and forth. The 1973 edition of *Open Doors* reported that 34,218 U.S. students were "enrolled as full-time students in institutions of higher learning abroad" during 1971–1972. It did not specify how many of these students were undergraduates, how many were graduate students, how many were seeking the foreign university degree, how many were earning credit as part of their U.S. degree studies (independently or as part of a U.S. program), or how many were enrolled as visiting students with no expectation of being able to transfer credit to their U.S. institutions.

There was a hiatus of five years during which IIE did not collect any information from abroad, most likely due to the fact that IIE realized by then that more and more students enrolled in "special programs" rather than directly matriculated at host institutions. Consequently, the next phase of data collection, from 1979 to 1986, focused instead on

Part I: Education Abroad as a Component of U.S. Higher Education

program sponsors and domestic institutions sending their students abroad. IIE recognized all along that it was probably missing a large segment of the U.S. overseas population enrolled in summer options, attending branch campuses, or participating in other types of study abroad programs.

In 1986 IIE devised a new system, still used for the most part today, based on the recommendations of the Inter-Associational Data Collection Committee. Made up of representation from the American Association of Collegiate Registrars and Admission Officers (AACRAO), NAFSA's Section on U.S. Students Abroad (SECUSSA), and IIE, this advisory group focused on how to get better and more complete study abroad information. It advised IIE to collect the information needed via "a national survey of colleges and universities that allow students to apply credit earned overseas toward their own home campus degree studies." As described in *Open Doors* in 1986–1987, this is "not a survey of study abroad programs to determine the number of students enrolled in them and to obtain other information about them," but rather a record of students earning credit, institution by institution, and in the aggregate. As *Open Doors* states, "Although less than complete, [it] offers the first comprehensive analysis of a major sector of the study abroad population." This comprehensive survey was conducted biennially until 1994 when IIE began circulating it on an annual basis.

Overview of IIE's Open Doors Methodology and Results from 1986–2002

The IIE *Open Doors* survey continues to be an essentially demographic survey circulated each spring semester to more than 1,200 institutions that have shown previous activity in study abroad for credit. To date, it is the only inclusive survey that exists in the field. It is designed to gauge study abroad participation during the academic year that ended the previous August. The reason for this delay is to accommodate those institutions whose students transfer credit throughout the fall and early spring from programs that took place during preceding semesters (fall, spring, or summer). The survey tallies the total number of students (U.S. citizens or permanent residents) sent by each institution and tracks some programmatic and demographic information on each student's experience. It does not track the number of international students who might be studying abroad as part of their U.S. degree studies. Since 1986, *Open Doors* has provided the following information:

- Program information

  Type of program (through home institution or through another institution or organization)

  Duration of the program

  Host country of the program

- Student information

  Academic level

  Major or majors

  Gender

  Ethnicity

The *Open Doors* survey also includes some questions on institutional policies regarding financial aid and safety and liability.

Among the challenges facing institutions that receive the survey is how to include every student on the campus who received credit for education abroad activity. Not all campuses centralize the collection of this information, yet IIE sends only one survey per institution. Therefore, there must be collaboration on a campus to pull together the statistics needed for the survey. (Some recommended approaches to collaboration can be found later in this chapter.) Program providers, unless they are campus-based, do not participate in this survey, since this would lead to double-counting or students not being counted by either the home institution or the program provider. If the program providers are campus-based, they are instructed to count only their own students studying abroad, not those enrolled from other institutions. Each year, many campuses are slow to respond, given the complexity of combining all data. Nevertheless, the majority of the contacted institutions eventually submit the requested information.

Profile of Education Abroad Students

The number of students abroad, as reported by *Open Doors*, has increased greatly over the years, from 48,483 in 1985–1986 to 174,629 in 2002–2003. Likewise, the numbers of institutions reporting has risen from 709 to well over a thousand, showing how education abroad is becoming an integral part of higher education today. However, although the total numbers have more than tripled in seventeen years, certain elements have remained fairly steady. Almost three-quarters of the students participate in programs administered by their own institutions, whereas a little over a quarter of the students access programs provided by other institutions or organizations.

The trend in participation by gender has remained almost constant over the years, with female students accounting for almost two-thirds of study abroad participants, and males accounting for one-third. Although multiple theories and conjectures abound, no research has been undertaken to identify any overarching reasons why the gender breakdown for education abroad is not parallel to the gender balance on U.S. campuses. The breakdown of the academic level has also remained very constant over the years, with an average of 17 percent seniors, 41 percent juniors, 13 percent sophomores, 3 percent freshmen, and 8 percent graduate students (with the rest unspecified). The ethnic profile of study abroad participants has remained fairly constant over the years as well, with an average of 85 percent white and 15 percent from various minority backgrounds. Asian-Americans and Hispanic-Americans are involved in study abroad in greater numbers than African-Americans. However, due to concerted efforts to guide students of color to education abroad, there has been a small increase in the number of African-American students participating in a wide range of programs overseas.

Trend Toward Shorter Programs in More Diverse Disciplines and Locations

In addition to the large increases in overall participation by both students and institutions, the survey shows trends toward shorter programs and more diverse locations and disciplines.

Duration

In a sixteen-year period, the percentage of students participating in academic-year programs has dropped by more than half—from 18 percent to less than 9 percent—while the percentage of students participating in short-term programs of less than a semester or quarter has gone from 28 percent to 50 percent. Some of this increase is due to the new and innovative 'niche' programs that run less than eight weeks, either between terms or as part of an on-campus course. It is interesting to note, however, that the absolute number of students doing academic-year programs has increased slightly, despite the drop in the overall percentage rate. Interestingly, the proportion of students on semester programs has remained fairly constant, at an average of 38 percent of the total.

Diversity of Discipline

Significant efforts have been made over the years to encourage students from diverse academic backgrounds to study their disciplines abroad, resulting in some significant changes. Whereas business and management students once accounted for only 10 percent of the total, today 18 percent of students studying abroad are business students. That does not necessarily mean that all these students are taking courses from a business curriculum while they are overseas, but it does suggest that there is a supportive environment for them to take courses toward their degrees overseas, even if those courses are in general education. This is a change in perspective from the mid-1980s. And while the number of foreign language majors has dropped by half, the percentage of students in the sciences (physical, mathematical, health, and engineering) has almost doubled in that same period. It is not surprising, therefore, that the number of students abroad who come from a social science or humanities background is increasingly a lower percentage of the overall pool.

Diversity of Locations

In addition to encouraging students from diverse disciplines to study overseas, the field has actively pushed them toward branching out beyond Western Europe. At one time, Europe accounted for 80 percent of the total enrollment of U.S. students abroad; today the figure is almost 20 percent lower. Where are the students going instead? With political stability returning to most of Latin America during the late 1980s and early 1990s, a plethora of new programs have opened up there. This has resulted in the doubling of the percentage of students selecting programs in that region, amounting to 15 percent of the total. And the addition of programs in Oceania has meant a meteoric rise in the number of students choosing that region for study abroad, from a few hundred to almost 11,000 students (7 percent of the total). The number of students studying in Africa has also increased each year to a new high of 4,633. Asia has seen small, steady increases as well.

The efforts of the education abroad field to increase programming, provide better advising, and offer improved safety and security orientation have made a difference in making developing countries viable options for U.S. students who want to study abroad. If this trend continues in the coming years, U.S. students will not remain clustered in Western Europe, as they do now. In 2001–2002, the United Kingdom drew almost one-fifth of all U.S. students studying abroad; Spain and Italy each attracted one-tenth of all U.S. students studying abroad.

SECUSSA/IIE Data Collection Initiative 1999–2002

During the past decade, education abroad professionals began to look at data more carefully, particularly given the call to get a wider range of students abroad to a wider range of places. Markers were needed to gauge progress in these proactive efforts. By the end of the decade it was clear that the field needed a renewed focus on the importance of data collection, to assist IIE in improving its survey efforts. In 1999, SECUSSA created a standing committee to work with IIE and U.S. campuses to make further improvements in national data collection on education abroad activity. This large working group of almost thirty individuals devoted four years to devising strategic goals and methods of improved data collection. The goals of the group included (1) increasing awareness in the field of the *Open Doors* survey and its methodology; (2) acquiring more accurate data by adding institutions to IIE's survey list and by improving the response rate of participating institutions; (3) adapting a standardized formula for estimating participation rates; (4) categorizing top institutions by variables (e.g., duration and participation rate) other than global totals; (5) improving the *Open Doors* survey instrument itself; and (6) devising more sophisticated data-collection techniques (e.g., via e-mail or the Web), with the aim of conducting more frequent and more focused surveys of leading institutions.

The data committee appeared at regional and national conferences all over the country from 1999 through 2003, making presentations on various aspects of data collection. At these and other focus sessions, it became clear that many advisers and administrators confront data challenges on a daily basis. Many international education professionals, particularly those at decentralized institutions, did not understand or accept the responsibility for collecting data for all students abroad, regardless of the student's program choice or whether the student remained registered at his or her home institution or took a leave of absence while studying abroad. Many did not have the resources (e.g., staff, technology, ability) to tackle data collection in an accurate and inclusive manner. Many requested guidance or offered suggestions regarding the *Open Doors* survey instrument. The committee collected these various experiences and began to tackle ways to satisfy the various levels of need in the field.

The first task was to collaborate more closely with IIE on *Open Doors* issues such as the design of the instrument, its dissemination, follow-up contact with unresponsive institutions, and so on. The data committee and IIE staff started off by clarifying the wording in various sections of the survey and having a subcommittee create a set of policies regarding difficult issues such as how to account for students doing two programs in the same year or those participating in programs that are organized according to a calendar year rather than an academic year. IIE also invited the chair of the data committee to co-write the cover letter of the survey, in order to make clearer to the field that IIE was partnering with AACRAO (American Association of College Registrars and Admissions Officers) and SECUSSA in sponsoring the survey. Each year, members of the committee divided up the list of unresponsive institutions and followed up with e-mails and phone calls to encourage institutions to submit their data, in order to improve the overall response rate.

The committee also conveyed to IIE staff the longstanding desire of international educators to have the survey data presented in ways that would more clearly represent institutional profiles. The committee requested that IIE consider creating and reporting participation rates (i.e., the estimated number of students from an institution who will have had an education abroad experience during their academic careers) to counter the trend of creating a ratio out of the number of students abroad over the number of students enrolled in colleges and universities at any given time. The latter makes it seem as if only one percent of students from U.S. institutions of higher learning ever go abroad. Since the vast majority of students tend to study abroad only once in their college career of four to five years, the value is actually more like 4 to 5 percent. The participation rate is a better gauge of the number of students who will have had an academic experience abroad once during their degree program.

However, *Open Doors* is currently a snapshot of those students abroad in a given year rather than a snapshot of a graduating class. Devising a participation rate through the national survey is difficult, and requires significant estimating since the cohorts being considered are different. The committee offered a methodology in 2001 that IIE has adopted (Hoffa 2001). Although it can never be 100 percent accurate for a number of complex reasons, it comes closer to the reality than the traditional method. IIE and the committee continue to refine the methodology and encourage campuses to calculate accurate participation rates by counting the number of graduating students who have a study abroad experience on record. In fact, *U.S. News and World Report's* annual survey of U.S. colleges and universities now requests that institutions report the study abroad participation rate for their campuses. The current challenge facing the committee and IIE is how to disaggregate the graduate students from the undergraduate students when reporting participation rates. Such a distinction is necessary because at research institutions with large graduate student enrollment, the estimated participation rate is skewed downward when all degree recipients are factored into the formula, because study abroad tends to be more of an undergraduate activity. In 2001–2002, IIE reported undergraduate participation rates for the first time, but only for selected institutions because not all institutions break down their data into class standing.

The data committee also requested that IIE create institutional rankings based on program duration, to give a better sense of the type of programming in which institutions are engaged. It has long been believed that ranking institutions only by the global total of students abroad overlooks the fact that this approach gives equal measure to students who go abroad for a two-week intersession program and those who go abroad as part of a twelve-month program. Ranking by global total also encourages competition among institutions, since it focuses on the quantity of students abroad rather than the quality of the experience. Many professionals are of the opinion that the quality is correlated to the length of time abroad and the level of integration in the host culture. Duration charts serve various purposes and recognize that there are different resources and philosophies regarding different types of programs. To date, the duration charts have been available only online and not in the published version of *Open Doors*. The charts are accompanied by an overview of different perspectives on the impact of duration (Hoffa and Spencer 2004).

The committee quickly realized the necessity of creating a central Web site through the SECUSSA homepage where educators could look for guidance

One of the first resources the committee created was "Data Collection Frequently Asked Questions," a document related to data collection in general and the *Open Doors* survey specifically. The committee methodically made more resources available online as the initiative moved forward, including articles on the subject of data collection that were published in NAFSA and IIE publications (Sideli and Koh 1999; Sideli, Vande Berg, and Sutton 2001; Sideli 1999a, 1999b, 2000a; 2000b). These articles went far towards achieving the first goal of the initiative—to raise the level of awareness in the field about data collection.

IIE and the committee also put together a few electronic surveys. They targeted the top 100 institutions in the field, which accounted for almost 50 percent of the students abroad, asking a series of questions on various topics including insurance requirements, internship tracking, and so on. The results are available online at the SECUSSA data collection Web site. IIE has since developed Web surveys for the entire field that have replaced the e-mail surveys.

INITIATING AND MANAGING CAMPUS DATA COLLECTION

It is clear that complete and accurate data collection is not possible without having methodical systems in place within various offices of a home institution. Such systems are only possible when all the stakeholders on a campus are consulted and involved. Individuals on decentralized campuses need to make contact with any offices that have knowledge of students abroad (e.g., admissions, schools, registrar, academic departments) in order to determine how best to collect data on those students. A basic census form can help in these efforts. (An example is available in the Data Committee area of the NAFSA Education Abroad Knowledge Community Web site.) For campuses where students who choose external programs must apply for transfer credit through the office of admissions or the registrar, a solution might be as simple as having the responsible office send the study abroad office a photocopy of each transfer agreement or report. Some offices have devised a zero-credit enrollment process for students who choose outside providers, a process that allows the institution to track such students electronically.

In each of these cases, capturing information such as the student's name, major or majors, study abroad term or terms, and the student's study abroad location and provider goes far in putting together a data-tracking system. Many education abroad providers will provide lists of students who are on their programs, grouped by the name of their home institutions (a practice that is strongly encouraged by the profession). If outside providers do not provide student profiles automatically, it is recommended that institutions establish communication with the providers so that such information can be requested on a regular basis. If students on faculty-led programs fall outside the education abroad office's purview, a dean or administrator should be enlisted to require that faculty report the students to a central location, either the education abroad office or another central unit on campus.

Once a determination is made about the best way to pool information about the students who participate in education abroad programs, a decision can be made about the technology to be used to automate the way data is captured. International educators have often clamored for a standardized database software package that would automatically produce reports designed to respond to the *Open Doors* survey questions. There are some database packages that can be purchased to serve this purpose but most education abroad offices have had to design systems that best serve their specific needs. Others have partnered with their institution's technology unit to ensure that the data collected by the university system includes the information required by the education abroad office for various purposes.

To make data collection a routine task, it is critical to include the responsibility for data collection as part of someone's job description. If data management and reporting becomes a regular part of an office's systems and structure, then data collection will not pose a challenge, as it often does in offices that assign data-collection duties only when an outside survey arrives. As argued at the beginning of this chapter, data collection at its best ensures the academic integrity of education abroad programs, serves to protect the safety of the students and the liability of the institution, and allows education abroad professionals to advocate on behalf of their enterprise.

OTHER DEMOGRAPHIC STUDIES AND RESOURCES

Although the *Open Doors* survey is the only nationally conducted survey on education abroad in the United States, many university systems, regions, consortia, and institutions collect and publish data on a regular basis for multiple purposes. For example, the University System of Georgia has been conducting a system-wide data-collection project for a few years, tracking a number of variables, including student outcomes. The International Office of the University of Texas at Austin publishes a comprehensive data analysis of all areas of international education at the University of Texas and circulates it widely to the field (2003). The Study Abroad Advisors Group of New England (SAAG) combines and shares institutional data across the region for benchmarking purposes. The Big Ten institutions (more formally known as the Committee on Institutional Cooperation, or CIC), annually pool their *Open Doors* survey results to share their institutional profiles with each other. The State University of New York (SUNY) system also does a thorough data analysis across the system, tracking students within the system as well as students outside the system who go abroad through SUNY programs. The University of Minnesota's Learning Abroad Center (formerly The Global Campus) regularly compiles statistical analyses to share with colleges and schools within the university to keep deans and departments informed about study abroad movement. These are just a few examples of successful data-collection projects across the United States.

Of course, surveys on educational mobility have been conducted in other countries around the world by organizations such as the Higher Education Statistics Agency (HESA), Canadian Bureau for International Education (CBIE), and IDP Education Australia, to name just a few. Oftentimes these organizations' surveys are considered more thorough than U.S. surveys because they include U.S. students who are pursuing full degrees in other countries whereas the *Open Doors* survey targets students who are doing education abroad as only a portion of their U.S. degrees.

Since third-party provider data has not been included in the *Open Doors* survey since 1986, the SECUSSA data committee encouraged the development of a survey of providers to see what the data revealed. Nine third-party providers—American Institute for Foreign Study (AIFS); Arcadia University's Center for Education Abroad; Brethren Colleges Abroad; Council on International Educational Exchange (CIEE); Institute for the International Education of Students (IES); Institute for Study Abroad at Butler University; International Studies Abroad (ISA); School for International Training (SIT); and Syracuse University—jointly developed a comprehensive survey to collect data on 2000–2001 and 2001–2002 students. They funded the project themselves, hired an external consultant to collect the data, and reported the data only in the aggregate to one another and to the public. The decision to report the data in the aggregate was to prevent the data from being misused, particularly for marketing advantage.

What made the survey exciting for the field, but complicated to complete and compile, was the inclusion of information not normally requested by demographic surveys like *Open Doors*—home college type, types of housing used, types and amount of financial aid, various program models involved, language requirements, and so on. The survey included over 18,000 students. As this book goes to press, the data are still being analyzed, although the initial report, *Survey of Third Party Providers: Final Report*, is available. The survey was the first large survey of education abroad among U.S. students after the terrorist attacks of September 11, 2001, and it showed that there was still an increase in the number of students going abroad, although not the typical double-digit seen in the years before the attacks. There have also been recent discussions about collecting data on noncredit work and volunteer experiences. The Education Abroad Knowledge Community's Committee on Work, Internships, and Volunteering Abroad is contemplating a provider-based survey of students participating in these important education abroad endeavors.

New Resources for Supporting Data Collection

In 2001, a new organization called The Forum on Education Abroad was established to tackle a series of activities and projects in the field of education. It was designed for institutional membership, with the intention that colleges, universities, and organizations would get involved with the array of important projects envisioned. A recent data survey of The Forum's membership shows that after its first official year as an organization, The Forum's membership extended to institutions and organizations that account for approximately 50 percent of all students going abroad

Data collection was established as one of the five pivotal goals of The Forum (2004). Education abroad professionals have longed for sophisticated data analyses of various dimensions of the education abroad experience, even if the analyses cannot include the entire spectrum of students participating in programs. The Forum plans to coordinate statistically reliable, focused studies on segments of the population, and will pursue grants in order to accomplish such studies. Its advisory council has a standing committee devoted to data collection, whose membership is comprised of advisory council members and other experts in the field.

The projects planned for outcome assessment studies and curriculum development and academic design, two other major goals of The Forum, will collect data as part of their focus. One of the first challenges of these projects will be to develop a typology of education abroad programs, which will open pathways to data studies because the field to date has no agreed-upon terminology in this area. The Forum will organize and obtain funding for the projects, and disseminate the project results to its membership and the education abroad field.

The Research Roles of International Educators

A quick review of the history of our field reveals copious articles and references to the need for research into all facets of education abroad. Recently, there has been an increased focus on the need for additional research and on the dissemination of already-available research. This agenda goes back to at least as early as 1951, when the Council on Student Travel (which became Council on International Educational Exchange in 1967) was formed. The fifth of its five goals, more than fifty years ago, was to "assist with or conduct research that will clarify the conditions under which educational travel could most effectively contribute to international understanding and education." (Mikhailova 2002, 4). The need for research has continued as the number of programs and students participating in those programs have grown exponentially over the past fifty years. It is not surprising that there are more and more graduate programs in international education, such as those at the School for International Training, University of the Pacific, Lesley College, University of Minnesota, Boston College, SUNY Buffalo, and Columbia University. International education graduate programs are fertile fields for budding scholars and professionals, and every year interesting theses and papers emerge from such programs.

This combination of interest and productivity resulted in the need to update the original annotated bibliography in the field, *Research on U.S. Students Abroad: A Bibliography with Abstracts* (Weaver 1989). In 2000 the SECUSSA leadership team accepted proposals to update the bibliography. Maureen Chao's *Research on U.S. Students Abroad: A Bibliography with Abstracts*, volume II, 1988–2000 (along with the original Weaver bibliography) is available at the Web site of The Center for Global Education at Loyola Marymont University, Los Angeles and can be accessed through the Education Abroad Knowledge Community homepage. Chao's bibliography is categorized by topic, including cross-cultural issues, evaluations, guides, impact studies, language acquisition, general overviews, program descriptions, research, and theoretical presentations. A bibliography by Philip Altbach, *Foreign Students and International Study 1984–1988*, containing resources related to international students, is also available on the Web site.

David Comp of the University of Chicago has continued the bibliography project and updates the online resources on a regular basis. He has also created an annotated bibliography on the subject of diversity, which includes categories for minority students; students with disabilities; gay, lesbian, bisexual, and transgendered (GLBT) students; adult learners and professionals as students; community college students; business students; education students; engineering students; science and technology students; human and social service students; medical and nursing students; and articles on underrepresented student groups.

When her update to Weaver's original annotated bibliography was released, author Maureen Chao wrote in the online announcement:

> There are many ways practitioners can benefit from accessing these various bibliographies and examining the valuable research that has been conducted in the field of study abroad. Research results can be used to provide support for campus advocacy efforts and budget struggles. Ideas can be garnered for new program planning and development. Administrators can find assessment and evaluation tools that have been tested in the field. Advisors can find useful information on marketing programs to nontraditional students. Many of the documents also include addendums such as sample forms, course syllabi, survey instruments, and bibliographies. Together the bibliographies provide hundreds of references for articles, dissertations, papers, guides and other documents related to study abroad, most documenting research studies. (2000)

(It is obvious that professionals in the field are doing a better job of making current research accessible, but there is an ongoing need for additional research. As previously mentioned, there is a continuing need for serious outcomes-assessment studies. The Forum on Education Abroad has conducted roundtable discussions on this topic, posted position papers on assessment, and completed a survey of assessment projects being conducted by Forum members. Research is an area that is finally receiving a lot of attention in the field. From these rountables and other interactive sessions, The Forum's Committee on Outcomes Assessment has narrowed down a number of variables that should be tracked by means of assessment studies: language acquisition, cross-cultural skills, acquisition of discipline-specific learning, and emotional intelligence.

Questions regarding potential research topics often reach leaders in the field. The Education Abroad Knowledge Community's Committee on Data Collection put together a list of potential topics that includes study abroad and security issues, work abroad, career-related outcomes, destination choices, the nature of study abroad programs (e.g., study in English or second language, fields of study while abroad, fully integrated in foreign university, island program, or other), and international student participation, to name just a few. These "Data Collection Related Research Topics" can be found in the Data Committee area of the Education Abroad Knowledge Community Web site. The range of potential topics is almost infinite, so future scholars should not limit themselves to these suggestions. People interested in doing research in the field can contact the Education Abroad Knowledge Community Research Committee for advice and guidance.

Part I: Education Abroad as a Component of U.S. Higher Education

Summary

Professionals in education abroad today should collect and report data on their students as well as engage in, support, and follow other data-related research. The reasons for quantifying not only the students but also their programs and overall educational and personal experiences are multiple. In order to ensure the academic integrity of education abroad programs, promote safe and responsible behavior among students and staff, and successfully advocate among various constituencies on behalf of education abroad, it is essential that education abroad professionals devise accurate data-collection techniques. This has to happen not only within individual institutions and organizations but also on a national level. We can look to our predecessors for encouragement since data collection has long been a goal of professionals in the field of international education.

Even our predecessors were aware that the challenges posed by the complexity of education abroad programs and the variation among institutional environments create barriers to developing perfect data-collection systems. Nevertheless, improved technology and multiple pressures have contributed to the success of recent efforts to engage in more and better data collection. The eyes of the public are on the education abroad field today, sometimes because of the demands of globalization and its impact on higher education, other times because of occasional tragedies that befall students who study abroad. In all cases, the more accurate a picture we can present of who our students are, where they come from, where they go, what they study, and what they gain from the experience, the more successful we will be in our efforts to send more students on higher-quality programs with appropriate support and funding from our institutions, our states, and our government.

CHAPTER 4

Education Abroad in the Campus Context

Contributors: Maryélise S. Lamet, Mell Bolen

Did you work on admitting a student, giving academic advice, resolving billing issues, advising on a health issue, transferring a course credit, or designing a curriculum today? Many education abroad offices do all of these things and more, and if not daily, then certainly in the normal course of their work. Basically, international educators run a university in miniature, with the added complication that the locations are far away from the home campus. No one office or person can do all this independently. It is necessary to use the systems that already exist and to integrate education abroad into the appropriate departments and offices. This both prevents reinventing the wheel and makes international education a central and integral part of the institution's academic and administrative identity.

Education abroad, as a component of U.S. higher education, represents a diversification of the undergraduate curriculum and a broadening of liberal education. The major goals of education abroad—whether academic or experiential—are pedagogical. These goals stem from two basic convictions: first, that students who have experienced living and learning on the social and educational terms of a foreign culture will be broadened in ways impossible to achieve on the home campus, will benefit academically and culturally, and will be better prepared to face the challenges of the globalized future than students who do not have these experiences; second, that students who participate in programs that may not achieve these academic and cross-cultural benefits, due to their brevity or other emphases, will nevertheless profit from being exposed to other cultural norms and are more likely to return for cultural immersion at a later time.

Education abroad improves returned-students' classroom performance, assists students' development in positive ways, and makes students more likely to become contributing and empathetic citizens of the world. The value of these educational goals, in the context of the often narrow and isolationist strains of traditional American culture, cannot be overestimated. Twenty-first century higher education must prepare students to live in a world

Part I: Education Abroad as a Component of U.S. Higher Education

shaped by global considerations in every way. Education abroad provides a dynamic tool in achieving that important goal.

Whatever education abroad means for U.S. students and however profound its potential impact, it functions as an institutional activity. It lives within the pedagogical, political, and economic realities of the individual colleges and universities. While national organizations are useful to education abroad offices in providing evidence and support for study abroad, they will never determine what goes on at individual campuses. Education abroad belongs to all members of the institutional academic community.

The successful international educator maintains the challenging balance of being fully aware of the goals, values, and culture of the U.S. institution of higher education (the subjective context), while at the same time being imbued with the vision that international opportunity and global perspectives are critical to the formation of successful lifelong learners (the universal principle). The strongest development of education abroad in the campus context occurs when this balance is negotiated successfully at all levels—from the articulation of the institution's mission statement to the coordination of arrangements for credit transfer and student leave policies.

Education abroad advisers and program administrators who forget or ignore this contextual truth are likely to be frustrated and ineffective. International educators face the perennial challenge of maximizing, by conscious and enlightened on-campus planning, what and how students learn outside the campus environs, and ensuring that everyone involved understands and values this educational opportunity—formally or informally—as part of the academic process. This process includes students, parents, and other university faculty and staff. "Think globally, act locally" should be emblazoned over the desk of every education abroad professional.

Administration of education abroad programs occurs in a truly remarkable variety of organizational contexts. Some colleges are entirely new to the field and are tentatively finding their way. Others have in recent years made an initial institutional commitment, establishing a few programs and priorities, yet know that they want to be doing more. Still others exhibit a long history of program development and activity and have reached what may be a real plateau of commitment and activity, or, conversely, a period of stultification, requiring additional thought and institutional commitment.

Institutional settings for education abroad activities range from an individual faculty member's office, to the large single-purpose education abroad office, to the comprehensive international education office that serves the needs of short- and long-term foreign students and scholars, as well as U.S. students and scholars seeking overseas opportunities. The responsibilities range from advising only to all aspects of international education advising, program development, and administration. Even within the full-service office there may be no common ground as to staffing levels, reporting lines within an institution, or even objectives and mission statements. A successful education abroad professional not only knows the field of international higher education but is also fully engaged with campus policy and politics.

INSTITUTIONAL CHARACTER

International Mission and Curricular Orientation

Careful identification of the mission, characteristics, dynamics, and structures of the institution provides the first step in the development—as well as the continuing viability—of education abroad on any campus. The mantra "know your campus" cannot be repeated too often. Many institutions do not mention international education in their mission statements. Others mention international education, but say nothing specifically about education abroad. If education abroad is well established, there may already exist a clear understanding of the particular desired outcomes for education abroad within the educational framework of the institution and a well-articulated mission statement related to those goals. If it appears that such a contextual awareness of purpose does not yet exist, it is important to clarify the institution's international goals.

The benefits of achieving high-priority status for education abroad in an institution's mission cannot be overemphasized. When a global perspective involving education abroad is designated as integral to the undergraduate mission, the institution as a whole and the education abroad office are partners, and solving the challenges involved in sending students abroad is part of everyone's job. Since all colleges and universities evolve over time, education abroad advisers and program administrators must also remain in tune with shifting institutional priorities and realities.

While U.S. higher education presents a dizzying variety of types of colleges, universities, institutes, etc., the central purpose of all institutions is the education of individuals through suitable curricula designed by faculty and administration. The demands of the twenty-first century world call for intentional articulation of international perspectives and experiences with these curricula; the modes of activity will vary as much as do the institutions themselves. The types and locations of programs appropriate for any institution to use or develop will flow naturally from the academic departments present on campus and, among other things, the emphasis of those departments on teaching, hands-on learning, language facility, research, and so on. Only as the curricular connection is secured will the ongoing international education of students be assured.

Another way of looking at the institutional context issue is to pose a series of leading questions, such as those outlined below. The answers to these questions will not only help to formulate an action plan (by identifying the offices to work with most closely), but may also determine the most appropriate location on campus for the education abroad office, if this is negotiable. Learning the campus context is the beginning point for each education abroad professional. Following accepted patterns will in time open doors to developing new international initiatives as the campus code is deciphered.

- What are the subjects taught at the institution? How are students taught—in small classes, large lectures, through hands-on experiences?

- What are and who controls the key academic gates; for example, curriculum development and approval and credit transfer?

Part I: Education Abroad as a Component of U.S. Higher Education

- What currently drives study abroad at the institution? Is it an overall mission statement, student interest, or the existence of a minimal resource allocation to allow a basic level of advising?

- Who supports study abroad on the campus? Is it a few faculty and administrators, or are there broad bases of support among faculty, staff, and students?

- Who on campus has trouble with education abroad? What is the reason for their opposition?

Administrative Organization and the Education Abroad Unit

Large or small, private or public, the administrative character of the institution will be reflected in the development of education abroad policies and programming. The services offered by the education abroad office are usually suggested by its location on campus. Most offices are located in one of two divisions: academic affairs or student affairs. Within academic affairs, the office may be an autonomous unit that reports directly to the academic dean or provost; part of a unit overseeing all international programs (including services for foreign students and scholars); part of academic advising; part of one or more academic departments (usually languages) or area studies programs; or part of the college of liberal arts. Some argue that the location within academic affairs attracts more prestige within the institution and greater support from faculty, and that any office dealing with the academic aspects of a student's collegiate experience—whether on campus or abroad—should be located in academic affairs.

Within student affairs, the office might be an autonomous unit within the campus international center or house, part of the student union, or part of an office in charge of career counseling, placement, and other off-campus studies. On some campuses, education abroad programming has developed in the continuing education division, along with other off-campus activities. In short, the office that has primary responsibility for overseeing education abroad advising, and perhaps also education abroad programming, can exist in a number of campus administrative contexts.

Excellent education abroad offices are found under both the academic affairs and student affairs administrative umbrellas, but both have inherent strengths and drawbacks. Certain fortunate education abroad offices are located within a freestanding international programs unit whose director reports to the campus chief executive officer (CEO) or a senior administrator within the CEO's staff. This latter location may be ideal in that it reflects the fact that the full internationalization of an institution of higher education permeates both academic and student affairs from its core.

In small institutions, there may be no office per se, but rather the responsibilities for education abroad advising may reside within the responsibilities of a designated person within academic affairs or student affairs, or both. In such cases, the person in charge of education abroad advising and programming may not work full-time. This individual may have a split appointment as a faculty member or staff member of a student-services unit. The demands on such a person and the need to interact effectively with all other dimensions of the campus, however, are just as great as they would be at a larger institution.

Regardless of the reporting lines, remember that the range of services will differ from one office to another, and that no single office or individual will be able to offer everything to everybody. Offices located within student affairs may be limited to general advising and travel services, seldom becoming involved with program development, recruitment and selection, or academic credit. The academic education abroad adviser may have responsibility for only language and other academic programs, with financial resources, time, and institutional pursuits precluding the adviser from offering advice or programming in the fuller range of education abroad opportunities, such as work, community service, and internships abroad.

Whatever services the education abroad office offers, they must be clearly defined relative to its position in the institution and must accord with the perceived needs of students and faculty. The closer these services connect to the institution's academic mission, the stronger the foundation for the office's support and funding is likely to be. Only when the administrative position of the education abroad office and its relationship with and to other campus offices is clear, is it possible to begin to build a political support structure that can affirm and sustain its role.

Setting Campus International Education Goals and Policy

Of equal importance to the administrative position of the education abroad unit is the connection of international education to the institution's mission, goals, and policies.

When setting goals and policies related to education abroad, the education abroad administrator must think strategically about how best to integrate international education into the normal administrative priorities and processes of the institution. This allows education abroad to become a central part of institutional functioning rather than an "extra" or something separate from the home campus. While this involves a balancing act between the requirements of systems that function within the U.S. context and those with sufficient flexibility to meet the special needs of working with international systems, it is well worth the effort. International credit systems, currency exchange, and differing academic calendars constitute just some of the myriad areas where U.S. systems must be adapted.

The higher the institutional level to which an international administrator can take this integration, the better. If the board of trustees sets certain areas of policy for the campus then it is important to make sure that they also set international education policies in these areas. This will encourage the CEO and upper administration officials to view education abroad as an important and integral academic activity. Wherever possible it is preferable to use existing governance units or create subcommittees of them rather than form separate groups to oversee policies related to education abroad. This again will help faculty and others understand that international education forms part of the core educational mission of the institution. For instance, if the faculty senate sets all academic guidelines, then propose that they set the guidelines for international education. This will allow the education abroad staff to point faculty to the minutes or guidelines of the faculty's own committees, providing instant legitimization of education abroad policies.

Many campuses have a smoothly functioning system with one or more special governance or advisory committees dedicated to education abroad. When that structure exists, the key is to work toward integrating them as much as possible as opportunities arise—something that may become possible when leadership at the upper levels of the administration changes or during a strategic planning phase. Another important integrating strategy involves someone from the education abroad office joining standing committees such as enrollment management, student financial services committees, emergency risk-management committees, international development committees, and so on. Of course, in one-person or short-staffed offices, not all meetings can be covered.

The administrator must strategically decide what are the hot-button issues to consider or which are the most respected committees to join. Joining appropriate committees or groups allows education abroad administrators to know the constraints of the other systems on campus and prevents them from proposing a policy that other offices might see as an imposition. Also, through administrative integration, students going abroad encounter a university administration with a broader level of understanding of their concerns.

To make this policy integration work, education abroad administrators need to be astute political players. They must consult with colleagues across campus and be seen to take the needs of other offices and departments into account when designing policies and procedures. Also, they need to provide key faculty members and committee members with information that explains why a certain policy works best for international education and can work for them. Talking with committee members regularly and keeping them updated on how policies are functioning will give leverage to the international educator when proposing changes. This will also give the committee members the context they need to make decisions that favor the positions of the education abroad office.

EDUCATION ABROAD AND THE ACADEMIC CONTEXT: CURRICULAR INTEGRATION

One of the most striking developments of the closing decades of the twentieth century has been the increasing movement of education abroad to connect with the core of the institutional mission of all institutions of higher education—the curriculum. The relationship between a period of study abroad and the curriculum of language departments, which sponsored some of the earliest formal study abroad programs, is clear. To a great extent the development of education abroad in the subsequent decades represented a dramatic mixture of integrated and peripheral models. On some campuses, faculty and departments created both traditional study programs and more varied experiential models, to fulfill particular curricular goals. On others, education abroad was viewed as an extra which, while enriching students in terms of personal development, had little to do with the prescribed curriculum for majors, minors, or general and core education requirements.

Currently, higher education campuses across the United States are grappling with the forces of globalization in the world around them, and the call to internationalize has grown louder and louder. At the same time in Europe, major efforts to encourage mobility and educate future "Europeans" outside the traditional national frameworks has created models of internationalization that focus on the core curriculum of the European student. Though the general education needs of postsecondary students are a growing concern in Europe, still the primary discipline of study forms the heart of higher education there. U.S. institutions and education abroad professionals can learn much by observing these developments.

Whether the U.S. student abroad enrolls in a traditional classroom, takes part in field-based research, or works as an intern, the curricular connection is of central importance. As students and their families invest more and more resources in undergraduate education, this becomes not only a pedagogical but also a financial necessity. Gone are the days of the 'eternal student,' for whom an extra semester was not a disincentive. For today's student, the efficacy of spending time abroad connects inextricably to the academic degree.

Many modes of integration and points of interface exist, but the key is for the education abroad office to be administratively and procedurally well connected on the campus. The office should offer opportunities abroad that have clear curricular connections to the areas of concentration (majors, minors, certificate programs, etc.) and the general and core education curriculum. Different program models will achieve the goals of different fields of study.

Since the core of all institutions of higher education is learning—immediate discipline-based and lifelong—the overarching goal of international educators must be to create a process that makes study abroad an integral part of this learning for all students regardless of their fields of study. All students should be able to say, "Study abroad is a natural part of my academic experience." This can be achieved through three basic steps:

- Streamline and clarify policies for all procedures for study abroad.

- Enhance and enable the recognition of study abroad course work for major, minor, and general education or core credit.

- Situate study abroad as a central part of the lifelong learning environment of the university and its departments.

When the upper administration has "seen the light" in terms of the priorities of the international educator, the mandate for curriculum integration will come from above. In such an environment, the multiple levels of potential interconnection between study and/or research and work abroad will be presented to the faculty and departments with a mandate that will make the work of the education abroad staff much easier. Yet grass-roots connections are what make it all come together for the student.

The smooth integration of education abroad procedures into the policies and procedures of the institution as a whole has been emphasized above. Along with the careful attention to the mechanics—course approvals, credit transfer, financial aid processing, etc.—the importance of creating clear roadmaps for students to see where the course work or field/internship experience can fit into the home campus curriculum cannot be overexaggerated.

The best approach to curriculum integration follows the organization of the institution—

department-by-department, division-by-division. International educators must learn the culture of each unit and respond by creating advising tools, programs abroad, and faculty opportunities that fit the unique curricula of each. In addition, if the institution has general or core education requirements, attention must always be paid to the committees, councils, task forces, etc., that maintain the curriculum.

Within the two or four years of an undergraduate degree in the United States, space can be found for a student in any field to participate in education abroad. For this to work, the education abroad adviser needs to understand the possible points of interface in the academic flow chart for a student in a given discipline. Ideally, the student begins to plan early and identifies, with the help of education abroad staff and department or college advisers, the potential matches between the home curriculum and what may be studied or accomplished abroad.

Even better, the departments and general or core education committee work with the education abroad staff to develop a mutual understanding of academic goals and curriculum components at home and abroad to ensure that the credits a student earns while abroad may be a part of the normal process of advancement toward degree completion. This may lead to collaboration on development or refinement of program opportunities to further this goal. These options should include as much variety as possible so that students at different points in their academic careers can find programs that suit their needs. For instance, summer programs for basic requirements could be recommended for students early in their academic careers and semester or yearlong options developed for advanced work in a field.

Of course, when the institution or academic department has a clearly stated pedagogical goal related to global or international education, it will more easily integrate study abroad components into their curriculum. This may be the case at an institution or for an academic program that either requires or strongly urges participation in education abroad—whether through purpose-designed programs or the identification of preapproved destinations or courses. Yet, even when this is not the case, education abroad staff can make the curricular connection for students by maintaining up-to-date knowledge of and good lines of communication with departments regarding their curriculum, advising culture, policies, and procedures.

Finally, curriculum integration involves not only the student's academic program—whether the field of concentration or general and core education—but also the formation of the lifelong learner. Teaching course content is not enough; rather, students must be taught how to learn throughout their whole lives. This powerful realm relates to the largely undeveloped area of preparation for and debriefing from the education abroad experience. During these "teachable moments," students learn how to observe, understand, and respond to the world outside of the United States.

While international educators accept the responsibility to prepare students through orientation sessions, they often limit the scope of such predeparture preparation to location-specific information. In order to situate study abroad as a central part of the learning environment of the university and its departments, strategies must be developed to integrate cross-cultural training,

Chapter 4: Education Abroad in the Campus Context

observation, and reflection into both the orientation and debriefing of all students participating in education abroad.

Many opportunities for curricular contextualization of this type exist for campuses of all disciplinary orientations and sizes, such as full-fledged courses, mini-courses, weekend retreats, and so on. By offering this type of learning, the education abroad office proactively embraces the underlying lifelong learning mission shared by institutions of higher education.

The more actively the education abroad office engages the core educational mission of the campus, the greater the success of curriculum integration. Because departments and institutional goals change over time, international educators can best mesh with this mission through an ongoing process of day-to-day alliance building across campus. When the campus community views education abroad staff members as trusted colleagues involved in the common academic and administrative effort—rather than slightly exotic folks who create problems by taking students to strange locations—students will be saying, "Study abroad is a natural part of my academic experience."

The Education Abroad Office in the Administrative Context

With institutional policy as a guide, the education abroad administrator must establish working goals and priorities for the day-to-day functioning of the office. The two most common are education abroad advising and the development and management of education abroad programming. Next, it is essential to define the academic, administrative, and financial contexts in which these functions can best flourish on campus.

Ideals and reality rarely coincide in institutional settings. Fiscal pressures on U.S. institutions are a fact of life; priority setting must take place everywhere and necessitates a healthy view of reality from educational abroad advocates. Conflicts may exist between institutional rhetoric and reality; between what some members of the academic community want and what seems to be immediately possible; and between national calls for increased participation in study abroad (or at the very least an individual adviser's commitment to education abroad) and real or imagined institutional fears, hesitations, and limits. Education abroad administrators must find a middle ground within these conflicts to move the institution in new directions. In this process, the office involved in providing services for international students and scholars should always be seen as an ally in the cause of internationalism.

Working Within Your Institution

The impact of education abroad programming on all other sectors of the university must be anticipated. Almost every office on campus will eventually be involved in some area of international education. Whether interaction involves a central part of program functioning or simply assuring smooth services for departing and returning students, offices from academic services to parking to financial services to risk management may play a role. There are four general areas where significant interaction will likely take place. These include academic, financial, student and administrative services and departments. U.S. campus organizational variety is vast, but regardless of exactly how the functions are lined up, they will be critical points of interaction for all education abroad offices.

Key players in each area must be consulted and reconsulted to determine how education abroad affects existing institutional priorities and programs. The education abroad administrator's ongoing agenda should be to initiate, understand, cultivate, and maintain relationships among the campus's academic, administrative, and service areas. The many people who have their primary responsibilities in each sphere must be continuously informed, cultivated, and sought out for their opinions and perspectives. Where the faculty and academic administrators stand on issues such as credit validation or transfer and residence and degree requirements will form the foundation that education abroad offices use to administer their programs.

It is essential that the education abroad office initiates the contacts. Perhaps the words "Be proactive" should be stenciled alongside the inscriptions mentioned earlier. It is important that the first interaction with other offices on campus not be because they have a problem or concern about an international education program.

As noted above, study abroad programs must be thoroughly integrated into the academic mission of the institution. If absent at your institution, this integration should be regarded as the primary personal and professional responsibility of the education abroad staff. The task cannot be done by one person alone, and it certainly cannot be imposed on the institution. Collaboration is crucial.

Academic Departments and Academic Services

This realm includes faculty, departments, registrar or records office, academic advising units, and so on. Maintaining regular and meaningful communication with all academic units, including both those perceived to have a vested interest in education abroad, such as the arts and humanities, and others not typically involved with education abroad, such as engineering, will greatly facilitate the credibility of the office on the campus. Working with key members of the faculty can also be critical for addressing academic policy (e.g., program structure or credit transfer). Faculty with expertise in area studies or languages can be especially helpful in addressing issues ranging from program development to student orientation. (See Part I, Chapter 5, "Faculty Roles.")

However, in order to encourage study abroad in as wide a range of disciplines as possible, it is best not to rely solely on area studies or language faculty for this support. Sometimes the most obvious faculty allies will be seen as already belonging to a narrow interest group. Ironically, they may be as concerned about losing students or allowing others abroad to teach key curriculum topics as their colleagues in fields such as engineering, business, or public health—or more so. International education can gain greatly when positive arguments come from faculty in sciences, economics, or other less obviously pro–study abroad disciplines.

Many of these faculty members have studied or conducted research abroad and if brought into the program design or approval process are likely to have strong interests in seeing their students' educations enhanced by an overseas academic experience. Specific academic departments will support the programs and activities of the education abroad office very effectively, once they see that their interests are not threatened by education abroad. Effective use of electronic communication can foster regular and efficient communication with faculty across the campus. If your institution has one or more academic advising offices, they can often complement faculty support. Sometimes faculty members cannot answer the detailed questions students have about studying abroad—for example, how credit transfer works.

At the very least, insure that the academic advising units and the registrar's office know to refer students to the education abroad office and work toward the goal that all academic advisers on campus encourage students to think about spending a period of time abroad. Advising offices, as well as academic departments, may be willing to assist international education by adding this to their periodic information series informing students about educational opportunities.

Regardless of the precise role played by the registrar or records office in approval of courses taken abroad for credit, the cultivation of a positive, cooperative relationship with this unit will greatly assist students, faculty, and the education abroad staff. The education abroad office often knows more about the credit systems of the countries where students are going to study, and it is desirable for the rest of the campus to view staff members as knowledgeable resources. Reach out to share that knowledge and learn who the other experts are on campus.

Financial Services and the Development Office

Think beyond the financial aid office and look at all aspects of financing education abroad. Student financial services, the controller's office, and the development office comprise the three main sectors international educators need to understand. Of course financial aid is also important. Higher education institutions are legally required to permit students receiving federal and institutional financial aid packages to utilize their funds to help pay for the costs of overseas study. Institutions have some leeway in interpreting this requirement because it relies on how the institution accepts study abroad credit. Because of this leeway, maintaining a strong communication link with key persons in the financial aid office will help advocate for the best possible situation for students abroad. The benefits of policies that allow institutional aid to travel abroad and provide special institutional awards for the period of study abroad cannot be overemphasized. These policies will be more easily achieved the more integrated education abroad is in the campus curriculum and culture, and should be goals for all education abroad administrators.

Student financing does not stop with financial aid packages, because those packages must flow through the loan office, bursar's office, or other student financial services before the students can receive their funds. International educators must work with these centers to insure that the processing of aid happens in ways that work for study abroad. For instance, can the bursar process aid refunds based on the academic start date abroad, not the on-campus date? Will the loan office allow early signing of loan papers so students can do this before they leave the country? Will the loan office make emergency loans for airfare, deposits, or other fees that will be due before a student's aid can be released? These are just a few of the issues that may arise in the flow of a student's financing through the campus systems. (See Part I, Chapter 7, "Financial Aid and Funding Study Abroad.")

Beyond the students' funds, the international educator must also work with the campus office of financial systems, especially if running programs. Since many aspects of working with international finance are likely to require exceptions to normal U.S. campus financial rules, a solid relationship with the controller's office is a must. It is vital that whenever possible the education abroad office's financial operations conform to on-campus rules even when these are tortuous. This will give the office respect among the accounting staff, which will stand it in good stead when asking for the inevitable exceptions. The controller will trust when the office really needs a special process and will be more likely to cooperate in the creation of what is needed.

Finally, the development office holds a central place in institutional finance and should not be unknown territory to the international educator. At the very least, education abroad staff should be knowledgeable about how to get approval for seeking donors. Generally, the board of trustees, president, and other high-level staff set the priorities for the development office's list of approved fundraising areas. It behooves the education abroad office to be on this list if at all possible. Even if no immediate prospects are in sight, when development officers receive proposals from donors for international funding they will be more likely to think of education abroad if they have met with someone from this office.

Student Services

Many education abroad offices rely heavily on student affairs offices to help students through the process of leaving campus and then returning to it. Services such as psychological counseling, health centers, or disciplinary review committees may be involved in providing information on students' applications either before or after acceptance to a program. Health centers may also provide travel medicine services and guidance to students on staying healthy during their overseas sojourn. While students are away, these same offices may provide advice to international educators dealing with students in crisis. Offices such as residence life and student programming are vital in reintegrating students into campus life when they return. Even less-central offices such as those issuing campus identification cards or parking permits often play an important role. The campus information technology center is also likely to receive questions from students and parents about how to maintain telecommunication access from afar and how to reconnect upon return.

The international student office and career services office merit separate mention. Resources available through the foreign student office include access to international students and scholars for study abroad program orientations, cross-cultural expertise, overseas contacts, and occasionally, shared fiscal and personnel resources. Foreign student offices and study abroad programs have many of the same academic aims and counseling goals. Cooperation between these two primary international units can forge a very strong and productive alliance.

Given the focus of students and their families on the career outcomes of higher education and efforts to measure investment by outcome, career offices have gained a more significant place in institutional priorities. Thus, the career office can be a strong ally in developing institutional support for international education if a collaborative relationship can be developed. The career services office can assist students by providing advice on what to do while studying or working abroad to increase the chance of finding work there later on, in preparing resumes that highlight students' overseas learning to potential employers, and in advising employers who hire for international positions. Also important for the education abroad office, career services can help in creating or advising on international internships that might be completed either in conjunction with an education abroad program or as a winter or summer break add-on to the students' studies overseas.

Administrative Services

Among the many elements of campus administration, three administrative services should be singled out as being of particular importance to the education abroad office. These include the admissions office, computer services, and risk management. The admissions office should be made aware of international opportunities for students in order to market these to potential applicants, especially if the international educator's goals include increasing study abroad participation and encouraging students' early planning and integration of education abroad into the home campus curriculum. Admissions officers can offer a great deal of assistance in publicizing the education abroad program and attracting students to campus who are already thinking about study abroad as an option. Because admissions officers are generally experienced in producing information about the institution, they are excellent resources to assist in assembling materials and developing a marketing plan for education abroad programs. Working with the admissions office can help integrate the concept of study abroad and international programs into the larger image of the institution.

The admissions office usually provides the first point of contact with the institution for both students and parents. As time goes on, the student becomes the key player in his or her life on campus. Nonetheless, parents resurface significantly when the student begins to plan to go abroad. It is very important for the education abroad office to understand the campus approach to parental relations, and respect both the individual student's right to privacy and the family's desire—and in some situations, their need to know—as plans to leave the United States are made and while their son or daughter is abroad.

In this day of widespread internet use and even a preference by students for electronic access to everything from applications to returning-student advice, the computer center plays an increasingly central role in international education. Its personnel can provide technical expertise in creating online applications, designing a workable and well-thought-out Web site, integrating international education record-keeping with institutional data, and a host of other office needs. If nothing else, they keep international educators' e-mail working, making dealing widely across the world faster and easier than in the past.

Finally, risk managers also need to be involved with education abroad program development and

Part I: Education Abroad as a Component of U.S. Higher Education

management functions. They can provide insurance standards and advice, serve on health and safety committees, and help the international educator understand the campus climate around risk. Does the campus have a sophisticated understanding of international risk or not? The education abroad staff need to know this so they can educate key people on campus about these issues and so they can feel comfortable that they have the backing of these people when making decisions about sending students abroad. Otherwise, the administrator can find herself or himself in the lonely position of having made a decision that does not conform to campus practices. The education abroad office, in turn, offers unique knowledge of international issues that affect students abroad and international students on campus, offering campus authorities a specialized understanding of travel advisories and in-country conditions.

development, curricular integration, and administrative functioning at every level from mission statement to registration forms. The examples included here represent some of the most essential and obvious, but education abroad staff members should realize that if it is important to the smooth functioning of the campus and to students and faculty, they need to know about it. Of course, no education abroad staff can do it all and thinking strategically about which areas to prioritize for immediate action and which to postpone will be vital to the ability of the staff to successfully complete any one of the three. To summarize:

- Think globally; act locally.
- Know your campus.
- Be proactive.

SUMMARY

The number and diversity of cross-campus alliances that will assist the education abroad staff is clearly vast. These alliances provide support in policy

CHAPTER 5

Faculty Roles

Contributors: JoAnn Wallace, Shannon Cates, Tom Ricks, Roy Robinson

At some institutions, it is a single administrator's knowledge, persistence, and enthusiasm that are responsible for the beginnings of "internationalization." At others, the push toward campus internationalization comes from the initiative of a president or chief academic officer. At yet other institutions, faculty members are the impetus behind or collaborators in the establishment of new programming, which can include study abroad opportunities and exchanges, the creation of special degree programs in international or area studies, the design of special language courses, the establishment of language houses and internationally themed dormitories, the hosting of international conferences, and the use of distance-learning technology and collaborative teaching across national borders.

Regardless of the origin of the initiative for international programming, the education abroad office needs faculty colleagues as advocates for, and contributors to, almost all institutional goals related to internationalization. In both the "top down" and "centralization" scenarios, the education abroad professional must engage in a process of careful learning about the programs and personnel, and must use diplomacy and compromise to effect needed changes. A patient and diplomatic approach will pay off in a strong and cooperative international community on campus. Any college or university that contemplates internationalization without the involvement of its faculty risks failure. Collaborative partnerships between academic departments and the education abroad office are essential to internationalization.

At almost all institutions, even though there may be a general faculty consensus for international programming, not all faculty members are equally committed. Those in the language departments, traditional backers of study abroad for their majors, are almost always supportive, whereas faculty in the natural or social sciences may or may not be. Those who themselves have studied or traveled abroad or are active in overseas research projects are likely to be among the strongest proponents of students being given such opportunities. Other faculty who would like to have an overseas experience may find that the workload or promotion and tenure system does not easily allow participation in international activities. Young faculty in particular, who can be natural and energetic program leaders, are frequently afraid to be away while tenure is being decided. Older tenured faculty may have research and service workloads that leave little time for new ventures.

When academic departments run study abroad programs, overseas leadership positions may be treated as if they are part of a tenure benefit, with program leadership rotating around the department more because "someone needs to go" than because an individual is either competent or interested in being with a group of students. As a result, students may have an incredibly knowledgeable and experienced program leader or one who neglects them to concentrate on personal relationships and research. When an international office is established, faculty members who have been "in charge" may be reluctant to relinquish this role.

One cause of faculty indifference or even opposition to education abroad programs is that these activities may not be perceived to be relevant to or supportive of the faculty mission, as noted in numerous recent national manifestos on the need to internationalize U.S. campuses. Often, education abroad involvement is not taken into account as a part of the administrative or faculty reward system, and plays little or no role in tenure or promotion decisions; or, when involvement with programs abroad cuts into student numbers in advanced level courses or the faculty member's publication and committee service record, it may even be viewed negatively. Even dedicated and committed internationalists may feel that their international activities are neither recognized nor rewarded.

In spite of these limitations, significant campus internationalization can be concretely implemented only with a proactive and committed faculty. Faculty have important roles to play, as

- members of international education policy and advisory committees,
- international consultants to other campus committees,
- general advocates of education abroad and promoters of campus-sponsored, campus-affiliated, and other international programs,
- advisers and evaluators of transfer academic credit,
- resources in program selection, development, and administration,
- area studies resources for predeparture and reentry programming,
- administrators of departure and reentry programming,
- overseas program directors,
- instructors in programs overseas and participants in faculty exchanges,
- leaders of short-term programs, and
- partners in grant writing.

The challenge for the international education administrator is to identify the supporters and win over the doubters and detractors. While language and area studies faculty have traditionally been leaders and partners in international education, it is important to seek out faculty in other disciplines whose international interest and expertise is likely to have an impact on students in areas of study not traditionally associated with study abroad. The chemist who did graduate work with a French colleague and the historian who studies the Irish and Scottish roots of Appalachian culture are equally able to be collaborators in education abroad.

Faculty may come to these responsibilities with significant international experience, but without much practice or background in international education administration. The challenge is not to supplant what faculty are trained to know and to do, but to complement it with the evolving professional pedagogy, principles, and pragmatism of international educators.

One of the most important jobs of the international education professional on campus is, therefore, to work with the president, deans, provosts, department heads, and others, whenever an opportunity presents itself, to encourage, expand, and reward high-quality faculty participation. The 1995 American Council on Education report, *Educating Americans for a World in Flux: Ten Ground Rules for Internationalizing Higher Education*, written by a commission of college and university presidents and chancellors, suggests that administrative support for the internationalization of faculty should include the following actions:

- Encourage faculty to develop expertise in the global dimensions of their discipline.

- Encourage interdisciplinary study.

- Give weight to international experience, skill, and foreign language competence when hiring new faculty.

- Provide faculty and staff with opportunities to develop their own international and language skills.

- Include international service or study among the criteria for tenure or promotion.

These same points were made more recently in the NAFSA Strategic Task Force Report on Education Abroad, *Securing America's Future: Global Education for a Global Age* (2003).

The education abroad or international office can contribute to faculty development by assisting with or providing a variety of activities, such as

- including faculty teaching or research exchanges in institutional exchange agreements,

- providing information or financial support for faculty international travel or research,

- encouraging participation in Fulbright and other professional development opportunities,

- connecting international and departmental objectives to support growth of departmental resources via speakers, Fulbright scholars, international personnel, etc.,

- developing faculty-led study abroad— both short-term, discipline-specific tours and semester or year programs, and

- sponsoring visits to campus-sponsored or campus-affiliated programs.

Education abroad administrators can help "educate" faculty through dialogue, as well as by directing their attention to online networks on education abroad, such as those of NAFSA, American Council on Education (ACE), Institute of

International Education (IIE), and the Forum on Education Abroad. This can serve to clarify administrative mandates. This avenue can also be used to disseminate information on grant opportunities and national and overseas developments that bear on education abroad programming. It is also important to invite faculty to share what they themselves learn from their own professional networks and overseas contacts.

Faculty contributions to the international arena need to be regularly recognized and rewarded. This can include sending regular thank-you letters to program leaders and evaluators, campus advisers, and committee members, as well as showcasing exemplary international research, publication, or leadership in a newsletter, Web site, news release, or presentation series.

Education abroad administrators and faculty need to see themselves as partners in the enterprise of providing meaningful intercultural learning experiences for students. Neither can do it alone. Education abroad staff need the expertise of faculty to create and sustain quality programs, and faculty need education abroad professionals to manage the administrative details of these complex endeavors and to work directly with students. The on-campus roles of faculty are many.

On-Campus Roles

Advising

Overall, faculty work with students most closely and are the academic specialists in student advising, counseling, and evaluation. Ideally, education abroad advising takes place within the context of degree planning, and emphasizes the connection between academic work pursued on campus and that pursued overseas.

A study abroad experience may be incorporated into degree planning in any of the following ways:

- As a supplement to courses available on campus. Faculty members understand the "holes" or gaps in their own departmental offerings. Education abroad can both fill the gaps and enhance the institution's academic strengths.

- As a substitute for courses on campus, matching their content but offering students the added benefit of study in a cross-cultural setting.

- As a "flex semester," allowing students to pursue language or culture studies outside of their majors. Early intercession to include education abroad in the degree planning process may help students in underrepresented fields of study, such as the natural sciences and engineering, to preserve flexibility in their schedules.

- As summer or winter break programs designed by faculty and incorporated into departmental offerings.

- As a required language or cultural experience.

At some institutions, faculty have direct advising contact with students from the beginning, and the well-informed adviser can and often will incorporate study abroad into the degree-planning process. At other institutions, it is the lower division advising

Chapter 5: Faculty Roles

office that begins the degree-planning process, which is then passed on to departmental advisers when the student declares a major. Understanding your institution's degree-planning process and providing comprehensive information and support to the right people are essential to effective study abroad advising and recruitment.

Recruitment

Because of their frequent contact with students, faculty are uniquely positioned to recruit for education abroad programs. To contribute most effectively to the visibility of education abroad programs, faculty need to be equipped with accurate, up-to-date program information. The education abroad office may disseminate its program information by creating summary charts detailing the unique points of affiliated programs, or by meeting regularly with undergraduate advisers to discuss changes in program offerings and application processes. Because print recruiting materials as well as oral presentations can constitute contractual agreements, all disseminated information must be accurate and consistent.

The education abroad office can also support faculty recruiting efforts by coordinating events at which faculty can share their expertise, such as a region-themed film and discussion series, symposia on world issues, or informal country-focused gatherings.

Faculty recruiting may encompass scenarios, such as

- mentioning a program course in the on-campus classroom,
- inviting returned study abroad participants to speak about their experiences in class,
- encouraging students to include an international experience when discussing degree planning,
- disseminating information about events such as study abroad fairs, international visitors, and speakers, and
- facilitating connections with international exchange students.

On-campus faculty can support the safety plans of off-campus study programs by helping create realistic expectations among program participants prior to departure. The setting of behavioral standards begins in the recruiting process, when students receive their first impressions of the program.

Admissions

Academic staff are valuable resources during the program admissions process, and may contribute by evaluating students' academic backgrounds, and also by assisting with the applicant review process. Strategies for incorporating faculty expertise into the admissions process include

- seeking out faculty advice on a case-by-case basis depending on the student's major or majors,
- soliciting a dean's approval for a faculty appointment to a committee to review all student applications, and
- requiring students to submit letters of reference from academic staff as part of the program application.

Each institution should evaluate its needs in developing admissions and credit-approval processes. The role of the faculty member is essential to the process, and it is important to keep in mind the other academic and nonacademic burdens on the faculty member's time and interests.

Orientation and Reentry

Faculty members are often willing to contribute to information, planning, and orientation meetings set up by the education abroad office. The involvement of faculty in discussions regarding academic goals and systems of education overseas underlines the academic nature of the experience. Those who have lived abroad can also provide helpful insights on history, social patterns, and tips for survival and daily living. They may demonstrate support for the discipline of cross-cultural training by participating in group-building activities and cultural simulations. Students and faculty can benefit from the exchange of values and information, as well as the opportunity to see each other in different settings and roles.

Faculty who have spent time abroad can supplement the reentry programming offered by the education abroad office in a number of ways. For example, they can be enlisted to debrief returnees in postprogram exit interviews. Faculty can also support returned students by inviting them to talk about their experiences and new expertise in the classroom setting. Because of their frequent contact with individual students, faculty can also be encouraged to alert the education abroad office when students appear to experience difficulties during the transition back to campus life.

Program Selection and Affiliations

Many colleges and universities depend on affiliations or consortial exchanges to broaden the opportunities available to students. Such relationships, which are governed by contractual agreements, typically allow students from one institution to participate in programs offered by other colleges or third-party providers. Before entering into an affiliation, the education abroad office, usually in cooperation with an international education committee, will review the proposed program's academic offerings, student services, and safety protocols. Faculty involvement in this process is essential, particularly in terms of establishing curricular compatibilities. It is also important that individual faculty members are made aware of the affiliate review process, to minimize the risk that well-intentioned individuals may enter into agreements on behalf of the institution without considering issues of sustainability and reciprocity.

Program Design

Faculty, particularly those who are internationally educated, are excellent resources in the selection, planning, designing, networking, and implementing of overseas programs. Their insights into the functioning of overseas universities at which they may have studied or taught is similar to a "voice within the system." Overseas universities have administrative and academic systems that differ widely from those at the traditional U.S. college or university. Potential differences include the hierarchy of authority within the administration; the roles and functions of the faculty within departments, colleges (faculties), or the university as a whole; and the methods of grading, assessing, and evaluating students' in-classroom and out-of-classroom work. Again, as partners in overseas programming, faculty need to be intimately involved in the planning and implementation of an institution's programs—consulting on the types and varieties of courses offered, academic field trips, internships or service learning, and the development of independent studies or tutorials.

More often than not, establishing overseas centers necessitates the inclusion of faculty from a variety of disciplines and colleges. In order to justify the typical outlay of expenses, faculty time, the education abroad office's commitments, and the university's liabilities, faculty members need to be an essential part of overseas center planning and implementation. In many cases, faculty also assume the roles of overseas directors or academic advisers who need to take time from their campus obligations to insure the credibility of the academic enterprise. Because new programs require such significant institutional commitment, it is important that the education abroad office counsel the program designers about existing programs run by other institutions or departments. Frequently, student and departmental needs can be met by affiliating with an existing program, rather than "reinventing the wheel." (See Part III Chapter 1 "Program Designs and Strategies," for more on this topic.)

Short-term summer programs can be excellent venues to teach a course in an overseas setting. They are conducive to hands-on experience, they can introduce underclass students to new languages, or they can serve as attractive in-country orientation programs for intermediate and advanced language learners. Indeed, more often than not, well-planned short-term programs encourage enrollment in upper-level courses and embolden the students to try longer overseas program stays in their junior or first semester senior years. Such programs, however, should not be hidden in corners of the university where the light of safety and liability protocols does not shine. To make sure they are not thought of as the "personal property" of individual faculty (or the bright idea of a travel agency that offers free airfare to any faculty member who can get 10 students to pay for a trip to Timbuktu), an institution-approved and faculty-supported program approval process is crucial to protect the institution, the students, and the faculty. (See Part III Chapter 2, "Short Term Programs Abroad," for more information on this topic.)

Almost every college and university employs a slightly different program proposal and development model. In some cases each program is initiated and run by one individual who is in charge of both the academic and administrative responsibilities. This model is frequently employed in the development of short-term programs. Such programs are often highly specialized, reaching a particular subgroup of the student population. They frequently involve intense mentoring relationships between the director and participants. However, they are also marked by challenges related to sustainability, risk management, and the relationship between the program and the education abroad office.

The office can mitigate those issues by providing training and support for all directors of overseas programs. At a minimum, a program proposal process should provide a structure for feedback from academic departments and consultation on program design, budget, safety and liability, and student affairs issues with the education abroad staff,

Part I: Education Abroad as a Component of U.S. Higher Education

financial officers, university counsel, risk management office, and student services office. This process can assist with focusing the scope of the program; it can also document campus-wide support for the responsible faculty member. A comprehensive director handbook or manual should include university policies, procedures, suggested practices, and on- and off-campus resources.

Suggested topics for a faculty program director handbook:

- Academic issues, such as

    Teaching responsibilities

    Academic calendars/schedules for the program

    Host university courses open students on the program

    Cultural factors affecting teaching and learning at the host institution and on the program

- Host institution issues for the program, such as

    Exchange agreement stipulations and limitations

    Financial arrangements

    Offices/contact people for the program

    Organizational chart for the host institution

    Library/computer resources available to the program

- Home institution issues, such as

    Academic policies

    Understanding of how the program fits with degree requirements

    Registration/credit procedures

    Hiring and compensation procedures for directors and staff

    Internship protocols for students

    Budget and banking policies

    Contact numbers—phone Tree

    Emergency protocols and procedures

- Contract information (if not included in the previous categories), such as

    Compensation

    Faculty enforcement of university policies and regulations

    Sexual harassment and non-discrimination policies

    Faculty workload

    Faculty housing

    Faculty per diem

    Office space

    Facilities and equipment

    Insurance

    Tax liability

    Spouse/partner participation policies

- Student affairs issues, such as

    Housing or Homestay policies, selection, assignment, monitoring

    Detailed description of what it means to "wear all the hats"

    Names and contact numbers for local, English-speaking medical and counseling facilities/personnel

Student records, FERPA and related confidentiality issues

Predeparture orientation contents

Guidelines for on-site orientation

Safety manual

Contact numbers for the U.S. Embassy/Consulate and instructions for registering the students

- Cross cultural issues, such as

    Cross cultural theory

    Culture shock

    Local culture

    Specific information for women, gay students, students with disabilities in the host culture

    Case studies for further training

Grant Writing and Research

Research collaboration between education abroad professionals and faculty frequently yields powerful results because of the different strengths the two constituencies bring to the endeavor. Whereas the education abroad administrator can assist faculty with making research connections abroad, the faculty can contribute expertise to projects involving grant writing, data collection, and publishing.

Faculty-level international exchange can support the mission of individual departments by facilitating innovative and collaborative research; it also can support the interests of the education abroad office by encouraging the development of international expertise among faculty participants. Teaching and research options can be incorporated into institutional exchange agreements. Such opportunities can help build faculty confidence in exchange relationships as a whole, making those relationships more sustainable.

Faculty are valuable and essential resources in the grant process. Many academic staff members have significant experience with grant writing in association with their own research. Their participation in international education grants is often required by grant makers and donors. Faculty can contribute valuable expertise not only during the proposal phase, but also during the assessment phase.

Over the past decade, international educators have been asked to be more proactive and skilled in assessing the value of their work, the academic growth of their students, and the internationalization process in their institutions. The faculty role in designing research surveys and data collecting instruments is *essential* for two reasons:

Many have been trained in field work methodologies. As such, they are prepared to collect and assess data, and then analyze the findings within various theoretical frameworks.

Trained faculty are excellent evaluators of the data and analyses collected and shaped by international educators, and are able to recommend ways of editing and publishing such data.

Participation on Committees

The international education professional needs to be aware of the dynamics of the service component of a faculty member's job. At each institution, teaching, service, and publications are valued in different proportions. The willingness and energy with which faculty members will participate in committees is often determined by their perception of the importance of committee participation in the promotion and tenure process.

Having a functional faculty committee associated with education abroad and other campus international aspects is essential. Models for these committees vary with the make-up of the institution and the size and strength of its international efforts. In larger institutions, there may be several regional committees. For the education abroad office, a faculty advisory committee can be of tremendous help in establishing policies that will be followed and respected by the faculty, creating and affiliating with programs that will support and be supported by the curriculum, disseminating information to faculty and students, and dealing with appeals and problems that inevitably arise in the selection and evaluation of students for study abroad.

The committee should include representation across disciplines and a mix of seasoned international veterans and newcomers anxious to develop international expertise. It is good to include the student services, enrollment, and financial offices, too. Many colleges also appoint returned study abroad students and international students to the international education committee. While the chief international officer or education abroad adviser should have a role in the selection of committee members, it is best to have them appointed by the chief academic officer so that service in this capacity can be valued equally with other committee work.

On a campus just beginning to internationalize, the international committee can be instrumental in developing a strategic plan, presenting the rationale and action plan to the administration, and winning over its colleagues to the benefits of internationalization.

Advocacy

The role of advocate for international education comes naturally to many faculty members who see the overarching importance of internationalizing their institution's staff, faculty, courses, and campus. Faculty are key advocates within departments for shaping the hiring process in favor of candidates with international interests and experience. The same role can be critical within college deans' meetings, or within ten-year accreditation committees. Faculty are natural allies in encouraging students to include education abroad in their four-year plans, and can act as education abroad promoters within public forums and their own departments.

In addition to having advocates who serve on the education abroad advisory committee, it is good to have faculty friends on other committees such as budget (to make sure that education abroad is adequately funded), financial aid (to preserve student aid for the year or semester abroad), curriculum (to have a sympathetic ear for proposed new overseas program credits), student academic appeals (to hold the line on admissions standards or behavioral expectations for programs abroad), strategic planning (to be sure that internationalization has a prominent place in the institution's goals), and promotion and tenure (to encourage support and recognition of faculty international activities).

As researchers and lecturers, many faculty have accomplished public relations and communicative skills that work very well in on-campus contexts, such as a Parents or Candidates' weekend, during Alumni week, or in an interview with local media or their national affiliates. Many faculty appreciate being included in the education abroad office's orientation sessions for education abroad, as well as in welcome-back sessions. Meeting and talking with students before and after an experience abroad can be an eye-opening experience for faculty.

Overall, the on-campus roles of faculty are many and diverse. The international educator may need to be imaginative in seeking out faculty to assist in the multiple tasks faced daily by the office of international programs. Faculty members as colleagues, allies, and advocates enrich and enhance international programs, and generally contribute to the professional development of international educators.

Faculty Roles Overseas

Whether an institution runs stand-alone programs or works with overseas institutions or agencies to provide programs for its students, faculty may be called upon to assume a range of important overseas roles. Such roles can range from assuming full administrative and academic responsibility for a program, to monitoring the academic credibility of a host institution's curricular offerings, to simply teaching as part of an established program. What faculty do overseas largely depends on the nature and purpose of the program, along with its design and structure. For example, a six-week study tour for an institution's own students dictates a much different set of responsibilities for the faculty leader than does a full-year residential program in which one or more faculty members may teach a course or provide academic counseling to students from a variety of institutions. (See Part IV, Chapter 2, "The Overseas Program Cycle and Critical Components," for a fuller treatment of the responsibilities of on-site program management.)

In his article, "It's Like Wearing All the Hats" (1995), John C. O'Neal, professor of French and director of the Hamilton College Junior Year in France, provides an insightful account of the demands of directing a full-year program. Serving a fourth year as director of the Hamilton program, O'Neal likens the overseas experience to being college president, dean, academic adviser, lecturer, psychological counselor, accountant, and even, in some cases, repairman. He describes these multiple roles as a series of constantly shifting responsibilities for which adequate prior training is likely to be minimal and on-the-spot problem-solving ability critical.

What is crucial in each and every overseas instance is that faculty clearly understand what their institution demands of them before they are asked to accept these responsibilities, and that the duties and the lines of authority and responsibility are reviewed and understood by all concerned, well in advance of departure. Additionally, there need to be unambiguous channels of communication with both the home institution or provider and the host institution, as well as a lucid understanding of the resources available at the program site. Flexibility is essential. Faculty will need to be available around the clock to deal with the unexpected, and must consider how comfortable they will be spending considerable amounts of time with students, local faculty, and administrators. It is also important for faculty to understand that their pursuit of scholarly research while abroad must often be subordinate to their prescribed teaching, advising, and administrative duties.

Part I: Education Abroad as a Component of U.S. Higher Education

Although it can be trying at times, the opportunity to assist students through their experiences abroad and watch them grow both academically and personally can be extremely enriching for faculty. At the end of the academic year, overseas faculty may find themselves both exhausted and invigorated, and they may return to their home campuses with new perspectives and a new sense of energy towards working in their departments and in their courses. They will invariably have new contacts and ideas for research collaboration with overseas colleagues.

Program Director

The U.S. faculty program director has both academic and administrative responsibilities. In a stand-alone program or within a university or provider program, these duties may vary and overlap. Program directors have short-term appointments, usually one year, but the term can be somewhat longer. Many faculty program directors rotate with home-campus colleagues on a regular basis. (See Part III, Chapter 1, "Program Designs and Strategies" and Part IV, Chapter 1, "The Program Director and the Program," for a discussion of the work of overseas resident or program directors. Such positions may be short- or long-term, and are filled by a U.S. national or a host-country or host-institution national who works for the program or provider on a contractual basis.) The degree of contact and collaboration between the program director and the 'home office' varies significantly from program to program. Some directors are completely autonomous, others must strictly adhere to policies and procedures. The following discussion assumes that the director has a great deal of autonomy.

Academic Responsibilities

The program director is responsible for the academic quality and integrity of the program and generally acts as the academic liaison between the home institution or program provider and the host institution or locally employed faculty and staff. Depending on the type of program, the job may require simply relaying academic information from the home institution or provider to the host institution or local staff, and assuring that the expectations of both the participant and home institutions are being met. The director may also find himself or herself developing curricula, working with the host institution and local staff to make various curricular changes, and hiring local faculty to teach specific courses.

The program director's familiarity with the local culture, the curriculum, and the credentials of the local or visiting teaching staff is critical. Coordination of the academic program may require reviewing the curriculum, selecting and reviewing local faculty, designing new courses, and learning the local academic system. In some cases where local faculty must be hired to teach courses, the program director may need to provide training in order to make local faculty aware of the background and learning styles of U.S. students.

If the program is not directly integrated into a host institution, the program director may have to create the academic calendar and the course schedules. This will require close collaboration with the home and host institutions. In addition, the host institution may ask the program director to give lectures for local students and faculty on his or her area of expertise, or to discuss other fields, including U.S. culture, perspectives, and values.

Chapter 5: Faculty Roles

Administrative Responsibilities

In many cases, the administrative and academic responsibilities of the program director will merge. In addition to teaching and academic oversight, the program director is often responsible for the direction and day-to-day functioning of the program—and running a program that appears seamless can be a very difficult process. The quality and thoroughness of the orientation and information provided by the education abroad office are key elements in the success of an overseas program leader.

Upon arrival on-site, program directors should meet with the host institution staff to learn local protocol and how to work through the host institution's offices, hierarchy, and service units so that both parties clearly understand the expectations, responsibilities, and available resources for the program. When problems occur, the program director should know the appropriate person or office to contact. This is not always outwardly apparent at each institution. It is important to develop open communications from the beginning.

Arranging or coordinating student housing is among the many administrative responsibilities that begin before the students arrive. All housing should be visited by someone associated with the program to assure that it meets the program's requirements. When the students are placed in homestays, the program director may be working with a local homestay coordinator, who selects and prepares the host families for the arrival of the U.S. students and monitors the living arrangements for the duration of their stay. In the absence of a homestay coordinator, that role falls to the faculty director.

The safety and well-being of the students should be a major concern of the program director. He or she will need to be prepared to respond to emergencies and have systems and resources in place to effectively deal with any physical and mental health problems that may occur. (See Part II, Chapter 5, "Health Issues and Advising Responsibilities," for sample policies.) Another important function is dealing with disciplinary problems. The program director, the home institution or provider, the host institution, and the students should understand the behavioral expectations, policies, and procedures of the homestay program. This information should be plainly articulated to students during the on-site orientation. (See Part II, Chapter 6, "Advising Students on Safety and Security Issues.")

On their home campuses, students are provided with an abundance of support services and offices. While abroad, however, this is not always the case. Therefore, the program director is often looked at as a "one-stop shop" for all student needs. The 1994 September/October issue of *Academe* is an excellent resource for faculty considering overseas program leadership. "It's not a Sabbatical" by Roberta L. Krueger, "The Toughest Job You'll Ever Love" by James F. Hornig, "The Challenges of Directing a Program in Jordan" by Mohammed Sawaïe, and "It's Like Wearing All the Hats" by John C. O'Neal give first-hand accounts of the joys and challenges of program leadership and provide excellent ideas for coping with "wearing all the hats."

Student questions may relate to issues as diverse as registering for courses, locating research materials, a request for departure before the end of the program, negotiating curfew with a host family, or communication problems with a boyfriend or girlfriend at the home campus. Because of this it is very important that the program director be comfortable spending considerable amounts of time with students and that those students feel comfortable with the program director. Established office hours provide students with an opportunity to meet with the program director at regular times. However, the program director needs to be flexible and should be able to meet with students at almost any time, because problems will often occur outside of office hours. Overall, the program director needs to be flexible enough to deal with whatever may occur, including issues that may be of a very personal nature.

The program director may be asked to create or participate in the creation of the budget before departure, including the negotiation of financial agreements with the host institution and the establishment of bank accounts. Similarly, the program director may be asked to make payments to the host institution for local staff, services, or student costs. The program director will need to work closely with the home institution or provider to have a clear understanding of the financial expectations. The amounts and types of payments should be plainly defined and understood by both the home institution or provider and the host institution.

As the program provider's representative on site, the program director may negotiate agreements and contracts between the home institution or provider and the host institution. (See Part III, Chapter 1, "Program Designs and Strategies," for further information on contracts.) If a program offers internships, the overseas director may need to make contacts in the local community for possible internship sites, to educate the local community and contacts on the role and responsibilities of both the intern and the internship supervisor, and to act as internship evaluator or liaison to the home school. It is important to keep in mind that the creation and administration of internships can be a very time-consuming responsibility.

Formal and informal responsibilities will often overlap and the program director will be expected to supervise field trips, host dinners, and organize social functions. The program director should be aware of these expectations and should honor local standards without violating institutional policy (e.g., use of alcohol at social events with students).

Teaching

Program directors often teach one or more courses. Visiting faculty members teach courses at a host institution or program but do not take on specific programmatic responsibilities. However, visiting faculty members should be aware of the same issues as the program directors, including salary, housing, office space, facilities and equipment, and tax and insurance questions.

Faculty

The expectations and responsibilities of faculty can be quite different abroad. For example, students will look to faculty as local cultural experts, whether or not the faculty have particular expertise in that area. Even if a faculty member is not a local expert, he or she may want to incorporate local institutions and sites into his or her lectures to provide local content to bolster the courses when appropriate. The host institution may view faculty as an additional resource and ask them to provide lectures for local students and faculty. This can be a wonderful opportunity to collaborate with colleagues on projects and future research ideas.

Faculty who are asked to teach local students as well as visiting students will need to have a background in the local teaching culture. In many parts of the world this style can be quite different than that of the United States. Along with the teaching culture, access to libraries and other resource materials may be quite different than in the United States. The requirements and expectations of both the faculty and the students may need to be adjusted.

Visiting faculty can expect students to ask the normal questions related to the academic content and administration of their courses. It is important to understand both the home and host institutions' academic regulations. Student questions may range from wanting to know the add/drop period or the final exam date, to asking about the rules of the library system, to identifying the office they should visit to find help with a particular problem.

Role of the Faculty Spouse or Partner

Spouses and partners often accompany faculty abroad and can play a very important role in the administration of the program. Often the partner will find himself or herself responsible for various ad-hoc program activities. In many cases, the partner may be viewed by students as a father- or mother-in-residence and may be asked to advise students on a host of issues. Not only does the faculty spouse or partner provide valuable assistance to the students, but he or she can also be a vital extra set of eyes and ears for the program director, and can help gauge how things are functioning from both the students' and program director's perspectives. It is essential that the home institution or provider, the host institution, and the faculty spouse or partner have a clear understanding of the spouse's or partner's formal and informal responsibilities. If the spouse or partner will be assuming formal responsibilities, the responsibilities should be outlined in a contract with the home institution or provider. Formal responsibilities may include counseling students, organizing activities, managing the program budget, or translating on behalf of the group.

Regardless of the spouse's or partner's responsibilities, it is essential that he or she and the home institution or provider understand the visa, insurance, and legal issues involved with accompanying a faculty program director abroad. Again, these issues should be clearly understood and agreed upon by the home institution or provider and the faculty spouse or partner.

On-Site Orientation

Before arriving on-site, students should have received a predeparture orientation, either from the education abroad office at their home institution or from their program provider or, ideally, from both. Even when students have received a predeparture orientation, the on-site orientation is vital to help the students adjust to their new country and culture as well as to communicate the expectations of the program director and host institution. If the program recruits and accepts students from other institutions, the program director may be faced with a student population with various levels of orientation and preparation. This on-site orientation can reinforce the information given during the predeparture orientation, correct misinformation,

Part I: Education Abroad as a Component of U.S. Higher Education

and bring those who did not receive predeparture orientation up to speed. The quality of the on-site orientation sets the tone for the rest of the time abroad. (See Part II, Chapter 7, "Predeparture Orientation and Reentry Programming" and Part IV, Chapter 2, "The Overseas Program Cycle and Critical Components.")

Advising Students

As previously stated, students will assume that visiting faculty members are experts regarding the local institution and culture. Therefore, it is important for the program director to be comfortable in the local culture and to understand the academic regulations at both the home institution and the host institution. These may range from the add/drop period and course prerequisites, to registration schedules and procedures, to grade and credit translations. In some programs, faculty may have to know multiple home institutions' academic requirements and how those translate to the local institution.

Directing a study abroad program for participants who most likely have limited experience in a new culture (and who come from diverse campus cultures) presents a range of advising challenges that go far beyond what might be required on the home campus. Students will see the program director as someone who can alleviate the initial confusion and disorientation that confronts them, and then guide them along the paths of new knowledge and cultural integration. It is very important to understand the variety of motivations that encourage students to study overseas. Not all students will be as academically focused as faculty would prefer. Indeed, a student's desire to escape from the academic pressures of the home campus may be as fundamental as the student's desire to test himself or herself in a new and foreign environment. Successful advising therefore must take into account this complex combination of student hopes and desires, balancing the twin academic and experiential bases of international education.

Faculty need to take into account that overseas academic advising occurs in a cultural setting that, because it is by definition foreign, can be both liberating and threatening to students. Further, students abroad seek counsel and advice that likely addresses the "whole person" of the student, in comparison to the more limited version of themselves that students share with faculty domestically. Advising for the semester after the overseas program and dealing with financial aid issues may require frequent contact with the home institution. Emotional and mental adjustment problems can be a major challenge. A director can address these adjustments and transitions by offering frequent group advising and office hours for those students who are more comfortable with private conversations, building group cohesion, creating opportunities to interact with peers in the local culture, establishing a sensible pace for program activities to reduce fatigue, and providing sensitive leadership. Early impressions are important, and faculty will be looked upon as advisers, counselors, friends, and administrators. In these roles, faculty need to be firm and flexible.

As students grow and learn throughout the semester, faculty advisers will notice a change in the students' questions and demands. Slowly, the students will become more independent and less reliant on advising and assistance. As their familiarity with their new surroundings increases, students who had adjustment problems may ask their directors to recommend the best way, for example, to travel independently. Maintaining a resource library of books on travel, local and regional culture, and available community services is a good way to respond to the students' seemingly endless questions. Here, the key is to challenge students to try to integrate what they experience outside the classroom into their primary educational goals for being abroad, and not to see that experience as something extraneous to what the program asks or offers.

Preparing Faculty for Leading Programs

Education abroad administrators and advisers have a broad range of responsibilities, not the least of which is helping train faculty before they depart the campus with a group of students. It is crucial that faculty who are to lead programs be properly and thoroughly trained for all of the challenges they and their students will face. As noted elsewhere in this volume (see especially Part IV, Chapter 1, "The Program Director and the Program," regarding the work of the overseas resident director), the faculty member's work abroad is far more varied and demanding than teaching courses on the home campus, and faculty must understand this fact well before departure. The job of the education abroad administrator is to assure that faculty are appropriately prepared for their overseas responsibilities and are able to provide support to the students while maintaining communication with the home institution, especially during emergencies.

Of course, the program director cannot be expected to perform all the duties that a range of domestic student services administrators perform on the home campus. However, the program director does need to be briefed on issues such as student health, safety, security, and handling individual and group crises. The education abroad office is the appropriate venue for the development of a comprehensive manual and an orientation program that can be updated each year. Many of the necessary resources for training faculty can be found through national professional organizations and networks. Other offices on the home and host campuses should be consulted and invited to contribute to the orientation and ongoing support of faculty working overseas. (See Part II, Chapter 5, "Health Issues and Advising Responsibilities," Part II, Chapter 6, "Advising Students on Safety and Security Issues," and Part III, Chapter 6, "Maximizing Safety and Security and Minimizing Risk in Education Abroad Programs.") Concerns about liability exposure have led college and university administrations to centralize and standardize procedures and expectations for faculty leading groups abroad. Faculty need to be fully informed about such issues. (See Part III, Chapter 7, "Legal Issues and Education Abroad.")

Every overseas program leader, with the possible exception of those who were born and educated at or near the program site, needs a "culture bridge," a local contact who is regularly available to provide advice on everything from academic and social culture, to safe and unsafe places, to how to get from one place to another. The culture bridge person may also make introductions and open doors to professional and social settings that may not be easily accessible to foreigners.

Part I: Education Abroad as a Component of U.S. Higher Education

Summary

A wise and experienced education abroad adviser once said, "If you don't have the faculty on your side, then you're running a travel agency, not a study abroad office." There is much truth in this admitted overstatement. The range of challenges associated with dealing with faculty is broad. Particularly with programs abroad, the liability climate demands that education abroad offices have the authority, or be connected to those who have the authority, to create processes and protocols that will assure "reasonable care" in a legal sense, as well as quality and excellence in academic and student services. Education abroad professionals are central to the development and support of a strong, well-informed, and effective overseas faculty community who in turn select, negotiate, design, and support high-quality overseas programs.

CHAPTER 6

Credit and Grades

Contributors: William Cressey, Sara Dumont

In a past era, the international education staff member's main concerns were winning acceptance for overseas study options and finding ways to overcome objections. These concerns were reflected in professional publications and in the training offered to new staff members. In the last two decades, however, international education has become part of the mainstream of U.S. higher education. Although it would be wrong to think that the advocacy goals of education abroad professionals have been totally met, it is appropriate to shift emphasis and view the main task now as one of refining and selecting available options overseas so that an institution's international education program is in consonance with its overall mission.

WHAT STUDY ABROAD PROFESSIONALS NEED TO KNOW ABOUT CREDIT AND GRADES

Education abroad professionals need to have a good understanding of U.S. higher education values and norms related to academic credit and grades so that they can help evaluate their institution's own programs, other programs under consideration by their institution, policies and procedures used or suggested by overseas staff, proposals submitted by students, and more generally, the academic viability of any study abroad program or of any single component of a program, such as an internship option. In order to adequately represent an institution and help faculty and academic administrators make decisions about education abroad, study abroad professionals need to think and talk about credit and grades in ways that will both resonate with the institution's points of view and inspire confidence in faculty and administrators. Two dimensions are involved: the academic basis for credit and appropriate handling of grades in a study abroad context, and the mechanics of getting study abroad credits and grades accepted and correctly recorded at the student's home institution.

Academic Credit

What Is Academic Credit? What Is It For?

Academic credit is a measure of academic work, learning, achievement, or progress towards a particular degree. The exact definition of the first word, "academic," varies somewhat from institution to institution and even from program to program within an institution, but almost everyone makes some sort of distinction between academic learning and other forms of learning. For example, educational institutions are unlikely to consider learning how the streets and avenues of New York are laid out, which blocks are long and which are short, what streets are one-way, etc., to be academic learning. In addition, most academics today will agree that a credit-worthy form of learning differs from other forms of learning by being structured in certain ways and organized into coherent blocks of facts and concepts that are related in meaningful ways. Thus, while a study abroad participant (or a tourist for that matter) wandering around the streets of Paris for an afternoon might learn a number of interesting facts (about that city's language, history, sociology, popular culture, food, and economy), any one of which might under certain circumstances be included in an academic course, the random and disconnected nature of what has been learned would, in the minds of most academics, disqualify the experience as a credit-bearing one.

Study abroad professionals are fond of saying that what students gain just by being overseas is so valuable that any deficiencies in the academic portion of a program are more than made up for by the experiential (wandering around) kind of learning. An argument of this sort is useful and persuasive in some quarters but falls on deaf ears in others. The decision of whether or not to use such an argument will depend on the local situation. But whatever is decided, an education abroad professional's standing in the eyes of faculty and academic staff will be enhanced if he or she can demonstrate understanding of the distinction between academic and nonacademic learning.

There is a good deal of variation concerning how the second word, "work," should be quantified. Is it a measure of effort? Seat time? Achievement? Knowledge and skills acquired? In a study abroad context, this question becomes even more complicated because various cultures do not have identical views of the purposes of higher education, the nature of classroom and out-of-class work, and the relationship between various levels of achievement and the amount of credit assigned. Essentially, an education abroad professional is faced with the task of mediating between U.S. and host-country definitions of credit.

How Credit is Reckoned at Most U.S. Institutions

Although the task of defining credit is a daunting one, and one that will differ in crucial ways depending on which foreign country is involved, a useful starting point is understanding a typical U.S. definition of the amount of work associated with a certain amount of credit, for example, three semester hours.

In the United States, three semester hours of credit usually implies that the course

- constitutes approximately one-fortieth of a student's baccalaureate degree,

- constitutes approximately one-fifth of a full-time student's program for one semester,
- entails approximately 115 hours to 135 hours of academic work, including classroom contact hours and all other academic work done by the student for that course, and
- involves approximately thirty-eight to forty-five (fifty-minute) classroom contact hours.

Among most other countries, there will not be as much concurrence concerning these criteria. For example, the required ratio between hours in class and hours of outside work varies considerably from country to country. Therefore, which criteria to apply in determining the correct credit value of a specific overseas course is a judgment call. A recommendation as to how to quantify work that does not strictly adhere to U.S. conventions is more likely to be accepted if the professional making the recommendation comes across as knowledgeable about how the judgments are derived at home.

It is useful to consider the practical application of what is known about academic credit from a U.S. perspective when organizing the material in two partially overlapping but distinct roles: the overseas program operator who is involved in the design and implementation of an overseas program, and the academic staff member (e.g., director, assistant dean, adviser) who is involved in evaluating programs, helping students make their plans and successfully carry them out, and helping faculty and other staff assess students' work and decide on credit issues.

The Role of the Overseas Program Operator

Study abroad programs are managed on site in a number of ways and by various management entities. Although there is usually some degree of cooperation between a U.S. entity and a local institution, the actual structures and people assigned to carry out various roles vary significantly. In some cases, an individual or a department of the host institution may be assigned to manage everything. In other cases, all tasks may be assumed by one or more officers of the U.S. institution that "owns" the program. In all cases, the on-site program operator serves a number of administrative functions, which run the gamut of services provided by various departments (e.g., the academic vice president's office or the maintenance department) of a typical college or university. The top person at a study abroad location is usually called the resident director (RD). As one RD in Paris describes the job, "It's like wearing all the hats." Although all the hats are important, the focus of this chapter is the hat that corresponds to the registrar at a U.S. college or university.

Looking specifically at credit and grades, it's important to understand what the RD *must do* and what the RD *should not do*. The RD's main function in relation to grades and credit is to ensure that an accurate record each student's achievements is transmitted back to the U.S. academic institution or institutions that will post the credit on each student's transcript. The respectability of study abroad credit and grades depends on maintaining the confidence of faculty and administrators in the integrity of the data reported by the study abroad program. The good recording practices that are common in the United States should be followed at study abroad sites: a registration record for each student's coursework should be put together at the beginning of the term, and rational deadlines concerning when a student can change from one course to another or withdraw from a course should be established and adhered to. At the end of the term, the RD's role is to record the grades given by each of the professors, and in some cases, to convert those grades from a foreign system to a U.S. system.

Unless the RD is the primary professor for a specific course, the RD should *not* be determining who gets what grades or influencing the professors' judgments. Nor should the RD include considerations about how hard or easy a particular teacher is. There should be an official grade-conversion table for the program and the RD should apply it mechanically to all grades.

The Role of the Study Abroad Office

Study abroad must be administratively feasible in order to have support on campus and for students to have confidence in the experience. This means the study abroad office needs to work closely with the other units on campus that have responsibility for various aspects of students' study, such as the offices of the registrar, the bursar, and financial aid. Because academic credit and grades are the most crucial components leading to a student's eventual academic success and graduation, these parts of the study abroad experience must be seamlessly worked into the institution's administrative structure. It is the role of the study abroad office to ensure that this happens.

The study abroad office should develop policies and procedures that are congruent with the institution's existing ones for corresponding situations on campus. This not only facilitates data entry and paperwork, but also demonstrates to other administrators that study abroad can be an integral part of the institution's standard academic offerings. The institution must first develop a mechanism to maintain an appropriate enrollment status on the home campus for students who are studying abroad There will still, however, be much about study abroad that will not fit into standard administrative procedures, because the variety of study abroad programs usually means the administrative system will need to accommodate a variety of registration and billing instructions. The study abroad office should negotiate carefully with other key administrators to develop the necessary flexibility in the system for accommodating study abroad. Before entering these negotiations, education abroad administrators should investigate how their institutions' registration and billing procedures actually work.

Determining what study abroad experiences are creditworthy and how courses abroad relate to coursework on the home campus are other key issues for the study abroad office. In some institutions, study abroad office staff make these decisions; in others, the registrar's office or the faculty make them. When individuals other than faculty make these decisions, however, difficulties in promoting study abroad can emerge. This is because determining what is creditworthy, especially what is creditworthy within a discipline and according to a department's own approach to the discipline, is really an academic decision.

If determining what is creditworthy is left up to administrators rather than appropriate faculty members (e.g., the chair, the director of undergraduate studies, or an academic adviser), study abroad is likely to encounter resistance from the faculty at some stage. This approach also exposes the study abroad office to disputes from students and faculty concerning the kind of credit awarded for courses taken abroad. Therefore, it is in the study abroad office's best interest to develop a procedure for faculty involvement and approval for determining credit for study abroad. The study abroad office should still remain the central liaison among students, home institution faculty, and the study abroad program or host institution, in order to answer the many questions concerning the differences in educational systems and to maintain consistency in the conversion of credit and grades from abroad.

Types of Creditworthy Activities

The college years comprise learning, growth, and development of many kinds, and not all kinds earn credit. In the U.S. higher education framework, academic credit is typically associated with specifically structured and organized learning usually related to one or more of an inventory of academic disciplines, and it involves particular types of learning activities through which the student acquires knowledge, synthesizes facts and concepts, develops critical thinking and the ability to analyze, and perhaps conducts original research.

The range of activities for which academic credit is granted varies considerably from one institution to another. Whereas one college or university may insist on a classroom setting for the award of credit, another may apply a much broader standard and include other activities such as internships, field seminars, and service learning experiences. As exponents of the value of international education, education abroad professionals are often in a position to urge their colleagues in other branches of an educational institution to take a wider view and award credit for nonclassroom activities through which a participant gains international awareness.

There is ample anecdotal evidence to suggest that through study abroad a participant gains important insights outside of class that students who stay at home will never fully understand. Almost all former participants of study abroad programs rank the experience as one of the most life-changing parts of their undergraduate years. But since the same could be said of participation on an athletic team, volunteer service in Appalachia, playing a major role in a political campaign, or even singing Mozart's *Requiem*, education abroad professionals will achieve better results if they base their credit proposals on forms of learning activity that are accepted by the institution in a domestic setting. For example, if a college grants credit for service learning carried on in the United States, then it makes sense to argue for credit for overseas service-learning activities.

Often, the education abroad professional's most effective approach is to recommend credit for types of activities that have gained wide acceptance in the past, such as

- traditional classroom activities, including lecture and discussion coupled with reading and writing assignments, capped by a final examination;

- laboratories and practicums, in which students learn primarily by carrying out some specified activity under the supervision of a qualified academic with teaching experience in the relevant discipline (in activities of this type, more hours per credit are typically required than in classroom-based activities);

- independent study or directed tutorials, in which a student meets regularly with a faculty member and carries out a well-structured program of reading, writing, and sometimes research activities (in these activities, the contact time with the faculty member is usually less than the usual fifteen hours per credit, and this is compensated for by the fact that it's one-on-one time, and presumably the main learning activity is the reading/research);

- internships, which are typically structured opportunities to work several hours per week in a company or other institution; usually the work is uncompensated and the presumption is that the intern benefits from the experience and learns from an on-the-job mentor. When an internship is combined with a well-designed and directly related academic module, some, but not all, institutions will grant credit for the learning experience; and

- field seminars and other nontraditional teaching modalities, which can range from courses held in museums (which differ very little from traditional classroom-based courses) to expeditions to historically significant locales such as archeological sites.

Institutional reactions to these kinds of learning experiences vary considerably. In general, institutions are more likely to grant credit if the activities included hang together in a way that resembles the content of a course and allows for the sort of intellectual integration that should be expected in an academic course. For example, several guided visits to Moorish architectural sites in southern Spain, conducted by a professor in an appropriate discipline and focused on a theme such as how Moorish influences have contributed to Andalusian culture, might be accepted for credit, whereas visits to Notre Dame, the Eiffel tower, and other Parisian tourist attractions conducted in the style of a commercial tour operator probably would not be accepted.

Finally, the award of credit is most readily accepted by faculty if a student's achievement of the activity's learning goals can be objectively measured. Measuring acquisition of knowledge is fairly straightforward. Cross-cultural understanding, on the other hand, is difficult to pin down. The field of education abroad is striving to develop reliable instruments to document a student's growth and development in this domain, and perhaps once a credible methodology has been established, the less-traditional learning activities associated with education abroad may gain acceptability.

The Concept of the "School of Record"

The concept of a "school of record" is common to many educational activities that involve a student enrolling in more than one school. For example, the school district of Round Rock, Texas, which apparently allows its students to take courses at more than one school, defines the term as follows: "The school where a student's official records are maintained is the student's School-of-Record" (Round Rock Independent School District, 2005). In study abroad, the concept has a narrower meaning that is linked to a specific academic term. For many purposes, the most important of which are

Chapter 6: Credit and Grades

transcripting and financial aid, a student who is attending classes and making progress towards a degree must always be enrolled at some specific degree-granting institution.

By enrolling a student for a specific term, an institution is agreeing to do the following:

- maintain the student's enrollment status during that term, and certify to federal financial aid authorities, for example, whether or not the student is enrolled full time;

- accredit the instruction that the student is receiving that term (i.e., represent to the rest of the academic community and to the general public that the courses and other academic activities undertaken by the student meet the academic standards of the institution); and

- receive the student's grades from professors and record those grades on a "transcript," certifying the credits and grades thus earned as its own (as opposed to transfer credit, for example). In study abroad, this concept is extremely important but, unfortunately, not completely understood by everyone involved.

A study abroad professional who is approving a student's plans on behalf of that student's home school—the school from which the student expects to graduate—needs to be sure the student has a true school-of-record for the session spent overseas. If the home school is not willing to be the school-of-record, then another academic institution must be identified to serve this function. In most cases, the school-of-record will be a U.S. degree-granting institution. This is particularly important in the case of students attending programs run by third-party providers.

The Role of Non–Degree-Granting Third-Party Providers

Although many study abroad programs are operated by U.S. colleges and universities, or by consortia of colleges and universities, there are also many excellent programs that are operated by organizations that have come to be termed "third-party providers." (The student is the first party and the student's home school is the second party.) Third-party providers can carry out many of the functions associated with running a study abroad program, but there are some functions related to credit and grades that they should not attempt to fulfill. Specifically, third-party providers should not serve as a student's school-of-record during the session spent overseas. This means, among other things, that third-party providers should not call their in-house grade documentation a "transcript." If a third-party provider receives a true transcript from an overseas university, the provider may forward it to the student's home school without question. If a third-party provider writes up and delivers its own record of what the student has achieved, the document is properly called a grade report.

Transcripts Versus Grade Reports

A transcript is a document issued by a degree-granting institution; a grade report is any document that serves to report a student's grade or grades to an authorized academic officer or a student. Although the two documents serve similar functions and are often equally reliable, the distinction is important because a transcript has an officially recognized status that a grade report lacks. The distinction may be important for students going on to graduate school. If the student's home institution records the study abroad credit as "transfer credit," a graduate admissions officer may ask for a copy of "the original transcript" as supporting documentation for the work done overseas. Documents produced by third-party providers are often not accepted as original transcripts. Study abroad professionals helping students need to be sure that, one way or another, some institution will issue a true transcript of the student's work.

How U.S. Institutions Record Credit on Transcripts

Most U.S. institutions use a credit-hour system to track and record credit, and require students to complete twenty-four to thirty credits in an academic year to maintain full-time status. Other institutions may use a course-credit system, which requires that students take eight to ten courses in an academic year. Study abroad programs administered by U.S.-based institutions usually record credit hours on their transcripts. Foreign institutions, however, may use systems that are very different from those used in the United States. The study abroad office will need to provide its registrar's office with an appropriate "translation" of the credit earned by study abroad participants to the U.S. or institutional credit system. It is generally assumed that a full courseload of classes taken abroad, however the host institution defines it, will come back as a full load of credit on the home university's transcript. How exactly these credits appear (i.e., assigned to which course equivalencies) is a matter for the study abroad office to determine in consultation with the faculty.

Types of Credit

The study abroad office must develop a policy for what type of credit students will earn on study abroad. Whatever policy is chosen should be based on academic considerations, and should be applied consistently.

Home Institution Credit

In this system of credit, the study abroad courses are given course numbers and titles in the home university's system, and students receive credit just as if they had taken the courses on the home campus. This system may be used when the home university is operating and teaching its own program abroad with its own faculty; it may also be used when the faculty of the home university evaluate and equate into the home system all courses students take abroad at a host university or with a host program. The advantage of this system is that study abroad courses are thoroughly integrated into the academic structure of the institution, thus allowing students to apply study abroad courses to their academic requirements. It ensures students will continue to receive all financial aid and scholarships. It is also the system with the highest level of consistency, because all courses a student takes as part of his or her degree program are treated in the same way on the transcript.

Transfer Credit

In a transfer-credit system, study abroad courses taken at host universities or while on host programs are reported as transfer credit. The procedure may be exactly the same as for domestic transfer credit, or the study abroad office may develop a separate evaluation process for courses taken abroad, to effect the appropriate transfer of credit. The advantage of this system is its simple administration. One disadvantage may be that students at some institutions will not be able to use study abroad courses to fulfill academic requirements, and another disadvantage is that most U.S. institutions have strict regulations concerning how many transfer credits may be applied towards a degree. There is also a lack of consistency in the treatment of students who are doing very similar things. For example, one student who studies abroad on a program administered by the home institution may be granted home credit, whereas another student doing a very similar program run by another institution may receive transfer credit. Using transfer credit for study abroad may also adversely affect students' eligibility for financial aid and scholarships.

Credit by Examination

In certain academic areas, some U.S. institutions will not grant credit until the student takes an oral or written exam administered by the home institution to determine precisely what the student learned. Credit by examination is most commonly used for foreign language courses and in disciplines that must meet requirements set by U.S. accrediting agencies, such as engineering, business, and health sciences.

Grades and Grading Policies

The Arbitrary Nature of Grades

Imagine yourself (those of you who still eat red meat) in a steak house ordering a fine porterhouse steak. Your waiter will probably ask how you would like your steak "done." Typical choices are rare, medium, and well-done, often with intermediate possibilities such as medium-rare. But how do you know that *your* conception of medium-rare (sort of pink) is the same as the chef's (really pink)? Without a description in the menu or an explanation when you order, you may get a much different steak than one you thought you had ordered.

It's the same with grades. Everyone knows that an A is better than a B, and so on. But does it actually establish what a specific student has achieved if he or she has been awarded a B or a B-minus by a professor? The precise meaning of each of the grades commonly used in U.S. colleges and universities varies from college to college, from teacher to teacher, and even from course to course taught by the same teacher. In spite of these variations, however, there is at least an approximate common understanding of the meaning of the grades A, B, C, D, and F. When a student has received a specific grade in a course, it is possible to at least form a vague idea of the characteristics of that student's work.

In a 1993 article in *The Teaching Professor*, J. H. Williams suggests some descriptors that can be used to understand the rough meaning of passing letter grades. For each grade, the author describes the student in terms of attendance, preparation, curiosity, retention, attitude, talent, and results. Consider for example the attitude descriptions for A, B, and C: "A-students have a winning attitude. They have both the determination and the self-discipline necessary for success. They show initiative; they do things they have not been told to do…. B-students desire to master the course material. They are active participants, they occasionally show initiative and seek out additional topics related to the course…. C-students are not visibly committed to the class. They participate without enthusiasm. Their body language often expresses boredom" (Williams 1993). While a reader may not agree entirely with every point, these characterizations do enable a reader to understand that A and B grades are both positive, and that the big break is often between a B and a C.

Problems with Overseas Grades

A general problem with overseas grades is that the differences between the United States and other countries are often significantly greater than internal differences within the U.S. higher education community. There are three sorts of problems that typically arise and that make evaluation of a student's work overseas difficult: (1) systems in some countries (e.g., France, Chile, United Kingdom, Australia) are based on completely different qualifiers, which are difficult to translate into U.S. letter grades; (2) countries that do use letter grades similar to those used in the United States may use them in radically different ways; and (3) study abroad grades can be either too severe or too easy depending on many circumstances and local attitudes.

Totally Different Systems. Chile grades from 1 to 7 with 3 being the lowest passing grade. Chilean students often say that the 7 is reserved for God, the 6 for the professor, and that, therefore, a student who receives a 5 has really done an excellent job. Yet would a "natural" grade conversion chart convert a 5 to an A? France grades from zero to 20, with 10 and above usually considered passing. Use of the higher numbers is very restricted, and some would consider anything above 14 to be an A. The U.K. system, used in many parts of the world, makes a fine distinction among various types of "honours" grades, while the only other passing grade is simply called "pass."

Clearly this system is designed to make some distinctions that are quite different from ours and it is not at all clear that translations to U.S. letter grades can be accomplished at all.

Grades That Are Too Severe. A mechanical division of the range of possible passing grades in a particular country into four groupings assigned to A, B, C, and D, respectively, may often result in grades that are too severe from a U.S. perspective.

Grades That Are Too Easy. The opposite occurs as well. Often, local professors have low expectations for U.S. students because of what they have observed in the past. They may think, "These students are not really here to study hard," or "These students are here to learn about the culture and to experience our country." Locally hired teachers may place a high value on pleasing the students and the program operators, and may mistakenly think that if they are too strict with the students they might lose the program. It is often difficult to help such teachers bring their grading practices into alignment with what the profession would like to see. It won't do to simply say, "Please grade these students as you would your own students." Just about any U.S. student in a foreign college will have much less background in the history, literature, etc., of that country than a local student entering the same college. To ask a professor to grade a U.S. student in a course on the *Quixote* using the same standards he or she would apply to Spanish students would be inappropriate. On the other hand, if education abroad professionals can help professors with descriptors such as those mentioned in the Williams article, more favorable results may be obtained.

Grade Inflation in the United States. Grade inflation in U.S. colleges and universities is a well-known and much-discussed phenomenon. Grades of

B-plus, A-minus, A, and even A-plus are much more commonly awarded in the United States than in other countries, and grades of C, D, and F are much less common. It is wrong to assume, however, that the level of grade inflation is consistent among or even within U.S. institutions, or that it is nonexistent abroad.

Grading scales do not only differ between countries. There are grading differences among various types of institutions, fields of study, types of work being graded (e.g., final exam, research paper, in-class quiz), and types of courses taught by the same instructor (e.g., large introductory lecture, seminar).

Grade inflation is now an issue in other countries, with educators from Europe and Australasia making many of the same observations as educators in the United States. In addition, instructors at foreign institutions may grade their U.S. study abroad students more leniently, on the assumption that if the students were performing at the same level on a U.S. campus they would receive higher grades than are typically awarded to students on the host campus.

For these reasons, it is important for international educators to understand that grades are not simply numbers to be calculated, but messages about student performance that need to be understood in order to be correctly interpreted (Haug 1997).

Who Assigns Grades and Who Can Change Them

As in the United States, the faculty members who teach the courses abroad are the ones who award the grades. This means, of course, that many students will receive grades determined within an academic framework quite different from that used in the United States. Students should have a clear understanding of their host institution's grading system, and how those grades will appear on their home institution transcript, before applying to study abroad.

The U.S. institution must decide how to treat grades awarded within another country's academic system; that is, whether or not to "translate" them into the U.S. grading system. Some foreign universities convert their own grades into the U.S. grading scale for their study abroad students; others may provide a preferred grade translation scale along with their transcripts. Commonly used grade conversion scales for universities around the world are readily available, for example, from World Education Services (WES).

As noted earlier, many foreign universities rarely award grades that are equivalent to an A in the United States, and indeed may tend to cluster their grades at the level of a C. If this is left unexplained, good students may be deterred from studying abroad for fear their GPAs will suffer. For this reason, many U.S. schools simply report pass/fail or credit/no credit, instead of an actual grade, on the home transcript. This approach, however, penalizes the good student in other ways (for example, their eligibility for honors) and may encourage a less-motivated student to take study abroad courses less seriously.

A more satisfactory approach is to convert the grades earned abroad into the U.S. system. This does, however, require much more work on the part of the study abroad office. International educators will need to understand the various systems used by universities abroad and what the grades actually mean; that is, what message about the student's performance the grade is intended to convey. Only once that is properly understood can a fair interpretation and translation of the grade occur (Haug 1997, see also Feagles 1999).

On occasion, a student may contest a grade awarded abroad. The standard practice in such circumstances is for the student to go through whatever procedures the host program or institution has in place for contesting a grade. Most U.S. institutions will only consider changing a grade awarded abroad in cases where there has been a clear institutional problem with a course abroad, or severe extenuating circumstances beyond the student's control (such as serious illness or a death in the family). Procedures for adjudicating grade appeals vary widely from campus to campus; however, the education abroad office is usually involved. If the education abroad office is asked to play a role in the process, someone from that office should make sure that both the host institution or program abroad and the appropriate faculty at the home institution are consulted.

Options for Transcripting Study Abroad Grades

The home institution transcript should always note the dates and location of the study abroad program, the name of the institution issuing the original credit, the number of credits earned, and the titles of the courses taken. Beyond that, there are several options the home institution may choose for reporting the grades students earned abroad.

Conversion to U.S. Grades with Inclusion in GPA. This is the most fully integrated method of transcripting study abroad grades. With this method, courses taken abroad are treated exactly as if they were taken on the home campus. Institutions using this method typically have significant faculty involvement in and support of the study abroad program. Students are able to fulfill academic requirements with study abroad courses, remain eligible for honors, and receive all scholarship and financial aid monies to which they are entitled. Students are also encouraged to consider the academic component of their experience abroad much more seriously when they know the grades will appear on their transcripts and will count toward their GPAs (Merva 2003). There are, however, certain issues that need to be addressed. One is whether or not the institution as a whole, or academic departments individually, wishes to limit the number of courses a student may take abroad and still receive a diploma from the home institution with a major from the department concerned. Another is that the administrators at some institutions may hold strictly to the notion that home credit and grades should not be granted for any courses not taught by the institution's own faculty.

Conversion to U.S. Grades Without Inclusion in the GPA. This option is a compromise to conversion with inclusion in the GPA. Some institutions may adopt this system in the belief that it is not fair to calculate the grades earned abroad into the student's GPA, because the grades were originally determined in another country's academic system using teaching methods that may have been alien to the student. The institutions do, however, wish to report the grades so that students will approach their academic work abroad seriously, and so that students will have a record of their true performance.

Host Country Notation Only. Some institutions simply transfer what appears on the host institution's or program's transcript onto their own transcript. The grades are not calculated into the student's GPA. While this method has the attraction of simplicity and avoids any of the gray areas associated with grade translation, it can be problematic. Grade notations abroad can differ widely from those used in the United States. For example, in Australia the grade of D is a high grade, indicating "Distinction." A student with an Australian D on his or her transcript may be penalized after graduation when applying for jobs or for graduate schools, if individuals unfamiliar with foreign grades are evaluating the student's transcript.

Credit Only (Pass/Fail). This is the least-integrated method of transcripting study abroad grades. The transcript shows only the courses the student has passed to a minimal standard. At many institutions, the student must earn grades equivalent to at least a C or a D in order to receive the transfer credit. While this method, like the one above, has the merit of simplicity and a certain ease of administration, it is also the one with the least academic weight. Study abroad courses are not integrated into the home institution's academic program, but remain something outside the system, considered to be of lesser academic importance. Students may not be able to use courses taken abroad to fulfill academic requirements, or to count them for honors.

Some financial aid offices refuse to award federal aid for periods of study where the credits and grades are not counted the same as on the home campus. Posting passing grades only also means that students' academic programs and performance abroad may not be fully recorded. If a student receives a failing grade in a particular course abroad, that course may not appear on the transcript at all, as if the student never took it. This may encourage students to take their work abroad less seriously, because they know there will be few consequences for poor performance (Merva 2003). And this in turn may lead to the faculty and the administrators at the home institution viewing study abroad in a less favorable light.

Summary

Academic credit and grades are at the heart of any academic program. In the case of study abroad, which is strongly supported by most faculty but not universally supported, it is especially important that records be handled with precision and integrity at every step of the process. A good knowledge of U.S. values and practices regarding credit and grades is an essential part of an education abroad professional's preparation for the tasks to be undertaken in the job. Making sure faculty members see that professionals in this field understand these principles and apply them correctly is essential for successful outcomes.

CHAPTER 7

Financial Aid and Funding Education Abroad

Contributors: Brad Lauman, Nancy Stubbs, Charles Gliozzo, Elizabeth Lee

Prohibitive cost, real or imagined, is one of the reasons students do not consider education abroad when planning their undergraduate careers. The bad news is that study abroad can be much more expensive than the usual cost of education at the student's home campus. The good news is that more and more students can use campus financial aid programs to help pay for the experience.

Some students may not realize that financial aid resources can be used to make an overseas experience affordable. Others may think there are endless scholarships out there waiting to be tapped for that experience in England. The education abroad adviser is increasingly called upon to both provide access to affordable programs and be an expert on how students can obtain financial assistance. At a minimum, an education abroad adviser needs to be able to answer the following questions:

- What is financial aid?
- How do students qualify for it?
- Can financial aid be used for study abroad or for other forms of education abroad?
- What must the campus do to help students use aid for education abroad?
- Are there funds specifically for education abroad?
- Can money be raised for this purpose?
- How can the education abroad office help students find inexpensive programs?
- Can the education abroad office assist students in investigating scholarship opportunities for study and research overseas?

This chapter will provide ideas about how to learn about financial aid, make it available to students, develop aid specifically for education abroad, and help students shop for the best education abroad bargains.

Financial Aid and Study Abroad

Financial aid can be broadly defined as any assistance that does not originate with the student or his or her family. Financial aid comes from federal and state governments, institutions of higher education, foundations, ethnic groups, clubs, religious groups, associations, and private and public organizations.

Federal and state government aid is

- funded by taxpayer dollars, or sometimes by revenue-raising devices like lotteries;

- most often need-based (the student must demonstrate financial need to qualify), but can also be merit-based (the student must show some special quality such as superior academic ability or exceptional skill in art, athletics, or other cocurricular activities);

- sometimes targeted to special groups (ethnic minorities, disabled or other nontraditional students, or students entering certain professions such as teaching); and

- in the form of grants, scholarships, loans, or work-study.

Federal financial aid is governed by Title IV of the Higher Education Act of 1965, which is reviewed and reauthorized every five years by the U.S. Congress. In the 1992 reauthorization, language was inserted stating that it is legal to use federal aid for study abroad if the credit earned by the student is preapproved by the home institution.

Institutional aid is

- any aid funded by the student's educational institution;

- based on need or merit, or both;

- most often awarded as a scholarship, which is typically a tuition discount;

- sometimes targeted at special groups (ethnic minorities, students from particular areas of the country, certain majors, first-generation college students, etc.);

- sometimes awarded only to students enrolled at the institution; and

- sometimes restricted for use only on the home campus or in the home state because of funding restrictions or institutional budget constraints.

Because of the latter two stipulations, students who are heavily subsidized by institutional scholarships often cannot afford to study abroad, even if the term abroad costs less than a term at the home campus. This unfortunate fact sometimes clashes with an institution's stated goal of providing international experiences to all students. On more enlightened campuses, all financial aid is usable for education abroad as an entitlement of enrollment in good standing.

Private aid is

- aid whose source is neither governmental nor institutional;

- usually available as scholarships or grants;

- most often awarded directly to the student, who then uses it to attend the institution of his or her choice; and

- sometimes includes requirements that it be used for specific colleges or geographic regions.

Because of the last limitation, private aid may not be available to use while studying overseas. Private aid has the most diverse eligibility requirements and sources of funding.

Types of Aid

There are several types of aid: grants and scholarships, loans, and work-study or subsidized work. Grants and scholarships are most desirable because they do not have to be repaid. Grants are need-based; scholarships are generally merit-based and are often awarded to people who demonstrate a special ability or belong to a specific group. Most students receiving grants must meet some minimum standard of academic progress (e.g., enrolling at least half-time during the term the grant is used, maintaining a minimum grade point average, etc.). Scholarship awardees sometimes must undertake specific activities (e.g., competing in a sport or making presentations or appearances for the scholarship sponsor).

Loans generally have low or fixed interest rates with long repayment periods. Repayment on student loans of which the student is the borrower does not commence until after graduation (unless the student drops below half-time enrollment). Interest on some loans is paid by the government while the student is in school. The student may not need an established credit rating; for example, federal student loan programs do not require a credit check or a cosigner. Many loan funds are self-renewing, meaning that the money repaid by former students is lent to new students. Loans are also routinely made available to students' parents or guardians, though at less favorable terms and with a required credit check.

Loans have become a major part of the standard financial aid package. This trend worries financial aid administrators because of concern that students are borrowing too heavily and will graduate with insupportable debts. Education abroad advisers must consider whether borrowing heavily to study abroad is in the student's best interest. At the very least, advisers must help students understand the implications of borrowing large sums of money.

Work-study, or subsidized work, is based on the premise that subsidizing student salaries allows an employer to hire more students. Most work-study programs are government-funded and require a student to show financial need. Work-study can be used while studying abroad if program administrators develop an appropriate process for employing and supervising overseas work. Students may work for the study-abroad program or may be placed with nonprofit or governmental agencies. Since the extra effort and paperwork required to comply with federal or state regulations for hiring, supervising, and paying work-study students can be formidable, these opportunities are usually quite limited.

Where Can I Learn More About the Aid Available on My Campus?

The campus financial aid office is the first and best source of information on all the kinds and sources of aid available at an institution. The office provides information that outlines the types of institutional aid available to students. Funds available through academic departments may be listed, if not, the departmental Web pages may have this information.

For a basic primer on federal government programs, obtain a copy of *The Student Guide* (2005) published by the U.S. Department of Education. *The Student Guide* and other resources are available through the Federal Student Aid Web site (2005). These information sources, which are updated regularly, define federal aid programs and provide information on eligibility requirements and responsibilities of the student and the institution.

Most students receive a combination of governmental and institutional aid, and no two students are likely to receive the same package. The campus financial aid office is also the best source of information about the often-bewildering variety of private aid available to college students. Many universities now provide a search service for students who want to see if they can qualify for private aid. This is usually a low-cost alternative to the many commercial scholarship search services. Education abroad professionals should find out if their institutions offer such a service and how it works so that they can share the information with education abroad students.

What Financial Aid Can Be Used for Study Abroad?

The ideal answer to this question is "everything the student would normally receive, plus any special study abroad scholarships that can be found." Using all types of federal financial aid for study abroad is perfectly legal as long as the student is eligible and the institution has approved the courses taken abroad for credit. Many states pattern their financial aid rules and regulations on federal statutes and regulations, so that aid can also be used for study abroad. However, institutional and private aid may or may not be available for study abroad, depending on the restrictions placed on the award. This is a problem for students attending private schools where large scholarships are awarded. All institutional and private aid should be made equally available for overseas study as long as students are participating in legitimate, approved programs and receiving credit toward their degrees. Denying this support to needy students sacrifices the principle of equal access to all academic opportunities.

On campuses that do not allow institutional aid to apply to travel abroad, education abroad professionals should consider carefully the impact of changing the policy, and be prepared to present the case to key administrators for using institutional aid for study abroad. The financial aid office and the bursar's or business office can help the education abroad office determine the cost impact for the campus, since failure to address the impact of using institutional fees to pay for expenses must be addressed elsewhere.

What About Financial Support for Other Kinds of Education Abroad?

Most undergraduate aid is geared toward helping students make progress toward their degrees. If the overseas activity involves work, internships, field experience, or volunteer activities, most federal, state, or institutional aid cannot be used. An exception can often be made when the activity generates credit. If internships, service learning, or field experiences are allowed to earn credit on the home campus, the education abroad professional should find out how that credit is arranged and see if international experiences can be added to the list. The other exception is private aid designed to encourage an international experience even if it does not include formal study. Some funding resources for international scholarships includes grants for travel, social work, undergraduate research, the exploration of architectural trends in major world cities, and unpaid work at various ecological or biological research stations.

Common Policies Used as Excuses for Not Allowing Aid to Be Utilized Abroad

Federal and State Regulations Allow Aid to Be Used Only on This Campus

Federal law says that students cannot be denied aid just because they study abroad, as long as the course work is approved for academic credit by the home institution. Federal regulations provide for the use of agreements to contract out a portion of the student's education, thus allowing students to study abroad or even to study at a different U.S. institution.

Our Campus is Tuition-Driven, So Aid Must Be Used to Support This University, Not Some Campus in Another Country

This argument is improper with respect to federal aid. Congress made Title IV federal aid available to help individual students pay for their educations, not to support colleges and universities.

We Don't Have Enough Aid for Students Who Are on Campus, Let Alone for Those Who Study Abroad

An important principle of federal and most state aid is that all eligible students must have equal access to that aid. To deny aid to students engaged in a preapproved educational activity would violate the principle of equal access.

It's Too Hard to Track Students Who Leave Campus; Giving Them Aid Would Cause Problems During an Audit

U.S. Department of Education audits are conducted at all institutions that award federal aid. If too many errors are found, the government can restrict or even refuse further aid appropriations. Denying aid for study abroad programs if the credit is preapproved by the institution is against federal law. Special arrangements must be made to properly track students and their aid. Education abroad professionals should ask the financial aid office what special information is needed to process aid for study abroad students and should keep accurate records. Often, all that is needed are simple things like program start and end dates, the estimated cost of education, and whether there is a written agreement with the program provider.

Part I: Education Abroad as a Component of U.S. Higher Education

It Takes Too Much Extra Work to Handle Study Abroad Students

A lot of extra work *is* often involved. But extra work is often required for other groups of students, too. This is not a valid reason to deny access to aid. It is not in an institution's financial or academic interest to deny aid for study abroad. Students and parents are increasingly aware that federal aid can be used for study abroad, and are far less likely to accept excuses. As the study abroad administrator, education abroad professionals are responsible for helping their institutions understand this. Education abroad professionals need to educate financial aid administrators and help develop adequate standards and controls to ensure that aid is properly awarded, disbursed, and tracked. Education abroad administrators can and must be involved in this process, both to help students and to help financial aid officers fulfill their legal obligations.

Is Awarding Aid for Study Abroad More Difficult?

Three financial aid processes become more complicated when students study abroad: qualifying for financial aid, disbursing financial aid, and applying for financial aid while overseas.

Qualifying

- Students must be enrolled in a degree-seeking program to receive federal and most state aid.

- Students must be enrolled for a certain number of credit hours during the terms they receive aid, usually at least half time.

- Study abroad courses must be preapproved for credit by the home institution before the student leaves. Preapproval must be defined on each campus, and an appropriate process for preapproval must be devised.

- The 1992 reauthorization of the Higher Education Act allows the "reasonable costs of study abroad" to be used to determine how much aid a student should receive. Students attending low-cost institutions can qualify for more aid if the cost of study abroad is higher. Budgets may be quite comprehensive, including estimates for travel, personal, and other expenses. Each campus should have a consistent policy regarding what is and what is not included in a student's budgeted cost of attendance.

- Study abroad budgets must be devised, and the cost of each study abroad program must be documented.

- Data the student submits on aid applications must be verified, sometimes with source documents like tax records and sometimes by verification from the study abroad office. This may occur after the student has left for the study abroad site or may be part of the required financial aid application process.

Disbursing Aid

- Students must sign award notices, loan applications, promissory notes, and other official forms.

- Federal and most state aid cannot be disbursed more than ten days before the beginning of the term.

- Federal and state grants and some kinds of loans (e.g., Perkins loans) are applied to the student's account at the home institution.

- Some other loans (PLUS and Stafford loans) and private scholarships may be disbursed in check form. It is possible to designate a power of attorney to pick up endorsed checks, including federal loan checks. Many loans are now disbursed electronically to the home institution and then credited to the student's account.

- Refunds may be disbursed upon the student's request after home campus fees are paid. Some institutions electronically deposit refunds in students' accounts. Refunds may also be sent to the student's permanent address or to the host institution to pay for study abroad charges, if the student authorizes the home school to do so.

- There are federal rules governing whether aid must be repaid if students withdraw in a certain period of time. If a student withdraws from his or her study abroad program or drops below half-time enrollment, the financial aid office should be notified immediately.

Applying for Aid While Overseas

- Students have to reapply for federal and state aid each year, and for some kinds of institutional or private aid. Satisfactory academic progress must be shown each term, typically by getting passing grades for a full-time credit load.

- Award notices and other documents must be sent to students for their signatures, or must go to a predesignated person with a valid power of attorney.

- It may be necessary to allow forms and other documents to arrive after normal deadlines to allow for international mail delays. The student may need to make individual arrangements with the financial aid office and other offices.

HOW CAN FINANCIAL AID BE MADE MORE AVAILABLE?

To help make financial aid more available to students, an education abroad professional must employ knowledge, communication, and cooperation. Knowledge of what aid is available and how it is awarded is necessary to understand how aid might be used by education abroad students. Communication with several offices, including financial aid, the registrar, the bursar, and academic

Part I: Education Abroad as a Component of U.S. Higher Education

departments, is needed to coordinate special policies and procedures for awarding aid to education abroad students. Cooperation is required to properly award aid, verify its use, and avoid violating federal and state law. Education abroad professionals must also be determined and resourceful activists, lobbyists, and proponents for using current funds and finding new funds. Without active leadership, opportunities for growth may be lost.

Where does an education abroad professional begin? First, the professional must accept the fact that financial aid for study abroad will probably involve more work for him or her and for the education abroad office, as well as for several other administrative offices on the campus. The extra work is generated by the need to create new procedures. The following questions will help define where new processes or procedures are needed on a campus:

- Who decides if the study abroad program provides credit acceptable to the home institution? What procedures and forms must be developed?

- How are study abroad students identified and registered on the aid-giving campus? (Many state loan agencies that monitor the use of student loans now have direct access to campus computer records.)

- Who determines the budget for a study abroad program?

- What if the study abroad program begins earlier or later than the date federal aid can be legally disbursed?

- How are refunds disbursed to students? Should refunds be paid to another institution if it administers the program?

- Who shows students how to get powers of attorney and how to use them for loan checks and refunds?

- Who notifies the financial aid office if the student withdraws?

- Who monitors academic progress and records grades and hours once the program is finished?

- What should be done if the grades are not received from abroad before the beginning of the next academic term?

- Who communicates with the student or his or her parents if there are financial aid problems while the student is away?

- How does the student get aid applications for the next academic period? Should application deadlines be extended for study abroad students?

- How will study abroad payment schedules be altered to allow students to receive their financial aid before paying for their study abroad program?

- How must computer systems be altered to allow for the special needs of study abroad students?

- Who is going to pay for and do all the extra work?

These questions can be even more complex when the student wishes to go on a program sponsored by another institution. There is a way to contract out part of a student's education and still give that student federal aid. Financial aid regulations devised by the U.S. Department of Education's Federal Student Aid Office allow for the use of consortial or contractual agreements (most recently referred to as "written agreements"). These allow students studying for a limited time at another college or university to use federal aid, for that study. While a written agreement will answer some of the questions listed above, it will also require another layer of procedure.

One of the best resources for establishing new procedures is networking. Contact other institutions and see how they have solved similar problems. Call nearby institutions that run study abroad programs. Contact NAFSA for a list of institutions with large education abroad programs, or go to regional or annual NAFSA conferences and meet other education abroad professionals. Send out an inquiry on SECUSS-L, the listserv for study abroad professionals. Remember, each campus has individualized systems, so there is never one perfect way to award aid. Even the best advice will have to be molded around an institution's policies, which will require knowledge, communication, cooperation, and skill on your part. The members of SECUSSA's Financial Aid Resources for Study Abroad Committee and the committee's area on the SECUSSA Web site provide additional resources. (It is anticipated that in late 2005 these resources will be moved to the new NAFSA Education Abroad Knowledge Community Web site.)

Finding Low-Cost Programs

In addition to financial aid, there are a number of other possibilities of funding study abroad, for example, using low-cost programs.

First, define "low cost." A bargain for one student may be a burden for another. Realistically, low cost will mean something different for each institution. In fact, the criteria change for each student. The study abroad adviser really needs to know three things to identify the "good-quality/lower cost" programs for a particular student at a particular institution.

- Know the home institution.
- Know the student.
- Know the possibilities.

Know the Home Institution

What is the cost for a similar term of study at the home institution? What items are normally considered part of the cost of education? For instance, are travel costs considered for all students? Can a budget be adjusted to include travel costs for study abroad students in instances where that cost is not usually considered (e.g., for students who are in-state residents)? Can the budget include the cost of local transportation for students studying abroad in large metropolitan areas where public transportation is a necessity?

What is usually considered reasonable for personal expenses at the home institution? An allocation of $800 per semester may work in a regional city, but it would not be enough in London, England. How much flexibility does the institution have in this area?

What is the institution's aid policy? How much aid might a student "lose" by going abroad? What amount of cost reduction from the usual cost of education is necessary?

Know the Student

Is the student adept at managing a limited budget? With the growing number of nontraditional students going abroad, many have budgeting skills well beyond what is expected of a "typical" undergraduate.

What is the student's travel experience? Is this a student who will need a lot of support abroad, or can this student take advantage of the often less expensive option of enrolling directly in a host institution?

Does the student know how to arrive at a realistic cost assessment for study abroad? Be sure the student includes the costs for such things as a passport and visas, local transportation, insurance appropriate for studying abroad, optional field trips, additional meals, internship placement, and even clothing appropriate for the climate, travel gear, and communications.

Is the student using a payment plan or other outside source of special funding that makes it necessary to consider when certain funds will be available?

Education abroad professionals should work to place the responsibility for cost management in the hands of the student. At the same time, the student should be given the tools necessary to effectively fulfill that responsibility. Start by preparing a budget at the beginning of advising, perhaps even showing the student how to prepare a budget. A "comparative" budget worksheet, showing the costs for the home institution as compared with the costs for studying abroad, is often an effective way to illustrate the process. It is probably a good exercise for all students to complete such a budget as a part of creating reasonable expectations for the study abroad experience, and budget planning can be productively incorporated into the advising and preparation process for all students. A clear statement of the institutional financial aid policy, contact information for the financial aid office, and an outline of the process (including the payment process) should also be available to the student from the beginning. With these details in mind, there are often ways to lower the cost of studying abroad.

Know the Possibilities

Exchange programs sometimes permit the student to apply his or her institutional aid (or even tuition remission) to an exchange when such aid cannot be used on other types of study abroad. If an institution does not want to manage direct exchanges, it might explore the International Student Exchange Program (ISEP) instead. This program, established in 1979 under the authority of the Fulbright-Hays Act and incorporated as an independent nonprofit organization, facilitates international exchange among universities worldwide. Students at member institutions have access to many different exchange partners. Because all fees, including room and board, are paid at the home institution, the basic cost of studying abroad remains constant. For more information on the ISEP program visit their Web site.

A brief search of study abroad programs in major cities will identify many programs utilizing classes at the same "host institution" abroad, but costs for those programs may vary widely. Education abroad professionals should, of course, always caution students to carefully consider what the "cost" of a program includes when comparing programs. A lower cost may actually mean less value for the money. Students need to understand that value lies in support services as well as such items as housing and meals. However, there will be instances in which two programs really are comparable (and the classes are the same because they are provided by the same host institution), but the price of tuition for one program is higher than the price of tuition at the other program.

Some programs pass along the institutional "in-state" tuition savings to study abroad program participants. In other words, there may be some advantage for a student to apply to a program sponsored by a state school in the student's home state.

Sometimes a consortial or affiliation agreement between institutions will provide students with access to lower fees, travel grants, scholarships, and so on. If there is a particular program to which a home institution frequently sends students, perhaps a formalized association between the two institutions could be beneficial.

Often, a student can meet academic and personal goals for study abroad in more than one geographic location. Changing location slightly can sometimes bring study abroad into a student's affordable range. For instance, it is almost always less expensive to study outside a capital city. Thus, studying in a regional center may be less expensive and just as cross-culturally stimulating. Also, some less traditional study locations, for example in Central Europe, may offer a significantly lower cost of living, which is then reflected in overall savings in the cost of housing, food, and personal expenses.

Direct enrollment in a foreign university, as opposed to application through a U.S.-based program, may offer a significant savings. However, some level of support to the student is usually sacrificed in using a direct enrollment option, so this is best reserved for more independent and experienced students. It also requires that the adviser have a good working relationship with and knowledge of the international office abroad.

Of course, the length of study will change the cost, but a shorter program is not always less expensive. For one thing, short-term programs less frequently qualify for aid. On the other hand, a full-year student may be better able to directly enroll in the foreign institution (with an associated cost savings) or may qualify for less-expensive housing.

Two publications from the Institute of International Education (IIE), *Academic Year Abroad* and *Short-Term Study Abroad,* have indexes in the back that list programs by cost range. However, few similar short cuts exist, and even these indexes can serve only as a starting point since they are intended for "approximate guidance only." Program listings can also be found in the Peterson's guides, *Study Abroad* and *Peterson's Short Term Programs*. There are also numerous Web resources. Some of the largest are IIE Online, Peterson's Guides, Studyabroad.com, and GoAbroad.com.

Don't hesitate to consult the experts: study abroad professionals. Posting a question about programs to the SECUSS-L e-mail list may yield the name of just the program an adviser is looking for. Faculty at one's own institution may have contacts in foreign institutions that have not yet been considered.

OUTSIDE FUNDING AND SCHOLARSHIPS

The financial aid discussed in the preceding paragraphs can be applied to the costs of studying abroad as part of federal support for undergraduate study. This funding, however, does not specifically

Part I: Education Abroad as a Component of U.S. Higher Education

represent a federal commitment to support overseas study. The American Council of Education (ACE) notes that, "one of the most critical and contentious issues today is the cost of higher education and related concerns about student financial aid" (2001). Even with greater access to federal and state aid, numerous students still do not qualify for need-based financial aid and yet also cannot find an extra $1,000 to $4,000 to participate in a study abroad program. This section will specifically address alternative means of financial aid for undergraduate overseas study.

Primary causes of this lack of sufficient aid include reduced state and federal government support, increased tuition costs, the high cost of technologies, and increased salary competition for quality faculty. These factors have a direct impact on study abroad. This view was corroborated in recent NAFSA workshops of study abroad advisers and their financial aid counterparts at Brown University, Xavier University, University of St. Thomas, California State University at Sacramento, San Diego University, University of Texas, Austin, and the University of Georgia. A major concern among the workshop participants was how to obtain overseas study grants and scholarships, since traditional financial aid sources are limited when applied to the increasing costs of overseas study.

Assisting Students to Compete Successfully

Assisting students in locating viable sources of financial aid is perhaps the easier half of the challenge. What remains is the need to work with them to make effective and potentially successful applications, knowing that they will be competing with similar students from other institutions. Competing for scholarship support can be time consuming, and even plenty of hard work does not guarantee success. Thus, before the education abroad office becomes involved in advising students about scholarship opportunities or administering such scholarship competitions, it is worth spending some time thinking through what is involved with such endeavors.

Administering scholarships for study and research abroad can be rewarding to an education abroad office, can bring it into contact with students and faculty who might otherwise not come within its scope, and can bring a certain degree of prestige, if the institution takes seriously the benefits of having scholarship winners from its campus. Although there are students who can, with almost minimal help, turn in applications that have "winner" stamped on them, experienced scholarship advisers know that most scholarship applicants, successful and otherwise, need some degree of advising. The education abroad office should consider whether it has the resources to provide this kind of support, and explore whether the institution already has a scholarships adviser charged with helping students apply for prestigious national, international, and other "top" scholarships. If not, the education abroad office may have to try to convince the institution that additional resources are required.

It is no less true for scholarship administration than it is for study abroad in general that faculty support and involvement is often necessary to produce successful applicants. Faculty support can take a number of possible forms, including the following:

- forwarding the names of students regarded as strong applicants for a particular scholarship (the education abroad office may have to elicit this information);

- advising students on award-selection criteria and helping students prepare their applications (for example, faculty members may know which physics departments in France are the most appropriate for study in certain fields);

- serving on or chairing interview panels, since many scholarships require an on-campus review process (it is very important to decide on the intent of any campus interview and make the purpose clear both to the applicants and to those on the committee; accordingly, ask faculty to serve who can best meet the objective of the interview); and

- writing strong letters of recommendation and support, which are often the sine qua non for student success.

Equally important is securing an unequivocal institutional commitment to having students win prestigious awards, an honor that not only assists the institution economically but also augments its academic reputation. Such proactive commitment encourages the campus community to provide students with the guidance they need at various stages of the application process.

Because sources for extra funding are limited, the education abroad office must consider two primary strategies: (1) identifying those funding sources that do exist and assisting students in securing them; and (2) developing additional funding sources for the campus.

Identifying Funding Sources

Every campus should have a library of books that describe all scholarships that exist in support of undergraduate study abroad. Many of the basic international funding books include a few entries for undergraduates. Listings of these books can be found in "Study, Work, and Travel Abroad: A Bibliography." (Currently on the SECUSSA Web site; beginning in late 2005, see the Education Abroad Knowledge Community area on NAFSA's Web site.) Make these books available to students in the study abroad office, or ask the campus library to stock the books in the reference section. A good general resource for financial aid is "The SmartStudent™ Guide to Financial Aid" on the FinAid Web site. This free resource on financial aid for higher education lists advice and general information about aid, and even has a special section for financial aid for study abroad.

Other sources of funding are the general grants, loans, or fellowships awarded by private organizations, businesses, churches, and others. Scholarships that can often be used for study abroad may be awarded on the basis of personal attributes (ethnic or religious background, parents' field of employment, children of veterans, descendants of immigrants from specific countries), or of academic focus, major, or career path. The challenge for the education abroad office and for students is to locate appropriate and relevant funding for the student's specific need level.

To find this appropriate financial aid, students do not necessarily have to pay the high fees that are sometimes charged by commercial search services. Most financial aid offices or campus libraries have resource books that list private scholarships. Many

Part I: Education Abroad as a Component of U.S. Higher Education

financial aid offices offer their own search services, which cost less than those offered by commercial companies. Students can do their own free search using a Web site called fastWeb (Financial Aid Search Through the Web). This site allows students to search a database containing more than 180,000 scholarship and loan opportunities.

Federal and State Scholarships

David L. Boren Undergraduate Scholarships. This National Security Education Program (NSEP) scholarships administered by IIE, supports U.S undergraduates studying languages and cultures currently underrepresented in study abroad and critical to U.S. national security. Study in Western Europe, Canada, Australia, and New Zealand is excluded from this program. Information from the NSEP Web site states that an NSEP scholarship is a "source of portable financial assistance that can be used to support study abroad through an established program, direct enrollment in a foreign university or an individually arranged study." (FAQ's, #10) Note that scholarships cover only a portion of the student's costs and are based on financial need. "The maximum award is $10,000 for a semester or $20,000 for a full academic year." (General Information: Scholarship Benefits)

NSEP also offers Boren Graduate Fellowships. Recipients of the Boren scholarships incur a service requirement.

Benjamin A. Gilman International Scholarship Program. Only U.S. undergraduate students in good standing in a two- or four-year institution receiving a Pell grant during the applicant's academic term are eligible for a Gilman scholarship. Administered by IIE, the Gilman scholarship awards amounts up to $5,000 to defray eligible student expenses. "These include program tuition and fees, room and board, books, local transportation, health insurance, and international airfare."

Federal Aid Agencies. In addition to providing Title VI funding, the federal government offers study abroad funding incidentally through its aid agencies that provide economic assistance to developing countries in the form of consulting services. Faculty members and graduate students from the United States may be hired as consultants. These agencies include the U.S. Agency for International Development, the Canadian International Development Agency, and multicultural development organizations such as the United Nations, the World Bank, and the International Monetary Fund. Although the funding comes from project grants, programs offered by these organizations provide unique field work experiences that enhance the students' professional development and provide significant career opportunities.

State Governments. Student study abroad advocacy groups, when backed by institutional support and allied with state legislators, represent a powerful constituency in obtaining funds. The Wisconsin and Texas state governments have taken a prominent role in establishing study abroad scholarships, at least partly in response to the efforts of student advocacy groups. The Wisconsin governor, with the approval of the state legislature, allocated two million dollars for study abroad scholarships for two years (2001–2002). The allocation was renewed for 2003–2004. Scholarship money was allocated to each state university based on the size of its student population. Eligible recipients must be Wisconsin residents and must demonstrate financial need. Since 1993, the state of

Texas, on the initiative of Texas students, enacted a student fee of $1 specifically earmarked for study abroad scholarships. In 1999, the student body at the University of Texas, Austin, agreed to increase the amount from $1 to $3. Two dollars goes into the scholarships and the other dollar goes into an endowment fund. At public institutions in the state of Georgia, out-of-state students pay reduced tuition when they participate in faculty-led study abroad programs. What an incentive to promote recruitment for overseas study!

International Friendship Organizations. Many cities have branches of international friendship organizations, such as Alliance Française, Goethe Clubs, the Dante Alighieri Society, or the League of United Latin American Citizens. Many such organizations have modest programs that aid students who study or do research in their countries of interest. Education abroad professionals may be able to work with an organization that doesn't have a scholarship program to start one.

Program Sponsor Support. Most of the large study abroad program providers have scholarships available. Students should check eligibility requirements. Some scholarships are merit-based, others need-based, and still others are for specific programs. Program representatives can provide information about available scholarships and eligibility criteria, as well as the number of scholarships granted and the average scholarship amount. Program-provider scholarships typically range between $500 and $3,000.

Special Aid for Underrepresented Student Populations. Federal and organizational funds are available to assist underrepresented students who are enrolled in overseas study programs. Special grants or scholarships are specified for this purpose.

The Minority International Research Training Grant, offered by the National Institutes of Health, is one example. These grants increase minority student participation in the health research sector in the United States and abroad. Underrepresented minorities who become fellows of the Institute for International Public Policy are given funding for language training, study abroad, and internships (in the United States or abroad) as part of the program's five-year funding cycle. The Institute's goal is to increase the representation of minorities in international service.

The Social Science Research Council offers minority incentive predissertation awards for research in Asia, Africa, Latin America, the Caribbean, and the Near and Middle East. Awards include language training and appropriate course work. The American Institute for Foreign Study offers scholarships for minorities studying on their programs. Nontraditional students who aspire to go overseas should seek information from appropriate academic units to determine if they are eligible for overseas study scholarships. Criteria might vary with institutions and program-sponsored organizations.

Private Sector Corporations and Foundations. Now more than ever, study abroad is generating good press and a corresponding positive environment for fundraising. Study abroad administrators should take advantage of these opportunities to pursue private sector funds. The private sector represents an additional and frequently lucrative source of funding for study abroad. Private sector aid supports both need-based and merit-based scholarships.

The disastrous events of September 11, 2001, have made corporations more aware of the importance of providing U.S. students with an international education. These organizations realize that U.S. leadership in the international arena of trade and commerce is dependent on the educational training and preparation of U.S. students. In contrast to past decades, corporations are now more apt to provide funding for study abroad and area studies. Specifically, the Amoco Foundation, the Daimler-Chrysler Corporation, the Coca-Cola Foundation, and the Lear Corporation, are just a few examples of companies providing study abroad scholarships. Typically, grants are offered through the student's home institution rather than directly to the student. If the granting organization is a corporation, it will dispense funds through its foundation. Foundation priorities usually focus on a field of study or a specific geographic area (city, state, or region), or they focus nationally and internationally with specified types of support (endowment, international studies, seed money, and operating support).

In order to effectively leverage this new source of funding, the education abroad office should partner with the campus development office in seeking funds. The institutional advancement unit should have a database of foundations and corporations, as well as a list of international alumni, for informational purposes. Development officers act as an important liaison between study abroad units and the private sector. Many universities have individual development staff members whose sole purpose is to raise funds for international studies and programs. Development units can enlist institutional support from central administrators, who are vital in obtaining private sector funding.

Service, Governmental, and Nongovernmental Organizations. Rotary International has an annual competition for students who wish to engage in study or research abroad. The Rotary International Ambassadorial Scholarship is a well-known example of support for undergraduates and graduates going abroad. Local Rotary Clubs can provide details on how students can apply for the scholarships. Local branches may consider creating a special award for local high school graduates who study abroad.

The German Academic Service offers undergraduate scholarships for study abroad, language summer courses, senior thesis research, and internships in Germany.

Freeman-Asia awards, administered by IIE, are offered to U.S. undergraduates or permanent residents in good standing at the time of application who wish to study in East or Southeast Asia for a minimum of eight weeks up to an academic year. Students must currently receive financial aid or have verifiable need for financial assistance." Awardees must fulfill a service requirement to promote study abroad in Asia at their home institution and share their knowledge with their community. See the Web site for more information.

Bridging Scholarships are administered by the Association of Teachers of Japanese to U.S. undergraduate students or permanent residents who wish to participate in study abroad programs in Japan. Students in any field of study are eligible and Japanese language study is not a prerequisite. Stipends range from $2,500 for semester programs to $4,000 for academic-year programs.

Aid from Foreign Governments

An untapped reservoir of fundraising is in the category of foreign governments. For example, the Japanese government offers one-year scholarships to undergraduate students who participate in exchange programs at Japanese universities—Association of International Exchange, Japan (AIEJ). Current AIEJ scholarships are for students participating in exchange programs between U.S. and Japanese schools.

Institutional Fundraising

Building a Campus Scholarship Fund

An education abroad scholarship fund can be created by raising funds through the campus community. The campus development office may be able to work an appeal into its annual fund drive, perhaps targeting alumni who have studied abroad. Working with the development office allows the education abroad professional to get expert advice about raising money, plus access to mailing lists, postage, the alumni magazine or newsletter, and the local community. A campus scholarship fund would help ensure that academically qualified and interested students are not denied the educational and career advantages of an overseas experience because they lack money

Some education abroad offices set up program budgets that generate some funding for students already receiving financial aid. Others charge an administrative fee or surcharge to all students studying abroad, some or all of which is put into a scholarship fund. Several study abroad offices use commissions from the sale of Britrail and Eurail passes and International Student Identity Cards (ISIC) to fund scholarships. Another source of financial support is multinational organizations that own and operate firms in the community and region (each state's Department of Commerce can provide a list of organizations in the state). Many of these companies will contribute to a scholarship fund in the interest of promoting community goodwill, particularly if the scholarship goes to help students who will participate in overseas study programs in the contributor's home country.

By contacting former overseas study students, study abroad offices have been successful in raising revenue through organized telethons and mail campaigns coordinated with the development office.

Any university-sponsored fundraising campaign should have a study abroad or international relations component. As an example, study abroad scholarships are a top priority at Michigan State University (MSU), and they are an integral part of any fundraising campaign that is fully endorsed by the university president and central administration. Institutional support from the higher echelons of administration cannot be underestimated. To assist students in locating appropriate sources of funding for study abroad, the MSU Office of International Studies and Programs published in collaboration with the MSU library in 2004, *A Student's Guide to Scholarships, Grants, and Funding Publications in International Education and Other Disciplines,* an annotated 228-page comprehensive directory of information of Web sites and reference works.

MSU also established an Overseas Study Endowment Fund. The monies for this fund come from former student participants, faculty, and corporations. Since the endowment fund is permanent, the interest accrued annually goes for study abroad scholarships. Moreover, more revenue is generated as the principal increases.

Matching funds are another potential source of corporate funding. Corporations such as Coca Cola usually request matching funds from the grantee of a study abroad award. Study abroad units, in concert with the development office, can tap departments

Part I: Education Abroad as a Component of U.S. Higher Education

that sponsor overseas programs as a source for matching funds. Scholarships would be offered to the department's students as an incentive for providing funds. The matching gift concept doubles the amount of scholarship money and is symbolic of an institutional commitment to study abroad.

At some academic institutions, a "senior gift" funded by collected donations is made for a specific project or projects selected by the graduating seniors. Efforts can be made to have the senior gift become a source of funding to establish overseas study scholarships or an endowment.

Sometimes funds can come from unexpected sources. The Michigan State University Federal Credit Union pledged two and a half million dollars for study abroad program scholarships. When fully funded in five years, stipends from $500 to $2,000 will be given to qualified students, independent of class level and degree program and will be used by the recipients to help offset additional costs associated with overseas studies.

Boston College offers another innovative approach to fundraising. The institution focuses on an interdisciplinary approach to Irish studies, involving the departments of political science, education, and business studies. Support for its Institute of Irish Studies comes not only from the British, Irish, and U.S. governments, but also from the private sector (e.g., IBM) and from organizations such as The Ireland Funds, the International Fund for Ireland, and the Irish American Partnership. The Institute of Irish Studies administers approximately twenty-one programs that involve hundreds of individuals from Northern Ireland and the Republic of Ireland, as well as many Boston College students. Boston College's faculty are involved as well, serving as consultants to Ireland in areas such as marketing tourism and establishing corporate child care. Boston College emphasizes an academic strength in Irish studies and utilizes the entire campus in furthering that objective. Fundraising activities are quite extensive, involving governments, the private sector, and sponsored organizations.

International Alumni Donors

The increased pressure on universities to generate new avenues of revenue and to meet challenging campaign goals has led fundraisers to contact international alumni for support. Media reports heralding sizable contributions to institutions such as the Massachusetts Institute of Technology, University of California at Berkeley, and Princeton University have substantiated the view that international alumni constitute a "major revenue stream." Yet study abroad advisers and development officers must recognize that the task of soliciting donations form international alumni is not easy. Major cultural differences in how countries do business and tax restrictions on donations can adversely affect results. The problem of maintaining an adequate up-to-date alumni database can also hinder fundraising efforts. International educators need to understand that other cultures may view philanthropy differently than the United States. The key in courting overseas alumni is to maintain patience and to cultivate a partnership. This means responding to their concerns, enhancing their professional development, and awarding incentive benefits such as recognizing distinguished alumni. International alumni as a primary fundraising resource for study abroad scholarships cannot be underestimated. International alumni want U.S.

students to study their respective cultures and languages. Thus, they are highly motivated to give donations for this purpose.

Program Tuition Surpluses

Finally, education abroad practitioners should examine institutional policies for charging study abroad students tuition or other fees. Does the campus make money on study abroad because students are charged normal tuition for the privilege of being enrolled while abroad or for having credit transferred back? Is that tuition then used to pay for the students' program costs and perhaps to fund the education abroad office, or is there a portion that reverts to the college's general fund? If the latter is the case, build a coalition of students, faculty, and perhaps alumni who are interested in seeing some of that money used to fund scholarships for education abroad. This would be an equitable way to, for instance, help offset the loss of other institutional funds that cannot be used for study abroad. If surplus funds are generated from program fees, a portion of those funds could be allocated for student scholarships for the department or college that accredits the overseas study program.

Grant Writing

The campus development office can assist study abroad administrators in grant writing to raise money for students or programs. Increasing awareness of the significance of study abroad has generated more revenue for student scholarships and grants. As study abroad advisers become more knowledgeable about fundraising, they become invaluable resources in helping students go overseas. Study abroad advisers must be diligent in working closely with their development colleagues. Concurrently, they must be continually active in obtaining institutional support for study abroad programs.

The following tips can help enhance grant writing techniques:

- Include a concise and comprehensive summary of the project goals in the abstract. The abstract becomes the window to the proposal and it is the first item that grantors read. A badly or hastily written abstract will automatically eliminate the proposal from consideration.

- Adhere to the grantor's guidelines and criteria. Ignoring these items can put the proposal at risk of elimination.

- Know the interests and background of the donor. Does the donor corporation or foundation have influential members who are alumni of study abroad? Is the corporation or foundation restricted to granting its funds only within a specific community or state? Although many corporations and foundations go beyond community and state boundaries, they will be more sensitive to a grantee's proposal if the funds will go to a community-oriented initiative; for example, funding local students to study overseas.

- Address the "need" for study abroad. What impact will a bicultural study abroad experience have on faculty and students? Is it language competence, enhancing professional development, or educating a cadre of internationally minded citizens of the twenty-first century? Any or all of these objectives are possible themes that can be emphasized.

- Include other key components in your proposal, such as a problem statement or needs assessment, objectives, timeline methods, evaluation plan, and a narrative budget. The proposal should focus on programs, but more importantly, it should emphasize results and outcomes.

- Communicate with other grantees who have been successful in obtaining foundation funds for study abroad. Gleaning information from successful grantees will enhance the proposal, and make it more likely to achieve positive results.

- Become acquainted with the granting organization's annual reports, tax returns, newsletters, press releases, and grant lists as potential prospect lists. Many university libraries maintain an index of foundation directories, indices, and guides that can help study abroad advisers who are writing grant proposals. Frequent contact with the potential donor through the development office can reap beneficial results, particularly if the donor's first reaction to the proposal is positive.

The key to successful fundraising is the exploration of sources of study abroad funding, including faculty, international alumni, the private sector, governments, organizations, and agencies. Key to any proposal is the confident assertion that an educated overseas study student dispels parochialism; that study abroad programs enhance the university, the students, and ultimately the country; that government and private organizations benefit from a student's broader world view; and that the education of future citizens is enhanced, as is the academic excellence of our institutions, by making available more economic support for education abroad.

SUMMARY

The lack of adequate funding for education abroad is of course related to the national problem of how to guarantee equal access for all students to all of U.S. higher education. While this reality remains, and thus major economic barriers continue to exist for many students, the most important duty of the education abroad administrator is to do everything possible to make study abroad a viable alternative for as many students as possible. With a thorough knowledge of what aid is available from public, private, philanthropic, and corporate sources, and through effective communication between the education abroad office, other campus administrators, students, faculty, and alumni concerning the need for more financial support, regular and alternate sources of financial aid can usually be found to help students afford the costs of

Chapter 7: Financial Aid and Funding Study Abroad

study abroad. The time and effort involved may seem daunting, but the rewards to students make the effort worthwhile. Always remember, education abroad professionals have an experienced and resourceful team of colleagues in the education abroad and financial aid fields prepared to assist with developing a strategy for growth and increased access for students to embark on a twenty-first century international educational opportunity.

CHAPTER 8

Technology and Education Abroad

Contributors: Lisa Donatelli, Katherine Yngve, Mona Miller, Jim Ellis

Where is the wisdom that we have lost in knowledge?
Where is the knowledge that we have lost in information?
—From T.S. Eliot, Choruses from "The Rock" (1934)

Over the last twenty years, the telecommunications revolution has transformed higher education. It has done so by creating new learning environments, new communication tools, and new means of information dissemination. The internet, e-mail, cell phones, personal digital assistants (PDAs), digital cameras, laptops, video and satellite conferencing, wireless data networks, and smart classrooms are now an integral part of the "interconnected world" in which our students live. Although these technologies have connected many of us in new and meaningful ways, they have also caused the phenomenon known as information overload. To overcome this sense of overload, students, faculty, and administrators must become more adept at organizing vast amounts information and discerning the relative importance of that information.

For education abroad administrators, the telecommunications revolution has provided the opportunity to rethink the very nature of their jobs.

At the highest levels of the university, technology is a valuable advocacy tool. Using technology to compile and present important institutional data is often a critical mechanism through which the mission of international education can be advanced both on campus and nationally. At the same time, technology has also made routine many of the administrative tasks associated with administering education abroad programs enabling education abroad professionals to redesign processes, redistribute their time, regularize communication with students, parents, and campus constituents, improve efficiency, and enhance student services.

Given the rapidity with which new technology emerges, this chapter focuses on the macro, or meta, issues of technology facing today's education abroad professionals. More specifically, it focuses on how the evolving telecommunications environment impacts the goals and outcomes of programs abroad as well as professionals working in the education abroad office Detailed technical information (e.g., regarding hardware, software, security, cost, and internet resources) is provided in the bibliography.

The Telecommunications Revolution and Education Abroad

Improvements in telecommunications technology have resulted in corresponding challenges. Education abroad professionals are plagued by issues of resource allocation for technology, training of staff, maintenance of information systems, appropriate use, and the broader legal and ethical issues of technology. Educators are now being challenged to move from *understanding* technology to *managing* technology. In addition to these challenges, the current generation of students is exponentially more technologically savvy, consumer-oriented, and environmentally conscious than preceding generations. These factors alter the role of advisers and program developers, and change how an ever-evolving telecommunications technology shapes the process of campus internationalization and contributes to the global outreach of U.S. students.

Generation Y: Recognizing Student Expectations

The discussion of technology and education abroad often begins with defining the relationship the current generation of students has with technology. U.S. demographers Howe and Strauss (1991) are said to have been the first to systematically describe the generational model, which is considered a theory of social history. Each generation is given a designation such as "Baby Boomers" (those born between 1943 and 1960) or "Generation Y" (those born between 1982 and 2000) and characteristics are assigned to each. Although generational models are somewhat useful in creating a context in which to discuss technology and today's students, such models should not become ideals to which to cling too tightly. The generational models are still untested, for example, in contexts outside the mainstream U.S. culture, and were not designed to take into account cultural or national differences.

Nevertheless, while it would be unwise to categorize all students around the world under the Howe and Strauss generational model, experience with non-U.S. nationals studying in the United States, as well as anecdotal reports from students and colleagues in Europe, Australia, and some Asian nations, suggest strongly that certain characteristics brought forward by this research model are broadly applicable (at least among educated elites) beyond the U.S. context. Research and our own experiences have shown us that this generation of technology users has several characteristics:

- *They are technology veterans.* Today's students have grown up in the age of computers, cell phones, video games, and multimedia software. Unlike many in their parents' generation, they do not see technology as negative or fear its impact on their lives.

- *They are socially conscious and service oriented.* Students today wish to make a difference in the world, and to give back and contribute to society. The difference between today's students and previous generations that exhibited social activism is that today's students seek to integrate service into their undergraduate experience in a much more formal way.

- *They are savvy, informed, and driven by choice.* As the first true "cyber generation," today's student population understands the enormity of the amount of information available to them. All of this information has shown students that there are many choices, and freedom of choice has become something this generation values greatly.

- *They are overcommitted and pressed for time.* Always on the go, today's students are active in maximizing academics, social events, and resume-building activities (Beck 1997; O'Keefe 2002; Cobb 1998).

These values and characteristics clearly affect the way education abroad offices present their material and advise students, the curricular focus and location of the programs they provide, and the infrastructure they build into each of their programs. Subtle adjustments that recognize the special characteristics of today's technology-savvy students, such as providing multiple sources of information, balancing face-to-face events with virtual ones (such as online orientations), and designing multi-dimensional programs (academics with service and internship, for example) will most likely enhance the entire education abroad experience for students.

The Digital Divide: Access and Use of Technology

Few observers question the existence of the digital divide between the estimated 500 million people with access to the internet and the part of humanity that has yet to have the opportunity to make a phone call. Although primarily described as a worldwide tension between those who have technology and those who do not, the digital divide also applies to the access and use of technology by students participating in education abroad programs compared with what is available to them at home and on most U.S. campuses. While the largest differential may exist for students from fully wired U.S. campus who are living and learning in less-developed regions of the world, gradations of a divide affect most students studying abroad. Nearly all will experience a gap or shift of some sort as they move into countries with a different technological infrastructure.

Far more challenging than preparing students to recognize the gap is preparing them to use and adapt to the available technology in a culturally sensitive way. Appropriate use of technology for business, academic, and nonacademic purposes—as well as simply understanding its relative importance—is vital to navigating a new culture successfully. Thus, technological differences between home and abroad often need to be included as part of education abroad advising and programming. Students should be prepared to question their methods of communication, and they need to be informed about what is and is not available in the country where they will be studying.

Internet and Technology Use and Cultural Immersion

It is rare these days to find an education abroad professional who has never wondered whether modern education abroad participants are impairing their immersion into the host society through the frequent use of modern communication media such as cell phones, e-mail, and the World Wide Web. Indeed, as the telephone and the used bookstore did

Part I: Education Abroad as a Component of U.S. Higher Education

for previous generations of students, electronic communication options can and do serve as a "protected space" or treasured link to the home culture for students who have not yet acquired the necessary comfort level or the social network to engage in meaningful interaction within a new cultural environment. For the on-site adviser or program administrator, this poses the very real dilemma of setting reasonable limits for students who may be accustomed to full-time, unfettered, and usually cost-free access to technology. When does the frequent use of these communication tools evolve from being a reasonable and even appropriate temporary reaction to culture shock into becoming a psychological crutch that impedes the learning experience? There are several issues to consider when dealing with the challenges of balancing internet use and cultural immersion. (Note: The following discussion points are based in large measure on conversations that took place over SECUSS-L—a study abroad–related e-mail discussion forum sponsored by the NAFSA Education Abroad Knowledge Community [formerly known as SECUSSA]—during the early weeks of July 2003.)

First, and most obviously, it seems important to emphasize that notions of what constitutes "too much" time spent with technology vary radically according to the educational situation and age of the user. Students who have grown up since the explosion of the internet are for the most part much more accustomed than earlier generations to relying on technological tools for meeting their research needs, locating and arranging entertainment or weekend travel options, and sharing information and feelings with their peers.

Unlike the previous generation (which includes many program administrators), today's students do not view technology as an impediment to human interaction but rather as an important and even necessary tool for enhancing interpersonal relations. Therefore, it can be appropriate for program administrators to encourage study abroad participants to make frequent use of telecommunications technology inasmuch as it allows students to forge higher-quality interactions with and immersion into the host culture, particularly in locations where internet use or instant messaging is a common tool of social interaction or information gathering, such as among college populations in Japan, South Korea, or Western Europe.

Conversely, in nations or subcultures where internet access or cell phone ownership is exceedingly uncommon or not yet a part of the typical daily routine, students from nations where technology is ubiquitous will need thoughtful advising and orientation as to the current role of communications technology (or the lack of such a role) in their host countries, and may even require a planned or graduated program of "weaning" from their own dependence on telecommunications apparatus.

Second, and equally important when seeking to define what constitutes excessive use of communications technology, it is important to remember that the idea of immersion into another culture (which requires cutting at least some of one's ties to the home culture) implies a high degree of independence and personal autonomy, both of which are values that are culturally specific to certain groups, but which are not necessarily as highly regarded in other cultures. As education abroad professionals strive to increase participation in education abroad among diverse populations, including students of color, refugees, or recent immigrants, they would do well to remember that other cultures, among them minority members of a given country's populace, may place a much higher value on family connections or on collectivist values than is the societal norm. For such students, integrating into and making meaning of an education abroad learning environment may well require a higher degree of (electronic) sharing of the experience with the folks at home than previous conceptual models of immersion have considered.

On the other hand, while wanting to encourage students to use all possible methods to integrate into the host culture and make meaning of the educational experience, international educators are correct to be wary of becoming, in a sense, "enablers" of what might be called technological escapism. Many of today's students need to become familiar with the true costs of internet usage and better acquainted with the fact that, for most of the world's users of modern communications technology, internet access is both inconvenient and infrequent. As today's working professionals know, even in the United States and other first-world nations, most internet users who are not in college must either visit the public library for free access or pay an hourly or monthly fee for personal online access, whether at home or at a cyber-cafe. Therefore, in places where local students or residents have only limited access to the internet, programs should encourage participants to conform to local internet usage standards, perhaps by making on-site computer stations available for academic and research purposes only, while encouraging participants to find access in a student-oriented cyber-cafe for personal correspondence.

Finally, to return to our conflicted education abroad adviser's dilemma about balancing technology use and cultural immersion, a few words need to be said about the phenomenon popularly known as 'internet addiction.' By and large, the phrase itself has been widely discredited in the scholarly world, though it remains a useful metaphor in popular usage. Educators and psychologists now agree that there is neither a clinical nor a qualitative way to measure "grossly excessive" technology use in modern society, and that surfing the Web yields neither a physical addiction nor a psychological effect such as the adrenaline rush widely described in chronic gamblers. That being said, recent research does clearly show a demonstrable connection between clinical depression and higher-than-normal use of the internet as an escape mechanism (the research also shows a similarly higher incidence of other reclusive activities such as television watching and reading) (LaRose, Lin & Eastin 2003).

In the education abroad context, this research suggests two conclusions: (1) that study abroad participants who exhibit a somewhat high initial internet usage level may be having a perfectly normal reaction to the stress of culture shock; and (2) that, conversely, study abroad participants who maintain a greatly increased rate of internet usage over a longer period than their peers, or who immediately exhibit a nearly exclusive desire to spend time at a computer terminal, may also be demonstrating significant depressive tendencies and may be in need of intensive counseling and advising to overcome culture shock before adjusting to a more culturally appropriate level of internet use.

The question of appropriate technology use and access is vitally important from an administrative standpoint as well. Education abroad professionals can play a part in alleviating the frustrations of their students by understanding their own campus administrative processes. Online registration and housing assignment often occur without accommodation for the student studying off campus. Education abroad professionals should work with the relevant campus offices to insure that students are aware of the technology requirements necessary to perform these processes while away. If the technology does not exist (and it should never be assumed that it does), an appropriate alternative should be implemented.

Technology and Global Competence: Impact on Program Design and Outcomes

Since its beginnings in the 1920s, study abroad has been seen as a way of encountering "the other," accomplished by living and learning in a country that is not home, through an in-depth exploration of a new language or culture. In the popular view, however, the computer is seen as a device that makes it possible to access a wide variety of written and visual artifacts from other cultures, with minimal face-to-face interaction or personal involvement. Given this dichotomy, international educators might consider themselves justified in wondering what purpose technology can serve in the educational context of intercultural understanding. Others may wonder what "global competence" means and what purpose education abroad serves in an age in which technology allows us to access and interact with other cultures with such ease and in an era in which the nation-state is widely believed to have met its functional demise. In this respect, technology and globalization pose challenges to anyone designing international programs in terms of student learning styles, curriculum, and outcomes.

For the purposes of the following discussion, the term global competence is used to signify the desired pedagogical outcome of education abroad programs; that is, successful "internationalization," or the capacity to become a functioning "global citizen" in the modern world. While definitions of global competence vary even within the restricted field of education abroad, the following list reflects common traits of global competence:

- general knowledge of one's own culture, history, and people;

- general knowledge of cultures, histories, and peoples other than one's own;

- fluency in a world language other than one's native tongue;

- cross-cultural empathy;

- openness and cognitive flexibility;

- tolerance for ambiguity, perceptual acuity, and attentiveness to nonverbal messages; and

- awareness of issues facing the global community.

Student Learning Styles

The twenty-first century student is a very different creature than the mid-twentieth century student or the student of the 1980s. A generation raised on electronic gaming and internet research has developed new capacities and some surprising capabilities. Specifically, as recent research in the developing field of literacy studies has shown, these emerging literacies include:

- visual literacy (primacy of images over print information),
- intertextual literacy (nonlinear thinking),
- analytical or critical literacy (data synthesis and problem-solving skills),
- communicative literacy (facility of written expression), and
- surface familiarity with the cultures of other nations, primarily popular culture.

Through internet research and e-mail use, today's young people are mastering collaborative skills and general knowledge of other peoples and cultures, while videogames, computerized simulation worlds, and online chat rooms teach them problem-solving skills and expose them to the value of adaptability and multiple perspectives. Observant international educators will spot a fair amount of overlap between these emerging technological literacies and the global competence skills that study abroad is designed to foster.

What do the new literacies mean for education abroad programs? They suggest that international educators should try not to rely exclusively on teaching techniques that favor alphabetical literacy over, for example, intertextual and visual literacies, and that educators may want to emphasize in recruitment materials or in orientation the ways in which today's students have already begun to master the skills needed to succeed in an intercultural or global context because of their familiarity with technology. In cases where students are expected to take course work in another educational system, particularly via direct enrollment, education abroad offices should take pains to sketch out the cultural context of the educational environment and point out how students can adapt their own technological literacy to the practice of learning in the host society. For example, intertextual and analytical literacy might be helpful in encounters with non-Western cultures such as those in Kenya, China, or Japan, where information dissemination and decision-making have often been characterized by newly arrived Westerners as either "circuitous" or "inscrutable."

Curriculum

The second difficulty that technology poses to international education arises from technology's role as a catalyst of globalization. Globalization presents challenges to education abroad, particularly in the area of curriculum, as it becomes increasingly clear that societies no longer interact in an exclusively bidirectional or nation-state mode. Although education abroad still thrives on the paradigm of a culture-to-culture exchange of knowledge (in terms of its curriculum and its raison d'être), it also often fails to look at the evolving global economy and address the shifting role of national governments in world affairs. Therefore, the key question for curriculum development in twenty-first century education abroad is how to help our students come to grips, as our area studies and international relations colleagues in the professoriate have had to do, with the redefinition of communications, geography, and distance that the new technology is bringing about in the modern world? In addition, the profession needs to help students overcome the assumptions that other countries should remain de facto museums, historically pure and monocultural, as well as untouched by anything as modern or Western as computers or cell phones.

The first pitfall to avoid is inadequately considering the effects of communications technology in weaving together all of today's societies. Globalization demands, and will continue to demand, that intercultural educators remember to explicitly give students the cognitive tools necessary to apply the lessons and cultural competency skills learned in a particular host society to a broader international context, whether during the actual study abroad program or as a part of a comprehensive reentry curriculum. Faculty across the globe who are forging new interdisciplinary fields such as transnational studies and media communication studies can help education abroad professionals define an appropriate educational approach to this dilemma.

Second, education abroad professionals need to be mindful, in designing contemporary programs, of the practical individual consequences of the so-called digital divide, which may cause adventuresome students to search out ever-more-remote destinations in order to have a technology-free and more "authentic" intercultural encounter. There are real benefits to living and learning in a remote area in the age of globalization, but it can be a disservice to the host society as well as to the sending society if students are allowed to enter into education abroad in a spirit either of boldly going where no student has gone before or of helping those less fortunate than themselves. As recent sociological theory is beginning to demonstrate, the globalizing forces brought about by the current technological era are now allowing nations and individuals to define their cultures and cultural heritages in ways that are both more fluid and more situational than national borders might dictate Teaching students to let go of the desire to search for "authentic" cultural immersion, where "authentic" means conforming to historical preconceptions about underdeveloped societies, is, therefore, a necessity.

For the reasons noted above, the twenty-first century international educator would do well to add specific orientation modules and course options that examine the impact of technology on the specific host culture or region. Not only will such options give students insights into what distinguishes the modern host society from its historical stereotype, but it will also force U.S. students (in particular) to confront false notions of the United States as the world's sole, and relatively benign, technological superpower. Students of non-U.S. origin who study abroad, either in the United States or in another country, must also be given the tools to understand globalization in a more nuanced manner, forsaking the tendency to characterize globalization's effects as Western hegemony.

For example, a good orientation will, in terms of information technology, seek to counter notions about traditional European or Asian societies by including information on the surprising (particularly to U.S. students) rates of technology usage among the youth of nations such as Japan, Korea, and Norway, and the sociological and practical impacts of these changes. To suggest a few examples of curricular options, an appropriate technology-related course could offer a perspective on how the rise of technology has affected global trade patterns and economic bust-and-boom cycles (and, not incidentally, caused much resentment against the

United States and the rest of the West), or might examine how internet communication is allowing diasporic communities to have an effect on both world politics and the local community.

Finally, given that long-term, immersive, and language-intensive study abroad will inevitably be feasible for only a comparatively small percentage of a nation's population, as many European educators have already realized, the twenty-first century international educator will need to actively employ technological tools as a means to deliver a wide variety of internationalization options to a broad public and to better prepare and reintegrate short-term sojourners. Among the panoply of possibilities that could enhance education abroad programs, only computer-assisted language learning (CALL) has been widely accepted into current program preparation curricula. A starter set of ideas that ought to be more frequently explored in education abroad includes the directed use of e-mail as a journaling device, use of e-mail or chat rooms to discuss cultural mindsets and values with host country students, delivery of a required science course to students overseas via Web interface, use of videoconferencing to deliver lectures from host country experts to participants either prior to or as a follow-up activity after a short-term education abroad experience, and development of computer simulation games that replicate the learning environment of commonly used intercultural training tools and games.

Outcomes: Technology and Global Competence

The final challenge that technology poses to education abroad arises from the emerging notion that global telecommunications and the global economy are forging a homogenous "global culture" (even if only among elite nations or classes). When Bengali techno-pop and Patagonian handicrafts are readily available over the internet, the nature of intercultural exchange has changed irrevocably. Perhaps the next half-century will reveal to international educators that to mourn the nature of the immersion experience in its mid-twentieth century study abroad form is in some senses to mourn the passing of the dinosaur, which although certainly a powerful and awe inspiring creature, was one whose time of influence in the world has long since passed. How do education abroad professionals ensure that study abroad itself does not become as irrelevant as the Hadrosaurus in an age where nearly every commonly listed global competence skill listed by Lambert (1994). might conceivably be acquired easily and more cheaply via technological means than by expending the time and money to go abroad?

International educators must remember that although today's nations and societies are sharing information, commerce, and cultural artifacts more freely than ever before, the forces of globalization are also causing an increased interest in tradition and cultural heritage and a strengthening of ethnic bonds within individual societies, in diasporic ethnic communities, and in cross-border special-interest groups. To the extent then, that international educators let students believe in the chimera of a global monoculture, they are betraying the founding principles of international education. Educators must remember, and teach, that each culture and subculture globalizes itself, or refuses to globalize itself, in a different and locally meaningful way, and equip students to fully experience this.

In addition, and most critically, globalization exposes two flaws in the current global competence paradigms of the educational outcomes desired by the education abroad profession: (1) a failure to acknowledge the importance of the affective or experiential component of education abroad in fostering transnational proficiency, and (2) the fact that "holistic, traditional immersion in the language and culture of another country may no longer be possible" (Hoffa 2003), for many study abroad participants for a variety of reasons. When teenagers in Italy and America grow up watching a translated Japanese cartoon series daily, educators need to examine whether being made to struggle with daily life in another country can continue to create the all-important encounter with otherness that forces a shift in perspective and results in true intercultural expertise.

International educators may find that they have already reached the stage when immersion in the twentieth century sense is insufficiently educative for some students. Recent research in attempting to measure the global competencies of returned study abroad participants indicates that relatively few undergo measurable development of intercultural sensitivity. Educators need to acknowledge the important learning outcomes of the experiential component of education abroad and use pedagogical tools that deepen the experience beyond the impact of a long-term travel experience. Otherwise, educators may risk the very real possibility that significant intercultural learning will increasingly take place only by happenstance or across an electronic interface.

Technology and the Education Abroad Office: Taking Stock, Assessing Needs, and Pooling Resources

Most education abroad professionals will agree that technology has drastically changed, and primarily improved, the administration of education abroad programs. The ability to access, store, share, and distribute information has improved educators' ability to communicate with and serve all of their constituents—students, parents, faculty, and colleagues. In addition to improved communication, the tedious aspects of administration such as mass mailings, tracking student forms, generating statistics, and designing the budget have been greatly improved with the advent of various word processing, database, and budgeting software. Overall, technology has made education abroad professionals more efficient administrators than they were before. International educators are now able to do more for less, and with fewer human resources.

Most of the technology needed for the daily tasks associated with program administration is readily accessible and requires minimal training. However, achieving sophisticated goals such as integration with other campuswide systems and wireless networking requires a deeper level of technical expertise. Whether an educator seeks that skill set externally, within the campus technology department, or within the education abroad office will depend on the institution and resources that are available.

Information and Data Management for the Education Abroad Office

Student Databases

Use of a student database will assist education abroad offices in efficiently managing all aspects of their operations. Databases are designed based on criteria specific to the needs of a particular office, and are far more useful than as simply a tool for making lists of student names and addresses for merge capacities. Databases should not be confused with spreadsheets, in which general student information is entered to track participation. Databases should not be viewed as merely a means to store and retrieve information about students. A quality data management system can serve multiple functions.

As an Advocacy Tool for Staffing and Program Development. Maintaining information and statistics on students engaged in international education on your campus makes it possible to demonstrate growth, which can support, for instance, a request to enhance staffing levels. It can also provide documentation for program evaluation, and generate data for university reports, public relations, and the *Open Doors* survey.

As a Tool for Marketing and Communication. A good database will allow the education abroad office to generate a list of e-mail addresses for students, overseas contacts, and parents. The database should have the ability to generate mass e-mail address lists as well as criterion-specific address lists. Ideally, the database will also have the ability to integrate with your office e-mail software, allowing addresses stored in the database to be added instantly to any e-mail you compose. Simple queries to the database should allow users to inform students quickly about a special program meeting, predeparture orientation, or instructions on registration for their return to the home campus. A database can also facilitate the marketing of various programs to students, by tracking how a student learned about a specific opportunity (e.g., via a faculty member, study abroad office advertisement, study abroad fair, high school visit, etc.).

As an Administrative Tool for Increased Office Efficiency. A good database will allow education abroad professionals to access, distribute, and compile the information they need to work efficiently in their positions. Having important information such as student biographical data, academic records data, education abroad program information, credit information, as well as emergency contact information readily accessible is helpful in increasing efficiency. In addition, a database allows users to share information quickly with other colleagues within their own offices, among university colleagues, and with their education abroad program contacts.

Planning for a Database or Information System

Workflow and Long-Term Planning and Reporting. The most important aspect of designing or purchasing a prepackaged database is clearly outlining the office workflow. The key is to work backwards over the last several years of the office's work and to carefully plan and anticipate future needs. It is far better to have capabilities that may not be utilized immediately than to wish for certain capabilities down the road. Develop a list of what the office does on a daily basis, what information must be collected, and what is done with the data

Part I: Education Abroad as a Component of U.S. Higher Education

once it is collected. Review existing required student forms to identify potential data fields. What types of reports must be generated on a regular basis? What types of data are requested by the university administration each year? Beyond data, what are the processes required to manage study abroad programming?

A well-designed student database will facilitate administrative functions and should include the following, as applicable:

- *Compilation of biographic, contact, and academic information.* Information pertinent to the student such as permanent, local, and abroad contact information (including e-mail addresses); gender; ethnicity; resident or nonresident status; student identity numbers; parent or guardian contact information and release permissions; date of birth; passport information; grade point average (GPA); year in school; majors, minors, and department or college affiliations; and financial aid and scholarship awards. The accuracy of the information will greatly enhance the flow of communication among students, parents and guardians, international partners, and university administrators.

- *Program information.* Program details specific to each student should be added to the database. Relevant details include program name; type (exchange, home institution study abroad, third party, faculty led); duration (summer, year, semester, quarter, short term, January term); country and city where study abroad will take place; and contact information for the program sponsor (if different from the home institution's education abroad office). Information tracking will facilitate the management of exchange program balances, document the duration of a student's program and his or her destination abroad, and facilitate contact with the program sponsor (for financial aid breakdowns, transcript requests, or other needs).

- *Student tracking and other administrative paperwork.* A database should track students through the various stages of the study abroad process from inquiry to application, acceptance, participation, and return from abroad. Tracking the distribution of paperwork and its submission by each student is also possible. The database can assist in generating the necessary forms (thus assuring efficient distribution to the appropriate students), track when the forms have been submitted, and assist in sending reminders to students who have documents still outstanding.

- *Credit information.* A database can assist with the issuance of credit after completion of an education abroad experience, by tracking each student's courses, grades, and number of credits earned. The database can include the list of courses taken abroad and their home university equivalency. This information will facilitate the issuance of either resident or transfer credit (if this is a function of the education abroad office); analysis of a student's GPA before and after study abroad; and verification of full-time status.

- *Office and staff information.* A database can help manage staff time through tracking of student appointments, staff time spent on specific tasks or programs, and walk-in traffic. In a time of dwindling university resources, documenting the need for staffing for education abroad is vital. University administrators are more apt to adequately support operations and staffing levels in offices that have ready statistics that demonstrate the number of students affected by the office's work on a regular basis.

- *Billing and payment details.* The billing and payment processes of the education abroad office can be expedited with the help of a database. The office usually must compile fee information for billing and must track payments, whether the office does the billing directly or transmits the information to the bursar's office. A quality database can reduce this cumbersome process from days to hours if properly maintained and managed.

Choosing a Data Management System. Once the need for and advantages of having a student database for education abroad management have been acknowledged, it is important to choose the database that will serve the office's specific needs. There are database programs already developed specifically for education abroad offices, or an office can design its own, using existing database software such as Microsoft Access, Foxpro, Sybase, MySQL, or Oracle.

There are several important considerations to guide the decision about whether to purchase an existing database or design a unique one. What database software does the institution support? Contact the technology department and ask. What are the knowledge and expertise levels in the education abroad office? Will training be available through the institution? Will the database be compatible with the office's current word processing and spreadsheet software? Should the database link with the university-wide student record system, for ease in merging letters and forms and sharing financial documents? One advantage of downloading student data is the elimination of duplicate entry, thus accruing greater efficiency of time and information. A disadvantage might be that information obtained directly from the students is more current, and therefore periodic downloads may delete the updates. Will the database be linked to the registrar's and bursar's record systems? If direct linkage might be problematic, consider whether there are other ways of generating data reports that will be more easily transferable. As new versions of software are introduced, will the database need to be upgraded? Will the education abroad office have network capabilities, so that two or more staff members may use information simultaneously (consider, for example, a situation in which a receptionist is entering student appointments while an education abroad professional is processing application letters)?

Prepackaged Software. There are existing databases that have been designed by study abroad professionals in collaboration with software specialists. These databases can be purchased by the education abroad office and then customized to respond to the specific requirements of the institution. The processes of study abroad office management and data needs are established, although each office will need to adapt the prepackaged software to the processes and data needs which are specific to the office's operation. The list of majors, minors, departments, required forms, and other items will then be added to the database lists. While a ready-made program will save substantial time and money in the design process, initial time will be required to customize the database and to transfer existing data into the new software or enter it from existing paper files.

Building a Database. The education abroad office may decide to design its own database and build the database to its own specifications. Unless someone in the education abroad office is highly skilled in using the software selected, it is strongly recommended that a computer programmer be tasked with building the database. Although it may seem like a cost savings to ask a student computer class to assist with the project, keep in mind that these students may not have a clear understanding of the needs of the education abroad office or the skills required for a long-lasting database program, and they may not be available down the road as questions or concerns arise. Verify that the software of choice can be maintained and adapted to changing needs. Techies may have a tendency to recommend software they are familiar with rather than software that will best serve an office's or an educator's particular needs. If the technical coding is so complex that only the builder can generate reports, download information for merge documents, or make corrections and additions, the database will quickly lose its effectiveness with staffing transitions.

Data Integrity and Security

A database will only be as good as the information that it stores and organizes. It is essential that staff be trained on how the database functions, to appreciate the need for consistency in data entry. Standardized drop-down lists of choices should be built into appropriate fields to assure such uniformity. For example, if one person enters the major as "Foreign Languages" and another enters it as "For. Lang." (or any other variation), the reporting will be skewed. The queries for information may entirely overlook this record, leading to errors in administration and reporting. All study abroad staff should feel comfortable with data entry, appreciate the benefits of the database, and be expected to actively maintain the accuracy of information, but one person should be designated to periodically monitor the data entry and manage the database. With some basic training it is not difficult to verify tables of information on a bi-semester basis to verify the accuracy of the data. Also consider what kind of access the staff, students, and other departments should have to the database. Some individuals should have sophisticated editing access; others should have only reading capability.

In summary, the question is not whether the education abroad office will design, build, and implement a student database, but when the office will integrate the database into its annual office management objectives. The process will require a substantial time commitment in early stages, so plan accordingly and do not expect immediate results.

But the long-term savings in terms of staff time, office efficiency, and student support will be well worth the initial investment. What are the financial implications of a ready-made versus self-designed database? Will the institution charge for support? If the office is a large one, will a study abroad staff member be hired and charged with managing and maintaining the database program? What is the cost of ready-made software support?

Course Databases

Course databases are a separate type of software that may or may not be integrated with a student database. Integration will facilitate the student's search for education abroad programs that provide courses specific to his or her needs. A course database is usually an integral part of third-party program Web sites and can be a tool for an education abroad office Web site. The courses available through each study abroad program should be classified by discipline and country so that the database's search engine can retrieve the program name when key words are entered by the student.

The Cost of Replacement Cycles and Staying Current

Most institutions are implementing or already operating on a three-year replacement cycle for computers, printers, and other major peripherals used by departments and offices. For large institutions or institutions just beginning the replacement cycle on a small scale, it may take several years before all departments and offices receive upgraded hardware. In this respect, one rarely has to worry about purchasing hardware for staff members from the office budget.

It is important, however, to have a clear understanding of the priority that the education abroad office has in the replacement cycle schedule. Academic departments are traditionally given priority over administrative departments. Educating the campus technology department on the nature of the services education abroad offices provide and how heavily the education abroad office relies on technology may be key in securing more priority in the replacement cycle—assuming that the cost of replacement is not something that must be absorbed by the education abroad office alone.

Additionally, it is very important to be clear about how many computers will be replaced. It is not uncommon for the technology department to replace the computers of full-time staff and faculty first, disregarding student workstations or other workstations not fully occupied. In these situations, the education abroad office may be left with less-than-ideal computers as student workstations, or with the prospect of replacing these computers from its own operation budget.

Training Staff on New Technology

Time must be set aside to train staff on new technology. The biggest error is thinking that successful training can occur when the administrative cycle has slowed and quiet time is available. Ideally, training should be done when there is an opportunity for immediate transfer of learning, and staff can return to the office and apply the knowledge they have gained. Most importantly, documentation should be provided as part of the training.

Directors and professionals in the field have begun to discuss the need for technical expertise within the education abroad office. Several offices have begun to hire their own technical gurus to manage the data and systems they have put in place. Large and small offices alike may wish to assess the time spent dealing with technology problems. The decision to designate a specific staff member as the "coordinator" of technology should depend on several things, including

- the level of support and responsiveness of the technology department or help desk,
- the reliability of hardware and the network, and
- the education abroad office's reliance on the technology in use.

If productivity can be improved by having a resident expert or liaison to deal with networking, printer, hardware, and software issues, it may be worth the investment to train a staff member. If staff time is not available, consider discussing the designation of a student worker from the technology department or arranging for direct access to one of the technology specialists.

INTEGRATING WITH THE WIRED CAMPUS

Integrating the education abroad office's systems and processes with the wider technology world on campus has several definitive long-term benefits: the community comes to understand the office's responsibilities; the technology department considers international education in discussions of future technology use; and through integration, data are shared between the education abroad office and other key departments on campus. The education abroad office must start by internally exploring the role of its office and the institution in the digital age. It must then look externally at the systems in use around campus.

Building Your Integration Plan and Your Knowledge Base

The education abroad office can begin building an integration strategy by following these steps:

- Identify guiding policies currently in use. What are the campus policies for use and application of technology? What are the appropriate use policies for faculty and students and what are the licensing requirements for software purchased by the university?

- Assess the current condition (age, operating system version, processor speed, etc.) of all technology systems in the office, and closely examine the office's technology infrastructure. This technology assessment includes items such as hardware, software, printers, networking, connectivity, and remote (off-campus) access.

- Analyze the office's present and future needs. Don't just look at tomorrow; look at the future one year, five years, and ten years out.

- Construct and implement a pilot test. Put a small pilot in place that represents the larger scale integration the education abroad office seeks. Try it, grow it, test it, break it, and then reexamine it.

- Evaluate the office's integration plan. What happened with the pilot or with the integration efforts that are underway? What is good, bad, or ugly about the plan or the pilot?

- Maintain and support the integration plan. One of the key aspects of any planning is developing an understanding of not only the short-term needs but also the long-term needs. Is there adequate support in the office's budget? Does the technology system allow for change? Most importantly, does the system allow for the transmittal of information to the appropriate places? Will the education abroad office receive resources and support for the integration project?

As a next step, education abroad professionals should review their understanding of the campus technology systems in use. The major products used by academic units, student affairs, financial aid, human resources, can be broken down into several categories.

Off-the-Shelf Products

Off-the-shelf products are typically purchased from a vendor, and range from the standard desktop operating systems offered by Microsoft and Apple to very large and intricate data management systems such as those produced by companies like PeopleSoft and SCT (Banner, SCTR Plus, etc.) for admissions and registrars' offices and human resources offices. On the academic side there are products such as WEB CT and Blackboard as well as a range of other classroom applications. E-mail systems such as Novell GroupWise, Microsoft Outlook, and Eudora are good examples of products typically used in the communications area. And of course there are the popular office applications such as the Microsoft Office suite of products (Word, Excel, Access, FrontPage, PowerPoint, Outlook) and the WordPerfect Office products (Wordperfect, Quattro Pro and Presentations).

In-House Systems

The university likely employs in-house technology staff that write programs, code, and so on, and support a customized series of data systems. The design and support of university Web pages as well as the support of free standing department specific databases are examples of typical in-house systems.

Hybrid Systems

A hybrid technology system is perhaps the most common method of data system management on campuses. Often, a university will purchase a commercial product that is essentially ready to use, and adapt it for internal use through the intervention of programmers and technology staff.

Another element of campus systems that education abroad professionals should consider is the test environment. The test environment is often a parallel world for the systems noted in the preceding paragraphs. It is where patches, fixes, new versions, and all the related software issues are experimented with, to see the impact any new additions will have on the various linked systems, and more specifically on the data contained in the systems. Making a simple patch on one data element can literally trash all the data related to the element in the system. Testing should always take place in a *test* environment and not in the *production* environment (or the 'prod,' as it is called by those in the technology field).

There are many types of data sources in a technology system. However, remember that in the simplest terms there are only two types of core data to look at in the systems discussed above: (1) real-time mainframe data and (2) data warehouse information. Real-time data are most often found in student information systems, human resources systems, and other core systems. Real time refers to live data that monitor the day-to-day activities of the university. The data warehouse (in its most basic sense) is a snap shot of the system data and is stored independently so that institutional planning people can take a look at the state of the university data in a longitudinal way. These data are often frozen in time only once, twice, or three times per term.

By reaching an understanding of campus technology systems and their levels, the education abroad professional will gain an idea of who has access to the data elements and various systems. The basic question that needs to be asked is "Who puts the data into the systems and how?" This is a crucial question because data integrity can become compromised when multiple units, including colleges and departments, have access and perhaps even update capability. Admissions offices are often the first level of data entry, and that data can be broken down by undergraduate and graduate programs. The human resources office may have its own accounting or business systems and may also have its own data system. But most campuses these days have only a campus wide student information system, which feeds data to all the other systems (with each department or office adding data to its own subsystem). So the information networks are linked and the source of the data may have some commonalities. Examine the data already in the system and determine whether the education abroad office can access it to avoid a duplication of effort. In short, make the existing system work for the education abroad office.

Once admissions, student, human resources and accounting data are in the system, determine how they are manipulated, massaged, reported, etc. Often, campuses have one office that reports institutional data. This office is sometimes called the Office of Planning and Analysis, the Office of Institutional Research, or something similar, and it is often part of the President's Office. The staff in this office help report data to professional, state, and federal agencies. The Office of Institutional Research can support the education abroad office in submitting data for the Institute of International Education's *Open Doors* report, or submit it on behalf of the education abroad office and the institution. Educators should find out how the institutional research office on its campus can assist with data requests for *Open Doors* and other, mandated reports. The research office may already be assisting other departments and offices with similar data requests.

Reaching Out to the Community

Once an integration plan and knowledge base has been established for internal use, education abroad offices must then try to become integrated with the world of the wired campus, that is, outside the education abroad unit. Education abroad professionals would be well-served by creating a list of questions that can be asked of a variety of people such as department heads, technology staff, and colleagues responsible for the reporting of institutional data. Questions to be answered include:

- Who is responsible for management of the campus technology infrastructure? Is there a committee for the management of technology on campus? Educators might be surprised at how centralized such management can be!

- Who is responsible for actually processing information on your campus? Who inputs the data? Who corrects the data?

- Where is the (student) data held? And even more importantly, what data are already held?

- Who else on campus uses or needs access to the same data that you use?

- What does the technology department do, who staffs the department, who does staff report to at the institution? Get to know them. Speak their language and help them learn the language of education abroad!

- What data does the campus already report electronically, for what purposes, and to whom?

Have a list of questions to show others to elicit their opinion on how your office can achieve its technology goals.

Beyond these systems questions, there are also important *data* questions which need to be asked.

These include questions such as:

- Who is officially responsible for the electronic reporting functions of the university?

- Who is officially responsible for the security of the electronic records and reports, and what are the security policies related to the records and reports?

- Where are electronic records held? What kinds of systems are used?

- What support is there for shadow data systems and where do the shadow systems exist on campus? Shadow systems are generally those data, e-mail, and other systems that are not centrally maintained but which may pull or access data from core systems.

- What data do the shadow systems maintain?

- How are the shadow systems linked? Do the shadow systems actively retrieve data from one source?

- How do shadow systems report data to the university system?

- What percentage of the information needed by the education abroad office is already captured in an electronic format? How can the education abroad office get these data so that double entry is avoided?

- What is the education abroad administration doing to get the office included in the university technology system?

Achieving Integration in Stages

It is often best to achieve integration slowly, so there is minimum disruption to the education abroad office's own processes. Consider the following education abroad office components and processes for integration:

- *Hardware.* How is purchasing handled? Is there a lease program? Is there a central repair function? Does the education abroad office or the institution have service contracts for repairs and support or help desks for software and data assistance?

- *Software.* How is purchasing handled? Do you have campus wide licenses for "office bundles?" Is there one e-mail system for the entire campus? What operating systems and networks are supported?

- *Data.* Where do student or faculty data reside for those who participate in education abroad programs? For the international student and scholar community? Where does the information come from for campuswide crisis management?

- *Reports.* Who generates the lists of students abroad? Programs abroad? Faculty with international experiences? Campuswide agreements? International students and scholars? International employees? Who wants or needs to see this information?

- *Visioning.* What are the campus plans for the future? Where are the technologies going? What is the future of distance technologies? Classroom technologies? The wireless world? Cellular technologies? Campus committees are looking at these technologies and planning for them.

The key element is to get maximum support from an integrated approach. Moving away from proprietary or shadow systems within the education abroad office, and toward an integrated approach, is a first step in gaining support and interest from the technology expertson campus In some ways, integration is hardest on the international education unit because it must adapt to the bigger picture, and often the office can feel as though it is being held back because of the limitations of the big systems. In the long run though, being integrated gives the education abroad office a voice in campus decision-making and allows others to represent the education abroad office in institutional matters.

Linking with the campus technology department requires that the education abroad office know its data and its technology system or systems, participate on the relevant committees, and teach their own administration about the need for their support in getting better specialized support, training programs, and policies that address the administration of international education in the mainstream of the campus education mission. The education abroad office can also look outward and educate NAFSA and other professional organizations such as EDUCAUSE (a nonprofit association whose mission is to advance higher education by promoting the intelligent use of information technology) and other technology organizations.

Legal and Ethical Issues of Technology and Its Use

Technology has greatly improved the administration of education abroad programs and communication among colleagues and students around the world, but international educators cannot overlook the important legal and ethical issues raised by its use. Online resources that detail a code of ethics for computer use for educators and professionals now abound. In cyberspace, terms such as 'cyber-citizenship', 'cyber ethics', and 'netiquette' have emerged to help society define appropriate cyber social behavior. Most institutions provide its employees and students with institutional guidelines for technology use. Even with guidelines provided, many of the legal and ethical aspects of technology use are still open to interpretation. Regardless, there are several aspects of responsible technology use that all education abroad professionals must consider:

- Appropriate use: Use technology responsibly and in a manner consistent with its intended use.

- Copyright and fair use: Be informed on current copyright laws. Abide by institutional guidelines for fair use of technology for educational purposes.

- Privacy: Respect the students' privacy, especially educational records and personal information, when collecting or distributing information. Respect for students privacy applies to student lists and other information posted on the institution's or education abroad office's Web site. Where federal laws exist to protect the privacy of student educational records (e.g., the Family Educational Rights and Privacy Act, FERPA in the United States), education abroad professionals should understand their institution's policy on how and under what circumstances information may be shared within the campus community and with parents or third parties.

- Access: Be proactive in assessing whether the technology being used in the education abroad office (or by students) is accessible to students with disabilities. Consider whether appropriate access exists for all technological processes that students must complete during the education abroad experience (e.g., registration, housing lottery).

- Internet/intranet/e-mail: These mediums are not considered confidential forms of communication. Exercise good judgment when communicating via e-mail, and when storing, sharing, or sending files via the internet.

- Social consequences: Consider the consequences when using technology or generating reports. As an educator, you should use technology in ways that benefit society, for positive (not negative) outcomes, and in a manner

Part I: Education Abroad as a Component of U.S. Higher Education

which represents yourself and your institution appropriately.

- Professional responsibility: Maintain and expand professional competency through continuous training in the technologies used in the education abroad field and, when applicable, within higher education in general (Adapted from Bequette et al., 2001).

Technological advances have provided us with instantaneous voice and data communication from almost anywhere in the world with almost anywhere else. Education abroad professionals now face the challenge of advising and preparing a technologically savvy generation for an overseas experience. Professionals will need to consider how technology is (or is becoming) part of the local culture overseas and prepare their students to understand and adapt to it. They must consider technology's impact on cultural immersion, global competence, and student learning styles. In addition, the education abroad office must take stock of its own use of technology within the office, and must seek ways to integrate its systems and processes with the wider campus technology infrastructure. In doing so, avenues for sophisticated data generation and institutional advocacy can emerge. Finally, education abroad professionals should be aware of the standards of appropriate technology use and the potential pitfalls in generating and distributing sensitive data.

Summary

Technological advances have provided us with instantaneous voice and data communication from almost anywhere in the world with almost anywhere else. On the one hand, this has allowed for closer collaboration between U.S.-based program administrators and their colleagues in study abroad programs overseas. On the other hand, it has allowed students to remain in much closer contact with their family and friends at home than ever before. Ease of access to home, family and friends through technology can make cultural adaptation more difficult, in that students (or faculty) do not feel the need to make new friends. Yet, no matter where a program is located, the locals will be talking on mobile phones and using the internet. Education abroad professionals will need to consider how technology is (or is becoming) part of the local culture overseas and prepare their students to understand and adapt to it. Similarly, the education abroad office exists within the technological culture of the institution. Being a 'resident' of this culture, requires the same cultural adaptation skills (flexibility, empathy, cross-cultural understanding, sense of humor, etc.) needed to integrate into any foreign culture.

CHAPTER 9

Education Abroad and Community Colleges

Contributors: Rosalind Latiner Raby, Geremie Sawadogo

Because of a misunderstanding of the role of study abroad programs at community colleges, several myths concerning study abroad's context and history, duration, logistics and programming, and administrative support and funding have emerged. The current high level of study abroad activity at many community colleges belies most of these myths. Such activity provides evidence of the role community colleges are playing to reduce the elitism that is traditional in U.S. study abroad. As do four-year institutions, community colleges believe in the benefits gained from studying abroad for all students, and especially for underrepresented students. Benefits include definite changes in perception and attitude towards global relationships, increased empathy toward politics and social service, significant learning curve growth in interpersonal skills and academic performance, and reduction of cultural stereotypes. Although short-term programs generally do not allow beginning language learners to gain comprehensive proficiency, such students still gain much from studying in another country. In adhering to the community college "open door" philosophy, study abroad programs include all ages, aptitudes, and backgrounds without sacrificing academic standards.

What is the Community College?

More than half of all U.S. students pursuing postsecondary education are enrolled in the 1,200 community colleges across the United States (Raby 1999). These institutions have a dual mission: to prepare students to continue their education in a four-year institution, and to provide critical training for direct application in the work place. Historically, several factors contributed to expansion of community colleges. These include the great need for trained and qualified workers for the nation's expanding industries, the Morrill Law of 1862, the lengthened period of adolescence that mandated longer custodial care for youths, the quest for social equality, and the GI bill of 1944. From 1901 until the 1940s, all community colleges were known as junior colleges. In the 1960s a national network of 457 community colleges emerged. By the 1970s due to changing emphasis of need, almost all junior colleges changed their names to community colleges (Cohen and Brawer 1981). The states with the largest number of community colleges are California (108), Texas (67), and North Carolina (59).

Typically, community colleges (formerly called junior colleges) are publicly supported institutions, accredited to grant short-cycle certificates, award associate degrees as their highest degrees (although some now offer Baccalaureate programs), and prepare noncertificated graduates for mid-level labor markets. Although each community college is unique based on its geographic location and the public education laws of the state in which it is located, four characteristics are shared by all community colleges.

Community colleges exist between upper secondary education and university education, and although they are included in state education plans, each community college may have a curriculum, budget, and mission that express localized connections.

Community colleges offer educational programs that emphasize technical, occupational, vocational, in-service retraining and training, or remedial programs; define a preuniversity or lower division academic instruction in liberal arts and sciences; provide socio-cultural acculturation programs, including adult education, English and citizenship for recent immigrants, and community services for lifelong learning (Cohen and Brawer 2002; Raby and Tarrow 1996; Vaughan 1998).

Community colleges may not share the prestige that is given to universities and they are frequently poorly supported financially. Tuition at community colleges is consistently lower than at universities, yet can still be out of reach for many students. Recent enrollment increases multiply overall costs that continue to make finances a critical issue (O'Banion 1997).

Community colleges embody an ideal that low tuition accentuates open accessibility, which in turn perpetuates educational and thereby economic democracy. Community colleges' open-access policies decrease the social gap by assisting with transfer between secondary schools, postsecondary institutions, and the job market; allow for an alternative route and a second-chance opportunity for postsecondary education; increase the availability of educational choices for disadvantaged populations and encourage greater participation in the overall economy; provide flexible programs in terms of requirements, admission, quality, and output of education opportunities; and build and maintain democratic overtures in relation to societal change (Raby 1996).

For the most part, community college students are age seventeen and older, and are admitted regardless of educational attainment, age, or socio-economic status. In 2004, 44 percent of all U.S. undergraduates attended community colleges and 45 percent of first time freshmen are in community colleges (AACC 2005). Traditionally, community college students were first-generation attendees or those who were labeled as academically and socio-economically at risk. Today, however, a range of students are choosing to attend community colleges because of the low tuition, strong academic and counseling support, and smaller class sizes. One of the largest groups of community college students comprises those who choose to complete their lower division course work and then transfer to a four-year school, in an effort to significantly reduce the cost of a four-year degree. Another notable group comprises those students who already possess a bachelor's degree but attend community college for instruction in differential work skills needed for job promotion. The tremendous diversity of students, therefore, does not fit a traditional higher educational profile (Cohen and Brawer 2002), as community colleges have become the place to expand opportunities and challenge the notion of higher education as an elitist venture intended for only a few.

Community colleges serve local community needs and in turn, design specific programs for older, place-bound, part-time students who have jobs, families, and other obligations that compete with academic requirements. The student population mirrors a multicultural and multiethnic mixture of local communities. Therefore community colleges tend to serve a greater proportion of lower income and minority students than in any other postsecondary institution. More than two-thirds of all community college students attend part-time and more than 80 percent balance education with full- or part-time work. Most importantly, of all students nationwide in higher education, 46 percent of African-American students, 55 percent of all Latino students, 46 percent of all Asian and Pacific Islander students, and 55 percent of all Native American students are enrolled in community colleges (Chancellor's Office, California Community Colleges [COCCC] 2002).

Community colleges are accountable to local universities because they provide an accredited preuniversity curriculum. Community colleges are also connected to local businesses because they design their curricula and programs to relate to the economic, social, and political needs of the community. Community colleges pride themselves on providing educational choices that reflect student and community needs. In spite of a rich educational tradition, community colleges only began to embrace international education in the mid-1960s. Most community colleges nationwide now sponsor international educational initiatives that bear many similarities to those offered by their four-year counterparts. These programs include internationalized classroom instruction and off-campus programs that combine different types of pedagogy. Study abroad is one such initiative.

Education Abroad and Community Colleges

The demographics, academic focus, and economics of community colleges necessarily result in a different study abroad profile than that of four-year institutions. Overseas programs for community college students nevertheless range from single-subject, one- or two-week courses for minimal credit to summer and full-semester programs with a full academic load. As is largely true of the national profile, instruction is primarily in the arts, world languages, humanities, natural and physical sciences, social sciences, and occupational fields. Travel and living arrangements are typically arranged by the college, a third-party provider, or both, as is the case elsewhere. In short, study abroad programs in which community college students participate offer an accredited academic curriculum that frequently matches transfer requirements of four-year institutions, as well as state mandated funding requirements in terms of weekly student contact hours, average daily attendance, full-time equivalent student counts, etc. Similar to study on campus, study abroad provides the college with state funding based on an established ratio of faculty-to-student contact hours. As such, study abroad class hours must match the state-mandated measurement of faculty-to-student contact hours per unit per semester.

Typically, any community college student in good academic standing must be admitted to that college's study abroad program. In some states, California for example, it is a state law. Thus, if a student is eligible to attend on-campus classes and programs, the student is also eligible to attend off-campus and overseas programs. The 1960s image of community-based institutions as "people's colleges" persists. As such, community colleges continue to provide for many students the only form of higher education that they will ever obtain. Open admission thus extends to study abroad programs, making such activities open and accessible to many who would not otherwise participate in educational endeavors overseas.

Context and History History of Community Colleges

Study abroad traditionally has been seen as the sole domain of four-year colleges and universities. Prior to 1967, community college institutional and student participation in study abroad was in fact negligible (Hess 1982). Both the embryonic state of the community college system and the philosophy that these colleges were not appropriate mechanisms for study abroad impeded development of study abroad programs at community colleges. Even today, there are many community college stakeholders who still define the role of community geographically. Moreover, many stakeholders also have an outmoded concept of education abroad as a set of highly selective and prohibitively expensive semester-length programs for traditional-aged students at four-year institutions, and thus well beyond the reach of community college students. By designing study abroad programs that are open to all students and through which all students can benefit, community colleges uphold their defining characteristic of open access to the broadest spectrum of society (Raby 1999). In doing so, community colleges have transformed the "junior year abroad" experience into one with democratic undertones (Greenfield 1990; King and Fersh 1992).

Starting about 1967, there have been three phases of study abroad program development (Raby 1996). During the period of 1967 to 1977, community colleges began to recognize that study abroad was possible for their students. The first community college study abroad programs were offered in 1967, and the first office dedicated to study abroad was established in 1969 by SUNY Rockland Community College. In 1971, the American Association of Community Colleges (AACC) established an office for international education that included study abroad as a priority. In 1973, the College Consortium for International Studies (CCIS) pioneered cooperative study abroad efforts with a tri-state consortium. By 1977, an AACC survey noted that 300 community colleges listed study abroad as an important component for their colleges (Shannon 1978).

Between 1980 and 1994, many community colleges established campus international committees and study abroad offices; some offices with full-time directors emerged. Some institutions linked study abroad to already existing international development and programs internationalizing curricula. Because smaller colleges found study abroad logistics costly, regional and state consortia were developed. By awarding an international studies group projects grant in 1976, the U.S. Office of Education validated community colleges as federal grant recipients. Federally funded program development and the mandated dissemination of project outcomes helped to solidify the role of community colleges in study abroad, address the concerns of study abroad opponents and furnish "how-to" guidelines for colleges interested in creating new programs or expanding on existing ones (Raby 1996). Consortial newsletters and brochures have also contributed to the growth of study abroad at community colleges and the increased number of options available to students. Member colleges can list their programs either to announce that these are open to students from other campuses or to invite the collaboration of other faculty or study abroad offices. In general, this type of resource sharing became the foundation upon which many colleges were able to establish their own programs without "reinventing the wheel."

Since the mid-1990s, community colleges have augmented the American Council on International Intercultural Education (ACIIE) 1994 "blueprint for the future." Community colleges have clarified their international education goals, explored how international themes and concepts could be integrated, and envisioned imaginative funding responses (Elsner et al. 1994). The result has been more funding for study abroad programs and augmentation of existing programs in terms of course offerings, geographic locations, and the active recruitment of underrepresented students. A 2001 AACC survey of 1,171 community colleges, with a 26 percent response rate, noted that 78 percent provided study abroad opportunities, an increase of nearly 30 percent since 1995 (Blair et al. 2001).

The key to success for the short-term community college program is whether or not it contains a defined purpose and maximizes the learning potential of the overseas environment. Students who attend programs that offer little interaction with the local population and who maintain weak language skills often reinforce their own ethnocentrism and even experience negative problems related to culture shock. In order to avoid these "island" experiences, wherein U.S. students live together, take courses in English, and rarely mix with the local culture, many community colleges sponsor programs that house students and faculty with home-stays, and design elements of the program to specifically encourage a real-life experience, no matter how short the program duration. The majority of community college students receive performance grades rather than a "credit or no-credit" option for study abroad. In many programs, students must sign contracts stating that their intention is to pursue academic work and that they understand that if they do not engage in academic work, they face the risk of being sent home.

Currently, the worldwide recession is affecting the number of community college students and faculty who can afford to travel abroad. Global terrorism and health crises such as AIDS and SARS have also caused some students to question whether they should go overseas. Severe cuts in community college budgets and the general economic slowdown are placing existing programs in jeopardy and causing archaic interpretations of the community college role in study abroad to resurface.

In spite of these obstacles, changing local socio-economic needs and the emergence of

Part I: Education Abroad as a Component of U.S. Higher Education

Table 1. Historical connections: case study profiles from Arizona (Maricopa Community College District [MCCD]), Pennsylvania (Community College of Philadelphia [CCP]), and California (California Colleges for International Education [CCIE])

First programs offered	MCCD: Initiated first summer programs to Mexico in 1984
	CCIE: Before 1976, only five colleges offered summer programs. The first semester-long programs were offered in 1977 by El Camino, L.A. Harbor, and Santa Monica colleges
	CCP: Initiated first summer programs to London in 2001
State laws	California state law first allowed state apportionment for community college study abroad in 1976. Proposition 13 (1978) drastically reduced public education funding, and peripheral programs such as study abroad were subject to budget cuts and program eliminations. Consequently, all future programs were forever linked to the state's economy.
Growth	CCIE was established in 1983 with twenty-one members. In 2000, ninety-four of the state's 108 community colleges offered study abroad options
Augmentation issues	CCIE: 1988 saw the expansion of course locations as the first programs were initiated in China, Ukraine, and Vietnam
	CCP: Will soon initiate programs in Japan, China, and Italy
	Throughout the 1990s, emphasis at all community colleges grew on academic standards, health, safety, and legal issues and serving underrepresented students

Source: Original survey research conducted for this chapter by Rosalind Raby, PhD, 2003.

neighborhoods that reflect multicultural diversity are forcing community colleges to rewrite their mission statements. Mandates are being put into place that will ensure that students have increased global competencies and a sensitivity to local, national, and international issues. AACC maintains that "it is increasingly evident that community colleges are strategically positioned and experienced to educate and train individuals to function successfully in a multicultural and advanced technological environment that crosses all boundaries of education, communication, language and business" (Boggs and Irwin 2003). Research indicates that success in preparing students for transfer, as well as students' success in workforce training, is enhanced by securing international literacy skills. One of the more effective ways to obtain this literacy is through study abroad, which Oberstein-Deballe (1999) notes is an integral component of international education within community colleges (Scanlon 1990; King and Fersh 1992; Raby 1996; Boggs and Irwin 2003).

For first-generation or immigrant students, all forms of study abroad provide an opportunity to re-learn their own cultures and histories. For students who have not traveled beyond their own neighborhoods, studying abroad can be a life-altering experience (Oberstein-Deballe 1999). Many program evaluations illustrate that community college students who participate even in one- to three-week programs have a renewed interest in their education, and that their academic performance improves significantly after their return. Study abroad therefore is a recognized investment in the future ability of all students, teaching them to interact in a multicultural world (Carew 1993). In sum, what benefits there are for four-year college students via study abroad also exist for community college students.

Although the Institute of International Education's (IIE) *Open Doors* survey has collected data from community colleges for many years, it did not offer a break-down of community college numbers until spring 2003. Still, IIE data for the 2001–2002 academic year come from only 180 of the nation's 1,200 community colleges. Of these, only ninety-one indicate that they sent at least one student abroad. The national total is given as 3,941 students. There is good reason to believe that the IIE figures greatly underrepresent actual totals. For example, whereas *Open Doors* reports that twenty-eight California colleges sent 1,516 students abroad, the CCIE *2001 Annual Report* indicates that fifty colleges sent over 4,250 students abroad (Raby 2002). Even then the CCIE numbers probably are low because many non–CCIE members send students abroad on CCIE programs. Hence, while the total number of reported community college students being sent abroad nationwide is indeed low, it is likely that the *Open Doors* numbers reflect an extremely conservative estimate.

Duration and Content

Community college student participation in year-long programs is rare. But the widely held belief that community colleges only offer summer programs is not the case. In addition to summer programming, community colleges offer semester and short-term (often course-related) programs. Because *Open Doors* reports summer and short-term programs (defined as less than eight weeks) together in a single category, concrete data on how many students participate in each of these types of programs are unclear. Community college winter intersession and spring break programs (typically one to three weeks in duration) tend to offer courses in the natural and physical sciences. Summer programs (typically three to eight weeks in duration) tend to offer courses in world languages and civilizations, followed closely by courses in the natural and physical sciences. Semester- or quarter-long programs (typically ten to sixteen weeks in duration) tend to offer courses that satisfy general education requirements.

Many community college students typically complete their general education requirements at the community college before transferring to a four-year school? By taking some of those requirements abroad, students do not lose opportunities in their future academic majors (Altshuler 2001). Rather, community colleges epitomize Marcum's (2001) call to integrate study abroad into lower-division curricula and majors. Furthermore, because of the short-term nature of many of the community college programs, studying abroad does not preclude participation in most college activities; students can still work for the college newspaper, be active in student government, and participate in clubs.

The field of international education in general continues to struggle with the question of how to determine the optimal length of a study abroad experience. Two conflicting views exist. One view is that length is a deciding factor in determining a study abroad program's pedagogical value; specifically, that students need to live and learn long enough overseas for the foreign environment to have a significant effect on their learning. Another view acknowledges that although a longer duration program may provide an optimal learning experience, participation in a program of any length is better than having no overseas experience at all.

Short-term programs have become especially appealing to both two- and four-year students who

Table 2. Program duration: case study profiles from Arizona (MCCD), California (CCIE), Illinois (College of DuPage—COD; and Illinois Consortium for International Studies and Programs—ICISP), and Pennsylvania (CCP)

	Program duration		
	Summer*	Winter/spring break†	Semester‡
MCCD	3–4 weeks	NA	NA
CCIE	4–6 weeks	1–3 weeks	10–16 weeks
COD/ICISP	5–6 weeks	2–4 weeks	14 weeks
CCP	4–6 weeks	NA	NA

NA indicates not applicable.
* In 2002–2003, MCCD offered 17 summer programs, CCIE offered 71, COD/ICISP offered 8, and CCP offered 2.
† In 2002–2003, CCIE offered 12 winter/spring break programs and COD/ICISP offered one spring break program.
‡ In 2002–2003, CCIE offered 71 semester or quarter programs and COD/ICISP offered one semester program.

Source: Original survey research conducted for this chapter by Rosalind Raby, PhD, 2003.

feel many pressures and know that time is often a valuable commodity. Short-term programs are often the only viable choice for many community college students, given their family and work obligations. For Middlesex Community College, MA, students, a three-week program is optimal, whereas for Maricopa Community College District (MCCD), AZ students, a four-week program has proved to be the preferred choice. It is important for each institution to design programs that fit the needs and lifestyles of the students. Table 2 illustrates some examples of the different approaches to study abroad program duration.

Typical Community College Programs

Community colleges typically offer one or more of four different types of programs:

Faculty-led programs in which individual faculty design, coordinate, market, and lead their programs abroad. These programs can be accomplished with the assistance of a study abroad office or by an individual faculty member working alone. The latter option is encouraged by some colleges, and discouraged by others because of college liability issues. The unique nature of the relationship between faculty and students at community colleges increases the popularity of faculty-led programs, and strong evidence exists that demonstrates that students are more likely to participate in study abroad when the programs are run by the faculty who teach them.

Faculty-led programs with logistics coordinated by third-party providers, in which a third-party provider assists faculty with program design, then coordinates and markets the programs. Faculty members, however, still teach the classes in the program. In many states, such as California, community college faculty are not allowed to coordinate their own travel arrangements and must use a third-party provider because of college liability issues. In states with such requirements, study abroad directors are highly encouraged to collect bids from third-party providers in order to select the best provider for each individual program.

Third-party provider centers or institutes, in which a college sends its students to established centers or institutes without college faculty involvement. Some colleges have established working relationships with various organizations and have had campus curriculum committees approve courses offered by these organizations so that students can receive college credit from course work taken while abroad.

Chapter 9: Education Abroad and Community Colleges

Consortia-led programs, in which clusters of colleges work together to design, coordinate, and market programs, share costs, and accept the transfer of credits from students enrolled in consortia-sponsored programs. Some consortia, such as CCIE, exist solely as a clearinghouse for advocacy and collaboration, whereas other consortia, such as CCIS, arrange all aspects of a study abroad program. Mini-consortia have recently become popular and are organized locally or by state. As the overhead costs for logistics increase, many colleges have found that working with mini-consortia is more economically feasible than working with large consortia. Two mini-consortia models exist. The first model designates a "lead college" that designs a program, sends its own faculty to lead the program, and receives all average daily attendance funding from students attending its program from other colleges. The second model changes the "lead" college annually to allow each consortia member an opportunity to send its own faculty abroad and receive average daily attendance funding. The benefit of the mini-consortia is that member colleges have an opportunity to send just one student abroad and still, without overhead costs, be involved in promoting study abroad.

Funding and Administrative Support

The best indicator of the extent of support for education abroad at community colleges lies in the large number of thriving programs and increasing student enrollments. It is unfortunately true for the time being, with the current budget crisis, that study abroad is sometimes still viewed by community college administrators and boards as dispensable, and that it is often among the first programs eliminated in times of crisis. Nonetheless, national surveys consistently cite chief executive officer or trustee support for study abroad. While there is a dichotomy in many institutions between verbal and actual support for study abroad, there are six criteria that can help define institutional commitment. Few colleges support all six criteria, but the more of these criteria that are backed, the less peripheral study abroad is.

Mention of international education in general, and study abroad in specific, in college policy, mission, master plan, and annual priorities. If international education and study abroad are included in college documents, support is evident (at least on paper) and study abroad options become more secure.

Connective tissue between study abroad and other college programs. If study abroad is part of the total college environment, it is less likely to become a stand-alone program. With integration into the college environment, both the study abroad funding and overall support become more secure. Study abroad participation is bolstered if academic programs require or encourage a study abroad option.

A campus study abroad committee that includes representatives from throughout the campus environment, the faculty senate, or from selected departments. Such a committee can help select participating faculty, interview third-party providers, and be involved in all aspects of curriculum planning and pedagogy affiliated with study abroad programs. Because a campus study abroad committee typically draws on representatives from throughout the campus, the presence of study abroad becomes institutionalized.

A line item for study abroad in the college budget. Constant and secure funding is essential for

Part I: Education Abroad as a Component of U.S. Higher Education

Table 3. Logistical connections: case study profiles from Arizona (MCCD) and California (CCIE). The MCCD material comes from their office and the CCIE material comes from the annual reports.

Arizona: MCCD	All programs are faculty led. Most faculty who develop study abroad programs do so because of academic interest or as a result of participating on faculty exchanges during which the faculty develop collaborative agreements with host institutions.
	Several of MCCD's partnerships with educational institutions overseas have helped to establish study abroad programs at sister institutions in Mexico, China, and Australia.
California: CCIE	International education is mentioned in 57 percent of member colleges' mission statements, master plans, college policies, or annual priorities. However, few actually mention study abroad in these documents. 69 percent of member colleges receive no funding to run their programs. Of those that do receive some funding, none have study abroad listed as a line item in the college budget. 25 percent of member colleges have visible offices with adequate clerical assistance. 75 percent have offices, but lack secretarial or technical support, including copying machines.
	34 percent of member colleges have full-time people working with study abroad; 26 percent have part-time people working with study abroad; and 40 percent have faculty or administrators whose job description dictates that either 0 FTE (which indicates that study abroad is not part of the job requirement) or between .2 and 1.5 FTE (which indicates that study abroad is but a small part of their job requirement) of their job is allotted to study abroad responsibilities.

Source: Original survey research conducted for this chapter by Rosalind Raby, PhD, 2003.

any program to thrive. A known line item in the college budget is the best way to secure funding. Because of changing administration, college politics, or budgets, invested and thriving programs can be entirely eliminated, while "peripheral" programs survive, if there is no assured financial support.

A secure, visible office with adequate clerical assistance and a full-time coordinator. In community colleges, the concept of an "office" ranges from a traditional, stand-alone office to a corner of a faculty closet. The key is whether or not this "space" provides a link between study abroad and other college programs. It is necessary for the study abroad office to establish a working relationship with college counselors and the registrar's office, and to be able to list programs in the college class schedule. Most importantly, the office must be in a viable location where students and staff can obtain additional information. The definition of "adequate clerical assistance" for campus offices also varies from institution to institution. Very few colleges have full-time clerical support for their study abroad offices. Some colleges have part-time student help, but most have no assistance. Finally, it is not uncommon to find study abroad duties included in the job requirements of deans, department chairs, and faculty. In some colleges, these individuals receive release time during which they may perform their study abroad duties; in other colleges, study abroad duties are assigned without any release time. There is seldom a requirement that one must be a professional international educator to serve as a coordinator of study abroad activities. A correlation exists between the size of a program and the number of released or full-time office support staff assigned to coordinate and direct programs. When compared to the resources for study abroad at four-year universities, assistance for study abroad duties at community colleges is notably absent.

Availability of counseling services and student advising services. Because community colleges emphasize counseling and student support services, which includes financial aid, these offices become important contact areas for study abroad. Therefore, staff from the counseling and student support offices must be educated on the benefits and availability of study abroad programs, and encouraged to play an integral part in the marketing strategies of the study abroad programs to encourage students' participation.

Community colleges are bound by their mission of open enrollment to offer high-quality academic programs at as low a cost as possible, so as to provide opportunities for all students to participate. Some community colleges annually send their programs out to bid to a variety of third-party providers to assure the highest academic quality at the lowest cost. Utilization of home-stays and dormitories also can help keep costs down. The average cost for a summer program ranges from $180 to $5,000, and a semester program ranges from $3,000 to $8,000. Despite the affordable tuition, loss of employment and estrangement from family still make study abroad prohibitive for many students. Therefore, proper planning and active financial aid and scholarship coordination are required for study abroad program success. It is not uncommon to find a significant number of students doing extensive advance planning in order to go abroad. Some students start planning for their study abroad experience one to two years before actually going abroad. Table 4 depicts the typical costs of CCIE, MCCD, and COD programs.

According to the 2000 ACE report, "Promoting Internationalization of Undergraduate Experience,"

Table 4. Sample study abroad tuition range, 2002–2003. All costs include visa, airfare, lodging, food, tuition and local campus enrollment fees.

	Summer session	Fall or spring semester	Winter or spring break
Low	$ 550 (Baja) $ 1,824–$ 2,200 (Mexico)	$ 1,370–$ 2,399 (Costa Rica) $ 3,687 (Madrid) $ 1,670 (Mexico)	$ 330 (Baja) $ 1,475 (Belize)
Average	$ 2,650–$ 2,800 (Spain, Paris, Czech Republic) $ 2,620 (China) $ 2,670 (Costa Rica) $ 4,900 (China)	$ 4,300 (London) $ 4,600 (Japan) $ 4,800 (Vietnam)	$ 2399 (Thailand) $ 2,550 (Cuba)
High	$ 2,995 (Vietnam) $ 3,195 (Munich) $ 3,290 (Japan) $ 3,315 (Florence) $ 3,999 (England)	$ 5,950 (Florence) $ 6,195 (Paris)	$ 2,600 (Fiji) $ 3,900 (Florence) $ 3,300 (Nepal)

Source: Original survey research conducted for this chapter by Rosalind Raby, PhD, 2003.

30 percent of U.S. students who study abroad receive financial aid (ACE 2000). The CCIE *2002 Annual Report* notes an average of 36 percent of semester-long program participants receive financial aid and 21 percent receive scholarships. It is not uncommon for CCIE member colleges, to have more than 75 percent of their semester study abroad participants receiving financial aid. At times this can reach 100 percent. An average of 13 percent of summer program students receive financial aid and 11 percent receive scholarships. Some colleges, such as Middlesex Community College, add a specified amount to all student fees or secure a percentage of student fees for the purpose of supporting study abroad (Falcetta 2003). It is, thus, not surprising that financial aid is the primary form of funding of study abroad for community college students.

The Role of the Community College Study Abroad Office

Each community college has its own structure. As noted, most community colleges do not have a formal study abroad office staffed with one or more full-time people. Nonetheless, be it in a fully defined office or via less-specialized oversight, someone must be involved in advising and programming, which also means that person must know about legal issues, travel advisories, and related administrative procedures. For some community colleges, there is a chain of command that faculty must go through to get approval for their programs. For example, MCCD faculty must submit their proposals to the relevant administrators, including the department chair, the dean of instruction, and the president, before the proposals are forwarded to the district's international education office for final review and approval by the vice-chancellor for academic affairs. When programs are carried out in collaboration with service providers, selection and approval of the providers must be obtained through a competitive bidding process. At other community colleges, colleges faculty submit their proposals to the international education office, which then shares the proposals with the campus international education committee. Regardless, the more people involved in the selection process, the more institutionalized the study abroad program becomes; it is no longer the whim of a renegade faculty member. Table 4 depicts the different ways study abroad programming is overseen at MCCD and CCIE.

Student Eligibility and Admission Requirements

The open admissions policy and mission of community colleges extends to study abroad. Some colleges no prerequisites as to age, class standing, required course preparation, or GPA. Other community colleges accept only students who are officially enrolled into their study abroad programs, whereas others accept high school students who are concurrently enrolled in community college classes. Prerequisite knowledge, such as language skills, cannot be reinforced, because the community college must offer the same experience abroad that it offers on campus. Issues of compliance for students with disabilities also surface, because although community colleges cannot reject disabled students from a program, even if their disabilities prevent them from full access to program components, the college can advise students as to the most appropriate program to fit their abilities. Finally, while some community colleges have instituted a GPA requirement, others argue that even students with GPAs as low as 1.5 can have life-altering experiences as a result of studying abroad. The most important aspect of designing a study abroad program for a community college is to ensure access for all students (Falcetta 2003).

Health, Safety, and Legal Issues

Community college stakeholders recognize the importance of establishing health, safety, liability, and legal policies related to study abroad. Thus, education abroad professionals at community colleges should inform themselves and work with their campus administrative structure to implement appropriate policies and procedures for health, safety, emergency response, risk management and related issues. (See Part II, Chapter 5, "Health Issues and Advising Responsibilities," and Part II, Chapter 6, "Advising Students on Safety and Security Issues.")

Predeparture and Reentry Programming

Community college predeparture programs can be a few hours of time during orientation just prior to departure, a specifically focused four-hour presentation, or spread out over a few weeks and including an on-campus class component. Orientation programs may be administered by the college, a third-party provider, or both. A typical predeparture program includes basic information about flights, ground and public transportation, home-stay, climate, excursions, packing, passports, telephone and internet access, and money; information on health and safety issues; helpful hints for making the most of the abroad experience; specific information on geography, culture, and socio-economic issues, gender issues, social life, and activities in and near the program site; and local laws. Provision of such information enables students to optimize academic and cultural learning during the time spent abroad. Predeparture orientation programs are particularly useful as a tool to help deepen students' cultural skills and competencies in the short-term programs typical at community colleges. MCCD's predeparture program, for example, includes research and discovery assignments, and addresses theoretical frameworks related to the program.

Many predeparture programs also include information on the host institution or university center. Some colleges have programs that use the internet to allow students to engage in direct communication with host country staff or student peers. Colleges located in areas with a significant host country immigrant population can organize cultural learning encounters between students and that population. While the open door policy of the community college can present some challenges for a predeparture orientation program, the ultimate goal is to equip students to use the overseas program location as a context for implementing and applying the ideas, frameworks, and concepts presented to them before their departure. Generally, the more thorough the predeparture orientation, the more likely it is that students will experience meaningful learning.

Part I: Education Abroad as a Component of U.S. Higher Education

Reentry programs also can range from a few hours of evaluation done while abroad or upon return, to a defined workshop, to concluding the course on campus. Reentry program components help students process and give context to learning and experiences that occurred during the overseas experience. Given the short duration of many community college study abroad programs, it is crucial to create a framework that allows participants to process their experiences in order to maximize learning. By employing an experiential learning cycle that reviews the entire program and draws useful lessons and generalizations, students can be encouraged to take specific courses in subsequent semesters that emphasize their learning experiences. Students can also be counseled on how the new skills acquired abroad can be used to reach individual educational and professional goals. Reentry programs are important, but they are difficult to administer since not all program participants go to the same college and many do not return to a college after completing a study abroad program. For these reasons, reentry programs frequently consist of evaluations that are given on-site abroad rather than after the students return home. Furthermore, if the study abroad director position is a release-time position, then providing a reentry program becomes very difficult. (See Part II, Chapter 7, "Predeparture Orientation and Reentry Programming.")

Table 5. CCIE, MCCD, and COD nontraditional academic-based programs.

Discipline	No. of programs
CCIE	
Art History	11
Humanities	10
Marine Biology	8
Geology	3
Biology	3
Political Science	3
MCCD	
Environment/Geology	2
Interior Design	2
Marine Ecology	2
Natural History	2
Theater	2
Culinary Arts	2
COD	
International Business	1
Fashion Design	1
Sports Medicine	1
Architecture	1
Math	1
Archeology	1

Source: Original survey research conducted for this chapter by Rosalind Raby, PhD, 2003.

Work Abroad and Other Education Abroad Opportunities

Altshuler (2001) assertion that community college students are unable to obtain work-study or internships abroad is far from the truth. Since 1996, a few community colleges have offered a variety of work-study abroad programs. Some programs include short professional internships in industries, businesses, and organizations. Some programs are solely work oriented, whereas others combine work with a study component. Most work-study programs

Chapter 9: Education Abroad and Community Colleges

Table 6. Programmatic connections: case study profiles from Arizona (MCCD), California (CCIE), Illinois (COD and ICISP), and Pennsylvania (CCP)

	Summer	Winter/spring break	Semester/ quarter
MCCD			
Europe	7	0	0
Latin America	5	0	0
Australia/Oceania	2	0	0
Asia	1	0	0
Canada	1	0	0
CCIE			
Europe	46	1	48
Latin America	19	7	4
Australia/Oceania	2	1	1
Asia	6	2	4
Canada	0*	0†	0‡
COD and ICISP			
Europe	5	1 (spring break)	0
Latin America	1	0	1 (semester)
Australia/Oceania	0	0	0
Asia	3	0	0
Canada	0	0	0
CCP			
Europe	1	0	0
Latin America	1	0	0
Australia/Oceania	0	0	0
Asia	0	0	0
Canada	0	0	0

* CCIE also offered summer programs to the following nontraditional sites: Argentina, Bali, Brazil, Cambodia, China, Costa Rica, Cuba, Greece, Guatemala, Japan, Peru, Turkey, Thailand, and Venezuela.
† CCIE also offered winter and spring break programs to the following nontraditional sites: Australia, Cuba, Japan, and Vietnam.
‡ CCIE also offered semester/quarter programs to the following nontraditional sites: Argentina, Bali, China, Costa Rica, Russia, and Vietnam.

Source: *Open Doors 2001–2002.* IIE NETWORK "Open Doors: Community College"

are located in England; however, many colleges are expanding their work-study programs to other countries. The Santa Rosa Junior College (CA), for example, has a program that includes a work-study and internship program in the wine region of Australia.

International visitor programs allow students to travel to prearranged lectures and work meetings. The goal of these programs is to expand and enrich the participant's course work by adding a focused practical international component to it. The programs are short, focused, and almost tailor-made to enhance the professional training of the participants. International service programs take the already-existing opportunities for community college students to conduct community service, volunteerism, or field education, and place that experience abroad. Given the required level of advance activity planning and organization, the best way to succeed in such endeavors might be through partnerships with overseas institutions, thereby insuring that participants are assigned tasks and activities that can result in meaningful learning and service rendered.

Part I: Education Abroad as a Component of U.S. Higher Education

Table 7. Ethnic Breakdown of Students Enrolled at Community Colleges and Four-Year Institutions.

Ethnic group	Percentage in community college programs	Percentage in four-year college programs
African-American	4.2	3.4
Hispanic-American	11.5	5.3
Native American	0.1	0.5
Asian-American	4.3	5.3
Multiracial	0.8	3.5
White	79.1	80.0

Source: *Open Doors* 2001–2002.

DISCIPLINES AND LOCATIONS

While the majority of community college study abroad programs take place in the same countries and regions where other study abroad programs are located, and offer course work in most of the same academic disciplines, some community college programs reflect the socio-cultural interests of their local domestic communities, faculty, and students. In addition to programs in humanities, arts and architecture, natural and social sciences, community college also offer programs abroad that focus on such topics as interior and fashion design, sports medicine, and culinary arts to name a few.

Community colleges continue to offer programs in Western Europe, but many are now augmenting the European programs with others in Latin America, Asia, and Oceania. Since 1983, CCIE member colleges have sent students to 50 countries worldwide. The number of programs in Africa and the Middle East, however, remains low. Table 5 depicts some of the nontraditional, academic-based, study abroad instruction offered in 2002–2003 by CCIE members, MCCD, and COD.

STUDENT DIVERSITY

Since underrepresented students attend community colleges in high numbers, it is not surprising that large numbers of students of color and lower income students also participate in study abroad through community colleges. Moreover, *Open Doors* reports confirm that community colleges send a more diverse range of students abroad than any other type of postsecondary institution. (See Table 7.)

Community colleges now have a solid foundation in the field of study abroad. Though the overall percentage of students who study abroad through community colleges is decidedly lower than the percentage at four-year institutions (especially affluent private colleges and universities and flagship public institutions), community college numbers continue to grow. With special reference to programming now underway in Arizona, California, Illinois, and Pennsylvania, this chapter has demonstrated the tremendous diversity in type, content, and duration of study abroad programs offered by some of the nation's leading community colleges. Additional work is needed, however, to document on a national level the range of programs and activities that fall under the heading of community college study abroad endeavors.

Summary

Nationally, more undergraduates attend community colleges than any other type of postsecondary institution. Community colleges continue to grow in popularity, in large part because they are

- less expensive and more accessible than universities,

- adaptable to providing product-oriented and transferable curricula,

- flexible in providing short-term programs that address the varying interests of the community, and

- able to meet the demands of emerging local population and regional needs.

Successful study abroad programs at community colleges are no different than those at other U.S. institutions of higher education. They benefit from the full support of the faculty, administration, and students. Unfortunately, in many community colleges too few students and staff view study abroad programs as an integral and essential part of the institution's educational mission. Although study abroad is widely recognized by educators as one of the best avenues to develop international competency, there is often limited support for it at community colleges.

To correct this situation, community colleges must concentrate their efforts in two areas of educational and policy reform. First, there is a need to address the persisting argument that study abroad diverts the community college from its mandate. As discussed in this chapter, nothing can be further from the truth. Nonetheless, there is a need to address the low level of awareness for the rationale and benefits for study abroad. In an effort to build and bolster local coalitions, some community colleges are now seeking partnerships with those local businesses that might benefit from hiring employees with international and intercultural competencies. In turn, such connections can help to solicit funding scholarships to help support the study abroad programs.

Community college administrators, faculty, and staff must be educated about the conditions and support needed to ensure high-quality study abroad programs. Sharing information is needed on all levels. On the campus level, there is a need to

- ensure a line item for study abroad in the college budget,

- support a visible office with clerical assistance and a full-time coordinator,

- make connections with counseling services and student advising,

- form campus-based study abroad committees and find other ways to connect study abroad with other college programs,

- establish educational policy that supports study abroad, and

- develop broad-based coalitions with regional and national support and advocacy groups such as NAFSA's Education Abroad Knowledge Community (formerly known as SECUSSA), and the newly formed SECUSSA-CC (for Community College).

Part I: Education Abroad as a Component of U.S. Higher Education

On the program level at community colleges, there is a need to

- identify how to establish study abroad programs,
- ensure the development of policies on health, safety, and legal issues,
- arrange for the transfer of academic credits, and
- arrange for availability of financial support.

Finally, on the student level, there is a need to

- provide accessibility to campus- and consortia-based study abroad programs, and
- establish measures to help overcome barriers to participation by all students.

Although community college study abroad activity is much larger than is generally recognized, community colleges must do a better job of educating their own constituencies regarding the benefits of study abroad. They must also design program content with a particularly strong focus on international service learning and professional internships to attract both participants and potential funding sources in the business community. Community colleges must use partnerships and collaborative agreements overseas as avenues to implement safe and affordable study abroad programs. In an increasingly multiethnic, multicultural, and multilingual world, a higher education structure (such as the community college model) that acknowledges, endorses, and respects diversity, must produce more and better study abroad advising and programming.

Note: The authors express their sincere appreciation to the following individuals who provided invaluable support, feedback, and information essential to the creation of this chapter: Zinta Conrad, director, international education, College of DuPage; Marion Froehlich, international education coordinator, San Diego City College; and David Prejsnar, director, international education and studies, Community College of Philadelphia.

Part II
Campus Advising

II-1
Advising Principles and Strategies
Lynn C. Anderson, Christina S. Murray

II-2
Integrating Intercultural Learning into Education Abroad Programming
Joseph G. Hoff, Barbara Kappler

II-3
Reaching Underrepresented Constituencies
Carol J. Lebold, Amy Henry, Pamela Houston, Marilyn Jackson,
Michele Scheibe, Scott Van Der Meid

II-4
Whole-World Study
James L. Buschman, Rebecca Hovey, Gurudharm Singh Khalsa, Rosa Marina de Brito Meyer,
Michael D. Monahan, Joan A. Raducha

II-5
Health Issues and Advising Responsibilities
Joan Elias Gore, Judith Green

II-6
Advising Students on Safety and Security Issues
Patricia C. Martin

II-7
Predeparture Orientation and Reentry Programming
Stacey Woody Thebodo, Linda E. Marx

II-8
Work Abroad and International Careers
William Nolting, Martha Johnson, Cheryl Matherly

Introduction

Patricia C. Martin

The chapters in Part II discuss advising skills, principles of intercultural communication, the changing nature of the types of students served by education abroad professionals on campus, the expansion of locations and types of options offered (including work abroad), preparing students for the abroad experience, and assisting students upon their return.

Part II, Chapter 1, "Advising Principles and Strategies" covers the fundamentals of advising, students' expectations of the advising process and how those expectations change over the course of students' educational careers, and the knowledge base that advisers must have. Because one of the fundamental goals that institutions hope their students will achieve in studying abroad is the development of cross-cultural knowledge and skills, Part II, Chapter 2, "Integrating Intercultural Learning into Education Abroad Programming," addresses intercultural communication theory, ways to integrate intercultural learning into predeparture and reentry programming, and program design.

Given the importance of making education abroad available to all students, Part II, Chapter 3, "Reaching Underrepresented Constituencies," explores barriers to participation (both real and perceived), and potential solutions for several groups now underrepresented in overseas enrollments. Those underrepresented groups include ethnic and racial minorities; students with disabilities; students with financial concerns; students pursuing certain majors; gay, lesbian, bisexual, and transgendered students; athletes; student leaders; nontraditional students; and students interested in practicing their religion abroad.

Because it is critical for our country to have an educated citizenry with an understanding of the world's many cultures and languages, Part II, Chapter 4, "Whole-World Study," presents strategies for encouraging more students to pursue education abroad opportunities outside of Western Europe. It also explores the challenges and benefits of study in non-Western locations and suggests ways in which advisers and institutions can develop the knowledge, experience, resources, and commitment necessary to increase student participation in those areas.

The health, safety, and security of study abroad participants are primary concerns for all education abroad professionals. Part II, Chapter 5, "Health Issues and Advising Responsibilities," and Part II, Chapter 6, "Advising Students on Safety and Security Issues," provide detailed information on how to prepare students for healthy and safe experiences abroad, with an emphasis on prevention and student responsibility. These chapters should be used in conjunction with Part III, Chapter 6, "Maximizing Safety and Security and Minimizing Risk in Education Abroad," which focuses on managing safety, security, and risk through program planning and management. Part IV, Chapter 2, "The Overseas Program Cycle and Critical Components," details resident directors' responsibilities for keeping students safe and healthy, and managing individual and group crises.

In Part II, Chapter 7, "Predeparture Orientation and Reentry Programming," readers will find a discussion of the theory and practice of developing and conducting predeparture and reentry programs, both of which are essential components of the education abroad learning cycle and thus important to the education and well-being of study abroad participants.

Finally, Part II, Chapter 8, "Work Abroad and International Careers," provides an overview of overseas opportunities that feature internships, work placement, volunteer service, or other forms of practical training that may or may not involve the awarding of academic credit. It also addresses the relationship between an overseas living and learning experience and the pursuit of a career in the global economy.

Chapter 1
Advising Principles and Strategies
Contributors: Lynn C. Anderson, Christina S. Murray

Education abroad has the potential not only to help students make memories but also to create meaning in their lives and to help them gain a sense of belonging within the world community. For students to realize this potential, high-quality advising must not be marginalized but instead recognized as a key responsibility for education abroad professionals and a vital resource for students. Advisers must work across the campus spectrum with students, faculty, departmental advisers, campus administrators, and other education abroad professionals to make the education abroad experience as academically integrated and administratively seamless as possible. Just as in the African saying, "It takes a village to raise a child," it takes a campus of caring individuals to educate a student.

The wider the range of educational opportunities available and the greater diversity of the students seeking those opportunities, along with their various motivations, makes what was once a more straightforward advising endeavor significantly more complex. Advisers must know more about their advisees and their goals if they are to counsel them responsibly and well. Although many participants still fit the profile that dominated education abroad in the last century (European-American females with significant second-language skills, looking for a junior year abroad in language and culture), more and more of today's undergraduates interested in studying abroad represent a far wider range of characteristics and interests. Advisers assist first-year Asian-American mechanical engineering students interested in heritage experiences in Hong Kong along with course work in engineering, and second-year male Latino interior design students eager to go to Australia, and third-year, first-generation college students who are paper science and engineering majors who want internships in Finland. Students also select education abroad programs based on the availability of cocurricular opportunities. Are there excellent art museums in the study abroad region? Are there any gym facilities and are they included in the program fee? Are there opportunities for rock climbing, bird watching, kayaking, piano lessons, or classes in languages other than the host-country language? While students may still focus on studying in a particular location and meeting degree requirements, increasingly they seek education abroad programs that meet their needs in a holistic fashion.

Therefore, advisers must be knowledgeable about education abroad opportunities and the curricular and degree requirements of the majors and minors on their campuses. They must be firmly grounded in student development theory and ready to assist students by drawing upon a full set of tools in their "toolboxes." A hammer is no longer sufficient. The student development theory needed by the education abroad advising community has been researched through educational psychology departments across the country and is widely used by collegiate and departmental advisers. The National Academic Advising Association (NACADA) offers regional and national workshops, along with publications, that are extremely beneficial for education abroad advisers. But although the core of what advisers need is readily available, it must be modified to apply to education abroad, and advisers must partner with NACADA to create a special interest group for education abroad so that members of the two organizations can learn from each other.

Education abroad advisers must develop and continuously adapt service delivery models that are responsive not only to students' changing needs and aspirations, but also to the home institutions' policies and practices. Policies and procedures applied to study abroad (e.g., regarding grading, transcript entries, and financial aid) must be coordinated with campus policies. The education abroad office can ensure academic viability and a smooth administrative process by facilitating communication and cooperation with departmental faculty, academic advisers, and administrators across campus. Just as importantly, by keeping education abroad program managers informed about students' aspirations and interests, as well as about changing degree requirements, cross-campus integration provides valuable information for maintaining high-quality, academically relevant, and developmentally appropriate offerings for students.

To integrate education abroad into the students' academic plans (thereby preventing graduation delays and additional expenses, along with the attendant lost-opportunity costs), education abroad and campus administrators must invest in education abroad advising positions, training, and ongoing development. Appropriate levels of staffing and training allow the education abroad office to meet the changing needs of students. The quality of education abroad advising is linked directly with the rest of student services on campus. High-quality advising is central to good student services and is increasingly seen as a distinguishing selection feature for prospective students.

Student Development Theory and Its Application to Education Abroad Advising

Student development theories help advisers understand why students behave as they do and can help advisers make sense of the patterns they observe. Knowledge of theory can often help advisers understand and react appropriately when they are perplexed by a student's comment, question, or reaction. Theory allows advisers to be proactive in designing and implementing developmentally appropriate student services and education abroad programs. But while other professionals on campus are likely to already consider student development theory in their work, education abroad has not fully realized the potential of the theory. Awareness and application of theory to education abroad is an important professional competency. It enhances education abroad advisers' credibility within higher education, and allows education abroad advisers to work across campus and across institutions using the same principles that are used by all institutional academic advisers.

Of the many student development theories that have been published, three examples that are particularly applicable to education abroad will be discussed here. These theories are often used in academic adviser training across the country, and perhaps they will inspire education abroad professionals to consider the implications of theory for their work.

Schlossberg's Theory of Mattering

According to Nancy Schlossberg's (1989) simple but powerful notion of "mattering," each person needs to know that he or she matter to others. One way of signaling that someone matters, Schlossberg notes, is to address that person by name. Students who are known and addressed by name by one faculty member, adviser, staff member, or administrator on campus are usually retained on that campus, because the students realize that someone on campus knows and cares about them. Mattering matters. Small campuses pride themselves on knowing their students, and they understand Schlossberg's principle intuitively. Larger campuses must take whatever measures possible to help recreate this small-campus feeling for students by creating smaller communities within the larger campus through honors programs, student organizations, advising offices, and departmental functions.

Education abroad advisers show students that they matter by doing simple things like introducing themselves, thus signaling the beginning of a relationship with the students, rather than a bureaucratic processing of their questions. Advisers can also show students that they matter by stopping conversations with colleagues as quickly as possible when a student comes into the office. Students matter enough for advisers to take notes on each interaction with them. Advisers can keep paper or electronic records about students, and refer to those when continuing a conversation with the student or responding to an e-mail or phone call. Advisers can connect students to other campus resources relevant to education abroad, and thus help the students understand that the adviser knows that studying abroad requires liaison with many campus offices. Advisers should not gossip about students, since that is not only unprofessional but also dehumanizing. Advisers can greet students on campus. Even if the adviser can't remember the student's name, a smile does wonders. All of these examples of mattering might be considered just good manners but, unfortunately, students too often report that they are not treated as individual human beings on their campuses. An education abroad office that signals in all of these small ways that students matter is a place where students know they will be treated as individuals and with respect. It's also much more rewarding for advisers!

Schlossberg's theory of mattering suggests that advisers can gain developmentally useful clues about students through observation and conversation. Regardless of the size of an adviser's campus, this is information that he or she is otherwise likely not to know about the student and that is not shared across various campus offices. An adviser needs to ask the student whatever questions the adviser feels will elicit the information that will allow him or her to help the student. This information can inform program-selection advising and help find an education abroad match that is developmentally appropriate, in addition to all of the other factors normally addressed by education abroad advisers (e.g., language, major, location, grade point average [GPA], class standing, cost, extracurricular interests). Here are some examples of questions that advisers can ask to illustrate the application of Schlossberg's theory to program-selection advising:

1. Has the student shown a preference for working with only one staff member in

the education abroad office, or is he or she comfortable with whoever is available at the time? The answer could help the adviser understand whether the student will need a program with more or less staff support abroad, whether the student may flourish on a center-based program with lots of ready-made friends, or whether the student will fare best on an integrated program where he or she must take the initiative to get to know host-country students.

2. Has the student moved to campus and already left family and friends, or is the student commuting? If the student is commuting, he or she may be more relationship dependent and therefore want to participate in a program with others from his or her home campus, or even in a faculty-led program. Or the student may have different reasons for commuting, such as not having the funds to live on campus or having a job near home.

3. Does the student already have a good relationship with a mentor or two on campus? If so, it may mean that the student would benefit less from large lecture classes abroad than from a well-supervised internship, a closely monitored volunteer position, or a job with mentoring.

There are no magic formulas here and this is just a taste of the questions that could be posed to a student pursuing a study abroad experience. What is important is for advisers to recognize that there are touchstones that can help inform an adviser's judgment or lead to more conversations with the student to gather additional information.

Perry's Nine-Stage Theory of Cognitive Development

William Perry's (1970) nine-stage theory of cognitive development is broadly accepted in the fields of education and psychology, and has been applied widely to academic advising. Perry's theory has enormous untapped potential for general education abroad advising and for program selection as well as program development. His theory assumes that development occurs through interaction with others and is sequential, hierarchical, and irreversible. Perry urges that a combination of support and challenge from advisers is needed for students to move to the next stage. The nine stages of Perry's theory fall into the following four categories (St. Edward's University, Center for Teaching Excellence 2003):

1. *Dualism*
   - Knowledge is absolute.
   - Authority (e.g., the adviser, the professor) is the source of knowledge.
   - It is Authority's responsibility to provide true knowledge.
   - Facts and right answers are desired.

2. *Multiplicity*
   - Multiple perspectives on both true knowledge and morality exist.
   - All perspectives are equally valid.
   - Authority represents a perspective, but with no greater validity than any others.

3. *Relativism*
   - Knowledge is relativistic and contextual.

Chapter 1: Advising Principles and Strategies

- Authority is valued for its expertise but not depended on exclusively.
- Need for creating order out of diversity is recognized but not always realized.

4. *Commitment Within Relativism*
   - Relativism demands individual choice and responsibility.
   - Initial personal commitments are made in areas of both academics and lifestyle.
   - Personal strength is recognized and risk-taking is possible.

Perry's theory can help advisers understand why students behave in particular ways, gives advisers tools to help students find good education abroad matches, and allows advisers to anticipate reactions and plan a service delivery model proactively. Here are some thoughts about and examples from each of the four main categories.

Dualism

Advising freshmen, who are typically in the dualistic stage, requires that advisers meet their need for authority figures and concrete information. Though more often characteristic of freshmen, anyone in a new situation may revert to the dualistic stage for a while. (Think of when, in your mid-20s or 30s, you started graduate school or a new job and asked questions about what to wear or how to behave.) Students with high GPAs, who seem mature, sometimes perplex education abroad advisers with simple questions about the process of education abroad program selection. They may ask if their application must be typed and if so, in what font. Or they may want the adviser to pick a program for them. In response, the adviser may suggest a short list of programs (based on what is understood about the students' needs and wishes) and ask them to choose from among those, using a factor analysis model that the adviser teaches them.

In a simple factor analysis, students list the characteristics of factors about study abroad that are most important to them (e.g., cost, location, courses offered, language of instruction, length, housing options) in one column; weight the importance of each of the factors relative to the other factors in another column; see if the potential program meets their desired characteristics for each factor; and then decide if the factors that cannot be accommodated by a potential program choice can be dealt with in some other manner, or whether another program must be selected.

Additionally, advisers might ask students to review program evaluations that other students have written, to get a clearer picture of the program from a student perspective. Providing students with a process to follow and evaluations to read meets their need for concrete information. Generally, advisers must provide students with the support and challenge they need to move to the next developmental stage and become more autonomous learners who take responsibility for their own educational experiences. Advisers can provide students with options and illuminate possible implications, but the students must make the decisions.

Students in the dualism stage typically are most successful on a faculty-led short-term program or an island program, although they may also be ready for a highly structured study abroad center program. (See the discussion of program typology below.)

Multiplicity

Advising students in the multiplicity stage requires advisers to be able to discern how well the students can identify multiple and sometimes conflicting perspectives, and how they react to them. For example, an adviser might evaluate the student's adjustment to life in his or her residence hall and to a shared-living situation by considering such questions as "How well does the student adjust to individuals who are different from him or her?" and "How does the student resolve conflicts with roommates?" Information about how well the student adjusts on campus will have direct application to potential living options for the student abroad. It will tell the adviser if the best match might be in a dorm with other host nationals, a home-stay, or an independent apartment.

Other clues from students might help advisers ascertain how ready students are for the academic components of their study abroad programs. For example, the student who is perplexed and even angry that what the professor says doesn't match what is in the book has not yet reached a stage of multiplicity that may allow him or her to successfully integrate his or her own experiences, beliefs, and knowledge with what he or she may be exposed to abroad. Such a student may flourish in a more structured study abroad program but be unhappy and unsuccessful in a less well-structured program. Students who become discipline problems during a study abroad program may be stuck in the multiplicity stage and may not see the value of listening to a program director about cultural norms. The student may feel that all perspectives are equally valuable, including his or hers, even though he or she has only recently arrived abroad. Why listen to an authority figure? Recognizing the behavior doesn't always give advisers an answer about how to proceed, but it helps them understand the student's perspective and may help them formulate a response.

Students in the multiplicity stage will need some assistance with the process of program selection, but once that process is described, they will be much more autonomous than students in the dualism stage. Students in the multiplicity stage typically are ready to move beyond island and short-term programs and tackle study abroad center-based programs, internships, and exchange programs that offer support to international students, but may not be ready for integrated or research programs that require a high level of independence.

Relativity

Students in the relativity stage are trying to integrate the multiple perspectives that they encounter, but are not always successful. They may understand that the right answer depends on who is asking the question and for what purpose. During the program selection phase, and afterward, they may value an education abroad adviser's advice but may also seek opinions from other students, advisers, and faculty. Education abroad advisers ought not to feel threatened when students seek other opinions. The students are listening to the education abroad adviser, but also to many others. They are able to gather information and make their own informed decisions about program selection. Advisers need to provide these students with the process for gathering information but will not need to provide as much support in the decision-making process.

To determine if the student is in the relativity stage, consider how the student is integrating past beliefs and knowledge with new, challenging perspectives from classes, readings, faculty, and classmates. Is the student thinking carefully about what a professor said about Judaism in her "Bible as Literature" class, or does she feel that her religious upbringing is being threatened? If the student is rooming with a student from a very different background than his own, does he feel threatened by this difference or is he eagerly learning about other lifestyles and perspectives? The responses to these kinds of questions may indicate whether the student is ready for exposure to different perspectives with minimal support from the on-site education abroad program. The students' answers may help the adviser decide how psychologically "far away" their education abroad program can be.

Students in the relativity stage generally will be successful in programs with less structure and more challenge than is required by students in the dualism or multiplicity stages. These students may be ready and eager for internships, field study, independent research, and integrated programs.

Commitment with Relativism

Students in this stage celebrate the diversity of perspectives they encounter, are not threatened by them, and make decisions for which they take responsibility. They not only make considered decisions about their intellectual, social, political, and emotional lives but can also articulate why they made these decisions. Students in the commitment with relativism stage know who they are, and are comfortable with the consequences of their choices. Not all students reach this stage in college. Some people never reach this stage.

At this stage, students are able to analyze and synthesize what they are reading, hearing from professors, and learning from other students. These students are more likely to take on leadership positions or be responsible for group work. The students' responses to the education abroad adviser's questions about their living situations, classes, and on-campus involvement will quickly tip the adviser off to how successfully the students are managing commitment with relativism. The responses will be thoughtful, sophisticated, and nuanced, and the students will be open to other perspectives. Students in this stage often require very little support from advisers, and quickly take over the program selection process. They only need to be pointed in the right direction.

These students are ready for integrated study, as well as independent research abroad, and internships, work abroad, and exchange programs. They will flourish, despite lots of ambiguity and little support. They are like kites that just need a light hand on the string.

Chickering's Seven Vectors of Development

Unlike Perry's theory, which combines emotional, intellectual, social, and political growth as one moves through the nine stages, Arthur Chickering's theory (1969) is grounded on the notion of monitoring all of the "vectors" by discerning and attending to the emotional, intellectual, social, and other needs and stages of the students. Growth must be tracked through the intersection of several variables. Students on education abroad programs are dealing with differences overseas that can impact every aspect of their lives. That is why Chickering's theory seems particularly applicable to education abroad.

The vectors involve cycles of differentiation and integration in a person, and are constantly moving toward more complex levels of self-knowledge. Development is not automatic but instead depends on the stimulation available in the college environment. Chickering's seven vectors of development include developing competence, managing emotions, developing autonomy, establishing identity, freeing interpersonal relationships, developing purpose, and developing integrity (St. Edward's University, Center for Teaching Excellence 2003). What are the implications and applications of Chickering's vector analysis for education abroad advising?

Part II: Campus Advising

As education abroad advisers attempt to discern a student's development in relation to Chickering's vectors, advisers can consider, for instance, how the student managed the transition from high school to college, and from the hometown to the college town. There may be ways that the student coped that will be useful in his or her transition to a new environment. Advisers should talk with students about how they managed their emotions, the intellectual challenges, and the social adjustments of coming to college. Advisers can remind students that they already know the process of adapting and can apply those skills in a new setting abroad.

To determine how well students are developing competence, advisers might talk with them about their successes and ask them to describe an accomplishment that has made them proud of themselves. Students who respond that they are pleased to have mastered the campus bus system are in a different place than students who say they can use the library well or those who cite their involvement in student government.

Participation in education abroad usually requires that students function autonomously, and also improves their ability to do so. Students must have a certain level of independence to be able to successfully negotiate the challenges of an education abroad experience. Advisers hear time and again from returnees how they have grown in their ability to manage almost any challenge on their own. Education abroad programs can be placed along a continuum from lower to higher levels of required autonomy. Like Perry's stage theory, an adviser's sense of a student's ability to function autonomously will allow the adviser to help the student find a good program match. For instance, an adviser can gauge a student's ability to function autonomously by asking what he or she did upon encountering a problem in the residence halls. Did the student go to the residence hall director immediately, or did the student try to resolve the situation on his or her own? Also, how students move through the education abroad selection process gives advisers a good sense of their ability to function autonomously.

Finally, advisers may gain a sense of how students are developing a sense of integrity by asking them how they responded to situations when they realized that what they believed or thought they "knew" was not accurate. Gentle questioning can help advisers determine if the students admitted to themselves or others that they were wrong, and whether or not they learned from that situation and were able to move on. Students whose beliefs were challenged and who responded maturely will weather the challenges of education abroad, adjust as needed, and keep their values intact.

THE ADVISING PROCESS

An international experience is increasingly understood as an integral component of higher education in the twenty-first century. Students arriving on U.S. campuses are more likely than ever before to have had an overseas experience prior to their matriculation. This climate means that advising for education abroad is a multidynamic process, with an arc that extends from before the student arrives on campus until after the student graduates. In addition to understanding and applying student development theory, advisers must also understand and respond to each phase of the student's process of program selection and reentry.

Students' expectations of the advising process change over the course of their educational careers. This process can be roughly divided into four periods:

1. Formative, for prospective students and freshmen.
2. Program selection, which may begin in the freshman year and extend to the sophomore or junior year.
3. Practical preparation immediately prior to departure, which may take place in the sophomore and junior years.
4. Reentry, for assistance in integrating experience back on campus, and beyond graduation.

Formative Period

Increasingly, education abroad advisers find themselves talking with students (and sometimes with students' parents) who are interested in education abroad opportunities when they are in the college selection process. Of utmost concern to these students and parents is the availability of programming, the quality and scope of those programs, and the advising service they will receive.

For students newly arrived on campus and interested in study abroad, it is important to establish a relationship to ensure that they understand that assistance is available. At this stage, students want general guidance and encouragement on how to begin the process. They may or may not have selected a major and may not have considered how to integrate language study into their academic goals. It is vital at this stage to be able to refer them to academic advisers who will be able to assist in these areas, and who will advise that the students include education abroad in their planning.

Students at this point may find a general overview of the systems and procedures required to participate in education abroad most helpful. It is also ideal to provide printed information that they can take away with them and refer to later, along with a list of Web sites to browse. Most students will also have questions about financing education abroad. A general description of financial aid policies and scholarship resources is helpful.

Education abroad advisers should listen to the questions the students ask and determine what other issues are behind the actual questions being asked. More specific information can be provided to students who are able to be specific about their education abroad goals. To give more information than is requested may overwhelm students at this stage, so it is wise to be judicious but not superficial. The most important advising goal is to establish a welcoming and connected relationship with students; that is, to ensure students feel that incorporating education abroad is a reasonable goal, and that people and resources are available to support them in achieving that goal.

Program Selection Period

Students in this stage begin to research programs and resources. The education abroad office is responsible for providing students with the information and advice they need to make sound educational decisions, but the decisions are the students' to make. While advisers provide a process for students to follow in the program selection period, students do the research. Some students will require very little direction as they set off to find a good program match for themselves. Others will require more encouragement to take responsibility for this process. It is helpful to provide students with printed materials, names of resource people, Web resources to draw upon, and a clear road map of expectations. Here are several key issues for advisers to keep in mind when advising students on program selection.

Part II: Campus Advising

Wealth of Information about Education Abroad Programs

The variety of programs and information sources has increased exponentially in recent years. As more institutions offer education abroad programs to students at other institutions, advisers are deluged with a variety of materials to promote study abroad programs and destinations. The Institute for International Education's annual publications, *Academic Year Abroad* and *Short-Term Study Abroad* and the annual Peterson's *Study Abroad* guides are probably the most useful resources for many study abroad offices. Instructions in the front of the guides explain how to use these comprehensive listings of education abroad opportunities.

New media outlets, most prominently Web-based resources, are increasingly attractive to the technology-savvy students of today. The internet provides a wealth of easily accessible information on education abroad options, and advisers should suggest appropriate search engines for student research. Most resource centers designate at least one computer terminal specifically for this purpose.

Advisers should keep track of those programs in which past students have participated, and keep in touch with students who have returned. Returnees' evaluations and willingness to talk with students in the program selection stage are valuable resources for students.

Federal Financial Aid

Federal financial aid regulations require that institutions "preapprove" the education abroad programs for which students are allowed to receive loans and grants. Institutions are left to define what the preapproval process is. Some institutions have a formal vetting procedure that includes an articulation of credit. Others simply check to ensure that the institution issuing the transcript is regionally accredited in the United States or is officially recognized by the Ministry of Education of the host country. Once a program is chosen by a student, the student will have to receive preapproval for the credit, to the extent that he or she is able to identify specific courses prior to departure. (For more information on the approval process and the use of financial aid 'consortial agreements,' see Part I, Chapter 7 "Financial Aid and Funding Study Abroad" and Part III, "Chapter Planning, Budgeting, and Implementation.")

Institutional Policies

Advisers must be familiar with the curricula of the various majors of their institution. Although not a substitute for departmental and collegiate academic advising, knowing the parameters specific to one's institution enables the adviser to assist the student in identifying programs appropriate to their needs. As much as possible, advisers should get to know their advising colleagues in the academic units on campus. Education abroad and departmental advisers have a shared responsibility to assist students in the selection of a good education abroad match and to talk through the implications of that selection for major and degree requirements. Some majors may be more restrictive about allowing students to study abroad than others. Some majors will be subject to professional as well as regional accreditation. In these cases, the accrediting body will generally provide guidelines on transfer of credit, and may have articulated policies related to the internationalization of the professional content area. Some accrediting bodies now urge that students participate in education abroad. Advisers should also be aware of any particular application requirements that specific majors might have (e.g., audition tapes for music majors, and portfolios for art and design majors).

Individual Considerations

Advisers need to discuss with students any issues that are unique to the student. For instance, does the student have health or access issues that figure in program selection and must be addressed? Does the student have a learning disability? Is the student a parent who wants to take his or her child or children along? Does the student have need of regular appointments with a psychologist or psychiatrist while abroad? Does the judicial affairs office have information about the student that the adviser and program provider need to be aware of during program selection and placement? While these factors need not be barriers to education abroad, they may inform program choice.

Program Typology

In order to sort through the mounting number of programs available to students, advisers must understand how elements of each program type may match the degree of ambiguity and consequent level of autonomy that a student is prepared to handle. The typology offered below can help advisers understand the characteristics the programs share, and make it easier to explain the similarities and differences to students. Students should be encouraged to challenge themselves in order to maximize the potential for a meaningful cross-cultural experience. The categories below range from the highest to lowest levels of autonomy, followed by a discussion of hybrid programs. Although these are the traditional categories for education abroad programs, programs have evolved to include so many different features that it is often difficult and inappropriate to label a program as a particular type. Education abroad professionals, students, faculty, and academic advisers would be well served by a national discussion and subsequent standardization of the terminology used to characterize education abroad programs and their features. (See Part III, Chapter 1, "Program Designs and Strategies," for more discussion of program typology.)

Independent study and research programs allow students to work in labs, participate in field study, pursue topics of their own design, and participate in home or host faculty research projects abroad. Typically, the content and structure of these programs require a high level of independence, maturity, and flexibility.

Direct enrollment or integrated study, means enrolling in the host institution as a local student would to obtain credit in the host-country system, and then transferring the credit back to the home institution. This type of program exposes the student to all of the cultural dynamics of the international educational system, and support is frequently provided through service facilities available to local students and, increasingly, through specialized international student offices.

There is a high degree of ambiguity associated with this choice, as students may not be able to identify specific courses for preapproval. Nonacademic student services are based in the host-country culture, and may not exist to the same extent as at the home institution. Credit may take extra time to process, as the host institution may have to set up special procedures for producing a transcript, and the home institution would need to have a process for evaluating the credit as well.

Students frequently will be required to have a high degree of facility, if not fluency, in the language of instruction. This may be ideal for students who aim for fluency, but may be prohibitive for those students who do not have the language capacity sufficient to function in a native environment. Direct enrollment for students without a high degree of fluency may be an option for students who are not capable of taking courses in another language, though, if opportunities exist at host institutions to take some course work in English.

Traditional exchange programs are set up on the basis of direct enrollment. Each participant pays a set fee to the home institution for tuition and fees, and sometimes for room and board. These funds remain on the home campus to provide in-kind benefits to the incoming student, thus creating a one-for-one swap. Because exchanges mirror the cost of on-campus study, they are an affordable option for students for whom financing is a concern. Students will want to investigate the level of services provided on the prospective host campus.

Study abroad centers are resource-rich, locally organized programs that give students the opportunity to take courses taught by local faculty in the host language or in English. Fellow students may come from other institutions in the United States and possibly from other countries. Centers may provide students with the opportunity for direct enrollment in courses with host-national students for one or two of their classes if the students have the appropriate language ability. Centers may also arrange for use of the local gyms, piano lessons, studios for art majors, internships, and so forth. Housing options may include family stays, apartments, and residence halls. Center-based programs often provide greater opportunity for involvement with host-country nationals while still providing the support some students find necessary.

On island programs, the home campus is recreated in an overseas location. Often, courses regularly offered at the home campus are replicated abroad by instructors from the home institution. Programs may be offered for a semester or a full year. These programs may have prerequisites (e.g., prior relevant course work). They generally do not, however, provide direct acculturation through the academic component, and care should be taken to ensure that students have the opportunity to experience the host culture through nonacademic components, including activities and housing, or cocurricular components such as internships.

Short-term programs are increasingly attractive to students, especially students who may be more comfortable with a short, faculty-led introduction to study abroad. Such programs typically are of six weeks' duration or less, and can take place during intersession, spring break, or the summer months. Since programming does not coincide with any host-country academic calendar, these programs are typically similar in structure and function to island programs. Care should be taken to ensure that the student understands the qualitative differences between short-term and longer programs. Advisers can encourage students to think of a short-term program as the first step toward a semester or year abroad.

As noted above, increasingly programs will take elements from one or more of the types described above to make hybrid models. Programs may offer courses through a local institution and also by professors accompanying the group. Internship offerings may be combined with an island program. On some exchange programs, students may receive a high level of support from the host institution. Increasingly, prospective international partners will offer a wide variety of language support, enabling a wider range of students to attend their institutions through direct enrollment. More often than not, a program type is not set in stone, and advisers are urged to use care when assessing programs and describing them to students and colleagues.

Practical Preparation Period

Institutions should offer a comprehensive group orientation to students who have applied to education abroad programs well in advance of their departures, and additional advising should be available to individual students on an as-needed basis as issues arise.

Family members and friends will have questions about what to expect and how to support their family member or friend while he or she is abroad. Some universities provide a Web site or a handbook with tips, and still others invite family members and friends to the student orientation or to a special orientation. The federal Family Educational Rights and Privacy Act (FERPA) requires that students' academic records be kept confidential. Advisers cannot discuss various aspects of a student's participation in a program with a third party unless the student has given written permission. Talking with family members and friends in general terms often answers their questions without violating data privacy.

Students will often inquire as to how to make the most economical travel arrangements possible, particularly if flight arrangements are not included in the program. Some education abroad offices offer comprehensive advising that includes information on travel, while others refer students to the Web and to local travel agencies. Advisers should provide students with contact information on local and national student travel resources. Advisers should also help students understand the benefits of the International Student Identification Card (ISIC): discounts on transatlantic and in-country travel; entry to museums, movies, and concerts; and travel insurance. Many institutions issue these cards on site.

Students may also inquire as to the availability of ground travel and in-country air travel specials.

The travel industry is constantly changing and it is important to keep abreast of these changes as they occur. Some campuses offer travel services to students or point them to agencies specializing in student travel.

Assisting students in securing the proper immigration documents prior to departure is of the utmost importance. For many, participation in an education abroad experience is the reason to obtain their first passport. It may be helpful to keep a supply of applications on hand, or bookmark the Web documents if computer-based advising is utilized. Some institutions arrange for an event at which the students can apply for their passports, and some actually pay for the cost of the passport as an incentive for students to go abroad. Although it is impossible to keep up on every immigration detail for every country, a general grasp of the most common destinations' requirements is important, as well as information on embassies, including contact information.

Some other general areas of inquiry may include finances, health and safety, registration for the semester upon return, and how to communicate with friends, family, and the education abroad office while abroad.

If the education abroad program is offered through a third-party provider, it may be necessary to assist the student by using the orientation materials provided by the program.

Reentry

As with orientation, organized reentry events are a standard aspect of all education abroad offices. It is important to note, however, that students vary widely in their reactions to reentering the home environment and returning back to the home institution. Some students may seek additional opportunities to share their experiences; others may need assistance in processing their emotional reactions to their return. Some offices offer reentry student organizations, run by students, or offer returnees the chance to talk with students who are in the selection process. Some campuses offer reentry courses (participation is required on some campuses). The adviser's role is to help students anticipate and plan for the reentry process by providing them with resources and options to consider. Advisers may want to ask students to send them an occasional e-mail or postcard to help bridge the abroad and home-campus experience (and it's fun and instructive to hear from the students while they are abroad). (See Part II, Chapter 7, "Predeparture Orientation and Reentry Programming.")

Through education abroad, students often gain enhanced personal skills: deepened self-knowledge, maturity, adaptability, ability to deal with ambiguity, ability to take reasonable risks, and willingness to take initiative. These skills enhance a student's ability to live and work abroad successfully, an increasingly important requirement for new employees since disciplines recognize no national boundaries and many companies are multinational. But to take full advantage of their experiences, students must be able to synthesize what they have learned in an appropriate and meaningful way on their resumes and in their applications for graduate and professional schools.

MULTIADVISER OFFICES AND GROUP ADVISING

As education abroad continues to grow, many universities are now faced with the need to manage that growth in terms of office staffing and responsibilities. In some cases, that may include separating the advising function from the office and program administration functions. Offices may divide advising responsibility by region of the world, language of instruction, or by college or academic department. It is vitally important that office standards are clearly understood, preferably articulated in writing, to ensure uniform quality in advising. It is also important that advisers have a basic understanding of the primary academic issues that students face (i.e., registration, calculation of grades, and credit transfer), so that uniform information is conveyed. Regardless of division of duties, all advisers must be generalists and have a basic knowledge of each other's content areas so that students directed to the wrong adviser can be redirected efficiently, and so that advisers can cover for one another.

Group Advising

Many education abroad offices offer general information meetings either at the beginning of the term or periodically throughout the year. To provide comprehensive information, offices may find it helpful to include key members of the academic community, a representative from the financial aid office, and returning students. Such meetings need to be widely publicized to ensure the greatest possible participation, including faculty, collegiate and departmental advisers, and student organizations. A well-rounded and substantive presentation will allow personal advising to commence at a more advanced level.

Small group meetings allow for dissemination of information of a general nature, or may address specific content areas, majors, or destinations. Such sessions may take longer than an individual session, but will cut down on the number of sessions necessary. These sessions may also include returning students and international exchange students, as well as campus resource persons able to address the specific issue at hand.

Peer Advising

Peer advising is an increasingly popular means to make the initial general advising contact. Interested and committed students can be the best ambassadors for the programs in which they participated, and for education abroad in general. It is important to be judicious in the selection of peer advisers, as some students have difficulty drawing appropriate generalizations from their own experiences. It is also important to have established written policies and procedures and a thorough training process, to ensure that peer advisers are clear about where their responsibilities end and a professional adviser's responsibilities begin.

PRACTICAL APPLICATIONS OF THEORY FOR EDUCATION ABROAD ADVISING SERVICES

Education abroad administrators are responsible for creating infrastructures on their campuses that support and integrate education abroad advising, as well as for creating and improving the student services models in their offices.

Principles for Creating an Infrastructure for Quality Education Abroad Advising

While on some campuses the education abroad office enjoys a strong reputation, on other campuses it may be marginalized. If education abroad is to be an integral part of the educational experience of undergraduates, the education abroad office must be centrally located, adequately funded, and its staff included on campus committees and in discussions that impact education abroad.

Specifically, education abroad advisers must advocate on campus for quality education abroad advising. This has both an external and an internal aspect. Advisers can help administrators across campus understand how quality education abroad advising helps them achieve their goals (e.g., the admissions office wants higher quality students; the financial aid office wants students who have properly prepared their paperwork; academic departments want education abroad to comply with degree requirements; and the housing office needs to know who is going to be abroad and when). Advisers can also underscore the importance of education abroad advising by getting education abroad program managers involved in the advising, if they are not already. This involvement will help them stay current with student issues surrounding program selection and will help advisers, who may not be program managers, stay current with programming offerings and issues.

Principles for Developing or Improving a Student Services Model

Student development theory helps advisers work with individual students and it can help advisers structure and improve their advising services. If education abroad advisers are to bring their advising in line with other on-campus advising so that students see advising on campus as a holistic experience, education abroad advisers must partner with other advising offices. There are many ways for advising colleagues to partner on campus.

Consider hiring advisers with graduate degrees in student development theory, who have studied abroad and advised in collegiate or departmental advising offices. Short of that, train advisers by linking them with faculty who teach student development theory or with colleagues who use such theories in their work. Hire advisers who are energized by talking with students, and train them in the theory, information, and practical techniques they need to be successful. Provide ongoing support and professional development opportunities. Help advisers develop a network of colleagues within and outside the campus.

Compare students' needs with staffing availability. Students' needs generally outstrip the resources available, so design a flexible and efficient student services model. Such a model balances information sharing (via the Web and publications) with advising (in small and large groups, in individual appointments, and through shorter walk-in, phone, and e-mail contacts). If the education abroad adviser is the sole adviser in the office, decide what portion of each day or week will be given over to each type of advising. In order to prepare advisers to help students consider multiple education abroad opportunities in their planning, ensure that adviser training and the education abroad office's Web site and print materials show potential pathways linking study, work, volunteer programs, internships, and graduate fellowships abroad.

Generally, half of all students want a relationship with "their" advisers and the other half want good advice but are less concerned about having a specific adviser. Determine ways to connect students with an education abroad adviser as early in the program-selection phase as possible. Make sure that written or computer notes provide a record of each conversation and a bridge to future conversations with the education abroad adviser or other advisers. Written records make it easier for advisers to track previous conversations with students and move forward with each student efficiently. They also underscore for students that they matter.

Prepare group presentations about the process of program selection. Decide what information can be presented in groups, such as an overview of the education abroad selection process or an overview of resources available to students, including resources outside the office (e.g., parents, returnees, departmental and campus advisers), and always allow time for questions. Students may not know what to ask and can benefit from hearing each other's questions. Some campuses mandate attendance at this kind of first-step meeting, so students will have the tools they need, presented in an organized format, with appropriate print materials distributed as well. Having a requirement like this also means enforcing it in a way that helps students understand that attending this meeting will benefit them and ensure that they receive the information they need.

Offer meetings about specific programs that include information such as location, housing, courses available, and admission requirements. This is an economical use of staff time, allows students to benefit from each other's questions, gets students thinking about issues, and gives students a sense of bonding and energy—"Other students are doing this too, and have questions and concerns!"

Develop and use a set of frequently asked questions for programs, financial aid, registration and grades, and so on. This will save staff time and give students something in writing to reference and show to family members and departmental advisers.

Provide faculty and advisers on campus with information about the education abroad office's services so that they can appropriately refer students, and also provide them with information targeted to their majors and advisees so that they can include it in newsletters (electronic and print), post it on bulletin boards, or send it to e-mail discussion lists.

Many students come to college aware of their preferred learning style. As advisers develop or improve their advising processes, they should be attentive to how they present information. Providing a reasonable balance of mediums for students will allow them to absorb information in a manner that is most effective for them. An advising manual that advisers can point to and students can reference is particularly useful in helping students understand the service model. The manual might contain information on topics such as resources, education abroad programs, funding education abroad, and steps to choosing an education abroad experience, among others.

Offer walk-in advising for students who have been through the introductory general meeting. Walk-in advising is ideally suited for quick conversations (less than ten minutes) about an aspect of education abroad selection. Helping students and colleagues around campus understand the place of walk-in advising in the education abroad office's service model requires good publicity (via paper and the Web) and patience. Students who want to learn about, and decide upon, their education abroad programs by using only walk-in appointments must be gently but firmly helped to understand the other steps that are necessary before and after walk-in advising.

Offer individual appointments for students who may be stuck in the process of program selection, have special considerations, or want some one-on-one time with an adviser after a group meeting. Training is essential to help staff know when this is appropriate. Information in an advising handbook will help students understand when to request an appointment.

Offer follow-up phone and e-mail advising as a means for students to get answers to quick, factual questions or to clarify something that was discussed previously. E-mail is an excellent way to track students' questions and the education abroad office's responses. Consider developing an electronic database of responses to frequently asked questions that advisers can access as needed, and tailor to quickly respond to a student. Advisers should be careful of responding via e-mail to students with whom they have not yet worked. Advising by e-mail as a first contact with students is much harder because of the lack of context. It is easier to miss the students' real questions, and since tone is completely neutralized, advisers may miss the students' anxieties or fears that must be addressed. Again, advisers should include this information in an advising handbook.

Principles for Adviser Development

There is no one way to advise. Through training and experience, advisers will develop styles and techniques that fit them best. As advisers become even more experienced, they will broaden their approaches and become optimally effective with a wider range of students. The advisers' focus shifts from themselves ("Am I advising correctly? Do I know the information the student is going to ask me?"), to the students ("What does this student need?" "What approach might work best with this student?").

Ethically, regardless of where advisers have gone and what they think are the "best" kind of education abroad opportunities, advisers must always focus on what the best match is for each student. Advisers can certainly urge students to select a program that will challenge their abilities and sensibilities, but advisers must also guard against setting students up for failure. Suggesting that a student consider a year-long program rather than a semester-long program may give the student permission to consider something he or she wasn't sure he or she was capable of managing. Wondering with the student if he or she could directly enroll in a course or two at a university near the center-based program site, might encourage the student to investigate that possibility.

Ascertaining when to challenge and when to support a student is a skill that develops through reflective experience. Advising is an art, not a science, and advisers must give themselves permission to experiment and learn.

Just as students develop over time, so do advisers. L. Lee Knefelkamp (1987) describes three stages that advisers go through in their own development: (1) learning the student services model, (2) internalizing the model, and (3) moving beyond the model. Within these stages, advisers move from an ability to manage a limited amount of information within a few settings, to a wider range of information in a single setting, to a wide range of information in multiple settings. For instance, a new adviser might offer a group information session, following a prescribed script. This is one type of advising setting using concrete information. That adviser might then be trained to use this same basic script but increase the variety of settings by offering education abroad information sessions to prospective students in freshman seminars, or to parents. Knefelkamp's theory can help structure ongoing adviser training, and the stages may be helpful to share with advisers so that they understand their own development and the manner in which their responsibilities will change.

No matter what theories or practices are utilized, if advisers are not keenly interested in students and committed to assisting them with their academic planning, they will not be good advisers. Authentic communication is a key aspect of quality advising since it impacts the adviser's interactions and effectiveness with students. Advisers must recognize the strengths and pitfalls of their communication style and strive to improve. It is often easy for an adviser to ask a supervisor or colleague about information that the adviser does not know. It is often much more difficult, but crucial, for the adviser to ask for feedback on his or her style of advising. Supervisors can assist in this process by observing advisers in a variety of settings and providing them with constructive feedback. Advisers can also benefit from observing each other and discussing what they observed with each other afterwards. This creates strong interpersonal relationships among advisers and enhances advisers' abilities to consult each other about not only the "what" but also the "how" of advising.

New and experienced education abroad advisers would benefit from participation in NACADA workshops and regional or national conferences, and from reading NACADA publications. NACADA's Statement of Core Values of Academic Advising is worth including in all adviser training. In addition to the core values, the statement includes information about the power of academic advising, beliefs about students, and why core values are important. Advisers can increase their knowledge and improve their skills by participating in conferences and reading publications from organizations like The Forum on International Education, the Society for Intercultural Education, Training and Research (SIETAR), the National Association of Student Personnel Administrators (NASPA), and the American College Personnel Association (ACPA).

Students should be given the opportunity to evaluate the education abroad advising services, and those evaluations should be made available to advisers and supervisors. Evaluation can take the form of a quick questionnaire at the time of service, a focus group, phone interviews, or a comprehensive evaluation of services at the point of departure or return from an education abroad experience. Many universities have assessment offices that can assist education abroad offices in developing instruments and making sure they conform to university and

Chapter 1: Advising Principles and Strategies

federal regulations about human subjects. Some offices request the services of outside reviewers to periodically assist them with assessment. Not only do evaluations let students know that education abroad advisers are accountable for their services and eager to improve them, they also provide excellent feedback for individual advisers and help offices and individuals fine tune their advising models.

Training, Support, and Further Education

As the field of education abroad grows, there is an increasing variety of resources available to ensure that advisers can keep up to date in their training. Supervisors have an obligation to provide advisers with ongoing professional development. NAFSA offers a series of workshops for professional development on many essential topics, including advising and workshops in "Financing Education Abroad," "Health, Safety and Liability," and "Short-Term Programs," among others. NAFSA's regional and national conferences offer a wide variety of sessions and workshops to assist in keeping abreast of the latest developments in the field. NAFSA's Education Abroad Knowledge Community's (formerly known as SECUSSA) e-mail discussion group, SECUSS-L, is open to anyone who wishes to join. It provides an effective forum to publicize programs, as well as invite discussions, on relevant topics and emerging situations. NACADA also offers regional and national conferences and workshops that will help study abroad advisers enhance their general advising skills.

Advisers, particularly those new to the field, are encouraged to seek out colleagues in their college or university, state, and region. Many institutions have working groups to discuss issues specific to the regions in which the institutions reside.

SUMMARY

Education abroad advising principles and strategies must be student-centered and holistic, and based on theoretical principles. Education abroad advisers should create an environment within their offices and on their campuses that is supportive of quality advising. Advisers are responsible to the students they serve, the campuses on which they work, and to their own professional development. NAFSA's Education Abroad Knowledge Community is responsible for underscoring the importance of education abroad advising and for forging closer ties with organizations with similar objectives, such as NACADA.

CHAPTER 2

Integrating Intercultural Learning into Education Abroad Programming

Contributors: Joseph G. Hoff, Barbara Kappler

The number of students studying, working, and volunteering abroad from U.S. higher education institutions continues to increase on an annual basis, and more of these students are choosing less traditional destinations outside of Western Europe. Given the rise in the overall number of education abroad students and the establishment of institutional goals for education abroad, attention is focusing more than ever on the outcomes of the education abroad experience. A highly accepted goal of education abroad by members of the international education field is to obtain cross-cultural knowledge and skills—also referred to as intercultural competence. This goal is described in various ways in the literature but ultimately focuses on the development of intercultural competencies that allow an individual to function in a different culture (Fantini 1995). In this chapter, intercultural learning refers to the process of developing intercultural competence in the course of the education abroad experience. Intercultural training is the vehicle for facilitating the development of intercultural learning.

Administrators in the field frequently cite anecdotal evidence from students concerning the positive outcomes of education abroad programs, including awareness of other cultures and the acquisition of intercultural skills. Given that many students do not receive extensive training in intercultural learning, the development of effective intercultural training materials and orientations has become a priority in order to affect change in intercultural understanding and intercultural competence. Until recently, training materials specifically related to and designed for education abroad programming have not been widely available. Materials from intercultural communication form much of the basis of what is now available for program administrators to utilize in their own intercultural training.

Intercultural competence, sometimes referred to as intercultural communication competence, is defined as "the ability to relate and communicate effectively when individuals involved in the interaction do not share the same culture, ethnicity, language, or other salient variables" (Hains, Lynch, and Wintons 1997, cited in Milagros and Reese 1999). Intercultural competence involves one's motivation, knowledge, attitudes, behaviors, and skills (Martin and Nakayama 1997). The acquisition of intercultural competence depends on a number of variables, one of which is the preparation and training of students. As La Brack notes, "it has been proven that properly designed and conducted orientation programs do assist participants to achieve positive intercultural adjustments" (La Brack 1993, 242). In most university study abroad programs however, relatively little attention is given to intercultural training in predeparture orientations, either while overseas or upon the students' return to the home culture. Unless students enroll in a special course before departure or while abroad, such as an intercultural communications class, they may take little initiative to reflect on their intercultural interactions and other experiences abroad. In order to assist students to achieve the goal of becoming interculturally competent, more effective materials and systematic approaches to training must be employed.

As noted above, one of the critical variables that affects the development of intercultural competence for education abroad participants is intercultural training, either in predeparture or on-site formats or both (Larsen 2002). Martin (1989) notes one of the reasons students do not always achieve the benefits of education abroad is the lack of training for the intercultural experience. A major report on the study abroad field states that in determining necessary program characteristics, an important feature of study abroad programming should be the "careful preparation and orientation of students for study abroad so that cross-cultural differences, dissimilar approaches to teaching and to students at the host institution and inadequate foreign language skills do not impede the Americans' international learning" (Carlson et al. 1990, 121). To understand other cultural differences, Kohls (1979) notes that we first need to understand our own cultural baggage through intercultural training in order to be aware of how culture affects our perspective. Brislin and Yoshida (1994) state that cross-cultural training should assist people in overcoming cross-cultural obstacles so that they can become more effective in cross-cultural situations and cope with any stress experienced from cross-cultural encounters. Brislin and Yoshida maintain that the result of cross-cultural training is the acquisition of knowledge of the informal guidelines that make certain behaviors appropriate in cultures.

Culture-general learning skills can be enhanced through training. Bennett (1993) also posits that intercultural training can assist individuals in progressing along the continuum of ethnocentrism to ethno-relative worldviews. Another assumption is that by teaching culture-general learning skills, education abroad participants will be able to use the strategies developed in any culture worldwide. As Juffer notes, by providing training that teaches students to learn how to learn about a new culture, we are "teaching strategies to enable sojourners to become independent cross-cultural learners" (Juffer 1993, 202).

The idea that the education abroad experience by itself will bring about better international understanding in students and develop intercultural competence is now being challenged by studies that prove otherwise and call for effective preparation and training of students. Laubscher's (1994) study of out-of-classroom learning in study abroad students is one of the first studies that focuses on the process that generates the outcomes rather than on the outcomes themselves. The study concludes with a call for a more systematic approach to teaching cross-cultural skills in order to achieve more success in out-of-classroom learning. Bacon questions the legitimacy of a one-time predeparture or on-site orientation for study abroad students in her case study of the cultural adaptation learning process of a British student in Mexico. She maintains that "mere competence in an area is not sufficient to guarantee success, minimizing the usefulness of a better orientation or more background information" (Bacon 2002, 645). Instead, Bacon calls for a way for study abroad students to talk about or write about critical incidents as they happen while abroad and therefore analyze their initial responses, learning more and more about the culture and language in the process. Lundy Dobbert adds a twist to this concept with her statement concerning the fact that not all individuals have the natural propensity to be able to adjust to a different culture successfully. Therefore "the university's job is to prepare students and faculty prior to their internships [sojourn abroad]" (Dobbert 1998, 65). La Brack states that the field now realizes "just how much more effective and relevant the overseas experience can be made by providing participants a well-designed orientation prior to immersion" (La Brack 1993, 242).

Based on office and staff resources, education abroad advisers must determine to what extent it is possible to integrate intercultural training into programming both at home and abroad. Incorporating intercultural training into programming and creating an environment for ongoing learning, not only for students, but also for education abroad personnel, is essential and should be done in a systematic way. Equipped with intercultural learning skills, students are positioned to gain the most from their academic and extracurricular education abroad experiences. How education abroad professionals and international educators frame the process of intercultural learning will affect the learning outcomes of the students.

Frequently Asked Questions about Intercultural Learning and Intercultural Training

Don't Students Learn Intercultural Concepts On Their Own?

Some students have a greater aptitude for learning languages or subjects such as mathematics than others. The same is true for understanding the breadth of difference that may occur between cultures. If students are given the tools to learn about different cultures and a "mindset of inquiry" then they are apt to learn more. This is especially true when exploring those cultures that are initially taken to be somewhat similar to U.S. culture, such as those of Australia or the United Kingdom, where students' expectations tend to downplay any differences.

Teaching Intercultural Communication Concepts Is Extra, Only if I Have Time, Correct?

Intercultural learning is a goal of study abroad. Learning how to learn will prepare students for future careers in a very diverse world. The realities of time, budgets, and staffing affect all of us. With the increase of study abroad–related intercultural learning materials, integrating intercultural training into orientation programming has become easier. As international educators, we must study the best practices in the field and look for ways to apply them to maximize students' intercultural learning. The current climate—the demonstrated need for intercultural training, the desired outcomes, and the variety of students' cultural experiences—demands that we take the strongest educational approach to study abroad and do all that we can to integrate intercultural learning into our programs.

Should I Teach Culture-General or Culture-Specific Concepts?

According to Lustig and Koester (1993), culture-general concepts refer to generic skills for developing intercultural competence as opposed to culture-specific learning, which refers to learning perceptions and behaviors that are unique to specific cultures. Because within each nation state there are multiple cultures and each person can be a member of multiple cultures, the primary focus should be on culture-general concepts. Still, you can teach the culture-general via culture-specific examples of any particular culture. The precise balance between culture-general and culture-specific concepts in your intercultural training will depend on the amount of time available and the purpose of the orientation.

If you are conducting a general orientation for students going to many different parts of the world, then culture-general concepts may be taught, focusing on one's own culture in order for students to begin to think about what culture means, using their own cultures as reference points. If you are conducting an orientation for a group of students traveling to one country only, then both culture-general and culture-specific concepts may be taught. When teaching culture-specific concepts it is best to relate them to culture-general concepts in order for students to have a depth of understanding of why people from the culture may behave as they do, rather than simply noting behavioral differences. For example, when teaching about differences between usage of the Japanese and English languages, such as the use of honorifics in Japanese or the comparative linearity and directness of English (culture-specific), it is possible to also relate these concepts to differences in the communication goals of both parties in the situation (e.g., efficiency or relationship-building), as well as the inherent values involved (e.g., hierarchy and equality).

What if I Don't Have the Background to Teach Intercultural Communication?

Study abroad administrators may find resources such as *What's Up With Culture?* (University of the Pacific 2003) and *Maximizing Study Abroad: A Program Professional's Guide to Strategies for Language and Culture Learning and Use* (Paige et al. 2002) helpful in teaching intercultural communication. Resources for students are also readily available. *What's Up With Culture?* is appropriate for student use, and there is a student version of *Maximizing Study Abroad*. Other helpful resources for students include Storti's *Art of Crossing Cultures* (2001), *The Art of Coming Home* (2001), *Figuring Foreigners Out* (1999), and Hess's *Whole World Guide to Culture Learning* (1994) and *Studying Abroad/Learning Abroad* (1997). Moreover, many higher education institutions across the country offer intercultural communication courses. Specific institutes such as the Summer Institute for Intercultural Communication at the Intercultural Communication Institute at Pacific University in Oregon, and the Summer Institute at the Center for Advanced Research on Language Acquisition at the University of Minnesota offer intercultural communication or study abroad-specific workshops to assist professionals in developing skills for the facilitation of intercultural learning.

What if Students Resist Learning Intercultural Communication Concepts?

Understanding the underlying reasons for student resistance is critical in order to understand how to respond to this resistance. Often, resistance is a symptom of offering information that has little meaning at the time. Therefore, it is important to consider what to offer in predeparture orientations compared with on-site orientations. For example, it may be more beneficial to focus on the students' own culture(s) before they leave the country as a focus point when teaching culture-general concepts because they can understand what is being discussed. Once overseas, new concepts such as different values or nonverbal communication may be more evident to the students as they experience the host culture. Some of the common reasons for resistance are highlighted below, as well as strategies for working more effectively with such resistance.

Resistance: Students are experienced and don't want to sit through another presentation on culture shock.

Strategy: Consult Bennett's (1993a) *Content and Process: Balancing Challenge* model and Section III of *Maximizing Study Abroad: A Program Professional's Guide to Strategies for Language and Culture Learning and Use* (Paige et al. 2002), to find guidance on how to shape a program that encourages experienced students to develop skills rather than simply acquire knowledge.

Resistance: Students are too busy.

Strategy: Require attendance and make the program dynamic and worthwhile. Students will make time for what is essential. They will have very valid reasons for not attending things that are not absolutely critical to their lives. Tell them if you are piloting a new program and invite their feedback. Always ask students to evaluate orientation programming. Incorporate this feedback into future sessions in order to improve your program.

Resistance: Students do not expect to encounter great differences; they think, "We are all more alike than different so let's just go and be ourselves."

Strategy: Bennett (1993) provides study abroad professionals with a model of how students respond to cultural difference, and suggests how to approach training based on the level of the participants' development as it pertains to intercultural competencies. For example, if students are at a point of being defensive against differences, then highlighting differences in a training session—a common reaction by educators—may actually be counterproductive. For this stage, Bennett recommends focusing on similarities. In later stages, focusing on differences is more productive.

Resistance: Students feel that since they are just going for a short time and will not really be interacting with the culture they don't need much training.

Strategy: Certainly, different experiences need different depths of intercultural training. (For a discussion of intensity factors, see Paige 1993 and Paige et al. 2003.) However, simply because an experience is short does not negate the need for training. Runners must train for the 50-meter dash as well as for a marathon!

The most challenging aspect of resistance is not necessarily that it exists, but that it can come to life in forms that are intense and thus difficult to cope with and that it can be difficult to gauge just how widespread the resistance is. For example, a student who "rips apart" the adviser on the evaluation form is remembered for months while a student who was pleased may be forgotten. This example is meant not to diminish the importance of resistance, but rather as a reminder to carefully assess the depth of the resistance.

There is also a quieter voice that is often forgotten in the face of resistance. Students, when only provided with a brief packet about practical registration information, logistics, and cross-cultural adjustment theory and tips, often wonder why the program advisers don't take a more serious approach to preparing students for study abroad. They may express feeling "duped" if they were told that study abroad would be educational but instead they get the impression from the abroad office that it's really an excuse for a vacation abroad. These students want an educational approach and they want to be taken seriously. They look to their education abroad advisers to provide the educational framework. In short, advisers must not let the students who express the most resistance to intercultural learning preparation determine the extent to which the advisers make their programs as educational as possible for all involved.

Learning Styles, the Learning Cycle, and Intercultural Learning

During orientation programs, education abroad professionals stand before a group of students who are diverse in so many ways: life experiences, second language competencies, and motivations for study abroad, just to name a few. While the degree of attention education abroad professionals give to any one of these issues may depend upon their specific programs and personal experiences and motivations, professionals also need to understand and integrate the different learning style preferences of the students into program planning. While learning styles have been analyzed using a number of typologies, Kolb's (1984) approach to learning styles will be used here.

Learning style preferences represent how a person feels most comfortable when entering a learning situation. For example, if you were to learn a new computer program, how would you start? Would you call a trusted friend who had recently gone through this experience? Read the manual? Enroll in a mini-course taught by an expert so that you could learn how the program can be integrated with other technologies you are using? Or would you just simply launch the program and start "playing"? Your initial reaction can be telling of your preference. If you prefer to learn through personal connections and feelings, you are a concrete experiencer; if you want to reflect upon material before acting upon it, you are a reflective observer; if you most enjoy analyzing models and connections between the things you are learning, you are an

Chapter 2: Integrating Intercultural Learning into Education Abroad Programming

abstract conceptualizer. If you learn best by trying things out (and wanted to skip your own orientation prior to study abroad), you are an active experimenter. (For additional background and to take the Kolb's Learning Styles Inventory, contact Hay/McBer Resources Direct.)

Certainly, neither educators nor students simply use one style. Chances are, we have skills in each of the styles even if we maintain an inclination for one or more styles. Further, we have hopefully had an encounter in which we had the opportunity to experience the powerful learning that occurred when connections were made among the learning styles. For example, you may have heard a trusted colleague discuss a great new activity they incorporated into their predeparture orientation (concrete experience). You then attend a NAFSA conference and have a chance to experience the activity yourself (active experimentation). At this point you are tempted to jump right in and add this to your own orientation program. However, you are a bit uncertain about how well the activity will work given the time constraints (reflective observation) so you read more about the specific activity (more reflective observation). You conduct the activity (active experimentation) but are not quite comfortable with how the debriefing went (reflective observation). You contact your trusted colleague and discuss the experience (concrete experience). She recommends some additional reading on the underlying theories involved in the activity. You read a bit more about these theories (abstract conceptualization and reflective observation) and set up a new plan for how to facilitate the activity next time. The second time with the activity, you feel much more comfortable with not simply the logistics, but how the overall debriefing went and how well the students responded to the activity. You realize your success is not simply that you conducted the activity twice but that you stepped outside of your comfort zone (concrete experience) and challenged yourself to complete a cycle of learning by using all four styles throughout the experience.

Study abroad presents one of the most powerful opportunities for fully engaging in learning precisely because it affords the opportunity to utilize all four learning style preferences. Because study abroad occurs in a new context, engages the students inside and outside of the classroom, and often forces students out of their learning style preference comfort zone, they are apt to need to utilize all four styles.

Yet simply using all the styles does not necessarily mean that students will encounter the connections among the styles, as was the case in the example of the program professional conducting the experiential activity. It's quite possible that students may encounter an activity that requires a different learning style than they are normally comfortable with (for example, if reflective observers are asked to do a more active experimenter activity such as finding a language partner at the host institution) and may consequently resist the activity. However, if the students either challenge themselves or are challenged by an educator to make connections among the styles, the subsequent learning that takes place can be impressive. For example, even the fairly simple activity of working with language partners, if taken through the four styles, could be transformed from simply a language activity into a meaningful intercultural exchange:

- Students are required to meet once a week with a language partner from the host institution (active experimentation).

- Students record their emotional reactions to the first meeting with their language partner as part of a required

Part II: Campus Advising

   journaling activity (reflective observation).

- Students share their reactions in small groups (concrete experience) and an educator facilitates a discussion about language anxiety, cross-cultural adjustment, and specific strategies for engaging in conversations with native speakers (abstract conceptualization).

At future meetings with their language partners, the students are encouraged to share comments about their adjustment to the host culture (concrete experience) and to invite their partners to reflect upon whether or not they have had similar adjustment experiences. The students can share photos of things that most surprise them about their experiences in the host culture or that make them homesick (the act of taking the photos involves reflective observation). Sharing the photos gives the language partners an opportunity for reflective observation as well as an opportunity for the partners to share their own perspectives on the photos (concrete experience).

Similar interactions can be facilitated for international students in the United States. Transforming a one-style activity into a cycle of learning is precisely what makes the education component of international education come alive. It's why we do what we do.

INTERCULTURAL COMMUNICATION: WHAT TO TEACH

As is evident in Part III, Chapter 7, "Predeparture Orientation and Reentry Programming," and Part IV, Chapter 2, "The Overseas Program Cycle and Critical Components," deciding what to include in predeparture and reentry sessions is a balancing act. The following section focuses on fundamental concepts and tools for facilitating intercultural learning.

Where to Begin?

A common starting point in facilitating intercultural learning is to begin with definitions because it provides learners with an opportunity to consider the complexity of culture. That is, how culture differs from personality and other influences on behavior, and that we are all members of more than one culture. This last point is critical as so often U.S. students assume that topics involving culture or diversity are about "the other" rather than about themselves. Several textbooks provide straightforward approaches by first defining culture, then defining communication, and from these definitions, they define intercultural communication (Ting-Toomey 1999; Gudykunst and Kim 2003; Lustig and Koester 2003). Culture has been defined in many ways, from holistic definitions such as "culture is everything and everywhere" (Samovar and Porter 2003a) to more of a reductionistic approach in which lists of what makes up culture are presented (e.g., values, beliefs, traditions, behaviors, nonverbals). Intercultural communication is then defined as occurring when a member or members of one culture interact with members of other cultures.

In contrast to presenting definitions, educators may first prefer to have students experience some aspect of a cultural difference so that they experience a feeling of belonging to a particular culture or explore a specific difference (consult Intercultural Press for numerous resources on activities). One advantage of such an approach is that in the debriefing, educators can focus on the importance of guessing, developing an hypothesis, and being comfortable with ambiguity—critical skills in intercultural communication. This also provides a tangible link with what is easy to miss in an introduction to intercultural communication—a discussion of the effort involved and what it means to be interculturally competent.

International educators commonly assume that learners will understand the importance of working to be successful at intercultural communication and moreover, that they will understand what it means to be interculturally competent. Educators should offer examples from real life regarding these two specific topics. For example, regarding the amount of work involved in intercultural communication, educators could relate student testimonials about the efforts the students undertook to understand the host culture and alternatively how the students helped their hosts to understand U.S. culture. To help students understand what being interculturally competent means, international educators should help students set their own goals for achievable outcomes for their education abroad program and also challenge them by providing a number of clear and varied outcomes achieved by others.

Why So Much Attention to Difference?

At this point in the facilitation of intercultural learning, we typically focus on either culture-general or culture-specific differences. A common question from educators and students alike is, "Why do we have to pay so much attention to differences?" The logic is that similarities do not cause as many difficulties as differences, but it is also true that we might assume similarity when in fact it may not be present (Bennett 1993). However, just presenting the categories of similarity and difference does not provide enough of a framework for understanding human behavior and motivations. Educators should consider the following typology and share it with students, thereby helping them to examine their experiences beyond the initial "we are alike" or "we are different" mentality.

People from Different Cultures Can Have Similar Motivations, Expectations, and Assumptions About Similar Behaviors

Where there are differences, there may also be similarities. Two Japanese students, Mariko and Kentaro, and two U.S. students, Jack and Anita, are working together on a group project. Mariko and Jack agreed to have their portion of the group's papers written and sent to the group on Friday. When Mariko and Jack were late handing in their work, both Kentaro and Anita responded with "That's okay." When the group discussed the project after it was completed, Kentaro and Anita confessed that they were bothered that Mariko and Jack were late, but that they had decided they did not want to address the conflict directly while the group was in the middle of the project. In this manner, both Kentaro's and Anita's motivation to avoid direct conflict and their behavior of saying that being late was okay were similar, even though they were from different cultures.

People from Different Cultures Can Have Different Motivations, Expectations, and Assumptions About Different Behaviors

Differences can run deep. An Estonian student, Rein, comes to talk to a program administrator and complains that not only do his U.S. friends not accept his silence, they constantly ask him to explain his silence. The administrator explains that she often interprets silence as lack of interest or a sign that something is wrong. Rein explains that this is not the case—he just does not like to talk a lot and enjoys being silent. Not only are the language behaviors of Rein and his U.S. friends different (i.e., more use of silence compared with more talking), but Rein and his friends also appear to have different assumptions about what silence means among friends.

People from Different Cultures Can Have Similar Motivations, Expectations, and Assumptions and Have Different Behaviors

Whereas a common goal can foster unity, different behaviors can cause confusion. Samantha, a U.S. student studying in Italy for the fall semester, buys her Italian friend Angela a gift for Christmas, to express how much Angela's friendship has meant. Angela, also wanting to express how much the friendship has meant, consciously decides to not buy a gift for her friend Samantha. They are motivated by wanting to express what a friendship means, but they do so with different behaviors. Angela views gift giving as possibly creating an obligation on the part of the person receiving the gift, whereas Samantha sees gift giving as representative of the feelings associated with the friendship the women have formed.

People from Different Cultures Can Have Different Motivations, Expectations, and Assumptions About Similar Behaviors

Things may not appear to be what they seem. In the previous example, Samantha sees gift giving as a sign of a friendship, whereas Angela sees the gift as creating a potential obligation. If Angela had given Samantha a gift, Samantha might have assumed that Angela did so for the same reason Samantha did—as a sign of a close friendship. Likewise, Angela might not have understood that Samantha's gift was intended to be a sign of a close friendship and not one of obligation.

International educators and students are encouraged to look beyond the obvious and to look for similarities and differences in not simply behaviors, but also in the motivations, expectations, and assumptions that give those behaviors their culturally driven meanings.

I Don't Have Much Time Available for My Predeparture Orientation; What Should I Cover?

Doing something is better that silence on the subject, which can give untended messages to your students such as intercultural understanding is not the focus of your program, or that it is easy to achieve, or that it is not that important. Use whatever time you have for your program to discuss the main components of successful intercultural learning: the process of discovery, understanding the tangible differences among cultures, and establishing a framework for a lifetime of learning.

Demonstrate That Intercultural Learning Is a Process of Discovery

Think back over your own intercultural experiences. Can you pinpoint the moment when you truly understood yourself as a cultural being and when you felt competent in another culture and language? Chances are there is no one specific point in time to refer back to, but rather a series of discoveries that built upon one another. Encouraging students to understand intercultural learning as a process will provide a foundation for them to use the learning styles in a cycle of reflection, experimentation, experience, and reconceptualization.

Personal stories from students and staff can demonstrate key discovery points about how an understanding of one's self and the host culture develops over time. If you have time, facilitate intercultural simulations, which will give students the opportunity to experience the process of discovery.

Establish That There Are Tangible Ways in Which Cultures Can Differ

Knowing exactly how students from different cultures will interact in a future situation is impossible to predict. However, it is possible to understand that there are demonstrable differences among cultures in areas such as values and communication styles (these differences are explored in more detail in the next section). The goal is not to stereotype any one particular cultural group, but rather to give students the tools to recognize possible differences as they experience them. For example, if we teach that Chinese students are collectivists and are very group oriented, how will the U.S. students understand how to recognize Chinese students who may be more individualistic than the U.S. students are themselves?

Regardless of the amount of time you have to present your program, you can require that participants do some background reading. Consider Storti's *Figuring Foreigners Out* (1999), Kohls' *Survival Kit for Overseas Living* (1979), or textbooks such as Martin, Nakayama, and Flores' *Readings in Cultural Contexts* (1998), and Ting-Toomey's *Communicating Across Cultures* (1999). You can also discuss actual critical incidents that have occurred during the course of the study abroad program that highlight ways in which the culture or cultures of the U.S. students may differ from that of the host culture.

Establish a Framework for Ongoing Learning

It is clear that educators cannot accomplish all that needs to be done to prepare students for intercultural learning in a single orientation (Bacon 2002). Instead, education abroad professionals are setting a foundation for the learning process that students are challenged to follow throughout the education abroad experience, including reentry into the home culture. Each program must consider how to integrate ongoing learning directly into the program structure, as experience shows that intercultural learning may not occur without structure. Consider offering credit for an on-site class in which students can debrief their learning experiences. Share excerpts (with permission) of students' journals in which they detail their own learning, to demonstrate the value of writing and journaling as a vehicle for ongoing learning. Integrate culture-general concepts whenever possible into on-site language classes or ongoing orientations, excursions, newsletters, or regularly scheduled meetings. Students who have not studied intercultural communication previously may not have the interest or expectations needed to learn the different concepts on their own. As mentioned previously, this may be especially true for students studying in countries where they perceive the culture to be similar to that of the United States. The assumption is that the more intercultural learning takes place, the easier it will be for students to adapt to the host culture. Therefore, incorporating intercultural concepts into regular programming should assist study abroad administrators and on-site directors with student adaptation problems as well as provide the foundation necessary for ongoing intercultural learning.

What Intercultural Topics Should Be Included in an Intercultural Orientation?

Excellent resources are readily available that offer detailed background information on common topics to include when facilitating intercultural learning. These topics include perception (Singer 1987, 1998), communication styles (Storti 1999; Ting-Toomey 1999), values (Kohls 2001; Stewart, Danielian, and Foster 1998; Ting-Toomey 1999), nonverbals (Samovar and Porter 2003b), and adjustment (Bennett 1998; Storti 2001).

Three topics for intercultural orientation programs—values, communication styles, and nonverbal communication—are explored in the following paragraphs.

Values

One methodology in intercultural training is for educators to present lists of what particular cultures value. While this list approach can provide some initial insights, it falls far short of preparing sojourners for actual experiences. Consider the following scenario, taking into account that it's common to hear that U.S. citizens value their time: Renee, an international student adviser, is walking across campus and is a bit late for a meeting. She sees an international student in the distance. It is Givi from Georgia, with whom she worked several months ago. He is dressed in a suit. Renee has never seen Givi dressed in a suit before and wonders where he is going. She is aware that she is late. Does Renee stop and talk to Givi?

This question has been posed to hundreds of training participants, and many have been quite confident that they know whether or not Renee will stop. They have explanations both for why she would not (U.S. citizens value time) and why she would (she is too curious). At this point, training administrators usually emphasize that participants cannot use a list of values to determine Renee's specific behavior. To know what Renee would do, one would have to ask Renee. What can be discussed with participants is the following question: What might make a difference in whether or not Renee stops and talks? The responses to this question (Renee's personality, what the meeting is for, how she feels about being late, what her status is at the meeting, etc.) can reveal much about Renee's decision-making and potentially the decision-making process of others with similar backgrounds. In short, people don't act based on their values lists, instead, they have complicated systems of decision-making.

The critical point of this story is that cultures themselves are systems for decision-making, and no one particular value ever operates alone. Cultural information can be used to make informed guesses about a particular human behavior, but such information will not reveal for certain why a specific action has been taken. Taking a systems approach allows for much more complexity and thus, promotes intercultural learning at a deeper level than can be achieved by using lists.

Communication Styles

As with values, it is important to look beyond simple comparisons to help explain why individuals communicate the way they do. For example, in preparing a group of students to go to Japan, educators may be tempted to portray Japanese students as having an indirect style of communication. While this may be a helpful introduction, it should be supported with much more elaborate information about the contexts in which Japanese students might be direct, what values might come into conflict when Japanese students choose to be indirect or direct, and some of the ways Japanese students express themselves in a direct manner (all cultural groups have rules about how to be direct and what level of directness will be tolerated in specific situations). Educators are encouraged to consider that their role is not to supply the specific answers about why a person behaves in a certain way, but rather to offer questions and suggestions about how students can develop skills in understanding differences as they experience them.

Nonverbal Communication

Nonverbal communication—including everything from touch to tone of voice—consists of the little things that can make a big difference in successfully understanding other cultures. Because of the specific nature of some of these differences and the fact that they are not necessarily spoken differences, it can be quite challenging for U.S. students to consider the importance of the differences. Educators should present students with key differences that they might encounter in another culture: differences in gestures, eye contact, sense of personal distance and space, touching, nonverbals used in host-country greetings, and pauses and silences in communication.

Tools

There are a number of effective methods available to help students to develop their intercultural learning strategies. As is to be expected, different strategies will resonate with different students and the educator's role is to encourage students to use as many strategies as they have access to—not just those strategies with which they are most comfortable.

Iceberg Metaphor

In *Maximizing Study Abroad: A Student's Guide to Strategies for Language and Culture Learning and Use* (Paige et al. 2002), the iceberg metaphor (Weaver 1986) is not presented in a lecture format (as is typically the case), but as an activity in which students are asked to read a true story of a student's experience in Venezuela. Students are then asked to identify the observable aspects of the situation (i.e., what's above the waterline) as well as the deeper cultural and personal differences that might contribute to the challenges in the story (i.e., the larger part of the iceberg that is not visible and rests below the waterline). The idea of learning through specific stories has been found to resonate with students. Educators can introduce the iceberg metaphor via very specific and tangible examples of student experiences so that students see the benefit of the metaphor and understand the areas in which their understanding of cultural differences is lacking (e.g., values and communication styles). This way, students learn how to apply the metaphor to their own experiences abroad.

The Description, Interpretation, and Evaluation Exercise

The Description, Interpretation, and Evaluation exercise (D.I.E.) assists students in interpreting critical incidents experienced while abroad (Bennett, Bennett, and Stillings 1977). First, students must objectively describe the critical incident. Then with the assistance of a cultural informant from the host culture (if one is available), students attempt to think of possible explanations for what was observed or experienced. Finally, students evaluate the experience focusing on their own feelings along with those of the member or members of the host culture who was involved. This activity attempts to teach students to consider multiple perspectives and interpretations.

Journaling

Journaling allows students an opportunity to reflect on their experiences and note their progress while abroad. Journaling on a regular basis does take some effort and time, however, which must be stressed in order for students to be successful in this activity. Encourage students to try out different journaling styles. Most students are familiar with a chronological approach in which there is an entry for each day's events. It can be easy to fall behind with this approach and feel overwhelmed. Alternative approaches include more free flowing journaling or to separate a journal into different sections for various elements of intercultural experiences: identity, adjusting to the classroom, initial reactions, revisiting initial reactions, etc. When short on time, even listing words or phrases can be an excellent way to trigger memories and reactions to significant experiences.

Students as Ethnographers

Students must be active in their approach to intercultural learning. In order to be effective, students can use the techniques employed by ethnographers (i.e., observation and informal interviews) to learn more about the host culture. One of the best ways to do this is to find a cultural informant such as a host family member, language partner, or friend at the local university. Discussions with a cultural informant will yield valuable information, keeping in mind of course that the informant's point of view is but one in a culture with many individuals and perspectives!

Summary

Intercultural learning is in essence what makes the education abroad experience unique and rewarding for students. By introducing students to intercultural learning concepts, education abroad professionals prepare them with the skills and knowledge that will be required to successfully live, study, and work in diverse or international environments, or both. Intercultural learning concepts will enable students to continue intercultural learning after they return to the United States or embark on their next sojourn abroad. The concepts and resources discussed in this chapter will assist study abroad professionals both at home and abroad to create intercultural learning environments. Resources are constantly being updated and created in the intercultural and international education fields. International educators have the responsibility of continuing to investigate ways to introduce intercultural learning to their students. By doing so, international educators will adhere to one of the goals of education abroad—that students become interculturally competent. Creating a more systematic approach to intercultural learning, from the predeparture stage to reentry, will ensure that students are prepared to understand and appreciate the multiple perspectives of different cultures in an increasingly interdependent world.

CHAPTER 3

Reaching Underrepresented Constituencies

Contributors: Carol J. Lebold, Amy Henry, Pamela Houston, Marilyn Jackson, Michele Scheibe, Scott Van Der Meid

Increasingly, colleges and universities seek to expand international education opportunities to all undergraduates. The overall number of students participating in education abroad programs has increased over time, yet international educators continue to struggle with issues of inclusion and participation for many underrepresented groups. In NAFSA's *Strategic Task Force on Education Abroad* (2003), the goal to extend study abroad opportunities unequivocally to the "broadest possible spectrum of students" is identified as a national priority. The challenge extends to education abroad initiatives that specifically address ethnic, socioeconomic, and gender diversity, as well as overseas study opportunities and curricular integration for students in mathematics, sciences, engineering, and business. In order to achieve the goals for study abroad participation stated in the task force report (i.e., 20 percent of U.S. students studying abroad by 2010 and 50 percent by 2040), proactive approaches for reaching underrepresented groups are essential.

The mandate is clear. It is imperative that the education abroad community identifies and addresses specific access issues for underserved constituencies in order for international education to move away from an elitist experience for a small percentage of students to an achievable choice for the majority of undergraduates. Collaboration across campuses and state and regional sectors must proactively address the needs of all students. Not only do students and campuses benefit from such inclusion, but also participants who are more representative of the U.S. population provide a more accurate picture of the richness and complexities of the diverse peoples of the United States to their overseas hosts. Participating students benefit from opportunities to explore other approaches and world views with respect to race, ethnicity, class, and nation by living and studying outside the home context.

NATIONAL TRENDS IN U.S. HIGHER EDUCATION AND UNDERREPRESENTATION

"The most racially and ethnically diverse generation in U.S. history" referred to as the "Millenial" generation is now enrolling in colleges and

Part II: Campus Advising

universities across the country (Howe and Strauss 2000). U.S. high school graduates are entering colleges and universities in record numbers despite the alarming rise in the cost of higher education. The percentage of students identified as nontraditional has been estimated to be as high as 75 percent according to the National Center for Education Statistics (2003). Nontraditional students in the general university context include those who are 24 years old or older; those with disabilities (9 percent report some type of disability that has an impact on learning); those with dependents (27 percent have dependents); and those who work (80 percent work while attending college, with 39 percent working full time) (United States Census Bureau 2000). The need for financial assistance is at an all-time high, with financial aid supporting 63 percent of undergraduates in the 2003–2004 academic year (NCES 2005).

The communities and homes from which students come reflect some of the changes within the United States. Only 24 percent of households in the United States are defined as traditional, if traditional is taken to mean married heterosexual couples with children. Latinos and nonwhites account for nearly 36 percent of the 18-years-old-or-under population, with one in five of these households having at least one immigrant parent, and one in ten with at least one noncitizen parent. Latinos now comprise a larger percentage of the U.S. population than blacks (United States Census Bureau 2000). Half of the rising immigrant inflow to the United States is from Latin America (one-third from Mexico alone). Another one-fourth of the immigrant population is from Asia. In spite of security-related restrictions, immigration accounted for over 42 percent of the recent population explosion in the United States. U.S. campuses have the most diverse students in history.

WHO IS STUDYING ABROAD?

One trend in education abroad is that students tend to choose programs that are shorter in duration than in the past. In 2002–2003, 93 percent of American students who studied abroad did so for one semester or less (*Open Doors* 2004). Another trend is that more financial aid and scholarships are available, and a third is that there is greater participation by students from community colleges and technical schools (see Part I, Chapter 9, "Education Abroad and Community Colleges"). Despite these trends, which meet the recommendations made over the years by those engaged in reaching out to underrepresented students, the traditional profile of who is studying abroad has not changed significantly over time. The typical study abroad participant is a female (64.7 percent), Caucasian European American (83.2 percent) in her junior or senior year (58.2 percent), and is studying in the humanities or social sciences (34 percent, though business now ranks second). She is most likely to study in Europe: the United Kingdom is the most popular destination (more than 20 percent), followed by Italy and Spain. As in the past, she still pursues language study, though her interest in studying a foreign language abroad has decreased. While she still may choose to study for one semester and sometimes a full year, she is more likely to attend a short-term program, unlike her international student counterparts, who typically enroll for a full degree when studying in the United States (*Open Doors* 2004).

Encouraging students from underrepresented constituencies to participate in education abroad programs is not simply a matter of replacing one type of student with another. Rather, the challenge is to support those who traditionally apply for education abroad programs, while increasing enrollment among those groups of students who do not typically seek to participate.

As indicated above, in terms of gender, race, and ethnicity, the profile of education abroad participants has not changed dramatically over time. However, students in business, the sciences, and engineering are enrolling in international education programs in increasing numbers and the destinations of choice of study abroad participants have expanded dramatically, even though Western Europe continues to dominate as the largest region in terms of overall education abroad participants.

International educators must understand the complexity of issues facing students on campuses, in communities, and within society. The fact that the overall number of participants in education abroad programs has significantly improved, but that there has been no appreciable change in the diversification of our student ranks, is a challenge that must be addressed in new ways. While educators continue to struggle with documenting the actual participation of underrepresented students, the crisis of inclusion and equity remains real and must be addressed with renewed commitment and advocacy on every level.

How Can Underrepresented Constituencies Be Defined in the Context of Education Abroad?

NAFSA's Committee on Underrepresentation in Education Abroad focuses attention on the need to both define and provide advocacy for those groups of students who are underrepresented in education abroad. In general, the underrepresented population has included but is not limited to ethnic and racial minorities; students with disabilities; students in academic disciplines such as business, engineering, education, nursing, medicine, law, agriculture, and sciences; men; students attending community colleges, technical schools, historically black colleges and universities, and tribal schools; student leaders; athletes; first-generation college students; gay, lesbian, bisexual, or transgendered (GLBT) students; and older students (over 24 years and often with dependents). In other words, the vast majority of undergraduates enrolled on U.S. campuses are underrepresented in terms of participation in education abroad opportunities.

To help refine their work and focus on specific constituencies, the committee, in recent years, has chosen to focus on the following specific groups:

- *Majors:* Business, sciences, math, technology, medicine, health sciences, engineering.

- *Nontraditional students:* Part-time students, commuters, low-income students, first-generation college students, older students, and those caring for dependents.

- *Gender:* Males.

- *Ethnicity and race:* Students of color (e.g., students of African, Latino, Asian, or Native American heritage).

- *GLBT:* Gay, lesbian, bisexual, and transgendered students.

- *Students with disabilities:* Physical, vision-related, auditory, psychiatric, health-related, cognitive, or a combination.

- *Religion:* Students with religious considerations and priorities as part of their social and cultural identities.

These groups of students require special attention in the recruitment, advising, program selection, and orientation phases, and also need in-country support as well. Each of these groups has specific issues that can and must be addressed by international offices in ways that encourage greater participation in education abroad opportunities. Some of these groups also share common concerns.

Not all groups of students who are underrepresented in general on U.S. college campuses are, in fact, underrepresented on education abroad programs. For example, Asian-American students participate in education abroad to a much greater degree than students of African descent. In some cases the data are simply not available to make a determination. Many students who have learning disabilities may, in fact, be studying abroad quite successfully. Gay students may be studying in record numbers but are "invisible" to education abroad advisers if resources and opportunities are not provided for them to discuss their concerns.

Outreach and targeted services at all stages of the education abroad process have proven successful in encouraging underrepresented groups to study abroad. Not all of the issues facing underrepresented constituencies are obvious and visible to the education abroad professional. Hence, it is the education abroad professional's obligation to collaborate with relevant campus offices and staff to ensure success in reaching these students.

Developing a Profile of an Institution's Student Body

The clearest solution for sending more students abroad will be based on the needs of each institution's underrepresented constituents and the institution's campus context. Education abroad professionals must investigate who is under-represented on their campuses, by examining what majors are offered, how diverse the campus is, and which students are not finding their way to the education abroad office or to education abroad programs.

Professional Profile: Who Advises and Administers Education Abroad

Successfully reaching students who continue to be left out of education abroad requires a close examination of the profile of the practitioners and directors managing our international programs. An education abroad professional's experiences, social identity, and his or her ability to advise, mentor, and be a role model for the students are important considerations for the profession. Diversity within the ranks, institutions, and professional organizations of the education abroad community must be sought if there is to be any appreciable change.

Little research has been done with regard to the profile of professionals entering the field and what kinds of experiences they bring to it. Research in other professional fields such as counseling, social work, teaching, and medical practice suggest the importance of identity issues for both client (i.e., students) and counselor (i.e., education abroad professional). In *Counseling Across Cultures* (1996), Paul Pederson and others suggest that, for those working in U.S. majority-culture institutions, differences between the counselor and the counseled intrude upon the overall interaction in ways that may negatively impact the overall experience. When applying his ideas to the profession of international education, we may recognize that a traditional approach to advising may also be unconsciously aligned with a Euro-American cultural bias. However unintended, some of the mainstream U.S. American values identified by L. Robert Kohls seep into study abroad advising. Optimism, individualism, egalitarianism, glorification of social mobility, encouragement of personal change, respect for individual self-determination and a belief in personal responsibility for one's own actions are values that are reflected in our approaches to advising. This partial list of U.S. American values is familiar to those educators who use adapted versions of L. Robert Kohls' *Values Majority Culture Americans Live By* (2002) in predeparture orientations. The relevance here is that while international educators apply these theories and knowledge to their work with students, educators rarely use them as a frame for interpreting their own responses to their work, their institutions, and the policies that they develop in education abroad.

In a small, informal study initiated in 2003 by the leadership of NAFSA's Section on U.S. Students Abroad (SECUSSA), entitled *Pathways to the Profession*, a profile of education abroad professionals began to emerge. Perhaps not surprisingly, early results indicate that the "who" in this field is strikingly similar to the profile of students going abroad from U.S. institutions. Men are less represented in entry- and mid-level positions. Those responding to the first informal survey overwhelmingly self-identified as white. While it is important to note that this study by no means represents the field as a whole, it still serves as a reminder of the importance of linking diversity and equity at the institutional level and also within NAFSA and specifically within the Education Abroad Knowledge Community. There continues to be a need for a proactive commitment to find new ways to include strong leaders from diverse backgrounds and experiences in the profession.

ACCESS AND EQUAL OPPORTUNITY WITHIN EDUCATION ABROAD

The commitment to nondiscrimination is a guiding principle in education abroad. However, although education abroad administrators and advisers would not purposely set out to discriminate against students with disabilities, program practices, policies, and perceptions about disability can unintentionally lead to exclusion. The same unintentional results can be found when education abroad offices and programs are run without regard to the specific needs of various underrepresented groups of students on the home campuses. Attending to the needs of students of color, students with disabilities, and other traditionally underrepresented groups will enhance services for all students.

Another unintentional exclusionary practice occurs when some international program offices simply do not capture statistical data that could assist in developing effective and strategic efforts focused on increasing minority student participation. It is safe to assume that many international education offices are understaffed, have insufficient budgets, and are overwhelmed with the requirements of daily operations. Increasing the participation rates of underrepresented groups could be low on the priority list because administrators are busy battling to preserve, protect, and justify resources they currently have. But there are ways to meet this challenge that require little resources and low maintenance.

How can education abroad administrators strategically approach the need to increase participation by underrepresented groups without having a quantitative gauge to measure their success and failure? Adding a statistics section to the information card that is given out to students inquiring about abroad programs allows offices to capture useful information. A statistics section on the application form, or on a postadmission form, yields further results concerning which students complete the application process and ultimately attend education abroad programs. Other questions to be asked are, "Which groups are being reached successfully and which are not being reached," "Which programs attract certain students and why," and "How do individual campus participation rates compare to national trends?" Administrators can also set attainable goals from term-to-term or year-to-year to increase the number of students in a given period. Although it may be unpopular to incorporate business strategies when dealing with students, a business model has much to offer, including strategies for meeting certain goals if the current approach is not yielding positive results.

The debates raging on campuses across the country on affirmative action policies, admissions standards, economic hardship, and the widening gap of income inequities seem somewhat removed from the arena of international education. Yet, in comparing "who" enrolls on U.S. campuses with "who" we send abroad, there is a clear need to examine policies and practices that are discriminatory and exclusionary, however unintended, as a part of the collective experience in education abroad.

Social Identity Models: Relevance to International Education

Educators must understand how the complex issues of race, class, gender, disability, sexual orientation, and other social identity factors of both students and professionals affect international educational endeavors. Pederson and others in the field of cross-cultural counseling and social-identity theory offer some insight into approaches that might assist international educators in achieving the goals of greater inclusion. Pragmatic approaches are useful in reaching out to students who do not plan to go abroad, and partnering pragmatism with deeper understanding of the issues facing particular constituencies may assist in truly broadening participation. As Pederson states, "culture impinges upon the person both across the globe and around the block" (Pederson 1996, 5).

The fields of multicultural education and psychology provide some guidelines for approaching the need to infuse our international offices and advising centers with more culturally pluralistic approaches. Social-identity research suggests that lack of awareness of one's own ethnocentric biases impacts professional settings (Adams and Bell 1997). This idea must surely ring startlingly clear to all international educators. Isn't ethnocentrism addressed when preparing students for their experiences abroad? Both "internationalists" and "multiculturalists" are engaged in work that enhances an appreciation of differences. International educators bring their experiences of other cultures to the campus context and enhance the definition of diversity on their campuses. By incorporating greater knowledge of and commitment to social justice, shared privilege, and inclusiveness, international educators may open the doors for more students to go abroad. Greater self-knowledge and education in the areas of white privilege, oppression, domestic nondominant ethnic cultures, and other forms of diversity will enhance the ability of international educators to work across campus with colleagues and students.

Social-identity development theory also has value in helping educators not only better reach diverse students, but also in preparing all education abroad students to live and learn in another culture. When confronted with different social histories and experiences across and between cultures with respect to privilege, race, class, and religion, how do students adjust their self-concepts in the face of conflicting information? How do issues of identity with regard to certain social reference groups enhance anyone's ability to cross into another culture? Where might there be indicators that such experiences may have specific challenges or difficulties? Better preparation for students in anticipation of differently constructed social identities in other countries will enhance the learning of education abroad's majority and minority students, regardless of program choice.

In reaching more students, what do education abroad professionals need to know about themselves? How can educators best understand, within their own cultural boundaries, the needs of their students before they leave home and how to serve diverse needs upon their return? What are the social and cultural realities of education abroad students in contrast to those of education abroad professionals, including generational differences? Social-identity theory has application across the constructs of race, class, gender, age, and other dimensions. It also has relevance when thinking about outreach and service to students in nontraditional majors (e.g., science and engineering). What is the "culture" of a scientist or an engineer? Do these majors primarily attract males? How does gender impact program choices? What relevance does this have for students in the sciences or engineering who are seeking a study abroad program? What questions are relevant beyond the specific curricular questions raised?

Taking advantage of the rich resources on the home campus that provide support, education, and awareness of the needs of an institution's diverse student body will enhance the efforts of those involved with international education. The intersection is not always clear, nor in all ways overlapping. Yet, in many ways, multicultural education and international education deal with common ideas found both in curricular activities and student advising and support systems (Bennett and Bennett 1997). Building strong alliances across campus promotes access to study abroad as well as building trust between the international office and other relevant units on campus.

IMPORTANCE OF THE CAMPUS CLIMATE TO EDUCATION ABROAD PARTICIPATION

Many campuses pay specific attention to the comfort and quality of life of students on the home campus. Retention rates, timely graduation, admissions policies that meet the demands of a diverse student body, federal regulations, and standards that impact services for students, all influence the local campus environment. Research conducted by the Student Affairs Research, Information and Systems office at the University of Massachusetts (University of Massachusetts Project Plus 1999) on retention rates suggests that innovative academic programs that improve campus climate include experiential learning opportunities, new student entry programs, freshman programming, residential life and residential

Part II: Campus Advising

academic programs, and curricular integration of international education.

Local context is extremely important. The campus climate is of particular importance for students who are part of a minority on their campus. How any campus provides support systems for its diverse student body has an impact on attrition and therefore on whether students stay enrolled long enough to participate in an education abroad program. Further, the connection between the comfort that a student has developed with the home campus, their consequent ability to leave campus in order to study abroad, and finally, their comfort with the readjustment process to the home campus, can result in their having an important and positive peer-group influence on future participation by other students. If students feel welcome upon their return, both on campus and within their communities, the power of persuasion and support that they can then provide as mentors to members of a group to which they belong or represent can be extremely influential.

How does campus climate impact participation in education abroad? Consider the importance of the campus environment for students in the outreach and recruitment phase of education abroad. Do students feel successful in the college environment? Does academic advising include discussion of study abroad as a viable option? Do social support programs and various student organizations feel connected to the campus as a whole? Do education abroad experiences tend to lead to greater retention and graduation rates? Finally, remember that the campus climate impacts faculty and professional staff as well. If faculty members are supported, encouraged, and rewarded for international work and achievements, they will be more likely to support education abroad.

Proactive Strategies at the Home Institution: Linkages

In order to diversify the ranks of students going abroad, leaders at the highest level of the institution must see the importance of education abroad opportunities for the entire student body and not simply for the privileged few. It is crucial to secure top administrative support for the following principles:

- Education abroad must be an integrated academic program on campus and open to all students.

- International education must be integral to the institutional goal of serving and contributing to a diverse campus community.

- Multicultural offices on campus should be starting points for support and collaboration.

- Every office should have some role to play in relation to education abroad and access for all students.

Faculty support is critical to efforts to increase the participation of students from underrepresented groups. Students are more responsive to guidance and encouragement from faculty members who represent the same underrepresented group. Advisers should link prospective education abroad participants with faculty who are able to talk to them about their own international experiences, their own views on the importance of education abroad, and their ideas about how international experiences benefit students. This encouragement can occur

Chapter 3: Reaching Underrepresented Constituencies

one-on-one, such as part of mentoring programs, or in large groups, such as a presentation at a new-student orientation.

Faculty members who are involved in efforts to recruit and retain students in underrepresented populations are likely to be good allies. Consider contacting faculty who teach courses that are known to be of particular interest to students who are not normally reached by the education abroad office's usual marketing and advising methods (e.g., courses that cover non-Western religions). Once faculty members are familiar with the institution's education abroad programs, they may share information about the programs in their classes and with their colleagues.

In addition to linking students and faculty, it is also important and helpful to link faculty directly to the education abroad office and its programs and activities. When looking for new partners and programs, faculty can offer advice about which universities or locations would be suitable academic links for the university. Their advice will not only help with program development, but will also garner their support for those programs. Education abroad professionals should get to know campus faculty through membership on committees, attendance at receptions, and other campus events. Reach out to faculty who are campus advisers to student organizations that serve underrepresented groups, such as minority student organizations and professional societies for engineering students. Be sensitive to important issues for faculty members such as workload, tenure, salaries, allocation of time between teaching and research, and diversity (NCES 2003). In all contact with faculty, education abroad professionals need to educate themselves about faculty views on education abroad, including why they may or may not be supportive. A prepared educator will arm himself or herself with reasons about why education abroad is important to the campus community and mission that go beyond "It's a great experience." (See Part I, Chapter 5, "Faculty Roles.")

On most campuses, policy discussions address issues of ongoing concern: curriculum content, student access to faculty and courses, the use of technology, and the availability of student support services. When considering additional factors reflecting the needs of a diverse student body in terms of factors such as age, gender, race, ethnicity, disabilities, socioeconomic background, academic goals, and work and enrollment patterns, the need to network across campus must be evident. The critical work that should be shared through close collaborations across campus cannot be emphasized strongly enough.

Staff in multicultural offices, student affairs, disabled student services, counseling services, and various special academic support programs already have relationships with the students that education abroad professionals want to reach. Partnering with these groups on campus will enhance students' comfort with the notion of study abroad and will provide valuable support from other offices on campus. Writing, mentoring, and peer counseling programs as well as any other programs that reach out to underrepresented students must be invited into the process. Meet students and staff in areas of support and comfort already established on campus and involve them in the creation of outreach and advising processes specific to certain constituencies. Consider ways to include them in program development, evaluation, in-country support, and in welcoming returning students back into their campus communities.

Attending events sponsored by underrepresented groups can help build trust that the education abroad programs are inclusive. It is important for students, staff, and faculty engaged in education abroad programming to meet and work with campus partners within the context of their areas of expertise. Networking with faculty, staff, and students across campus through existing committees, student groups, and organizations, can extend the work of the international educator in creative, supportive ways. While one person cannot attend all events, this important work of outreach can be shared among education abroad staff, administrators, and former participants.

Cross-Cutting Issues: Special Notes

For many students, barriers to study abroad are both perceived and real. If there is not a tradition of going overseas, either at the institutional level or from a student's personal or family experience, then participating in an education abroad program is perceived as a luxury rather than an integral part of the educational experience. Additionally, if professionals in education abroad offices do not come from a nontraditional background or have little experience in diverse settings, the perception may be that education abroad is not inclusive.

Family

Increasing the participation of students who do not come from backgrounds that traditionally support education abroad may require building alliances with parents and families from the beginning of the students' undergraduate careers. Partnering with admissions offices, new student programs, residential life programs, and other mentoring activities can be crucial to reach students traditionally left out of the loop. Ensuring that information on the benefits of education abroad participation is included in the many activities directed at families, both in the recruitment phase as well as in retention of students, can have long-term advantages. Creating a warm and inclusive welcome, recognizing that parents have fears and doubts, and working closely with extended family members can make a noticeable difference in participation rates.

There are numerous resources to offer parents, both formal and informal. Setting up parent-to-parent connections within a community can be reassuring and allows education abroad offices to draw upon the expertise families bring from their experiences. Directing parents to *Study Abroad: A Parent's Guide* (Hoffa 1998), as well as to Web sites specifically designed to address parents' questions, can be reassuring as well. The SAFETI Web site is one example of a Web site that offers information specific to family questions and concerns.

Finances

Income inequity continues to widen across the United States and the poverty rates remain high for large segments of many ethnic minority communities. Higher education continues to be a distant dream for most students from low-income situations. Frequently, those who attend school do so by studying part time and holding down full-time jobs. For these students to take time away from work and family requires extraordinary creativity, commitment, and support by the academic institution and the international office. (See Part I, Chapter 7, "Financial Aid and Funding Study Abroad.")

Being able to acquire financial aid for education abroad will make a critical difference for students. Many underrepresented students are typically dependent on financial aid to attend school. If financial aid is restrictive or does not take into account such basics as roundtrip airfare or a student's need to work part time, then education abroad experiences remain impossible. Additionally, some students simply need proactive assistance to locate scholarships for education abroad. Ignorance about scholarship opportunities is one barrier but so is the lack of time to investigate scholarships and to put in a competitive application (while studying full time and perhaps working full time as well). Many students are defeated before even attempting to put the pieces together.

Fear of the Unknown

Faculty mentors and peers with prior international experience can address questions that often go unasked. It is difficult to know what barriers may exist for specific students unless they are encouraged to articulate their concerns. Building relationships with student groups and student services professionals can help bridge knowledge and experience. Education abroad professionals can't presume that students will automatically find their way to the education abroad office, that they will perceive that they are welcome on education abroad programs, or that they will know whether the education abroad office provides individualized support and counseling that will address their specific concerns or needs.

SPECIFIC CONSTITUENCIES

It is impossible to identify a one-size-fits-all strategy for reaching all underserved groups of students. Therefore, some examples of issues, along with strategies for outreach and support of specific constituencies, have been chosen by way of example. Many of the examples offered later in this chapter in the section "Mobility and Disability Issues: Physical, Sensory, Psychiatric, and Learning," have implications for service to other groups.

Majors

Business Majors

According to trends revealed in *Open Doors* (2004), business and management majors are studying abroad in record numbers (18 percent reported in 2002-2003). The numbers can be deceptive. For example, are these students taking course work relevant to their fields? How many pursue a second language or integrated cultural experience? Are these opportunities integrated into the overall business or management degree on the home campus? Do more students participate in short-term programs rather than in semester-long programs? Can short-term programs offer sufficient depth and exposure to different business cultures, knowledge of languages, and other pertinent elements needed in an increasingly complex, global business world?

Science, Math, Engineering, and Technology Majors

How are science and technology students different from student with other majors? Because their programs of study are often so rigid and packed with specific, required courses (with very few electives), these students are likely to seek courses that fulfill degree requirements, although some, at the recommendation of faculty members, choose electives. It is important that education abroad professionals learn the academic details of these courses of study at their own institutions (e.g., how they are structured, the best time in the programs for students to go abroad, and which courses absolutely cannot be taken elsewhere) and about U.S.

standards and policies related to accreditation in these fields. Resistance and inflexibility on the part of faculty and preprofessional advisers can pose significant barriers to students interested in studying abroad, therefore education abroad advisers must work closely with academic departments and advising units to help identify programs that meet the academic objectives of the home institution. Education abroad advisers must familiarize themselves with the corresponding curriculum of partner or proposed partner institutions. It is also important to connect visiting faculty members from host institutions to the faculty on the home campus who share similar research interests to assist the ongoing dialogue about curricular issues.

Ask academic advisers and faculty on campus about the written standards and unwritten expectations of professional societies and accreditation bodies and research basic information about equivalent academic programs abroad. The Accreditation Board for Engineering and Technology (ABET), the American Chemical Society (ACS), the Institute of Electrical and Electronic Engineers (IEEE), and similar organizations have some of this information on their Web sites and available for purchase from their publication units. Articles published by professional societies and accreditation bodies such as those listed, speeches and statements made by business executives and companies, and faculty engaged in international activities, are all resources that can help education abroad professionals make the case to students and others about the relevance and importance of education abroad for science, math, engineering, and technology majors.

Students in preprofessional programs (e.g., pre-health and pre-law) have two added concerns. First, they must prepare for admission tests and this preparation, whether it is formal or informal, may typically take place during the time when students are most likely to study abroad. Second, admission to professional programs includes a thorough review of the student's academic history and therefore these students are often concerned about making sure that the study abroad program or host university abroad is highly regarded and that participation (including the grades received) will not negatively impact their applications.

Some institutions have made significant progress in opening up opportunities for science and technology students and increasing their participation in study abroad programs. The University of Minnesota's Curriculum Integration Initiative is one example of an institution successfully working to provide better advising and a variety of opportunities to its students in science and technology fields. U.S. universities that organize their own abroad programs for science and technology students and universities abroad that have special programs for these students may be interested in partnerships and can serve as resources to U.S. institutions that want to expand opportunities for their students.

Nontraditional Students

First-Generation College Students

First-generation college students are enrolling in higher education in record numbers. Students entering college from families with little or no experience with higher education have an enormous challenge. Culture shock and adjustment issues are prevalent in the first year, whether students commute from home or enroll full time as on-campus residents. The first big step away from home makes the further step of going abroad seem nearly impossible.

Total undergraduate enrollment in degree-granting postsecondary institutions has generally increased in the past three decades, and it is projected to increase throughout the next ten years. These increases have been accompanied by changes in the attendance status of students, the type of institution attended, and the proportion of students who are women. The number of students enrolled part time and the number enrolled full time, the number of students at two- and four-year institutions, and the number of male and female undergraduates are projected to reach a new high each year from 2003 to 2012 (NCES 2003).

Many first-generation college students may also be holding down part- or full-time employment. Add to this challenge, issues of family pressure to graduate on time or in record-time.

Program Type and Duration. Work abroad may appeal to these students, allowing a short leave from home and the opportunity to cover one's expenses. For similar reasons, short-term programs, including alternative spring break opportunities and January terms, may be of interest. The lack of financial aid for short-term programs is often a major issue, although many programs of short duration are affordable and allow a student with family and job responsibilities to participate.

Credit and Graduating On Time. Credit transfer within the context of degree completion may be a critical component for these students. Appropriate advising helps to assure students and their families that students can continue progress toward their degrees while participating on a study abroad program.

Affordability. Given possible limitations on family income and potential sacrifices already made, students and families alike welcome proactive advising on financial issues.

Family. Clear advice and guidance with respect to the rationale for study abroad may help families support what often feels like a luxury few can afford. Articulation of education abroad goals into the overall goals and mission of the institution helps families and students recognize the value of an education abroad experience in the pursuit of a global education for all graduating seniors as well as the enduring benefits to the future professional and personal lives of participants.

Student Leaders and Athletes

Student leaders and athletes must be encouraged and supported in order to participate in education abroad programs. Working with student leaders at host institutions overseas can lead to lifelong partnerships between the United States and the host-country students. Sharing ideas about running the student newspaper, organizing a student conference, or learning about why students may choose to go on strike for better access to resources can be life changing. Foster discussions with student organizations and their advisers on your campus to examine how students could take a leave from on-campus responsibilities. Discussions with coaches will lead to an understanding of when, during an athlete's career, the athlete is most likely to be able to participate in an education abroad program (and perhaps pursue his or her sport while abroad as well).

Gender

The most recent data indicate that women continue to study abroad in greater numbers than men and slightly more women than men receive bachelor's degrees. In the fall of 2002, 57 percent of all degrees went to women (Goodman 2002). There is, in fact, no real gap between traditional-age white male and female students attending colleges. The educational gap appears to be a matter of race and class. More low-income women attend college than do low-income men. It is also true that among African-Americans, two women for every man graduates from college (Goodman 2002). It's worth noting that low-income and minority men are less likely to be enrolled in college at all, let alone to be found studying abroad. The gender imbalance is important, but it may be addressed as education abroad professionals get better at attending to all underserved constituencies. If educators better serve students in the technical fields (83 percent of engineering majors are men), then more male students will be reached. In addition, as opportunities are created for students of color, including young men, the number of males participating in study abroad should also begin to rise.

Ethnic and Racial Diversity

Asian-Americans and Study Abroad

While the percentage of Asian-Americans that participate in study abroad programs corresponds closely to the percentage of Asian-American students enrolled in colleges and universities in the United States, closer examination reveals that study abroad participation rates vary among different Asian ethnic groups as reported in a study conducted by J. Scott Van Der Meid, "Asian Americans: Factors Influencing the Decision to Study Abroad" (2003). It is therefore misleading to classify all Asian-American students together. Students who are first-generation immigrants are likely to have different expectations and goals for their educations than those who are second-, third-, or fourth-generation immigrants. Evidence suggests that those students who have resided in the United States for only a short amount of time are less likely to study abroad than those who have lived in the United States for a long time. Asia continues to be a less-sought-after destination overall for study abroad; however, 37 percent of Asian-Americans who studied abroad, studied in an Asian country (Van Der Meid 2003).

There are several implications for education abroad. First, developing and promoting opportunities to study in more locations in Asia, specific to particular majors, may encourage more students to participate in programs abroad. Second, while Asian-American students are not underrepresented overall in study abroad participation, the advising and support needs of these students are not well understood. The myth of the "model minority" continues to plague this group. The fact that Asian-American students reflect a broad and deeply varied range of populations "...from fourth-generation, upper-middle-class Japanese Americans to newly arrived Southeast Asian refugees on welfare" (Lott 1998, 27–28; cited in Van Der Meid 2003) offers unique challenges to the international office. However, education is clearly an important value for the Asian-American students who do attend colleges and universities, and therefore connecting study abroad advising with academic advising is essential when working with these students.

While some students are heritage seekers (see "Heritage Seeking in Education Abroad"), more often than not students will choose a location based on their academic needs or personal interests. Thus, increasing participation in Asian locations is only part of the picture. Advising suggestions include (1) listening to the students' needs and interests, (2) learning about the Asian communities represented on campus, (3) assuring that the education abroad office environment is inclusive and welcoming, and (4) linking staff and students to Asian and Asian-American support groups on campus to assure that specific needs or barriers are addressed.

Students of Color

There is an abundance of literature that speaks specifically to the benefits of study abroad for minority students (see Anderson 1996, Carew 1993, and Craig 1998). Mattai and Ohiwerei (1989) state that a returning study abroad student will benefit his or her African-American community. Widening the circle of benefit, Talburt and Stewart (1999) state that having an African-American student on a program to Spain benefited the white students, because through listening to the black student's experiences with racism in Spain, the white students were confronted with the significance of racial differences, racism, and outsider status. The white students were able to think about this reality outside their own culture in neutral territory and it had special meaning because in Spain they also experienced feelings of being "different" and "outsiders."

Ethnic-minority students make up 29.9 percent of students enrolled in higher education institutions and an even smaller percentage (16.8 percent) participate in education abroad programs (U.S. Census 2000). Without a doubt there are practical issues that prevent students of color from studying abroad. Among those issues are lack of funds, not meeting curriculum requirements, and fear of delaying graduation. Additional issues may have to do with retention rates and graduation. If a disproportionate number of students of color leave their institutions after the first or second year, they miss the opportunity to participate in an education abroad program.

Given the diverse communities within ethnic and racial groups, and the continuing influx of immigrants from Africa, Latin America, the Caribbean, and Asia, the needs of these students and their families must be addressed with local communities in mind. Different experiences within families influence the choice of whether or not to participate in an education abroad program. For example, teachers who have immigrated from Haiti or Ethiopia can have a great influence on arousing the global curiosity of African-American students within the black community. Likewise, recent immigrants and children of immigrants from Mexico will have an impact on Spanish-speaking communities, both on and off campus. First generation immigrants as well as first-generation Americans are likely to get their international perspectives from close family and community. The needs of first-generation immigrants vary considerably yet many of these students experience similar challenges in terms of access to education abroad programs. In some parts of the country, Latino communities are predominantly Puerto Rican, in others, Mexican, while in other more diverse communities there is an even broader range and complexity to what is meant by "Latino" or "Chicano" or "Hispanic." The point is not to label but rather to refine understanding of the needs of individual students while recognizing the communities to which they belong.

An additional barrier to participation by many students of color may involve their major course of study. In a study conducted by Michigan State University (Hembroff and Rusz 1993), there was some evidence to indicate that African-American students are more likely to select majors that are underrepresented (in terms of availability on education abroad programs) in comparison to the majors of students who study abroad overall.

Many issues that students of color face are not specific to them and many universities already address these issues for the general student population. For example, many schools have instituted policies whereby students pay the same tuition when they study abroad as they do when they study on the home campus, and students can use their financial aid to finance study abroad on selected or campus-approved programs. Approved programs should offer opportunities to a wide variety of majors and skill levels so many students can not only qualify for participation, but can also make progress toward graduation while studying abroad. Thus, financial barriers to study abroad or a fear of delayed graduation are eliminated. The Michigan State University study found that students of color were only slightly less likely to know about study abroad programs and financial aid opportunities than other students, but were significantly less likely to participate (Hembroff and Rusz 1993).

For black and Latino students, the issue is often what Marilyn Jackson of San Francisco State University calls the "Not for people like me" syndrome. It is important to be mindful of and to address the factors that contribute to the lack of participation of minority students in education abroad programs. The following challenges are also access issues, because even though they may seem intangible, they are real barriers to participation.

Historical Exclusion. In many upper middle class, predominately white families (especially on the east coast) there is a long-established tradition of sending young people to Europe for "finishing." Back in the 1800s, in some circles the travel abroad experience was preferable to college or formal education for marriage preparation. The value of traveling abroad may not be a familiar concept in the families of some underrepresented constituencies.

Family Support. Family support is crucial for education abroad participants, particularly for first-generation college students. Many first-generation college students and their families have not traveled outside North America and it is uncommon for a minority student to have a family member who has studied abroad. Families may struggle to send their child to college and may therefore view education abroad as a frivolous luxury. Immigrant families may have sacrificed to come to the United States and may consequently not comprehend why their sons or daughters would want to leave the United States. They may view studying in another country, especially outside Western Europe, as less prestigious than studying on the home campus. Families also fear that their children will suffer racism, be exposed to health, safety, and security risks, and not have a family network to protect them.

For Latino students, particularly young women, the connection to family and community can be very strong. Participation in an education abroad program requires an extended period away from home. Therefore, short-term programs that offer an opportunity to study abroad without the long-term commitment of being away from home, may be good options for some students from this underrepresented group.

Peer Group. Just as their family members probably have not studied abroad, it is statistically unlikely that members of the students' peer groups would have studied abroad or in some cases even traveled abroad. Friends might not understand why the student would "abandon" them to go somewhere else (Malone and Craig 1996). In addition, Latino students may tend to deselect themselves. They don't consider study abroad because they already consider themselves bicultural. Education abroad professionals may want to consider advising friends together and holding group meetings with food and social activities.

Mentors. Mentors to minority students may not have studied abroad, may not see the value in it, and may not think about mentioning it to their advisees (Monaghan 1994). Consequently, there is generally very little word-of-mouth information about

Chapter 3: Reaching Underrepresented Constituencies

education abroad programs in the world of minority students.

Media Images. Media has a strong influence on youth. Media images of Americans traveling overseas tend to reflect typical education abroad participants—white, privileged young women going to European destinations (consider, for example, films such as *What a Girl Wants* and *The Lizzie McGuire Movie,* and the Mary-Kate and Ashley Olsen films set in several different countries, among others). Movies that depict African-Americans abroad are harder to find and depictions of Latinos are often based on stereotypes. When you do find them, the characters usually have no choice about going abroad, and are very likely depicting travel in relation to the military.

Insensitive Advisers. Minority students are often overlooked and therefore not seen as potential education abroad candidates. Advisers may make quick assumptions about which programs a minority student might be interested in (e.g., making the assumption that an African-American student would only be interested in studying in an English-speaking African country) and not present the full range of opportunities to the student (Carter 1991).

English as a Second Language. Students who grow up in a home speaking a first language other than English, and who choose to study abroad in their "first language," may be unprepared for the linguistic and cultural experience abroad. Many students seek a heritage experience but are not aware of the depth of the language challenges. They are fluent when speaking about everyday topics (e.g., family life and food) but do not have academic or business vocabulary or experience speaking their native language in a formal setting. When Latino students choose to study in locations other than Spanish-speaking ones, they are often pleasantly surprised by the experience. Students both overestimate and underestimate their language abilities. Many students may choose to learn a third language as part of their overseas experience.

Lack of Travel Experience. In the Michigan State Study, African-American students had less domestic and international travel experience than their white counterparts. That may lead to more anxiety about traveling in general and more specifically, traveling to a foreign country (Hembroff and Rusz 1993). For students with little or no international travel experience, short-term programs may be a more viable introduction to education abroad. Creating short-term programs for ethnic minority students, as well as freshmen and others, can offer opportunities at a relatively low cost.

Fear of Racism. Students have coping methods at home, but may have a fear of "unknown" racism. The prospect of facing racism without a support system can be a barrier.

Personal Concerns. Some minority students become less enthusiastic about study abroad when they realize, for example, that it may be difficult to find hairstylists who are familiar with handling their texture of hair: no one wants to have every day of their education abroad program be a bad hair day (Malone and Craig 1996). These personal factors often become real concerns for minority students who have to consider giving up everything familiar in their lives in order to study abroad.

Religion. Not being able to attend familiar religious services may be a deterrent to study abroad participation (Malone and Craig 1996). Additional concerns may also be related to religious practices and freedom from discrimination. Orthodox and conservative practices on the part of some students may keep them close to home (see section below, "Religious Issues").

Destinations. Advising students on appropriate study abroad destinations, including those literally all around the world, can be inspiring for students of color. Joy Carew (1993) describes the experience of African-American students from a predominantly black college studying for three weeks in Russia as exciting and liberating, both for the students and their Russian hosts. Tapping into student stories about their experiences in specific destinations can be inspiring and can encourage students considering education abroad to learn more. Materials that are specific to country, region, and city, and that address the local culture with attention to race, immigration, and other diversity issues can give students the assurance that they need.

Partners in locations around the world offer unique and invaluable insights on the experiences of diverse people within the local context. Destination-specific material can point students toward in-country communities and opportunities that might be surprising. The African community in New Delhi, India, for example, may offer a haven and unique connection to Africa for the black American, just as the Spanish-speaking neighborhood in Copenhagen, Denmark, can be a delight for Latino students. Muslim worshippers can find solace and connections in the heart of London, England. Students of color will be better prepared for the possibility of experiencing racism in Australia if they connect ahead of time with American students of color who studied in Australia and who can't wait to return there.

Recruitment and Marketing. To attract students of color to education abroad programs, education abroad professionals should create an atmosphere where minority students can feel comfortable. Students prefer that recruitment efforts offer substantive information. Students want explicit information that helps them recognize the real value of study abroad for them, including helping students deal with difference in supportive ways, even at the initial phases of marketing and recruitment (Mawila, unpublished study 2001). Consider the following:

- Decorations should go beyond Western European art and study abroad posters. Represent cultures and locations from around the world.

- Create visuals like a photo board, showing diversity among the participants so students can see "someone like me" reflected in the pictures.

- Hire staff and recruit student workers and volunteers who reflect the diversity of the campus community.

- Publish materials on special topics (e.g., hair care, religion, and race issues).

- Provide articles about students of color studying abroad in the education abroad library and on your office Web site (link to other appropriate offices on campus and to important resources).

- Create a video of participating or returning study abroad students and create a resource library of other appropriate videos.

- Create a mentor program and develop a network of role models. These can include past participants, faculty, and staff with international experience, as well as college alumni with international careers and parents of past participants.

- Provide information about famous Americans of color who studied or lived abroad (e.g., W.E.B. DuBois, James Baldwin, Angela Davis, and Maya Angelou).

- Create support systems such as advising in groups. Create advising sessions on specific related topics. Ask students to bring a friend.

- Network with already formed groups on campus (i.e., student clubs, student organizations, or associations).

- Connect prospective study abroad participants to exchange and other international students on campus.

- Create an advisory council to help with recruitment issues. If somebody asks, "Why don't you send more students of color abroad," ask them to help with recruitment.

- Be yourself and be sincere. Don't overcompensate or patronize.

- Be honest. If you don't have an answer, refer them to someone who does.

Heritage Seeking in Education Abroad

The primary motivation of some education abroad participants is to explore their cultural roots, whether racial, ethnic, or religious. While this is a rewarding experience for most students, many are surprised that they are seen as "Americans" rather than as long-distant relatives of the host country people. Such experiences can be particularly painful if students presumed a shared culture and history with host-country nationals and thought that they would receive a welcome "home" with open arms. On the other hand, the rewards are nearly indescribable and students should be encouraged in their search for their cultural roots. Some programs are designed with these considerations in mind and students who have assistance in the predeparture phase of preparation, as well as on site, may have extraordinarily rich experiences. Mentoring from past participants can provide specific guidance and caution with respect to expectations.

Families may also be supportive of, though often fearful for, their children who seek to return "home." Outreach to parents and communities may alleviate some fears and draw on additional resources. Finding ways to link global and local study experiences by reaching out to local ethnic communities provides rich experiences for all students.

There are creative models that bring students and community members together for a short-term study tour. Teachers, artists, community leaders, and community-based service organizations, among others, provide unique study opportunities for institutions. Joint programming with local communities and organizations can further enhance the experience for underserved students as well as provide a bridge between university and community (e.g., nurses and nursing students traveling to Ghana or business faculty members and computer science students studying in Jamaica).

Gay, Lesbian, Bisexual, and Transgendered Students

While it is difficult to know the sexual orientation of students, it is important for education abroad professionals to recognize the need to provide appropriate advising and resources to students who identify themselves as gay, lesbian, bisexual, or transgendered (GLBT). Identity issues are profound for college students and life-changing events occur for many students during their education abroad experience. For students who may also be facing sexual identity issues, study abroad opportunities must be offered with as much supportive information as possible. Conceptualizing "gay culture" can help advisers understand the issues facing GLBT students. The Rainbow special interest group (SIG) of NAFSA has a rich collection of resources available on the NAFSA Web site. The Rainbow SIG recommends the following strategies for education abroad professionals looking to reach out to the GLBT student population:

- Include and prominently position a diversity statement in all education abroad materials, including a statement specifically in support of GLBT students, so that all students know the education abroad office is a safe, inclusive place.

- Coordinate orientation activities with the GLBT center on campus.

- Collect and make available materials (e.g., guidebooks, articles, and bibliographies) as well as information from returning students, staff, faculty, and exchange students about GLBT issues that may be encountered overseas. Include a section on the program evaluation that allows students to share GLBT resources with other students.

- Include information on HIV and AIDS, which must be available to all students, gay or straight.

- Provide a list of Web resources for students, including the NAFSA Rainbow SIG Web site.

It is important for education abroad professionals to recognize that personal development and self-awareness are particularly relevant with respect to sexual orientation. Whether students are openly gay or not, it is important for them to consider the differences across cultures with respect to homosexuality. Issues of personal safety take on additional meaning for GLBT students, including the understanding of behavioral nuances and differences, along with different cultural norms with respect to sexual orientation. Physical harassment, assault, and rape are issues for all students to bear in mind. Incorporating open and clear information with respect to GLBT issues overseas allows education abroad professionals to encourage all students to pay attention to their surroundings.

GLBT students may well find the experience of being somewhere foreign very liberating and transforming as it affects their own self-awareness and the "coming out" process. Providing information on support mechanisms and program- or country-specific information will be useful to GLBT and other students. International educators, too, will benefit from learning about GLBT issues both at home and abroad. Consider the following statement from NAFSA regarding the creation of an inclusive and meaningful study abroad experience for GLBT students:

> International educators need to be informed and sensitive to the needs of GLBT students involved in international educational exchange. To be effective, the international educator will need to gather as much information as possible and increase his or her knowledge about the topic of homosexuality. The international educator will need to examine his or her own personal values and beliefs to know where she or he stands on specific issues and their willingness to be open. She or he will need to remember that gay, lesbian, bisexual, and transgendered students are individuals, each with

different experiences and each at his or her own level of development. It is through this understanding and application of ideas that the international educator can begin to aid in the establishment of a college and university environment that is inclusive and accepting of diverse sexual orientations (NAFSA 2003).

Educators should talk with students about their priorities with respect to study abroad, including their personal as well as academic goals. Remember, students may not reveal sexual orientation but may very well be in need of information related to sexual identity. The education abroad professional's role as a source of information and ongoing support throughout all phases of the education abroad preparation process is very important.

Mobility and Disability Issues: Physical, Sensory, Psychiatric, and Learning

In his book *Moving Violations,* John Hockenberry speaks to his intercultural interactions in the Middle East as a National Public Radio (NPR) correspondent who uses a manual wheelchair. One quote is quite retelling:

> After enough experiences with the chair in this new place I discovered that having a disability offered an advantage in seeing some of the more subtle differences and similarities between Arabs and Jews. There were vast differences in how Palestinians and Israelis reacted to disability. The simplest tasks were rich with cultural commentary. Far from disabling me, being in a wheelchair allowed me to discover deep truths about Arabs and Jews much more quickly than from the sole vantage point of a journalist outsider. Those truths were not news, but they did allow me to acquire a familiarity with both Israelis and Palestinians that I never imagined achieving when I first arrived (Hockenberry 1995, 257–258).

All cultures have complex belief systems related to disability and have their own explanations, roles, and expectations for people with disabilities. The United Nations' *Standard Rules for the Equalization of People with Disabilities*, as well as regional treaties and legal changes in many countries, are widely reshaping the places where differently abled students may choose to go. These changes have been a part of a global grassroots effort by people with disabilities to gain greater access to all sectors of society, including higher education, transportation systems, and places of employment.

Nongovernmental organizations of people with disabilities can give insight into the local context, disability laws, attitudes about different types of disabilities (e.g., what is and isn't accessible), and to the networks available to assist students with disabilities. For instance, blind students studying overseas may receive orientation and mobility training from local blind organizations upon arrival—services that are readily available to the local population.

People with disabilities do not always face negative challenges abroad; some discover that the differences are beneficial. Things that are barriers in one country may not be a problem in others. Consider the following examples:

- A student whose systemic disability caused her to have low energy and be tired some days, found that living with a home-stay family in Spain was a good fit with her abilities. The host mothers in Spain tended to do their adult children's and guests' laundry, cooking, housecleaning, and other daily tasks, which allowed the student to avoid doing those regular things that normally taxed her energy. This freed her up to do other things such as study or explore the new culture. The siesta and late morning class schedules helped her as well.

- A student with a learning disability commented that the informal conversational structure of her language classes in Mexico and the fact that tests were not timed helped her to better keep up with her class lessons and classmates. She didn't need taped textbooks or to make arrangements for extra time on tests like she did at home.

- A deaf student on an internship in Costa Rica found that for the first time he could join his friends to watch a new movie released in the local theatre. This was because the U.S. movie had subtitles for the general audience members who didn't know English. It also helped the deaf student to improve his Spanish reading skills.

Some barriers that students may not have experienced at home may arise while they are abroad. While at home, power wheelchair users may be able to access toilet facilities independently. While abroad, they may need to request a personal assistant, if the bathrooms are inaccessible and not adaptable. Replacing or repairing medical or adaptive equipment overseas may be more complicated abroad than it is at home.

Students with hidden disabilities may expect a certain level of confidentiality as well as set procedures for requesting accommodations and informing faculty, while the host country approach may focus more on fostering relationships to achieve a desired outcome. Deaf students may not be able to access local sign language interpreters (if they exist) if they were not able to learn the new sign language before going abroad. They may need real-time captioning instead to assist the classroom translations, even though they may not use this service at home. In all these cases, advance planning is necessary in order to think through the differences and the corresponding needs.

Students with disabilities may also experience increased staring, negative stereotypes, or unsolicited assistance from strangers abroad. It is important for students to focus on learning from another culture and not make value judgments about the way other cultures deal with disability. This is a lesson Pamela Houston, who has cerebral palsy, learned while living on a small Pacific island:

> As the weeks passed, I became more accustomed to the rhythm of family and village life. I learned that laughing, joking, and poking fun at others is central to interpersonal communication in Kiribati culture. I learned that guests are honored by being allowed to eat first, that staring is a way of being with someone, of learning about who they are. I discovered that the countless offerings of unsolicited help were not meant to demean me.
> Rather it is the way Kiribati families and communities work. It is how their people have lived on these little, isolated, central Pacific islands for generations (Houston, 2003).

For advisers, informational sheets about what differently abled students can do to prepare and modify their expectations while abroad can be found in publications and through Web site resources created by Mobility International USA/National Clearinghouse on Disability and Exchange, Access Abroad, and other projects that focus specifically on this topic. Included in these resources are tools and processes that the education abroad office can implement to be better prepared for answering questions differently abled students may have about the overseas site. Examples include collaborating with disability service providers, utilizing peer mentors, conducting assessments of host sites, and coordinating site visits and training of overseas staff. All of these will help the educator understand the similarities and differences associated with disability in the local context.

Advising and Accommodations

A guiding principle of education abroad must surely be inclusion of all students. However, inexperience may lead to unintentional exclusion, reflected in the policies or practices of the international office. Examples of such practices and policies may include holding meetings, interviews, and orientations at inaccessible venues or not budgeting for reasonable accommodations such as sign language interpreters. The definition of reasonable accommodations varies considerably and is not easily transferable from one cultural and legal context to the next. Rather than become fearful of legal implications, education abroad professionals should work with students, families, and overseas partners to identify ways to provide appropriate accommodations for disabled students.

Consider the following examples of exclusionary perceptions:

- "Athens, Greece, is not a disability-friendly place." What does that statement mean? Does it mean that a person with any type of disability will find Athens to be too difficult a place to live and study? How about someone who sometimes uses a wheelchair versus someone who always uses a power chair and has a personal assistant? How about someone who has a mobility impairment but is ambulatory? How about a student with diabetes, or a student with low vision, or a student with dyslexia? There could be two students with very similar disabilities but one could be very flexible and have a strong sense of adventure and the other might not be open to doing things in a different way. The outlook of the participant has a strong bearing on the quality of his or her education abroad experience.

- "We can't take responsibility for the student's safety." This statement assumes that students with disabilities will be more vulnerable to injury, accidents, and illness than other students. Students with disabilities have the same drive toward self-preservation as other students. They will benefit from the same health and safety policies, orientation, and availability of counselors that benefit all students. Depending on the student's disability, it may be necessary to modify specific safety procedures and plans to be sure that the person is aware of emergency situations and receives the support that he or she needs to be safe. It is likely that some thought has already gone into this, as any student can become injured in an emergency situation and will need assistance to get to safety.

- "We don't have the time and resources to assist a student with a disability." It may take some extra time and effort initially, depending on the student's accommodation needs and on prior experience and proactive preparations made by the program. Enlist the collaboration of the student, the disabled student services office, and overseas counterparts. This will help ensure that all bases are covered. It also encourages team learning, creative problem solving, and it spreads the work around.

One guiding principle when working with students with disabilities is to be careful about making assumptions. Just because a student has a disability does not mean that they will take more time to assist than a student without a disability. No generalizations should be made about an individual based on their having or not having a disability.

A second guiding principle, especially in working with students to select programs, is to focus on the individual. A student with a disability is not the disability, but rather the person. What skills, interests, experiences, and personality traits make the person a good candidate for the program? The impact a disability has on a person will be individual too. Some wheelchair users are able to stand and walk short distances. Some people with visual impairments have excellent mobility skills, enabling them to confidently learn their way around a new place; others are more easily disoriented. Some deaf people are adept at using a variety of communication methods. Others are more comfortable with one or two methods. Talk with each student about how his or her disability impacts mobility, communication, energy level, and learning style. Advisers can help guide a student in selecting a program based on the whole person. In addition, education abroad programs should establish procedures and best practices that will streamline the program selection process for students with disabilities and their advisers.

Learning Disabilities and Dyslexia

Since many students receive credit at their home school for study abroad programs, it is important for them to be able to access the same level of learning abroad as at home. While the education abroad staff may know more about the overseas situation, the disability services staff on campus may have more ideas about alternative accommodation possibilities. They will also be able to explain to overseas institutions the U.S. system of providing accommodations, which could add insight into planning discussions with the student and the host program.

There is no worldwide standard for the documentation of learning disabilities. In some cases students have been denied or approved services (e.g., extended time on tests) based on the host country's acceptance or denial of the U.S. documentation. It is important for disability services staff in both countries to work together and with the international education offices to ensure that it is clear what type of documentation is needed. If documentation from the home institution is not accepted, the student may be required to have an assessment done in the host country. Such testing is expensive and time consuming for a student who will only be studying in the host country for a semester. Additionally, determining how to interpret the quality of assessments done in another country and what services and adaptations will be provided (if any) as a result, often come into question. Disability service providers at the host campus, rather than study abroad advisers, make these determinations. All of these issues and expectations should be worked out before the student goes overseas. This will help to resolve discrepancies in expectations and services before the student arrives.

Some of the other issues that a disabled student can discuss with their study abroad advisers include what, when, and where accommodations will be provided; who will the student contact overseas if they have questions about their disability services; and how will his request for accommodations be shared, and with whom, and who will cover any related expenses? Also, study abroad advisers should discuss with the student the classroom setting and physical environment in the host country and how they may be different from those of the home university. For example, some students with learning disabilities may benefit from a foreign language teacher who uses a highly structured, multisensory, and explicit approach that helps students see and understand how language is structured and provides ample opportunity for practice. Some classroom locations may be subject to more street noise and the walls may not have sufficient insulation, so the classrooms may be louder and more distracting than what is expected in U.S. classrooms.

Another issue that may affect disabled students while they are abroad is the way in which the instruction and assignments are different overseas than in the U.S. educational system. For example, some classes require little reading or a lot of note taking. This may impact what services a disabled student would need. Some disabled students may have questions about the technology they use for adaptation, while others will want to know if tutors could be made available. Open the discussions with students early so sufficient planning can occur.

Psychiatric Disabilities

What do Abraham Lincoln, Ernest Hemingway, and Vincent van Gogh have in common? Each made a significant contribution to our world yet each was diagnosed with a mental illness. Many education programs have concerns and questions about whether people with psychiatric disabilities can have a successful experience abroad. Of equal concern are the challenges that dealing with psychiatric illness can pose to both the sending and host country programs. Success, as in other arenas, has to do with open communication with students, advisers, and overseas partners, as well as appropriate in-country support.

According to some estimates, as many as one in five people will experience mental illness in their lifetime. Given the predominance of mental health issues for colleges, it is inevitable that students with psychiatric disabilities will go abroad. Providers may be concerned that these students won't be able to manage in the new environment or worry that extraordinary measures must be taken to accommodate them. Most programs routinely establish components like predeparture orientations and on-site contingency plans for all students because it is known that the majority of participants will experience stress and culture shock. These same plans and procedures can be used for students with psychiatric disabilities with great success. As with other services, it is important for the individual and the international program staff to discuss what types of services are used at home and what services are available abroad. Acknowledging the need for mental health and psychiatric services will benefit all students, not simply those with identifiable issues.

Part II: Campus Advising

Consider the following ways to help students with mental illness enjoy a successful study abroad experience:

- Include disability statements in brochures, handbooks, and other materials. Clarify cultural differences and language differences with respect to psychiatric or mental health services and the provision of such services.

- Encourage self-disclosure in all acceptance packets sent to students. Include information that encourages students to disclose any disability information, including mental health. Make clear that this information is confidential and is being collected for purposes of assuring appropriate services and accommodations. Allow participants to clarify health insurance coverage for such services, if applicable. Approach psychiatric health issues in the same way that physical health issues are managed so that knowledge is shared, not hidden.

- Collaborate with advising staff at host institutions and programs to identify resources for any student exhibiting psychiatric or mental health issues while abroad.

- Provide information on in-country services, counseling centers, health centers, and other similar services for students who experience psychological issues abroad. Many students, both with and without documented disabilities, have need of such resources while adjusting to a new environment.

- Gather information about free or low-cost support groups and local telephone crisis hotlines, along with other community resources.

- Advise students to bring an adequate supply of medications, if possible—generic rather than brand names. For further information see Part II, Chapter 3, "Health Issues and Advising Responsibilities"). Students should be encouraged to bring updated information from a medical or counseling chart to facilitate ongoing care, should it be needed.

The National Clearinghouse on Disability and Exchange (NCDE) has many resources for advisers and staff, including individualized contacts for several countries upon request.

Fears

What are some of the fears that students with disabilities may experience beyond the common worries of all students? Study abroad advisers are well practiced in alleviating student worries. However, if the program staff has had limited experience working with students with different types of disabilities, they may feel some concern about issues that may emerge for these students.

Students may be concerned about not having access to the health-related, structural, psychological, and informational support systems that allow for maximum independence. Many students feel some insecurity about being accepted and making friends in a new situation. Having a disability may sometimes seem like an additional barrier to fitting in with a group. If a disabled student is fearful of not being accepted by his or her study abroad or host-country peers, talk with the student about his or her current strategies and successes at making friends and finding a niche. If the student is comfortable with the idea, perhaps he or she could be given some time during orientation to talk with the group about what support is needed from the group and about all the things that the student expects to contribute to the study abroad experience.

Many people are inexperienced at communicating with people who have speech impairments or who use sign language, and may have difficulty understanding those with such a disability. Another aspect of misunderstanding comes from societal misperceptions about disability. Peers who are not disabled may assume that the student with a disability is less capable and less intelligent. In situations where there may be communication issues, education abroad professionals should work with the disabled student to strategize a variety of ways to communicate with peers and participate fully in the program. The student may be accustomed to using adaptive equipment or sign language interpreters. NCDE offers resources about finding and funding interpreters. Consider incorporating information into program activities about books or presentations that address disability rights philosophy and etiquette. Connect students with local disability organizations for peer support while abroad.

Students may be concerned that they will not be respected for what they can contribute to the group, the experience, or the project. The education abroad staff should review the different activities and expectations of the program with the student, resident advisers, and the disabled student services office with the goal of determining where the challenges might lie, so that those areas can be addressed beforehand. Some activities can be easily adapted, and some project tasks can be modified. Preparation, flexibility, and creativity are key.

The disabled student participant may be unsure of how the new environment may impact his or her health or disability condition. Go over possible concerns. Issues may include diet, weather and climate, fatigue, academic procedures, and language learning. Work with the student to research the reality of the situation and the resources needed to help manage challenges. For example, if the student feels exceptionally anxious about learning the language, would it be possible to secure a tutor while abroad? Could the student take steps to learn some of the language before going abroad? What strategies does the student already use to deal with anxiety?

Allow students to be open to leaving the program early if needed. Knowing that early departure is a possibility may reduce the pressure a student feels before committing to going abroad. The participants may be worried about knowing the ropes for solving disability-related problems in a different culture. Link the students with relevant disability organizations in the host country before the start of the program. Encourage them to utilize NCDE's Peer-to-Peer Network. It can be helpful to talk with someone who has a similar disability and who has been to the same country. Establish a connection between the disability service office as well as the international education office abroad with the appropriate office or offices back home so that all concerned parties can communicate effectively if mediation is needed.

Arranging Accommodations

Involve Students with Disabilities in Arranging Accommodations. It is important to establish open communication with disabled students and share the responsibility for preparation and planning. Education abroad professionals should not feel that they have to work out all of the details and accommodations on their own. Education abroad professionals have expertise about education abroad in general, about particular programs, and about the host country. Individuals with disabilities know themselves, their disability, and how to deal with many disability-related challenges. Together, the educator and the student can be an effective and efficient planning team. The Mobility International USA/NCDE publications, *Building Bridges: A Manual on Including People With Disabilities in International Exchange Programs* and *Survival Strategies for Going Abroad: A Guide for People with Disabilities* can be consulted for support and ideas. Through these publications, educators can learn from people with disabilities who have successfully participated in all types of education abroad programs.

Accommodation Forms and Other Information Sheets for Students. Develop accommodation forms to assist with planning; however, the student should be asked to complete the form only once he or she is accepted to a study abroad program. A useful form will break down the different components of programs. The form to request accommodation for different types of disability should be used to further discussion with students and to aid in planning accordingly. The form can also help education abroad professionals learn what a student already does or what services he or she already uses to meet challenges. A good example of an accommodation form can be found on the Access Abroad Web site. Students are asked to evaluate the ease or difficulty with which they are able to accomplish tasks. NCDE has information sheets about traveling with medications, traveling with a service dog, working with personal assistants, and much more. Advisers can use and adapt the information to fit their programs.

Collaborations: Disabled Student Services and Education Abroad Offices. Disabled Student Services (DSS) offices or independent living centers (ILCs) have extensive resources about different disabilities and about typical accommodations. DSS and ILC professionals are generally accustomed to working within tight budgets and may have creative ideas for low-cost disability-related accommodations. Education abroad professionals should meet with DSS and ILC professionals to brainstorm tangible and financial solutions to identified barriers (some education abroad and DSS offices have collaborated to share the financial costs of sending a differently abled student overseas). A DSS office may simply agree to transfer the student's services abroad. It may not be any more expensive to contract with a note taker, reader, or sign language interpreter overseas, than it is on the home campus, and the DSS office would pay for those services anyway if the student were taking classes at the home campus. Seek the expertise and input of DSS professionals or general counsel in developing and revising policies and procedures to be sure they are not unintentionally exclusionary. Provide the DSS office with an in-service training program about the value of education abroad. Make sure the DSS office is on board and that they promote education abroad programs to the students who use their services.

Site and Partner Selection

Whether working with long-established program partners or developing a new program site, education abroad professionals must be sure to discuss their institutions' commitment to inclusion, foster open dialogue about possibilities, and proactively brainstorm solutions to barriers. *A Practice of Yes! Working with Overseas Partners to Include Students with Disabilities* (McLeod and

Scheib 2005) is a resource for overseas counterparts. This toolkit describes various concepts to consider when receiving disabled participants (e.g., how to arrange disability-related accommodations and services, creative ideas on how to make the program fully inclusive, and understanding cultural differences around disability).

By developing a survey of important characteristics, resources, services, and cultural information for program sites with overseas counterparts, education abroad professionals can provide a baseline of information for students and for administrators. Students, disabled students, host-country staff, and disabled people from the community can be enlisted to assist with surveys. Samples of site visits done by Access Abroad and the Catholic University of Leuven, Belgium, are available on the Access Abroad Web site.

National or local disability organizations in program countries may be able to assist with providing referrals to local disability-related resources: locating personal assistants, sign interpreters, and orientation trainers for people who have visual impairments; finding accessible housing or host families; and providing insight for site evaluations. NCDE offers an online searchable database of disability organizations worldwide and has developed country sheets on a range of countries from every continent. For example, the country sheet for Australia includes a list of disability services offices for each territory, information on a variety of national disability organizations, information on taking a service dog to Australia, and more. These sheets can give education abroad professionals a place to start in considering new sites as well as the resources available in countries with long-established programs.

- With a baseline of what the disability-related resources are, the education abroad office and its overseas counterpart can design a plan for making changes and adaptations. It will be less overwhelming if the projects are broken into categories, such as:

- What is readily doable?
- What will take some planning and a little more work?
- What will take significant planning, work, and some funds (but is doable)?
- What is impossible at this time?

Site visits can be rounded out with information about cultural values and attitudes about disability and relevant laws. Good sources for this information are The Center for International Rehabilitation Research Information and Exchange (CIRRIE; it provides information on culture and disability) and the Disability Rights and Education Defense Fund (a comprehensive database about disability law in various countries).

Finances

Money is a worry for most students—often more so for students from underrepresented populations. Students with disabilities may have additional expenses for items and services such as personal assistants, repairs for adaptive equipment, or taxi use for non–program-related activities rather than taking public transportation.

Many of the accommodations made for disabled students are cost-free but some can be quite inexpensive. The key to finding low-cost solutions is to foster open communication and a process of investigation with the exchange participant. Think broadly about the possibilities and resources available to the organization and the student. For example, a program can make a tape recorder available for note taking to participants with visual impairments, certain types of learning disabilities, or those who have difficulty writing. A few steps into a classroom or regularly used building can be temporarily, but sturdily, ramped using locally available materials.

Do not be surprised if disabled participants do not require any special accommodations at all. Some will; many won't. Those people with disabilities who do use adaptive equipment usually own the equipment they need for everyday life and will need only minimal, if any, additional assistance or information from others. Sometimes the resources or services they'll require can be found at the host university or in the local community. Remember that each individual participant will have a unique approach to his or her own disability. Chances are, the individual has an already demonstrated the ability to meet challenges and barriers with creativity and flexibility—characteristics that an education abroad coordinator would hope for in any participant.

Budgeting. Incorporating a disability accommodation line item into every program budget is the most reliable way to ensure that resources are at hand to include people with disabilities. Based on twenty-one years of experience conducting international education programs for people with and without disabilities, Mobility International USA (MIUSA) recommends using a percentage formula to determine disability accommodation expenses in budget requests. Mobility International USA has found that allocating 5 percent of the program budget will be adequate for meeting most disability-related accommodation needs. Another way to handle budgetary matters is to share the expense among the offices concerned—the study abroad office, the disabled student services office, the U.S. program (if working with a third-party provider), and the overseas host institution. Sharing expenses in this way can assist all sides to be prepared for participants who need disability-related accommodations.

Supplemental Funds. Organizations may also create a supplemental fund, perhaps dedicated to expenses such as personal assistants, which participants would ordinarily be required to cover on their own. Service clubs, foundations, corporations, and private donors interested in reaching underrepresented groups tend to be responsive to appeals for donations earmarked for making programs accessible to people with disabilities. Contributions could also come from allocating a set amount to the fund out of participant fees, thus ensuring that each participant shares in the costs of making the program inclusive.

Targeted Scholarships. When procuring funds for scholarships, it may be useful to allocate at least one scholarship specifically for participants with disabilities. Some individuals with disabilities may self-select out of applying for an education abroad program. A targeted scholarship allows potential participants with disabilities to see that the sponsoring education abroad programs welcome them and that participation is not just for their peers without disabilities.

Participants with hidden disabilities who may not have disclosed their disabilities to the program staff in advance may do so in order to apply for the scholarship. This assists the education abroad staff in having more time to plan for needed services or accommodations and reduces the possibility of being surprised by the needs that must be addressed once the student is overseas.

Students with disabilities who must pay for the cost of disability-related services (e.g., personal aids), may receive funding from state agencies or other sources at home for these personal aids, and that financial assistance may not travel with them overseas. Scholarships could offset such costs.

Some college and university students with disabilities receive funding for their education from the state Vocational Rehabilitation (VR) Department. Students who receive VR funding and plan to study abroad should work with their VR counselor to add the study abroad experience to their vocational plan. If VR has already approved funding for tuition, books, fees, a personal care attendant, adaptive equipment, or a note taker, it may be possible to use those funds to cover the same costs while studying abroad.

If an individual with a disability receives Supplemental Security Income (SSI) benefits and has the opportunity to participate in a study abroad program, he or she should apply to have those benefits continue while abroad. There is a little-used SSI provision that allows for the continuation of benefits while participating in an overseas educational program. This provision makes it possible for people with disabilities, who financially need to continue receiving SSI benefits, to gain the international experience needed to meet their vocational goals. Encourage disabled applicants who use either one or both of these resources to contact NCDE for more information.

Budgeting for inclusion of people with disabilities and looking at all of the funding options is a proactive goal that all organizations that are committed to diversity and concerned about resources can embrace. Be sure to have information about disability-related scholarships and grants available for students. With funding established, international education organizations will be able to respond positively and creatively when outreach efforts pay off and qualified disabled study abroad applicants, job applicants, volunteers, or home-stay hosts come knocking at the door. By investing wisely in the full participation of individuals with disabilities, international education organizations take powerful steps toward reaching even broader diversity goals.

Religious Issues

Education abroad advisers should be mindful that a student's religion can affect his or her choice to study abroad, the location where the student would feel most comfortable, and the support he or she desires when overseas. If a student makes his or her religious background known and inquires about the religious climate in the desired host country, the education abroad adviser has a responsibility to provide the student with appropriate resources. Because some students may not make their religious affiliation known to the education abroad adviser, it is important for general information to be provided to all education abroad participants on the host country's dominant religion or religions, religious freedom, access to various religious communities, and the reception of visitors who are not members of the dominant religion or religions.

Even if such information is not site specific, it can be an important tool that helps students to explore religion in the host country on their own. General information about various religions, religious freedom in specific countries, and adherents to particular religions by country can be obtained through agencies such as the U.S. State Department's Bureau of Human Rights, Democracy, and Labor, and the Religious Resource and Research Center at the University of Derby in the United Kingdom.

In addition to general advice about religion, some students need very specific information about an education abroad program's ability to meet their dietary needs and about their access to a specific

Part II: Campus Advising

religious community in the host country. It is important to ask each student at the beginning of the advising process or during the application process if the student has special dietary, religious, or worship requests, so that the education abroad adviser and student can work together to determine the best program to meet the student's needs. For example, some Jewish students may want to know which programs use Jewish host families or offer reasonable access to kosher foods.

Most religions have Web sites that include contact information for places of worship around the world as well as how to access other members of the same religion in various countries. A newsletter specific to the needs of faith-practicing students is available through the Education Abroad Knowledge Community (formerly known as SECUSSA) Web site on underrepresentation.

Summary

Diverse environments help all people to thrive and transform themselves beyond predictable limits. With care and attention to inclusion of all students in various education abroad experiences, all participants will benefit on multiple levels. Participants without disabilities may be sensitive to issues of cultural difference and outsider status when they return home. Many argue that having diverse students on an education abroad program benefits the host country because these students bring with them a unique American perspective that is often ignored or portrayed very negatively in the media. The same can be said when hosting international students on U.S. campuses. The exchange of ideas, cultures, and life experiences—all within a diverse learning environment—must be accessible to all students.

Carter (1991) makes a bold and compelling argument. She asserts that the goals of international education (i.e., helping students understand another country's history, geographic environment, values, and traditions in order to foster better cultural understanding and world peace), will never be met if cultural diversity in these programs is ignored. Internationalism and domestic cultural diversity are concepts that should be compatible. However, many minority communities speculate that Americans are more comfortable looking outside U.S. borders for international cultural understanding rather than dealing with the "international" cultural diversity represented by ethnic communities in our own hometowns (Carter 1991). She suggests that if there is a true commitment to the concept of internationalism, it must be linked to a commitment to acknowledge, respect, and teach the benefits of cultural diversity in our society.

Every student needs access to international opportunities to develop the understanding, skills, and perspectives necessary to be a global citizen. The task can seem daunting. Outreach to all students, linking with colleagues across campus and in the local community, seeking financial support, and broadening advocacy efforts throughout the campus in support of education abroad opportunities will result in opening up opportunities for all students. The rewards of this effort will be felt by every single one of us.

Note: Special thanks to Inge Herman, University of Pennsylvania, and Dawn Anderson, Northeastern University, co-chairs for the SECUSSA Committee on Underrepresentation in Education Abroad, 2003–2004.

CHAPTER 4
Whole-World Study

Contributors: James L. Buschman, Rebecca Hovey, Gurudharm Singh Khalsa, Rosa Marina de Brito Meyer, Michael D. Monahan, Joan A. Raducha

Whole-world study is a growing trend on U.S. campuses as a growing number of students and faculty look to non-Western nations and societies for international learning experiences. In many ways, this trend reflects the impact of globalization and the understanding that the economic and political realities that shape students' worlds and future careers include the many diverse cultures and nations outside of the traditional U.S.–Europe nexus. Calls within the higher education community to internationalize the curriculum reflect this concern to broaden the scope of academic knowledge in a way that integrates a global understanding of the world, and the myriad interconnections between its peoples and cultures, into the traditional knowledge base of the academic disciplines. The literature on internationalizing the curriculum is vast. See specifically, *Internationalizing the Campus* (NAFSA 2003); the *Journal of Studies in International Education* (Association of International Education Administrators, fall 2002); *A Research Agenda for the Internationalization of Higher Education in the United States* (Burn and Smuckler 1995); and *Internationalizing the Undergraduate Curriculum: A Handbook for Campus Leaders* (Pickert and Turlington 1992).

On some campuses, the goal of internationalizing the curriculum has resulted in revised mission statements that include preparation of a global citizenry as a goal for higher education (Lutterman-Auilar and Gingerich 2002; Edwards and Gaventa 2001).

It is within this context of shifting world geopolitics and an increased emphasis on internationalism within U.S. national education policy that advising for whole-world study assumes a critical role in shaping students' educations.

This discussion intensified in the post–September 11 era, as U.S. policy makers and academics argued that U.S. higher education was not producing a professional workforce adequately prepared with political, historical, cultural, or linguistic knowledge of diverse regions of the world. The challenge has been portrayed as a national security issue in some circles, augmenting an already-existing concern that the United States lacks the human resources needed to compete economically in the global economy of the twenty-first century (American Council on Education 2002). "The nation learned on September 11, 2001, that we must become much more sensitive to the rest of the world. We are four percent of the Earth's population, yet we are the military and economic giant. We slowly have come to understand that in administrations of both political parties there have been awkward and stumbling moments, caused not by ill intent, but by a lack of understanding both by leaders and the public" (NAFSA 2003, ii).

Advisers who work with students interested in studying in nontraditional locations are in a unique position to contribute to efforts to internationalize the curriculum, to address the national security and human resources issues of national education policymakers, and to help broaden the U.S. worldview through an appreciation of other cultural realities and their accompanying perspectives on the U.S. presence throughout the world. NAFSA and the Alliance for International Education and Cultural Exchange issued a white paper in 2000 and again in 2003 calling for a national international education policy. The objectives included the promotion of diversification of the study abroad experience, including increased study in nontraditional locations. The mission of the Strategic Task Force on Education Abroad, spear-headed by NAFSA, is to "articulate such a policy.... It is a political and educational roadmap of how to get there" (NAFSA 2003, 2). This is an inspiring challenge for advisers, one that ranges from the understanding of the larger policy realm to the day-to-day logistics of safety, travel preparations, predeparture orientation, and support, as students return to the home campus.

Academic Context for Whole-World Study

International and Global Studies

At one time, nontraditional locations for study abroad seemed best suited for the nontraditional student, but in 2001–2002, 37 percent of U.S. college students studying abroad did so outside of Europe. Overall, the number of U.S. university–level students who receive credit for study abroad continues to grow (4.4 percent increase from 2000–2001), as does the number of students studying in less traditional locations. The percentage of all students going to Latin America has more than doubled since 1985 (an increase of 4 percent over 2000–2001). There have also been increases since 2000–2001 in the number of students going to Oceania (up 18 percent), Africa (up 2 percent), and Asia (up 18 percent); however, there has been a decline in the number of students studying in the Middle East (down 21 percent) (*Open Doors* 2003).

Of all U.S. students studying abroad in 1981, those known to be going to destinations other than Europe accounted for only 5 percent of the total. In the post–Vietnam War era, support for Area Studies courses at U.S. universities proliferated, as did awareness of the realities of developing countries and an interest in new nation-building among the postcolonial nations of the third world. In the early 1980s, international educators saw a need for support of nontraditional locations for study abroad (*Frontiers* 2000). In 1984, the Whole World Committee was formed as part of NAFSA, and by 1985, 25 percent of all students studying abroad chose to study in non-European countries (the reported increase was due in part to improved data collection methods) (Sommer 2000).

An awareness of the globalization debates on U.S. campuses is critical for study abroad advisers' roles in helping students and faculty assess their academic options abroad. These debates are reflected in new theories, approaches, and knowledge constructs of the academic disciplines. Kennedy notes that the internationalism associated with the Area Studies period prior to the 1990s is greatly different from the new Global Studies focus, and sees these as two distinct eras in international studies:

> Globalization, as a knowledge culture, is based above all on the decreasing significance of political boundaries and the diversification of knowledge flows around the world. Area Studies was founded in a security culture that emphasized the importance of contextual expertise, and its associated concerns with grounding and translation (Kennedy 2003).

The support of international study, especially in nontraditional locations and cultures, is not just a question of supplementing existing knowledge of the world, but transforming that knowledge through interdisciplinary inquiry, which the knowledge flows noted by Kennedy can foster. Mestenhauser argues that a knowledge gap between "what is known and what needs to be known" (2002) is crucial to the distinction between international education (the Area Studies focus) and internationalization (the Global Studies focus).

> ...[G]lobal changes are so dramatic that the existing frames of reference are not adequate to respond to them... Internationalization involves not just a simple transfer of knowledge from one country to another, but the use of that knowledge to produce new knowledge (Mestenhauser 2002, 170–171).

(See also the special issue "The Meanings of Globalization for Educational Change" *Comparative Education Review* 2002; 46:1, and the editorial essay by guest editors Martin Carnoy and Diana Rhoten.)

Witnessing this change in forms of academic knowledge and disciplines is exciting and stimulating, but it does ask that the study abroad adviser be able to set aside his or her own preconceptions of the key issues or subjects for a given major. Relationships with faculty are important and students may sometimes need to be encouraged to visit several different faculty members to determine the merits of a given program. For example, a faculty member who holds a more conservative view on international relations may not be supportive of a program with courses such as "The Politics of Transnational Identity in South Asia," whereas a different faculty member who has recently taught or conducted research in the region may see the value of such a program to the students' overall degree goals.

Along with an awareness of the changing dimensions of international and global studies, understanding aspects of non-Western educational practices and approaches aids educators in both advising and preparing students for the different learning processes they will encounter in these locations. The most critical distinction made between Western and non-Western views on education is that whereas Westerners typically equate education with schooling, other cultures tend to view cultural practices and community and family life as important forms of social learning in addition to schooling. The ability to value the learning that takes place outside the classroom is not just a question of developing appropriate cultural sensitivities (although this is a desired outcome). The appreciation of oral traditions or the structures of extended family networks also gives the U.S. student an understanding of how knowledge is transmitted, shared, and validated within the host culture (Reagan 2000).

As education abroad offices provide detailed information on curriculum offerings in non-European countries and themes relevant to those cultures and regions, the education abroad staff can play a valuable intermediary role in bringing together faculty, lecturers, study abroad representatives, and returning students to share the new areas of knowledge emerging from whole-world study. In the end, these are academic decisions approved by the campus international education or study abroad committee, faculty, and department chairs. However, this critical role offers study abroad advisers an exciting opportunity to take part in the internationalization of the curriculum debates and initiatives.

> College policies, albeit often unconsciously, discourage study abroad more than they encourage it. Colleges must take a hard look at the possible institutional barriers that stand in the way of study abroad, which may include: a lack of leadership on the part of senior campus officials, faculty indifference, rigidities in the curriculum, anachronistic rules, ineffective enrollment management, program designs that are inaccessible for nontraditional students, and a lack of predeparture and preparation and reentry assistance (NAFSA 2003, 8).

Mestenhauser's work on systems and structures of internationalization in higher education is a helpful guide in thinking about how to assume this role in promoting nontraditional international study (2002). He describes seven learning domains with the university:

- international studies or international relations,
- area studies,
- foreign languages,
- international dimensions of academic disciplines,
- student and scholar educational exchanges,
- intrauniversity development contracts, and
- university organization, policies, administration, and governance.

Education abroad advisers are key stakeholders within this system perspective, and by learning to operate within these structures and systems, they and the education abroad office can promote whole-world study and provide the support needed to ensure students' success in what can often be an extremely challenging learning experience.

Nontraditional Destinations

Education abroad programs in nontraditional destinations include programs in modern cities with rich histories stretching back to antiquity, such as Cairo, Jerusalem, Beijing, and Bangkok. They also take place in regions inhabited by ethnic or linguistic groups considered minorities by a country's dominant culture. Although stereotypical thinking often labels such locations as third world, many countries—Brazil, Thailand, and Indonesia are prime examples—are highly sophisticated and developed societies in terms of urbanization, industrial output, and technology. In other nontraditional education abroad locations, millennia-old subsistence farming practices continue virtually unchanged. Opportunities exist for students to study in rural Kenyan villages, modern, skyscraper-filled Singapore, and many other areas exhibiting a range of development.

Study abroad in any country challenges students to learn about themselves. In non-Western cultural settings, however, everyday life is likely to be radically different from anything a native-born U.S.

student will have experienced. Such differences, small and big, nuanced and dramatic, create a multifaceted learning environment that stimulates intellectual and personal growth of an order different from what is often possible in more culturally congruent surroundings. Academic learning in such sites can be greatly enhanced by daily recognitions of cultural difference, as well as by unexpected similarities in values and behavior. This is a point made by almost every student returning from a nontraditional study abroad experience.

Whole-World Issues for Study Abroad

As the range of possible study destinations widens, so too does the range of topics that can be appropriately studied in classes abroad. In addition to the study of languages, a number of critical world issues are particularly well suited to studies in sites outside Western Europe, including biodiversity, environmental studies, global communications, international finance, migration and refugee issues, natural resource management, non-Western religions and cultures, peace studies and conflict resolution, public health and epidemiology, social movements, sustainable development, transfer of technology, women's studies, and world trade.

Certain sites offer unique experiences for particular majors. For example, a political science major may have the opportunity in Accra or Delhi to view institution building firsthand or observe how a government deals with issues pertaining to globalization, such as the migration of minority groups. Students may have the opportunity to meet leaders, visit political institutions, attend relevant conferences, and see change in the making. Students in Cairo or Hanoi can explore the effects of development on a society or explore specific linguistic, historical, or cultural interests.

Language Study

The American Council on Education (ACE) reports in *Mapping Internationalization on U.S. Campuses* that:

> Collectively, U.S. colleges and universities reported teaching more than 40 languages, including courses in Asian and Middle Eastern languages. Very few offered any African languages....Spanish was by far the most commonly offered language, with French and German second and third, respectively. The fact that Japanese was the fourth ranked language and that Chinese was the sixth suggests that Asian languages are not being neglected. The percentage of institutions offering Arabic was about seven percent; African languages were available at only 1.5 percent of the institutions surveyed (ACE 2003, 22).

ACE also suggests that "While student attitudes about the importance of foreign language were positive, actual foreign language study at higher education institutions presented a different picture. These data suggest that without a major push by institutions, the percentage of students taking languages will remain low and constant at about 8 percent of total course enrollments—as it has for the last 25 years" (ACE 2003, 23).

The education abroad field should carefully assess the relationship between language classes offered on the home campus (and enrollments in those classes) and student choices for study abroad. Institutions need to determine ways to address the fact that students recognize the importance of studying another language, but in reality choose to do so in small numbers. For those students who do choose to study in less traditional locations, programs should provide (if not require) the opportunity for students to pursue local languages while abroad. It is ideal if the students have the opportunity to begin that language study on their home campuses prior to study abroad, and if possible, students should be offered the opportunity to continue the study of these less commonly taught languages after returning to the home campus.

Institutional Strengths and Goals

A critical issue to the success of developing education abroad opportunities for students in nontraditional locations or encouraging students to attend programs sponsored by other institutions, is how study in nontraditional destinations fits into an institution's goals. One approach is to very directly and deliberately link the institutional mission to study abroad in nontraditional destinations. In practice, this may require a careful review of what the institution aims to accomplish through internationalism. It may mean an emphasis on medical research in developing countries, a stress on understanding the development process, or on teaching students to learn "in the field" about cultures that are radically different from their own. Some institutional missions may focus on foreign language and area studies or stress an intellectual effort to understand and analyze globalization or environmental sustainability.

In any case, institutions interested in study abroad in nontraditional destinations may do well to "build by strength" rather than to encourage student participation or program development in areas where the home campus has no interest or expertise. The rationale for this approach is to strengthen learning in a more cohesive, sustainable, and in-depth way by linking study abroad curricula and learning to on-campus education. Study abroad should build upon on-campus learning, rather than provide a hiatus from it.

Education abroad professionals must therefore be intimately familiar with the academic and cross-cultural strengths of their institutions. This often involves compiling an inventory of international expertise and interests, assessing the inventory in light of the institution's education abroad needs, and strategically targeting priority interests. It also involves building incentives for faculty to become more directly involved in education abroad, often through professional development, contacts with counterparts abroad, and opportunities to enhance teaching and research.

There are more than 100 campus-based Title VI National Resource Centers located around the country. A primary mission of these centers is to establish, strengthen, and operate undergraduate and graduate centers in a particular region of the world, focusing on language and area or international studies. Most of the centers also have an outreach mission, so education abroad professionals are encouraged to consult the centers for advice on orientation programming or on ways to establish contact with specific faculty experts. Some of the resource centers are located at universities that operate study abroad programs in nontraditional study destinations, and which are open to qualified students from other campuses. A list of the Title VI centers can be obtained from the Center for Education of the U.S. Department of Education.

Education abroad professionals may not realize the resources available to them right at their own institutions. Individual academic departments, area studies programs, and other thematic or interdisciplinary programs are excellent places to search for information on appropriate study sites and foreign universities for direct enrollment. International studies, foreign language, and area studies faculty are often deeply familiar with universities abroad and can offer both general guidance and specific suggestions on courses of study.

Program Selection and Advising

Adviser Knowledge

Education abroad advisers have an important role to play in providing the information and encouragement needed by students who are considering study abroad in an unfamiliar location. It is very hard to be able to paint a picture of the sights and sounds, program or university, educational system, and people of a nontraditional location if the adviser has not visited the location. Additionally, advisers should have knowledge of the culture or cultures, the religions, and the social, economic, political, and environmental conditions of the region, particularly those that may directly impact the student. When hiring new advisers and program managers, directors should consider the diversity of staff in terms of the languages they speak, the countries where they have lived and studied, their academic disciplines, and their prior work-related experience.

Education abroad offices should budget for their staff to visit sites where their students currently study, as well as locations where they would like their students to go. To gain experience, advisers should consider participating in site visits sponsored by education abroad programs. Advisers benefit from an arranged visit, and some of the travel expenses may be covered or subsidized. Another long-term benefit of making site visits is the development of relationships among the site-visit participants, who can then serve as resources for one another when advising students. Faculty and other university staff who might travel independently to the education abroad locations should be encouraged to add a site visit to their travel plans.

Advisers should link up with the faculty and staff at their institutions with members of the local community, and with education abroad advisers at other institutions who also have an interest in a particular geographic area or university abroad. Institutions can form consortia to conduct education abroad programs jointly, share other resources such as host family coordinators, or collaborate on the organization of excursions for participants or the joint purchase of computer equipment.

For educators and advisers who are interested in gaining in-depth experience in a particular region of the world, the Fulbright Scholars Program, administered through the Institute for International Education (IIE), offers lecturing, researching, or consulting awards in 140 countries. Traditional Fulbright awards are available for a period of two months to an academic year and longer. The Fulbright Senior Specialists Program offers grants for opportunities that range from two to six weeks in duration. The Fulbright International Education Administrators Program invites applications for summer seminars of two or three weeks in Germany, Japan, or Korea. (See Part I, Chapter 2, "The Profession of Education Abroad.")

Advisers can participate in a number of workshops sponsored by NAFSA and other organizations. Every year, NAFSA's Education Abroad Knowledge Community's (formerly known as SECUSSA) Whole World Committee offers a workshop at the NAFSA national conference specifically designed to address the issues associated with study in nontraditional locations. NAFSA offers country- and culture-specific workshops that may relate to nontraditional destinations.

Advising Practices

Students may sometimes be unintentionally discouraged from pursuing study in nontraditional locations. Education abroad advisers should review their advising practices, and those of their campus colleagues who advise students:

- Are students receiving adequate information about education abroad opportunities?

- Are students receiving reliable information about health, safety, and security?

- Are new concepts introduced to students, or are students simply advised about the program or programs they ask about?

- Does the education abroad office possess and make available to students photos, student evaluations and testimonials, videos, and travel literature related to less traveled program sites?

- Does the university offer less commonly taught languages and if so, are students encouraged to learn them?

- Are students who have returned from study abroad encouraged to pursue higher-level courses in the language or languages that they studied abroad?

- Are students offered the opportunity to connect with past participants; international students, faculty, and staff; or other members of the college community who are from or who have an interest in regions not typically chosen for study abroad?

- Do the education abroad programs include independent study or research options, or internships, and does the institution award credit for these options?

- Does the education abroad office link its Web site to the Web sites of appropriate majors and minors on campus (and vice versa)?

- Are students encouraged (both before and after studying abroad) to participate in internationally oriented extracurricular activities (either on campus or in the community), such as buddy or language partner programs? Does the education abroad office contribute to the development of such programs?

Academic Standards

Respect for U.S. higher education can frequently mean that study abroad programs are welcomed into the best universities, particularly those in the developing world. U.S. institutions that seek to establish programs abroad may have access to brilliant faculty with international reputations and to qualified, bilingual, cross-culturally experienced staff. Advisers should determine whether the programs they investigate rise to such standards. They should cultivate a network of knowledgeable faculty and administrators at their own institutions, or at other institutions in their region.

Program Assessment

There are a variety of issues to keep in mind when assessing overseas programs, depending on the location and type of program. (See Part III, Chapter 5, "Program Assessment and Evaluation.") Consider the following:

- What are the academic and cross-cultural strengths of the program?
- What unique study, field research, or internship opportunities does the program offer?
- What kind of orientation is provided by the program?
- Do students receive adequate information concerning local health, safety, and security issues?
- Does the program have the faculty and staff expertise to deal with rapidly changing situations?
- If classes at a local university are canceled, is the program prepared to organize special classes or develop special project opportunities so that students do not lose academic credit?
- What is the nature of the health support infrastructure?
- Does the program have a plan for evacuating a seriously ill student if necessary?
- Does the program make sure that students are registered at the U.S. embassy and that the program is included as part of the warden system, so that staff and students will receive any notices the embassy wants to convey to U.S. citizens?
- Are there any particular issues related to course registration or the timely issuance of transcripts?

To help assure the quality of a direct enrollment study abroad experience, and the safety of U.S. students who participate in direct enrollment opportunities without a third-party provider resident director, education abroad advisers should consider the adequacy of the local support infrastructure:

- Does the university have a foreign student office? If so, what services are provided there?
- Does the university have a history of closing due to student, faculty, or staff strikes, or government-imposed closures?
- Does the city or region where the university is located have a local group or center that can act as a contact for U.S. students on nonacademic areas of the experience? There are many cultural learning centers around the world that are staffed by local people or expatriates, who have long grappled with cultural learning issues.

Factors that Contribute to Program Selection and Participation

While some students enter the education abroad adviser's office still open to a range of possibilities for study abroad, many others have already decided on their destination. Their selection of a specific program may hinge on course offerings or program reputation, or on less academic factors such as cost or the recommendation of fellow students. Increasingly, undergraduates may possess previous international experience through high school programs or from traveling or living abroad with their parents. Some students who seek to study in Africa, Asia, Latin America, or the Middle East are looking for a heritage experience, the chance to explore a culture and a people related to their own ethnic origins. (See Part II, Chapter 3, "Reaching Underrepresented Constituencies.") Students who seek to study in non-Western parts of the world are often experiential learners who prefer tactile, field-based programs that present significant cultural challenges.

"Is it Right for Me?"

The following advice for students who ask, "Is it for me?" is available on the Education Abroad Knowledge Community Whole World Web site:

> In deciding if studying abroad at a less traveled destination is for you, you must review your objectives for your semester abroad, your sense of adventure, your ability to deal with ambiguity, and how open minded you are. If you are a person who must have every detail laid out ahead of time, an experience in a less developed world may not be for you. Circumstances of infrastructure development and poor communications systems may mean that things that would be easy to accomplish here may not be done so easily while abroad. The degree to which these traits are necessary is dependent on the program model. Stand-alone programs or those with less reliance on the local structures will be less impacted by outside influences and so the need to be flexible and patient may be less important.

> Programs where students are joining locals in their schooling may require more. It should be understood, however, that regardless of program model, daily life could be very difficult and tax the most patient among us. It is important to remember that a stranger to our ways may feel the same when confronted with similar issues in the United States (Vande Berg and Leonard 2003).

Advisers should ask students use the following questions to evaluate their motivation for non-traditional study abroad:

Personal

- How flexible can I be, and in what aspects of life?
- Do I find new and different types of food interesting? (A student who is a vegetarian may have no problem studying in India in a Hindu community, but may find it difficult to manage food preferences in a Muslim setting unless he or she is willing to compromise on diet for the duration of the program.)
- What are my everyday necessities and what can be forgone? (Students may need to do without creature comforts such as toilet paper, or they may have to do without regular electricity or work supplies.)
- What are my needs related to privacy? (In some cultures, young people who want or need privacy may find themselves ostracized and labeled "antisocial.")

- How accepting can I be with regard to different gender role expectations?

Academic
- What is it, precisely, that can best be learned at this particular site?
- How well can I adjust to classes, learning a new language or languages, and possibly conducting research? (Classes may meet for a longer period of time, and may feature less discussion and more lecture, as is typical in many non-U.S. academic institutions.)
- How will I adjust if computer facilities, e-mail and phone access, the library system, availability of books, and other learning resources are inferior to those on the home campus?
- Will I be able to focus on my academic work while adjusting to different ways of living, transportation challenges, a different diet, and an unfamiliar housing situation? (See Part II, Chapter 1, "Advising Principles and Strategies.")

Negative Stereotypes

Regardless of the reasoning behind their selection, many students are powerfully influenced by the stereotypes they hold. Negative stereotypes may lead students or parents to rule out study in certain countries or parts of the world; for example, the Middle East is violent and dangerous; Africa is disease-ridden and primitive. Other stereotypes may actually influence a student to select a particular site, yet the stereotypes must be confronted as false and misleading if the student is to maximize his or her in-country experience; for example, every Brazilian loves samba and soccer; every Chinese is hard-working and smart. Advisers need to point students to accurate information about the culture or cultures of their destination, and if possible to host-country informants. This can be a tricky venture, since naive student questions, asked out of ignorance, for example, "Does your family have electricity?" can come across as insensitive and offensive in certain situations. The education abroad adviser should seek ways to prepare students and informants for such encounters. Advisers should invest time in their own education as a means of overcoming their own knowledge gaps.

Parents

The student and the adviser must involve parents in the beginning stages of program selection, and in all subsequent phases of the program. While some parents are knowledgeable and supportive of their son's or daughter's decision to study in a nontraditional location, many others are lacking in knowledge and are likely to have the same stereotypes as their children. Unless parents can be brought on board early in the selection process, the student may face so much resistance to their plans that they may ultimately have to eliminate certain program sites from consideration.

The images Americans have of nontraditional destinations are based to some extent on the media coverage of such regions: spectacular natural disasters, major health crises, and political instability. Little news space in the U.S. press is devoted to the broader context and history of these problems, and they are often generalized to include whole countries or even continents, even when the actual impact is limited to a specific geographical location. It is therefore not surprising that the general public in the United States, including many parents of prospective study abroad participants, have a less-than-positive reaction to the thought of their child living in a nontraditional study abroad location.

There are, of course, real challenges in developing countries, including, for example, shortages of food, water, and electricity, and bona fide concerns about health care. However, well-constructed study abroad programs address these issues and create a healthy working environment for participants. Students and their families should be made aware that some less traditional sites offer all of the conveniences to which students and their families are accustomed.

It is important to have information available for parents who are concerned about their child studying in a part of the world that may seem (and be) so remote from their own experiences. There are several ways to address parental concerns. Advisers can make themselves available to answer questions; organize an information session on study abroad designed specifically for visiting parents; provide accurate and well-written materials on programs in nontraditional locations; and establish a database of former students and their parents whose phone numbers and e-mail addresses can be shared. Carefully prepared information can address the concerns of many parents. Providing information to parents establishes a line of communication that may be very helpful in case of a real or perceived crisis concerning their son or daughter.

Impact on Career

Given the recognized need for college graduates to have global competency skills, including the direct knowledge of other cultures and languages, an overseas educational experience is a great enhancement to a student's application to graduate school or for employment. Fewer students choose to study in nontraditional locations; therefore, the ones who do are of interest to employers who seek to recruit individuals who are flexible, willing to take risks, adapt to new work environments, deal with ambiguity, and have complex problem-solving skills.

Financial Issues

Although many of the financial questions about study abroad in nontraditional destinations are similar to those regarding study abroad elsewhere, there are a few special concerns and opportunities education abroad advisers may wish to highlight when advising students interested in nontraditional study destinations. For example, immunization and international travel costs may be higher for students heading to nontraditional sites, whereas daily living expenses (e.g., room, board, local commuting) may be lower. Educational costs vary greatly, depending on, among other factors, whether the selected program's fees are based on local or U.S. tuition and administrative expenses. As with any study abroad program, a comprehensive budget and cost analysis should be made available to prospective participants.

With regard to special funding opportunities, students should be encouraged to consider scholarships and grants designated for the study of "critical" languages and study in less traditional locations. Students should also be encouraged to research study abroad programs that offer scholarship opportunities. Some countries have developed scholarship programs to encourage U.S. students to study in their countries. Students should also review community resources. In some instances, emigre communities may offer financial support for students to study in their countries of origin.

Education abroad advisers can refer students to funding opportunities such as those offered by the Freeman-ASIA Program, whose primary mission is to increase the number of U.S. undergraduates who study in East and Southeast Asia. Awardees are expected to share their experiences with their home campus, to encourage study abroad by others and to spread understanding of Asia in their home communities. For information on the David L. Boren Undergraduate Scholarships for Study Abroad, the Gilman International Scholarship Program, and the Rotary Foundation, all of which offer grants and funding for students to study in nontraditional destinations, see Part I, Chapter 7, "Financial Aid and Funding Study Abroad."

It is important that the education abroad office work creatively to secure special funding for study in nontraditional destinations. This might include, for example, a strategic focus on direct reciprocal exchanges with selected universities beyond the common destinations, scholarships for the study of less commonly taught languages, or other grants strategically committed to building incentives for study in underrepresented areas of the world. The selection criteria of existing scholarships might also be reevaluated to include a preference for nontraditional destinations.

Types of Programs

Direct Enrollment in a University

One of the most stimulating forms of study abroad is to become a student in a university in another country. Ideally, this involves living among local students in a residence hall, or in a home with a local family. Students typically select their courses from the regular university offerings, sit alongside the local students, and compete directly with them. This is an enormous challenge, even more so when the university's instruction is in a language other than English. Many U.S. students, even those raised speaking another language at home, will need special preparation to confront such an environment. The academic culture of the university can be equally daunting. Students who are used to small classes, clear and explicit directives from the professor, and earning all As and Bs, may need to develop a very different set of expectations. Classes in a foreign university may be in the form of a lecture to 100 or more students; the professor may offer little or nothing in writing as a syllabus to guide the student; and the average grade may be the equivalent of a C in the United States.

Reciprocal Exchanges

Exchange programs represent a commitment between two universities, and may include any of the following: exchange of undergraduate or graduate students, staff, or faculty; joint research efforts; or other types of collaboration. Student participants benefit from the wealth of information about the host institution built up over time at the home institution (and vice versa), and from the relationships between faculty and staff that contribute to sound advising, support, and often, academic and extracurricular opportunities that might not be available otherwise. Exchange programs are very rewarding but are also very demanding in terms of the commitment of time and resources of faculty and staff at both institutions. Colleges and universities that choose to develop exchanges need to make sure that there is sufficient commitment among the faculty and administration, that the exchange supports the educational mission of the institution, and that there is an appropriate infrastructure in the education abroad office to support the activities of the exchange.

Hybrid Model

Some study abroad programs offer a sort of interface between the directly enrolled U.S. student and the foreign university. Small, interactive seminars may supplement the lectures and some professors may be encouraged to provide American-style syllabi. Special courses may be organized for the participants for language study or on special topics, often designed to encourage discussion and to provide an ongoing venue in which students can process the learning that takes place both inside and outside the classroom.

Island Programs

U.S. students may know shockingly little about the environment in which they choose to study. Sometimes, specially designed programs offer a more realistic academic experience for such students than direct enrollment in a university, since the content of a specially designed class can be tailored to the background of the target group. For example, in a university class in Hong Kong covering the history of China, the instructor might presume that students have learned the basics of this subject in earlier schooling. Such a presumption would probably not be valid for U.S. students enrolled in the class. Those students may be better off in a specially taught class that includes an introduction to the basics of Chinese history. Island programs can structure portions of many courses to be taught in situ, in settings ranging from art museums to battlefields and other historic locations. Such programs need to overcome a natural isolation of their students from the local culture. This can be accomplished through forging contacts with local residents, especially local students, and by ensuring that students live in home-stays rather than as a U.S. group. Students should also be encouraged to take part in local activities. In this way, island programs can establish links to the cultural mainland and might be more accurately described as "peninsula" programs.

Independent Study and Research

Programs at foreign universities may include a field work component or independent research project as part of the academic program. Students can expect to interact with the local community to a greater degree than they would in a traditional program. There may also be potential for contact with authors, community workers, and government leaders. Conducting research in another country is very challenging for a student who is likely to have little to no experience with field work methodologies. There may also be barriers related to the lack of knowledge of the local language or languages, not to mention cultural differences. Some U.S. institutions provide training for their students before the students leave for direct enrollment study abroad, and some programs offer on-site training, which may include course work on field work methodologies. Some students may continue with the research that they started abroad as part of their senior thesis after their return.

Short-Term Programs

More than 50 percent of undergraduate and master's degree candidates who studied abroad in 2002–2003 participated in programs of eight weeks or less duration (i.e., summer, January term, internship, and other short-term programs) (*Open Doors* 2004). Some students and their families are more willing to consider studying abroad in a destination that is unfamiliar to them if it is for a relatively short period of time. Short-term programs to less traditional locations provide a variety of opportunities and challenges. When there is a great contrast between the U.S. culture and that of the host country, as is often the case with less traditional locations, there is great potential for students to be able to discern and therefore start to contemplate and absorb information about the host culture. As is the case with all short-term programs, it is extremely important that the program design allow for a maximum amount of interaction with students and other host-country nationals, to avoid academic tourism. (See Part III, Chapter 2, "Short-Term Programs Abroad.")

Preparing for Whole-World Study

Predeparture orientation sessions present an opportunity for students and parents to confront any remaining fears regarding traveling to and living at the program site. Orientations conducted by knowledgeable staff can provide reassurance that all necessary steps are being taken to ensure a successful semester abroad. Some programs provide orientations in the United States prior to departure, some provide orientation upon arrival in the host country, and some provide an orientation in both locations. Minimally, orientations should include past participants, international students, and other resource people who have spent time in the region, and will include a discussion of health, safety and security issues, how to handle emergencies, and basic information on academics and appropriate cultural behavior. In addition to the information provided in Part II, Chapter 7, "Predeparture Orientation and Reentry Programming," the subjects discussed in the following paragraphs may be particularly applicable to students who study in less traditional locations.

Advisers need to confront students who have been accepted into less traditional programs with the need to learn more about the place where they are going. Select internet resources can provide extensive and multidimensional information. Advisers should guide students through a systematic review of their destination country's significant events and resources. This review can involve English-language sites for better understanding, but should also include resources in the destination country's language, as students learn to master it. Internet resources published by the U.S. government should be required reading for all participants, including the country-specific U.S. Department of State Consular Information Sheets and relevant public announcements and travel warnings. In cases where the home campus imposes travel restrictions based on advisories issued by the U.S. Department of State, education abroad advisers need to be sure that the information they give to students is consistent with the institution's policies. Another invaluable internet resource is the Travelers' Health portion of the Centers for Disease Control and Prevention (CDC) Web site, which features destination-specific information on how travelers can stay healthy.

Americans Abroad

It is often observed that many U.S. students become a minority for the first time when they study abroad. In the case of study in less developed countries, students frequently find themselves members of a privileged, envied, and sometimes-resented elite. As citizens and representatives of the world's only remaining superpower, U.S. students in such countries may encounter local fascination with American culture and prominence. In many cases, students' hard currency U.S. dollars, when exchanged, will give them buying power well beyond the local currency. Students often interact with local elites or even with members of the international diplomatic community, an irony since many students choose such countries expressly to learn more about poverty and underdevelopment. Relatively wealthy families often volunteer as home-stay hosts, granting students immediate entrée into their social circles. Often, the student's first encounter with the poor is through interaction with the domestic servants of a home-stay family, where rigid but unspoken class expectations govern the relationship and create confusion for inexperienced students. Resolving this rich-poor paradox can be one of the most powerful and insightful experiences of the abroad experience. In caste societies, students may have severe adjustment issues. Local administrators should be alert to the adjustment issues experienced by these students, and be available to help them cope. At times of medical or police emergency, the "elite" status of students can be a distinct advantage to them and to administrators, as it may grant them access to scarce resources not available to the average local citizen, thus bringing some program sites closer to the home university's health and safety standards.

A distinct advantage of many sites in Africa, Latin America, the Middle East, and Asia, especially university environments, is the relative ease of interaction with local students. In contrast to Western Europe, where U.S. students frequently encounter difficulties in establishing friendships with their peers, students in developing countries are often quite eager to meet Americans. On-site staff can take advantage of the situation as a means of immersing U.S. students into the local culture. However, students should be cautioned that just as in the United States, particularly in urban environments, not everyone who is friendly to them is to be trusted. Students should be wary of people who may want to exploit them by attracting them into inappropriate relationships (e.g., marriage proposals for the sake of getting a visa to the United States are not uncommon in some sites).

Academic Resources

Advisers need to alert potential participants to the lack of certain resources at universities in developing countries, notably library collections, science facilities, and computer networks. In many cases, however, the opportunity to experience a country's educational system or cultural traditions may make up for inadequate resources.

Strikes and Political Instability

A particular problem in some countries in Africa and elsewhere (strikes also take place in Western European countries) is the possibility of university shutdown. Regular university operations, including classes, may be halted by student strikes, discontented faculty, or governments seeking to stifle university-based dissent. Experienced programs have contingency plans that may involve independent studies, classes for U.S. students taught away from the campus, and other options designed to safeguard the U.S. students' course credit. In turbulent political and social contexts or in areas of potential environmental disturbance, some programs also prepare alternate study sites, where an entire program might be continued on short notice, rather than be forced to suspend operations.

Health, Safety, and Security

At a time when concerns of health, safety, and security abroad are high, students and parents with limited information often conclude that study destinations in less developed world regions must be risky and unwise. Such a conclusion is unwarranted. Experienced advisers know that all forms of study, including those on the home campus, involve risks that must be calculated and managed. The situation in the resource-poor areas of the world is no different. The experience of U.S. students in these regions can be quite different from what they would experience in Western Europe, however, as are the strategies for developing and maintaining high-quality academic programs that place student welfare as a top priority.

Health

It is absolutely indispensable to have qualified medical personnel provide health orientation to education abroad participants. Most program managers with experience in programs in the developing world say that students who follow health guidelines provided by the Centers for Disease Control (CDC) and the program administration rarely become seriously ill. It is not uncommon for students to experience simple diarrhea while adjusting to a new diet and the local water, but it need not lead to anything more than a few days of mild discomfort.

Prevention of illness should start before the students leave home. Students should obtain the appropriate immunizations and learn about prophylactic drugs, such as medication for malaria. Although use of prophylactics does not ensure that students won't contract malaria, students should be informed of all precautions that might lessen the likelihood of contracting the disease.

Once abroad, students may be able to avoid many of the ailments often encountered in developing countries, by following guidelines regarding drinking water and food, and by using preventive measures such as sleeping under a mosquito net and applying insect repellent. Students can, and regularly do, return from programs in nontraditional locations as healthy as they were when they left. (See Part II, Chapter 5, "Health Issues and Advising Responsibilities.")

Emergencies

On-site orientation should include information on what to do in various kinds of emergency situations, particularly those situations that are known to be potentially volatile (e.g., natural disasters, health crises, university and labor strikes, political turmoil, or real or threatened terrorism).

Travel Safety

More U.S. citizens are harmed in road accidents than in any other way while living abroad. Factors leading to road accidents include different driving styles, poor road infrastructure, and poor maintenance of vehicles. Students should be cautioned about driving in countries where traffic travels in the lane opposite to where it travels in the United States. Some programs specifically forbid students to rent or purchase vehicles while they are studying abroad. Detailed information about general and country-specific road safety is available to students, advisers, and program administrators through the Association for Safe International Road Travel (ASIRT). (See Part II, Chapter 6, "Advising Students on Safety and Security Issues.")

Crime

Petty theft is a problem that students will often encounter, particularly if they are studying in a relatively poor country. Prevention can go a long way toward avoiding being the victim of a crime. Students can help to ensure the security of their belongings by storing valuables in a locked cabinet, not wearing jewelry when traveling, and carrying wallets where they are not visible or easily reached in a crowded area such as on a bus or train. Other preventative measures are traveling in pairs and learning about the city or town so as to identify areas to avoid. Personal crimes are usually no more common in poor countries than in many U.S. cities, but since U.S. students are more visibly foreign, particularly right after arrival, they may be especially vulnerable. Predeparture and on-site orientations should provide information on the level of crime in the area, any known incidents that affected prior participants, known places to avoid, and any other site-specific information related to avoiding being the victim of a crime.

Security

Program administrators should provide students with information about how to register at the U.S. embassy or consulate in charge of U.S. citizens in the program region, or they should facilitate students' registrations. Students should be advised about how to obtain, on an ongoing basis, local and international news. In the event of a security situation that affects people residing in the area where the program is located (or in locations where program-related travel or activities will take place), students should follow the advice of their program or local university, as well as information that is given by the local government to everyone residing in the area affected by the security situation. There should also be a plan for how students are kept apprised of general notices issued by the U.S. Department of State concerning the well-being of U.S. citizens throughout the world and what security precautions they are expected to take. (See Part II, Chapter 6, "Advising Students on Safety and Security Issues.")

Program administrators should clearly state their expectations for students' behavior, monitoring of news, and handling of any health, safety, or security matters while students are traveling independently on weekends or during breaks.

Communication

Following years of technological development, communications systems are now greatly improved in many countries of the world. Most regions have reasonable phone, fax, and e-mail service, and courier-packet facilities. Nevertheless, programs and administrators vary considerably in the nature and frequency of their communication with the home campus or office. Regular office-to-office communication prior to the semester's start helps ensure the availability of appropriate housing, awareness of special medical or dietary needs, and a good match between available classes and students' intended enrollment selections. During the semester abroad, regular communication keeps the home office informed on student progress and any special situations. In crises and emergencies, good communication plans keep students, parents, administrators, and other concerned individuals fully aware of the nature of and developments in the situation. Programs that employ only sporadic communication with the home campus force students to be more reliant on themselves and on local resources. Education abroad advisers need to consider the appropriateness of the communication networks in place at the program locations under consideration by their students.

Students should be informed of their level of access to resources such as e-mail and cell phones. In many sites, students have more than sufficient access to these resources, and in other locations, access is limited. Depending on the philosophy of the program, students may find that e-mail and cell phone use may be actively discouraged or actively encouraged. (See Part I, Chapter 8, "Technology and Education Abroad," and Part III, Chapter 6, "Maximizing Safety and Security and Minimizing Risk in Education Abroad Programs.")

Living Arrangements

Programs in nontraditional destinations offer housing choices that run the gamut from home-stays, to apartment living, to dormitories, just like study abroad programs in other parts of the world. Many students have relished the relationships they developed with other students in dormitory situations, or getting to know the local food vendors and marketplaces when they lived independently. Home-stays are often encouraged in nontraditional program locations, at least at the start of the program. Students who are accustomed to independence may balk at the expectations of a host family, whether the issue is curfew, neatness, or attendance at meals. Most students who live with a family for at least part of the time they are abroad find that the cultural benefits, the language-learning opportunity, and having the necessities of life managed by someone else, are reasonable trade-offs for any limits on their freedom. In urban areas, getting to know a family often offers students an opportunity to understand the relationship between rural and urban segments of society. Students often meet visiting relatives and sometimes meet household help who have relocated to make a living wage.

Gender Issues

Gender- and age-specific behaviors are defined differently by various cultures. Some students may be concerned about how they will be treated in a nontraditional program location, and in what ways they will be expected to alter their behavior to comply with cultural or societal norms. Experiencing differences in norms is an important source of learning in the study abroad experience. Before they depart the United States, students should be encouraged to read novels and newspapers and view films about the program region, to identify local norms they may encounter and find unsettling. Students should find opportunities to meet with past program participants, and with exchange students, international students and scholars, faculty, staff, or members of the community who are either from the region or have direct knowledge of it. This knowledge will help students adjust their expectations so that they can derive maximum benefit from their time abroad. Students must be prepared to be sensitive to different cultural norms (e.g., those concerning dress and behavior) as well as stereotypes of or past experiences with Americans that may impact how U.S. students are viewed and received by people in the program region.

Pace of Life

Students can expect the pace of life to be different than what they are used to in the United States. Life may be much more hectic for a student from a rural or suburban U.S. town who has chosen to study in a densely populated major urban center. On the other hand, students may find themselves in a much quieter or slower situation than they are used to, requiring that they place a high emphasis on developing relationships with their fellow students, people in the community, and with their host families.

Arrival Adjustment

Some students' first reaction to the overseas site may be negative, and it is important for such students to know that the situation can be managed and can be enriching if they are prepared to be open-minded and adaptable. Students may need to be encouraged to give themselves time to put their initial experiences into context. What may seem like an insurmountable problem on the first day, when the student is recovering from jet-lag, can soon become a humorous memory.

Languages

Many nontraditional program destinations use a European language as the language of instruction. Students should be encouraged, however, to study a local language. Such study can open whole worlds of culture and ideas. In some countries such as India, multiple languages (e.g., Hindi, Gujurati, and Punjabi) are spoken among the local population. In a country where English is not the language of instruction, students may find themselves studying in one language and speaking outside the classroom in another (e.g., in Senegal, instruction may be in French and students may learn to speak Wolof or another local language outside of the classroom). These multilingual environments are both challenging and stimulating, and are often more representative of the world than are monolingual environments. Local inhabitants are unlikely to think that their native language will be mastered by short-term visitors, but they do appreciate visitors' attempts to learn the language.

Students with Disabilities

Students should consult carefully with the education abroad office and the particular program in which they are interested, to determine if the program and the program site have appropriate resources and can adequately accommodate their special needs. (See Part II, Chapter 3, "Reaching Underrepresented Constituencies.")

Gay, Lesbian, Bisexual, and Transgendered (GLBT) Students

GLBT students may face greater challenges in less traditional education abroad destinations, or, conversely, they may find that there is a particularly welcoming community in some program locations. Students should be aware of the host-country laws concerning homosexuality, and they should be provided with information about how accepting or restrictive the host culture might be. Information on these topics and on GLBT organizations and support resources, norms and styles of behavior, GLBT media, and so on, can be found on NAFSA's Rainbow Special Interest Group (SIG) on U.S. Students Abroad Web site. (See also Part II, Chapter 3, "Reaching Underrepresented Constituencies.")

REENTRY

Returning students are usually the best advocates for study in less traditional locations. Advisers should organize reentry activities that give the students who have studied in nontraditional locations the opportunity to talk about their experiences. The students should be asked to serve as spokespersons at study abroad fairs, information sessions for prospective participants, and at orientation sessions. Advisers should look for ways to connect these students with other people and units on campus (such as the Area Studies program, the special events office, guest lecturers, and international students) that are relevant to their particular area of study. Returned students should be asked to complete a program evaluation, review program literature and handbooks for accuracy, and for suggestions. After being immersed in a new culture, students may be interested to find resources back on their home campus that will further their academic goals, and they may be interested in how they can return overseas to work, study, volunteer, teach, or travel.

Advisers should also research additional opportunities for students to integrate their experiences after their return. One potential resource is the NAFSA Cooperative Grant Program. This program offers grants that may aid in developing new outreach efforts between the campus and the greater community. In some cases, returned students may have the opportunity to connect with people from the region of the world where they studied, and there may be opportunities for students to volunteer with these groups, enabling them to put their newly developed cross-cultural skills to work, or to apply their language skills in their home community.

Summary

Today's increasingly interconnected world requires an educated citizenry prepared to live and work in complicated multicultural and multinational environments. The gradually increasing number of students who choose to study abroad in non-Western nations and societies represent both opportunities and challenges to education abroad advisers and program providers.

> We are unnecessarily putting ourselves at risk because of our stubborn monolingualism and ignorance of the world. As strong as our country and economy are, we cannot remain prosperous and secure if we do not understand the words and actions of our international neighbors. We need soldiers, diplomats, and business executives who speak Arabic, just as we need speakers of French, Spanish, Chinese, Swahili, Russian, Korean, Farsi, Hindi, and dozens of other languages. To successfully navigate the new millennium, we will need leaders who are able to understand global crises not only from an American vantage point, but also from those of our allies and our adversaries (NAFSA 2003, 2).

CHAPTER 5

Health Issues and Advising Responsibilities

Contributors: Joan Elias Gore, Judith Green

Many students who study, work, or travel abroad are less prepared than they should be for the possibility of sudden injury, illness, depression, or other health contingencies. Although most students will face few health issues abroad, to minimize risk it is best to prepare students before they leave home, and encourage them to be proactive, not fearful. From the first discussions about study abroad, students should be encouraged to take responsibility for their own health. At the same time, advisers and program managers are responsible for helping students do so, by informing them of problems they may confront and by coordinating an effective program of support. Clear institutional policies, sound operating procedures, and responsible programming decisions will go far in answering health and safety concerns.

RESPONSIBILITIES OF EDUCATION ABROAD ADMINISTRATORS

Health Information

The responsibilities of education abroad administrators vary depending on whether the home institution operates its own programs or whether the administrators are advising students attending programs run by other institutions. For programs run by the home institution, administrators should develop an entire set of procedures including thorough and up-to-date information on health and safety issues as well as carefully checked lists of health care and emergency contacts in the program region; well-designed information packets to guide students in every step from preparation to reentry, and plans for ongoing communication with students and parents.

For programs run by outside institutions or third-party providers, it is still beneficial for education abroad administrators to collect as much information as possible about current health and safety risks around the world. Administrators should communicate fully and accurately with students and parents concerning the responsibilities they assume and the challenges they face. It is important to offer students general information packets on health and safety abroad months before they embark on their journeys, even if specific contact names and numbers cannot yet be provided.

Education abroad advisers should build-up a library and compile a reference list of books about travel health issues, and advisers and students should become acquainted with Web-based resources for international health information. NAFSA offers a thorough and extensive Web-based booklet aimed at improving the quality of health care provided for students studying overseas, *Optimizing Health Care in International Educational Exchange* (Rogers and Larsen 2003). There are some basic resources that every student, no matter what her or his destination, will find useful, such as the Travelers' Health portion of the Centers for Disease Control and Prevention (CDC) Web site. (Please note that the CDC site contains much technical information and can sometimes be confusing to a lay reader.)

The U.S. Department of State hosts a constellation of Web sites with information on traveling and living abroad. Each February, it sends an announcement to college and university newspapers, alerting American students who intend to travel in the spring and summer (primarily those undertaking short-term travel), about any conditions that may affect their safety or welfare. This information, along with additional information for study abroad participants, including "Travel Tips for Students" is available on the U.S. Department of State Web site. Education abroad professionals should subscribe to the free subscription list for the U.S. Department of State's travel advisories. This e-mail list provides travel advisory updates whenever they are posted nationally.

The health and safety committee of NAFSA's Education Abroad Knowledge Community (formerly known as SECUSSA) conducts workshops on health and safety issues, and committee members serve as resources for the education abroad community. The Education Abroad Knowledge Community also maintains an e-mail discussion list, SECUSS-L, and maintains useful links on its health and safety Web site.

Safety Abroad First—Educational Travel Information (SAFETI) is an extensive Web site developed by the Center for Global Education at Loyola Marymount University devoted to health and safety issues. The Center for Global Education also publishes a subscription On-Line Newsletter with articles and updates on health and safety issues in the field of education abroad. For both health policy and specific health information, there are a number of printed and downloadable publications on health and insurance issues available from NAFSA, the Council on International Educational Exchange (CIEE), and the American College Health Association (ACHA), among other organizations.

A number of medical insurance companies, including some that specialize in student insurance, have Web sites that include information and resources for overseas travel. Advisers should check with the education abroad office's insurance company, and with the student health administrators on campus, to see if this resource is available to students. Students covered by private policies should also check with their insurers for more information.

Printed Information for Participants

The more information education abroad advisers can provide in written form to students the better, either in print or posted on the education abroad office's Web site, or both. Some printed booklets and pamphlets are available for the asking from international education organizations. Others can be easily downloaded and printed from the internet. Advisers may also prepare their own written material. Whatever form the information comes in, students should be strongly encouraged to pack all relevant information and carry it with them as they travel. Advice that seems irrelevant when read in the comfort of home may mean something entirely different when read by a student in a panic who is worried how to respond immediately to real health and safety issues.

Students should be provided with the following printed material:

- Cautions about alcohol and drug abuse. Material should emphasize that alcohol and drug use customs differ from culture to culture; that laws controlling drugs and alcohol in the host country are likely to be different from those in the United States, and that penalties for breaking the law may be severe.

- Descriptions of persistent and epidemic diseases with information on their transmission, prevention, symptoms, and treatment.

- Information about the physiological and psychological consequences of changes in routine that a traveler might encounter: jet lag, culture shock, homesickness, loneliness, changes in diet, lack of exercise, and so on.

- General instructions for emergency medical situations, beginning with the contact information of any program coordinators abroad. Many regions use an emergency telephone system like the 911 system in the United States, and students should also know how to call an ambulance, hospital, or doctor in their area. Students should carry the location and phone numbers of the nearest U.S. embassy or consular office. In an emergency, a student can contact a large hotel nearby to ask for the name of the hotel's physician, who will likely be used to working with foreign visitors. The International Association for Medical Assistance to Travelers (IAMAT) provides a list of English- or French-speaking doctors worldwide, and students should be advised to obtain IAMAT's free listing of participating physicians.

- General advice on nutrition, including ways to supplement dietary deficiencies.

- Advice for students with disabilities on adjusting to accessibility issues and on cultural perceptions of various disabilities. (See Part II, Chapter 3, "Reaching Underrepresented Constituencies")

- Gender-related information, including personal safety issues, how dating behavior differs in the host culture from that in U.S. culture, and date-rape risks.

- Full health and accident insurance policy coverage information and identification. These notes should contain special

Part II: Campus Advising

limitations or instructions on applicability and instructions for filing claims while overseas.

- Region-specific health information, which can be obtained from international travel health centers, the CDC Web site, or other sources. Third-party program providers should be able to supply the education abroad office and the students attending their programs with health information specific to their program regions. Education abroad professionals should be able to receive their own copies of the predeparture information provided to program participants.

Advising and Student Conduct

During early information sessions for students planning to go abroad, health matters should be one of the topics under discussion, and handouts should provide health-related information and also encourage students to gather information on their own.

Education abroad students may hold unfounded assumptions that can contribute to health and safety problems. For example, they may believe that clean water and sterile food preparation conditions exist only in the United States, or, alternatively, they may not recognize how different food preparation habits influence health and disease. Students may be model citizens on the home campus and believe they will know how to behave abroad, but the experience of being in a foreign land can be unsettling, with its tricky combination of new social demands and freedoms. Sometimes making good decisions about health may be more than a student can handle on top of all the other changes. Thus, aberrant or unexpected student behavior patterns, by U.S. or foreign standards, are not uncommon in education abroad.

The issue of appropriate student conduct during times of stress while abroad can and should be addressed during advising and orientation. Students who make sound health preparations for travel will significantly improve their overseas experiences. Advisers have a key role to play in raising awareness of specific health issues, providing resources and information, establishing a system of response and support, and motivating students to take charge of their health and well being. Advisers should make every effort to create an environment at home and abroad that encourages students to raise health concerns without risk of discrimination and that accommodates those students with special needs.

Ultimately, it is the student who must bear the responsibility for healthy travel. If faculty or staff members can guide the way but leave the work to the student, it is more likely that the student will take authority over her or his own health, thus taking one of the many steps toward maturity that education abroad can offer. (See Part II, Chapter 6, "Advising Students on Safety and Security Issues.")

Student Applications

During the application phase, education abroad advisers should encourage students to be as honest and complete as possible in their descriptions of health needs and problems when they fill out their forms. Some students may worry that by revealing a health problem, they are reducing their chance for admission. Advisers should reassure students that by disclosing their health issues, they are increasing the chances that they will receive the best attention and help possible as they travel abroad. If an adviser senses any particular health care concern on the part

Chapter 5: Health Issues and Advising Responsibilities

of the student, a frank discussion of risks and possibilities should take place as early as possible. Advisers should check, too, with the legal office to find out what the legal obligations are regarding knowledge of student health information and how it can be shared. The Health Insurance Portability and Accountability Act (HIPAA), federal legislation passed in 1996, protects individuals against the inappropriate release of private health information.

Some programs and visa applications require a physical examination, which may or may not be arranged through campus health services. For stays in some countries, visa applications may also require chest x-rays or HIV/AIDS testing. Students must be informed about all such requirements as early in the advising process as possible. Perhaps advisers can include such information as part of the study abroad planning handbook, to give students time to make appointments and get shots, if necessary. Advisers should review program and visa application rules carefully during predeparture orientation, to be sure that every student has followed them.

Predeparture Orientation

In many ways, predeparture orientation is a culmination of the advising process. Administrators should consider that they are responsible for providing a thorough orientation for all students going abroad and not just for students attending programs sponsored by the home institution. Students who have paid attention to earlier advising sessions and are planning ahead should find few surprises. Much of the information reviewed and the materials distributed during the predeparture orientation should not be news by then. Such information is certainly not intended to alarm students or parents, but rather to guide them toward intelligent, rational preparation for study abroad.

Health and safety issues should get serious attention during your predeparture orientation program. (See Part II, Chapter 7, "Predeparture Orientation and Reentry Programming.")

Predeparture Medical Examinations

Students need to think ahead and complete all medical appointments, immunizations, and assessments of special health problems well in advance of the program departure date. They also need to take care of any gynecological, optical, and dental check-ups that would fall within the time they plan to spend overseas. Students should obtain copies of important health records and carry the copies while traveling (e.g., records on blood type, electrocardiograms (ECG/EKG) and x-rays when relevant to a student's medical situation; their doctor's statement about any special health problems; dental records, particularly if special procedures or medications are indicated). Along with those records, a student should carry information on how to contact his or her health care provider at home (i.e., name, address, and phone and fax numbers).

What to Pack

Students should create a small first aid kit to take along while traveling. A typical kit would contain adhesive bandages, antibiotic ointment, aspirin or another painkiller, antidiarrheal medicine, and, depending on the region being visited, water purification tablets, antihistamines for allergy relief, skin moisturizer, lip moisturizer, insect repellent, sun block, and sunburn ointment. Students who wear glasses or contact lenses should bring back-up pairs as well as a written prescription for the lenses. Waterless hand sanitizer is always a good idea, too.

Part II: Campus Advising

Students who need prescription drugs should take enough of a supply of the drugs to cover the time they will be abroad, particularly if it will be difficult or impossible to obtain an additional quantity in the host country. Prescription drugs should be carried in their original containers along with copies of the prescriptions, which should state the drugs' generic names. The prescription and the supply of medicine should be packed in different places, ideally not in luggage that might be lost or stolen. Any necessary nonprescription drugs should be obtained in the United States.

Students who use syringes for administration of prescription drugs and who are traveling to areas where there is a high incidence of blood-borne illness, should consider bringing a supply of syringes and sterile latex gloves. Diabetics, in particular, may want to bring a full supply of syringes. Those students who are traveling to countries where the blood supply is not thought to be safe and where syringes might be reused should do the same. Rules governing the import of medicines and medical apparatuses vary from country to country. All students should research the laws in the region where they will be studying, and carry a doctor's note authorizing the use of the medications or equipment that they will carry with them. Students should also travel with their "yellow book" official record of immunizations, provided by the health care professional who administered the immunizations.

If the water supply in the study abroad program location is contaminated, students must be prepared to boil it, filter it, or treat it with appropriate chemicals, or buy safe drinking water. Water-treatment equipment (e.g., filters) can be obtained from outdoor equipment stores.

Accessing Health Information While Abroad

In many study abroad destinations, students will have easy access to the internet and to telephones from which they can make international calls (many students will have their own cell phones as a means of communication). However, in some locations, it will be more difficult to gain computer or phone access. All students going to locations with less ready access to technology should receive information from their program directors about how to receive and send communications and how they are expected to communicate in an emergency. (See Part II, Chapter 6, "Advising Students on Safety and Security Issues.")

Information for Parents

Advisers of undergraduates going abroad may want to create a packet of handouts and brochures about health and safety concerns, and predeparture and program information to send to parents and guardians at least two to three months before their children are due to travel. Students must be given an opportunity to indicate if their parents are not to receive information about their activities. (Many parents will request advice or information about health insurance for their children going abroad. See the section on "Medical and Accident Insurance" below. Some institutions devote a part of their Web sites specifically to information for parents of students going abroad.

It is valuable, too, to warn parents about what to expect in the early days of their child's visit abroad. If parents hear ahead of time that many students feel lonely, afraid, anxious, tired, and even confused during their first week abroad, they will feel more able to advise their children wisely and calmly. They

Chapter 5: Health Issues and Advising Responsibilities

should expect a few frantic or unhappy phone calls and recognize that these calls are a normal reaction to adjusting in a new culture. It is prudent to provide parents with a few pointers to help them recognize cues from their child that something is wrong, and that action is warranted. Parents need to receive an information sheet with emergency contact information. The program administrator can provide the actual names and numbers of appropriate program contacts at the home institution and abroad. Advisers of students going abroad with other programs can create an information sheet for parents that contains basic health and safety information, suggestions for what information parents should look for from the study abroad program provider, and the adviser's contact information. One comprehensive source of information for parents is *Study Abroad: A Parent's Guide* (Hoffa 1998).

Responsibilities of Program Providers

For those programs sponsored by their institution, the responsibility for collecting, maintaining, and distributing accurate and ample information on health and safety issues is typically shared by the faculty director of the program and that university's education abroad adviser. For programs sponsored by other institutions or third-party providers, campus-based advisers should request that the program's sponsor provide the relevant health and safety information to the students and also keep a copy in their files. Information should include the structure of the host country's health care system, the function of pharmacists, and the specific expectations of payment for health services (cash upon treatment is not unusual in many regions). Advisers should help students understand their role in obtaining reimbursement, which may include submitting an insurance reimbursement claim form and all pertinent receipts. The program director or sponsor should determine what health-related information should be imparted to students before their departure and what information is better delivered to them on-site. (See Part III, Chapter 6, "Maximizing Safety and Security and Minimizing Risk in Education Abroad Programs" and Part IV, "Overseas Program Direction.")

COLLABORATION WITH HEALTH CARE PROFESSIONALS

Developing Partnerships with Health Care Professionals

Talking honestly with students about health concerns is essential, but there are limits to the medical counsel an education abroad adviser can provide. Advisers are not expected to be health care experts, have training in medicine or psychological counseling, or make judgments about an individual student's medical history. The primary role of advisers is to develop partnerships with individuals and organizations who can help with the many aspects of health care advising for students going abroad. Advisers should determine the baseline of information that must be collected and the time frame for collecting it, then develop approaches and materials that meet any additional needs.

A good way for advisers to start the task of health care information collection is by forming a partnership with the student health services office on the home campus. Ongoing dialogue with that office may lead to their becoming involved with study abroad health orientations or in modifying insurance policies to meet the needs of students going abroad.

Part II: Campus Advising

Such dialogue will also keep student health personnel attuned to the special needs of students going abroad and informed of the education abroad office's activities done on their behalf. The education abroad office's strong partnership with the student health services office will be vital for students when they return from their abroad experience, since they may need treatment for illnesses contracted abroad. Advisers should form partnerships with public agencies in the college area, too, such as public health services and international travel clinics. These organizations will prove to be valuable resources for advisers who may need to refer students with specific health-related questions.

Students and other travelers may want to consult a medical travel specialist, because other types of health practitioners may not be familiar with travel-related issues, particularly with regard to rapidly changing health advisories in the case of an epidemic. The home institution may also retain medical professionals who specialize in geographic medicine or who operate a travel clinic where immunizations for foreign travel are administered. Students should consult the medical travel specialist about what special conditions apply to the overseas areas where they will be traveling. The briefing should include information on the recommended and required immunizations for those areas. The earlier students get this information, the better, because some immunization requirements involve a series of shots over an extended period of time. Students must then arrange to receive the appropriate immunizations at the student health services office, their doctors' offices, the public health service office, or the office of the institution's medical travel specialist. When students receive their immunizations, they should also obtain prescriptions for any medications (e.g., malaria prophylaxis) or medical equipment (e.g., syringes) that they must take abroad, either because of in-country health requirements or recommendations or because of students' individual health needs (see the section, "What to Pack," earlier in this chapter).

Resources in the Community

Advisers can make their jobs easier by identifying the consultants and experts in their communities who can provide help and information about travel health. Advisers should get to know the resources of their colleges or universities. As already mentioned, the student health services office, student counseling office, and travel clinics, will be important allies. Institutions that include a medical school, or those that are located near a medical school, may be able to gain access to faculty experts on international health issues. The community public health service may also provide travel health services, as well as administer many of the inoculations necessary for international travel. Doctors in the community who have studied, lived, or traveled in foreign countries can also be valuable resources for advisers and their students.

WORLD HEALTH PROBLEMS

Travelers should seek advice and assistance in considering any special medical problems they might encounter while traveling to particular destinations. Such matters might include the prevention and treatment of malaria, traveler's diarrhea, insect-borne diseases, HIV and other sexually transmitted diseases, sunburn, and altitude sickness. Whether any one of these afflictions might concern a particular student will depend on that student's itinerary. The two most common health problems for world travelers are diarrhea, experienced almost

Chapter 5: Health Issues and Advising Responsibilities

anywhere, and malaria, experienced in regions where the disease remains prevalent. Mild forms of diarrhea are readily treated, but severe dysentery can have long-term effects. Malaria continues to be endemic in tropical regions, despite an increase in community preventive measures. If students will be in Africa, Asia, Oceania, Central America, or South America, advisers should alert them to these problems and give them information on prevention, symptom identification, and treatment. The CDC Web site offers up-to-date, specific information on health conditions in all parts of the world, as well as recommendations for vaccinations and prophylaxis.

Sexually transmitted diseases such as gonorrhea, syphilis, herpes, and Chlamydia continue to pose health risks for travelers in virtually any country. The HIV virus, which is responsible for AIDS, is not only transmitted sexually but also through contaminated hypodermic needles and blood supplies. In some developing countries, health care providers may reuse needles. Students, especially those who self-medicate with injections (e.g., diabetics), should carry a supply of syringes that will last their entire stay abroad. Students should also understand that contracting hepatitis or cholera is a possibility in countries with untreated drinking water.

The yellow fever vaccine is required for entry into many countries in sub-Saharan Africa and equatorial Latin America. It may also be required for travelers who pass through those regions on their way to other countries. Other vaccines, although not officially required, are important in preventing infectious diseases such as hepatitis A, hepatitis B, typhoid fever, and others. Note that people with cancer or other diseases that compromise their immune system, and pregnant women, may receive different recommendations than the rest of the population. Students who will be visiting areas where tuberculosis is common should have a tuberculosis skin test prior to departure and, if it is negative, be retested upon their return to the United States.

Given the potentially grave physical consequences of contracting such diseases, students should learn about transmission routes and appropriate preventive measures to avoid and, if necessary, treat these diseases. At the same time, advisers need to couple their warnings with encouragement, allowing that health risks abroad, even in developing countries, are not always dramatically greater than those in the United States, provided that travelers be informed, follow recommended guidelines for prevention, and stay alert while abroad. Advisers must also keep students from assuming that foreign health care is inferior to that available at home. As with other advice given, a balanced approach is the best.

In some areas, the water supply may not be safe to drink without the possibility of suffering intestinal upsets and other maladies, and food preparation may be contaminated. Students traveling in countries where this is the case should be advised to

- consume only beverages that have been made with boiled water (e.g., coffee and tea), or ones that are canned or bottled;
- avoid unpasteurized milk and milk products;
- eat only food that has been cooked or fruit that the student has peeled;
- avoid beverages with ice (unless the ice was made from purified water);
- drink only those fruit juices that are made with purified water;
- avoid consuming food from food stands and restaurants unless the student can

be sure that the food was prepared safely. Check the overall appearance of the restaurant and staff for attention to cleanliness. When in doubt, order food that is cooked just before serving.

Medical Concerns

Preexisting Physical Problems

Students with known and ongoing medical problems, such as allergies or diabetes, must take special precautions to manage their situations overseas. They need to anticipate how their new environment and the stresses of study abroad might impact their health. Each student's situation may be different, as each individual's set of health concerns interacts with that student's travel destination. For example, a student with allergies needs to ensure that specialized medications will be available, and she needs to learn the foreign names for those medications. A diabetic student needs to consider the consequences of contracting malaria. Because advisers cannot and should not specifically address every student's medical needs, students must be prompted to obtain medical advice from someone who knows their medical history, and combine that advice with information about the host country from someone who is familiar with conditions in that region. In such a situation, the consultants in an international travel center can be especially helpful. Students with common and foreseeable medical problems need to know that adequate treatment will be available to them, and they need to know how to procure such treatment. Information about a student's medical conditions that may have a bearing on the student's experience abroad must be conveyed in an appropriate manner to the host program site and to the appropriate staff members.

Ideally, physical handicaps should not restrict a student's participation in an education abroad program, but each case needs individual consideration, taking into account the particular needs of the student and the accommodations available in the chosen destination. Any limitations should be addressed at the earliest stages of the advising process, well before orientation. Students with disabilities must be sure at the outset, even before the application process, that adequate facilities and personnel exist at their chosen destination overseas, that they will be welcomed, and that their special needs will be met. Mobility International USA (MIUSA) is a nonprofit foundation that provides information and guidance and actively encourages programs and campuses to serve students with physical handicaps. MIUSA can help identify programs that have the will and ability to assist students with their specialized needs. Students know what their needs are, and they primarily seek assurance that those needs will be met so that they can participate fully in their chosen program. Program administrators should check with university counsel to ensure that their institution's education abroad programs are in full compliance with the Americans with Disabilities Act (ADA), which codifies the obligations of institutions to people with disabilities.

Substance Abuse

Some students, once freed from U.S. laws and mores regarding the use of alcohol, will slip into or maintain patterns of alcohol abuse while abroad, regardless of how they behaved while attending school on U.S. campuses. Alcohol abuse occurs for a variety of reasons: students may have a mistaken impression of how alcohol is used in the host country, alcohol may be cheaper in some countries than in the United States, the host country may have a lower drinking age or more lenient laws against drunkenness, or the student may simply have a desire to experiment or fit in.

The education abroad office's orientation program should address alcohol issues head-on, and present clear information about the use of alcohol in the host country. The orientation should emphasize that the abuse of alcohol in any cultural setting can result in disruptive and offensive behavior and can bring on or exacerbate serious academic, psychological, or health problems. Program expectations regarding alcohol consumption should be determined in consultation with the home campus's legal office and should be clearly stated, as should the consequences for abusing the rules. Some students may already attend Alcoholics Anonymous (AA) meetings in the United States; those students should be encouraged to call AA or visit the AA Web site to learn what services are available abroad, the meeting times and locations of meetings, and the language in which meetings are held. Advisers should encourage students to disclose their AA membership to overseas program administrators, who will take AA members into consideration when planning social functions.

Although most countries tolerate social drinking, with the exception of those with religious prohibitions against alcohol, the use of inebriating or hallucinogenic drugs is seldom allowed anywhere, under any circumstances. Drug abuse, while less commonly reported among education abroad participants, carries immeasurable health risks and serious cultural and legal consequences. The risks are complicated by impure drugs, shady and often criminal contacts, and rigid legal systems that impose severe penalties on those caught with drugs. The prevalence of designer drugs and date-rape drugs makes it imperative that students be counseled to avoid situations in which they may come under the influence of such drugs. Students should be encouraged to look out for the well-being of their fellow students and to never leave behind another student in a situation where drugs or alcohol are in use. Institutional liability arises in the arena of student drug use as well. The risks justify a careful consultation with university counsel to ensure that the education abroad program complies with the 1988 Anti-Drug Abuse Act (specifically the provision relating to drug-free workplaces), and other federal legislation regarding illegal substances.

Nutrition

Living in another culture necessarily entails a change in diet, eating routines, and assumptions about food. These changes are usually beyond students' control. Some students find that their diet abroad is considerably healthier than the one they followed at home. People in other countries may generally eat less and more healthily and have a more active lifestyle than Americans do. As students encounter a new culture, they may feel confused over new body image assumptions, which can have an affect on eating habits in the host country or upon return home, or both. Changes in body image and eating habits can sometimes even lead to the development of an eating disorder. Advisers should discuss cultural assumptions about body image and eating habits with students before their departure. Overseas resident directors should be aware of the signs of eating disorders and the steps to take to help students who develop problems with nutrition or other eating disorders while they are abroad.

At the other extreme, some students may find that their diets change for the worse during their time abroad. In poorer countries, the variety and quantity of food may be limited, food may be prepared in unsanitary ways, and students might suffer from vitamin deficiencies. Students faced with such situations should be encouraged to pay attention to ways they can adjust to their new diet while knowledgably supplementing it, to ensure themselves the full nutrition they need to remain healthy and strong. Whatever the situation, advisers can be sure that what students eat, do not eat, dream about eating, or hate eating, will be a very important part of their thoughts and conversations while they are abroad, and will form an important aspect of their memories of education abroad for years to come.

Students should understand from the beginning that it is not feasible, or even advisable, to try to impose American eating habits on a foreign culture or to expect to find American foodstuffs abroad. It is possible for an adviser to learn what the diet consists of in a given foreign country, and use that information to give nutritional counsel to students in advance. Such information should be readily available on-site for an institution's programs; otherwise, advisers can obtain the information from program representatives or people who have lived in the program locations. Because students from one institution may well be going to many different countries, advisers should keep dietary information relevant to each country in their education abroad libraries, and try to provide some sound general nutritional guidance during predeparture orientations. The institution's student health services office or counseling center may have nutritionists and eating disorder specialists available for consultation.

Emotional and Mental Problems

It is normal for students to feel a little insecure about traveling abroad. Jet lag is a very real physical phenomenon that can contribute to a person's sense of disorientation and physical discomfort. Education abroad advisers should inform students about ways to prepare ahead of and during travel to minimize jet lag, such as being well-rested when embarking on travels, immediately shifting to the new time zone's eating and sleeping schedule, and avoiding alcohol consumption during the adjustment period.

Culture shock can be temporarily shattering and disorienting, even in the most self-confident students (an in-depth discussion of culture shock can be found in Part II, Chapter 7, "Predeparture Orientation and Reentry Programming"). It is a real and very normal adjustment phenomenon that everyone will go through, with predictable psychological and social dimensions. In almost all cases, students can be primed to move gracefully through culture shock with proper predeparture and on-site orientation.

Students who develop longer-term mental and emotional problems raise more serious concerns for education abroad advisers. Students who carry serious, unresolved emotional problems with them overseas can jeopardize themselves and their programs. As with substance abuse, although the individual student feels the immediate impact of the problem, side effects can affect others and may even extend to an entire group. The challenge to advisers and program administrators is to know how to prevent the situation from happening, and what to do if and when it occurs.

It is not always easy for students or their families, let alone education abroad advisers, to predict who will suffer emotionally while abroad. It is clear, however, that preexisting emotional difficulties are often intensified by living in a foreign culture. Many students and their parents seem to think that an overseas experience might be just the thing to cheer someone up, but in fact a stressful experience in foreign surroundings can have just the opposite effect. On top of that, there may be few resources in foreign settings to help a student deal with emotional problems.

As discussed in Part II, Chapter 1, "Advising Principles and Strategies," every education abroad adviser should stress the importance of students having a clear and positive motive for choosing to study or work abroad. Students need to know that going abroad just to get away from something does not make sense. Advisers should take the time to schedule one-on-one counseling sessions with every student applicant. Personal conversations offer an opportunity for advisers to judge the emotional stability and maturity of most students. Reservations about a student's ability to enjoy a successful study abroad experience should be shared openly and directly with the student.

Unfortunately, students who will not admit psychological problems face-to-face are also likely to disguise the problems on their applications. Most letters of recommendation ask for comments on a student's emotional, as well as intellectual, maturity. But only the especially astute faculty member may discern such characteristics and then willingly state them for the record.

If the student does not exhibit any obvious problems, if the student is determined to hide problems, or if the student genuinely does not recognize or acknowledge emotional problems, the adviser may feel that he or she has no choice but to proceed as if no problem exists. Advisers whose instinct tells them that a particular student's participation might not be beneficial to the program or the student, may wish to consult university counsel and professionals at the health services office or counseling center about the right approach to take. Privacy and confidentiality are difficult issues, particularly when decisions may be based on instinct or hearsay. An education abroad professional must be ready to work closely with counseling centers to make sure that students with difficulties are not peremptorily excluded but rather are given sufficient opportunities to discuss the kind of stress and strain that can accompany studying overseas. To search or probe further (for example, to inquire at the counseling center if a particular student is in therapy) may constitute a breach of the confidentiality of student records.

It is possible to require, as part of the postadmission process, that any student who is in counseling provide a note from the counselor to the education abroad office, indicating that the counselor is aware of the student's plan to study abroad. This approach is similar to the typical requirement that a medical history from a physician be submitted to the education abroad office, to verify that the student's health will not be placed in jeopardy by his or her participation in an education abroad program at a particular site. If a student's health care provider, advisers, or parents are concerned about the potential well-being of the student, and whether adequate counseling or medical facilities (or both) will be available, the student should be encouraged to give written permission for the appropriate parties to consult with the student and one another, particularly since all parties will need to work together to ensure a healthy and safe experience abroad for the student. In rare cases, the student and other concerned parties may agree that it is not in the student's best interest to study abroad at a particular time, in a particular location.

This is another situation in which institutional partnerships can work to an adviser's advantage. Advisers who have already connected with the counseling center, to ask for advice on the counseling and orientation provided by the education abroad office, can acquaint the center with the emotional risks associated with study abroad, and invite a representative from the center to lead a group discussion about the mental health issues students may face overseas. Send the counseling center a copy of the list of education abroad participants, in the same way the registrar and the housing office are informed. Knowing the special needs and concerns of the study abroad constituency will enable the counselors to act appropriately and sensitively on the information provided by the education abroad office.

Reentry and Health Concerns

Many students returning from overseas study fail to consider that the jet lag and reentry culture shock they may experience are potential health issues. They are surprised to find themselves emotionally drained and physically enervated shortly after their return. Advisers can prepare students ahead of time by telling them that they will need time and care to adjust to their own native culture, just as they did to the foreign one. And just as their bodies needed to adjust to jet lag upon arrival in the host country, the same is true upon return to the United States.

Returning home may involve other emotional stresses for some students. Advisers would do well to warn students of this possibility and also to keep in touch with returning students, watching for signs of distress. Some students may find that problems they left behind have not yet been resolved. For other students, it may be hard to fit back into a social group that has evolved without them. Friends may change, and family members may find it hard to accept the new, more mature, and independent person who comes home. Students need to be assured that the bad feelings associated with reentry are usually temporary, but they should be encouraged to get professional counseling if the problems seem extreme. Likewise, advisers shouldn't ignore the possibility that reentry symptoms are masking a more serious medical condition that genuinely needs professional attention. Advisers who have any suspicions that a student has returned with a medical problem should not hesitate to encourage the student to consult with a family or student health care provider. (See Part II, Chapter 7, "Predeparture Orientation and Reentry Programming.")

Foreign Medical Practice

Many countries differ from the United States in their medical practices. How medical help is obtained, the way patients are treated, the conditions of the facilities, the method of payment for health care—all these things can vary greatly from country to country. Students need to be prepared for the reality that U.S. health care values, assumptions, and methods are not universal, and that even the definition of illness, including the answer to the question, "When is expert attention required," is to some degree a cultural phenomenon.

In some countries, medical standards will turn out to be superior to those in the United States in effectiveness and cost. In other countries, however, standards are low enough that some medical needs cannot even be met. The key is to know, in advance, which of these two situations students will face and to be sure that every student is prepared for all contingencies.

The availability of emergency medical help is a particularly important area of concern. In the United States, children are taught early in life to know what to do and whom to call in an emergency. Overseas, students need to learn these basics again for their new, temporary, home country. The orientation materials prepared by the education abroad office should offer general principles for finding emergency medical help and information. Encourage all students to think through and write down their emergency medical procedures, before they even start to travel. Students should then refine those notes with information they gain once they get to know their new home countries.

Insurance

No college or education abroad program should allow a student to travel without sufficient medical insurance coverage for all possible medical needs, including medical evacuation and repatriation of remains. Health, accident, and life insurance are fundamental. Many institutions can arrange to extend coverage of the policy that already covers students on campus, although there may be an extra fee. Also, extension of coverage may apply only to programs sponsored by the home campus. A number of national agencies sell medical and accident insurance policies designed specifically for participants of education abroad programs.

It is the education abroad adviser's job to work with others at the home institution to make important decisions about insurance. What sort of coverage does the institution want for its students? How do students acquire the insurance? Will the institution make the cost of insurance part of its student fees? How will the education abroad office ascertain that all students sign up for insurance and understand how it works? Often, parents will be involved in the discussion about health and life insurance, so advisers should be sure to communicate with parents about the rules and requirements regarding insurance coverage for education abroad. If students are still covered by their parents' medical insurance policies, they must verify that the coverage meets the education abroad program's requirements and that the coverage is valid overseas.

The International Student Identity Card (ISIC) provides its holders with emergency services and basic sickness and accident travel insurance. Some institutions provide the ISIC to their students, or they recommend or require that their education abroad participants purchase the ISIC to obtain a minimal level of coverage. If repatriation or medical evacuation costs might be higher than what is provided by the ISIC, students should be advised that additional insurance is necessary.

OVERLAPPING HEALTH AND SAFETY CONCERNS

The Student's Role in Minimizing Health and Safety Risks

Travelers should take special precautions to avoid accidents overseas, and there are many pieces of common-sense advice worth giving students on this subject. First, when students arrive in a new country, it is important for them to note any conditions that might compromise their safety, such as driving on the opposite side of the road or the use of bicycles in unfamiliar traffic patterns and rights-of-way. Students should be alerted to the following good practices:

- Follow traffic rules and use seat belts whenever possible.

- Make sure that equipment, such as bicycles, mopeds, motorcycles, or cars, is operationally safe.

Part II: Campus Advising

- Inquire about driving regulations and laws governing legal operation of a motor vehicle (note that driving is discouraged or forbidden by many education abroad programs).

- Study the symbols on road signs and other details that native drivers take for granted, and learn their meaning, in order to make quick driving decisions and drive or walk safely in traffic.

- Be very cautious when swimming, especially in large bodies of water. Find out about tides and currents before jumping in.

- Be aware that electrical appliances may operate differently from those in the United States, and may operate on a different voltage. Make sure equipment is suited to the local voltage (which may require a converter as well as an adaptor to fit the electrical socket). Don't use poorly wired or exposed electrical equipment.

Natural Phenomena

Students must be alerted if they are going to be studying in a region prone to typhoons, hurricanes, tornadoes, blizzards, or other extreme weather and natural phenomena. Students should also consider any special pollution issues in the program region. Just as students pay attention and respond to environmental and weather patterns at home, so should they do so whenever and wherever they travel.

Terrorism

Today, the news is filled with information about terrorism and the potential for terrorism. Sometimes terrorism is directed at a particular country or region, but it is often nonspecific in nature. All responsible education abroad programs should provide students and their families with concrete information about any possible threats in the program region, as well as the procedures for dealing with the threat of or actual terrorism.

First, and perhaps foremost, education abroad advisers must remember—and may want to also remind students and parents—that ongoing exposure to media coverage about terrorism can contribute to anxiety. Often, media coverage of terrorism has no direct bearing on students' education abroad programs or regions. Anxiety related to media coverage of terrorism can be especially acute in people who find themselves in a new situation where they do not recognize social, political, and cultural cues. Advisers should firmly advise students not to wallow in speculation. If students have concerns about terrorism, they should speak directly with the program director. Students should feel free to ask questions and get facts. (See Part IV, "Overseas Program Direction.")

Second, students should be told to follow the simple precautions recommended in the United States to minimize the risk of and be prepared for acts of terrorism. Students and their parents can be advised to refer to the many useful information sources that now exist on this subject, including the book by Senator Bill Frist, *When Every Moment Counts* (2002), and the U.S. Department of Homeland Security Web site. Both resources provide basic information on actions to take and items to keep on hand to create a cushion of safety and health (e.g., keep extra prescription medications accessible and ensure an adequate supply of food and drinking water).

Finally, advisers should remind students that the odds of being involved in a terrorist attack are small. It is much more likely that a student's education abroad experience will be interrupted by something the student has to be personally responsible for, such as his or her health, food consumption, and choices regarding alcohol and drugs. Making the best decisions about these aspects of their lives, and employing everyday safety practices, are the best things students can do to keep strong and ready for adventure. (See Part II, Chapter 6, "Advising Students on Safety and Security Issues.")

Summary

Students have the right to expect a safe and healthy experience during their time abroad. The world beyond U.S. borders sometimes poses health and safety problems unlike those found at home. There is no way that all dangers and risks can be eliminated, nor will students always act in their own best interests. In a sense, the risks that students face abroad are part of the important learning process associated with study abroad. An adviser's responsibility is to help students face those risks with knowledge and wisdom, by ensuring that students receive appropriate information and assistance, and giving them responsibility for maintaining their own health and well-being. Advisers can meet their responsibility to the students and the institution by seeing that their programs comply with relevant statutes and regulations, and minimizing liability through careful planning. As the saying goes, an ounce of prevention is worth a pound of cure. Good advising, planning, and program management make for great education abroad experiences.

Note: Special thanks for assistance and advice on issues in this chapter go to Dr. Richard Pearson, Professor of Medicine and Pathology in the Division of Infectious Diseases and International Health at the University of Virginia's School of Medicine.

CHAPTER 6

Advising Students on Safety and Security Issues

Contributor: Patricia C. Martin

Conveying the significance of safety and security issues to education abroad participants and instilling in them the need to take responsibility for their preparations and actions are two of the most important challenges facing advisers, program administrators, and on-site staff. This chapter reviews recommendations to students and families from the publication *Responsible Study Abroad: Good Practices for Health and Safety*, and reviews safety principles and security issues. Details on health precautions and preparations are provided in Part II, Chapter 5, "Health Issues and Advising Responsibilities."

GOOD PRACTICES FOR HEALTH AND SAFETY

Responsible Study Abroad: Good Practices for Health and Safety (2003—hereafter referred to as *Good Practices*), was drafted by the Interorganizational Task Force on Safety and Responsibility in Study Abroad, now known as the Interassociational Advisory Committee. *Good Practices* provides guidance to program providers, students, and families or guardians of participants.

This chapter will focus on how the good practices outlined in that publication form the basis for how advisers, program administrators, and on-site staff can prepare students for the overseas experience in terms of safety and security concerns, and also instill in them the importance of personal responsibility for their own well being. Advisers and program providers are encouraged to incorporate these recommendations into their program literature, Web sites, and information and advising sessions with students.

The recommendations for parents from *Good Practices* are noted in italic throughout this chapter.

Good Practice:
Students are advised to assume responsibility for all elements necessary for their personal preparation and participate fully in orientations

Frequent and consistent messages throughout the recruitment, advising, application, and post-admission phases of the education abroad process, verbally and in writing, will help students to absorb over time the level of responsibility that they must undertake to satisfy the regulations and expectations of the home campus and the host institution abroad, and to have as healthy and safe an experience abroad as possible. It should be made clear to students what information will be provided by the abroad program and what information must be obtained by the student. For example, one study abroad program may collect student passports and apply for visas for entry to the host country, whereas another program may make it the responsibility of the students to request visa applications and instructions from the host-country embassy and submit the visa application and required documents on their own in a timely fashion. Advisers and program managers should be aware that if they handle a lot of administrative details that could be done by the students, the students might take a less active role in their preparations because they may feel that everything is being taken care of for them. Conversely, if a program requires that students handle many of the administrative details that are not familiar to them, advisers and program managers should provide an adequate amount of information and support so that students will be successful in the tasks before them.

Details about orientation programming are provided in Part II, Chapter 7, "Predeparture Orientation and Reentry Programming," and Part IV, Chapter 2, "The Overseas Program Cycle and Critical Components." Advisers should provide a predeparture orientation that includes basic safety and security principles for all students, whether they will attend home campus education abroad programs, or take leaves of absence and attend programs provided by other institutions. If a student attends a program run by the home institution, the orientation should cover not only the basic administrative details of participating in an education abroad program, but should also include detailed information about the program and the overseas site, including relevant information on safety and security.

Whenever possible, the predeparture orientation program should be coordinated with the on-site orientation program. Sometimes, students will choose not to attend orientation because they can get a cheaper flight if they fly a couple of days or a week later, or they may want to travel ahead of time with friends, or they may have another event in their lives that they decide is more important to attend. Attendance at orientation should be mandatory, and advisers need to determine in advance how to enforce participation and the consequences of nonparticipation. Students who do not attend the on-campus and on-site orientations are likely to miss critical safety and security advice. Students must be made aware through recruitment literature, advising, and orientation programming of any in-country conditions that present a particular health, safety, or security risk to the students. This would include information on incidents that have affected past participants. For information on what safety and security topics to include in orientation programming see the sections below on "Safety Principles" and "Security Issues."

One way to ensure that students are taking an active role in their preparations is to give them orientation topics that they must research and prepare and then present to the group. Students can also be given a self-orientation manual that consists of questions only. They can then use their program literature, handbooks, the internet, and discussions with past participants, international students, other advisers, and faculty to obtain the information they need to complete the manual. This technique is particularly useful as an alternative orientation method for students who cannot attend scheduled orientation programs. Lecturing to students in a large group is likely to be the least effective method of conveying information if the goal is to get the students actively engaged in their preparations to go abroad. Depending on the amount of time and resources of the education abroad office, advisers should consider offering orientation programs on special topics, thereby ensuring that a sufficient amount of time can be devoted to in-depth discussions of varying topics; resource people from other offices can be asked to participate. Sample topics for these sessions could include programs for students who have not traveled abroad; gay, lesbian, bisexual, and transgendered students; the experience of being a religious or ethnic minority abroad; travel options in specific regions; women's issues; and staying healthy abroad. (See Part II, Chapter 7, "Predeparture Orientation and Reentry Programming.")

Good Practice:
Students should read and carefully consider all materials issued by the sponsor that relate to study, health, legal, environmental, political, cultural, and religious conditions in the host country or countries

It is extremely difficult to verify if students have read the program materials provided to them. Some program administrators read certain information out loud during orientations, particularly liability waivers, to assure that the students have thought about the content of such important information. At a minimum, advisers and administrators should require that liability waivers and behavioral contracts are signed by the students, indicating that it is their responsibility to read program handbooks and any other required information.

Good Practices *recommendations to parents, guardians, and families: Obtain and carefully evaluate participant program materials, as well as related health, safety, and security information.*

Some programs will routinely send information to parents (students should be notified if this is the case), and others consider it the student's responsibility to share information with his or her family. One alternative is to post information on the education abroad office or program Web site, where it will be accessible to anyone. Some institutions design Web pages specifically for parents.

Good Practice:
Students are advised to conduct their own research on the country or countries they plan to visit, with particular emphasis on health and safety concerns, as well as social, cultural, and political situations

Students should be encouraged to conduct their own research on the host country. In some cases, program admission requirements include prior language study or appropriate area studies courses that help students to focus on their targeted country for study abroad. Education abroad offices should keep a library of culture-specific and related books, articles, magazines, student evaluations, photos, and videos for students to use in the office or take out on loan. The education abroad office or program Web site should also contain links to sites where students can get detailed country and culture information, including health, safety, and security information. Students should be encouraged to become familiar with the resources of the U.S. Department of State Web site, among others.

Good Practice:
Students must consider their physical and mental health, and other personal circumstances when applying for or accepting a place in a program, and make available to

Part II: Campus Advising

the sponsor accurate and complete physical and mental health information and any other personal data that is necessary in planning for a safe and healthy study abroad experience

Students may be reluctant to be forthcoming about a disability. Therefore, it is important to provide information about learning, physical, or psychological disabilities as they pertain to the education abroad experience, and to encourage students to discuss their needs with their education abroad adviser as soon as possible in the advising and program selection process. The education abroad office and abroad program Web sites should include information for students with disabilities and should link to other on-campus offices that provide services to these students (ideally with joint statements). The forms that students fill out prior to advising, and the program application, should request information about any special needs that the students might have. Students may still choose not to provide information at this stage of the process. As part of the postadmission process, students should be asked to complete forms that again ask them to declare any disability, dietary need, etc., that may have a bearing on the overseas experience. Once the need has been indicated, the adviser should discuss the disability, health condition, or other special need directly with the student. The student should give written permission in order for the adviser to discuss the student's record with the disabilities office on campus or with their physician or counselor or psychiatrist. Ultimately, determining whether participation is advisable and whether appropriate accommodations can be provided on the education abroad program should be a collaborative endeavor including the student, the disabilities services advisers, health providers, and education abroad offices both on-campus and at the program site.

Students may also be concerned about how they will be received in the host country due to their race, religion, gender, sexual orientation, citizenship, or some combination of these or additional factors. Again, students may or may not be forthcoming with questions related to these factors. (See Part II, Chapter 3, "Reaching Underrepresented Constituencies.")

If the program has any specific physical requirements (e.g., students must be able to swim or hike long distances) they must be made clear in the program literature. Environmental factors that may have a bearing on a student's participation should also be indicated (e.g., severe air pollution), as should information on local health conditions (e.g., the need for immunizations and medication to prevent illnesses such as malaria). If it may be difficult for some students (e.g., vegetarians) to maintain a healthy diet, that information should be shared as well. Basically, any situation or condition that students have found to be a challenge in the past should be evaluated, and disclosed to potential participants if it is likely to be a recurring issue. Information on these topics should be included in orientation programming.

Good Practice:

Students should obtain and maintain appropriate insurance coverage and abide by any conditions imposed by the carriers

Students must have health insurance that will cover them adequately while they are overseas. Unfortunately, the coverage that the student has in the United States may not be adequate. Additionally, students should have sufficient medical evacuation and repatriation insurance. Institutions address this need in a variety of ways. Some institutions require that the students purchase a particular insurance policy and may build the cost into the program fees. Others will put the responsibility entirely on the student to obtain insurance but will assess the policies, which students must submit for approval. Still others will place the responsibility solely on the student to assess their current insurance policy and obtain additional insurance as needed. Some go midway and provide travel insurance, such as that provided by the International Student Identity Card (ISIC). However, the insurance provided may not cover all the expenses related to medical costs, including evacuation and repatriation.

Students should be aware of what their responsibility is in terms of evaluating their insurance policies, and may need guidance to determine what is and is not covered and whether their policies are adequate for the overseas experience. Advisers should keep in mind that students may not be familiar with the details of their insurance policies. For example, some policies exclude coverage for what is defined as participation in extreme sports, such as water activities, bungee jumping, or skiing. Students should also be advised to maintain their U.S. coverage and to make sure that they have insurance coverage for all countries they will visit, and for times when they are in transit. It is important for students to be aware that they may need to pay cash up-front for services rendered; some local or travel insurance policies provide that service as part of coverage. Students should also be given an estimate of the desired level of coverage for medical evacuation and repatriation insurance.

The following questions may be useful to students and their families when reviewing an insurance policy for education abroad:

- Will the plan cover hospitalization for accidents and illnesses for the entire period while I'm abroad? (Some policies may cover brief stays but not the entire duration, and may only cover emergency treatment.)

- Will the plan cover doctor visits and medication prescribed abroad?

- Is there a deductible? If so, how much?

- Is there a dollar limit to the amount of coverage provided?

- What are the procedures for filing a claim for medical expenses abroad? Do I need to pay for expenses up-front and then submit receipts to the insurance company for reimbursement? (Make sure to get full information from your insurance provider about how to arrange for routine treatment and medical emergency procedures, and what is required to pay for services or be reimbursed for a claim. Many overseas health providers will not process U.S. insurance claims, and will expect payment at the time of treatment. Students should have access to funds—either credit cards or traveler's checks—in the event that medical treatment is required while they are abroad. Students must remember to obtain a receipt to submit with the insurance claim for reimbursement.)

- What if I don't have enough money to pay cash up-front?

- When does the plan begin and end?

Part II: Campus Advising

- What do I use as proof of international medical coverage (if I need to use the insurance or if the host government requires documentation)?

- If I am not a U.S. citizen, will I be covered by the plan? (International students might need to arrange for coverage with a company in their home country. Most policies do not cover international students traveling in a country other than the United States.)

- Will this insurance cover me in the United States for the insured semester if I decide, for medical or other reasons, to return before the end of the program?

Good Practice:
Students should inform parents, guardians, family members, and any others who may need to know, about their participation in the study abroad program; provide those people with emergency contact information; and keep them informed of their whereabouts and activities

Advisers need to let students know that they expect students to discuss their plans to participate in an education abroad program with their families, or others who need to know, as early in the process as possible. As indicated above, some home campuses will send information to this effect, directly to parents or guardians, after notifying students that it is their intention to do so. Students should set up a regular system of communication with their families and should inform them of their travel plans away from the education abroad site. This is important not only in the event of a safety or security issue affecting the student, but also because it is important that there be a way to contact the student if there is an emergency affecting a member of the student's family.

Good Practices *recommendations to parents, guardians, and families: Be informed about and involved in the decision of the participant to enroll in a particular program. Be responsive to requests from the program sponsor for information regarding the participant. Keep in touch with the participant. Be aware that the participant rather than the program may most appropriately provide some information.*

Good Practice:
Students must understand and comply with the terms of participation, codes of conduct, and emergency procedures of the program

A thorough discussion of terms of participation, codes of conduct, and emergency procedures are presented in Part III, Chapter 6, "Maximizing Safety and Security and Minimizing Risk in Education Abroad." These are the most binding aspects of the program and students should be required to sign off on them (parents or guardians should also sign if students are under 18 years old). These documents usually contain references to safety and security policies regarding student conduct, academic integrity, adapting to local conditions and customs, risks of study abroad, medical treatment, restrictions on travel within the host country or to countries in the region, withdrawal or program cancellation, insurance, emergency procedures, and limits of responsibility.

Good Practices *recommendations to parents, guardians, and families: Engage the participant in a thorough discussion of the safety and behavior issues, insurance needs, and emergency procedures related to living abroad.*

Chapter 6: Advising Students on Safety and Security Issues

Good Practice:
Students must be aware of local conditions and customs that may present health or safety risks when making daily choices and decisions, and they should promptly express any health or safety concerns to the program staff or other appropriate individuals before and during the program

Students should be made aware that they are responsible for all of their own decisions and actions, even if they find their decisions to be in conflict with the program. For example, should a student feel uncomfortable with a program activity because he or she does not feel safe, the student should discuss his or her concerns with the home campus representative and the resident director. It is important to emphasize that individuals have choices and do not need to "go along with the group." This should include any element of the program, from excursions to home-stay placements. Some campuses have instituted self-assertiveness training for students, to help enforce the concept that students do not have to do things that they do not want to do and to recognize when their behavior may put them in risky situations.

Any known health or safety risks that the students may encounter in the host country should be made known to the students in written materials and during orientation. Students should be made aware of when certain aspects of their behavior, or even their clothing or body language, could be construed as disrespectful. Additional suggestions concerning appropriate behavior are indicated in the "Security Precautions" section of this chapter.

Good Practice:
Students must accept responsibility for their own decisions and actions

One of the most important points that advisers, program administrators, and on-site staff can make to students is that they are responsible for their own decisions and actions. This should be emphasized through all stages of the abroad process, and reinforced through program policies and procedures. All staff working with students should familiarize themselves with student development theory. (See Part II, Chapter 1, "Advising Principles and Strategies.")

Good Practice:
Students must obey host-country laws

Programs should provide information about host-country laws that they know to be different from U.S. laws, and that may affect the experience of the program participants. Among the possible differences are laws pertaining to alcohol and drug purchase and use, the carrying of weapons (including mace and pepper spray), and photographing government installations. These differences should be introduced in predeparture information and elaborated upon during the on-site orientation. Students should be aware that they do not maintain the civil rights of a U.S. citizen while abroad, but are subject to the laws of whatever country they visit. They should also be aware of the severity of the consequences of violating certain laws.

Good Practice:
Students should behave in a manner that is respectful to the rights and well being of others, and encourage others to behave in a similar manner

Expectations for student behavior should be made clear through all phases of the education abroad process, including recruitment, advising, and on-campus and on-site orientations. These expectations should be codified in the "code of student conduct" that is signed by the participants. If students remain registered at the home institution, then the existing on-campus codes of student conduct and academic integrity can be enforced. Students should be made aware if they are subject to more than one code of conduct and if one set of regulations may supercede the others. For example, if a student is caught cheating at the host institution, they may fail a course there and could possibly be expelled. What would be the corresponding action at the home institution? Similarly, if a student is considered to be disrespectful to a faculty member at the host institution, and then expelled for that behavior, what would be the position of the home campus? What action would be taken if a student sexually harasses another program participant? It should be made clear to students, in writing, that there are circumstances in which they could be sent home.

The importance of both on-campus and on-site orientations that cover administrative details and responsibilities, in addition to cultural orientations that cover expectations for student behavior and how to show respect in the new culture, cannot be overstated. If students have a record on the home campus of violating the on-campus code of conduct, the student conduct office should evaluate whether or not the student has served his or her "sentence" for the violation and if the student is eligible to participate in the overseas program. Some programs have successfully used behavioral contracts that allow students to participate. A behavioral contract can also be used for situations in which a student's health must be monitored.

Good Practice:
Students are expected to avoid illegal drugs and excessive or irresponsible consumption of alcohol

Very few people think that all students will avoid alcohol if it is legal to drink at their age in the host country. It is therefore important to have policies in place that bear that reality in mind. As always, students should be counseled to act responsibly. They should be made aware of the possible consequences of drinking to excess, including that they are more likely to make poor decisions that could make them vulnerable to those who might want to prey on them (e.g., theft and sexual assault), and that they are much more likely to get into an accident, particularly involving motor vehicles. The training of on-site staff and resident directors should include the program's alcohol policy. Staff should not host events where unlimited amounts of alcohol are served.

Students should be cautioned against illegal drug use, and should be made aware of host-country laws and punishments.

Good Practice:
Students should be encouraged to follow the program policies for keeping program staff informed of their whereabouts and well being

The education abroad office and the overseas program representative need to make clear to

Chapter 6: Advising Students on Safety and Security Issues

students what their expectations are in terms of notification of student travel plans before, during, and after the program. Some programs may not require any notification of travel plans, and others may require full details whenever a student travels away from the program location. The policies of most programs probably lie somewhere in between, and may vary according to the level of tension surrounding local or international security concerns. Some institutions, such as the University of Michigan, have instituted an online registration system that makes it relatively easy for a student to report their travel plans. Travel plans can be registered through the U.S. Department of State Web site.

Good Practices *recommendations to parents, guardians, and families: Discuss with the participant any of his/her travel plans and activities that may be independent of the study abroad program.*

Good Practice:
Advise students to become familiar with the procedures for obtaining emergency health and legal system services in the host country

Resident directors should provide students with information about obtaining emergency medical and legal services in the host country. In cases where students are directly enrolled in an institution, and do not have a resident director, education abroad programs should steer students toward the services of the U.S. embassy or consulate, which can provide information on where to turn for legal advice and how to replace a lost or stolen passport, and which will have lists of health care professionals in the region. In addition, many insurance companies offer, as part of their policies, emergency services to travelers, which typically include a hotline that students can access for information on where to turn for assistance with an emergency situation. Students should be referred to the many resources for travelers available on the U.S. Department of State Web site, including *Tips for Students*. (See Part II, Chapter 5, "Health Issues and Advising Responsibilities," for information on emergency services.)

Safety Principles

This section contains suggestions on safety and security topics to include in program literature and orientation programming. In addition to the information provided here, a wide range of information on safety principles is available on NAFSA's Education Abroad Knowledge Community's (formerly known as SECUSSA) Web site and on the SAFETI Web site. The latter includes information adapted from the Peace Corps. (See Part II, Chapter 7, "Predeparture Orientation and Reentry Programming," and Part IV, Chapter 2, "The Overseas Program Cycle and Critical Components.")

Predeparture

Securing Documents

Students should be familiar with the U.S. Department of State Consular Information Sheet for their host country and any other countries they plan to visit. Predeparture orientation should include information on obtaining and securing important documents, such as a passport or any required visas. Students should make sure that they have signed their passport and filled out the emergency contact page. Students should be instructed to make extra copies of the passport data page and to leave copies of their itinerary, passport data page, and visa or visas with family or friends who can be contacted in the event of an emergency.

Protection Against Theft

Students should not bring more luggage than they can personally manage. They should be advised about obtaining travel gear like money belts and locks for their luggage. Expensive jewelry, watches, and clothing should be left at home and students should avoid carrying large sums of cash or unnecessary credit cards. Copies of credit card numbers should be left with someone at home and students should know the telephone numbers to call to report lost or stolen cards. Should students decide to bring an expensive piece of equipment such as a laptop computer, they should be advised to make sure that their parents' homeowner's insurance policy covers their personal possessions while abroad, or they should obtain appropriate insurance. If personal liability insurance is available in the host country, students should be advised to purchase it, since it can cover any number of situations in which the student may do harm to another person or someone's property. Some program sites recommend personal alarms among other safety precautions for women. In most cases, any recommended gear of that sort can be purchased on-site.

Travel Safety

Orientations should include a walk-through of the procedures required upon arrival at the airport in the host country, and getting to the program site or to the home-stay or program accommodations, if the student is not going to be met at the airport. Students should be advised about the documents they must have when entering the country and that they must keep such documents readily accessible with their passport. Advisers or past participants should describe to students what it will be like to go through immigration, collect their luggage, and meet up with whoever is picking them up. If students will not be met at the airport, they should be advised on how to choose safe transportation from the airport. Advisers should emphasize to students the importance of keeping an eye on their luggage, backpacks, and handbags. Students should be alerted to any specific airport conditions that could affect their safety, including the possibility of scams (e.g., offers of help with their bags or of rides from unlicensed taxis).

In-Country Safety Procedures

Road Safety

Road accidents are the number one cause of injury and death to U.S. citizens abroad. The Association for Safe International Road Travel (ASIRT) provides information for students and program providers concerning how to travel as safely as possible in many countries throughout the world. Students should either be provided with this information or they should be advised on how to obtain it. Students should be alerted to the safest modes of transportation in the general area where the program takes place and for travel throughout the country. Some students rent cars or actually purchase "junk" cars to use for the duration of their overseas experience. Program advisers and administrators must carefully consider how to talk with students about personal transportation, and determine what actions to take if they decide that purchasing or renting cars places the students at increased risk for injury.

Chapter 6: Advising Students on Safety and Security Issues

Women

Students should follow all of the regular safety precautions that they would take in a U.S. city, and they should be advised to not let their guard down at any time. Female students must be encouraged to not put themselves in situations that host-country women their age would not be willing to find themselves in. Again, an emphasis on the importance of good decision-making, thinking ahead, not making oneself likely to be a victim of a crime by using drugs or abusing alcohol, dressing in a culturally appropriate manner, and not being alone with people who may get the wrong message about what being alone means, are all important points to make to female program participants.

Sexual Harassment

Students should be informed of any cultural differences in behavior that may be perceived as sexual harassment. Unwanted male attention to female foreign students is quite common in some locations. However, students should let the program staff know of any behavior that crosses the line from annoyance to a situation where a student is fearful for his or her well being. Additionally, anyone employed by a U.S. institution should be informed of the on-campus or program sexual harassment policy and should be held to that standard. Students should be informed of how to file a sexual harassment complaint.

Recreational Hazards

It is of course impossible to cover all potential hazards involving personal recreation. However, common hazards should be shared with the students. Examples include the dangers of swimming or surfing in unmarked waters, or canoeing or white-water rafting in areas where emergency medical care and rescue systems are inadequate.

Emergency Procedures

The following information should be provided during the on-site orientation and in writing to participants, as applicable to the program site:

- Procedures for making local and international phone calls, and the best place for making them (if students do not have cell phones or phones in their rooms or the residence building).

- The local equivalent of 911, or how to phone the police, fire department, and hospital. When emergency phone service is not available, students should know how to explain to a driver how to get to an appropriate hospital.

- What to do in case of earthquakes or other natural disasters, or severe weather, if the program is located in a region prone to these activities.

- How to communicate basic needs in the local language, if the students are not fluent in that language. There are international symbols for some common needs.

SECURITY ISSUES

Security issues can be divided into two categories when advising students: (1) local or national situations that affect all citizens in the region in question, and (2) local, national, or international situations that may be targeted toward specific groups of people, specifically toward foreigners or U.S. citizens.

Host-Country Security Concerns

If there is a security situation in the host country, students should follow the advice that is given to local residents. Resident directors and students should monitor local and international news sources, including local newspapers, radio broadcasts, and local government emergency services and other internet news sites, on a regular basis. Students can be given information about reliable sources of information in their orientation programs (predeparture and on-site), and in their program handbooks. Information about the internet site for the local U.S. embassy or consulate should be included. U.S. embassy sites are a wealth of information for U.S. citizens residing abroad. In addition to registering with the embassy (which can be done individually or coordinated by the resident director), students should also register to receive announcements electronically from the embassy, if the embassy offers that service.

Periodic e-mail messages to students from resident directors and from study abroad advisers (these messages should be coordinated for consistency), or local briefings, can serve as reminders to students about establishing good habits in terms of staying abreast of the news and knowing what to do in the case of an emergency. Examples of emergencies of this type include natural or manmade disasters, disruption to transportation services or public utilities, university strikes, civil unrest, health epidemics, and accidents involving planes or mass transit. Students should be advised that they should always get in touch with their families as soon as possible after such an event, even if they were no where near the incident, so that their families will not worry about their well being. Students should carry a set of emergency contact phone numbers with them that includes contact information for the resident director and host university, home campus numbers, and the U.S. embassy or consulate. Cards with emergency information should be provided by the home campus and usually are provided by the education abroad program as well. Students should add contact information for insurance companies and any other information that would be critical in an emergency situation.

Security advisories that are general in nature are familiar to U.S. citizens now that the United States has its own domestic system of alerting the public to the possibility of a terrorist action. The public is made aware through radio and television news broadcasts of the level of threat that is perceived by the government, and the steps that the public is advised to take to prepare for a potential incident. Individuals are reminded to be aware of their surroundings and to report any suspicious activity. As general preparation for any kind of emergency, households are advised to have extra provisions on hand, to have extra funds and copies of important documents, and to have a communication plan in place so that family members will know how to contact one another and where to meet up should it not be possible to communicate with one another.

Preparedness at the overseas site is similar to preparedness in the United States. However, it may be the case that students are used to letting their families and colleges or universities concern themselves with most aspects of the students' security. As with all aspects of participating in an education abroad program, advisers must emphasize that the students, and the students alone, have the primary responsibility for their well being.

Therefore, taking the time to think through and establish emergency plans early in their stay abroad, is an important responsibility for all students.

U.S. Department of State Notices

Should the government have knowledge of a potential threat to U.S. citizens residing abroad, the U.S. Department of State will issue either a Worldwide Caution, or a Public Announcement or Travel Warning for a specific country or region. Education abroad advisers and resident directors are expected to monitor these notices and should register to receive them electronically from the U.S. Department of State. Students must then be alerted to these notices, preferably by sending students the full announcement. During orientation, there must be a discussion as to the nature of these notices, so that students are not shocked to receive them, especially without the proper context in which to read them. But, given that Worldwide Cautions tend to be updated frequently, it is important to make sure that students realize that they should take such notices seriously, and that the notices serve as good reminders for students to review their personal and program emergency procedures.

Precautions

Advisers and program administrators have a responsibility to do their utmost to provide a secure and unthreatening environment in which students may learn, but that goal must be balanced with the reality that the possibility of terrorism exists both in the United States and abroad. Therefore, programs and host universities must develop appropriate policies and procedures and contingency plans with this reality in mind, and students must be prepared to abide by those policies and plans. The following list of safety precautions for students abroad is adapted from the U.S. Department of State Web site and the University of Pennsylvania handbook, *The Practical Penn Abroad*.

- Keep a low profile and try not to make yourself conspicuous by dress, speech, or behavior in ways that might identify you as a targeted individual.

- Avoid crowds, protest groups, or other potentially volatile situations, as well as restaurants and entertainment places where Americans are known to congregate.

- Be wary of receiving unexpected packages and stay clear of unattended baggage or parcels in airports, train stations, or other areas of uncontrolled public access.

- Report to the responsible authority any suspicious persons loitering around residence or instructional facilities, or following you; keep your residence area locked; use common sense in divulging information to strangers about your study program and your fellow students.

- Register upon arrival at the U.S. consulate or embassy having jurisdiction over the location of your foreign study.

- Make sure the resident director, host family, or foreign university official who is assigned the responsibility for your welfare always knows where and how to contact you in an emergency, and your schedule and itinerary if you are traveling, even if only overnight.

- Develop a plan for regular telephone or e-mail contact with your family, so that

Part II: Campus Advising

in times of heightened political tensions, you will be able to communicate with them directly about your safety and well being.

As a regular part of safety preparedness, students should carry the standard and emergency phone numbers, and the e-mail addresses, of the following people and offices with them at all times (as applicable):

- Resident director
- International programs office of the host institution
- International programs office of the home campus
- U.S. embassy or consulate for any country that the student visits
- Family members and other personal contacts (home and work)
- Travel agent

Summary

Advisers, program administrators, and on-site staff must emphasize to students the importance of taking responsibility for their program preparations and for their personal actions throughout their education abroad experiences. This is critical not only to their development as adults, but also to their safety and well being throughout the program. In retrospect, many returning students say that one of the major benefits of the abroad experience was the personal growth that came as a result of taking responsibility for their own decisions and well being throughout their stay abroad.

CHAPTER 7

Predeparture Orientation and Reentry Programming

Contributors: Stacey Woody Thebodo, Linda E. Marx

Education abroad advisers and administrators have a responsibility to prepare student sojourners to make the most of their international experiences. It is now widely accepted in the field that the education abroad experience is a continuum, and that advisers play an important pedagogical role before, during, and after the time spent overseas. The education abroad experience begins when students first consider going overseas. When students attend advising sessions, they start the process of learning general information about the host country or city and its people, and the education abroad process in general. Predeparture orientation sessions give a needed perspective to the planning process, and help prepare students for the experience. Reentry programming, a vital part of the education abroad continuum, facilitates the reflection aspect of the students' learning process. Well-designed predeparture and reentry programs assist students in the development of adjustment skills and intercultural competencies and therefore may make the difference between the success and failure of a sojourner's education abroad experience.

This chapter focuses on practical guidelines for advisers conducting predeparture orientation and reentry programming, and provides some theoretical background for programming. Advisers should consult Part I, Chapter 8, "Technology and Education Abroad;" Part II, Chapter 1, "Advising Principles and Strategies;" Part II, Chapter 5, "Health Issues and Advising Responsibilities;" Part II, Chapter 6, "Advising Students on Safety and Security Issues;" and Part III, Chapter 5, "Program Assessment and Evaluation." On-site orientation and reentry preparation are discussed in Part IV, Chapter 2, "The Overseas Program Cycle and Critical Components."

PREDEPARTURE ORIENTATION

Goals and Objectives

The goals for predeparture sessions, and the design of the program (including the format, content, and process), must be established in advance. A balance must exist between the practical and the philosophical, and between culture-general and culture-specific issues.

Part II: Campus Advising

Orientation sessions often relieve many concerns of student sojourners and their families. Staff members can be introduced and students can meet one another. During these sessions, students will learn to make effective plans and begin to temper some of their own potentially false expectations. Activities should safely and ethically allow the students to become more aware of themselves as cultural individuals, and to learn how the study abroad experience may affect them. Well-planned sessions will save some of the education abroad staff's precious time, because questions are generally answered in a group format, and important forms may be explained and completed immediately.

Major goals for predeparture orientation are to

- provide essential, practical information;

- motivate student sojourners to learn more about the host culture, and about themselves and their home culture, prior to departure;

- familiarize the student sojourners with the process of cross-cultural adjustment (including reentry) and the concept of culture, cross-cultural adaptability skills, and developing intercultural understanding;

- help student sojourners gain a better comprehension of world issues and their role as global citizens; and

- assist in reviewing each student's overall objectives and how the overseas experience fits into his or her long-term personal, professional, and academic goals.

Predeparture Program Design

Content

The program content needs to fit the goals for orientation in a creative way. A thoughtful agenda should include academic and practical issues. If orientation sessions will be provided at the study abroad location, it is beneficial to determine what topics will be covered abroad, in order to avoid duplication and so advisers can be sure to include in their hand-outs any material that students will not receive on-site. Advisers should strive to provide complete, current, and unbiased information in their orientation program.

It can be beneficial to enlist others on campus who may be available to help with orientations. For example, area specialists, former Fulbright participants, or Peace Corps returnees from the faculty or staff, may be willing to assist with history and culture segments. On-campus health care workers or local health department professionals, counselors, or financial aid personnel may be resources to tap for various content areas of predeparture sessions. Former education abroad participants and international students and scholars are excellent resources both for topic-specific panels and to answer students' questions.

Most seasoned professionals agree that it is a good idea to require that students attend the predeparture orientation sessions. This, however, can be challenging because advisers must institute a penalty (that they are willing to enforce) for students who do not attend. The most severe consequence, of course, would be to prohibit a student from participating in a program if he or she fails to attend mandatory predeparture sessions. Another option would be to require successful completion of a writing assignment for students who choose not to attend. In any case, it shows a lack of seriousness and commitment on the part of the student who does not attend orientation. Advisers may wish to provide some sort of enticement to boost attendance at orientation sessions, such as giving out the predeparture packets and forms at the meeting (rather than sending them beforehand), and, of course, offering snacks at the meeting.

Format

Decisions on the design and format of the predeparture orientation will depend on budget, staffing, and time limitations (the adviser's and those of the student sojourners), as well as the institution's educational philosophy. There are ethical issues to consider in preparing for orientation sessions, in particular, the need for appropriate professional training, planning, and preparation. Predeparture programs can be designed that are only one or two sessions in length. Some more ambitious approaches are to offer weekly sessions over a whole semester, a weekend retreat, a complete academic course, or to offer Web-based orientations (see "Sample Orientation Programs" below). If the home institution allows students to participate in many different types of overseas programs in various locations, including programs operated by outside sponsors, advisers should consider holding some sessions that are general in nature, along with others that are country- or region-specific, or even topic-specific (e.g., women abroad; being an ethnic minority abroad; gay, lesbian, bisexual, and transgendered issues abroad; and religion abroad). This approach will save time and repetition, provide large- and small-group interactions, and will provide the students with a comprehensive orientation.

In considering the format for predeparture orientation sessions, advisers can consider intercultural training techniques in two dimensions: (1) didactic versus experiential, and (2) culture-specific versus culture-general (Cargile and Giles 1995). Bearing in mind the first dimension, didactic versus experiential, advisers should consider pedagogy (methods to impart knowledge) and andragogy (the process used to train adult learners) (Arnold and McClure 1996). Because students are often caught up in the practical details of study abroad during orientation, perhaps the use of adult-learner techniques (i.e., where the focus is on life tasks and situations, and the instructional format is group-oriented and participatory), mixed with traditional pedagogical techniques (i.e., where the focus is on content and data, and is instructor dependent), will facilitate a viable, real-world focus that will keep the sojourners active and interested and will enable the learning process.

Experiential learning activities that can be employed in predeparture orientations include icebreakers, simulations, role-playing, films, video clips, games, and field exercises. Many resources are available through NAFSA (see NAFSA's Web-based *Intercultural Activity Toolkit*) and the Intercultural Press. The Peace Corps and the School for International Training (SIT) are also excellent sources for experiential learning activities. Advisers should be aware that since experiential activities require more active participation and risk-taking for students, advisers may encounter some learner resistance. However, most advisers and participants find that using experiential techniques holds students' interest and provides learning that will stay with the students for the long-term.

Providing time at the end of the session for evaluation of the predeparture orientation will help facilitators see what is effective and what is not for future sessions. Sufficient time for questions and answers should also be allotted.

Part II: Campus Advising

Sample Orientation Programs

Evening Session

If students will be studying abroad on several different programs, it may be beneficial to hold several shorter sessions on different evenings, with each session focusing on a specific country or region. With careful planning and facilitation, each session can be done in one-and-a-half to two hours, and still be quite effective. It is recommended that advisers carefully select a few articulate and enthusiastic education abroad returnees to attend each session, to contribute to discussions and share their perspectives and experiences.

A sample two-hour evening session might be broken down as follows:

1. Welcome, introductions, review of agenda and purpose of orientation;
   7:00 p.m. – 7:05 p.m.

2. Practical details and logistics;
   7:05 p.m. – 7:30 p.m.

3. Small group activity;
   7:30 p.m. – 8:30 p.m.
   Topic: Addressing the Issues. The large group can be broken down into smaller groups of five to ten students. Each group can be assigned a different topic area (e.g., academics abroad, extracurricular activities, or how to get involved in the culture, health and safety, cross-cultural adjustment, identity issues abroad). Groups can spend five to seven minutes listing on a flip chart the issues related to their topics and any questions they may have (e.g., for the topic of academics abroad, one issue may be the grading systems used abroad). Groups can then bring their lists back to the large group, and go over the lists one topic at a time, for discussion and feedback from the adviser and study abroad returnees. This exercise is a good way to cover many different topics in a format that provides the opportunity for interaction and allows the adviser to cover all the necessary information. Another alternative for covering all of these topics in a one-hour time frame is to present a panel of returnees who can speak about the topics. The education abroad adviser can facilitate and contribute information as appropriate.

4. Short experiential activity;
   8:30 p.m. – 8:50 p.m.
   The activity should address one of the following areas: cross-cultural adaptation, value clarification, being an American abroad, identifying stereotypes, and so on.

5. Questions, concluding remarks, and evaluation of the orientation;
   8:50 p.m. – 9:00 p.m.

Full-Day Predeparture Orientation

A full-day orientation can be very successful if advisers have the time, budget, and staffing to devote to the event. Full-day orientations may focus on a specific country or region, or may focus on culture in general. One-day sessions can also be designed for large groups of students going to many different destinations abroad, with time allowed during the day for breaking up into smaller groups based on study abroad destination.

A sample full-day orientation might be broken down as follows:

1. Arrivals, registration, coffee, and bagels; 8:00 a.m. – 8:15 a.m.

2. Welcome, review of agenda, and objectives for orientation; 8:15 a.m. – 8:30 a.m.

3. Ice breaker; 8:30 a.m.– 8:45 a.m.

4. Practical details and logistics; 8:45 a.m. – 9:30 a.m.

5. Health, safety, and emergencies, possibly with a health professional as a guest speaker; 9:30 a.m. – 10:15 a.m.

6. Coffee break; 10:15 a.m. – 10:30 a.m.

7. Academic issues, including students' expectations, how students benefit from a different academic system, and so on; 10:30 a.m. – 11:30 a.m.

8. Identity issues, including discussions of gender, race, sexual orientation, and so on; this topic could be addressed in a large group setting or by interest group; 11:30 a.m. – 12:00 p.m.

9. Lunch; possibly seating participants with returnees, in groups based on region or country; 12:00 p.m. – 1:00 p.m.

10. Experiential activity or cross-cultural simulation; 1:00 p.m. – 2:00 p.m.

11. Processing activity and introduction to culture, possibly including a lecture or video, or both; 2:00 p.m. – 2:30 p.m.

12. Cross-cultural adjustment, including reentry; 2:30 p.m. – 3:00 p.m.

13. Coffee break; 3:00 p.m. – 3:15 p.m.

14. Discussion of how to learn about the host culture, including resources to consult prior to departure, techniques of observation and reflection, the use of journaling, and so on; 3:15 p.m. – 3:45 p.m.

15. Break out into smaller groups by region or country to address cultural issues, political and historical awareness, customs, academic differences, daily life, and so on; this portion of the day could take the form of a question-and-answer session with returnees or student panels organized by country or region; 3:45 p.m. – 4:45 p.m.

16. Remaining questions as a large group; 4:45 p.m. – 5:15 p.m.

17. Concluding remarks and evaluation of the orientation; 5:15 p.m. – 5:30 p.m.

Part II: Campus Advising

Academic Course

Conducting an academic course on predeparture is ideal in many ways, as courses can cover every predeparture topic in an in-depth manner. Predeparture courses, which are often taught by faculty in conjunction with education abroad staff, may include lectures, videos, experiential activities, and cross-cultural theory. Just as in any academic course, students are required to write term papers, exams, and other assignments. Predeparture courses can train students to write analytically about their cross-cultural experiences, which can aid them in analyzing cultural interactions and critical incidents and can prepare them for journal writing. For more information on using writing as a tool for cultural learning and helping students learn to write about their cross-cultural experiences, see *Writing Across Culture: An Introduction to Study Abroad and the Writing Process* (Wagner and Magistrale 1995), *Studying Abroad/Learning Abroad: An Abridged Edition of The Whole World Guide to Culture Learning* (Hess 1997), and *Study Abroad: How to Get the Most Out of Your Experience* (Dowell and Mirsky 2003). There are several campuses that have implemented excellent predeparture courses, such as the orientation course taught by Dr. Bruce La Brack at the University of the Pacific, the content of which can be found on the SAFETI Web site. A predeparture course taught by Dr. John Greisberger at Ohio State University, titled "Intercultural Experiential Learning," can be found on the Ohio State University's Office of International Education Web site. The Kalamazoo Program in Intercultural Communication (KPIC) of Kalamazoo College can be found on the Web site of the College's Center for International Programs.

Web-Based Orientations

Putting interactive orientation materials and even complete predeparture courses on the Web is a cutting-edge practice that several institutions have successfully implemented. Online predeparture and reentry modules developed by the Peace Corps are available on the SAFETI Web site, along with "What's Up With Culture," an online resource for education abroad students. The Montana State University Arabic instruction program is a pioneer in the creation of Web-based orientations. Web-based interactive predeparture materials or courses, or both, have been developed by the Office of International Studies and Programs at Central Washington University, the International Center at Macalester College, the Center for Study Abroad and Interdepartmental Programs at the University of Rochester, and International Academic Programs at the University of Wisconsin Madison. Considering today's computer-savvy generation of college students, it is useful if predeparture handbooks and any pertinent predeparture forms or handouts are easily accessible online. Some institutions have gone a step further, including a required online component to orientation that covers more of the logistics and nuts-and-bolts of predeparture, and spending in-person orientation sessions covering more substantive topics such as cross-cultural adjustment and skills. Several institutions have developed complete Web-based orientation courses, which can be useful if there is a problem with student attendance at regular orientation meetings or if program participants come from several different colleges and universities. Web-based orientations can include compulsory quizzes and homework and even online discussions and student presentations. Programs can then register students

Chapter 7: Predeparture Orientation and Reentry Programming

as having completed required assignments. Popular instructional software programs include Blackboard and WebCT. Another possible medium for predeparture materials is an interactive CD-ROM. (Note that the use of any type of technology or software requires the assistance of the campus technology support staff, as well as an institutional commitment to renew software site licenses.) Many professionals agree that computer-based orientations should not completely replace in-person sessions, but Web-based material can provide an invaluable supplement to other predeparture activities, and can help ensure that students are actually reading the materials provided for them. (See Part I, Chapter 8, "Technology and Education Abroad," for further information.)

Practical Concerns

It is recommended that advisers incorporate all of the practical predeparture details into handouts or a predeparture handbook (and possibly into a Web page or other interactive medium, as mentioned), so that students will have the information in writing for future reference. Regardless of what format is chosen for orientation sessions, advisers should cover certain practical concerns, as outlined in the following paragraphs:

Logistics

- Passports and student visas
- International and local travel arrangements
- Packing and luggage issues
- International Student Identity Cards (ISIC) and rail or travel passes
- Housing and board
- Communications such as phone, e-mail, and regular mail
- Banking and finances
- Campus-specific issues such as maintaining student status, how to register for classes and arrange for housing after returning to the United States, financial aid issues, how and when to keep in touch with the home campus, and graduation arrangements

Health and Safety

For more information regarding health and safety issues for programs abroad, consult Part II, Chapter 5, "Health Issues and Advising Responsibilities," and Part II, Chapter 6, "Advising Students on Safety and Security Concerns."

- Predeparture medical and dental check-ups
- Resources for determining required or recommended immunizations for the host country (e.g., the local health department, the Centers for Disease Control, and the home campus health center)
- Prescriptions and over-the-counter medications
- HIV/AIDS and sexually transmitted disease information
- Medical insurance coverage
- Alcohol use and abuse issues
- First-aid kits
- Information on illnesses endemic to specific regions

Part II: Campus Advising

- Food and water purification procedures
- Special student health needs and how they relate to services available or conditions in the host country

Each sojourner should be encouraged to confer with his or her family physician or personal health care facility in regard to health issues. Sojourners need to be aware that traveling abroad is not going to cure any preexisting physical and emotional health issues. In fact, travel often exacerbates problems such as eating disorders, smoking, alcohol and drug abuse, and other health problems. Students should honestly assess their own health needs, particularly if they have allergies, disabilities, dietary requirements, or are undergoing psychological treatments, special exercise regimens, or physical therapy, or have other needs. It is vital that students share these needs as early as possible with the appropriate education abroad professional. An appropriate overseas doctor, health care practitioner, or self-help group may need to be identified before travel begins. In some cases, an abroad destination other than the one the student has chosen may be more appropriate given a student's health requirements, or, possibly, an education abroad experience may not be in a student's best interest at that particular time.

Predeparture orientations should include information about

- student responsibility for safe behavior,
- safety precautions students should take while at the program location and while traveling abroad,
- overseas emergency contacts and procedures,
- the U.S. Department of State and its resources,
- road travel safety,
- gender, race, sexual orientation, and religious stereotypes, and tolerance issues,
- women's safety issues and sexual harassment,
- dating and relationship norms in the host country,
- local crime statistics and laws,
- appropriate dress in social and academic settings,
- regional climate and weather conditions,
- political tensions and social and environmental issues,
- liability waiver and release forms, and
- program cancellation policies.

Academic Information

It is easy for students to get bogged down with the practical details of predeparture, and they may need to be reminded that if they are going overseas and earning credit, their education abroad experience is in fact *study* abroad and is fundamentally an academic experience. Therefore, it is crucial to include discussions of credit transfer, differences in academic requirements and policies, and language learning in the predeparture program.

Credit Transfer Issues. It is essential that advisers review any forms students may need to complete and inform students on how to get preapproval for their courses abroad. Advisers should also review course load and grade requirements, as well as procedures for transferring credit after students return to the United States.

Academic Differences Abroad. Preparing students for the sometimes vastly different academic setting they will find in the host country is a vital part of predeparture preparation. Students should be informed about the underlying educational philosophy of the host country, to provide a cultural context and reduce judgmental attitudes about differences. Most foreign educational institutions place more responsibility on individual students for their own learning than is the case in the United States. U.S. students enrolling directly in local universities will find this to be especially true, but even students enrolling in American-sponsored programs abroad will typically also be given more personal responsibility than they would on the home campus, as many programs include courses taught by local faculty. Advisers can prepare students to thrive in an unfamiliar academic environment by preparing them for the differences they may encounter. For instance, students can expect less frequent assessment (e.g., fewer daily homework assignments, quizzes, papers, etc.), and it is likely that a final exam or paper will have more emphasis abroad than it does on the home-campus classroom. Benefits of a system with less oversight include increased student responsibility and, perhaps, more academic freedom to pursue areas of interest to the individual student. Depending on the size of the student's home institution, he or she may need to be prepared for a different style of teaching (e.g., large lectures as opposed to small seminar classes). Preparing students for differences in faculty and student interactions, as well as the availability (or lack thereof) of different educational resources abroad (e.g., libraries, computer facilities, etc.) can help give students realistic expectations for their academic experiences. Students should also be educated about cultural aspects of conducting research abroad. At the predeparture program, study abroad returnees can explain the details of the academic program they attended and how they profited from experiencing a different educational system.

Language Learning. Many students choose to study abroad to improve their language proficiency. Indeed, language acquisition is one of the primary arguments often touted in support of education abroad. As such, it is important to address language learning in predeparture orientation. During predeparture meetings, advisers can begin to educate students about learning strategies they can employ to make the most out of their language-learning experiences abroad (e.g., in-class instruction and social and cultural interactions). The Fall 1998 issue of *Frontiers: The Interdisciplinary Journal of Study Abroad* was devoted entirely to the topic of Language Learning in a Study Abroad Context, and is available on the *Frontiers* Web site. Another resource for facilitating student learning abroad is *Maximizing Study Abroad: A Student's Guide to Strategies for Language and Culture Learning and Use* (Paige et al. 2002).

Cross-Cultural Issues

Culture is a major sociological concept that includes the standardized ways of feeling, thinking, and acting that persons acquire as members of a society. Culture has been defined differently by various academic disciplines. More in-depth information on definitions of culture may be found in *Learning Across Cultures* (Althen 1994), *Communicating with Strangers: An Approach to Intercultural Communication 3rd Edition* (Gudykunst and Kim 1997), and *Among the Interculturalists: An Emerging Profession and Its Packaging of Knowledge* (Dahlen 1997). Predeparture programs should begin by helping students to become aware of the features of culture (e.g., individualism versus collectivism, low-context [specific] versus high-context [diffuse] cultures, and monochronic [sequential] versus polychronic [synchronic] time-oriented cultures, etc.). Only then can the sojourner deal with examples of critical incidents and become knowledgeable enough to analyze intercultural interactions. More information on teaching about culture and the purpose of cross-cultural training programs can be found in *Improving Intercultural Interactions: Modules for Cross-Cultural Training Programs* (Brislin and Yoshida 1994). Edward T. Hall's books, such as *Beyond Culture* and *The Silent Language* are also good resources for teaching students about the various aspects of culture.

An effective way to introduce the concept of culture is the iceberg analogy: an iceberg has a small part above the water and a larger part below the surface of the water, comparable to culture having visible, observable aspects as well as a large component that is invisible, or below the surface (Weaver 1986).

Cultural issues are bound to arise early on in orientation sessions, even when the adviser is discussing practical and logistical details. For example, discussions of housing, academics, and communications all introduce cultural issues and necessitate an understanding of cultural context. It is impossible for advisers to cover all culture-specific issues during orientation, especially if students are going abroad to different locations; however, bringing up some of these particulars will allow students to see that these seemingly minor details will be a large part of their daily lives abroad. Students should reflect on the desired outcomes of the program and their role in achieving these objectives.

Cross-cultural Adjustment. Starting in predeparture orientation and continuing through the reentry process, advisers should educate students about cross-cultural adjustment and the concept of culture shock. Adjustment, which can cause great anxiety for students, is of a multidimensional nature, being both a task and an individually based process of change. When students cross cultures and interact with individuals who have been conditioned by a different culture, and when they encounter situations for which they do not have a set of ready-made definitions, they may experience feelings of insecurity, frustration, and uncertainty. Students may meet cultural differences that will be difficult to understand and which may cause reactions ranging from mild discomfort to deep disturbance (it is important to note that culture shock symptoms can initially be confused with mental health issues, and sometimes mental health issues that had not been previously identified can surface when a student is abroad). These feelings usually last until the students have lived in the foreign culture long enough to become accustomed to the new environment. There are a number of cross-cultural adjustment models; it may be useful to share one or more of these models with students during both predeparture and reentry training. One of the most commonly known theories is the "W-Curve" model of cultural adjustment (Gullahorn and Gullahorn 1963) which describes the emotional highs and lows experienced during the entire cross-cultural adjustment process in the shape of a "W." With any discussion of adjustment, advisers should take care to emphasize that culture shock is normal and to be expected, and not set students up to expect a negative experience. For a discussion of the W-Curve hypothesis (which includes reentry), see Art Freedman's chapter "A Strategy for Managing 'Cultural' Transitions: Reentry from Training" in *Cross-Cultural Reentry: A Book of Readings* (1986).

During predeparture and reentry it is very important to discuss with students the common signs and symptoms of culture shock: sadness, loneliness, aches and pains or other health problems, insomnia or the desire to sleep too much, depression, anger or irritability, resentment of cultural differences, feelings of inadequacy, extreme linguistic difficulties, and the feeling that minor tasks are overwhelming. A description of the process and symptoms of culture shock can be found in studyabroad.com's online handbook, *It's Your World: Student's Guide to Education Abroad.*

Have students brainstorm about the following ways to cope with and combat the stress produced by culture shock:

- Establish simple goals.
- Be patient.
- Maintain confidence.
- Look for help and establish support systems.
- Remember that the problem is not with the host culture but with oneself.
- Do not be negative or critical.
- Keep an open mind.
- Stay involved with the culture and do not become isolated.
- Practice a familiar sport or hobby or develop a new interest.
- Maintain a sense of humor.

Remember that although culture shock can sometimes be difficult, it can leave students with deeper insights and greater tolerance, as well as broader perspectives.

Predeparture sessions should also emphasize learning cross-cultural adaptability skills, such as personal autonomy, flexibility, perceptual acuity, and emotional confidence, as well as developing intercultural understanding and, ideally, ethnorelativism. Milton Bennett describes a continuum of stages of personal growth through which individuals progress in order to develop intercultural sensitivity. Using this developmental continuum, which begins with ethnocentrism and moves toward ethnorelativism, one can diagnose individuals' understanding and interpretation of cultural difference (1986). Beneficial experiential activities to help students acquire cross-cultural skills include those that help them develop empathy and sensitivity to and respect for differences, seek value clarification, and increase the capacity for self-reflection.

Personal and Cultural Identity. Education abroad advisers should be knowledgeable about student development, part of which includes identity development, in order to understand what stages or phases students are going through prior to and during the education abroad experience. Advisers can assist students in their progression through the various developmental stages by beginning to address identity issues with students in predeparture orientation. This task can be challenging in that students often do not see the importance of examining their own identities in relation to their upcoming cross-cultural experience. It can be useful for students to generate a list of different aspects of identity (e.g., gender, race and ethnicity, sexual orientation, class, religion, learning style, health issues). Advisers can then facilitate a discussion (and invite education abroad returnees to join in) of how different aspects of students' identities will affect and be affected by their experiences abroad. (See Part II, Chapter 1, "Advising Principles and Strategies.")

Culture is also a vital component of identity. Therefore, it is essential that students consider the concept of being an American (or whatever their cultural background is) abroad. For discussion, it may be helpful to use the list of commonly held American values developed by Kohls (1996), or Stewart and Bennett's *American Cultural Patterns: A Cross-Cultural Perspective* (1972). Students should be encouraged to think about and discuss how American values may be different from, and in some cases diametrically opposed to, those of the host culture. For the education abroad experience to be successful, it is essential that students reflect on the cultural baggage they are taking abroad with them and how it will influence their cross-cultural encounters. There are many experiential activities that advisers can facilitate in orientation sessions to address cultural identity and being an American abroad. Examples of these activities, as well as articles and other resources for helping students to examine their cultural or American identities, can be found in *Developing Intercultural Awareness: A Cross-Cultural Training Handbook* (Kohls and Knight 1994), "Body Ritual Among the Nacirema," *American Anthropologist* (Miner 1956), and *Manual of Structured Experiences for Cross-Cultural Learning* (Weeks et al. 1979).

Advisers should be prepared to address the topic of anti-American sentiment. Returnees can discuss their experiences with anti-American attitudes, and participants may find it helpful to brainstorm strategies for dealing with anti-American slurs and comments. A discussion of stereotype awareness can also be beneficial, so that students are conscious of the unflattering stereotypes of Americans that exist around the world.

Another component of the cultural-identity discussion should be to encourage students to expand their knowledge of the United States. Students are often astounded to discover that their peers around the world are much more knowledgeable about U.S. politics and history than U.S. college students tend to be. Moreover, students will be better qualified to make comparisons with the host culture if they are well informed about their own country.

Other cultural topics that should be included in predeparture orientations are the concepts of multiculturalism and responsibility in an interdependent world. Students should be prepared for living in a multicultural society abroad and in a heterogeneous setting; advisers may choose to address this issue in a discussion or activity about stereotype awareness. The issue of student responsibility in an interdependent world will inevitably raise ethical and political questions, which the adviser should be prepared to address.

Country- and Region-Specific Issues. In country-specific orientation sessions, advisers will have more time and will be better able to focus student interest on context issues. If time is limited and country-specific sessions are not possible, it may be best to emphasize why students should take the initiative to gain country-specific knowledge and how they may go about getting it. As previously mentioned, case studies, readings, videos, films, slides, experiential techniques, and presentations by experts, returnees, and international students or scholars can be very effective. The following information should be covered either during orientation or through the sojourner's own research: land and climate, history and art, population, predominant languages, religions, attitudes and appearance, customs and courtesies, patterns of daily and family life, dating, sexual norms, marriage, gender- and age-specific roles, food and diet, recreation and holidays, business, labor and government, foreign relations, transportation and communication, and education and health care systems. These topics are typically covered, if only superficially, by "CultureGrams," (published by Axiom Press) that may be purchased

Chapter 7: Predeparture Orientation and Reentry Programming

for education abroad libraries. The United States "CultureGram" may open students' eyes to assumptions made about the United States, and help them become aware of the nature of stereotypes. Another resource, the U.S. Department of State "Background Notes," is political in nature but may be insightful nonetheless. Advisers can also encourage students to conduct internet and library research on the host country, and interview international students or scholars who are from the country where the students will be studying. Ideally, before they leave, students should also have taken or be encouraged to take one or more courses that focus on the region to which they are traveling.

Students who are studying abroad in developing countries have unique preparation needs and may require a more extensive orientation. Areas of discussion may include issues facing developing nations, ethical questions regarding development, understanding and living with poverty, class issues and the variance between rich and poor, family and gender roles, environmental issues, and more. Again, it can be useful to rely on returnees and faculty with expertise in these areas. (See Part II, Chapter 4, "Whole-World Study.")

REENTRY PROGRAMMING

Reentry, which is sometimes referred to as return culture shock or reverse culture shock, is defined as the sometimes difficult and often unexpected transition process through which students progress when they return to the home culture after an education abroad experience. Reentry programming is an important component in the education abroad continuum and should not be neglected by the education abroad office.

Goals and objectives for on-campus reentry programs include the following:

- To assist students in their readjustment to the home culture and to college or university life after studying abroad.

- To help students learn to reflect on and articulate what they learned from their education abroad experience.

- To facilitate opportunities for students to incorporate their international experiences into their lives at home, both academically and personally.

- To help students identify ways they may use and market their international experience in the future.

Reentry Theory and Common Issues

As mentioned in the predeparture section of this chapter, there are a number of culture shock models, many of which include the reentry phase of adjustment. Just as during orientation sessions, it can be helpful to share different culture shock diagrams with students in reentry sessions as well.

One of the main factors that influences the intensity and nature of reentry difficulties for returned students is the unexpectedness of having to readjust to the home culture after living abroad. Most returnees do not expect to experience adjustment difficulties after their return home, whereas when they traveled abroad they were most likely prepared to experience some discomfort in making adjustments to the host culture.

The reentry literature suggests several useful hypotheses. (A thorough review of reentry literature is included in Nan M. Sussman's article "Reentry Research and Training: Methods and Implications" in the *International Journal of Intercultural Relations* [1986].) First, for many returnees, reentry shock is more severe and debilitating than the initial adjustment to the host culture. Second, those students who are the most successful in their adjustment and integration abroad often experience more severe reentry challenges than individuals who do not adapt well overseas. Some research, however, appears to contradict this hypothesis, suggesting that individuals who adapt well abroad also adapt well when they return home. The former theory, however, may be more applicable to first-time returnees having more difficulties, whereas subsequent reentry transitions may prove to be smoother and easier. A third hypothesis is that readjustment challenges can be related to the length of time spent abroad and how different students' host cultures are from their home cultures.

It may help students to know that the reentry process is normal and that it is common for students to experience an adjustment phase after they return from an abroad experience. Advisers should discuss with students the common issues that all education abroad returnees face, including personal growth and change, the acquisition of new knowledge and skills, a change in relationships with family and friends, lifestyle changes, feeling critical of the United States or American culture, decisions about careers and postgraduation plans, fear of losing the "international experience," and other emotional issues.

Personal Growth and Change

Students are likely to have experienced some challenges to their beliefs, attitudes, values, and worldviews while they were immersed in another culture. They also probably experienced more personal freedom and autonomy, and perhaps more academic independence. They may have experienced changes and challenges to their identity (see the predeparture section for a discussion of the aspects of identity). Students are likely to be more mature, self-confident, and self-reliant than they were before their abroad experiences. After returning home, students can have difficulty reconciling their new self with their old self, and they may experience feelings of alienation and loss of identity.

New Knowledge and Skills

Just as students' attitudes and worldviews probably changed while they were abroad, they also developed new knowledge and skills, such as learning to find their way around a new city, acting in a culturally appropriate manner, conversing about new subjects, and perhaps, developing foreign-language ability. Other new competencies may include knowledge about an academic field of study, and research and problem-solving strategies. Some returnees may feel frustrated if they perceive that their new skills are of little use in the home culture.

Changed Relationships with Family and Friends

Some returnees find that the most difficult reentry issue to deal with is the lack of interest that friends and family may have in hearing about their international experiences. Some returnees express irritation if they feel that their family and friends did not change at all while they were away. Moreover, some friends and family members may expect students to be the same people they were before they went abroad, and it can be difficult for some students to deal with this expectation. The School for International Training offers an online handbook, *Surviving Reentry: A Handbook for Parents of Study Abroad Students Returning Home* (Cavallero 2003), that provides student and parent perspectives and provides helpful insight into what parents can do to assist their children in the reentry process.

Lifestyle Adjustments

Returnees may have difficulty adjusting to a faster-paced lifestyle than the one they grew accustomed to abroad. This can leave students feeling out-of-control and unsettled, and they may have difficulty adjusting to the academic routine at the home school.

Feeling Critical of American Society

Travel abroad can open students' eyes to values, customs, and ideologies that may conflict with how things are done at home. Common issues include aversion to American materialism, consumerism, and wastefulness.

Facing Career and Postgraduation Decisions

For some students, the semester or year spent abroad was a time during which they did not think about their future plans. The return home, especially if study abroad was undertaken in the students' junior or senior year, can leave them panicked about suddenly having to plan for the future. In addition, education abroad often influences students to think about career paths they may not have previously considered.

Fear of "Losing" the International Experience

For some students, the education abroad experience feels far removed once they return home, and feelings of apprehension and frustration can result if students perceive that there is no way to incorporate the experience into their lives at home.

Other Emotional Issues

Typical feelings often reported by education abroad returnees include boredom, loneliness, isolation, anxiety, and irritability. Students may have difficulty articulating their feelings, and may feel disoriented and overly emotional. They may sleep too much or too little, or feel homesick for the host culture.

Benefits of Reentry

Advisers should point out to students that, although they may be experiencing difficulties with reentry to the home culture, there is a positive side to this stressful experience. For example, going through the sometimes-painful experience of reentry can help students gain perspective on their experiences and integrate aspects of their host cultures into their personalities and lives at home. Reentry can, therefore, be a period of immense personal growth and change.

Preparing Students for Reentry

Before Departing and On-Site

Much can and should be done to help students prepare for the reentry experience before they actually return home. As previously mentioned, when discussing cultural adjustment in predeparture orientations, it is worthwhile to point out that reentry is a normal part of the adjustment cycle. Even though the concept of reentry adjustment will seem far removed for students at that stage, mentioning it will perhaps cause students to recall the information later, thus alleviating some of the feelings of unexpectedness that students encounter when they actually return to the home culture.

As with predeparture training, much depends on the nature of the reentry program attended, including whether it is administered by the home institution or a third-party provider, or whether the program is offered by a local university in which the student is directly enrolled. Education abroad professionals will have some control over or input in the topics that the on-site program staff include in the reentry programming if the program is run by the professional's home institution. It is ideal if on-site staff can begin discussing reentry issues with students several weeks before their departure to the United States. As with predeparture sessions, reentry discussions should emphasize preparation, rather than set students up to expect a negative experience.

If students from the home institution are scattered on many different programs abroad, there are still steps that can be taken to prepare students for reentry. The education abroad office can send students a newsletter, e-mail message, or handouts that describe the reentry process, and that may include comments celebrating the end of the program or letting the students know that the home campus community looks forward to welcoming them home. Logistical details can also be included in this mailing, so that students returning to campus will be aware of any procedures they need to follow for transferring credit, obtaining campus housing, or registering for the next semester. Covering these details can assuage some of the stress associated with going back to the home campus. Another useful bit of information to include in a handout or letter for students is a summary of some of the ways the United States has changed while the students were away, which may help returnees feel less out-of-touch with U.S. culture.

After Returning to the Home Campus

When students return to the home campus, advisers should be prepared to make them feel welcome by holding some kind of event for the students, whether it be a welcome home dinner or reception, a formal reentry workshop, or some combination of these. The format of the event will depend on the staffing and budget resources of the institution and the make-up of the returnee group (e.g., group size, where they studied, duration of the abroad experience, etc.). Regardless of the format chosen, it is most beneficial if all the returned students have an opportunity to participate, discuss issues and problems, and ask questions. Advisers can use the event as an opportunity to cover basic concerns such as credit transfer, common reentry challenges and techniques for coping with them, and incorporating the international experience into life back home. Advisers may also choose to cover these essentials in handouts or in a special returnee handbook.

Sample Reentry Programs

Social Event

If the reentry activity takes the form of a social event, such as a dinner, pizza party, or reception, it may elicit more of a turnout than one billed as a workshop, and it will still be possible to discuss reentry issues at a social event. Faculty with international experience and interests, school administrators, and recently arrived exchange students may also be invited to participate. If the group of returning students is large, it may be broken down into region- or country-specific groups. An agenda for a social reentry event may be structured as follows:

Chapter 7: Predeparture Orientation and Reentry Programming

> **Evening reception and short program for returning students**
>
> 1. Social time with refreshments;
>   7:00 p.m. – 7:15 p.m.
>
> 2. Welcome home address by the education abroad office, and any announcements (e.g., regarding credit issues, photo contests, or other special events);
>   7:15 p.m. – 7:30 p.m.
>
> 3. Short speech by school administrator, faculty member, or returned student about coming home, dealing with reentry, and so on;
>   7:30 p.m. – 7:45 p.m.
>
> 4. Discussion of incorporating the international experience into life at home (this may be facilitated by the education abroad adviser in conjunction with a career services adviser or an administrator responsible for advising on postgraduate international fellowships and scholarships, or both);
>   7:45 p.m. – 8:00 p.m.
>
> 5. Additional social time;
>   8:00 p.m. – 8:30 p.m.

Reentry Workshop

If institutional resources and student interest allow for a full-day reentry workshop, such an event can be quite effective in helping students to experience a smoother and more edifying reentry. Advisers from area colleges and universities in Philadelphia, PA, and Boston, MA, have developed and executed successful reentry conferences that can be used as models. For information on the Philadelphia Reentry Conference, contact the Office of International Programs at the University of Pennsylvania. For information on the Boston-Area Reentry Conference, contact the Eastern Massachusetts representative for NAFSA Region XI.

> **One-day reentry workshop**
>
> 1. Arrivals, registration, coffee, and bagels;
>   8:30 a.m. – 9:00 a.m.
>
> 2. Welcome and introductions;
>   9:00 a.m. – 9:30 a.m.
>
> 3. Large and/or small group discussions on issues commonly faced by study abroad returnees and how to cope with reentry (possibly facilitated by study abroad advisers, counselors, etc.);
>   9:30 a.m. – 10:30 a.m.
>
> 4. Coffee break;
>   10:30 a.m. – 10:45 a.m.
>
> 5. Lectures and small group discussions on how to incorporate the international experience into life at home;
>   10:45 a.m. – 12:00 p.m.
>
> 6. Lunch, possibly in small groups by study abroad country or region;
>   12:00 p.m. – 1:00 p.m.
>
> 7. Marketing the international experience (possibly facilitated by study abroad advisers in conjunction with career services advisers);
>   1:00 p.m. – 2:00 p.m.

Part II: Campus Advising

8. Financial resources for additional study or work abroad experience (e.g., postgraduate scholarships and fellowships);
   2:00 p.m. – 2:30 p.m.

9. International career panel and discussion;
   2:30 p.m. – 3:30 p.m.

10. Coffee break;
    3:30 p.m. – 3:45 p.m.

11. International opportunities fair (which may include representatives from international agencies, nongovernmental organizations, graduate schools focusing on international affairs or international education);
    3:45 p.m. – 5:00 p.m.

Reentry Meeting

Even if they do not have the resources for a full-day workshop, education abroad professionals can still offer an effective one- to two-hour reentry session. If the group of returnees is not too large, this short session could be conducted as a discussion, facilitated by the education abroad adviser. Sample topics to cover include reentry issues, coping strategies, and finding ways to use the international experience at home.

Reentry Course

Some campuses have successfully implemented academic reentry courses for education abroad returnees. The content of a reentry course taught by Dr. Bruce La Brack at the University of the Pacific can be found on the SAFETI Web site. Kalamazoo College also has a formal structure integrating the study abroad experience into the curriculum, which includes a reentry seminar that can be found on the international programs section of the college Web site. Usually, faculty members teach these courses, sometimes in conjunction with study abroad administrators and sometimes as a continuation of predeparture courses. Courses typically cover the theoretical background of cultural adjustment and include term papers and assignments that ask returnees to reflect in an academic manner on their international experiences.

Counseling and Advising Issues

It is important to make students aware of the services available to them should they experience a particularly difficult reentry adjustment. Advisers should make themselves available and accessible to students to discuss reentry issues, and students should be made aware of any counseling services that the home campus offers. Advisers will find it beneficial to liaise with the campus counseling office and to include that office in the reentry programming.

Mental health issues, in general, should be addressed during the reentry program. Students may be experiencing many emotions and working through personal issues that surfaced while they were abroad or since their return home. For example, an eating disorder can begin or become aggravated when a student lives in a culture that has very different body image ideals than those in the United States. Conversely, an eating disorder can also erupt when a student returns to the United States, particularly if the student was more comfortable with his or her body image abroad than at home. Eating disorders can also be issues for international students as they cross cultures.

Students may feel less alone in the adjustment process if they can get support from other education abroad returnees and faculty and staff with international experience. In order to encourage this kind of networking, advisers can provide returnees with lists of students who studied abroad at their host institutions during the previous semester or year, and of current exchange students.

It is vitally important to help students seek out ways to continue their international experience and incorporate it into their life at home: academically, personally, and on their career paths. In counseling students about how to manage their reentry issues, advisers can implement or recommend a number of different practical techniques and coping mechanisms.

Academics

Professors on campus may find it beneficial to know which of their students studied abroad. They can then encourage returnees to use their international experiences in classroom discussions, papers, and presentations. During class registration time, education abroad advisers can suggest to returnees particular courses that are of broad international interest or that focus on the region of the world where students studied (e.g., Latin American politics, African music, European history, international economics). Many returnees find that writing can be enlightening, therapeutic, and a wonderful way to share their international experiences with the campus community and others. Students can be encouraged to keep journals and write articles for the campus newspaper or other university publications. Education abroad offices may consider organizing a writing contest for students to submit essays, short stories, or poetry about their international experiences. *Transitions Abroad* magazine holds an annual writing contest for students. Other publications, such as *Abroad View* and *Glimpse* welcome submissions from study abroad returnees.

Extracurricular Opportunities and Community Involvement

Students should be encouraged to network with one another. Some colleges and universities have residential settings where specific languages are spoken, or they have language-specific tables in the dining hall, and students may want to take advantage of these opportunities, which they may not have known about before studying abroad. Advisers can notifying students about clubs on campus that have an international focus or that are oriented toward intercultural issues (e.g., language clubs, Irish Society, World Dance Club, Habitat for Humanity, Amnesty International). Study abroad returnees can use their knowledge of and enthusiasm for study abroad to volunteer in the education abroad office, counsel peers, help with study abroad fairs or predeparture meetings, or perform administrative duties. Advisers can organize a study abroad photo contest, which is an excellent way for returnees to share their international experiences with the wider campus community (this is also great on-campus publicity for study abroad). Opportunities abound for returnees who are eager to get involved in the local community outside the campuses. For example, returnees can speak about their education abroad host country to local elementary students, volunteer to teach English to immigrants, or work with local refugee communities.

Postgraduate and Career Opportunities

Education abroad professionals can liaise with the career services office and with advisers for postgraduate scholarships and fellowships, to provide information for students who wish to pursue international opportunities after graduation. Education abroad professionals may wish to conduct workshops in conjunction with these people and offices, on how to market the international experience, highlight experience abroad on the resume, talk with potential employers, locate resources on employment abroad, find volunteer work, arrange to teach in another country, and so on. (See Part II, Chapter 8, "Work Abroad and International Careers.")

Evaluating the Overseas Experience

After students return to the home-campus environment, it is important that they are offered opportunities to actively reflect on their experiences and evaluate their study programs. Some study abroad offices require students to complete evaluation forms as a condition for transferring credit or obtaining a transcript. Other offices offer incentives, such as a free t-shirt, for students to complete evaluation forms. In any case, student evaluations are crucial to the education abroad office's ability to evaluate programs and advise future students. (See Part III, Chapter 5, "Program Assessment and Evaluation," for more information.) Evaluation forms should be constructed in a way that helps students reflect on the different aspects of their education abroad experiences (e.g., academic, personal, extracurricular, cultural), and puts their growth and accomplishments into perspective, which can ultimately aid in the reentry adjustment process.

SUMMARY

Predeparture and reentry meetings must be a vital part of the programming of any education abroad office. It is unfortunate, however, that empirical evidence evaluating the usefulness of intercultural training programs is rare. One area where future research is needed in the field is on ways to incorporate use of the internet and other technology into predeparture and reentry training. New training techniques and experiential activities can be developed to give advisers new and innovative ways to conduct predeparture and reentry sessions. Research on diverse populations and education abroad would benefit the field and help advisers address different students' needs for preparation for studying abroad and returning home. Outcomes assessment research can also inform advisers how to best prepare students for education abroad, and how to help them incorporate their experiences abroad into life at home. New developments in the curriculum design of programs abroad can help advisers, in their role as educators, manage the education abroad experience as a continuum. More research is needed regarding how predeparture and reentry programming plays into students' development of intercultural competencies. Education abroad advisers should continue to discuss and share good practices and develop materials for use in predeparture and reentry training. Any new research on education abroad can only help advisers in their predeparture and reentry programming, as they seek to help students.

CHAPTER 8

Work Abroad and International Careers

Contributors: William Nolting, Martha Johnson, Cheryl Matherly

Education abroad programming will probably always be dominated by credit-bearing study programs. But students learn in different ways and have many different needs, only some of which can be satisfied by educational programs that are purely academic in their structures, methods, and values. As an alternative to academic programs—or to expand their international experience—many students now seek opportunities abroad for work, internships, and volunteering, in part because of their belief in the intrinsic educational value of such experiences, in part because of economic advantages these opportunities sometimes provide, and in part for career preparation. All of these motivations are valid and need to be supported by advisers and institutions.

The term education abroad includes both classroom instruction and experiential, beyond-the-classroom education. The expression "experiential education" has many meanings that encompass a vast array of approaches to learning outside the classroom—sometimes complementing classroom-based instruction—such as field trips, research, and participant observation. This chapter focuses on experiential programs open to students and recent graduates for working, interning, volunteering, and teaching abroad. The term work abroad is used here to mean immersion in an international work environment with the educational value of the experience itself as the primary purpose, whether for academic credit or not. Career-related overseas assignments through one's employer and permanent jobs abroad will not be covered in this chapter. By design, work abroad programs are temporary, lasting anywhere from a few weeks to two or three years, and they may or may not be related to specific career goals.

History

Programs for working abroad have a tradition paralleling that of study abroad. It would be a major study in itself to document the worldwide, centuries-old history of apprenticeships in the trades, arts, and professions. Cluett (2002) cites examples such as Cicero traveling to Greece to improve his skills in rhetoric, and Peter the Great serving incognito as an apprentice in the shipyards of Amsterdam. The oldest program listed in the Institute of International Education's (IIE) education abroad guides is one for teaching abroad, Princeton-in-Asia, founded in 1898. Volunteer programs known as work camps started after World War I to promote understanding among the youth of war-ravaged Europe. Reciprocal work-exchange programs were founded after World War II (in 1946) in hopes of fostering peace, including the Fulbright scholarship and teaching programs along with the International Association of Students in Economic and Business Management (AIESEC) and the International Association for the Exchange of Students for Technical Experience (IAESTE) (both in 1948) and CDS International (CDS) internship exchange programs (1949). The idealism of the 1960s saw the inception of the Peace Corps (in 1961, inspired in part by Operation Crossroads Africa, founded in 1957), along with the BUNAC (1962) and Council on International Educational Exchange (CIEE; 1969) work abroad programs. Pioneers in international service learning along with classroom-based courses were Antioch College (1957), which included a broad variety of work abroad experiences, and Goshen College (1968), which focused on volunteer service. This model was later emulated and widely propagated by the International Partnership for Service Learning (1982) through conferences and publications. Steady expansion of study abroad—in numbers of both programs and participants—from the 1970s to the present has been accompanied by similar increases in work abroad. Since the 1990s this growth has been dramatic. Study abroad programs increasingly offered internships and service learning as an integral part of their curriculum. Nonsectarian volunteer abroad programs blossomed, often with a focus on social justice issues. Teach-abroad programs were developed to meet a worldwide demand for learning English. Overall, teaching English is one of the fastest growing sectors in education abroad.

Participation Data

How many students and recent graduates participate in programs for work, internships, and volunteering abroad? These data fall largely outside the annual IIE *Open Doors* survey, since by definition the survey counts only those students who receive credit at their U.S. home institution for study abroad, excluding participants in all other types of education abroad programs—even, ironically, recipients of such prestigious scholarships as Fulbright, Rhodes, and Marshall. *Open Doors* first asked institutions to report for-credit internships only starting in 1998–1999, yielding figures to date of only around 4 to 5 percent of total participants. Given that around 25 percent (1,418 of the 5,695 total) of all programs listed in the 2003 edition of IIE's study abroad guides offer internships, service learning, practical training, or student teaching, the *Open Doors* figure probably represents underreporting. William Nolting has surveyed a dozen of the largest not-for-credit work abroad provider organizations since 1998, and they report over 18,000 participants annually (academic year 2000–2001); the data is available on the Web site of NAFSA's Education Abroad Knowledge Community (formerly known as SECUSSA). The International Volunteer Programs Association (IVPA) surveyed 49 member organizations in 2000, which reported 15,000 participants annually; a figure twice as high—33,000—was reported by the authors of *How to Live Your Dream of Volunteering Abroad* (Collins et al. 2002) in their 2000 survey of a broader range of volunteer abroad programs. Adding the two smaller, conservative figures (with no double-counting of organizations) yields over 30,000 U.S. participants annually in educational, not-for-credit programs for work, internships, and volunteering abroad. A truly comprehensive national survey could easily yield double that number. As a last word concerning numbers of participants, *Open Doors* also does not track foreign participants coming to the United States in work exchange programs, which are often reciprocal—this number is probably two to three times higher than the number of U.S. students going abroad, according to reciprocal program providers.

Professional Associations and Standards

The growth in the work/volunteer/intern abroad sector of education abroad has drawn the attention of professional associations within the past few years. Established associations such as NAFSA, the National Society for Experiential Education (NSEE), and the European Association for International Education (EAIE) have created standing committees, professional sections, or interest groups devoted to issues in work, internship, and volunteer abroad programs. IVPA is a new professional association, dedicated solely to issues related to volunteering and service learning abroad. It lists standards for volunteer abroad programs on its Web site. Another organization, the Forum on Education Abroad, chose its name to indicate that its domain includes the full range of education abroad programs. Most education abroad associations have published statements of best practices for work or volunteer abroad programs, programs that can be expected to enter increasingly into the mainstream of professional discourse and practice within the field of education abroad. As one example, see the discussion by Lynne Montrose (2002) of the NSEE's *Principles of Good Practice of Experiential Education*. That article also discusses theories supporting experiential education. NSEE's principles concern the following areas: intention, authenticity, planning, clarity, monitoring and assessment, reflection, evaluation, and acknowledgment.

Research

While it is beyond the scope of this chapter to cover research in depth, some general comments are possible. Both academic study abroad and domestic experiential education have been extensively covered in theory and research literature. The literature base for study abroad is documented online in the regularly updated "SECUSSA Research Bibliography," by David Comp, Maureen Chao, and Henry Weaver, which is hosted on the Safety Abroad First—Educational Travel Information (SAFETI) Web site and can be accessed from the Education Abroad Knowledge Community area of NAFSA's Web site. For experiential education, NSEE has published several large volumes of theory and research, although little of it has a specifically international focus. While the literature in these two areas has much to offer, studies of internships, volunteering, teaching, and working abroad remain relatively rare. The handful of such studies that appear in the "SECUSSA Research Bibliography" are intriguing inasmuch as they generally agree in their findings that the benefits of such programs tend to be similar to those of study abroad, only amplified.

The Winter 2002 issue of *Frontiers* has the most comprehensive introduction to theories and research on international experiential education available. One article from that issue, both sophisticated in methodology and succinct, may stand here as representative of the results of most other studies. Michael Steinberg's article (2002), "Involve Me and I Will Understand," presents the results of several large-scale surveys conducted by the Institute for the

International Education of Students (IES) of participants in their internship programs (programs in which students also take courses), comparing this group with IES participants who studied abroad but did not do an internship. According to Steinberg, "The (2002) survey suggested that these students who participated in field placements learned more in the experiential aspects (i.e., internships, field placements, and living situations) of the programs generally than they did in either program or university courses" (Steinberg 2002, 215). Those who had an internship reported much greater gains in foreign language (where applicable), an assertion verified by IES using standardized tests. Additionally, students who had internships reported greater gains in knowledge of the society, work-related knowledge, and personal knowledge. IES also surveyed 3,400 alumni of their programs from the last fifty years. Steinberg sums up the results of the alumni survey as follows: "Students who participated in internships and field placements on IES programs were much more likely to say that study abroad ignited their interest in a career decision pursued after graduation" (2002, 218) (than did those who studied abroad but did not participate in an internship or field placement). In light of this and other factors reported on by alumni, Steinberg concludes that, "These findings suggest that experiential offerings have a significant and measurable long-term impact on those who have studied abroad" (2002, 218).

Several dozen additional studies focusing on participants in work, internship, and volunteer abroad programs may be in the "SECUSSA Research Bibliography." Interestingly, early studies often included work abroad alongside study abroad as a valid educational experience. Irwin Abrams (in articles from 1960–1980) assumed this broader perspective, as is evident in his 1979 article, "The Impact of Antioch Education through Experience Abroad," which reported on the results of a survey of 670 alumni, including those who studied and worked abroad, those who only studied abroad, and a control group of 200 students who did not go abroad:

> The work experience appears to have had a most important influence. The Antioch Experience Abroad (AEA) alumni who did not work abroad were less likely than those who did to finish their B.A. degree. They were less likely to be able to use a foreign language and less inclined to note an influence of AEA on their graduate school and job choices…In these areas and others, the AEA alumni without job experience [while abroad] look much more like those who did not go on AEA at all then they do those who went on AEA but held jobs. [...] In general, then, what seems to be the case is the more immersion, the more satisfaction and the more impact. To put it differently, the more a program overseas encourages involvement with the host culture in a variety of roles, with that of worker in the society very important among them, the more we can expect to find enduring [changes in] attitudes and behavior. (Abrams 1979, 184–185)

While the bulk of research over the last two decades has focused on purely academic study abroad, increasing numbers of studies have appeared that focus on the outcomes for participants in work abroad programs. Service learning (volunteering combined with academic course work) has been the subject of studies by Pfinister (1972, 1979), Pyle (1981), and Berry and Chisholm (1999). See also, other articles in the

Winter 2002 issue of *Frontiers* by Lutterman-Aguilar and Gingerich, Peterson, and Annette, and an article by Honigsblum that reports on a U.S.-sponsored study internship program in Paris. Many studies have examined internships abroad in specific disciplines, such as business (Toncar and Cudmore 2000; Feldman et al. 1998; Gonzalez 1993), engineering (Grandin 1991; Klahr and Ratti 2000), social work (Krajewski-Jaime et al. 1996), and teaching abroad (Mahan and Stachowski 1985, 1990; Roose 2001; Sussman 2002). Freyer and Day (1993) focus on the foreign language needs of MBA students doing internships in Spanish- and French-speaking countries. The Fulbright programs, which include teaching opportunities, have been the subject of studies by Burn (1982) and the U.S. Department of State's Office of Policy and Evaluation (Ailes and Russell 2002). Work exchanges supported by European governments (e.g., CDS) were evaluated in a doctoral dissertation by Thot (1998). A study of participants in a U.S.-sponsored study internship program in Australia was documented in a doctoral dissertation by Weiss (1998). Hannigan (2001) conducted perhaps the only study to date comparing participants in United States internships with participants in overseas internships. The conclusions of these studies are generally similar to those reported by Steinberg (2002).

INSTITUTIONAL SUPPORT

Although many institutions have been quick to incorporate service learning components into study abroad programs, relatively few have been proactive in establishing advising offices and support services that provide genuine encouragement and counseling for the full range of education abroad options.

Interestingly, the Faculty of Arts and Sciences of Harvard College, in a 2004 study of its curriculum, did endorse this broader view of education abroad:

> Because of the important contribution that an international experience can play in the education of Harvard College students, we recommend that there be an expectation that all Harvard College students pursue a significant international experience during their time in the College, and that completion of such an experience be noted on the transcript. [...] We would expect that study abroad for a summer, term, or year, as well as international internships, independent research, volunteer work, or employment abroad would qualify, but that travel for tourism or recreation would not." (Gross and Kirby et al. 2004, 40)

Despite the fact that work abroad programs are accessible to students from any college or university, work abroad has been relatively neglected at many colleges and universities because it falls into the bureaucratic cracks. Traditional study abroad offices have refrained from promoting work abroad opportunities because they do not view such programming as their responsibility. Most define their domain as providing access to credit-granting academic opportunities. While it might seem logical for career-planning offices to handle work abroad advising, such offices frequently lack the international expertise needed to advise in this area. It would behoove both study abroad and career offices to familiarize themselves with these work abroad experiences, as the job market is beginning to demonstrate that such experience is good career preparation in an increasingly globalized economy. Setting aside questions of turf, the bulk of this chapter is intended to introduce the education abroad adviser to the great number of work abroad options available to students and recent graduates, as well as to areas of possible cooperation with campus career offices. Please refer to the books and Web sites mentioned in this chapter for more in-depth information about work abroad opportunities.

Benefits of Working Abroad

Simply put, education abroad offices should advise on work abroad program options because some of the most significant outcomes of a study abroad experience are also among the main benefits of a work abroad experience. Some of the most common benefits that students report they gained from working abroad are reviewed in the following paragraphs.

Cultural Immersion

Most work abroad settings are, almost by definition, "full immersion." The work abroad participant is likely to be the only American, or one of a few, working and living in a fully indigenous setting. Most study abroad students have to work hard to break out of a comfortable American enclave where English is spoken and familiar customs and mores prevail; work abroad students have no choice but to do what the locals do.

Personal Development

Working abroad, like studying abroad, will challenge and usually strengthen a student's self-confidence, independence, tolerance, empathy, flexibility, adaptability, pragmatic know-how and cultural insights. Unlike typical study abroad programs, many (though not all) work abroad programs offer less in the way of handholding and oversight. Although such independence can be stressful, most students adapt readily, discover inner resources, and later identify overcoming this challenge as one of the primary benefits of their experiences.

Cross-Cultural Learning

The opportunity to meet host country nationals is assured in most work settings. What makes work abroad encounters different even from full-immersion study abroad settings, is that participants are more likely to experience differences of social organization, such as class and cultural distinctions, than would be likely in the relatively elite environment of the university. The significance of work in another culture, relations between managers and workers, and forms of gender, ethnic, or class stratification in everyday life may differ from those experienced in the United States. Firsthand experience of such differences may become a rich basis for later study or career work that involves other cultures.

Language Learning

The give-and-take, and the immediate feedback, of communication in a workplace can be enormously beneficial in learning a foreign language. Most work abroad participants demonstrate dramatic gains in their language skills, although they are more likely to learn the slang or dialects associated with everyday life and popular culture than the formal academic language. While language acquisition is certainly a benefit for students who choose to work abroad, advisers should caution students not to overestimate their communication skills and risk being unable to perform adequately in an internship or volunteer placement or find a job on their own.

Relevance to Academic Major

Students with certain majors can more readily arrange internships abroad than find a relevant study abroad program. Few study abroad opportunities exist in the engineering core curriculum, for example, because of problems in matching courses at overseas universities. Yet engineering internships are available in the summer for juniors, seniors, and graduate students, who can accept paid internships without delaying their graduation date. By contrast, relatively few work opportunities exist in the humanities, except in related applied fields. An English major can teach English as a foreign language, for example, and a history or political science major might do a parliamentary internship. In an effort to combine the best of the academic and work models, many colleges build evaluated-for-credit field experiences into their study programs. These experiences may take the form of job placements before or after a study term, volunteer activity during the academic year, or a field-based independent study built around an internship. For humanities majors, these for-credit field experiences present the broadest range of opportunities for a career-related internship.

Career Development

At the risk of stating the obvious, working abroad can benefit students' careers. For some students, such as engineers, business majors, and those planning a career in international affairs, the opportunity to gain practical experience can enhance employment and graduate school applications. Yet students working abroad, even in casual jobs, add a dimension to their resumes that they cannot add simply by waiting tables in their hometown. The kind of personal development that students experience when working abroad can make them very marketable to potential employers, regardless of the major. It is important, however, that students are advised about how most effectively to present their international experiences to employers on their resumes and in job interviews (see "Presenting the Abroad Experience on a Resume" below). Research, although limited, does suggest that working abroad provides concrete benefits to students' careers. In a study published by the RAND corporation and the National Association of Colleges and Employers (formerly the College Placement Council), *Global Preparedness and Human Resources: College and Corporate Perspectives* (Bikson and Law 1994) employers cited cross-cultural competency, which is enhanced by working abroad, as one of the four major sets of criteria used when hiring college graduates for a global job market. The other criteria were knowledge of a specific field; interpersonal skills such as problem solving, decisionmaking, and communication skills; and previous work experience.

Postgraduate International Experience

There are many reasons students might choose to go abroad for a period of time after graduation: they may wish to take a break before beginning graduate school; they may need to develop another skill, such as fluency in a language; they may hope to gain additional experiences that will make them more competitive in a weak job market; or, they may be given a unique opportunity that will be difficult to repeat once they begin a full-time job. Students looking for gap-year opportunities frequently explore working abroad because they can earn money and, depending on the program, even defer student loans while participating. Postgraduation scholarships such as Fulbright and Rotary are another excellent option that graduating students should consider.

Challenges of Working Abroad

Working abroad is not without its challenges, yet the challenges themselves may be included in the very factors that attract students to a particular program. It is important when speaking with students about working abroad that advisers be aware of certain issues, to help students set realistic expectations.

Loneliness

Depending on the design of the program, students may find that lack of a peer group is a challenge. Unlike a student who studies abroad, a work abroad participant may find that he or she is the only person in his or her age group at the workplace (though program structures vary—some may be very group oriented, offering projects or seminars for student participants). Local workers have their own families and personal lives, and a student can find himself or herself alone in the evening and left to his or her own devices on weekends. A common question during the interviews for the Japan Exchange and Teaching Programme (JET), for example, is how well the candidate adjusts to spending large amounts of time alone. Advisers may want to discuss ways that students can make friends outside of their jobs, such as participating in clubs, enrolling in special interest classes, or seeking out alumni of their university who are living abroad.

Costs and Benefits

Most work abroad options are substantially less expensive than study abroad options for the same location and length of time (except for university-sponsored study-work programs, which have the advantage of being eligible for financial aid). Students who work abroad, however, will be responsible for up-front expenses, which may include program participation fees, international airfares, and housing deposits. Students considering formal internships may object to having to pay to work, as will be the case while participating in many credit-bearing or unsalaried programs abroad. Other students may be disappointed to learn that international internships, especially in fields such as business and engineering, typically pay far less than equivalent internships in the United States. This is where a savvy education abroad adviser can discuss the students' work abroad experience as an investment in their future job marketability!

Location

The geographic location in which a student is interested can factor prominently in discussions about where a student can work abroad. There are some countries in which it is difficult or even impossible for a student to work. The decision about where to work may require that the student make compromises regarding the type of job he or she is willing to perform, and the amount of money he or she would like to earn. For example, a student who wishes to pursue a paid public health internship in Spain will have to choose priorities and examine options carefully. Spain's unemployment rate makes paid internships extremely rare, and the student might be advised to look instead at volunteer public health programs in Latin America and Africa that offer the kind of experience he or she is seeking.

Adjusting to the Workplace

In some instances, a student's overall cross-cultural adjustment takes a back seat to the adjustment of simply holding a job. For students with limited employment histories, adapting to regular work hours, reporting to a boss, or dealing with difficult coworkers can be overwhelming. Even students who have had previous internships may find it difficult to understand the cultural nuances that shape their workplace culture. These experiences can be further complicated if the supervisor has had little experience with U.S. students, or with any intern for that matter! Advisers who suspect that this type of adjustment might be an issue should be prepared to engage the student in a candid discussion about workplace expectations. The campus career center can provide good resources about adapting to a new job in any country.

Perceptions by Future Employers

It is a conundrum that, for every chief executive officer who proselytizes about the importance of international experience, a campus recruiter will rank it low in the criteria he or she considers when evaluating candidates. Students should be aware that their decision to work abroad might be perceived by a potential employer as having been made because they could not find another job or because they were not focused on a career. While this is less of an issue for students seeking internships, it can be a significant risk for students who seek "casual" summer jobs or overseas opportunities after graduation, particularly in conservative fields such as banking, or for students who have not had previous internships. Students who have had plenty of relevant work experience will likely not experience bias from potential employers, and there are certainly many companies who value students' international experiences. A student's effectiveness in explaining the value of his or her international experience to a potential employer is key. Advisers should be prepared to talk with students about how to present their international experience to future employers so that it is perceived as an asset rather than a liability (see "Advising Students When They Return" below).

Institutional Control

Unlike students who attend study abroad programs sponsored by their home institutions, many students who participate in work abroad programs do so independently. Education abroad offices may exercise some oversight by carefully choosing which work abroad programs they promote through the office (see "Types of Work Abroad Programs" below). This oversight may be compromised when individual academic departments develop international internship programs without consulting with the international programs staff. As with policy issues arising from study abroad advising and administration, advisers may find it useful to consult with university legal counsel or the risk management office to review procedures concerning the selection and administration of work abroad programs that are both reasonable and responsible.

Advising for Working, Interning, and Volunteering Abroad

Advising students for work abroad is different from advising them for study abroad, despite the many commonalities. Advisers may be hesitant to advise on work abroad opportunities, as they are often less familiar with the programs and issues, which are by nature highly diverse. It is extremely useful for advisers to be familiar with the main issues, organizations, and resources in work abroad. Ideally, advisers should make a variety of print and internet work abroad resources available to students, as the field has no single exhaustive directory comparable to the IIE guides for study abroad.

There are many available work, internship, and volunteer abroad options, which vary with respect to time, location, and program structure. But an unrealistic wish, such as a paid position in philosophy in Paris, may simply be impossible to fulfill. There are several essential considerations to cover when advising for work abroad that will clarify possible options and help students set realistic expectations. Readers are advised to use this section together with the section that follows, "Types of Work Abroad Programs."

Promoting Work, Intern, and Volunteer Abroad Opportunities

Raising awareness among students and the campus community may require little more than expanding current efforts to include a wider array of opportunities. Do you promote and discuss "study abroad" or use a more inclusive term such as "education abroad" or "international experiences?" Some easy strategies to incorporate these opportunities into an existing advising structure could include the following:

- Invite reputable work, intern, and volunteer abroad program representatives to existing events, such as a study abroad fair.
- Consult with the campus career office about the best strategies for providing international work resources and directing students to appropriate advisers.
- Incorporate sections on work abroad into reentry programming.
- Make students aware of programs or opportunities that can be coordinated with study options (e.g., a study program that incorporates an internship or service learning component, an opportunity to volunteer throughout a study semester or to stay on in the host country to work over the summer).
- Create a section of the education abroad office's existing library and Web site for materials specific to work, intern, and volunteer abroad programs.
- Develop advising guides or handouts highlighting considerations specific to work, intern, and volunteer abroad programs, and include checklists or a list of questions potential participants should ask to get started.
- Target students who are approaching completion of their degrees, to promote opportunities available to recent graduates.

Program Selection Advising

Advisers should begin by helping students define their goals for the abroad experience and consider their developmental readiness. Once the students' goals are defined, issues regarding program availability, support, preparation, and logistics can be explored.

Motivation

The motivations for a work or volunteer abroad experience can include professional development, cultural interest, academic goals, or a desire for language acquisition. Some students may desire a

Chapter 8: Work Abroad and International Careers

change of pace in which the demands of the experience, albeit cross-cultural, are not primarily academic. It's important that students' expectations match their experiences.

Navigating Terminology

Understanding students' use of terminology can be problematic: an engineering student and a sociology student may define an internship in completely different ways. What does the student mean when he or she expresses interest in an internship or work abroad opportunity? Often, the programmatic differentiations between work, internship, and volunteer programs are subtle.

Local Support

Some programs offer considerable on-site support and structure, whereas others offer far less of these. Students need to determine what level of support they desire or are comfortable with, and seek an appropriate experience.

Work Permits

A work permit is required in any country to pursue legal paid employment—a fact of which many students are unaware. "Off the books" work may be possible, but is inadvisable as it puts the individual at risk for exploitation, on-the-job injury without legal recompense, and deportation. Visas permitting work are usually far more difficult to get than visas for study or tourism, because many countries have a commitment to finding jobs for their citizens first (as is the case in the United States). Special work exchange programs, discussed later in this chapter, (see "BUNAC and CIEE Work Abroad Programs") are an important exception to this rule. Unpaid work, whether in an internship or volunteer capacity, may or may not require a work permit, depending on local regulations.

Location

Program options may depend on the region or country. In Western Europe, for example, numerous programs exist for paid short-term work in some countries (e.g., Britain, Ireland, France, Germany), but are scarce in others (e.g., Spain, Italy). In Asia and certain countries in Europe and Eurasia, programs that offer placements in teaching English as a second language dominate, though the placements offer vastly different rates of pay. In developing regions such as Africa and Latin America, study abroad programs that include an internship or service-learning component offer virtually the only realistic way for U.S. students and recent graduates to gain work experience.

Financial Realities

U.S. students are often unaware of the great disparities in living standards around the world. They may be surprised that they cannot expect a salary on par with U.S. salary levels when working in many regions of the world. Indeed, the cost of an airplane ticket may exceed a local citizen's annual salary. Thus, working abroad may involve program fees and living expenses, and sometimes may not pay at all, especially in less wealthy regions. In these areas, a U.S.-funded volunteer experience such as can be found through the Peace Corps (which covers all expenses and pays a $6,000 stipend at the end of two years) may be the best-paid job available to a recent graduate. Even in areas that enjoy a similar standard of living as in the United States, students participating in paid work programs will probably save less than they would in a summer job at home, simply because of the additional costs involved in program fees, traveling abroad, and settling in to a new environment. Those who earn wages while working abroad will still need to pay taxes in most cases (including in-country taxes), and should consult the Internal Revenue Service Web site and their work abroad program representatives for details. Health insurance is another essential expenditure that many students will not necessarily consider.

Eligibility for Undergraduates, Graduate Students, and Recent Graduates

Some work abroad programs are open only to those with student status or who participate within a semester of graduation. Other work abroad programs are open only to those who have a bachelor's degree, such as programs for teaching English abroad and long-term volunteer programs. Internships with major international organizations or corporations often require graduate student status or graduate degrees.

Duration

Work abroad programs last anywhere from a few weeks (e.g., volunteer work camps), to a summer or semester (e.g., internships and short-term work abroad), or up to a maximum of one, two, or sometimes three years (e.g., teaching English or working with volunteer organizations). Permanent work abroad is extremely difficult for most individuals to arrange.

Academic Credit and Professional Development

Internships, by definition, should provide experience in a particular profession. Undergraduates can receive credit for working abroad through academic internship programs that charge tuition. Such programs offer the greatest choice in terms of location and subject. Students need to check their own institution's policy towards credit for internships or other experiential learning. However, students who ask for an internship abroad may in fact not have any specific career focus, and may simply want some kind of work abroad experience. Students may also explore mechanisms for independent study that may allow them to earn academic credit for volunteer or independent opportunities by developing a research paper or other project. An internship in the United States with an international organization might be another option worth mentioning. Paradoxically, students may face a choice between gaining overseas experience in a job with little specifically international focus, or having an internship in the United States involving international issues and working with U.S. colleagues. Most work abroad options, like most study abroad programs, are not designed to be directly linked to a career field, but can provide overseas experience, which would be one of several steps towards an international career (see "Building an International Career," below). Prospective teachers might consider teaching English, or language and area studies majors might teach English as a means to improve their knowledge of a culture. Those interested in issues concerning developing countries would certainly want to consider a long-term experience with the Peace Corps or similar organizations.

Language Learning and Level of Proficiency

In places where the local language is one other than English, even nonprofessional jobs (i.e., work in restaurants, au pair work) will require a level of foreign language proficiency considered by Americans to be intermediate or advanced.

Conversely, for most overseas English-teaching positions, knowledge of the host country language is not required although it would definitely facilitate cultural integration.

Previous Work Experience

Any type of work experience beyond the purely academic is a plus when applying for work abroad programs. Obviously, for technical positions (such as engineering internships) there is no substitute for academic training, but even in technical positions, prior work experience is advantageous. For a parliamentary internship, prior experience working for a local politician or even in student government would be viewed positively. For positions teaching English as a foreign language, previous experience as a tutor or conversation partner would prove valuable. In general, students will find that the same hiring rules apply overseas as in the United States: previous related experience can help secure a similar position.

Citizenship

Some work exchange programs are open only to U.S. citizens or permanent residents; U.S. government internships are usually limited to U.S. citizens, as is the Peace Corps. One option for non-U.S. citizens is IAESTE, which can arrange for work permits in a third country outside the United States. Study-internships and unpaid internships rarely have citizenship restrictions.

Institutional Issues to Consider in Advising

Orientation and Reentry Programming

Participants in work abroad programs would benefit from the same kind of preparation for travel and living abroad as study abroad participants. Can work abroad participants be included in the orientations and reentry programs already provided for study abroad participants? Can a newsletter or flyers be used to invite returned participants to take part in orientation and reentry programs? Can advisers obtain participant information from the host programs to contact the participants directly?

Institutional Communication and Consistency

Campuses may unintentionally send mixed signals and conflicting information to students. Education abroad advisers should find out how the career advisers on campus counsel students who ask questions regarding international work experiences. It is important to determine whose office will have the primary responsibility for advising on work, intern, and volunteer abroad experiences. Career offices may offer a wealth of information regarding strategies for successful internships, but the staff may feel uncomfortable advising on the specific challenges of experiences abroad. Make a plan for working together.

Data Collection

Although *Open Doors* still does not include any data regarding the estimated number of U.S. individuals who participate annually in work, intern, or volunteer abroad programs, individual campuses can compile their own data. BUNAC, CIEE, Peace Corps, CDS, IAESTE, and other organizations all keep excellent participant data and are willing to share reports to help institutions track their students' rate of participation.

Part II: Campus Advising

Types of Work Abroad Programs

Programs designed for students and recent graduates make procuring a work abroad placement far easier than trying to line up a job abroad on one's own initiative, analogous to the difference between enrolling in a study abroad program and enrolling directly in a foreign university. Given the severe restrictions imposed by most countries on foreign workers, special work exchanges make feasible that which would otherwise be difficult, if not impossible. For advising purposes, it is useful to categorize work abroad programs into four types: (1) internships, (2) short-term paid work, (3) volunteering, and (4) teaching. A few major or unique organizations are listed here, and there are hundreds more listed in the Web and book resources section for this chapter. See the "Work Abroad and International Careers" information on the Education Abroad Knowledge Community's (formerly known as SECUSSA) section of the NAFSA Web site. In addition, there are several university Web sites that provide valuable overviews of all options for working abroad:

- University of California-Irvine, Center for International Education, International Opportunities Program, by Sharon Parks. Extensive work abroad listings by type with links.

- University of Minnesota Learning Abroad Center, by Martha Johnson. Searchable directories include programs for work, volunteering, and internships abroad, and related advising resources.

- University of Michigan International Center, by William Nolting. Articles and annotated guides to Web sites and books.

Internships

Advising Highlights

- Most direct connection to career tracks.
- Wide range of location and discipline, equaled only by volunteer options.
- Paid internships are fairly rare.

Internships can be found through three routes. First, colleges and universities offer study-internship programs that charge tuition and grant academic credit; these number in the hundreds and are available in countless disciplines. Second, specialized internship organizations such as AIESEC, CDS, and IAESTE offer placements into nonacademic internships, which may be paid or unpaid. Third, U.S. and foreign corporations and governments, and international organizations may be willing to take on interns (often unpaid). Some, such as the U.S. Department of State, have large formal programs.

Advantages

Internships give insight and, occasionally, entry into international careers. Even those who try out a career this way and decide against it feel the experience is valuable. Some internship programs offer a group experience, either in classes or through organized social activities. Academic credit and financial aid may be available for many university-sponsored internships.

Drawbacks

Assignments may be very demanding, leaving little time to explore the local culture. Conversely, the participant may be given busy work at the expense of professional tasks, or the internship may simply lack structure. The intern may have to demonstrate initiative before being given responsible assignments. Study-internship programs do not always guarantee placement into an internship. In some programs, an intern's social contacts may be limited to older professionals who are not interested in socializing outside the workplace. U.S. government internships overseas will be in a mostly American environment.

Application Requirements

The selection process for internships tends to be competitive, and the fit between an applicant's background and the job may be as important a factor in selection as a good academic record. Excellent command of the relevant foreign language is often essential if the internship is in a non–English-speaking country. Prior related work experience is very helpful. Watch for early application deadlines, such as the U.S. Department of State's early November deadline for summer interns.

Duration

Summer- or semester-long internships are typical; a few internships are longer. There are relatively few short-term internships (i.e., those lasting less than two months) available.

Location

Internship programs have long offered placements in Europe, where there is a tradition of providing internships in higher education. Increasingly, programs are expanding their placements to other world regions including Africa, Asia, and Latin America.

Sample Sponsoring Organizations

Universities. Hundreds of study-internship programs are offered by colleges, universities, and independent organizations. These programs are readily accessible in the many print and online study abroad directories, which are indexed for internships. Service-learning programs combine a volunteer experience with course work.

Reciprocal Paid Internship Organizations. There are several organizations that operate reciprocal programs, including the Association for International Practical Training (AIPT)/IAESTE, AIESEC, the American-Scandinavian Foundation, and CDS.

Governments, Corporations, and International Organizations. Internships with the following organizations are very competitive, sometimes for graduate students only, and often unpaid. These organizations are just a sampling of the many that provide internship opportunities overseas: The U.S. Department of State (more than 1,000 internships, half of which are abroad), Proctor & Gamble, CNN, and the United Nations.

Nongovernmental Organizations (NGOs). NGOs offer internships at their U.S. offices or, for the well qualified, overseas.

Guides to Internships

In addition to the previously mentioned study abroad directories published by IIE and Petersons, the following resources are essential guides to overseas internships: *Directory of International Internships*; the *Transitions Abroad* magazine and Web site; and the online directories iiepassport.org, goabroad.com, and studyabroad.com.

Short-Term Paid Work Abroad

Advising Highlights

- Most work is in typical summer jobs, such as working in a restaurant or as an office temporary, although enterprising students can find professionally relevant work.

- Offers best chance of paying one's way abroad for a short time, although there will be up-front costs.

- Participants report satisfaction with the degree of self-sufficiency they achieved.

- Participants experience rapid improvement in foreign language skills (where applicable).

- Locations primarily in Western Europe, Canada, Australia, and New Zealand.

There are essentially three options for short-term paid work. One is to go through a work permit program that provides students with work permits and some assistance in finding a job. This assistance usually takes place once the participant is in the host –country it is up to the participant to find the job. The second way to obtain short-term work abroad is to apply to one of several organizations that offer job placements overseas. A third way is for students to attempt to find their own position in advance (perhaps while studying abroad). Work permit programs such as those listed below (see "BUNAC and CIEE Work Abroad Programs") can help remove one of the major obstacles to getting an offer. Note that some institutions, such as Rice University, have established placement programs for their own students whereby the university arranges for job placements while using a work permit program for the work permits. A full list of reciprocal work exchange programs, which must operate under formal government approval, is provided on the Web site of the U.S. Department of State's Bureau of Educational and Cultural Affairs.

BUNAC and CIEE Work Abroad Programs

The BUNAC and CIEE programs can procure a short-term work permit (typically for three to twelve months, depending on the country) that allows students or recent graduates to enter a specific country and seek work of any kind. Outside these unique programs, work permits can be obtained only after receiving a job offer, which would usually not be forthcoming without a work permit! With over 6,000 U.S. participants annually (and far more overseas students coming to work in the United States), these programs have the largest number of participants. BUNAC and CIEE administer reciprocal exchanges with a limited number of countries, including Australia, Canada, Great Britain, Ireland, and New Zealand (check with the programs for changes in participating countries).

Advantages

The program fees are low, in the hundreds rather than thousands of dollars. Permits can be used for any type of work, including professional-type internships. Nearly all jobs involve total cultural immersion because work colleagues are usually local citizens. Social contacts tend to be with people from a variety of class backgrounds. Since students find their own jobs, they have control over their employment situation, and credit themselves with success. Although jobs are not guaranteed, few participants fail to find a job; average job-search time tends to be a week or two. Application is noncompetitive and can be done weeks rather than months in advance.

Drawbacks

The uncertainty of arriving without a job deters some students (and parents). Even under the best of circumstances, stress levels during the job and apartment hunt can be high. It can be difficult to find internship-like positions. Up-front costs include not only the modest program fees but also the cost of airfare, and usually at least $1,000 is required for initial expenses once the participant is on-site, before the first paycheck.

Application Requirements

Usually, applicants must carry at least an eight-credit-hour load (undergraduate or graduate) in the semester prior to participation. Participants going from the United States usually must be U.S. citizens, though some countries allow U.S. permanent residents to participate.

Other Permit Programs

Other organizations can also assist individuals in getting a permit, typically for up to twelve months, but they require that the individual have a job offer first. Job seekers can notify potential employers that the employer would be relieved of the burden of obtaining the work permit, which will increase the chances of getting a job offer. In practice, an employee is rarely hired sight unseen; therefore these permits are most useful for those individuals who are participating in a work abroad program and want to stay longer (although a return to the United States for the new permit is necessary), or for cases in which an individual has the necessary connections—perhaps made during a study abroad experience, through alumni, or even through e-mail contacts—to land a job offer. These organizations, all of which also arrange internship placements, include AIPT/IAESTE (worldwide), the American-Scandinavian Foundation (for Scandinavian countries), and CDS (for Germany and Switzerland).

IAESTE United States

This organization is worth special mention, given its unique capabilities as the U.S. affiliate of a network of 80 member countries that provides both internship placement and work permit services. IAESTE United States can assist students in most disciplines who have either located their own internships abroad or have been placed by another internship program, with obtaining the appropriate work documentation (IAESTE's placements are for engineering, science and technical students). Most permits are available for up to twelve months. IAESTE is the only program that can be used by international students studying in the United States who wish to obtain an internship in a third country. The parent organization of IAESTE United States, AIPT, also offers the "Americans Abroad" program, which offers work permit services for professionals (U.S. citizens under age 30) who wish to find placements in Austria, Finland, France, Germany, Malaysia, Switzerland, and the United Kingdom.

Placement Programs

It is possible to be placed into a paid, short-term, overseas job with the assistance of a number of organizations. The following organizations are just a few of many long-established U.S.-based programs:

- AIESEC, the American-Scandinavian Foundation, IAESTE, and CDS are reciprocal exchange organizations that offer placements into paid internships.

- InterExchange (since 1971) offers positions in Europe, including skilled

Part II: Campus Advising

and unskilled summer jobs, internships, au pair positions, and teaching English.

- The International Cooperative Education program (since 1971) offers paid, entry-level internships in Europe that require knowledge of German, French, or Italian.

- Center for Interim Programs (since 1980) offers nonacademic but structured opportunities, which may be paid or unpaid.

Work Without a Permit

Working for pay without a work permit is illegal. Illegal workers do not have any legal protection from exploitation or injury on the job, and they may be deported if discovered by the authorities. Student travelers do occasionally find casual work without a permit, usually of a menial and low-paying variety, but it is not recommended.

Guides to Short-Term Paid Work Abroad

Copies of the BUNAC and CIEE Work Abroad Participants' Handbooks can be requested by college offices; these are otherwise available only to individual participants. The magazine *Transitions Abroad* provides updates, and the book published by Transitions Abroad, *Work Abroad: The Complete Guide to Finding a Job Overseas* (Hubbs, Griffith and Nolting 2003), gives a worldwide overview of programs along with firsthand articles. *How to Get a Job in Europe* (Sanborn and Matherly 2003) gives in-depth, country-by-country coverage of programs, work permits, and prospects for employment in Europe from an American perspective. For the adventurous individual who wants to find a job on the spot, Susan Griffith's *Work Your Way Around The World* (2003) is a comprehensive source, though its advice, from a British point of view, may not always hold true for U.S. citizens who wish to work in countries of the European Union (European Union citizens can legally work in any member country). The Web site goabroad.com has a section for paid jobs abroad.

Volunteer Work Abroad

Advising Highlights

- Defined not by pay or lack of it, but by service at the grassroots level.

- Work is with ordinary local people rather than professional elites.

- Excellent career preparation for those interested in developing countries or nongovernmental organizations.

Traditionally, volunteer work abroad has been seen as service work, helping the underprivileged and powerless. Though this is still true, today most volunteer organizations see their role as one of solidarity with indigenous peoples, helping them to achieve their own goals. Sponsoring organizations run the gamut from the U.S. government's Peace Corps to independent nonsectarian volunteer abroad programs (the latter category has experienced rapid growth in the last decade), from large NGOs to religious organizations which may be virtually indistinguishable from NGOs or may have a missionary focus.

Volunteering is not necessarily defined by lack of pay. The Peace Corps, for example, covers all expenses, provides training and on-site support, and pays a "resettlement allowance" of more than $6,000 (in 2003) at the end of the two-year assignment. This benefit package far exceeds local wage levels in most developing countries. Other, mostly religious-based, organizations also support volunteers willing to make a lengthy commitment. Even short-term volunteer projects known as work camps provide room and board. But many programs are unpaid or charge a fee to cover the costs of supporting the volunteer. College-based service-learning programs combine volunteering with course work and provide academic credit in return for tuition. Community groups such as Rotary, Kiwanis, or religious organizations may be willing to help fund a volunteer's expenses. Repayment of educational loans may sometimes be deferrable for those participating in bona fide volunteer abroad programs. Expenses for volunteering abroad may be tax-deductible.

Advantages

Volunteers are needed for a huge variety of work, ranging from the unskilled to the professional, in virtually all areas of the world. Volunteering is frequently the only realistic possibility for individuals who wish to work in developing countries, and being a volunteer can provide essential career preparation for those interested in development or relief work. Most volunteers live and work with ordinary local people, rather than with the host-country elite, other Americans, or other foreigners.

Drawbacks

Service work is not for everyone. Idealistic individuals in particular may be frustrated at being able to do little about conditions they would like to change; successful volunteers tend to combine idealism with other goals, such as the desire to learn about other cultures. Cultural adjustment can be severe for sojourners to developing countries. Not every volunteer organization has a good support network.

Application Requirements

Application requirements vary widely depending on the organization and the duration and type of assignment. For example, screening for the Peace Corps is thorough and the application process can take nine months to a year. Organizations offering long-term positions often want volunteers with specific skills. For positions in programs such as work camps, applications are noncompetitive, and are accepted on a first-come, first-served basis. Organizations affiliated with religious groups may insist that applicants be members of the religion or at least exhibit a willingness to examine the particular beliefs of the religion; in such cases, applicants should be sure to find out whether or not proselytizing would be expected as part of the overseas assignment.

Duration

Most work camps last two to three weeks in the summer. Other volunteer possibilities may last from a few weeks to two or three years.

Locations

Short-term possibilities, such as positions in work camps, and a few long-term ones are available in Europe. The vast majority of long-term positions and some short-term positions are in less-developed regions.

Sample Sponsoring Organizations

Government, including the Peace Corps (3,000 to 4,000 new volunteers annually). For the United

Nations Volunteer Program, applicants who are U.S. citizens also apply through the Peace Corps.

Academic Institutions Offering Service Learning Programs, including Antioch College, Augsburg College, Brethren Colleges Abroad (BCA), the Higher Education Consortium for Urban Affairs (HECUA), the International Partnership for Service Learning, Goshen College, and the University of Minnesota Studies in International Development. (See Frontiers, Winter 2002, for articles on this kind of program.)

Nonsectarian Volunteer Organizations, including AFS, Amigos de las Americas, Child Family Health International, Cross-Cultural Solutions, Earthwatch, Mobility International USA (MIUSA), and Operation Crossroads Africa. (See "Teaching Abroad" below.)

Organizations with a Sectarian or Religious Affiliation, including American Friends Service Committee, Brethren Volunteer Service, Jesuit Volunteer Corps, and the Mennonite Central Committee.

Short-term Work Camps, including CIEE International Volunteer Projects, Service Civil International-International Voluntary Service (SCI-IVS), and Volunteers for Peace (VFP).

Best Guides to Volunteering Abroad

The outstanding book *How to Live Your Dream of Volunteering Abroad* (Collins, Dezerega, and Hecksher 2002) gives comprehensive guidance for those considering service work, including candid in-depth evaluations of 100 volunteer abroad programs. IIE's study abroad guides and the IIEPassport Web site list programs in an index for volunteer and service. The Web site of goabroad.com has a section devoted to volunteer abroad programs. The International Volunteer Programs Association (IVPA) sets standards for its members and lists its programs on its Web site.

Teaching Abroad

Advising Highlights

- One of the most accessible long-term (one- to two-year) options for recent graduates.

- Locations primarily outside of Western Europe.

- Previous teaching or tutoring experience is highly recommended.

In the late 1980s and early 1990s, political changes in Eastern Europe and strong economies in East Asia created a booming market for teachers of English—known variously as TEFL (teaching English as a foreign langue), EFL (English as a foreign language), TESL (teaching English as a second language), or ESL (English as a second language). Anyone whose native tongue was English could travel to these regions and land a job within days. This is no longer the case due to market saturation in popular destinations, such as Prague and Tokyo, and higher standards for teachers. Although teaching EFL remains one of the most accessible options for long-term work abroad, most positions now require a bachelor's degree and some experience teaching or tutoring English, even if only as a volunteer. Teacher placement programs and agencies can match the novice teacher with locales that still need EFL teachers.

Salaries vary, of course, depending on the local economy. Positions in some countries in East Asia (e.g., Japan, Taiwan, Korea) can pay well. If the position has been arranged by a sponsoring organization, airfare may be included and housing—

otherwise scarce and expensive—provided. If the position is found after arrival in the host country, beginning expenses can be very high, and may include airfare, housing (usually requiring a deposit of several months' nonrefundable rent), and a trip to another country to obtain a work permit.

In areas with less wealthy economies (e.g., parts of Central and Eastern Europe, China, South Asia and Southeast Asia, Africa, and Latin America), pay may be high by local standards but low in absolute terms, making positions in these regions, in effect, volunteer positions. Living expenses may be covered, but the cost of airfare probably is not. Many volunteer organizations provide placements and sometimes training.

Advantages

Teaching English is one of the few long-term overseas positions available to new graduates. Considerable cultural immersion is possible, especially for those who already had some knowledge of the host-country language before going abroad.

Drawbacks

Most of the working day is spent speaking English, which makes learning the host-country language difficult. For those with little knowledge of the host-country language, friendships tend to be mainly with other English-speaking expatriates. Many programs provide only limited training and on-site support; prospective teachers should bring their own teaching materials.

Application Requirements

In most cases, a bachelor's degree is required, and applicants must be native speakers of English. Formal TEFL credentials are not always required though some TEFL tutoring or teaching experience is a big advantage; volunteering as a tutor for one's own university's English program for foreign students is an easy way to get experience. No knowledge of the host-country language is necessary, though not knowing the language may prove to be a disadvantage in the long run.

Duration

Nearly all TEFL positions are for at least one year. A few summer- or semester-long placements are available.

Locations

Most positions are in East Asia (e.g., Japan, Taiwan, Korea, China) or Europe. Some are also available in Latin America and Africa.

Sample Sponsoring Organizations

Governments. The U.S. Peace Corps places teachers of EFL in many world regions. The Japan Exchange and Teaching Programme (JET) manages more than 4,000 positions annually and recruits EFL teachers through Japanese consulates. The French Teaching Assistant Program does the same for France, managing about 1,500 positions annually through French consulates.

Exchange Programs. Fulbright English Teaching Assistantships are available in locations such as Belgium, France, Germany, Hungary, Korea, Luxembourg, Taiwan, and Turkey; future teachers are preferred. The Austrian Fulbright Commission offers its own program for Austria.

Universities. Earlham College (Japan), Princeton-in-Asia (most of Asia), Marshall University, and Western Washington University

Part II: Campus Advising

(China) offer programs that place teachers into paying positions.

Volunteer Organizations. Many nonprofit organizations assist in placing teachers of EFL abroad. Teachers will be expected to cover the cost of airfare and a placement fee. Examples of such organizations include The Central European Teaching Program, Volunteers-in-Asia, and WorldTeach.

Private Language Schools. Several language school franchises recruit from the United States for their overseas branches, including AEON and GEOS (Japan) and Hess (Taiwan).

Best Guides to Teaching English Abroad

Susan Griffith's *Teaching English Abroad: Talk Your Way Around the World* (2003) is comprehensive, though its information on Western Europe, written from a British perspective, is best suited to European Union citizens. Also see the Web sites listed above, such as the site of the University of Michigan International Center, which includes a selected list of established programs for teaching abroad.

Professional Teaching Positions in Overseas K-12 Schools and Universities

A different realm of possibilities exists for those with certification to teach kindergarten through high school: teaching in Department of Defense (DOD) schools at overseas U.S. military bases; or teaching in private international schools, which are English-language schools for the offspring of expatriate diplomats and businesspeople. The easiest way to land a position in these types of schools is to attend one of the special job fairs for international schools. Major fairs are held in February, and a few smaller fairs take place in June. For more information, contact the two largest international school job fair organizers: International Schools Services and the University of Northern Iowa.

The Fulbright Scholars program offers overseas assignments for up to one year for university-level teaching or research, and the Fulbright Teacher Exchange does the same for community college and K-12 teachers. The Civic Education Project (CEP) sends holders of recent advanced degrees to teach in central European universities.

Building an International Career

There is a distinct difference between briefly working abroad and actually establishing an international career. An international job, loosely defined, is work that a person may do with the primary objective of supporting himself or herself while living abroad for educational purposes. The job may or may not be related to the person's long-term career plans. For example, a recent graduate may work as an au pair for a year in Spain in order to improve her Spanish. Many of the options covered in this chapter are available to students with little previous work experience, and are not especially competitive. Most students who go abroad, either for work or study, do not necessarily want an international career—that is, they do not intend to work overseas for the rest of their lives. What these students consciously seek is a serious, nonacademic, cultural-immersion experience; career considerations are secondary. Many who return from an extended period of working abroad, however, do go on to develop an international career, often by pursuing graduate study or a professional degree in business, public health or medicine, engineering or natural resources, law, or international relations, to name a few possible fields. Such a career, however, may or may not entail living overseas for an extended period, but will include a significant international component.

Ironically, Americans in international careers are usually based in the United States. In addition, international careers are competitive. Even an entry-level position may require a combination of education in a discipline related to the career, career-related work experience, overseas experience, and knowledge of one or more foreign languages. Not surprisingly, in view of this complexity, preparation for an international career is often a lengthy process. Those interested in an international career should begin by using the guides listed in the following paragraph to thoroughly research the career path of their choice. Campus career centers will likely have additional resources on international careers, and students may find it instructive to meet with a career counselor to develop a plan for pursuing work in an appropriate field.

This section is not intended as a definitive summary of all international careers. In fact, it is likely that in the near future all careers will have some international aspects and will perhaps involve working in a multicultural environment. This section is intended, instead, as a guide for advisers to use when talking with students about long-term career options. Students should be encouraged to use the suggestions in this section on developing an international career as jumping-off points for additional career research. Two particularly useful guides are *Careers in International Affairs* (Carland and Gihring, 2003) and *International Jobs: Where They Are and How to Get Them* (Segal and Kocher 2003). These books provide fully updated overviews of international career fields and how to prepare for them. A personal perspective on a life spent working in career positions abroad is found in *The Global Citizen: A Guide to Creating an International Life and Career* (Kruempelmann 2002). Additionally, the books *International Job Finder: Where the Jobs are Worldwide* (Lauber and Rice 2002), and *The Directory of Websites for International Jobs* (Krannich and Krannich 2002), online resources for exploring international careers.

Types of International Careers

Certain fields, including the ones listed below, offer particularly attractive international careers.

- Business, which includes international trade, banking and finance, economics, and consulting.

- Law, which usually refers to the practice of domestic or local law for foreign clients or the counsel given to a domestic client on the legal aspects of international transactions.

- Media and communications, which can include working as a correspondent for a newspaper, magazine, television or radio station, or wire service.

- Nonprofit sector, which includes opportunities ranging from analyst positions in think tanks to positions in issue-specific organizations, such as those that deal with relief and development work.

- Government and public policy, which includes positions with government and nongovernmental agencies involved with business, trade, and political concerns.

- Education, which refers to opportunities for certified K-12 teachers, as well as opportunities in higher education ranging from university teaching and research to international education advising and administration.

Part II: Campus Advising

- Health care, which includes public health, medicine, nursing, and social work.
- Science and technology, which include engineering, information technology, natural sciences, the environment, and natural resources.

Skills

Each career field requires different skills and a specialized graduate degree. Students should be advised to research these skills and qualifications thoroughly as part of their own career exploration. There are some skills, however, that are common for anyone who is interested in an international career:

- Language. Most people who prepare for an international career speak at least one foreign language fluently.
- Knowledge of another country or countries. International careers require that students develop an in-depth knowledge of another country or region of the world. Programs such as JET, through which students live and work in Japan, help students develop this knowledge prior to attending graduate school.
- Strong interpersonal skills. People in international careers tend to have interpersonal competencies in addition to technical skills.
- Initiative. International careers are competitive, and success demands well-honed personal drive.

Graduate Schools

Students planning for an international career may find that a graduate degree can significantly enhance their marketability. The most common degrees that students pursue are in business, law, education, medicine and public health, and international affairs. There are many good resources available on the internet for students to evaluate programs in these fields. US News & World Report's annual ranking of graduate schools is a good place for students to begin. The guide distinguishes programs according to their specialties, such as international business and law. Students interested in international affairs should look for information from the Association of Professional Schools in International Affairs.

Advising Students When They Return

Students who return from time abroad can become frustrated when they start looking for a job. Campus recruiters may not place a value on the time students spend abroad and, in some instances, may actually perceive abroad experiences as a distraction from more serious career preparation. This is an issue particularly when students focus so much on their experience abroad that they create the impression that they are only seeking work that will enable them to go abroad again. Most people who work in international education have data, as well as plenty of anecdotes, that illustrate the powerful learning opportunities available by participating in working or studying abroad. The key is for students to begin to think from an employer's perspective and present their experiences abroad in terms of the transferable skills for which a company recruits. The most common places that this presentation occurs are on the resume and in the job interview.

Presenting the Abroad Experience on a Resume

For most students, international work experience logically will be included in the "Work Experience" segment of their resumes. Students, especially those who had jobs that are not related to their academic major, should be encouraged to think of their experience in terms of transferable skills, rather than simply a list of their job duties. An adviser can ask a student, "What is it about your experience as a bartender in London that a future employer will find valuable?" This type of question can help students shift from writing about serving beer and scotch eggs to describing their role in training new employees and troubleshooting customer complaints. Students may also choose to list international work experience under the "Education" segment of their resumes, especially if they received academic credit for the experience. In this case, students would typically leave out any description of the nature of the work. Students who are pursuing an international career may also choose to create a separate block on their resume for "International Experience," and include within it all relevant information about their work abroad, study abroad, and foreign language experiences.

Discussing the Abroad Experience in an Interview

Most college recruiters use behavioral interview questions, which assume that how a student handled a situation in the past predicts how he or she will handle a similar situation in the future. Employers using behavioral interview questions attempt to get students to tell a story about themselves and relate it to the job for which they are applying. The behavioral interview presents a very good venue through which a student can make his or her international experience relevant for the employer. A very common behavioral interview question is, "Tell me about your most challenging situation while in college and how you handled it." A student who is able to discuss what he or she learned from a particular challenge associated with working abroad has, in this example, demonstrated to the employer how the experience helped developed his or her problem-solving skills. The most common mistake students make in interviews is to not relate an international experience to the job for which they are interviewing. The challenge, as with the resume, is to help students interpret their time abroad in terms of the transferable skills they developed. Most career centers have materials that include typical job interview questions, and it is a useful exercise for students to prepare answers using experiences from their time abroad as examples.

Cooperating with the Career Center

The staff in the campus career center can serve as resources for advising students about how to market their international experiences. The career counseling staff can assist students who are considering an international career as well as advise students who are simply looking for their first job after graduation. A good time to involve the career center staff is during a reentry program, when students are most enthusiastic about their time abroad. Whether the career center staff conduct a workshop on marketing international experiences or simply explain their services, involving them will draw tight the thread that links international experiences and career preparation.

Part II: Campus Advising

Leveraging Study Abroad Experiences

Only the most proactive students will plan ahead to take advantage of career development opportunities while abroad, especially in the heady days during which they are preparing to leave the country. Yet, as discussed in this chapter, studying abroad is good preparation for any career, and can provide some networking opportunities that may prove especially important to students considering international careers. Here are a few final tips on how students can leverage their time abroad; study abroad advisers might wish to incorporate these tips into predeparture orientations and advising sessions. These tips, while especially useful for students who wish to work abroad, reflect good habits in general for students seeking summer and full-time jobs.

- Make a list of alumni living in the destination country. The alumni affairs or career services offices can provide a list of university alumni living in the host country, and many overseas alumni organizations have their own Web sites. Overseas alumni can be useful resources for students to both learn more about particular career areas and obtain useful job leads for full-time or summer opportunities.

- Keep a contacts notebook. Students should be encouraged to develop a recordkeeping system to track the names, postal addresses, and e-mail addresses of people they meet while abroad. It is common occurrence that a student does not realize the value of a contact until after he or she has returned home.

- If participating in a home-stay, use every opportunity to talk with the host family about the local economy. The more knowledgeable a student becomes about the local market, the easier it will be for him or her to adopt a reasonable approach to finding a job.

- Pay attention to jobs listed in local newspapers and other local publications. These resources can be very useful for determining the employment sectors that have the greatest demand in a particular country.

- If considering graduate school in the destination country, obtain the application materials while abroad. Program representatives may be willing to meet with students to discuss particular degrees. Students who are considering applying for postgraduate scholarships such as the Fulbright should be strongly encouraged to research graduate schools while abroad.

- Find out how other people found their jobs. The best way to learn how to find a job overseas is to ask other Americans who have been successful in finding an international job how they did it. Alumni, of course, are good people to ask, but so are the other American expatriates whom students will meet in the course of studying abroad.

- Meet with the campus career center staff before leaving the country. The career services staff can advise students about how to manage the job, internship, and graduate school deadlines that will come about while they are out of the country. Additionally, a career counselor can help students devise a job search strategy to take advantage of contacts they make while abroad and how to best market their international experiences when they return.

- Keep in touch with useful contacts. E-mail makes it very easy for students to periodically touch base with the interesting people they met while abroad, to keep their network alive.

volunteer, and internship programs but remain, at present, largely uncounted in education abroad statistics. Education abroad offices, working in tandem with career services offices, should seek strategies to incorporate work abroad advising into their services, so that all students can benefit from the availability of the full spectrum of education abroad options, with the goal of enabling students to begin to shape their international futures.

Summary

Research demonstrates that the many benefits of participating in work abroad programs are very similar to those of studying abroad. Tens of thousands of students participate annually in work,

Part III
Program Development, Campus Management, Marketing, and Evaluation

III-1
Program Designs and Strategies
Stephen Johnson, Nana Rinehart, Leo Van Cleve

III-2
Short-Term Programs Abroad
Sarah E. Spencer, Tina Murray, Kathy Tuma

III-3
Planning, Budgeting, and Implementation
Susan Holme Brick, Lisa Chieffo, Tom Roberts, Michael Steinberg

III-4
Marketing, Promotion, and Publicity
My Yarabinec, Leo Van Cleve, Andrea Walgren

III-5
Program Assessment and Evaluation
Stacia Zukroff, Stephen Ferst, Jennifer Hirsch, Carla Slawson, Margaret Wiedenhoeft

III-6
Maximizing Safety and Security and Minimizing Risk in Education Abroad Programs
Barbara Lindeman, Natalie Mello, Joseph Brockington, Margit Johnson, Les McCabe

III-7
Legal Issues and Education Abroad
Gary Rhodes, Robert Aalberts, William Hoye, Joseph Brockington

Introduction

Joseph L. Brockington

The chapters in Part III focus on the design, implementation, and campus-based management of education abroad programs. The discussion takes us from program design to site selection, program length, budgets, marketing, assessment, safety and security, risk management, and finally to legal issues. While the primary focus is on programs overseas, each of the chapters also offers invaluable information directly related to the operation of the education abroad office on campus, especially in the areas of budgets, marketing, risk management and legal issues. In Part III, as throughout this edition of the *Guide,* we have endeavored to provide information and perspectives relevant to education abroad professionals who are not campus-based.

Chapters 1 and 2 cover the fundamentals of program design. Chapter 1, "Program Designs and Strategies," discusses the range of education abroad program models in use and considers the relative advantages and disadvantages of each. As its title suggests, Chapter 2, "Short-Term Programs Abroad," focuses on the range of issues present with faculty-led short-term programs.

Chapter 3, "Planning, Budgeting, and Implementation" looks at the financial structures of programs abroad and the campus contexts in which they operate. The chapter discusses items to include in a program's budget and also examines several models for funding education abroad programs. Chapter 4, "Marketing, Promotion, and Publicity," considers all aspects of the promotion of education abroad, from a single program of one's own to one's own students to a national marketing campaign. The also chapter includes helpful ideas for how to raise the visibility of the education abroad office on campus.

With Chapter 5, "Program Assessment and Evaluation" we take up the topic that has dominated much of higher education for the past ten years and will continue to do so for the foreseeable future. With both the regional accrediting organizations ask for outcomes assessment as an indication of student learning and funders (chief among them the U.S. government) demanding an assessment plan as part of every grant application, education abroad has no choice but to become part of this conversation. The chapter offers insights on assessing both internal (one's own) and external programs.

Chapter 6, "Maximizing Safety and Security and Minimizing Risk in Education Abroad Programs," considers the risk factors that affect safety and security in education abroad and discusses how campuses and program providers can work to reduce the risk associated with participation. The chapter also offers suggestions on developing an emergency response plan.

Part III: Program Development, Campus Management, Marketing, and Evaluation

Finally, Chapter 7, "Legal Issues and Education Abroad," examines the legal context in which higher education in the U.S. (and thus education abroad at U.S. colleges and universities) operates. The chapter pays particular attention to the concepts of duty and responsibility, both of which are associated with negligence. There is also a consideration of some of the implications that U.S. laws and regulations (the Americans with Disabilities Act or the non-discrimination clauses of Title IX, etc.) have on education abroad programs and offices.

CHAPTER 1

Program Designs and Strategies

Contributors: Stephen Johnson, Nana Rinehart, Leo Van Cleve

An institution's overall educational mission, philosophy, and goals inform the kinds of programs it provides its students abroad and at home, by defining the intended educational outcomes. Whether the goal is mastering a second language, conducting field studies, undertaking an intensive study of a specific topic "on location," engaging in service learning, exploring a discipline from another cultural viewpoint, or merely studying in an educational system different from one's own, the "perfect" program cannot be defined in the abstract. By matching an institution's resources and educational philosophy with the interests, learning styles, academic requirements, and welfare of its students, study abroad offices can design programs abroad that will provide a good fit between the institution, as program provider, and the student participants.

There are many reasons to offer a variety of programs ranging from summer programs to year-long opportunities, since what each student can afford in terms of academics and economics is likely to be quite different. Because students are at various stages of intellectual, intercultural, and academic development, a campus needs to have programs that are interculturally challenging, as well as programs that provide more support for those who require it. Some students will need to fulfill specific course requirements during their time abroad, whereas others will be eager to explore new academic areas. Finally, there will always be students seeking the challenge of learning new skills beyond an academic setting, as well as those who wish to experience living and learning independently on local terms, whether or not they earn credit for the program. By offering multiple education abroad opportunities (study, internship, work, and service-learning), an institution is better positioned to meet the needs of a diverse student body. Moreover, a broad variety of programs may lead students to consider more than one education abroad opportunity during their academic careers.

CAMPUS MISSION/EDUCATION ABROAD OFFICE MISSION

The design of education abroad programs begins with the careful consideration of the program's academic objectives as they relate to the overall mission and goals of the sponsoring institution or agency. The specific academic, experiential, and intercultural goals of the program must always be linked back to the program's overall mission statement, which in turn is linked to the institution's mission. Finally, the individual program activities should always support both one or more intermediate goals and the overall mission. By clearly establishing the relationship between activity and goal, education abroad professionals can avoid programmatic "non-sequiturs." For example, a program cannot claim to have an emphasis on language learning in a colloquial environment without a set of well-planned cocurricular activities where the students will use the language.

Ideally, the institution and the education abroad office already have mission statements and sets of goals and objectives for international education. These should be the guides for both the format of the program abroad as well as the content. It is very difficult to sustain a program that is at odds with the university's mission (and it is even harder to defend such a program in the event of a lawsuit). If the education abroad office or organization does not have a mission statement or goals and objectives to guide its policies and actions in regards to program development and implementation, it would be useful for an education abroad professionals to spend some time creating these. In so doing, they will need to work closely with faculty members and administrators to see that the final statement supports the internationalization objectives and academic goals of the institution, without causing financial or enrollment-management problems. It is equally important that education abroad professionals review the mission statement of the education abroad office regularly to ensure it continues to support the college's overall mission.

Finally, in planning and designing any education abroad program, education abroad professionals must consider the "what" of the program—that is, the academic and intercultural content—as well as the "how." If the program abroad is to be offered as part of a university's credit-bearing course structure, then the appropriate academic departments and faculty members must be involved in the process, because curricular issues are typically under faculty control. If the program is noncredit (e.g., an internship or a service-learning experience), it will still have a "what" component—that is, some content that will need both the approval and support of some person, office, or program, to be considered legitimate. Intercultural issues, which are often under no one's direct supervision, also play an exceptionally large role in the success or failure of a program. For example, an intensive language program with no opportunity for the students to use the language outside of the classroom would more likely fail than succeed. The education abroad office may choose to take responsibility for tracking and developing the intercultural aspects of a program.

If the abroad program does not use any local faculty, opportunities for students to hear from other academic and cultural perspectives may be reduced. If the program focuses on a particular topic or discipline, such as tropical ecology, the education abroad office will have to decide to what extent the program will consider the *people* who live in the area under study. Institutions typically must weigh the desire on the part of students and faculty for a home-campus-like atmosphere in the foreign country, against using the location to highlight and strengthen the academic content and achieve broader program objectives. In any event, it is typically the responsibility of the education abroad office to make sure all of the pieces fit and work together.

Education Abroad Nomenclature and Typology

Over the years, a variety of program types, as well as descriptions of these types, have emerged. For example, Goodwin and Nacht (1988) use a series of aquatic metaphors, ranging from "total immersion" to "staying by the pool" to "row your own boat" to describe various types of education abroad programs. John Engel and Lilli Engle (1999) propose a "classification of program types" based on "seven defining components:" the length of student sojourn, entry target language competence, language used in course work, context of academic work, types of student housing, provisions for guided cultural interaction and experiential learning, and guided reflection on cultural experience. Unfortunately, there has not been any systematic agreement within the profession of either definitions of program types or related program terms. To solve this, representatives from NAFSA's Section on U.S. Students Abroad (SECUSSA, which recently became the Education Abroad Knowledge Community of NAFSA), The Forum on Education Abroad, and other international education organizations have been working on a set of standardized definitions for education abroad terms and program types. In the meantime, we must continue to define our terms as we go.

Programs Sponsored by the Home Campus

Study Center Model

A study center is a program designed by the institution to allow students to take the same courses abroad as are offered at the home campus. A study center typically has a much narrower focus than the home campus and typically offers courses from a particular academic discipline or topic, such as language or art history, and a selection of general education courses. Because study center programs are often separate from local foreign institutions, they are sometimes referred to as "island" or "unintegrated" programs. Although some find the study center model closer to a tourist experience (albeit academic tourism) than a study experience, this model does serve students who may not be able to engage in a more integrated program, for academic, personal, linguistic, or financial reasons. When a study center is well designed and implemented, it offers opportunities for academic, cultural, and personal growth.

With a focus on a limited number of courses, study centers differ from branch campuses, which are designed to offer full degree programs from the home university intended primarily for students of the host country. However, one is hard pressed to argue that a university in a foreign country with a predominantly foreign student body and faculty is not in fact a foreign university, regardless of the curriculum and language of instruction. Nevertheless, education abroad terminology continues to distinguish between branch campuses and study centers.

Operating a study center means that the U.S. institution will be responsible for providing all of the academic and student services, administrative and financial infrastructures, risk assessment and management, insurance, medical services, emergency planning, crisis response, legal liability, human resources and labor issues, and possibly building and grounds maintenance. In short, operating a study center is like running a miniature university. The success of the study center will depend on close attention to all of these details. It is crucial to seek out the expertise and support of appropriate offices on the home campus, as well as in-country experts in these areas. The orientation of students and the training of faculty or resident directors are additional critical elements of a well-planned study center.

Basic Characteristics

Academics. Typically, the courses at a study center are drawn from the home campus's curriculum. These can be supplemented by specialty courses offered only abroad, such as a regional studies course focusing on the host culture or city. Unless the program focus is on language and culture, the language of instruction is most often English—although many study centers also offer courses taught in the language of the host country. The home institution's calendar (summer, quarter, semester, or academic year) is used at the study center, with accommodation made for host country holidays.

Faculty. The faculty who teach at the study center are hired by the home institution. Teaching at the center can be a faculty development opportunity for the institution's regular faculty. The center also hires local instructors to teach specialty courses. Typically, the study center has a resident director chosen from the campus faculty. The resident director often teaches, and acts as the on-site administrator and adviser for the program. The resident director (or the academic director of a large center) is responsible for local and home-campus faculty. If the center is large enough, there can be an administrative assistant and small staff of locals who, in addition to helping run the program, also provide a link to the local community. In the case of a small center, study center faculty and staff will report to the education abroad office at the home campus.

Participants. Students participating in study center programs are drawn primarily from the home institution—though some programs do allow participants from other U.S. colleges to apply as well. Students from the host culture are rarely involved in the study center's academic program, as it is designed to fulfill U.S. degree requirements, without offering a complete degree program. Most U.S. study center course credits cannot be transferred to a local university.

Admission Requirements. The home campus sets the admission requirements for the program. Requirements and eligibility criteria include a minimum grade point average (GPA), completion of a certain number of credits, perhaps a minimum proficiency in the foreign language, and specific course prerequisites. Application procedures vary greatly but typically include an essay or interview, in addition to a completed application form. Because this is a home-campus program, the application and selection process should also consider the student's campus conduct.

Student Policies. The home campus's policies on alcohol, drugs, sexual harassment, attendance, etc., apply to the program overseas. Care should be taken to carefully articulate the specific policies in effect for the program abroad, and the consequences for anyone (student or staff) who violates them. A student participation agreement and appointment letters for staff are essential.

Facilities. The study center operator will generally need to rent classroom, office, and faculty workspace from a local educational institution, a real estate agency, or commercial property management firm. Some U.S. universities with longstanding study centers have purchased or built the facilities that house their programs.

Housing. Housing options at study centers vary, and range from a dormitory attached to the center, to apartments, to rooms in a hostel or dormitory used by local university students, to even entire hotels. Some study centers have chosen to have long-term leases on apartments. Others prefer to work with a local rental agent on a year-to-year basis. Purchasing a number of apartments or an apartment building is also an option. Depending on local customs, U.S. students are sometimes placed with local families, thus lessening the island effect of the academic program. Home-stays are a particularly important component (perhaps crucial) of language programs, as they give students the opportunity to apply their language skills in an everyday setting. When home-stays are used, however, it is absolutely necessary to carefully screen and monitor the families, as well as the students living with them. Home-stay situations can range from a boarder living in one room of a large apartment to the student being accepted as a member of the family with full family (and kitchen) privileges.

Program Costs. Program costs generally include tuition, fees, room, and board, and any required excursions, such as field trips related to a particular class. Optional excursions, personal expenses, and independent travel are not included. Some programs include one-way or roundtrip airfare in the program fee. A program might arrange with a travel agent to offer a group flight, but not require students to use it. And an increasingly popular option is for the program not to get involved at all in the travel arrangements. In keeping with *Responsible Study Abroad: Good Practices for Health and Safety* (2003), students should be required to have medical insurance valid in the country overseas. For programs in the developing world, medical evacuation insurance is an important consideration. Typically, home institutions allow the full transfer of all institutional financial aid and merit scholarships for their students enrolled at the study center.

Advantages of the Study Center Model

Because it is under a high degree of institutional control, the study center model offers a number of advantages for faculty, administrators, and students of the home campus. The home campus develops the program, so all campus units can and should have input into the finished product. By having this front-end input, the study abroad office can help develop simplified processes for program administration and for students who are seeking academic, financial, and other kinds of support.

In the academic area, the home institution determines the focus and any specific themes of the program and sets all other policies. Since all courses are a part of the home-campus curriculum, there is no question of how courses transfer and no evaluation of unfamiliar transcripts. Academic standards for instructional time, class attendance, methods of examination, and grading remain the same as on the home campus. The program can be tailored to the home-campus academic calendar. All of these factors are helpful in marketing the program to students, who can know exactly what major or graduation requirements they are fulfilling and how their participation is likely to affect their GPA.

Another very practical advantage is that study center programs can accommodate large groups of students—anywhere from 10 to 200, depending on the structure. Because all the students going to the particular program can attend the same orientation programs and are required to hand in the same paperwork, individual advising time can be shorter and less formal than for more individualized programs. Placing an equivalent number of students directly into a foreign host institution can be very time consuming, by comparison.

The involvement of home-campus faculty can be another strength of the study center model. Teaching overseas creates an opportunity for faculty development; and it may be possible to "borrow" faculty from their departments at home, thus holding down program costs (provided the home-campus department will "loan" that professor's salary and fringe benefits to the study center). Aside from giving faculty members the opportunity to teach and sometimes conduct research in a new environment, this type of arrangement can increase general campus support for education abroad. When faculty members have had good experiences abroad, they become advocates in campus classrooms, who can talk with students about study abroad from personal experience.

Finally, study center models attract students who may not have the linguistic or personal self-confidence to participate in a less structured type of overseas study. First-generation college students, students from rural areas, or students who have simply never thought of themselves as the type to go abroad, may prefer a study center—not only because it does not require them to dive headfirst into an immersion experience, but also because it provides them with a "home island" from which to explore as they become comfortable in the host culture.

Drawbacks of the Study Center Model

Study centers require a high level of faculty involvement, strong administrative and staff support of education abroad, and institutional financial and administrative commitment from the home campus. If these do not exist, the home campus education abroad office and its staff will need to build them before launching a program on the study center model. Without the cooperation of home-campus committees such as the curriculum committee, and without support from home campus administrative offices such as the registrar, admissions, business services, risk management, and financial aid, the program will not get off the ground. Furthermore, most home-campus academic and student services need to be duplicated at the study center. If the education abroad office if the home campus cannot or chooses not to provide these services, it would be wise for the education abroad office at that campus not to pursue this model.

In order to run an effective study center program, the education abroad office needs dependable overseas contacts to make the necessary local arrangements. Even if the institution sends a faculty member to serve as resident director of the program, having an on-site liaison to deal with arrangements (such as arrival, orientation, housing, excursions, etc.) that need to be made or nurtured between terms is critical. For this reason, many study centers have a full-time local manager.

Because study centers typically depend on home-campus faculty involvement, the education abroad office must identify departments and individual faculty members who are dedicated to study abroad for their students, and to teaching abroad for themselves. As part of this process, education abroad professionals will need to find and remove any roadblocks to faculty participation in the program abroad, such as overseas teaching not being recognized in tenure and promotion decisions. In addition, fluctuating budget cycles in higher education may make it more difficult to gain the support of deans and department heads, particularly if part of the strategy for holding down costs for the study center includes having the study center faculty "loaned" to the program. If instead, the center has to pay the salaries of the U.S. professors, the costs may be too great for the program to be sustained.

Finally, study centers present a host of legal issues, as they are subject to both U.S. and local laws and regulations. Under U.S. Department of Education regulations, the study center may be considered a branch campus, and thus generate increased reporting requirements in such areas as campus crime, sexual harassment, discrimination, and Americans with Disabilities Act (ADA) compliance. Local laws will govern labor issues, workers compensation, taxes, insurance, as well as visas and work permits. Early consultation with legal counsel at home and abroad can save a great deal of frustration and money later.

In What Circumstances Should a Study Center Model Be Considered?

Study center programs work well when they serve one or several closely related departments or curricular areas. Study centers also work well when there is a large group of students with similar academic needs that must be met. Majors with strict course sequences (e.g., the sciences, nursing, social work, pharmacy, engineering), whose students may not otherwise be able to study abroad, are examples of these kinds of groups. Study centers can also provide opportunities for students to fulfill general education requirements. Humanities, social science, and cross-cultural requirements completed abroad may generate future interest in international education. Keep in mind though, that the institution will need to sustain its commitment to the study center over time, especially when there are multiyear leases or mortgages involved. Sustaining student numbers over time can also be a challenge, and care should be taken to assure that continuing student demand will be sufficient to support the ongoing fixed costs.

Education abroad professionals should be prepared to work with students and their parents, to set appropriate expectations of the program abroad. Unless their expectations are carefully managed, students and parents will expect that a program designed, operated, and staffed by the home campus will have all of the amenities of the home campus. The time and effort required to operate a study center may more than offset any time saved in individual advising.

Finally, in considering a study center as a program model, institutions will need to weigh the advantages of home-campus control over the curriculum, staff, and policies, against the relative isolation of the center from the host country's culture and institutions. Because a study center represents a large institutional commitment (especially a financial one), all of the program's stakeholders should be in agreement that this model represents an acceptable means to achieve the university's international education objectives.

Integrated Models

While the study center model basically exports part of a U.S. college's curriculum to a foreign country, an integrated study abroad program facilitates the participation of U.S. students in the local educational system of the host country through direct enrollment. Students take regular host university courses, but often bypass much of the regular admissions process of the host institution and are not matriculated in the same way local degree-seeking students are. To enroll in regular university courses, however, the visiting students must have the requisite academic background and language skills to participate fully in the foreign educational environment.

In some cases, direct enrollment is made possible by bilateral or multilateral reciprocal exchange agreements. In such cases, each institution sends and receives a designated number of students. (A full description of reciprocal options is given later in this chapter. See also, references at the end of the chapter to organizations such as the International Student Exchange Program [ISEP], which provides a clearinghouse for such exchanges.) In other cases, U.S. institutions organize integrated programs for qualified students at selected overseas institutions. There may or may not be an on-site adviser from the home institution for the U.S. students. In the case of reciprocal exchanges, where an international student office provides a campus adviser at each end, such support services usually do not add to overall costs.

Basic Characteristics of Integrated Models

Participants. If the program is an exchange between a U.S. institution and an institution or institutions abroad, U.S. participants will most likely be from the U.S. institution's home campus. On rare occasions, an exchange agreement will allow the inclusion of students from other U.S. institutions with the foreign partner. as well. At the site abroad, the home-campus students become part of a larger group of international exchange students and take classes with students from the host country, or take courses specially designed for international students, or both.

Admission Requirements. The admission requirements are set by the foreign institution, or, in the case of exchanges, are agreed upon by the participating institutions, usually in a memorandum of understanding (MOU). A typical exchange arrangement allows the U.S. institution to accept students conditionally to the program, but leaves the final admission decision to the host university. In return, the education abroad office at the U.S. institution reviews the applications of the students the exchange partner wishes to send to the U.S. school. Requirements often include a minimum GPA, completion of a certain number of credits, and specific course or language prerequisites. Many foreign institutions require U.S. students to have junior standing. Application procedures vary greatly and may include an essay or interview, in addition to a completed application form. In the case of integrated programs that are not exchanges, overseas institutions may or may not be flexible with regard to eligibility criteria. Some agreements leave the selection of the outbound participants to the sending institution, which is responsible for ensuring that each participant meets all necessary requirements, such as language ability or academic standing.

Faculty. Students take regular classes from local instructors at the host university, who judge the students' academic performance by local standards. It is thus very important that the visiting U.S. students fully understand and appreciate local attitudes toward teaching and learning, and that they know how their academic performance will be evaluated. In most other countries around the world, students are expected to be more self-motivated and self-directed learners than is usually the case in the United States.

Academics. Courses are chosen from the host institution's curriculum. In most other countries, students typically take most or all of their courses in their major field, the general education requirements having been satisfied at the secondary level. The U.S. institution may choose to institute some form of preprogram course selection and advising for participants, based on courses taken in the past. Students and their advisers will, however, need to be flexible in the course preapproval process, as the final listing of courses offered at the host institution may not be available until shortly before the semester begins, and detailed course descriptions are not always provided. U.S. students often have greater freedom in choosing courses at the host institution than the local students, because they are not preparing for a degree there. However, U.S.

students will find it easier to put together their course schedules if they select courses from only one or two departments, rather than several departments. In this way, their experience will more closely match that of their host institution counterparts, and they will realize academic as well as social benefits. It is also wise for students to get preapproval for more courses than they are actually going to take (or work out a virtual approval process), in case some are not offered, or turn out to be very different from what was expected.

Students obviously need to be proficient in the language of the host country in order to do course work in its higher education institutions. Students needing additional language training can benefit from an intensive language course prior to the beginning of the semester, and additional language training may be available during the term. Students spending a whole year abroad may be able to combine a first semester of intensive language study with a second semester of immersion in the host institution's regular academic program (see "Hybrid Models," below).

Increasingly, institutions in Europe, Africa, and Asia are offering courses from their regular curriculum taught in English, in order to accommodate international students and enable their own students to become proficient in English in their major field. In these instances, U.S. students can select from of a wide range of regular courses, doing all their reading and writing in English, alongside local students as well as other visiting students. Usually, these institutions offer courses on the culture, as well as language, of the country, that are designed for international students.

Grades are usually given according to the local scale of the host university, and a transcript of the term's work is sent to the home campus. The U.S. institution is responsible for establishing policies and procedures for translating the grades into home-campus equivalencies. The home-campus registrar and faculty will decide how course titles, credits, and grades will appear on the student's home-campus transcript.

A direct enrollment program runs on the academic calendar of the host institution. Full-year programs carry obvious personal and academic benefits, but semester options are available in most countries. In countries where the first semester does not end until late January, a second-semester exchange is usually the only option for U.S. students, although some host institutions may be willing to offer special examinations in December for visiting students. These types of special arrangements should be clearly stated in the exchange agreement or in the MOU.

Facilities. Typically, visiting students will have access to all of the facilities available to regular students at their host institution, in the same manner as the locals. In most cases, there will be an international education office on campus with special responsibility for foreign students, or a local faculty member who is the designated adviser for exchange students. This office (or person) typically provides an orientation program at the beginning of the semester and can generally refer students to the resources they need throughout the academic program. U.S. students should be forewarned that in many countries, student services are not as integral a part of higher education as in the United States.

Housing. Housing in integrated programs ranges from student residences (often located off-campus) to apartments on the local housing market. Student residences are typically home to international students and some host country students. The dorms are often "self-catering" flats, consisting of a number of single bedrooms with shared kitchen facilities. Home-stays and apartment options are sometimes available. Some institutions abroad are not able to guarantee or even provide university housing, either due to a shortage of dorm space or because housing is handled completely separately from the university. In such cases, students are advised to arrive several weeks early in order to find housing. Most universities will have some form of housing office, and will assist visiting students in finding somewhere to live.

Program Costs. Exchange programs are typically based on a waiver of tuition and certain (or all) fees. In other words, outbound students on both sides pay tuition and fees to their home institutions. Sometimes inbound students pay room and board to the host institution, or these can be included in the waiver. Some agreements allow the collected fees to be used to provide the same benefits to the incoming exchange students that outbound students would have received had they stayed at their home campus., with no funds exchanged between institutions. For integrated programs that are not exchanges, typically an inclusive or partial program fee is charged by the receiving institution, or the program fee is subject to negotiation as set forth in the MOU. Inbound students (or their institutions) are charged for tuition and fees, intensive presemester language training, orientation, plus, in some cases, the costs of extra administrative services, such as airport pickup.

Advantages of Integrated Models

A clear strength of an integrated model is the degree of immersion into the host culture available to visiting students. Even if there is an international office that visiting students can turn to for advice, the myriad of details of daily life is left to the students. They must learn to navigate a new academic system and foreign society with minimal assistance. When they need help, visiting students can turn to host country peers for guidance, building social relationships in the process. Such experiences promote a deeper and long-lasting understanding of the host culture.

Exchanges represent an attractive economic option. If the agreement includes an exchange (i.e., waiver) of tuition, fees, room, and board, the U.S. student pays the same basic costs that he or she would pay at home, making international airfare the only significant additional required expense. (The cost of sightseeing, etc., in the host country would be an optional expense.) If the exchange agreement involves tuition only, the actual cost depends on the cost of living in the host country. Nonexchange direct enrollment programs can also represent cost savings, in that the tuition charged by the foreign institution may be lower than the tuition at the home institution. In those countries where universities are fully subsidized by taxpayers, local students often pay no or very low fees. Sometimes visiting students are included in this subsidy. In other instances, only the local students' attendance is subsidized, and visiting students are charged full tuition. Because U.S. students are supported by the facilities of the host institution, the home institution does not have the overseas administrative costs associated with study center programs. Lastly, the integrated model puts all of the resources of the foreign institution at a student's disposal. Exchange students can usually take any course for which they have the necessary prerequisites, and thus expand their academic horizons or fulfill distribution requirements.

Drawbacks of Integrated Models

Integrated programs are not for everyone. Because students who participate in such programs need to be able to fend very much for themselves, the programs will only appeal to students who are already independent and self-confident. If, in addition to being on their own in a new academic system, students must also operate in a second language, such an option can be intimidating, causing students to opt out of study abroad if an integrated model is the only program choice.

Secondly, U.S. students often find it difficult to integrate into the new culture, even if social integration is necessary for survival. Friendship has different connotations in different cultures, and short-term, casual acquaintances or "friends" are less common in other countries than in the United States. Because the U.S. student will be at the host university for only a short time—be it a quarter, semester, or year—host country students may not go out of their way to befriend them. (U.S. students often treat the international visitors on their home campuses in the same way.) U.S. students, therefore, can find themselves by default in a social group of other Americans, or perhaps other international students. (Of course, many participants find the interaction with other international students to be an enriching aspect of their experience abroad.)

Although the wide range of course offerings may be appealing, it can also cause some problems. Because students may not know until they arrive at the program abroad exactly which courses will be offered in a given term, they need to plan for many different options before they depart. It is often impossible for the home-campus academic adviser to determine in advance how particular courses will transfer back. A course outline or syllabus may not be available until the student registers for classes abroad, if then. Students who need to fulfill specific requirements in a given term will find an integrated program less attractive.

If students register for courses that were not "approved" in advance, they will need to have those courses evaluated after the fact, to determine how much credit will transfer. Electronic communications have made it much easier than ever before for students to keep in touch with faculty advisers at their home institutions. (See Part I, Chapter 8, "Technology and Education Abroad.") If the home institution only grants pass/fail credit for work on exchange programs, students who can take only a limited number of such credits in their major may be deterred. On the other hand, if grade equivalencies are applied, students may not participate because of uncertainties as to how course work in an unfamiliar academic system will affect their GPAs. Delays in receiving transcripts from abroad are relatively common and can affect everything from financial aid to registration for the next semester.

Finally, integrated programs are time intensive on each end. Because each student is, in effect, planning an individualized study abroad program, a great deal of advising time can be required. Many of the advising issues for integrated programs go beyond the scope of the typical education abroad office and can require the assistance of offices across the institution, from the registrar to the academic dean. The posting of credit and grades after the student's return also requires individual review of the transcript and informed decisions regarding equivalencies of credits and grades. Students can facilitate the credit transfer process by familiarizing themselves with the academic system of the host country, discussing in advance with their adviser how course work abroad will fit into their overall academic program, staying in touch with their adviser while they are abroad, keeping all assignments and syllabi, and following directions for obtaining transcripts from their host institution. Finally, integrated models require that both sides have sufficient staff and expertise in the international student office for handling the myriad of intercultural, academic, and personal issues that come with studying at a new university. The best exchange relationships between the most prestigious partners can flounder because there are not enough advisers to handle the number of exchange students.

Hybrid Models

If integration into the host country academic system is used as a measure, the study center and integrated models are at opposite ends of the spectrum. As education abroad programs have evolved, many have attempted to combine the cultural advantages of more integrated programming with the pragmatic strengths and conveniences of study centers. Hybrid designs have evolved both from programs that began as study centers (and added opportunities for students to interact with the host culture) and integrated models (which have seen the necessity of providing more on-site support services or intensive language courses). Hybrid programs therefore are often offered by the U.S. institution in cooperation with a foreign institution, but are not necessarily fully integrated into the foreign institution's regular curriculum. They can also be offered in conjunction with a "foreign student institute" at the host university.

A first step toward a hybrid program is the addition of an on-site adviser to the program. The U.S. sending institution typically identifies and compensates a faculty member, from either the home or the host institution, who is familiar with the country and its higher education system and who can assist the U.S. students with academic and personal problems as needed. (Interestingly, it is extremely rare to find a foreign university making similar arrangements at a U.S. institution.) In another variation, such support services can be provided by the host institution (for an extra fee) by someone who is designated as an adviser or tutor to the U.S. students or to all visiting students. This person, who may or may not have teaching responsibilities, is responsible for the care and nurture of visiting students, and for encouraging their integration into their new studies and social life.

Other hybrid designs include program tracks geared to visiting students of differing backgrounds, educational needs, and motivations, and consist of courses developed specifically for program participants. In some cases this means special language courses. In other instances, it involves a set of related culture courses, coupled with the option of taking one or two regular university courses at the same time. In an academic year program, a language and culture first semester can be followed by an integrated second semester. Another variation involves establishing tutorials or discussion groups for visiting students, which can be independent of or connected with particular lecture and seminar courses. In each instance, the idea is to allow the U.S. students to move toward academic and cultural integration at their own pace.

Sometimes a foreign institution develops a semi-integrated program for outside students on its own (e.g., European ERASMUS programs for students from other member states, often offered through a foreign student institute), providing a set of courses for foreigners in a particular discipline or around a particular theme. These courses are taught either in the target language or in English, and often include language and civilization courses. Students who arrive with good foreign language proficiency or those whose language skills have advanced since their arrival are typically allowed into regular university courses, provided they score high enough on the qualifying language examination. Some agreements also include a waiver of the qualifying examination. Another hybrid model involves reciprocal enrollment in intensive language courses on both sides. This special curriculum and the faculty who teach it are usually described in university promotional materials, allowing credit transfer and equivalency issues to be determined prior to participation. Participants need to adjust to a new academic system, but faculty in such programs are generally more aware of and accommodating towards this adjustment than they might be in regular university classes.

Hybrid programs at their pragmatic best represent an effort to maximize the advantages and minimize the disadvantages of both island and integrated program models. Hybrids will not satisfy institutions that want their students to participate in only regular overseas university course work and social life. Nor, on the other extreme, will they satisfy institutions that wish to maintain full control over what students study and how they live overseas. Furthermore, what is possible in one country and university system may not be possible in others. Or they may turn out to be simply not affordable or practicable. Language proficiency is another barrier. Full integration at a university abroad is not possible for students who do not have university-level language ability; yet setting up a program that offers no language instruction and keeps U.S. students at a distance from their local peers and the cultural richness of the host country is also unappealing for many institutions.

Hybrid program models probably represent the mainstream of U.S. study abroad programming. They offer an institutionally defined blend of cultural enrichment and academic program that would not be possible at the home campus, yet meets the need for learning that is creditable toward undergraduate degree studies.

Independent Study

The fourth model program design for education abroad is independent study that is institutionally sponsored, approved, and directed. Despite appearing to be an oxymoron, institutionally organized independent study can be an effective program design. In this model, the home institution makes no effort to set up classroom instruction of its own, or to arrange for matriculation at a foreign institution, or to combine these program approaches in some hybrid format. Rather, independent study students assume the responsibility for learning largely on their own, carrying out projects that usually have been designed in consultation with home-campus faculty, have been preapproved beforehand, and are evaluated for academic credit when the students return to their home campuses.

Such an individual approach to learning overseas appeals to students wishing to deepen their understanding of a foreign culture by living and working in it, on its terms—something they feel that more formal program models often inhibit. Independent study also provides students with opportunities to develop particular technical, artistic, or career skills that they cannot pursue at home or in a typical study abroad program. The duration of the experience may be as short as a few weeks or as long as a year. Independent study can be done by itself, or as an extension of another type of education abroad program.

In order to receive credit for the independent study, students are usually required to show that they have engaged in serious intellectual reflection on and critical assessment of what they have learned, usually in the form of an extended essay or research paper. The standards and policies for awarding credit for the experience, however, remain those of each individual home campus. Here it is not simply a matter of awarding credit for the experience alone, but rather of recognizing that the experience likely inspired and stimulated a kind of learning not possible in a classroom environment. It is the responsibility of the students to demonstrate their learning by means of a thorough intellectual analysis, their performance, or some product.

Included under this rubric are such things as:

- Language-immersion experiences (usually short-term) with or without formal study, but evaluated on the home campus on the basis of a demonstrated gain in proficiency.

- Scientific research projects, designed beforehand but carried out in the field or in a laboratory overseas, with or without an on-site supervisor. The project is usually evaluated by home-campus faculty on the basis of a report and analysis of findings. If the research is done under the supervision of a foreign mentor, that person is often asked to contribute to the assessment of the student's work.

- Library research, often in the humanities or social sciences, utilizing holdings uniquely available overseas, and typically resulting in a lengthy scholarly paper or senior thesis.

- Participation in volunteer or service-learning programs, assisting foreign communities in humanitarian projects. These experiences are given credit by the home campus only if such experiences are allowable for credit back home. Typical credit requirements include keeping a daily journal, doing background research and analysis, and then preparing a longer reflective essay on the experience.

- Unpaid internships and other sorts of work experiences in foreign industry, commercial firms, diplomatic agencies, etc. Again, if such learning opportunities are eligible for credit on the home campus, then they should be given credit when undertaken abroad. (However, some universities have a policy that only unpaid internships can receive credit. If the student is paid, then it is a job, not a for-credit learning experience.)

- Creative work, with or without mentors abroad, in theatre, the plastic or visual arts, music performance, creative writing, photography, or art forms, the quality of which can be judged by the quality of artistic products or performance, upon return.

Basic Characteristics

Supervision. Independent learning abroad can take a myriad of forms. At its purest, independent learning involves students working entirely on their own while they are overseas, perhaps maintaining contact with home-campus faculty supervisors through periodic reports—now made even more feasible via e-mail linkages. In many instances, it is possible for students or institutions to arrange formal or informal on-site supervision and guidance, typically through faculty contacts, but also through the foreign partner universities.

In other cases, independent study may be connected with a group program led by a faculty mentor, in which students conduct independent research projects in the local community and then meet periodically with the faculty member to discuss their experiences. Examples of faculty-led independent study programs include archeological investigations, the study and collection of biological specimens, or the study of architectural features of various buildings and monuments. In this case, the faculty member functions as an on-site adviser, working closely with students to guide them in the early stages of their field work, as well as being a resource as they delve deeper into their research.

On-site guidance may also come from: (1) an overseas supervisor, tutor, or mentor, at the institution or agency where the student will be, who provides counsel and support; (2) an internship placement coordinator who negotiates the internship placements on behalf of the home institution; (3) a local instructor who helps structure a student's academic learning and who provides a preliminary assessment; or (4) a home-campus program staff member acting as an intermediary between the student, overseas contacts, and the faculty supervisor.

The evaluation and grading of the project can be handled by someone at either the home campus or the overseas study destination. If the overseas evaluator is not a member of the home-campus faculty, that person may need to be approved for adjunct status, or one of the home-campus faculty members may need to jointly oversee and review the evaluation of the project. The faculty supervisor and the student should work together to establish the guidelines of the research to be conducted and to clarify the requirements that must be completed in order for the work to receive academic credit. Some institutions may require that independent research projects be cleared through the university's human subject or institutional review board procedures.

Qualifications. Admissions standards vary, depending on the nature and duration of the independent study plan. In general, students need to be mature, independent, and highly disciplined. They also need to have a high tolerance for ambiguity and to be flexible in adapting their planning to the circumstances they meet. If the project takes place in a country where a language other than English is spoken and if its success depends on meaningful interactions with this culture, students must obviously be competent in the local language.

Academics. In order to offer meaningful and challenging experiential learning, the independent-learning project must clearly outline and approve student goals and the pragmatic means of achieving them, well in advance of departure. Part of the evaluation of the project should be the extent to which the student adhered to the goals and other requirements of the project. Students doing independent research are generally expected to gather information and perspectives, synthesize them, do further reading and analysis, and at some later point present in a predetermined format what they have learned. Requirements should be stated in a syllabus, prospectus, or other type of project description that outlines the specific criteria the student must meet, what kinds of group meetings or debriefing sessions will take place, whether additional readings or lectures will be required, and how grades will be assigned. At many institutions, requirements are encapsulated in a formal learning contract, agreed to by all parties, and sometimes filed with either the registrar or the department where the credit is sought. It is important for both the faculty supervisor and the student to follow the college's established policies on independent study in designing the project.

Practical Arrangements. Students are in charge of making logistical preparations, including identifying a particular study destination and corresponding with prospective hosts. If formal admission to a host institution (agency, laboratory, library, studio, natural preserve, etc.) is necessary in order to carry out the project, this is also the student's responsibility. Housing and meals will depend on the nature of the project, its setting, and duration. If the program consists of an internship in a rural setting, a home-stay can be an ideal option to enhance the student's interaction with the host culture. In the case of a short-term group program, housing usually consists of hotels or youth hostels. Other types of support services (e.g., transportation, visas, police registration, insurance, etc.) are also largely the responsibility of participants, but students will still depend, to some degree, on what the education abroad office or supervising faculty member can offer in the way of information and advice.

Program Costs. Most institutions allowing students to earn independent study credit have a per-credit fee schedule, and typically this applies to overseas studies as well. Additionally, students are responsible for finding out about and paying all other costs: airfare, housing, meals, in-country transportation, plus any tuition fees or costs charged by a sponsoring institution or agency. Some institutions process financial aid for such costs, whereas others do not. In general, because independent study requires the student to do much, if not all, of the work to set up the experience, it can be the least expensive form of education abroad.

Advantages of the Independent Study Model

Independent study overseas offers participants the unique opportunity to apply theoretical concepts learned in a more traditional academic setting to a "hands on" experience. Internship and field study programs provide students the opportunity to integrate more fully into one aspect of the daily world of the host culture, thereby enriching their understanding of the country in which they are living and studying. Because such programs are not necessarily tied to an overseas academic institution, they have greater flexibility in timing and duration. In countries that experience frequent campus closures due to funding shortfalls or political tensions, the independent study experience can provide the best way to offer students a meaningful and academically credible activity at that location.

For a student who is willing to undertake the proper preparation and arrange adequate support beforehand, and then invest the time and energy to gather together what has been learned at the end, an independent study project can produce truly impressive outcomes. Significant cross-cultural learning can take place, particularly where cooperative activity, either research or work, occurs while working alongside host country nationals.

In most cases, the independent study model requires only minimal assistance from the education abroad office. Because students work in cooperation with home-campus faculty members to establish project goals, a time frame, required written work, and the grading procedure, the education abroad professional's job may be mainly to help students learn how to prepare to go abroad. Once the students return to campus, they again work primarily with the faculty member to complete the necessary requirements. Credit is usually awarded under the rubric of "individual study" in the faculty adviser's department.

Drawbacks of the Independent Study Model

Relative to other types of education abroad, few students will be attracted to this type of opportunity, though strong institutional support can increase the numbers. Regrettably, only the best students are

Chapter 1: Program Designs and Strategies

capable of undertaking truly independent research abroad. Maturity, discipline, superior background in the research area, language proficiency, organization, cross-cultural skills, patience, and stamina are only some of the essential qualities students will need to possess.

For most undergraduates, independent projects are difficult to develop, and faculty who are called on to support these efforts are often skeptical of their outcomes. Unless either the supervisors at home or the overseas contacts are knowledgeable, they will not be able to say whether the data that a student wishes to study exist, or exist in an accessible form. If an independent-study project requires no regular and daily contact with the host culture, as for example in library research, opportunities for cross-cultural learning are sharply reduced.

Because overseas independent study still may involve several levels of on-campus administration, miscommunications and other breakdowns can occur, leaving the student frustrated and occasionally without direction or even approval for the project. In the case of internships, the work experience can be tremendously productive or quite menial, depending on a number of factors beyond home-campus control. Once they are overseas, students sometimes discover that a particular research project or internship experience is not realistic. This creates a period of uncertainty, as the student and the home-campus supervisor explore alternatives, often at the mercy of intercontinental long-distance communications.

Independent study experiences also run the risk of minimal end results, either because the student does not complete the required assignments or fails to take the reflective activities seriously. For students who find out too late that they need a more structured learning environment, independent study can lead to frustration, disappointment, and no credit.

The problem of supervision is often cited as the principal weakness of independent study abroad. Supervision of a research project from a distance is difficult in the extreme. Thus, faculty are often reluctant to supervise projects abroad unless they know the student well.

PROGRAMS SPONSORED IN COOPERATION WITH OTHERS

As a means of maximizing study abroad opportunities in the face of limited resources, cooperatively run programs can be attractive. Many U.S. colleges and universities use one or more of the three types of consortially organized programs. The first, often called a *partnership consortium,* is created when two or more U.S. institutions join forces to operate one or more programs abroad for the students of all member institutions. The second type, sometimes called an *agency consortium*, is run by an independent organization that acts on behalf of member colleges and universities to set up and administer one or more programs abroad. The last type is the *program provider*. A program provider takes full responsibility for the operation and maintenance of a program abroad. The relative advantages and disadvantages of these three types of consortia will be considered individually. Consortium programs are especially useful in serving student, curricular, or geographical needs for which insufficient resources or student numbers exist to support a program on a given campus.

Partnership Consortia

Partnership consortia can be structured in different ways. In one variation, two or more institutions share in the operation and administration of a study abroad program, and each member shares equally in the obligations (both financial and administrative) and benefits of the program. In other cases, two or more institutions agree to support the program, but one institution acts as a lead campus in carrying out the organizational and administrative tasks. The role of lead campus may also be passed periodically from one campus to another in order to share the burdens more equally. The terms of the partnership are usually set down in an MOU, and may include a formula that regulates the number of students participating from the cooperating institutions and spells out the financial obligations of each. More viable and effective study abroad programs can be possible for smaller institutions when they share resources and operational responsibilities.

Basic Characteristics

Programs run by a partnership consortium are generally open only to students from the member institutions, although nonconsortium students may also be eligible to participate under certain agreements. All facets of a student's participation in this program are handled as if it were a program organized by the home campus.

Admission Requirements. Member institutions determine and coordinate admission standards for the program. Special arrangements are made by the member campuses to facilitate credit and financial arrangements for participating students, and application procedures are generally coordinated to meet the needs of each member institution.

Faculty and Staff. Depending on the model, faculty may be drawn from the various member campuses, from only one campus, or hired in the host country. In some cases, additional overseas staff are hired to perform the local administrative and academic aspects of the program.

Academics. The academic structure of consortial programs can vary widely, depending on the goals of the program. All of the program types mentioned above, including independent study, can be organized on a consortial basis in order to broaden the pool of applicants and thereby sustain the program. The challenge for the consortium model is to coordinate credit arrangements with each of the member campuses. Because some institutions allow transfer credit from only accredited universities (and a few from only those with U.S. accreditation) the consortium may have a lead institution to generate transcripts. Other institutions prefer to have their students remain officially enrolled on the home campus while participating in the consortium program. Careful coordination in setting up the consortium agreement is absolutely necessary in order to ensure that participants receive credit upon completion of the program.

Facilities. Overseas facilities will vary widely, depending on the kind of program offered, the resources available, and the program model chosen. In some cases, classroom and faculty workspace will need to be rented, whereas in other cases the program may participate in an existing overseas academic structure and program. Depending on the nature of the consortium, it may be necessary to have additional staff in place to coordinate the needs of the member campuses and facilitate regular meetings of the key campus coordinators.

Housing. Depending on the program, housing may be in overseas campus housing, in home-stays, or in special housing designed specifically for the consortium program. The type of housing provided will depend on the program's model, goals, and duration overseas.

Program Costs. One of the chief reasons for colleges to form consortia is to ensure that program costs remain affordable to all member institutions. A consortium strives to have lower per-student overhead costs and a larger pool of potential applicants than the individual colleges on their own. If there is a special administrative fee normally charged to students using outside programs, this fee is usually waived or reduced for consortium programs. In some cases, the member institutions may decide to establish a reserve fund for miscellaneous administrative costs or to create a limited exchange agreement for students from the host institution overseas. In this case, a special administrative fee for the consortium program may also be created.

Advantages of the Partnership Consortium

The pooling of resources is an obvious advantage of this model because a single institution might not have sufficient numbers of students or faculty to mount a program on its own. This is particularly important when an institution wishes to operate a program in a country that may be a less popular destination for students. Furthermore, institutions in a partnership consortium avoid duplication of efforts in the host country. Each of several programs may hire the same language or content course instructor to teach the same course to three students; by combining their efforts, the various programs could have been able to offer three levels of the language or three different courses at the half the cost.

Where faculty go abroad as resident directors or instructors, it is always better to have a larger pool from which to select a teaching staff. Pooling resources in consortium-operated programs may be applied to expertise. One campus may have strong faculty expertise in the history of a particular geographic area but be lacking expertise in political science or anthropology.

By coordinating a faculty of expertise from among a number of institutions, stronger study abroad programs are possible. There is also an advantage in having a group of students abroad from a variety of U.S. institutions. The mix may help prevent the U.S. group from becoming too insular. Inasmuch as learning takes place between peers, diverse rather than homogeneous groups are preferred. Working together also provides some leverage when negotiating with foreign institutions over costs, facilities, courses, and support services.

The reduction of fixed program costs (as they are spread out over a larger number of student participants) tends to be the greatest strength of consortially operated programs. Fixed costs are those that a program must pay regardless of the number of students who participate (e.g., the costs of teachers, administration, and facilities overseas), or that change for a group of students, such as every eight students because that is how many can fit into the minibus. Variable costs are those tied directly to each student participant (e.g., tuition, some transportation, books and supplies, insurance, meals, excursions, cultural events, and lodging).

In general, where fixed costs are high relative to total cost, a consortium program will usually save money for the sponsoring institutions, but not necessarily for students. (See Part III, Chapter 3, "Planning, Budgeting, and Implementation," for a more detailed discussion of student fees and their calculation.) Where fixed costs are low relative to total costs (or perhaps even nonexistent, as is the case in some direct enrollment programs based upon reciprocity), it makes no difference financially whether a program is consortially organized, so long as institutions can find students to go.

Drawbacks of the Partnership Consortium

With several institutions, offices, and individuals involved in the operation of these programs, the flow of information may not be smooth or efficient. In addition, because the governance of the program's operation is shared among all of the participating institutions, more time is required to generate the information necessary for program operations. The problem of communication is compounded if the cooperating institutions are geographically distant. Holding joint predeparture orientation programs, for instance, becomes difficult if not impossible.

Consortially organized programs often involve the loss of some autonomy on the part of each participating college. Institutions may not, for example, be able to send as many students as they would like, because the numbers of participating students are often governed by an agreement among all the members. The shared governance of the consortium requires that representatives of the participating institutions meet periodically to set policies and in some cases to select students and resident faculty or staff.

Because of these drawbacks, many consortia choose to have the program administered out of a fixed office or location. This location might rotate among or remain at one of the cooperating institutions. In either event, all program matters are addressed to this central administrative office. If resident directors are sent abroad from the participating institutions, the directorship often rotates among the member institutions. Frequent changes in personnel or administrative operations at any institution, however, can also significantly compound even routine communication difficulties.

Working with an Agency Consortium

The second type of consortium assigns an independent agency (a nonprofit or profit-making organization) the responsibility for much of the logistical and academic details of establishing and maintaining one or more programs abroad. In this type of consortium, the agency works with the host institution to arrange housing, and provides on-site orientation and ongoing support services. It may conduct one or more predeparture orientation programs. In addition, some agencies also coordinate the academic program and the transfer of credit. The agency may be responsible for hiring resident directors (with the approval of member institutions) and monitoring the program on a regular basis.

Programs run in this way can follow any number of models: independent campuses for member-institution students only, direct enrollment into a foreign institution, or hybrid curricula that include both special and regular university course work. Students are drawn from the member institutions; and from the student's, as well as the home campus's point of view, it is a campus program.

Basic Characteristics

Faculty and Staff. Depending on the program model, the agency assists in recruiting faculty from the partner institutions, and supplements these hires with instructors hired on-site. In the case of an integrated program model, instruction is provided by the host institution or the partner institutions.

Academics. The academic structure of the program is determined largely by the agency, in cooperation with the member institutions. A variety of program models is possible, and programs are likewise determined in cooperation between the agency and the member institutions.

Advantages of the Agency Consortium Model

Regardless of the overseas program design, the agency consortium model has several domestic advantages. Membership in a consortium offers program choices far beyond those that a single institution is able to provide, especially if an institution has limited commitments to or funding for education abroad programming. Participating institutions are relieved of the burden of making the logistical arrangements abroad, and, in the case of study center programs, finding faculty each year who are willing to accompany the students abroad.

Because the central organization is also responsible for establishing and maintaining the programs abroad, students at the participating institutions have ongoing access to a wide variety of possible study sites, allowing the education abroad office to focus on advice, recruitment, orientation, and other on-campus support services. The agency can also effectively ensure that on-site orientation programs, advising, and classes meet the specific agreed-upon standards of the participating institutions as well as the academic and personal needs of students.

The costs of membership in an agency consortium vary quite a bit. Some agency consortia bring together public colleges and universities within a common range of tuition; others cater to private colleges and universities; some are established so that both public and private institutions find cost benefits. Some consortia have set a fee for the program, which includes all costs including airfare, orientation program, room and board, and excursions; others fix fees for only room, board, and tuition. Those with reciprocal agreements have participating students pay fees to the home institution, in addition to an administrative fee to the central organization. This feature is quite attractive to state institutions with low in-state tuition rates. Several agency consortia have special financial aid programs for qualified students.

Chapter 1: Program Designs and Strategies

Drawbacks of the Agency Consortium Model

Most agency consortia require an annual membership fee, and in some cases this is a significant amount, especially if few of an institution's students participate in the consortium's programs. In addition, many also have a per-enrollment administrative fee that is passed on to students, increasing their costs. If fees are set on the basis of private college tuition, public college students often find the costs unaffordable.

In an agency consortium, the home institution does not have complete control over the selection and placement process. In some cases, only a few students from each participating institution are eligible for certain programs. Where the consortium places students at several sites abroad, students may not be placed at the institution of their choice, or even placed at all. In sum, the admissions process can be lengthy and complex, and the results not always what students expected.

Finally, because consortia operate by consensus, with the agency simply administering these decisions, a given institution will not have its way on all matters. A program can easily get caught between consortium policy and the preferences of one administration. Matters such as the course content, the structure of the program, or the calendar can become divisive issues. If a given institution finds itself continually at odds with other members, however, it can always withdraw from the consortium. Whether it can take its programs along with it should be spelled out in the MOU.

Working with a Program Provider

The last type of consortium gives over to an independent organization, or program provider, the responsibility for both the operation and the academic content of programs abroad. In this type of arrangement, the program provider acts much like an agency consortium, in that it works with the contacts abroad to arrange housing and provide on-site orientation and student support services. The provider sends out predeparture information materials and takes responsibility for predeparture questions about the program. Most program providers assist with the transfer of credit, working with member institution representatives. The provider is responsible for hiring on-site faculty and staff and monitoring the program on a regular basis. Programs run in this way can follow any number of models: direct enrollment into a foreign institution, hybrid curricula that include both special and regular university course work, and island or study center programs. Most program providers also invite the participation of representatives of colleges and universities in some kind of program—both information-sharing and advisory forums. However, program providers differ from agency and partnership consortia in one important feature. In a consortium, the final decision comes from a consensus or a vote of the members. Program providers may call upon sending institutions for advice, but the final decision rests not with the members, but with the provider's executive director, chief executive officer, or board of directors.

Many institutions choose to establish a continuing relationship with one or more program providers, in order to facilitate academic articulation and administrative cooperation. Before making this choice, though, an institution should establish a policy on how it plans to cooperate with program providers. Among the many things to consider when establishing a policy on program providers are academic and programmatic issues such as language learning, level of integration in host country academic systems, credit for experiential learning, duration of the program, the qualifications of those who teach in the program, and finally, the academic and geographic distribution of program opportunities. A particular institution might not really need six programs in France. In addition, campus administrative and financial issues require consideration. Allowing students to participate in off-campus programs may affect revenues or expenses or both. (See Part III, Chapter 3, "Planning, Budgeting, and Implementation.") The education abroad office should work closely with its institution's faculty and administration to see that the providers and their programs under consideration aid the institution in meeting its internationalization objectives and academic goals without causing financial or enrollment management problems. Perhaps most importantly, student access issues (especially with regard to student finances) need to be considered when developing an institutional policy on providers. A program or provider that is available only to students with great personal or parental financial resources may conflict with other institutional values. This type of situation may open the education abroad experience up to charges of being peripheral to the institution, or elitist.

The senior administration of an institution may wish to delegate the process for recognition of program providers to a committee or to the education abroad office. Some institutions have created an all-campus committee to review and approve programs. Such committees often include a representative from the office of risk management and one from the study abroad office, faculty from various departments and colleges, a student (formally nominated by the student government organization) and, perhaps, others, such as the associate dean for academic affairs. At other institutions, such education abroad committees are only advisory in nature, with the actual authority resting with the director of education abroad. However authority is delegated, who decides what for whom must be clearly understood and documented. In any event, the more inclusive the review process, the broader based the support and the lower the risk that something will be questioned later.

Advantages of the Program Provider Model

Working with a program provider has a number of important advantages. By cooperating with one of these organizations, an institution can offer a wide range of programs without the commitment of resources necessary for belonging to a consortium or developing a program on its own. If the institution has one student in one year interested in the subject or region of the provider's program, it will be able to provide an appropriate education abroad opportunity without creating a whole new program structure. This type of arrangement is flexible enough to allow for an increase to ten students in one year and a decrease to one student in the next year. Because the central organization is also responsible for establishing and maintaining the programs abroad, students at the participating institutions have ongoing access to a wide variety of possible study sites, while the education abroad office can focus on advice, recruitment, orientation, and other campus support. The program provider also effectively ensures that all aspects of the program abroad, from on-site orientation programs to advising and classes, meet the provider's standards, the requirements of the sending campus, and the personal and academic needs of the students.

Drawbacks of the Program Provider Model

By working with a program provider that will draw students from dozens (maybe hundreds) of different institutions, an institution cedes academic control over the program to the provider. Good providers will be interested in each institution's comments and will strive to offer the best program possible. Still, there may be times when an institution will not be able to change or even influence some elements of the program. Furthermore, the education abroad office will have little influence or control over the selection and placement of its institution's students. While some providers may reserve a specific number of places for students from those institutions with a history of sending large numbers of students on their programs, others will admit students only on a first-come, first-served basis. Thus, while a particular student may meet the provider's eligibility requirements, the program may be already full.

Some program providers require an annual membership fee, and, as in the case of consortia, it can be significant. In addition, the cost to the student can be quite high, although it may be possible to negotiate a discount for large groups of students from the same institution.

Finally, while a program provider arrangement allows for minimal commitment of an institution's resources, it will also limit the ways in which key members of a campus community can be involved. Less involvement can translate into less support, if not managed correctly. The support of colleagues such as faculty, financial aid officers, and registrars can be critical in making a student's participation a success.

In sum, working with a program provider offers program choices far beyond those that one institution is able to provide, especially if the institution has a limited commitment to or limited funding for education abroad programming. The institution is relieved of the burden of making the logistical arrangements abroad, and, in the case of branch-campus programs, finding enough faculty members each year willing to accompany and teach the students abroad.

Reciprocally Organized Programs and Direct Exchanges

Any of the study abroad program models described above may be organized reciprocally. Reciprocity means that two educational institutions in different countries agree to some form of exchange. Typically, a reciprocal exchange involves an equal number of students or faculty taking each other's places over equal periods of time.

Originally, exchange programs between universities were based on the principle of student-for-student, one-to-one exchange, with each paying room, board, and tuition at the home institution and no monies changing hands. In practice, however, many universities have found it difficult to send an equal number of students in both directions in the same semester or academic year. Consequently, a variety of exchange mechanisms have been developed that are not limited to student-for-student reciprocity. Thus, reciprocity may now also involve asymmetrical numbers of students and unequal periods of time spent abroad; it may also include faculty members as well as students, with students exchanged for faculty and vice versa.

At the heart of strict reciprocity is the concept of a waiver of fees. This means that in the case of students, each of the students in the exchange pays the standard fees to the home university and then they trade places. Thus, reciprocity can occur only if each institution is able and willing to accept visiting students without an actual payment of tuition. In the case of faculty, the same concept applies, except that each side agrees to continue paying the faculty members as if they were teaching on the home campus. However, many U.S. colleges charge all incoming foreign students regular tuition and fees, regardless of whether they are visiting exchange students or regular degree seekers, making it necessary for the receiving college to grant the incoming exchange student a scholarship to cover the charges. Because of U.S. tax laws and various tax treaties, the foreign exchange student may be liable for U.S. taxes on the scholarship, but if the receiving institution increases the scholarship to cover the tax, things usually work out in the end. Some reciprocal exchanges include only tuition waivers; others cover room and board as well.

Usually, services beyond those that an institution regularly offers to its own students are not included in reciprocal exchange agreements. Thus, students needing significant language training, for example, might have to pay for that out of their own pockets. The additional costs besides room and board (travel, health insurance, and personal expenses) may put reciprocal exchanges to the United States beyond the reach of students from developing countries, unless they can obtain funding from other sources in their home country, from the Fulbright Commission, or from the receiving institution in the United States.

Creating a flexible system that allows the student or dollar balances called for in reciprocity agreements to be spread out over several years is helpful. This flexibility allows a system of credits and debits to develop, and provides time for the cooperating institutions to balance these credits or debits by sending more or fewer students in any given year to make up for previous imbalances. This adaptation works very well, particularly where room and board costs are covered directly by the participating students. In order to have this flexibility, an institution needs to have money available to cover costs for students from cooperating institution, either by accumulating fees paid by its own outbound students in previous years or by having a reserve fund to cover temporary exchange imbalances. Private institutions often have some advantages in these regards.

A third adaptation is based on exchanging a fixed ratio of students in staggered years. These exchanges begin in year one, with x number of students moving in one direction. This number becomes a base figure that dictates how many students the cooperating institution may send in a subsequent period. This mechanism works particularly well where the calendars of the two cooperating institutions begin during different times of the year. For illustrative purposes, assume a relationship between a U.S. and a Latin American university. The U.S. institution's calendar begins in September, and the Latin American's in March. They agree to exchange three U.S. students for one Latin American student. In September, the Latin American university sends five students to the U.S. university. In March, the U.S. university reciprocates and sends up to fifteen of its students to its Latin American partner. If it sends fewer or more, these gains or losses are simply transferred to the next cycle, with the exchange balanced in each succeeding year. The ratio of students sent between the institutions is determined by agreement and will depend on the respective services provided by each. This adaptation to direct exchange is particularly useful when room and board on both sides is delivered to the participating students.

Some reciprocal agreements are based on allocations of money rather than an exchange of students. Under these agreements, one of the cooperating institutions agrees to generate x dollars for each student it sends abroad, and to reserve that amount to support students coming from the partner institution. This kind of mechanism can easily be combined with those adaptations where uneven numbers of students are being exchanged. This approach simplifies the question of equity, and provides great flexibility to the institution that has received monetary credits in the foreign country. The institution can send students, but may choose to use the credits to support a single faculty sabbatical at the partner institution, an advanced degree for one of their students, or the purchase of equipment or library materials, and so forth. Obviously, these types of agreements must be specific on how financial credits can be used, because in most instances they do not represent actual funds that can be spent for salaries, equipment, or library books.

Reciprocal exchanges require that staff time be committed to the incoming exchange students. Ideally, the international student adviser's office and other offices on campus that provide services for students from abroad can do this work. If small numbers of students are exchanged, the education abroad office may be able to handle the responsibilities of arranging housing and meals, orientation, immigration, and academic counseling for incoming students, but—especially in view of recent and continuing changes in visa eligibility, immigration policy, and reporting requirements through the Student and Exchange Visitor Information System (SEVIS)—the responsibility is best handled by staff trained and assigned to work with international students. Even so, the education abroad office will still be expected to provide some support for incoming exchange students, whose needs are different in many respects from those of international degree-seeking students. Visiting students, however, can also provide valuable service by helping to promote exchange opportunities to U.S. students.

Advantages of Reciprocal Programs

Reciprocal exchange agreements offer significant advantages. Where the cost of launching stand-alone programs might be prohibitive, direct exchanges present low-cost alternatives. Because students from both sides remain registered at and pay tuition to their home institutions, federal and other financial aid can be applied towards the cost. For private institutions especially, the fact that there is no loss of tuition revenue and no need to pay out money to program providers for students with institutional scholarships is an important benefit. Because program costs are paid in the local currency, they are not affected by fluctuations in exchange rates, and, in countries where currency controls restrict the numbers of students studying abroad, programs organized reciprocally can provide some relief.

There are also significant advantages that are not financial. Reciprocity gives each institution a stake in the relationship, so that each works harder to make sure it succeeds. This networking tends to create additional activities, in some cases developing into additional programs (often for faculty), which further strengthen the links between the two institutions. When recruiting and conducting predeparture sessions for outgoing students, exchange students can serve as a valuable resource. Finally, reciprocity in education abroad programming diversifies the student body on a campus, often bringing to it students from countries who do not send many degree-seeking students to the United States (especially at the undergraduate level), and contributes to the international education of students who do not study abroad. Because exchange students are only on campus for a short period of time, they are often eager to become as involved as possible.

Drawbacks of Reciprocal Programs

Reciprocal exchanges place significant demands on institutional infrastructure. Hosting incoming students involves handling admissions, visas, orientation, housing, registration, and providing continuous academic and administrative support while the international students are on campus. Good liaison on the home campus between the education abroad office and the offices providing these services is essential; and when negotiating agreements, the education abroad office needs to ascertain that the receiving institution has sufficient resources to provide necessary services for students abroad. Different cultures have different expectations with regard to student services, and it is important to find a balance between ensuring that basic services are in place and preparing the U.S. students to accept a higher level of responsibility for their studies and daily lives than at home. (See "Integrated Models," above.) Good communication between the U.S. institutions and the overseas institutions is also essential in order to resolve difficulties or confusion regarding academic expectations, financial arrangements, or administrative support. Because exchange students are only on campus for one year, the education abroad office is constantly dealing with "first year" students, who must always start at the beginning.

It is possible to reap the benefits of reciprocal exchange and reduce the risk of imbalances and consequent financial liability by working through a state consortium (e.g., The University of North Carolina Exchange Program or the University of

Georgia System Consortium), a regional consortium, or an international network such as ISEP or the Consortium for North American Higher Education Cooperation (CONAHEC) among many others.

Summary

This chapter describes some of the major types of program design now in use, presenting the potential academic, intercultural, and financial advantages, as well as the corresponding limitations of each type of program design. Once education abroad administrators become familiar with the different types of programs and their advantages and disadvantages, they will be in a better position to give advice to senior administrators about designs that provide the best fit for the institution and its students. Moreover, consideration of the elements of these basic program types and their advantages as well as disadvantages can aid the education abroad adviser in helping students consider and select the programs that best meet their needs and interests.

CHAPTER 2

Short-Term Programs Abroad

Contributors: Sarah E. Spencer, Tina Murray, Kathy Tuma

Short-term program models can be found in abundance: a "Theatre in London" January course fulfills a fine arts general education requirement; a ten-day intensive program takes MBA students to Rio de Janeiro to study international business issues; a three-week May-term program with no prerequisites is aimed at first- and second-year undergraduate students, giving them an early option to study abroad; an eight-day study tour takes nontraditional students to Oaxaca, Mexico, as part of a spring semester language or sociology course. These examples point to the advantages of short-term programs abroad. Their short duration makes them attractive to students who don't have time in their academic programs for a semester or year abroad, or who must work to pay for college and can't afford to be gone for long. A change of majors, a double major, teaching certification, and varsity sports are among the reasons students commonly give for choosing a short-term program over a longer one. With short-term programs, it is also possible for students to participate in more than one program during their college careers; and some students will participate in a short-term program as well as a semester or year abroad program.

One of the most significant changes in education abroad in the last decade is the dramatic increase in the number of short-term programs and the considerable number of students participating in them. The context for the increase in the number of students participating in short-term programs is, of course, the reported overall increased participation in education abroad programs. In the ten years from 1993-1994 to 2002-2003, *Open Doors* data show that the number of students participating in education abroad rose from 76,302 to 174,629, an increase of 129 percent. In this same ten-year period, the percentage of education abroad students participating in short-term programs (i.e., lasting fewer than eight weeks) went from 1.7 percent of the total to 9.4 percent (an increase of 453 percent, and thus too large to represent on the chart below). Summer program participation has remained relatively level over the period, moving from 30.9 percent of the total to 32.7 percent (an increase of 8.3 percent). Likewise semester participation rose only slightly from 37.2 percent to 40.3 percent (an increase of 5.8 percent), while academic year participation declined from 14.3 percent to 6.7 percent (a decrease of 53 percent). Given these trends, it would not be surprising to see participation in academic year programs fall below that of January term programs (see Figure 1).

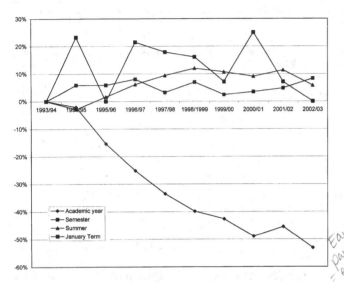

Figure 1. Percentage change in enrollment in education abroad programs from 1993–1994 to 2002–2003. Note: This chart does not include the 453 percent increase in participation in programs lasting fewer than eight weeks. (Dataset from Open Doors 2004.)

This rapid shift has left higher education celebrating the broadening of access to study abroad programs for students who otherwise would not have even considered it an option, especially those who are older than the traditional 18- to 22-year-old college student, are employed, or have limited funds. Institutions have also seen larger study abroad enrollments, more programs that integrate directly into the curriculum, and a more internationalized faculty. However, the overall growth in education abroad has also meant that education abroad professionals, university administrators, and faculty often must scramble to find sufficient resources and must implement appropriate academic, health and safety, and other policies in order to keep up with this expansion.

Within the higher education field, the definition of what constitutes a short-term program abroad has changed over the last fifty years. At first, yearlong study overseas was labeled short-term, as opposed to earning one's degree abroad. Later, a semester was considered short. Now, short-term programs are one to eight weeks in length (i.e., less than a term), are usually faculty-directed, and are typically sponsored by a U.S. university or consortium. The programs can be based in one city or one country, or travel to multiple sites or countries.

There is some evidence that students who participate in a short-term program early in college will feel more confident about enrolling in a longer program later. Furthermore, because short-term programs typically consist of only one course, they offer an intensive academic experience and, if properly designed, an intensive intercultural experience as well. Following a year of foreign language course work on campus, four weeks in a country where that language is spoken can go a long way to solidifying a student's proficiency and continued interest in the language. Many students are clearly drawn to a short-term program because of the content of the course as well as the location in which it will be taught. Because of their use of primary sources of information, lectures by prominent citizens such as politicians or human rights advocates as well as visits to rural communities, factories, artists and artisans, many short-term program courses focus on such contemporary issues as HIV/AIDS in rural Africa, Rainforest preservation and economic development in Central America, or the situation of refugees in any number of countries. Perhaps just as many take up topics ranging from the architecture of classical Greece to the zoology of the Galapagos.

Proposing New Programs

Anyone proposing a new short-term program abroad should be prepared to do two things at once: develop the academic rationale for the program and lay a solid foundation for the smooth administration of the program. A new program cannot be operated without the support of key campus administrators. But without a well-designed program, it will be very difficult to get that support. This chapter will look at issues of program development and design and consider how on-campus support for the program can be established. All of the topics presented in this chapter are discussed in greater detail in *The Guide to Successful Short-Term Programs Abroad* (Spencer and Tuma 2002).

Program Development

The preceding chapter, "Program Designs and Strategies," discussed the importance of having a solid academic design for any education abroad program. It is also very important to determine whether the course concept will make a feasible short-term program. Good on-campus courses do not always lend themselves to successful study abroad options, much less programs that can be sustained over time. Consideration of both academic and logistical issues throughout the design process will help determine the feasibility of a program. The following questions provide a starting point:

- What are the academic and intercultural learning outcomes for the program?
- How does teaching the course overseas enhance these outcomes?
- How is the instruction and learning environment enhanced by offering the program overseas?
- What facilities will be needed for delivering the course content? Are there special needs for classroom space and equipment?
- Will the program take place in one destination, or will participants travel to several destinations?
- How will transportation to and from the program's location and during the program be arranged?
- What arrangements will be made for housing and meals?
- What will and will not be included in the fees charged?
- What types of visits, excursions, and cultural activities will be included in the curricular portion of the program? When will free time be scheduled?
- Will additional support staff and faculty be needed? If so, how will they be compensated and their expenses provided?
- Are visas required?
- Are there any special medical requirements specific to location that should be addressed?

The Academic Program

Unlike its longer counterpart, a short-term program's academic content is typically designed and delivered by the home institution's faculty members. While the advantages of using home-campus faculty are clear, including their knowledge of curricular expectations and students, not all

Part III: Program Development, Campus Management, Marketing, and Evaluation

faculty realize that teaching a course off-campus in a short period of time differs greatly from the on-campus experience. Because short-term programs are sometimes perceived as "time off," or as being academically "lightweight," the program designer must clearly articulate to all stakeholders—colleagues, deans, the registrar, overseas partners, and especially, students—how the learning objectives, readings, excursions, and methods of assessment interface and integrate with the site abroad. The perception of the academic quality of the program will rest on how each of these is articulated throughout the course development and proposal process.

While all education abroad programs should draw their design, resources, and assignments from the unique opportunities offered by the site, the condensed timeline of short-term programs offers a greater challenge. There is not enough time for lengthy reading assignments during the time abroad. Moreover, traditional research methodology will have to be adapted to fit the time available. And intercultural processing time is so condensed that students tend to focus on what they see or do, and do not take time to reflect on what they are learning, unless they are motivated to do so through course assignments or instructor-led debriefing exercises. In addition, teaching techniques must be rethought and restructured in order to make the most of each short-term program. Cross-cultural methods such as interviews, academic journals, oral presentations, and frequent prepping, processing, or reflection can substitute and enhance the learning on-site, provided the students have the necessary proficiency in the target language.

Design Issues

In designing short-term programs, the following academic issues should be addressed:

Contact Hours. The common practice is to define contact hours as any activity in which students are engaged with the learning objectives of the program. Because of the nontraditional classroom and the unstructured schedule typically found in short-term programs, institutional policy must be clear regarding contact hours for these off-campus programs.

Site Visits and Excursions. Because short-term programs usually involve visits to various cultural, historical, governmental, or business sites, it is extremely important to the overall structure and academic quality of the program that students are well prepared. Each visit should be introduced beforehand, summarized, and reflected upon after the actual visit.

Readings. Assignments should be carefully chosen and apportioned in amounts that permit them to be read in the evening or during free periods of the day. If possible, materials should be distributed during orientation, and students should be encouraged (or even required) to do the reading before departure. This is particularly important if there are long articles or a book that must be read for the course.

Grading. While the basic form of assessment may be based on traditional methods (e.g., quizzes, papers, and exams), many short-term programs also include one or more subjective measures, due to their experiential nature. The grading policy must be clearly stated, including precise descriptions of the assessment of experiential components.

Learning and Intercultural Growth. The best short-term programs balance the experience itself with processing the experience. This leads to learning as well as to intercultural and personal growth. Kolb notes that without reflection, experience cannot be translated into learning (1984). Programs should be designed with sufficient time for students to reflect, especially outside of the defined class time.

Culture Learning. There is a risk in short-term, faculty-directed programs that the students will go abroad, learn the discipline-based content of the course offered, and return to the United States without having learned anything about the culture of the location where the program took place. It is important for the faculty directors to be taught how to facilitate culture learning. While this may be easier in some disciplines than others, it should be a priority for all programs.

As an example, an economics professor taking a group of students to the leading financial institutions in London needs to teach not only the fundamentals of the British economic system, but also the reasons why that system is different from that of the United States, what factors have caused this system to develop in the way that it has, and how the culture has contributed to these differences. In programs of longer duration, there may be time for students to realize some of these cultural differences on their own. However, in short-term programs, the cultural learning needs to be deliberate and carefully orchestrated.

Unstructured Time. Unscheduled time is a complex issue for short-term program design. Too much free time will raise questions about the academic integrity of the course vis-à-vis the amount of credit granted; too little free time could compromise the students' ability to learn and to participate in program activities, due to exhaustion and information overload. Programs should balance reading and writing assignments, program visits, and other activities, with time for rest, relaxation, and exploration for both students and faculty directors.

Group Dynamics. One of the greatest challenges for all faculty directors of education abroad programs, regardless of the program's duration, is group dynamics. In semester or yearlong programs, there is often time for the faculty member to let issues of group dynamics work themselves out without intervention. In short-term programs, group problems need to be dealt with quickly and decisively so that the more important business of learning can continue. If the program's success requires a cohesive group, the faculty director will need to be able to grow that kind of group, and should begin the process long before the group leaves the campus.

Obviously, interacting with a group of students in a classroom on campus requires very different skills than interacting with a group of students in an off-campus program. On-campus, the faculty member may see the students three or four hours a week. In a short-term program, they will be with the students twenty-four hours a day, seven days a week. Faculty directors will get to see all facets of their students, and probably all aspects of their lives, not just their appearance when they come to class. Education abroad administrators should not assume that every faculty member possesses the skills needed to direct a program abroad. Faculty orientation should include time for experienced and successful program directors to share with their newer colleagues various ways in which they have facilitated group dynamics issues and handled problems with students. Faculty directors should be advised to begin discussions about group dynamics in predeparture orientation with students. The students need to be made aware that, in many cases, they will be required to place the good of the group before their individual needs.

Orientation. While predeparture orientations and reentry programming are essential for all off-campus programs, they are especially critical for short-term programs, in order to avoid having any of the participants approach the experience abroad as superficial academic tourism. Before departure for the host site, students should receive an orientation that addresses topics such as academic course work, intercultural interaction, culture shock, travel and logistics, historical and cultural background information for the program's location, and group dynamics. This information should be repeated in a thorough on-site orientation. Both orientations should also discuss the student participation agreement, the code of conduct, and the sanctions for violations of any program policies. Reentry activities should focus on individual reflection as well as group discussion about the students' experiences and how they have used their experiences abroad in their studies at home.

Health, Safety, and Security

Information on health, safety, security, risk management, and duty and liability (see Part II, Chapter 6, "Advising Students on Safety and Security Issues;" Part III, Chapter 6, "Maximizing Safety and Security and Minimizing Risk in Education Abroad Programs;" and Part III, Chapter 7, "Legal Issues and Education Abroad") must be considered when designing and leading a short-term program abroad. Don't be fooled into thinking that a shorter duration means a lesser likelihood of any kind of emergency. The very nature of short-term programs, with their "hit the ground running and don't waste precious time" plan of action, can cause students, and sometimes faculty directors, to try to do too much too quickly, without taking the time to properly research and prepare. Following are a few things to think about when planning for short-term programs:

Health Issues. It is important for students and faculty directors to leave the United States healthy and stay that way overseas, as there is no time to be sick. If a student spends four or five days in bed with an illness, he or she may have missed as much as half of the program. Program directors should encourage students to rest well and take good care of themselves prior to departure. Program materials and predeparture orientation should provide as much information as possible about health risks that may be prevalent in the areas where the program will travel, and offer advice on ways in which they can guard against those risks and sources for more information. Students and faculty directors should be referred to a travel clinic for health information and immunizations before departing from the United States.

Safety Issues. Short-term programs need the same safety and risk assessments as their longer counterparts. (See Part III, Chapter 6, "Maximizing Safety and Security and Minimizing Risk in Education Abroad Programs.") It is especially important that at least one of the faculty directors of the program have recent experience in the location where the program will be based. If the program travels, then someone who will accompany the students should travel the program route in advance.

Because of time pressures and the tendency for students to try to do too much too fast during short-term programs, faculty directors must be especially attentive to the risks and hazards presented by the locale and activities. The rule of thumb in all education abroad programs is to plan for safety and stick with the plan. Predeparture and on-site orientations must include good information about safety risks and the consequences of certain behaviors. Program materials and the orientations must be very clear about the policy regarding alcohol and drug use and abuse.

Liability Issues. The need for all of the usual waiver forms and participation agreement forms is the same in short-term programs as in semester or yearlong programs. (See Part III, Chapter 6, "Maximizing Safety and Security and Minimizing

Risk in Education Abroad Programs," and Part III, Chapter 7, "Legal Issues and Education Abroad.") Many short-term programs are open to students from outside the home institution. Legal counsel and the risk manager from the sponsoring institution should be consulted to determine if visiting students are covered under institutional liability policies, or if special arrangements need to be made. University counsel and the risk manager should review all contracts with vendors and providers.

Legal counsel or the risk manager should also determine the level of protection that faculty have when directing a group of students off-campus. The duties and responsibilities that are required of a program director leave the faculty member open to a much greater risk of legal action by a student alleging negligence or breach of duty. It is crucial that the institution adequately protect its faculty members, or that the faculty directors obtain their own insurance. Faculty orientation sessions should identify situations where the institution's insurance coverage may not extend. For example, if institutional policy prohibits alcohol from being served at college- or university-sponsored functions, and the faculty member allows alcohol to be served at a group dinner abroad, he or she may not be covered by liability insurance because of noncompliance with official policy.

Faculty Roles

Part I, Chapter 5, "Faculty Roles," extensively discussed the roles that faculty can and should play on campus with regard to education abroad. All of these topics are equally important for faculty involved in short-term programs. Education abroad administrators should not make the mistake of assuming that a short-term program means that faculty need less preparation. In fact, most often, more preparation is needed. Faculty who direct short-term programs abroad must act not only as professors, but also as tour guides, nurses, personal counselors, intercultural advisers, psychologists, coaches, cheerleaders, dean of students, financial officers, bankers, and translators, and the list goes on. Faculty must be prepared to be on-call around the clock, every day of the program.

Program Ownership

In most cases, semester and yearlong faculty-directed programs are designed by an academic unit or area studies department; rarely are they the product of an individual faculty member. This is not the case, however, for short-term programs. Here, an individual faculty member is most often "the curricular architect of the program" (Hoffa 1998). Such individuals should be encouraged to share ownership in the short-term programs they will direct. It is important to strike a balance of ownership among the faculty member, the department, and the international office. While the faculty member may have complete control of the academic content of the course, and sometimes even the logistical arrangements, it is important for the international office to be actively involved in all off-campus programs. If for no other reason than to minimize liability to the institution, faculty should not be allowed to operate programs without institutional endorsement and oversight.

Program Providers

Given the increasing popularity of education abroad today, more and more organizations are offering to provide services in a wide variety of destinations on a fee-for-service basis. Frequently, such organizations, often called program providers, are able to provide a wide range of services in a cost-effective manner, because they work with a variety of institutions at the same time. Some providers will also provide assistance with publicity and curriculum design, which can be helpful to those education abroad professionals who are new to designing programs. Program providers can supply all or part of the travel arrangements, and may include the use of traditional travel agents, tour operators, and on-site service agents in their packages. Overseas institutions may offer services to short-term programs as a part of an overall institutional relationship.

Many institutions have rules and regulations regarding the procurement of and payment for services. Some also limit the types of vendors that may be used to make program arrangements. When designing a new program, it is important to know, understand, and follow the financial policies of the institution. It is important to receive a contract detailing the cost and type of services provided, as well as to note if the provider or agent is arranging the services itself, or subcontracting that task to others. The more detail received at the design stage, the lower the possibility for miscommunication during student enrollment and the time abroad. The contracts should provide for a minimum and maximum number of participants, and should also clearly explain cancellation procedures. For more information about program providers, see Part III, Chapter 1, "Program Designs and Strategies."

Program Administration

Historically, academic short-term programs abroad started with individual faculty members initiating ideas. In some cases, off-campus courses were taught with no institutional approval or administrative oversight. More recently, short-term programs have been offered as part of a deliberate institutional strategy, often in response to faculty or student interest. The support of the key offices on campus that will provide assistance in a wide variety of administrative details is critical to the success of a program. The following questions will help assure that the salient issues are addressed when the various campus offices are approached about supporting short-term programs abroad:

- *Deans, department chairs:* Is there support at all academic levels for short-term programs? Have academic units identified the appropriate student audience, curricular match, and faculty directors? What is the approval process for short-term programs? Who can propose a program? How long will the approval process take?

- *Registrar:* Will enrollment in short-term programs require special registration codes? Will the transcript reflect this type of study abroad credit? Who will be responsible for preparing transcripts for these off-campus students?

- *Business office:* Who will review budgets for accuracy? Who will review contracts? Who has the authority to sign contracts? Who will be responsible for collecting funds and paying vendors? How will budget deficits and surpluses be handled?

- *Financial aid:* Will students be eligible to receive financial aid for short-term programs abroad? Is there a separate process and application for the term off campus?

- *Risk management and legal counsel:* What are the federal, state, and institutional requirements concerning risk management? What are the legal issues? Will university legal counsel develop and review appropriate liability waivers for short-term programs?

- *Continuing education:* Are there policies for short-term programs already in place? Is there room for collaboration?

To avoid duplication of effort, the program administrator must research whether the college already has systems and procedures in place that could support short-term programs. It is also important to be sensitive to those programs already in existence elsewhere in the institution, as proprietary issues may arise.

Models of Short-Term Program Administration

Once the first short-term program has been approved, the number of other programs has a tendency to grow exponentially. It is essential to define and establish the procedures that will be used to administer these programs. Before setting up an appropriate administrative model, the program administrator must understand under what aegis the program will operate and how this will relate (if at all) to the education abroad office of the institution. Most administrative models can be defined as decentralized, centralized, or hybrid. (See Part I, Chapter 4, "Education Abroad in the Campus Context," for a more detailed discussion of these issues.)

Decentralized Administration. In a decentralized administration model, academic departments or individual faculty members design and administer their own short-term programs with little or no input from the education abroad office. This is a typical model for education abroad management at many institutions, particularly if the short-term programs are offered only in the summer. Even if semester and academic year education abroad programs are administered centrally from the college's education abroad office, summer short-term programs are often run by departments and individual faculty members. This arrangement is sometimes due to the fact that the education abroad office is open only during the academic year. It may also stem from the fact that the education abroad office does not have sufficient staff to run short-term programs in addition to managing its other responsibilities.

Institutions will want to avoid situations in which faculty attempt to develop and run programs without the knowledge of or input from the international office. This can be accomplished by having clear and well-published institutional policies, reinforced by a directive from the president or provost, that require all off-campus programs to be operated through or in collaboration with the international office.

Centralized Administration. As participation in education abroad grows, many institutions have found it advantageous to ensure a standardized approach to program development and management by employing a centralized administrative model for all education abroad (and often all off-campus) programs. In this model, the education abroad office is the venue for all phases of program development and operation, from evaluating designs and budgets, collecting fees and making payments, and recruiting faculty directors and students, to selection and enrollment, orientation and reentry, and the final reconciliation of accounts. A centralized approach to international programs administration underscores the understanding that international programs are an institutional activity and do not belong to any one department, college, school, or faculty member.

A centralized model of education abroad administration offers a number of advantages over a decentralized one. The standardization of policy and procedure, along with standardized predeparture and arrival orientations, can reduce the risk to and liability of the institution. Academic integrity can be strengthened through uniform course design and academic standards. A uniform process for selecting appropriate participants and faculty directors can be established. Centralization also eliminates the need for duplicate training and effort in areas such as financial management, logistics, and group travel.

The Hybrid Model. At some institutions, the level of staffing in the education abroad office may be inadequate to handle the management of all the short-term programs in addition to the office's normal responsibilities. In such cases, administrative tasks are often shared among several offices, such as continuing education, summer school, and academic departments. A hybrid model allows successful interplay among several different academic units, each with its own unique history, program model, and administrative needs.

As interest and participation in short-term programs increase, it is important to plan for growth management. If additional resources are not available, then the education abroad office will have to work with departments and faculty to develop a plan for keeping enrollments steady or to manage growth.

Program Approval Process

Every university has a policy and standard procedure for adding new courses to the curriculum. Typically, there is one procedure for permanent course additions and another for courses that will be taught only once or twice. Because short-term programs abroad are typically designed around a course, they are usually required to undergo the standard review process required of any new course. However, because the "course" will be taught overseas, there are other factors that must be reviewed in addition to the academic content. The issue for short-term programs then becomes which university committee, department, college, administrative office, or combination of these, must review and sign off on which parts of the short-term program for it to be offered.

Program review and approval should include an assessment of the academic components of the program, such as academic rigor, learning goals and objectives, faculty director qualifications, added value and benefit of the program's location or itinerary, admission requirements, and program size. Cultural and logistical components should also be considered, such as how the program incorporates the local culture into the academic and nonacademic aspects of the program; how international and local travel will be arranged; what type of housing options are available; whether support services such as computer support, health centers, and library facilities are available; what arrangements will be made for students' free time; and the degree to which faculty will be responsible for students' welfare after hours. Financial and risk management issues to review include the program's budget, the fees to be charged, student health, and possibly, medical evacuation insurance, safety plan, etc. (See Part III, Chapter 1, "Program Designs and Strategies;" Part III, Chapter 5, "Program Assessment and Evaluation;" and Part III, Chapter 6, "Maximizing Safety and Security and Minimizing Risk in Education Abroad Programs.") The approval timeline must allow sufficient time for the design, development, and review of the program. A period of at least twelve months is generally needed for development and approval of any new program abroad.

For a short-term program, the review of education abroad issues should come before the course goes to the curriculum committee. Of course, it is best if the faculty member or department proposing the course for the short-term program and the education abroad office begin their collaboration when the course and the program abroad are still in the idea stage. In this way, and by agreeing to frank and honest conversation as one of the ground rules, all of the component parts of the program can be arranged collaboratively, reducing the likelihood that one side will feel picked on or criticized by the other.

Ideally, the approval process for a short-term program abroad will be handled using a shared responsibility model. The education abroad office and the international programs committee share the authority and responsibility to review and approve all facets of any program abroad. The purview of an international programs committee typically extends to developing policy, establishing approval process, and reviewing and approving actual proposals. At some universities, the function of the international programs committee is to provide the director of the education abroad office with advice about programs and issues. At others, the international committee has full decision-making responsibility and authority for some or all of the university's education abroad programs. An international programs committee can be particularly helpful when it comes to issues such as how to manage growth, and, if there are more proposals than the resources can support, how to select from among several programs. The more centralized the institution's education abroad functions are, the greater the value of establishing a committee to review policy, procedures, and proposed program designs. As with any function in a university, review by a committee of faculty, students, and administrators will lend credibility to the process.

Policy Issues

When considering policies for short-term programs it may be possible to modify existing campus policies to respond to the requirements of a short-term program. Because short-term programs share many of the same issues faced by their longer counterparts, which are covered in other chapters in Part III of this book, only a few policy issues that may be unique to shorter programs will be considered here.

Faculty Director Salary

In many short-term programs, faculty draw their salaries from the income generated by the program, that is, from the tuition charged for the course, an off-campus program fee, a special fund, or a combination of these. If the program is offered during the regular academic year (in a January or May term), leading a short-term program may be considered part of the normal teaching load and, therefore, charged to the faculty member's department. It is important to have a clear and concise policy regarding faculty compensation in place so that faculty directors know how and how much they will be paid, before they spend time on course and program design.

Program Size

Setting the enrollment target for a program should be a collaborative effort of all people and offices involved. A new program may want to set a more conservative goal, in order to ensure that the program will achieve it. However, the relationship between the enrollment target and the cost to each individual student is an important consideration. If the enrollment target is too low, the individual cost will be too high. If the target is too high, it might not be possible to recruit enough students to operate the program.

Additional Staffing

One or more additional faculty members, staff, or graduate assistants can provide support to the faculty director and the students while abroad, and their presence can be crucial in the event of an emergency. It is important to define the duties, expectations, and compensation of additional staff members prior to their involvement in the program.

Nondegree Students

The sponsoring institution should set a policy regarding nondegree students participating in the program. Some institutions allow nondegree students to participate with the permission of the faculty director. Others may allow nondegree visiting students to participate if they will receive credit and a grade for the program, but may not allow students who have graduated or who are otherwise not enrolled at a college. The participation policy should be clearly stated in all program materials used in recruiting.

Family and Friends

Faculty directors and staff may ask to bring along spouses, partners, children, or friends for all or part of a short-term program abroad. The college may already have a policy with regard to the inclusion of friends or family in an off-campus program. If not, a policy should be developed to define who will cover the expenses of these additional people and whether the tagalongs will be required to perform any duties or participate in any or all of the program's activities. If the family member or friend has specific skills that can benefit the program, some colleges will allow their participation as an assistant. It is important to consult with the college's human resources department and legal counsel or risk management office with regard to issues such as health, accident and liability insurance, worker's compensation, and so on.

Policies and practices differ regarding the presence of children during the short-term program. Some institutions will allow children to accompany a parent if childcare needs are identified and taken care of well before the program begins. Others will not allow children under a certain age to participate, or will not allow children at all. The college's legal counsel and risk management office may already have a policy on children and will need to be consulted before promises are made.

It is important to remember that developing policies and procedures is a dynamic process. It is impossible to anticipate every need and situation, so a periodic review of policies and procedures is necessary. It is also important to maintain routine contact with key decision-makers on campus to ensure continued support of the institution for short-term program activities. Be sure to share the experiences of successful program directors and participants with the campus community, and especially with new faculty directors and program staff.

Financial Issues

Typically, short-term programs are required to be financially self-supporting. It is increasingly unlikely that a short-term program with a deficit will be approved for continuation. Moreover, most universities reserve the right to cancel a short-term program if the enrollment is not sufficient to meet expenses.

Once the basic design of the short-term program is established, the faculty director, international programs committee, and the education abroad office should begin work on the budget. It is important to clarify which expenses will be covered by the program fee and which expenses will be the responsibility of the students. For example, tuition, housing, and all costs for excursions might be included in the program fee, with the students responsible for airfare to and from the program abroad, all meals, and all personal expenses. The business office or other office that will handle fee collection and payments should be consulted, to see if the program will be charged for use of the business office's services as a type of overhead expense. If financial aid is approved for use with the short-term program, education abroad administrators will need to put together a comprehensive estimate of the total program cost. This estimate should also be included in all recruiting materials.

Fixed and Variable Expenses

When constructing a budget, it is often useful to distinguish between fixed and variable expenses. Fixed expenses are those that remain the same regardless of how many participants enroll, such as van and classroom rental costs, guest lecture stipends, insurance, recruiting materials, communications and other equipment, and all expenses of the faculty director and program staff (including transportation, room and board, salary, etc.). Variable expenses rise with an increase in the number of participants. Some examples of variable expenses include airline tickets, admission fees, arranged excursions charged on a per capita basis, and room and meal charges. The cost of an individual participant in the program is calculated by dividing the total fixed costs by the number of students and then adding the variable cost to that number. The following example uses a program with estimated fixed costs of $25,286 and a per-student variable cost of $2,145, with a participation of fourteen students: $25,286 divided by 14 equals $1,806.14 (fixed), plus $2,145 (variable), for a grand total cost of $3,951.14 per participant.

Contingency Funds — currencies, emergencies, etc.

Since the program fee must be established well in advance of departure, actual costs may be difficult to determine. In addition, currencies tend to fluctuate in value against the U.S. dollar. Thus, it is important to have an institutional policy for funding contingencies and emergency situations. Some institutions or the education abroad office have established reserves in order to provide funds for such situations. Others require that the individual program include a budget for contingencies. From the example above, charging the fourteen participants an even $4,000 will yield a contingency fund of $684, which is probably not enough. The estimate for the contingency fund should be included the budget, and can be listed as either a fixed amount (e.g., $5,000) or a percentage of the total program budget (e.g., 10 percent, which would be $5,421.60 using the example above). In addition, the program policy and materials should state that any amounts listed are estimates and that the final participant charge will be determined at a designated time prior to departure.

Additional Fees and Deposit

It is common for international offices to assess a fee to students who participate in short-term programs to defray the cost of implementation. This fee may be calculated either on the basis of a per-student charge or a percentage of the program's total budget. In addition, a nonrefundable application fee helps ensure that students who apply are serious about their participation. Moreover, requiring admitted students to pay a nonrefundable deposit to confirm their participation will further discourage students who are not committed to completing the program. The deposit is applied to the overall charge and used to cover program expenses (such as deposits to vendors or transportation companies) that must be paid before the program fee is collected from the students.

Collecting and Disbursing Funds

Most institutions have established procedures for procurement and payment of services. It is important that a short-term program abroad follow all established procedures. This will not only alleviate problems throughout the course of the program, but will also avoid duplication of effort. Making payments due prior to departure for the program will allow enough time to process invoices, reduce the amount of cash the faculty director will need to take overseas, and lessen the time the director must spend on financial matters. Some institutions have corporate credit card arrangements for making payments on-site. A provision will need to be in place to allow the faculty director to take funds abroad for program-related expenses. If the faculty director will be accessing funds from an automatic teller machine (ATM), this will need to be clarified beforehand with the business office and also with the college's bank, to be certain that the bank's ATM network can be accessed at all points on the program's itinerary.

Expense Reporting

It is extremely important to impress upon faculty directors the need to document expenses and keep receipts. Although in some instances it may be difficult to get a receipt, obtaining one is both an essential aspect of sound fiscal practice and typically a nonnegotiable requirement of the business office. The institution's procedures must be followed for expense reporting and reimbursements with respect to funds expended on-site. Typically, the program's expense report is due very shortly after the program's end.

What to Do with Leftover Money

It is important to decide well before program applications are solicited, what will happen to surplus funds. The college may already have a policy on surplus funds. Some program sponsors retain surplus funds to cover future deficits, contingencies, and emergencies. Others use the surplus for new program development or to provide scholarships. Sometimes, a program will refund the surplus to the participants.

Students and parents may ask where the money goes. Students, especially, are often more concerned with "getting their money's worth," than they are with their academic and intercultural program abroad. It is very important for the program to have a policy on how much financial information is communicated to students and parents. Too much information invites micromanagement; too little can lead to wild speculation. One possible solution is to consider the question, "Whose money is it?" And there is more than one possible answer. Certainly, funds collected for tuition payments belong to the sponsoring institution. The remaining funds are held in stewardship to provide the services and infrastructure needed to offer the present and future short-term programs. It is always incumbent upon the faculty director and the international program office to ensure the responsible use of the funds collected in support of program-related expenses. Moreover, the accounting and all transactions should be transparent and audited at appropriate intervals.

Marketing

After a short-term program has been developed, all of the academic and logistic decisions made, and a program fee established, students will need to be recruited. The strategies used in marketing short-term programs are similar to those used for longer study abroad options. (See Part III, Chapter 4, "Marketing, Promotion, and Publicity.") However, short-term programs present a few unique points. Frequently, students spend less time selecting and applying for short-term programs abroad than they do for semester or academic year programs. Whereas a student might take months to research, select, apply to, and prepare for a longer education abroad program, the same process for a short-term program may be condensed to a matter of weeks. As a result, the information contained in the program description and other recruiting materials must be thorough and complete, as it may be the student's sole source of information to use in determining whether to apply. The recruiting materials should fully describe the program, explain all policies and processes adequately, state all academic and other eligibility criteria completely, point out health, safety, and security issues, and include as complete and current an estimate of costs as possible.

It is also important that all program and marketing materials stress that fact that the short-term program is absolutely and unassailably academic in nature, if that is the case. Moreover, materials should point out how the program and the experience abroad are different from taking the same course on campus. All program materials and education abroad staff must emphasize that students are applying to an *education* abroad program, not a trip.

SUMMARY

Short-term programs are revolutionizing education abroad at a very quick pace, presenting both opportunities and challenges to U.S.-based and overseas professionals. More than ever, administrators must built collaborative relationships within the institution to support short-term programs, as well as effective partnerships with providers and colleagues abroad.

CHAPTER 3
Planning, Budgeting, and Implementation

Contributors: Susan Holme Brick, Lisa Chieffo, Tom Roberts, Michael Steinberg

Planning, development, budgeting, and execution are the nuts and bolts of any education abroad program. Although each institution will have its own unique systems and rules in place to accommodate the processes that the establishment of a new program abroad entails, there are many common issues that must be considered regardless of these particularities. This chapter begins with some insights on assessing the need for a new program and determining the program's feasibility in terms of staff and financial resources and the location overseas. It continues with pragmatic issues of program planning and a discussion of what will be necessary to move the program from an idea to a reality. Finally, the chapter examines some long-range considerations, including thoughts about the impact of education abroad programs on their host institutions and communities.

BEGINNING QUESTIONS

Why a New Program?

Today there are literally hundreds of study abroad options, encompassing a wide variety of geographic, curricular, and cultural approaches, and aimed at students at all economic and academic levels. Given this richness of programs already operating, the first question when thinking about a new program must be, "Is there a need for this program at all?"

Determining the Need for a New Program

Before going ahead with developing a new program, education abroad professionals should consider the following questions:

- How clearly are the academic and intercultural goals, objectives, and learning outcomes stated in the proposed program? How does the program plan to achieve these objectives? How does the program plan to assess achievement?

- How does the proposal meet the institutional mission and objectives? (Answering this honestly requires a hard look at the motives of the proposing group or individual and a close cost-benefit analysis.)

- How will the program serve student academic and intercultural needs that are currently either not well met or not met at all?

- How is the curriculum of the new program related to that of the home campus? Is this articulation possible or even desirable?

- How will the new program affect the enrollment in established campus-sponsored programs? Will approving the new program endanger their survival?

- Can the objectives of the new program perhaps be better met by existing providers or by joining a consortium of like-minded institutions?

- What type of program design (integrated, nonintegrated, or hybrid; see Part III, Chapter 1, "Program Designs and Strategies") best suits the institutional mission, the program's objectives, and the academic and intercultural goals and abilities of the students?

Examining the Motivations for the New Program

Ideas for new programs may come from upper-level administration, academic departments, committees of faculty (e.g., the curriculum committee or study abroad committee), or individual faculty members; and, of course, programs may come into being because of student interest. Projects abroad may even be the pet idea of a trustee. Finally, the education abroad office and individual advisers may be the initiators of a new program, or the idea for the program may come from a consortial arrangement.

While there may be agreement on the academic and intercultural goals for a new program, there are often secondary considerations that can vary according to the campus group discussing the program. Upper-level administrators might justify the institution's running its own program on the grounds of ensuring adherence to its own high academic standards, correspondence of course work to the home-campus curriculum, and reassurance to parents of the safety and welfare of the student participants. While these objectives can often be met by some existing programs (and sometimes more effectively), they provide strong impetus for the institution to embark on its own venture. Other powerful motivators include enhancing revenues (or at least stemming the outflow of tuition and financial aid from the home campus to other institutions); providing home-campus students increased access to highly popular overseas programs; offering low-cost study abroad options (especially for institutions with lower tuition and fees) to provide access for students of all economic levels; offering opportunities for study in areas not represented by existing programs; setting up bilateral exchanges to diversify the campus; providing faculty with overseas travel and research opportunities; and adding to the prestige of the institution.

Overarching all of these, money is often a powerful motivator. Although any study abroad program must be able to break even to be financially sustainable, institutions should not expect that study abroad programs (or the enrollment of students from other colleges and universities in these programs) will provide significant revenue enhancement. Furthermore, the issue of tuition drain must be examined closely to ensure that alternative options are actually financially sound and meet institutional objectives. It is rare that an institution will continue to fund programs in areas that are popular with students if these programs continuously lose money.

Aside from institutional objectives, each campus group has its own agenda and motivations for suggesting new programs. Faculty members often look at programs as a means to obtain an extended stay overseas, ideally in a region related to their academic expertise. Frequently, research interests are given as justification for the site, but the fact is that the demands of running even a short-term program effectively will typically hinder the achievement of any research goals, at least while the program is running. Departments proposing programs often reflect the motives of strong individual faculty members. A department may seek to strengthen its academic program by establishing a study abroad program that would serve primarily its own students. A program proposal may also come from a desire to "keep up with" another department's program abroad. Typically, these programs are set up with faculty members from the department leading the program in rotation each year.

Obtaining Input on New Program Ideas

The primary function of the curriculum and study abroad committees is not to initiate proposals for new study abroad programs, but rather to serve as a filter and quality control mechanism, to ensure that the proposed programs meet the institutional objectives. Ideally, the study abroad committee will receive and review the proposed program (and work with the program's authors to make all necessary changes) before it is formally submitted for approval. Although education abroad professionals are not typically members of the curriculum committee, their input should be solicited in the course of the committee's consideration of the new program.

The most challenging task of the curriculum committee (or other campus-wide course or program approval body) is articulating the proposed program courses into the on-campus curricular offerings—both those offered before the students leave, and those available to the students when they return. The matter of articulation confronts the curriculum committee with a paradox. Academic articulation can be extremely difficult when students are fully integrated into the curriculum of a university abroad, yet an integrated program has the potential for the greatest intercultural integration. Academic articulation is clearly easiest when the institution has great control over the content of course work taken abroad, whether those courses are taught by a member of the institution's faculty or by a local faculty member hired by the U.S. institution; yet students in these "island" programs often have great difficulty approaching and integrating into the local culture.

Because they will be both the participants and the beneficiaries of the new program, students should be given opportunities for input into the development of a new program. Prospective study abroad students may repeatedly suggest an academic or intercultural need that is not well met by the range of existing institutional options or those on the list of programs preapproved for transfer of credit, but that seems to be a valid option for a substantial number of students on the campus. Such expression of student interest should always be followed up with a more formal survey of students and professors to ensure that there is in fact adequate demand. A formal survey is always preferable to anecdotal reports, because data collected can be shown to senior administrators as part of making the case for the new program.

And a final consideration is whether the program being proposed is one that best meets the academic and intercultural goals of the unit that will be responsible for it. (See Part III, Chapter 1, "Program Designs and Strategies," for a taxonomy of program designs.) The choice of program type and design is an important issue, since it relates directly to the assessment of the quality of programs and control of curricular offerings.

Determining the Feasibility of a New Program

Assessing Resources

Having established a firm academic and intercultural justification for the new program, and having fully articulated the program with the on-campus curriculum, education abroad professionals are ready to be confronted with the cold, hard reality of resource allocation, otherwise known as "Can we afford to do this?" In determining the need for a new program, the education abroad office will no doubt have made a preliminary determination that the institution does indeed have such resources (or that it can obtain them) for the new program. It is possible, however, that the development process described above has been short-circuited by a more senior administrator who hands the education abroad professional an idea and asks him or her to take it and run with it. Either way, now begins the often-difficult task of identifying, and then obtaining, administration approval and commitment for the financial and personnel resources necessary to mount and sustain the program. As a theoretical construct, programs are relatively easy to design and develop. Once they become an agenda item in a budget meeting, competing with all of the other worthy projects fighting for institutional funding and staff resources, they must be shown to be financially feasible.

The type of program—long-term or short-term, faculty-led or program provider–led, integrated or nonintegrated, one-time or ongoing—will determine the resources needed to carry out the task. For purposes of this chapter, it is assumed that the institution seeks to establish a new program designed to suit institutional needs over an extended period of time, even if the leadership, length of program, and perhaps locale may vary from year to year.

If the institution is just beginning to get involved in running its own programs, it would be wise for an education abroad professional to undertake a survey of international expertise on campus—who studied or earned degrees abroad, who has conducted research, who has run programs or taken student groups abroad, etc. Educators may be surprised at what such a survey will yield, and it will provide them with a resource bank for program development.

If the institution has a decentralized model of program administration, the education abroad office may be setting up a program for a particular department that will select staff and faculty. The task of the education abroad office will be to provide orientation for the students and training of program directors. It is crucial to ascertain precisely the amount of actual departmental support or individual faculty commitment behind the program. How knowledgeable is the department or faculty member about the site involved, the skills necessary to manage the program, and the financial structure of the venture? Education abroad professionals must also be assured that the institution is fully behind the

Chapter 3: Planning, Budgeting, and Implementation

program (as demonstrated by the support of senior administrators). After all, any program will involve the whole institution in terms of budgeting and potential liability.

There are always financial and personnel restraints in all academic institutions. Therefore, it is important to ascertain how much money the institution is willing to commit to start-up costs, as well as to the long-term operation of the new study abroad program. For this reason, the plan should be approved at the highest levels, which may mean the provost, the president, or the board. The president may wax eloquently on the institution's general commitment to international education, but may not be willing to endorse the specific program unless the education abroad office can show that the program will, at the very least, break even financially.

The issue of the financial viability of programs abroad and the issue of institutional financial aid are covered later in this chapter, but careful consideration of the financial aspects when assessing resources for developing a program is vital. Public institutions in particular are faced with the necessity of ensuring a balanced budget within a particular academic or fiscal year, and often have great difficulty with programs that can project only potential break-even or surplus situations in the next year. That constraint also applies to the ability to buy forward in foreign currency or to invest in currency futures. While it may be possible to find funding for program development, it's rare to find grants, either from outside sources or from within the institution, to assist with program administration. Therefore, the program must be self-supporting, which means dependent primarily on student fees and perhaps also some tuition revenues (depending on the institution) to cover all of the program's expenses. A common error in planning programs is an overly optimistic estimate of the number of students expected to enroll. If revenues are budgeted too high (i.e., if enrollment is overestimated), the program risks being cancelled or losing so much money that the institutional commitment will disappear and the program will last only one term, if it is even permitted to run at all.

Deciding on a Location

Good site selection is central to a successful study abroad initiative, and location is undoubtedly (and too often, unfortunately) a primary consideration for students when choosing a program. By starting with a clear statement of the program's goals, objectives, and learning outcomes, the program's general location may quickly become clear. In determining which site is best for an institution and its students, education abroad professionals might try to capitalize on the institutional and individual professional international relationships that already exist on campus. A faculty member may have professional or personal contacts overseas that will facilitate the establishment of a program; a friend or trustee of the institution may have a connection with a country or city; perhaps there is a sister-city or sister-state agreement that can be expanded; an existing faculty research project or graduate exchange agreement may have strong contacts that could yield a fruitful undergraduate program. Finally, in selecting a location for the program, it is very important that careful attention is paid to issues of transportation, communication, health, safety, security, and risk management. The most idyllic and academically perfect spot is not necessarily the most safe or secure.

In choosing a site for a new program, education abroad professionals should be able to answer the following questions:

Part III: Program Development, Campus Management, Marketing, and Evaluation

How does the location support the specific goals, objectives, and learning outcomes of the program, as well as the mission of the institution? Why will this site serve your institution better than other possible sites?

Study abroad programs are costly and labor-intensive ventures with broad ramifications. Every institution will face a variety of priorities and interests in setting up a new one. The senior administration may place emphasis on a particular discipline (such as engineering) or a particular kind of experience for students (such as internships or community-based learning), which may or may not be easily developed at the site under consideration. A program in Guatemala may cost less to establish than a program in Spain, but if your Spanish department is particularly strong in Peninsular rather than Latin American literature, Guatemala may not be the best choice. Therefore, it is best to involve a broad range of constituencies (faculty, academic deans, risk management officials, legal specialists, and financial managers) when investigating possible program sites.

Will students want to study at this location? Will the students have a good intercultural as well as academic experience here?

Generally speaking, the best locations provide students with good educational resources, broad opportunities to interact with the host population, and, ideally, freedom to move about independently and with confidence—all at a reasonable cost. However, it is unfortunate but true that, for sojourns of a semester or longer, U.S. students tend to study at traditional sites in much greater numbers than at nontraditional sites. A relatively small number of students will choose a study abroad site because of a long-term academic interest in that site; generally, students' choices are more likely to relate to their career interests, their social commitments, or the popular image of a location. Countries where a widely spoken language is used are likely to attract more students than countries with less commonly used languages. Students tend to prefer countries with fast economic growth and good future prospects to countries with stagnant economies. Students also prefer locations that offer good travel possibilities. And of course, perceived safety is always an issue, especially to parents. Students are likely to be more flexible in their site choice for short-term programs, especially if a popular faculty member at their home university directs the program.

Does the institution have access to experts who know the country and city where the program will be set up?

Specialists will be needed to advise the education abroad office on location, help develop the academic program, smooth contacts with host universities and on-site personnel, and help navigate the uncertainty of a new cultural, political, and sociological situation. If faculty from relevant disciplines are involved in the initiative from the beginning, a ready core of experts should be already available. Like there campus-based counterparts, providers and consortia will need to have a way of tapping into the expertise of faculty from institutions with which they work.

What will the program cost at this location?

The best-designed program cannot succeed if it is cost-prohibitive to students or to the institution. Although each institution will have its own definition of what is cost-prohibitive, a number of factors should be taken into consideration. The number of students accepted into a program will impact the cost per student significantly. Will the program attract enough students to sustain itself? How much infrastructure will need to be provided? If staff and faculty are exported from the home campus, the program is likely to cost more than it would if local staff were hired. Personnel from the United States may require cost-of-living supplements, housing allowances, support for their children's private school enrollment, and moving expenses; and perhaps an additional salary will have to be paid to someone at home who will teach their home-campus courses. How much will it cost to rent space for the program's classes? If the U.S. institution is working with a host university, what are tuition charges for international students? Does the host university see the U.S. students as an important source of income? Is the U.S. institution expected to reciprocate in some way, for example by enrolling students from the host university at the U.S. campus or at another institution in a consortium? Will the U.S. institution be asked to make arrangements for the host university's faculty to come to the United States to teach or do research or even pursue graduate study? Will the host institution permit the U.S. institution's faculty to teach the U.S. students in the host country? Education abroad professionals should not assume that it will cost less to operate a program in a developing country than in a more developed one. While food and accommodation may be cheaper, the complete academic and student services infrastructure for the program may need to be provided.

Is there an academic infrastructure available to tap into?

If direct enrollment in courses is part of the program plan, the education abroad office will need to ascertain the language of instruction, the academic calendar, course timetable, qualifications of instructors, academic quality the courses, and, of course, the willingness of local institutions to accept the program's students. The education abroad office will also have to obtain the support of the relevant departments on the home campus (whose faculty, presumably, will at some point be evaluating the students' transfer credits). Will the local institution be interested in working with the U.S. institution, and if so, under what conditions? Can they provide office or classroom space? If the program will offer courses, are there local instructors available who can teach in the program and according to the U.S. institution's standards and expectations?

What kind of relationship, if any, should be developed with a host institution on-site?

In some countries, it may be desirable from a legal point of view to have a host institution provide the aegis under which a program will operate. Rather than go to the expense and difficulty of incorporating the program in the foreign country, a host university can pay the local employees and vendors. Working closely with a host university may provide access to courses, offices, housing, computer use for program administrators and students, library access, and other program needs. In countries where international students pay high student fees, this can be a purely cash relationship, but today most institutions expect some degree of reciprocity from their international partners. Reciprocity may involve a one-to-one exchange of students; however, there may be circumstances when this is not workable, or is prohibitively expensive for the U.S. program or institution. Proportional exchanges—for example, accepting one host university student for every five U.S. students sent—are a possibility in some circumstances. A host institution may ask the U.S. institution to organize a short-term program for a group of their students visiting the U.S. campus. Having faculty from the host institution teach or do graduate work at the U.S. institution is another possibility. In short, reciprocity can take a variety of forms; but in any case, negotiations will have to consider the program's needs and what the institution can afford.

How will the host country's academic calendar affect the program?

The academic calendars of institutions abroad often don't mesh easily with those of institutions in the United States. Foreign institutions may offer courses that last a full year, making it difficult for semester students to enroll. European fall semesters sometimes extend through January and into February; spring calendars may include study in July. Southern hemisphere calendars have their "summer" vacation from December to February, and begin their second semester in July. (This could be advantageous, however, for January short-term programs.)

What health, safety, and security concerns does the proposed location present?

It is essential to make a careful assessment of the health, safety, and security issues in any new location. It may be beneficial to retain a consultant firm that specializes in safety and risk assessment to help with site analysis. A site safety audit will include an assessment of crime rates, health conditions, access to hospitals and other health resources, fire codes, natural disaster hazards, safety of the food supply, and reliability and availability of civic services such as police, fire departments, transportation, etc. (See Part III, Chapter 6, "Maximizing Safety and Security and Minimizing Risk in Education Abroad," for a detailed discussion of risk assessment.)

How will the host country's political situation impact the program?

Political stability is an important precondition for a smoothly running program. Strikes by government and other workers will affect the program's students, and give cause for alarm on the part of parents who view the strikes on television back home. Faculty and student unrest can close a host university for long periods. Education abroad professionals should research the sentiment of the local people toward the United States, so they do not find that the program facilities or students become targets in times of political unrest.

Budgeting

Perhaps more than any other planning factor, the particularities of budgeting vary significantly from institution to institution; yet the issues surrounding the financial aspects of programs abroad are often quite similar among like schools (e.g., private versus public). The fact is that institutions of all types are subject to financial constraints, so even the most innovative and academically enriching program will be unsustainable if it is not well budgeted. In the following section, some of the major issues one must consider when establishing a new program abroad are addressed: working within the financial realities of one's institution, understanding the mechanics of cash flow, making a convincing cost-benefit analysis, and examining possible fee models (with particular attention to the education abroad offices at small, private colleges).

Working Within Financial Realities

Most education abroad professionals have little experience with budgets and other financial matters, though they may be required to develop such expertise quickly in order to make the case for the establishment of new programs overseas. Although it has become popular for senior university and college administrators to express a high level of commitment to international endeavors in mission statements and the like, the reality in these financially lean times is that decision makers must focus on the bottom line more than ever before. Therefore, education abroad professionals must know the financial profiles of their institutions, learn about internal funding mechanisms, and become acquainted with those who set priorities for spending. Some questions to answer when considering the financial realities of a new program are as follows:

- Must the new program be completely self-funding through student fees? If a third-party provider will be used, how do lost tuition revenues and institutional financial aid transfer factor into the break-even calculation?

- Will all or only a portion of student tuition be available for program expenses?

- Will the education abroad office receive an additional budget allocation to cover some program costs? If so, will this allocation vary depending on the number of program participants?

- If program revenues and budgetary allotments do not cover costs, how will shortfalls be met? Is the administration willing to cover shortfalls for a specified period until the program becomes self-sustaining?

- Is the education abroad office required to generate revenue beyond program expenses, in order to sustain itself or to contribute to institutional overhead? If so, is it reasonable to assume that the new program will meet these expectations?

- Does the institution have endowments or special sources of funding that can help defray the cost of financial aid that is sent to third-party providers?

Other questions may arise depending on the type of program and the institution's funding structure, but there is no doubt that making a case for a new program requires careful financial analysis as well as consideration of academic and other issues.

The Mechanics of Funding

Funding and Student Fees. Program budgets are typically divided into two sorts of expenses: fixed costs, which stay the same regardless of group size; and individual costs, which vary with the number of students on the program. Fixed costs may include facility rental paid to a host institution, rent on one's own facilities, instructor salaries, staff salaries, faculty director expenses, some field trip expenses (buses, guides), legal and bank fees, overhead costs of the sponsoring institution (e.g., the lead school in a consortium), costs for periodic program assessment, home university or provider charges to monitor the overseas program, advertising and student recruitment costs, administrative costs attendant on student admissions, postage, phone calls, office equipment purchase and maintenance, insurance for students, and liability insurance. Individual costs may include airfare, in-country transportation, housing, meals, registration fees, visas, host institution tuition, and some field trip expenses (admission fees, performance tickets).

Each institution will have its own model for funding programs. In some cases, the sponsoring institution will charge students regular tuition plus a program fee that covers individual costs. The education abroad office may receive all or part of student tuition revenues, which allows it to absorb some fixed costs such as instruction. In other cases, fixed program costs are part of the office's annual

Part III: Program Development, Campus Management, Marketing, and Evaluation

budget. Traditional exchange programs require students to pay tuition to their home institution and all other expenses to the host institution; some U.S. schools charge an additional study abroad fee to cover expenses that support these programs. Still another model involves dividing total fixed costs by the number of participants, and adding to that amount the individual costs. Institutions that send many of their students on third-party provider programs also use a variety of models involving combinations of home-campus tuition and study abroad fees. There are probably almost as many models of program funding as there are institutions that sponsor programs abroad.

Program Feasibility. If a college considers the study abroad experience to be an important part of its offerings, it will often transfer all of a student's aid to the study abroad program. By law, if students are receiving home college credit for study abroad, their federal aid is transferable to the study abroad experience (see 34 CFR 668.5, the Federal Student Aid Handbook 2003–04, and other Information for Financial Aid Professionals (IFPA) at the IFPA website). On the other hand, rules for state aid transfer vary considerably. Most colleges award institutional financial aid and merit scholarships as a tuition discount, rather than having a pool of cash from which to make the award. Thus, the transfer of institutional financial aid and scholarships may mean transfer of cash that was awarded to the student as a discount. This can be a major expense for colleges and will have an impact on overall college budgeting. However, if the college is strongly committed to study abroad as part of its overall academic program, the cost of aid transfer has to be a part of the cost of establishing programs abroad.

Enrollments are difficult to predict; numbers will invariably fluctuate, and it is possible that student fees will not cover program costs all the time.

Therefore, institutions need to have cash reserves to cover occasional deficits. In the long run, a program should ideally pay for itself and contribute to institutional overhead. However, some programs, like some college departments, may not bear their weight in the overall scheme. If the program forms an important part of the institutional mission, then a continuing subsidy may be justified. An institution then needs to balance money-losing programs with more financially successful programs that offset the losses. It makes sense to have criteria on which to base a decision about whether to abandon or maintain a program that continues to be a financial drain. These criteria should look at factors other than financial ones: Is the enrollment sufficient, for example, to offer a program that effectively serves students? Would important academic and intercultural aspects of the program be lost? Does the program address a need that is not met by other programs (e.g., serving an underrepresented discipline or providing geographic diversity)? Could the money spent on this program be better utilized in another program that would serve more students?

Colleges also need to be aware of the potential impact of enrollment abroad. A program that enrolls the greater part of the junior majors in a department has implications for the home campus offerings in that field. Students abroad can mean empty beds in student residences unless the college has planned for this by enrolling greater numbers of students, thereby planning that a certain portion of its students will always be abroad. Colleges often find it difficult to balance fall with spring enrollments, and this imbalance should be taken into account when planning new programs. In recent years, a number of colleges have been asking some first-year students to delay entrance until the spring semester to help to correct the imbalance between fall and spring, caused by study abroad.

Making a Convincing Cost-Benefit Analysis

In the field of education abroad, cost-benefit analysis is a method for determining the best choice among study abroad options by weighing the benefits (pros) and costs (cons), to determine whether or not to go ahead with the development of a study abroad program. The key problem in such an analysis is that costs and benefits must be quantified in order to be compared; yet many of the benefits of study abroad—educational, cultural, and maturational—are extremely hard to quantify.

Hardheaded, "no nonsense" financial analysts (who often begin the discussion with the phrase, "Academic considerations aside,") say that benefits that carry no dollar price tag must be excluded, and what is left is simply an analysis of income versus outgo, to get a "bottom line" rate of return. This is both too simplistic and unrewarding for study abroad, where the nonquantifiable benefits may be the most important for the university's objectives. Given the continuing financial constraints on higher education in the United States, the fiscal "hard-headers" may dominate any financial discussion. This situation means that education abroad professionals must attempt as much as possible to put a monetary value on intangible benefits. The only time this may be unnecessary is when trustees, presidents, faculty, and students clamor so stridently for a particular option, that the specific dollar return is not a factor.

The prestige and popularity of an institution's programs abroad may be considered quantifiable in terms of number of students attracted to the institution because of these offerings. A very few colleges and universities, when viewing the costs of study abroad in terms of loss of revenue for tuition or on-campus housing, simply decide to take in more first-year students to balance the loss of sophomores and juniors. This scenario assumes an applicant pool that is considerably larger than the number of annual acceptances, and it requires some creativity and cooperation on the part of the admissions and housing offices. It is worth talking with the admissions director to see if this addition to the school's "sales kit" will enhance the institution's attractiveness to good students.

As study abroad grows, becomes more publicized, and begins to be accepted as a part of the institutional mission, cost-benefit analysis becomes easier, because the value of nonquantifiable benefits is more likely to be recognized and accepted by the financial analysts.

Fee Models for Education Abroad and the On-Campus Office

Many colleges and universities in the United States (especially small, private colleges) administer few or no study abroad programs of their own, but instead rely heavily on sending their students to programs administered by other colleges, consortia, or education abroad providers. In order to ensure that all students on campus have access to such education abroad opportunities, many private institutions allow some or all of their institutional financial aid to be applied to the fees of programs administered by these third-party providers. Some institutions allow all institutional need-based aid and merit scholarships to be applied to the fees of selected study abroad programs, while others allow only need-based aid, or a portion thereof, to be applied. The challenge for institutions that allow home-campus aid to be spent off campus is to manage the fees and aid in a way that continues to provide all students access to education abroad programs regardless of financial need, while at the same time, avoiding a fee structure that makes it too costly in the long term for them to let aid "travel."

While some colleges and universities have special endowments that support study abroad, or view education abroad as so integral to the mission of the institution that they are willing to subsidize it, other institutions will insist that education abroad offices manage fees in such a way that there is no net loss to the institution. Some institutions may even expect that study abroad will generate additional revenue for the institution. The dramatic increase in study abroad participation in recent years has resulted in greater financial aid costs to the home institution. Consequently education abroad administrators have had to balance the level of study abroad participation against the financial aid cost to the institution. Even institutions that embrace study abroad with enthusiasm often begin to balk as rising participation rates mean increased real dollar expenditures due to institutional financial aid.

While there are many variations in the way institutions charge for education abroad, there are three general models commonly employed. Private institutions tend to show greater variation among institutions with regard to fee models than public ones. But there have no significant studies of this facet of education abroad. Determining which model will work best for an institution depends in part on the culture of the institution, the overall financial policies of the university and the particular financial structure of the education abroad office.

Two additional important factors affecting the fee structure for education abroad programs are the cost differential between the home-campus fees and the fees of the programs abroad, and the institution's discount rate. By using a tuition discount, rather than relying on actual dollars, institutions are able to greatly expand the number of students who are eligible to receive merit scholarships or need-based financial aid. Although tuition discounting, especially for merit scholarships has long be a practice at private universities, public universities are now engaging in the practice (Gose 2005, Sanoff 2004, Hebel 2003). In a 2003 study, the National Association of College and University Business Offices (NACUBO) found that the average discount rate for all institutions surveyed was 39.4% (Lapovsky and Hubbell 2003). Tuition discounting can have a significant affect on the financial base for education abroad, especially on the willingness of universities to transfer institutional financial aid to the program overseas. When a student with a large scholarship (in the form of a tuition discount) studies abroad at a program approved for the transfer of institutional financial aid, the university will have to make up the difference between the actual dollars received and the published fees for that university. This difference can be thousands of dollars for a single student (Brockington 2002).

Model No. 1: Flat-Fee Model

In this model, the home institution charges the students the actual fees of the education abroad program, plus a flat study abroad fee. The flat fee can be as low as $50 per semester abroad or as much as several thousand dollars per semester, and is retained by the home campus.

The flat-fee model has the advantage of seeming fair, because a student going to a location where the cost of living is high (e.g., London, England) will pay more than a student going to a location where the cost of living is low (e.g., Oaxaca, Mexico). Moreover, it provides more predictable revenue for the home campus—the home campus is assured of a certain flat fee per student abroad regardless of which programs are attended. It avoids the problem that the home tuition model has when the third-party provider program fees exceed the cost of the home-campus fees, which would result in the home campus subsidizing students who attend the higher-priced programs. The billing for the flat-fee model is also quite simple. The home campus simply charges whatever the program fees are to the students, plus the flat study abroad fee that the home campus retains.

The main disadvantage of this model is that for many institutions, the flat study abroad fee retained by the home campus may need to be quite high in order for that fee to cover all of the institutional financial aid that goes abroad. This will be especially true if the home campus has a high discount rate, or if high-need students have a high participation rate in study abroad.

Model No. 2: Home-Campus Tuition Model

In this model, the home campus usually charges the study abroad students home-campus tuition, plus program room and board fees. In a slight variation of this model, some institutions charge home-campus tuition and home-campus room and board, regardless of the actual cost of the education abroad program.

Proponents of the home-campus tuition model argue that charging home-campus tuition (or home-campus tuition and room and board) for all education abroad programs encourages students to select programs based on the academic merits of the program and not on cost. They assert that this fee structure is similar to what colleges already do when they charge students of all majors on campus the same rate of tuition. It is much more expensive to educate a chemistry major than it is to educate an English literature major, but students of all majors pay the same fees on most U.S. campuses. Institutions employing this education abroad fee model may realize considerable savings, especially if the programs their students attend are less expensive than the home campus.

There are a few disadvantages of this model worth considering. First, if an institution charges home tuition, students and parents may expect a level of service and quality of academic program akin to that of the home campus. Because the programs administered by third-party providers are not actually managed by the home campus, home campuses typically have little real input into how a program is administered, except perhaps in an advisory capacity. Moreover, many U.S. colleges have concluded that if they charge home-campus tuition, they are obligated to treat the education abroad credit as if it were credit earned on the home campus, and to average the grades into the home-campus grade point average. Faculty at some institutions may object to treating courses that are not actually taught at their institution as if they were. Billing is typically more complicated with this model as well. Many institutions that have adopted it have found that they need at least one additional part-time staff person to assist with study abroad invoices and with disbursing stipends to students for airfare, meals, etc.

Last, and perhaps most important, is the public relations problem that can arise from charging high home-campus fees for programs that are much less expensive. For example, a student paying $15,000 per semester in home-campus fees to the home campus for an off-campus program that costs only $8,000 will figure out quickly that other students on the program are paying $7,000 less for the very same program. For this reason, some institutions employing the home-campus tuition model provide airfare or cover the costs of some extras, such as excursions or language tutors, to make paying home tuition more palatable. In addition, those students who are more savvy consumers are likely to avoid destinations like Mexico, where expenses are low, if they know they have to pay the same high private tuition fees regardless of which country they choose. In other words, the model may have the unfortunate, unintended consequence of discouraging participation in programs at locations where the cost of living is low, which may mean fewer students on programs in developing countries.

Model No. 3: Combination Model

The combination model is a hybrid of model no. 1 and model no. 2. Some institutions, for example, charge home tuition, room and board, plus a flat study abroad fee. Others charge home-campus tuition and room and board for affiliated education abroad programs, but charge a flat fee if a student obtains approval to attend a program not on the college's affiliated list. Others charge home tuition, and let the students pay the cost of room and board directly to the program. The advantages and disadvantages of this model are the same as for model no. 2.

Analyzing which model suits an institution best will take some research and will require assistance from various offices on the campus, especially the business office. First, the financial implications of any model you are considering should be carefully evaluated, which means doing the mathematical calculations to see what the results would be under that model before making a change. When the trustees of one private college wanted to consider switching from model no. 1 to model no. 2, for example, the education abroad office used actual data from the previous year of study abroad participation to draw comparisons. By looking at the past year's study abroad program fees for programs attended, student financial aid awards, amount of home-campus tuition that year, and so on, the education abroad office determined that savings would have been nominal, had they used model no. 2 the previous year, because a number of the programs popular among their students were actually more expensive than home-campus fees, when living expenses and airfare were taken into account. (Some schools that have adopted model no. 2 get around the problem of subsidizing programs that are more expensive than the home campus by charging the fees that are higher—either the home-campus fees or the study abroad program fees.)

An essential consideration when choosing among the various options for education abroad program fees is to strike a balance between broad student access to the programs abroad and the institution's (and the education abroad office's) need for financial viability.

From Vision to Reality

Program Preparations

Once a site has been chosen, education abroad professionals will need to consider a range of technical and legal issues, as well as issues more specifically related to the academic development and day-to-day administration of the program.

Legal Issues

If the institution intends for the program to have an ongoing presence in the foreign country, the education abroad office will want to have expert advice on the legal status of the program in that country. It may be sufficient to operate under the aegis of the host university, or the program may have to incorporate or register as a nonprofit club or organization. The program's legal status will determine how business will be conducted on-site, including the handling of local taxes, bank accounts, remuneration of staff and faculty, insurance, and financial and personnel matters. While educational institutions are typically tax exempt in the United States, the overseas program may not be. For all of these questions, education abroad professionals should seek the help of local professionals and campus legal counsel and finance people. Local regulations governing labor practices in the host country can be especially complex. Labor laws often protect employees in other countries to a degree unknown in the United States. It may be impossible or extremely expensive to terminate employees, from professors to janitors, once they have been hired or have served a probationary period. Income and social security taxes can be complex and may require hiring local accountants. The legal status of the program may exempt it from certain transaction and value-added taxes.

In the early days of study abroad, issues of status and taxation were often ignored—largely because the programs involved were small, faculty-led and faculty-arranged, often one-time programs that were not officially recognized by their institutions. These programs were frequently developed in ignorance of local laws; and in several cases, institutions later found themselves embroiled in legal actions for failure to pay taxes, abide by local regulations, or exercise appropriate vigilance over the health and welfare of participants.

Regardless of the legal status of the program, education abroad professionals must take care that the disbursement of funds and the keeping of financial records are done according to the regulations of the university finance office. Programs of any size will draw the attention of university auditors, and records must be in good order. It is possible that local authorities in the host country may ask to see the program's financial records. Keep in mind that faculty often lack the skill and the patience to account for large sums of money. Hence, it may be wise to hire a local accounting firm—again, one that meets the approval of the home university auditors.

Interinstitutional programs will need carefully drawn contracts; this means working closely with legal counsel. While senior university officials (especially presidents) may feel that establishing agreements with other institutions by a handshake is sufficient, the hard work of making the agreement work will fall to the education abroad professional. Thus, the handshake will need to be followed up with a more formal agreement, often called a "memorandum of understanding" (MOU), which will be negotiated with counterparts overseas. Remember in working out details that room and board arrangements are often separately administered at universities abroad and may require separate contracts. Don't assume that the administration of a potential partner institution abroad is structured along U.S. models. Be sure the people being dealt with have the power to speak for individual departments; this is particularly crucial in arranging the important curricular aspects of the program.

In sum, there are four principles to keep in mind regarding the legal and technical aspects of program preparation:

Plan well in advance. In program development, haste does indeed make waste. It is not unusual for a new program to take several years from concept to student enrollment. Rushing a new program may expose students to danger, and the education abroad professional, and his or her institution, to litigation.

Cultivate and depend on the advice of local professionals, particularly on governmental, legal, banking, accounting, contractual, and general business issues. The cultural affairs office at the U.S. embassy or consulate can be helpful, as can the local

Part III: Program Development, Campus Management, Marketing, and Evaluation

U.S. educational adviser and the local Fulbright committee. By all means, consult with any established programs and associations of U.S. programs in-country.

Do a thorough risk and hazard analysis of the location and region where the program will be located. This information is necessary for a risk management plan, and it will also need to be disclosed to students and staff.

Be meticulous in cost estimates and projections about enrollment and budget. Revisit the cost-benefit analysis of the type of program being considered. After taking into account the various complexities, and attendant costs and risks, it may be necessary to rethink the best way to achieve institutional objectives.

Choosing a Program Director

The first task of management, after determining the type of program best suited to the institutionally defined objectives, is the selection of a program director. If the program being established will be separate from an overseas institution, the home university is faced with the question of whether to hire a U.S. person or a host-country national, academic or nonacademic, to administer it. If the students will be studying in an academic situation controlled by faculty hired by the home institution, it would be beneficial to look for someone who has strong administrative and student personnel skills rather than an academic background, since many of the critical issues faced by students while they are abroad are nonacademic.

On the other hand, the home institution may insist that the program be run by one of its own faculty members in order to ensure adherence to the academic standards of the institution, to provide overseas faculty and staff with a sound understanding of U.S. and institutional educational policies, and to reassure parents. (It should be noted, however, that local administrators will ordinarily have a better understanding of the host academic, cultural, political, and legal environment, and a better local network of contacts.) In the case of a faculty- or departmentally proposed program, the director may already have been chosen, but in some cases the education abroad professional may be asked to search for someone from outside the institution. Regardless of whether the person is a faculty member or an administrator, U.S.-based or in-country, the job description and qualifications should be agreed on through consultation with others on campus.

From this point on, one of the education abroad professional's most important tasks will be the orientation and training of the faculty member or on-site director. The individual selected to direct a program will be called on to use skills and knowledge often quite different from those called for in teaching or research. Training and orientation, particularly in the legal and technical issues previously discussed, and in issues of health, safety, security, and risk management, are of primary importance. Student affairs issues, such as personal and psychological, as well as intercultural, counseling, and student conduct issues, also loom large in the study abroad context. Most teaching faculty have not been trained to handle these situations.

Regardless of whether this is to be a repeating program with rotating faculty leadership, or a study tour, or an ongoing fixed base program, the program must have a complete operations manual. At a minimum, such a manual should include a discussion of the program's goals, courses, home university and program policies, risk assessment and risk management plans, and emergency plans and contact numbers. It is very important that the program director as well as all local staff receive a thorough initial training program from an experienced trainer. (NAFSA and its Education Abroad Knowledge Community—formerly known as SECUSSA—can help in this regard, with various Professional Development Program training and Professional Practice Workshops.) The initial training should be augmented with continuing in-service education in the form of yearly workshops at conferences, regular reading of journal articles, and campus and program visits. As the students change, as the political situation at home and abroad evolves, and as academic requirements change, education abroad office staff need to remember to keep the program staff updated.

Academic Parameters

The recognition and transfer of academic credit from a program abroad can be complex, and unfortunately, it can also quickly become a turf battle when departments see too many of "our" students taking too many of "their" courses overseas. The home institution, through its faculty senate, curriculum committee, or equivalent body, often determines the curricular focus of the program and even individual courses. At many institutions, there is a committee on programs abroad that conducts a preliminary review and makes recommendations to the appropriate body or individual. Typically, the education abroad office has either a representative on or a channel of communication to such committees. Turf battles with departments can be avoided or at least minimized by keeping departments informed about the programs abroad.

In addition, education abroad professionals must ensure that the program site has adequate resources to meet the academic objectives the program. In most cases, this means access to materials relevant to courses, either through a library or by computer.

Nonacademic Issues

Regardless of whether students directly enroll at an overseas university, enroll at a branch campus of the home university, attend an island program, or participate in a faculty-led study tour, education abroad professionals must assess the type and availability of support services the students will receive. U.S. campuses provide a host of student services that students have come to expect. Students will need to be informed of the level of care available, and education abroad professionals must either prepare students to operate in that environment or augment what is available locally. Few universities elsewhere in the world offer the level of personal, psychological, and academic attention, care, protection, and advice that U.S. students receive. A thorough assessment and disclosure of the resources available at the program location is necessary not only for the maximization of the study abroad experience, but also to reduce the legal exposure of the home institution. Nowadays, when students will have almost instantaneous contact with their parents and fellow students by cell phones and e-mail, education abroad administrators also must ensure a system of rapid and effective communication between the program office abroad and the home campus.

Program Mechanics

The following items are really the nuts and bolts of a program, and should be decided on in the initial stages as the program is established.

Part III: Program Development, Campus Management, Marketing, and Evaluation

Student Housing

Housing is a holistic part of the experience abroad; so, for many students, it is a top concern. Students want to know where they will be living and with whom, what the comfort level will be, whether they will have their own bathroom, whether they will have access to the internet, and how far will they have to travel to class, among other things. The best housing arrangements will reinforce students' cultural, academic, and, where applicable, linguistic experience. Conversely, an ill-conceived housing situation can serve to reinforce negative stereotypes of the host culture.

Finding out what kind of housing will be available to students should be accomplished during the planning stages of a program. The host universities with which the U.S institution is working may have housing for their own students or may offer housing for international students. If student housing is not available, the alternatives are housing the students in apartments, in home-stays, or in hotels or pensions, or allowing independent housing. Home-stays can be especially desirable when language development is an important program goal. Home-stays can also be an effective means of cultural integration, especially in non-Western societies. Students studying in English-speaking countries generally don't prefer home-stays, despite the cultural benefits, because they feel more independent (due to the lack of a language barrier) and are reluctant to sacrifice some of their freedom by living in a private home.

In locations where local students tend to live in apartments, this option may be best for U.S. students as well. Housing the program's students with local students offers an opportunity for more cultural integration than housing with other U.S. students. One possibility is to rent or purchase apartments and sublease some of the rooms to local students. In order to meet the home institution's own requirements for comfort and safety, the education abroad office may have to consider subsidizing rent for the host-country students, who may otherwise compromise on their living conditions in order to save money. An alternative is to find local students who are looking for roommates, and house the program's students with them. In this case, it is important to understand the local laws and practices. Students who sublet to other students may be required by law to report the income to the authorities and pay taxes, but may not wish to do so. The education abroad professional or his or her agent could become personally liable for nonpayment of taxes. Housing the program's students with local students in this manner requires local supervision of the housing arrangements and of the process to select and match the local students with their U.S. roommates.

Housing students together in a pension or hotel may be the easiest solution for short-term programs, but this arrangement may also create disciplinary issues that are less likely to occur if students are dispersed among locals. It is important that the program has clear conduct and disciplinary policies, especially with respect to alcohol and drugs, and mechanisms in place to enforce these policies.

Regardless of the specific housing arrangement, basic safety conditions pertain. Will students be able to get out quickly in case of fire? Are there smoke alarms present? If the program takes place in a region prone to earthquakes, are the structures built to withstand them? Is there appropriate security present? If students are being housed with host families, has a program staff member visited each home and looked at conditions? Will students have adequate quiet places to study? Has the family provided personal references? Is there someone to follow up with the families and students when they don't get along?

Courses

As mentioned previously, there are several course models: full immersion with host students, courses for foreigners offered by the host institution, special courses just for the program, taught by local professors or by the home institution's own faculty, or a combination of all of these. Taking courses with host students in a full-immersion situation may provide students with a more authentic cultural experience, but this option requires more independence and great linguistic competence on the part of the student and is not for everyone. Students at universities in other countries will have different preparation than U.S. students for classes, and the sequence of study is sometimes quite different, notably in science and mathematics courses. Likewise, courses in the humanities and social sciences may assume backgrounds that U.S. students lack, both in theory and in content. Even if the local calendar fits a program's needs, classes at some universities can be quite large and the faculty unapproachable, by U.S. standards; pedagogical methods may be tedious to U.S. students or rely on rote memory. If the program's students are used to an interactive classroom, they may not adjust readily to listening to long lectures. Academic demands can be quite high and there can well be a risk of failure for students who are unused to the system. Host country faculty may grade students down for grammatical errors, even if they have mastered the content. Many of these problems can be overcome by good orientation and tutorial support. The "sink or swim" approach in full immersion works best only for the most motivated, independent, and linguistically and culturally well-prepared students.

Overseas universities often offer special courses for foreign students, and the quality of these courses can vary a great deal from university to university. The greatest strength of these "foreign student institutes" is usually language instruction, and in some cases the emphasis in all courses may be on language development. In many respects, these foreign student institutes resemble intensive English programs in the United States. Universities typically do not use their regular faculty in these programs, and the training and qualifications of instructors can be quite varied. These programs need to be evaluated carefully for academic content and foreign language pedagogy before they are used, especially if credit will be given for this course work. It goes without saying that education abroad professionals will need to inform students that they will not be sitting in classes with host-country students.

Certainly, offering home-institution–sponsored courses gives the institution more control. Program administrators can hire the faculty, monitor the syllabi to ensure a better fit with students' home curricula, and enforce familiar policies regarding grading and attendance. The course requirements will be rigorous enough for the program's students and for their home colleges. More field study can be built into these courses than is ordinarily possible in regular host-university courses. At locations where tuition costs are high, offering home-institution–sponsored courses can also be a cost savings. The major disadvantage of such an arrangement is that students are likely to have difficulty meeting locals their age, unless the program deliberately makes such contact unavoidable, for example, by arranging housing with host-campus students.

A blended approach with a combination of host-university courses and the home-institution–sponsored courses can provide students with a more balanced academic and intercultural experience. The host university will provide a sufficient variety of course offerings to serve a diverse group of interests; and when U.S. students share classes with local students, they will get a taste of the flavor of the academic life of the host country. Home-institution–sponsored classes can serve as the tutorial and discussion sections of the host-university courses, and can also provide academic and cultural background that is not available at the local university, since local students already know the history, politics, literature, and sociology of their countries. As always, there is no overall "best" model; the preferred model will necessarily vary according to the values and needs of the sending institution, the goals of the program, the resources of the host site, and the budget.

Transcripts and Credit Transfer

Whether students are taking host-university courses, or home-institution–sponsored courses taught by local faculty, it is important that education abroad professionals understand the grading and credit system. Grades, even if they look like the grades at the U.S. institution, may mean different things in different places, and U.S. credit hours may have little meaning overseas. Thus, it's important for program administrators to develop a grade and credit translation system that will work for students from the home institution. Education abroad professionals can check with other programs in the area to see what they are doing. The home campus's international admissions office can also serve as a resource, since they deal with foreign transcripts on a regular basis. (See also the resources on the Web site of World Education Services [WES]) Steps should be taken to avoid having a situation, for example, in which two students from the same institution receive different credit and grades for the same course at a host country institution. If one institution sends students on a program organized by another institution, the sending institution should ask the host institution how it developed its grade and credit translation system, and ask to see syllabi for courses, to determine whether these are in accord with the sending institution's standards.

Office and Classroom Space

The home institution will need to find classrooms, and offices for its staff, if it offers its own courses. Many programs make agreements with local universities for office and classroom space. The advantages are that students will be going to class in a university atmosphere and will have access to university facilities. Students are also more likely to participate in extracurricular activities, which will facilitate their contact with local students. If the program is located at a university, part of the agreement may require that the program use the host university's faculty to teach courses, rather than use instructors from outside. However, the university may not have sufficient classroom or office space, or the space may not be suited to the program's needs. Classrooms or offices may be relocated on short notice, or classes may be scheduled at odd hours. Program administrators should expect to pay rent or provide some other equivalent benefit to the host institution.

Locating a program off campus will most likely cost more in rent, utilities, infrastructure (phone and internet), and, depending on the location, security, but may be the best way to obtain the needed space. If the program location is far from a university campus, more space (and financial support) will be needed for the program—for a library, lounge, computer room, and other amenities. Students on this type of program often feel isolated from the local student community. It is a sad fact that many U.S. students will not ride across town to take advantage of the amenities and services of a local campus.

Formal Institutional Agreements

A formal agreement with the host institution will help to avoid misunderstandings later on. The elements of an agreement will necessarily vary according to the nature of the sending institution's relationship with a host institution and the program being established. Such agreements typically include a statement of the nature of the relationship and the program, a detailed list of what the sending institution expects to receive from the host institution and what the host institution expects to receive from the sending institution, a description of any reciprocal understandings, financial arrangements, procedures and qualifications for selection and admission of students (including who makes the final determination of admission), student housing and meals, a procedure for amending the agreement, and either a specific termination date or a termination procedure. Institutional agreements can also provide for faculty and administrator exchange, joint research, procedures for publication and patents, etc.

Procedures for Application and Acceptance

Every program needs to set requirements for admission. The program wants to attract students who will be capable of doing the academic work and who will not bring down the general level in the classroom in either academics or linguistic competency. If the program is being organized in a country where the local language is not English, language preparation is a key factor if the courses are to be taught in the target language. If the local language is part of the academic program, then language-learning readiness might be a selection criterion. Applications should reveal enough about students so that informed admission decisions can be made: Are the students prepared for the program academically? Are they prepared socially and open interculturally? Are there other issues that should be revealed, such as a disciplinary record or medical issues, that will interfere with an applicant's ability to be a student on the program? (Note: The Americans with Disabilities Act [ADA] places certain specific restrictions on the use of certain questions and information in the admission process. The campus ADA officer and the legal department can help the education abroad office formulate questions and gather appropriate information. Asking students to voluntarily disclose any disabilities and accommodations the institution might have to make will aid education abroad professionals in making effective preparations for students' participation in an appropriate program.) Do the students have the necessary permissions from, for example, the academic adviser, registrar, academic dean, of dean of students, to study on the program? Will they receive full academic credit? Acceptance decisions need to be made at an early enough date so that students can apply for and receive passports, and visas if necessary. Alternatively, the education abroad office can require that students either have or have applied for a valid passport before they submit their applications. A student's citizenship may also be an issue in the institution's ability to enroll that student at the program abroad. It is important to remember that the number of international students participating in U.S. study abroad programs is growing, and that the lead time for visa applications for non–U.S. citizens may be longer than for their U.S. peers. (See Part II, "Campus Advising," for more information on student selection and preparation.)

Handling Finances

Generally, it is expected that local expenses will be paid for in local funds. Education abroad professionals should determine whether the institution's bank and business office can handle international wire transfers. If not, education abroad professionals will want to work with the business office to identify an appropriate bank or commercial firm that can pay the institution's local program expenses by check or wire transfer. It may be possible to set up a personal or business account at a local bank in the city where the program is located, but this may require formal incorporation in that country. While setting up a local business or personal bank account may seem to be a simple task, it can be enormously complex, involving a myriad of government regulations and the submission of several stamped and witnessed documents that are then certified by a consulate in the United States; and then there are the initial and continuing fees. Thus, a U.S. bank with branches, partners, or corresponding banks abroad may prove simpler and more cost effective. If a local account is set up in the name of the institution or an on-site staff member, consult the home institution's business office on its requirements for handling money and tracking expenses, such as requiring two signatories or a monthly accounting of all funds spent and on hand. Ordinarily, the host institution and vendors overseas will send an itemized invoice requesting funds. If the home institution does not have a staff member on site, it is essential to have one contact at the host university to whom finance-related questions can be referred. If the bulk of program expenses can be paid to local vendors ahead of time, it may not be worthwhile to establish an account for short-term programs. The faculty director should be able to receive a cash advance from the home institution and pay all other expenses in cash or by credit card.

Predeparture and On-Site Orientation

Orientation is a key component of an overseas program. (See Part II, Chapter 7, "Predeparture Orientation and Reentry Programming.") Ideally, orientation should begin during the advising and application process; it is much easier to correct misperceptions and misinformation before students apply to the program. A program-specific predeparture orientation will take place before the students leave the United States, and should include logistical, academic, and cultural information. On-site orientation is often provided to international students by the host university. Program participants should be required to attend, if at all possible. The program abroad can furnish the students with the latest academic information, introduce them to the staff, the city, and local culture, teach them how to be safe and stay healthy, and assist them in coping with new experiences. Ideally, the program will repeat this information a week or two into the experience, so that those students who were too jet-lagged to comprehend everything get a second chance.

Experiences Beyond the Classroom

Typically, students spend only 20 to 25 percent of their time in class. Thus, it is important for program administrators to consider what they want (or will permit) their students to do with the rest of their time. Most study abroad programs offer field trips, excursions, and extracurricular cultural programming (dancing, movies, cooking, calligraphy, etc.). Students will certainly travel on their own as well; in fact, this could well be their main reason for choosing the program. However, independent travel is likely to highlight tourist destinations and other well-known sites, rather than be a culturally or academically significant experience. Therefore, it is up to the sponsoring institution to provide field trips and field study that reinforce the goals of the program. Students who are abroad for a relatively limited time are less likely to independently seek out extracurricular activities that will add to their cultural experience by making them interact with the local students or townspeople. Offering students possibilities for volunteer activities, and facilitating (or even requiring) their interaction with local people will encourage more to get involved.

Experiential programming can be an important part of the students' academic and cultural experience. Experiential programs, such as internships, field research, or service learning, involve careful planning. It is essential to have a clear and defensible academic component if the experiential program carries academic credit. All experiential activities take time and require good local contacts as well as careful selection, preparation, and ongoing monitoring of both student and placement. University alumni can be helpful in this regard if they are well placed in international corporations or living at the program site.

Programming for the Long-Term

While a new program abroad may be considered a one-time endeavor, the investment of staff time and effort required to get a program off the ground begs the question of whether a program should be seen as a long-term venture right from the start. This chapter assumes that the establishment of a new program represents a long-term commitment of human, financial, and physical resources on the part of the sponsoring institution, and that such an undertaking is initiated only after thorough planning. Once a program is up and running and the initial (and inevitable) problems have been worked out, the challenging maintenance phase begins. Some of the ongoing issues to address include program assessment, the relationship with the host institution, financial solvency, and impact on the local (overseas) community.

Assessment

In the short term, education abroad programs are typically monitored through student surveys and directors' reports at the end of each program session. Some education abroad offices also conduct postprogram debriefings. This is especially common when problems have been reported during the term abroad, or when an institution sends its students on a program for the first time and wants to gain additional insights from the students and director by meeting with them in person after their return to campus.

Apart from these annual assessments, mechanisms should also be built into study abroad programs for a thorough review on a regular basis, perhaps every five years or so. During these long-term reviews, sponsoring institutions often look at issues such as the following:

- Are the goals of the program are being met?

- Is the curriculum still meeting student and institutional needs?

- What is the state of the facilities and technological resources?

- Is the housing still appropriate, safe, and congruent with program goals (e.g., cultural and linguistic immersion)?

- What new health and safety issues need to be addressed?

- Is the staff adequate for the program and are there any issues that need to be resolved?

- What is the state of the program's finances? Are there any significant upcoming expenditures that will need to be addressed?

Colleges and universities typically conduct periodic in-depth reviews of their own programs with a committee from the home campus. The committee is sometimes comprised of a group of faculty members from the academic department or departments sponsoring the program, or it might be a combination of faculty and study abroad staff. On some campuses there is a standing study abroad committee that oversees all study abroad programs and conducts ongoing assessments. In the case of study abroad programs administered by consortia, the education abroad program is typically managed and evaluated by a board made up of representatives from each of the member institutions. Whatever the review process, it will have greater credibility and generate broader support for any recommended changes if different constituencies, such as study abroad administrators and faculty in relevant fields, are involved.

Both the management structure and budget of newly established education abroad programs should include both yearly and periodic (i.e., every five years) assessments so that problems can be discovered and addressed quickly. This is especially important, for example, when programs are directed by faculty from the home campus, who may not have experience as on-site resident directors. Problems are much easier to address if there is an oversight body or committee already in place that has the authority to intervene. Because faculty are accustomed to a certain degree of autonomy, the study abroad office alone may have trouble effecting changes to programs led by faculty without the backing of a faculty committee. In some instances, the provost or dean of the faculty member may need to be consulted to help in the delicate diplomacy of providing feedback to an individual faculty member.

Another method for periodic review often employed by national study abroad organizations is to assemble a team of four to six outside reviewers. These review team members are typically study abroad coordinators from member schools, who are already serving on the advisory board of the study abroad organization; or they may be faculty in relevant fields, from member institutions, who are specially invited to take part in the review. The review team often travels to the program site for an intense week or so to scrutinize the program. They talk to students, sit in on classes, meet with staff and faculty, tour the program facilities and the city, look at student accommodations, and meet with host families to obtain a comprehensive view of the program. When the organization knows that the program has certain weak spots, the team may even be instructed to focus on certain areas, such as curriculum, housing, or staff. The teams are often given access to previous student surveys and directors' reports, and may even be given data on language acquisition or other skill areas, if the participating students were tested before and after the program. Reports from such reviews are typically distributed to program staff and to the representatives from the organization's member schools. Several study abroad providers post the results of these reviews on the internet.

The cross-pollination of ideas that results from the review process, particularly when outside reviewers are involved, is invaluable for infusing existing programs with new ideas. It also helps staff and faculty from home campuses to understand in greater depth the unique educational opportunities that particular programs provide. However, conducting reviews may be easier than actually implementing recommendations that result from the process. For that reason, it is advisable to set a time frame, such as one year, for implementing the changes suggested in the assessment report. (See also Part III, Chapter 5, "Program Assessment and Evaluation.")

Maintaining Relationships with Host Institutions

There are a number of key steps education abroad professionals can take when establishing a relationship with an institution overseas, that will help maintain a solid working partnership in the long run, such as the following:

- Identify the needs and goals of the partner institution abroad and build features into the relationship that will meet those needs.

- Build some sort of reciprocity into the relationship, if possible, and be creative about what sorts of exchanges can be established. The traditional exchange of the same number of students or faculty can be adjusted if administrations are willing to be flexible. For example, if the U.S. institution primarily needs local facilities and experts to assist with short-term programs, but the overseas institution wants to provide its students with more subsidized study opportunities in the United States, the U.S. institution may provide several semesters of tuition stipends in exchange for cost-free space and administrative support for its program abroad. Such an agreement meets the needs of both institutions.

- Ensure that the senior administration and the front-line staff at both institutions are on board with the new program.

- Designate a liaison at both institutions for the day-to-day operations of the program.

- Build periodic site visits into the budget of the program.

Understand that foreign partners will have certain expectations about how commitment to institutional relationships is demonstrated, and these expectations will depend on the culture of that country and the extent of the foreign partners' experience with U.S. partners. Typical expectations might be gift giving, holiday cards, invitations to university officials to come to the United States, etc.

Site visits between the United States and the host institution are integral to solidifying relationships and facilitating understanding between institutions. While e-mail, fax, and phone are essential for day-to-day operations, periodic in-person site visits demonstrate how the relationship is valued, and are often essential when thorny issues need to be resolved. Site visits should be made not only by those actually administering the program, but also by senior administrators, such as a dean, provost, or president, who can provide support from the top when problems arise, and whose presence provides evidence of broad institutional support for the endeavor. When programs are located in societies that are traditional and hierarchical, it is especially important for senior administrators from U.S. institutions to visit the host university periodically and to invite senior administrators from the partner institution to the United States, to demonstrate commitment to the program. Ordinarily, the hosting institution is expected to pay on-site costs of a visit.

It is important to be sensitive to how the relationship with the partner institution evolves over time. For example, one four-year liberal arts college in the northwest of the United States has had an exchange since 1982 for its alumni to teach English at universities in China. As part of the exchange, one Chinese instructor of English from those partner universities comes to the United States each year to take classes and learn about the United States. Because opportunities to travel abroad and to learn English have increased dramatically in China over the last 20 years, one of the Chinese partner universities recently asked to send its undergraduates to the college for a "study abroad year" rather than sending its instructors, because it believed its undergraduates today would benefit more from a year in the United States than their instructors. It is natural that the needs of Chinese universities have changed along with the rapid social and economic transformation of that country in the last few decades. International educational partnerships need to evolve according to new conditions that emerge in both countries over time.

Financial Considerations

Dealing with Financial Problems

A program needs to be monitored to make sure that it remains financially viable. If a program sustains an operating loss over several years, the future of the program will be very shaky. But before closing a program, it makes sense to contemplate changes that will restore it to significant health. These changes can be academic (adding new academic fields or areas of academic concentration, redefining the curricular focal point of the program, changing faculty) or financial (reducing overhead, negotiating lower tuition charges from host universities, negotiating lower housing costs). The program can revamp its approach to marketing through pricing techniques, positioning the program more favorably against the competition, developing more effective marketing materials, and providing special scholarships.

Financial problems in a program may be related to external factors such as world events, temporary political unrest, epidemics, and natural disasters, and it is useful to develop a financial cushion to sustain a program in hard times. However, some programs reach a stage where closing is advisable. Student interest may have moved permanently in other directions. Resources devoted to the ailing program may prevent the possibility of establishing other programs that will sustain themselves better and attract greater interest. Keep in mind, however, that there are financial costs associated with the closure of a program. Long-term staff members and faculty cannot be summarily dismissed, and there may be legally defined severance costs. Leases must be concluded or subleased; property needs to be repatriated or given away. If the sending institution's students have been directly enrolling at local institutions, it is good practice to help the partner universities find other partners or ways of continuing to attract students. The goodwill and credibility of an institution can rise or fall on the grace with which it suspends, relocates, or, if necessary, cancels a program.

Partner or Patron

Living, studying, and working in a foreign country has an enormous impact on the participants as well as on the programs' directors and faculty. However, the impact that U.S. students and their faculty and education abroad administrators have on local communities is not always factored into the equation when designing and implementing new programs abroad. To administer programs that will thrive in the long run, education abroad administrators must begin with a look at the long-term impact that their programs have had and will have on local communities overseas. Our success in increasing study abroad participation is coupled with the risk of having a negative effect on the local physical and cultural environments because of the presence of U.S. students, especially if the students arrive with a "tourist" mindset (i.e., the new location is there to provide light entertainment, attractions, and distractions). While the specific issues that study abroad administrators should be concerned about when assessing the impact on the local community or local university abroad will vary considerably from location to location, there are some general questions to keep in mind throughout the planning, budgeting, and implementation process.

Can the program be designed in a way that ensures that the host community or university abroad will gain something more than financial remuneration from the program's presence? Are there ways, for instance, for the program to ensure that the host nationals outside the university will also benefit educationally and culturally so that there are lasting and sustainable benefits?

How can the program ensure that it will continue to give participants an authentic experience of the local culture if the number of U.S. students in that location increases significantly?

For programs in the developing world, is paying tuition to the university adequate compensation when U.S. visiting students may be taking highly coveted places at the university away from local degree-seeking students, and draining scarce resources? Is there a way to build in additional reciprocity to benefit the partner university?

If the program includes a period of time in a rural area, what are the ethical and cultural ramifications of using a different village for home-stays each year, so that students have a "pristine" village experience? Or should the program remain in one village location over the long-term, viewing the villagers as partners, and structuring the program so that the villagers benefit in the long run?

In locations with cultures markedly different from that of the United States, can the program adequately prepare U.S. students for the social norms in the community abroad so that they will not make serious cultural mistakes that may do lasting damage to the reputation of an individual family or village?

What responsibilities does a program have to members of the local community, such as host families, who have become dependent on the income brought to the community by the program and the students, when the program sponsor considers it necessary to cancel or relocate it?

In Western Europe and Latin America these days, some universities have a high proportion of visiting students from the United States due to the popularity of certain education abroad locations. Some courses may even have a majority of students from the United States because they often gravitate to similar types of courses while abroad—Latin American studies classes in Latin America or Irish studies in Ireland, for example. Several unintended consequences result from the "Americanization" of such courses. First, the U.S. students will not have the kind of classroom immersion experience that is available in a classroom where most of the students are local. Second, the local faculty member may have to change how the class is taught in order to accommodate the largely foreign audience; this again alters the kind of classroom experience available. Recognizing these problems, some universities in Latin America are already limiting the number of visiting students that may enroll in particular courses.

Programs that have been established in rural parts of the developing world have other potential relationship problems. In these areas, where a few U.S. dollars can make a huge difference in standard of living, antagonisms can arise within a local community because the families selected to host U.S. students will reap significant economic rewards, whereas other families will not. While it is true that interactions with U.S. students will be an educationally and culturally broadening experience for local hosts in the developing world, the habits and material culture that these students bring with them can also affect a community negatively. One program located in a village in a developing country discovered that the U.S. students created a disproportionate amount of garbage because they tended to buy things that were disposable or had commercial packaging, whereas the locals reused nearly everything. The local village had not needed garbage service prior to the arrival of the U.S. students.

In essence, we are talking about "sustainable study abroad"—or how to ensure that the overall impact of having students in a locale is primarily positive. This is a relatively new topic in the field of education abroad but will undoubtedly grow in importance as study abroad participation increases in all corners of the world.

Summary

Anyone who has been involved in the establishment of an education abroad program knows that it is a huge, time-consuming, and multifaceted undertaking. And while careful and long-range planning is essential, it is also worthwhile to remember that one cannot plan for every eventuality, and that, as international educators tell their students, flexibility is key. But, regardless of the type of program or institution, each of the points raised above bears careful consideration in order to ensure a well-constructed program that will serve student and institutional needs.

CHAPTER 4

Marketing, Promotion, and Publicity

Contributors: My Yarabinec, Leo Van Cleve, Andrea Walgren

Few professionals in education abroad have a business or marketing background; consequently, commercial sales techniques are often alien concepts. Furthermore, other aspects of the job—advising students, developing programs, working with the faculty—often seem more important and enjoyable. Selling educational experiences may feel inappropriate. However, in order for education abroad to become a more viable, visible, and prominent part of undergraduate education, the field needs to learn to use appropriate promotion and publicity tools to build support in every way possible, on and off campus.

Promotion and Publicity on Campus

Convincing more students, faculty, administrators, parents, legislators, foundations, corporations, and the U.S. public to support increased overseas opportunities is both a political and rhetorical task in the best senses of these two words. That is to say, it requires education abroad advisers and administrators to attract attention to the value of education abroad through sound promotion and effective publicity so that students will be persuaded to participate, and can select programs wisely. Even today, the value of overseas programs often must be sold to many potential constituencies through persuasive and compelling arguments. Such efforts can be assisted by some basic marketing principles. There are three simple rules to successful promotion: variety, repetition, and appropriateness.

Repetition and variety go hand in hand. The first ad or brochure a student sees may not be effective, and multiple issuances of it will be perceived as dull and useless. A message repeated in a variety of formats is more likely to get a student's attention and get the message across. The student who passes a study abroad poster, then reads an article about study abroad in the campus newspaper, then picks up a free bookmark promoting the education abroad office, is more apt to realize the possibilities of overseas education and the potential that such programs offer—as is the student who sees a well-designed flier, then receives a brochure at student orientation, and then hears a classroom presentation.

Before deciding what is appropriate publicity, the education abroad office must clearly identify its audience. Advertising a study abroad program to students who do not qualify academically, cannot afford the cost, or are not free to go when the program is offered does little good. Identify target groups of students (e.g., science majors, minority students, classics students, students with a 3.0 grade point average, or fraternity or sorority members), and tailor the message accordingly. It is also important to ensure that the message reaches the faculty and parents who support the students. If education abroad advertising is not directed to a particular audience, program promotion may prove to be a frustrating and wasteful exercise.

Promoting the Education Abroad Office and Its Work

Most people are aware of the publicity required to ensure that a campus event is well attended or a worthwhile social cause is supported. Kiosks and bulletin boards crammed with fliers and posters, and ample ads and notices in the school newspapers are common on every campus. Making the campus community aware of the education abroad office and its services is an ongoing challenge. To succeed, education abroad professionals need to devise a conscious strategy to advertise the office's programs and to promote its services.

Although it can be counterproductive to promote education abroad to students before securing the broad support of the faculty and administration, demonstrating student interest can facilitate gaining such support. If the education abroad office already has the support of the faculty and the administration, but education abroad continues to have low visibility and low participation levels, the challenge is to reach students with the message that education abroad is possible for them. Even if the campus has many programs and a long history of involvement in international education, educators must avoid complacency and continue to work to attract students from a wider spectrum of the student body.

If the education abroad office is part of a larger entity—academic advising, student affairs, career services, or international programs—education abroad professionals may need to differentiate the office's services from those around it, through advertising and publicity. A higher profile will increase awareness of the education abroad office's services, remove misunderstandings about the office's purpose, and also make it easier for supporters and volunteers (as well as contributions) to find the office. A higher profile will also draw the attention of campus administrators who decide on the allocation of budget, personnel, space, and other resources.

Important Marketing Tools

Education abroad professionals cannot begin to advise students until they have demonstrated an interest in studying or working abroad, and have come into the education abroad office to look at materials and seek counsel. Thus, the challenge is to get students to this exploratory point.

College Promotional Materials

Increasingly, high school and transfer students are looking for education abroad opportunities as part of their college studies. It is imperative that an institution's overseas opportunities be a prominent part of any promotional materials sent to prospective students. The education abroad office should work with the admissions office to ensure that education abroad is promoted in an engaging but truthful fashion—in print, photos, and graphics—and that admissions counselors stress these opportunities at college fairs and in interviews with students. Education abroad office staff will want to meet regularly with the admissions office recruitment staff to let them know about new and continuing programs abroad. If the education abroad office has developed a general flier or poster, it should be on display in the admissions office. Campus tours for interested students and parents should pass through the education abroad office or building. Campus tour guides can, perhaps, identify the office as the "gateway to the world" or "gateway to "x number" of foreign countries," as represented by the campus-sponsored programs. The institution's admissions and public relations offices should be reminded, however, not to oversell the education abroad programs by promising more than can be delivered. Students who were "promised" during the admissions process that they could have a certain program abroad have long memories. Frustrated student expectations can lead to very unpleasant encounters with students and their parents.

New Student Orientation

Consider working with student services and academic affairs during the new student orientation, by preparing a presentation that will urge students to begin thinking now about how to include a study or work program in their undergraduate education. This is a good chance to distribute materials and to invite students to the education abroad office. Involving some enthusiastic and articulate returnees as part of the office's presentation can be especially effective.

The College Catalog

The education abroad opportunities and the services of the education abroad office should be prominently featured in any academic catalog and student services handbooks the campus publishes. This information should explain how to include overseas studies in a degree, and should feature the institution's own programs as well as the range of other programs available. Policies and procedures also need to be spelled out. If the institution offers financial aid for study abroad, or even if it only allows the application of normal aid packages, this should be made clear. In addition, departmental entries might indicate study abroad opportunities for majors, and the index should be cross-referenced to facilitate locating opportunities by country and language.

Fliers and Posters

Promoting education abroad can be much easier with a general information flier. This flier needs to be attractive (though not necessarily expensive); the language needs to be straightforward; and good graphics are essential. Likewise, developing an eye-catching poster for general use on campus is also a good way to call attention to the education abroad office and its services. The poster should highlight the excitement of studying or working overseas. By leaving a blank space at the bottom for date, time, and location, such a poster can also be used to advertise general information sessions as well as meetings about particular programs. It might also mention related products or services offered by the education abroad office (e.g., international student ID cards, rail passes, youth hostel cards, books). Using the school colors on posters emphasizes the connection of the study abroad program to the home campus. The design of the flier and poster can be an opportunity for collaboration between the education abroad office and students and faculty in the marketing/advertising program at the institution. Having advertising students design these materials will facilitate the connection to their

Part III: Program Development, Campus Management, Marketing, and Evaluation

peers; having the materials designed as part of a course will ensure a high level of quality. The education abroad office may want to consider holding a yearly campus competition for the design of the education abroad poster, and offer an appropriate prize such as a small scholarship towards participation in one of the programs abroad. Lastly, check the campus policy on putting up posters and bulletin board notices. Some colleges require that all items posted be cleared through the student activity or student life office.

General Information Meetings

Most experienced advisers and administrators agree that there is great value in hosting general information sessions or open houses for students exploring overseas opportunities. How the education abroad office sets up and publicizes these meetings depends on the size of the campus, the facilities available, what help the office can get from others, and a number of other variables. Meetings can be held at the beginning of each term. On some campuses general information meetings occur monthly; on others, weekly, or even two or more times per week. The education abroad office might consider having students attend a general information meeting as a requirement for admission to education abroad. Having supportive faculty, key administrators, recently returned students, and peer counselors participate will help create interest and enthusiasm. Being in a group and seeing that they are not "strange" or alone in their study abroad quest can also reinforce students' interest. Through these meetings, students can begin to make supportive contacts with their peers as well as with the education abroad staff. Although the education abroad representative's own remarks or those of the education abroad director will stress the academic and personal values of education abroad, as well as the institution's policies, the real goal is to encourage students to come to the office and use the office's advising materials to begin exploring their options. (See Part II, Chapter 1, "Advising Principles and Strategies.")

International Education Week

Since 2000, by presidential proclamation, U.S. campuses celebrate "International Education Week" as an opportunity to highlight the significance and importance of international education and exchange (see the International Education Week information on the Bureau of Educational and Cultural Affairs area of the U.S. Department of State Web site and also the International Education Week Web site). International Education Week is a splendid opportunity to put study abroad front and center in the consciousness of the campus as a key component of the institution's international mission. Some campuses organize a "World at a Glance" series, with special presentations on each of the overseas opportunities on a country or regional basis. Film, videos, student panels, presentations by knowledgeable faculty or former resident advisers can constitute a "World at a Glance" session. International Education Week is also an excellent opportunity to work with campus media on publicity and coverage. The education abroad office's publicity and information materials should be prominently displayed at International Education Week events. This will be an excellent way to promote education abroad services and programs to the internationally minded members of the campus and the community at large.

Education Abroad Fairs

Many campuses hold study abroad fairs as an effective way of publicizing education abroad to

Chapter 4: Marketing, Promotion, and Publicity

large numbers of students. Held annually or once each term, these fairs bring together in one large space—for an afternoon, evening, or an entire day—representatives and past participants of many different study and work programs. Interested students and faculty can ask questions and get further information. In addition to promoting particular programs, fairs also boost the idea of overseas study and highlight the variety of options. Though fairs are aimed at students, they also provide opportunities for faculty and administrators to get to know programs and to realize the diversity and quality of current international programming. Some fairs also include information on international work and travel. Others are conducted in conjunction with international student organizations, and celebrate global diversity.

Organizing and operating a successful fair is a major undertaking. It requires careful advance planning, good timing and publicity, and careful attention to logistical details. Education abroad professionals will need a great deal of help from the education abroad office staff and from other offices. Just deciding whom to invite (e.g., will the fair feature only the institution's own education abroad programs and returnees, or will it include other programs that are approved for credit transfer; will the fair be open to representatives from these other programs?) and how to arrange for their practical needs is a major task. But the cumulative impact of a well-attended fair can be powerful and long lasting. A fair—compared with most other means—can bring an extensive amount of information to a large number of students economically and efficiently. It will certainly boost the profile of the education abroad office. Strategies must also be developed for dealing with post-study abroad fair questions. Students often are confused by seemingly similar, yet clearly competing, options. By holding a raffle (for a t-shirt, perhaps), the education abroad office can obtain students' e-mail addresses to use for sending follow-up notes. Making sure that every visitor to the fair leaves with a card or bookmark with location, hours, and contact information for the education abroad office will also facilitate student follow-up.

Promoting Education Abroad Electronically

Internet services, which include e-mail and the World Wide Web, have added some exciting new tools for publicizing study abroad and disseminating useful—as well as much un-useful—information. (See Part I, Chapter 8, "Technology and Education Abroad.")

E-mail

E-mail allows rapid communication with potentially large numbers of people. One of the most useful functions of e-mail is the attachment of files that can be accessed on the recipient's computer. This function can be used to advantage in sending copies of press releases or any additional supplemental information to the targeted audience. However, because many viruses and so-called worms are sent as attachments, education abroad professionals will want to consider some of the alternatives discussed below, such as Web page downloads.

E-mail also allows users to create and use "address books," enabling them to send a single message to everyone, or only to certain individuals selected from the address book directory. The education abroad office's address book could include faculty and administrators, academic advisers, students who have contacted the office with a particular country or academic major interest, study abroad alumni and alumnae, campus media, student clubs on campus, etc. By targeting e-mails to one or more of these groups, the education abroad office would be able to easily notify a large number of people of its activities, information meetings, new programs, the study abroad fair, the visit of a program representative to campus, and the like.

Yet another useful function of e-mail is the saving of sent messages. This is particularly useful in that it allows users to retrieve a form letter and send it to new addressees in answer to common questions and requests.

E-mail also provides an excellent way to keep in touch with students overseas and to pass their comments on to other interested parties. For example, journalism majors who have been encouraged to serve as "foreign correspondents" for the campus newspaper can file their stories in this manner. If the university or program overseas does not have e-mail accounts available to students (although most do), the students should be encouraged to find a local service provider.

Finally, remember that most universities allow one or more e-mail accounts for an office. If the education abroad professional wishes to use e-mail to disseminate information about the office or receive inquiries from the general public, it is highly advisable to establish an office account separate from the professional's personal account. Also remember that just because an inquiry comes through e-mail, education abroad professionals are not required to respond to it in full detail. Some issues are too complex to resolve by e-mail messages. Instead, for example, the education abroad professional might respond by suggesting that the student come in to pick up some of the printed material, make an appointment, or attend an information meeting, and include in the message a schedule of the office hours and advising availability.

It is also important to remember that e-mail, though a highly popular communications medium among students, should be only one of the advertising and publicity strategies used by the education abroad office. Furthermore, remember that repeated unsolicited e-mail is considered to be "spam," and aside from being rude, may actually violate campus policies on electronic communication. Lastly, when sending out mass e-mail announcements to students or faculty, education abroad professionals may wish to use either the "blind copy" (bcc) function or the "recipient list suppressed" function to avoid inadvertently creating a discussion list that can be hijacked by a disaffected student, or seen as a violation of privacy.

The World Wide Web

The use and possible applications of the internet for marketing and publicizing study abroad programs are virtually unlimited. Surfing the Web has become second nature to most college-age students, and because it supports documents with a mixture of text and graphics, the Web can be both eye-catching and informative. The great strength of the Web is that large amounts of information can be included in a site either by posting it directly, or by linking other pages to the education abroad office's site. This allows students, faculty, and administrators to access information without additional effort on the part of education abroad staff. The chief drawback of the Web is that it is static; an outdated Web page is often worse than no page at all. Furthermore, people must seek out information and must know what questions to ask. When planning a promotional activity, education abroad professionals should consider carefully what information will be placed on the Web for reference, who will see to it that the information posted is kept current, and perhaps more importantly, how students, faculty, and administrators will be directed to the site.

A Web site typically begins with a "home page," usually the first page accessed. The home page identifies the university or office and provides a table of contents. Each item in the table of contents is a link to an appropriate page. In this manner, the Web site provides an informational hierarchy of sorts that allows the browser to go from the general to the specific—for example, from the university to the study abroad office to a specific program or supporting document.

Some of the specific applications of the Web for publicizing the education abroad office's program and services, and encouraging students to study abroad, include

- basic information about the program;
- important notices from the education abroad office;
- office location, hours, phone numbers, and e-mail addresses;
- staff listings, and perhaps short biographies;
- images of places where the study abroad programs go;
- study abroad program descriptions, and other information about the programs and services the office offers;
- links to other relevant information sources on the Web (e.g., Centers for Disease Control and Prevention, U.S. Department of State);
- "clickable" image maps;
- handbooks and policy manuals;
- predeparture information;
- reentry suggestions and activities; and
- university disclaimers and other required legal notices.

Interactive forms on the Web are becoming increasingly easy to make. They can contribute to the move toward a "paperless" office. Many universities already have online applications and other forms for study abroad programs. Interactive forms may also facilitate a student's application process. However, before the education abroad office goes completely paperless, it should check with university legal counsel as to how the required student signatures on applications, certifications, releases, and the like, can be collected. There should also be a ruling on how to file and archive electronic documents. And lastly, there is the question of who should be doing the printing of these applications and forms, and at what cost per page. A cost-benefit analysis may reveal that it is cheaper to have all of the forms duplicated at once, rather than printed out one at a time by education abroad staff.

Mobilizing Returned Students and International Exchange Students

Study abroad alumni are one of the most important resources for publicizing the study abroad experience on campus. These students can talk to classes and provide information to interested students. Returned students often represent a variety of majors and a variety of countries around the world. Their presentations complement and supplement other forms of publicity, and direct messages from experienced peers seem ideal in terms of appropriateness and credibility.

To best use this population, education abroad professionals should select and train study abroad returnees in some structured manner. A student organization or club for study abroad alumni is an ideal way to mobilize students who have returned from abroad. Often these "international student" organizations bring together study abroad returnees and both visiting and degree-seeking international students on campus. However, rather than just turning the alumni and international students loose, education abroad professionals would be well advised to meet with them—or even to select just a few students to meet with—and brief them on the message the education abroad office wants them to convey, and especially on the kinds of questions that should be referred to the office. Their energy is wonderful and can be quite invigorating, but they can also get carried away and promise things that the education abroad office will later have to either deliver or explain why it can't. Thus, it is good to provide these students with an outline of talking points and a list of topics that must be taken up with the professionals in the education abroad office.

Properly selected and trained, these students can contact faculty and make brief classroom presentations. They benefit by gaining practice in public speaking, enhancing their résumés, and having a captive audience for their photo albums. Some institutions also provide a modest honorarium or some other token of appreciation (e.g., food).

International student groups are particularly effective if they also include study abroad applicants and international exchange students. This provides a critical mass to the club, spreads the work and responsibilities, provides an opportunity for a greater number of students with leadership skills and other talents to participate, and, in general, is good for group morale and reinforcement. International students can also sit at information tables in well-trafficked public spaces on campus, and hand out study abroad information meeting slips and other promotional materials. Likewise, the international exchange students can hang fliers, distribute brochures, stock racks, design display cases, make room reservations, and organize activities. Don't forget that they also represent a number of talents and skills, such as Web site design, computer skills, graphic design talents for fliers and poster, etc. Additionally, having the various groups of study abroad alumni, study abroad applicants, and international (exchange) students working together provides opportunities for fertile interaction among these groups. Finally, having a student group officially recognized by the associated students (or equivalent student government organization) on campus can also often result in funds for activities from the associated students budget, thus providing a supplementary source of monetary support for the promotion of study abroad on campus.

Other Publicity Ideas

Piggybacking

If the education abroad office has kept abreast of other events on campus, it may be able to piggyback the education abroad message onto other international activities. For example, if international students give presentations in courses that focus on their home country, they could be encouraged to end with an invitation to study overseas and to visit the education abroad office to get more information. Similarly, if there is a foreign film series on campus, general brochures about the office could be left at the entrance to the auditorium.

Class Assignments

Another idea for promoting education abroad is to contact faculty in marketing, advertising, and public relations to ask whether the education abroad office can assign publicity projects. One institution gained a Web page, a study abroad logo, a new poster, and sample press release formats from such a project. The class assignment became a useful way of piggybacking on an existing activity.

All of the promotional opportunities listed above can greatly bolster the image of education abroad on campus. Ideally, these opportunities will prepare students to begin the advising process. Promoting particular program opportunities requires another set of strategies.

Publicizing Particular Programs

Getting the right students interested in the right programs is one of the major challenges facing education abroad advisers. To reach these students, education abroad professionals need to define and carry out a targeted promotion.

A targeted approach involves identifying a group of students that may be appropriate for a specific overseas program and then devising a publicity campaign aimed at the group. Some examples are a campaign to attract literature and history majors to an exchange program with an Irish university; a campaign directed at Latin American studies, public policy, or social work students (and those with African-American or Hispanic backgrounds) for an established program in the Dominican Republic, with good course work in urban studies and economic development and a social service agency internship; a campaign directed at Asian studies, architecture, and art history students to attract them to a program in Japan that focuses on traditional Japanese design. Each of these programs must be marketed in a way that will attract the desired audience. Promotional tools might include

- program posters, brochures, and other such materials distributed in areas frequented by the targeted students, including departmental libraries and hallways (with the proper permissions, of course);

- outreach to academic advisers and faculty in relevant subjects (personal visits, mailings, e-mail communications, and program materials);

- articles in department newsletters;

- classroom presentations;

- special mailings, e-mail communications, and meetings for students who have declared relevant majors.

In addition to directing promotional efforts at students with particular academic interests, the education abroad office can also direct campaigns at students seeking

- programs in particular geographic regions (e.g., Africa, Eastern Europe, or Southeast Asia);

- programs that are highly experiential or service-oriented;

- programs that require a lot of independent research or field study rather than classroom time;

- programs that are not located in English-speaking countries but offer a curriculum in English and the opportunity to learn the local language and live with families;

- programs that are able to accept students with physical or learning disabilities; and

- programs with moderate admission requirements or those that do not require a high GPA for admission.

If institutional fee policy permits, the education abroad office can publicize programs on the basis of their moderate or low-cost. Similarly, program length, time of year offered, the availability of scholarships, or the level of foreign language required can serve as the basis of a promotional effort. As a general practice, all publicity from the education abroad office should be designed to reach a broad cross-section of students and encourage them to consider a program abroad. It is especially important for education abroad offices to reach out to students of color, nontraditional students, as well as students in underrepresented majors, such as the natural sciences or engineering. It is equally important that all students be made aware of opportunities in nontraditional locations. The overarching goal is to make students aware that the education abroad office is ready and eager to talk with them about a variety of program possibilities.

Using the Media

Every campus has its own forms of communication, which may include a campus newspaper, a radio station, and a video channel. Although the campus-centered focus of these media will always dominate, there are many ways of getting these media to direct their attention to education abroad, and ultimately getting the attention of students. Since student media often have a commercial base, paying for ads in the newspaper to boost the education abroad office or its programs is one option that will raise the office's visibility, as well as its welcome at the newspaper. Make press releases appealing to student editors by making them easy to adapt for publication, and encourage follow-up features. The education abroad office might also host a reception for reporters from the paper, and use the opportunity to provide them with background information on education abroad programs and an opportunity to interview returnees. Also, be sure the media know about lectures and presentations given by international visitors to the campus community.

As advantageous as these strategies are, most education abroad offices do not have large discretionary budgets for advertising and hospitality. Another approach involves increasing personal contacts with editors, writers, and media managers. Why not meet with the faculty adviser and editors of the campus newspaper, offer to assist with articles, be available for interviews, make follow-up calls, or encourage students to submit articles about their experiences? When announcements and features begin appearing, always remember to thank the newspaper editors and staff. Send personal invitations to the media. It is surprising how often a specially invited reporter actually comes to events and programs. Finally, remember that no matter how the education abroad representative, office, and programs may be portrayed in the media, the education abroad representative and the office should always be cooperative and collegial.

The Campus Newspaper

The campus newspaper may appear daily, several times a week, or weekly, so knowing deadlines and timing a message for optimum impact is very important. In addition, education abroad professionals should be familiar with the various columns and announcements that appear regularly, and know who writes or edits them. Ask the newspaper's advertising department to send a new rate sheet whenever it is revised, and get the requirements for camera-ready copy.

Feature Articles. Features on international themes are desirable because they usually provide an implicit pitch for the value of education abroad, in addition to adding a human-interest element, whether through participant interviews or personal accounts. Such articles also remind all readers, including faculty and administrators, of the contributions the education abroad office makes to the campus community. The education abroad office can often be proactive in suggesting tie-ins between planned feature topics and education abroad programs. For example, most campus newspapers perennially run articles about love and dating for their edition on or near Valentine's Day. A possible tie-in could be a story on how some of the students currently abroad feel about the differences in dating practices between the home campus and the host country. Tie-ins and suggested story topics should always promote education abroad in general and the office in particular. Consider encouraging any students departing for an overseas experience to serve as "international correspondents" to the campus newspaper. This opportunity is of particular interest to journalism majors and is usually of interest to the campus newspaper as well.

The Calendar Section. Most campus newspapers provide a regular opportunity for disseminating campus information in a calendar section. Find out the requirements and deadlines, and submit announcements on a regular basis. Take advantage of this free service to announce meetings programs, deadlines for applications, visits by representatives from other programs, fairs, and other international events. Monitoring other international events listed in the calendar section can also help the education abroad office identify students who might be interested in an overseas experience. For example, a Japanese art exhibition or a guest lecture on international business is a prime opportunity to distribute fliers and brochures, provided this is acceptable to the sponsor, of course.

Letters to the Editor. Letters can be written by the education abroad professional, the education abroad office, or returned students in response to some related matter. Make sure that students identify themselves as alumni of the institution's education abroad programs. A letter need not be explicitly about overseas study or a particular foreign country. For example, an article about the business school could inspire a follow-up letter suggesting that study abroad will help make U.S. citizens culturally and linguistically more successful in pursuing careers in international business.

Personal Columns. Since students often read these, an occasional, cleverly worded message in the personals section of the campus newspaper may attract more curiosity and attendance at an event than a more expensive advertisement. For example:

"Darling, he suspects! Meet me at the Study Abroad Information Meeting, Next Wednesday, 7:30 p.m., in McLaren Hall. Your Turtledove."

Other Campus Publications

Education abroad professionals should not overlook opportunities to get a message into all campus and official university publications. Internationalism and internationalization are popular topics, and the education abroad office can be a rallying point on campus. Examples of campus publications include

- faculty and staff newsletters,
- department (including administrative departments) newsletters,
- alumni magazines and newsletters,
- any publications put out by the campus's international center,
- all admissions brochures, and
- the college's Web site home page.

Other Media Possibilities

The campus radio or television station may run (or be required to run) public service announcements. Advertising in periodicals that reach students likely to be receptive to education abroad should also be considered if the budget permits.

Points to Keep in Mind When Using Media On and Off Campus

Avoid confusing terms, as well as abbreviations, acronyms, and jargon. What may seem clear to an education abroad professional may be confusing to others. Make it as easy as possible for the writer or media contact to understand the point. The education abroad office or its representative should be readily available, respond quickly with additional material, offer to identify students for the article, and be understanding when its articles do not get published. Always be certain that announcements and articles include details about where to get more information, especially Web sites.

The chances of having an article published and published accurately will improve if the following tools are used.

The Press Release. Press releases should be provided for every suggested story and for every major event the education abroad office sponsors, to ensure that key information is included in the final version. Always remember to include who, what, where, when, why, and where to turn for more information. Try to limit the release to one page and always be sure to include a contact name and phone number of a person who will actually be available; reporters will not call back again and again. The campus public relations office, as well as the journalism program, can help with the basics of press release writing.

A Press Kit. This should include a cover letter (highlighting the essential elements of the story), the press release, an information brochure (if any), all pertinent information, photographs (if available), and the education abroad representative's business card.

Photos. These can be submitted with the press kit or sent separately, along with a caption. Photos with captions provide further interaction with the writers and editors. If the picture must be returned, make arrangements for this. Find out from area media if they prefer digital photographs to film, and if digital, at what resolution and in what format.

Follow-up. Give feedback to the media. Thank them for covering the education abroad meeting or printing a story about education abroad.

Other Methods to Get the Word Out

Using the campus media may be one of the best ways to launch a message, but a number of other means serve the same purpose, such as

- display cases (which are great for showcasing student projects as well as particular programs),
- fliers on campus bulletin boards (make sure these conform to campus regulations),
- banners (especially in the student union, dormitory lounges, and cafeterias),
- information booths outside cafeterias and snack bars,
- classroom presentations (especially in foreign language and area studies courses)
- representation at campus festivals and activities,

- exhibits of student photography and art from their programs abroad, and
- bookmarks and "table tents" (pieces of paper folded in a triangle shape) printed with the education abroad office's message.

COMMUNITY MEDIA

Members of a campus community do not live in a vacuum. They watch, listen, read, and notice what is conveyed to them by the local media. Utilizing the local media can be especially effective in smaller communities and should not be overlooked as a worthwhile promotion tool in urban environments. One advantage of dealing with community media is that the news and advertising staff are not as transitory as their student counterparts. This stability allows the education abroad office staff to develop personal relationships more likely to give a better return for their publicity efforts.

Initially, the local media should be approached with basic news stories, such as an article featuring students chosen for a particular study abroad program. In this way, study abroad is the story, rather than having to tie-in study abroad to some other article. When approaching the community media, use the standard tools of press releases, press kits, and so on. All earlier suggestions made regarding the campus media also apply to the community media. In addition, education abroad professionals should not be afraid of sending news releases on a regular basis; the local media are always looking for filler. The return is that the education abroad message is presented to a larger audience. Seek the assistance of the campus public information office, and keep it informed of the education abroad office's contacts with community media.

On occasion, the media will seek out the education abroad office, such as when there is civil unrest or a major disaster in a country where students from its campus are studying. These occasions cannot be anticipated, but given the number of students now studying and working overseas, education abroad professionals should be prepared for such situations and the ensuing media inquiries. Remember that anything said to the media will be taken as an official statement representing the institution. Therefore, education abroad professionals must be prudent, and work in cooperation with campus public information office and other appropriate university officials. Many campuses have specific protocols and policies for responding to media inquiries of any type, and such protocols and policies are especially important if the emergency overseas involves the institution's students.

Education abroad professionals should remain pleasant and fair at all times in their dealings with the media, never promising more than can be delivered, and considering carefully the confidentiality of the information being discussed. Nothing said to a newsperson is ever "off the record." An education abroad professional's ability to stay calm in times of overseas crises and to respond professionally to campus and media requests for information can do wonders for the reputation of the education abroad office. Mickey Slind's 1997 list of tips for "When a Reporter Calls" can also be useful when talking with the media, especially during an emergency. (See also NAFSA's *Crisis Management in a Cross-Cultural Setting* (Burak and Hoffa 2001); Part III, Chapter 6, "Maximizing Safety and Security and Minimizing Risk in Education Abroad Programs;" and the resources available from NAFSA's Education Abroad Knowledge Community's e-mail discussion list, SECUSS-L.)

Promotion and Publicity in Conjunction with Program Providers

Working with Program Providers

As student interest and participation in education abroad have grown, so has the number of programs and program providers serving these students. The term "program provider" includes independent programs based in the United States as well as overseas, foreign universities, nonprofit organizations, for-profit corporations, consortia, and U.S. colleges and universities. While foreign universities and program providers have long promoted their programs to other colleges and universities, a growing number of U.S. universities are opening their study abroad programs to students from other universities, thus becoming program providers in their own right.

This increase in the number of program providers, coupled with the increase in program advertising on the internet, as well as aggressive marketing on college bulletin boards by stapling services, have given students a much broader window on available program options. As a consequence, education abroad offices are fielding more requests for campus visits from program providers, and students are presenting more requests to participate in programs that they have learned about on the Web or from a bulletin board. When it works, collaborating with a provider to promote a particular program or group of programs can be both an enjoyable experience and a cost-effective way of recruiting students for education abroad. Because a number of provider organizations host conferences or site visits, collaboration may also lead to professional development opportunities. However, as in any successful collaboration, both sides must acknowledge and respect the limits of the other.

Campus Mission and Procedures

When a program provider of any type approaches a campus education abroad office, that office needs to have an understanding of how the program and its sponsoring organization fit within the mission, goals, and financial and staffing resources of the campus. Some campuses rely heavily on program providers to ensure a variety of opportunities for overseas study for their students. Other campuses have their own programs, and, for academic as well as financial reasons, place top priority on marketing their own opportunities to their students. In all cases it is critical that each institution has a clear policy and a set of procedures for handling the approval process for adding education abroad programs. If the institution chooses to use providers, these criteria will help the education abroad professional determine which ones best meet the needs of the students and the institution. Additionally, these criteria will automatically provide the professional and the institution with the guidelines for how to market programs offered by external program vendors to students and faculty. The key to any business relationship is for the professional to understand his or her own institution's philosophy, values, and priorities and then communicate these clearly to the vendors. This avoids misunderstandings and sets the tone for a constructive interaction among the institution, the education abroad office, the education abroad professional, and the provider organization.

Ideally, the institution already has a mission statement and a set of goals and objectives for international education that can inform any collaboration with a program provider. If this is not the case, then the education abroad professional should begin by taking a good look at the state of study abroad at the institution and the established institutional procedures for adding new off-campus programs, courses, or activities. A campus president, dean, or director of risk management, or the academic senate or department chairs, will be dismayed if they discover that, even with the best intentions, a study abroad adviser and the financial aid administrator have certified a new study abroad program without following the proper consultation procedure. As a general rule, the education abroad office should be in regular conversation with senior administration regarding the priorities and use of resources in assisting students to study overseas. They should hold regular discussions with faculty, both through formal consultative processes and informal processes, about their goals for their students who participate in study abroad. Such discussions will not only build support, but will also make education abroad a common educational experience for the institution.

The education abroad professional should research the institutional procedure for the certification of an outside agency for preapproval of academic credit and financial aid. If the institution has not developed one, the education abroad professional should urge that it establish a clear policy and procedure for approval of a program, with the agreement of all appropriate parties. (More suggestions on evaluating programs abroad for transfer of credit can be found in Part I, Chapter 6 "Credit and Grades" and Part III, Chapter 5, "Program Assessment and Evaluation.")

It is in the university's best interest to establish a continuing relationship with its program providers in order to smooth the academic articulation and administrative cooperation. It is impossible to sift through hundreds of program providers and thousands of programs on a regular basis. Thus, many campuses have developed a list of programs that are preapproved for the transfer of credit back to the home institution. Among the many things to consider when establishing a policy on cooperation with program providers are academic and programmatic issues such as language learning, level of integration in host country academic systems, credit for experiential learning, duration of the program, the qualifications of those who teach in the program, and finally, the academic and geographic distribution of program opportunities. For example, do the education abroad office and the college really need six programs in France? There are also campus administrative and financial issues to consider. Allowing students to participate in off-campus programs may affect the institution's revenues or expenses, or both. It is important to work closely with faculty and administration to see that the programs and providers under consideration assist the institution in meeting its internationalization objectives and academic goals without causing financial or enrollment management problems. Perhaps the most important issue to be considered when developing the institution's provider policy is student access—especially student finances. A program or provider that is available only to students with great personal or parental financial resources may conflict with other institutional values. It may also lead to the education abroad experience being viewed as peripheral or elitist.

With established institutional policies and procedures, the education abroad office can then set parameters for working with program providers. Program providers tend to use standard marketing strategies to promote awareness of their program on a campus. They must be made to understand that the campus priorities, and not those of the provider organization, dictate the structure of education abroad on a campus. Thus, it is the responsibility of the education abroad office to determine to what extent facilitating the work of a particular program provider (such as arranging for special presentations to students, meeting with key faculty, distributing their promotional materials, putting up posters) is an appropriate use of staff energy and scarce resources. While a campus may say "no," it also has the obligation to explain why a request would be inappropriate to the campus philosophy or procedures.

At the same time, program providers should take time to understand the institutional culture, goals, and procedures at work on each campus. The approach to use when working with the study abroad office at a state-funded university, where study abroad consists of a wide variety of faculty-led, short-term programs because many of students work part-time, will be very different from that at a small private liberal arts college that has few campus-sponsored study abroad options for its students.

Marketing Etiquette for Program Providers and Campuses

Although it may seem unnecessary to discuss proper etiquette between providers and campuses, a courteous relationship is very important. Both the program provider and the home institution have the shared goal of sending students overseas. Nowadays it is not unusual for individuals to have worked on a campus as well as with a provider in the course of their careers in education abroad. Thus, it is important to remember that all parties are professionals in the field of international education, and should treat each other with respect. Negative personal judgments about a particular organization or individual should be kept private. Campus-based education abroad professionals must not treat program representatives of providers like unwelcome door-to-door salespeople. And provider-based education abroad professionals must not treat their campus-based colleagues like curmudgeons or traitors to the field, just because they do not approve a particular program. Different institutions of higher education may have different goals and philosophies concerning study abroad. Professional international educators know that different is not bad, only different.

Campus-based education abroad professionals should strive to implement campus policies in a fair, open, and transparent manner. Remember, an approved program provider is helping the campus meet its objectives by providing opportunities abroad for its students. Plan campus visits deliberately and appropriately and use the visit to meet shared goals. Education abroad professionals should ensure that committee or faculty members who have oversight for or a particular interest in a program have a chance to meet the program provider representative. Campus colleagues should be encouraged to ask questions about the program. In addition to assisting in recruiting students to participate in study abroad, a well-informed representative can build confidence in the academic program and smooth the way for students who may need to fill particular requirements abroad. Arranging a meeting with students will give them an opportunity to have their questions answered by someone whose job it is to know the program abroad.

Program representatives are best served by establishing a positive cordial relationship with their on-campus colleagues. When arranging a campus visit, the campus should be given plenty of lead time. Program representatives should learn about the institution in advance, and be prepared with informed questions when they arrive. The more the program representative understands about the institutional priorities and how the programs fulfill some of the institution's specific needs, the more productive the visit will be. Respect campus priorities and understand that they were established to meet institutional objectives, and were developed through a process of shared governance and consultation. Although the campus-based education abroad professional may have significant influence over these, he or she may not have the freedom (or the desire) to change them. Program representatives should be sure to keep the study abroad staff informed of their plans to meet with faculty or other members of the administration. Refrain from pitting one education abroad office against another through references to the program provider's work at another campus. Each college or university has its unique characteristics. Working with so many different entities, adjusting to each one, and developing successful working relationships with each one is one of the challenges of being a program representative. Lastly, if a campus tells a program representative that a visit is not appropriate the point should not be argued. Move on to the next campus.

Finally, campus professionals and program representatives should try not to waste each other's time. Both groups have goals to accomplish and limited resources with which to do this. Campus education abroad professionals have an obligation to explain their institutional priorities to a program provider. This is particularly true if these priorities will result in little or no assistance to the program provider, or a refusal of a visit. While it may be pleasant to meet with representatives of programs and to learn more about their operations, if the education abroad office is unable to approve or promote the program, their limited time might be better spent in other ways. Similarly, if a campus representative has already explained the limitations, it is counterproductive for the program representative to insist on meetings that will not change the campus priorities.

Promoting Programs Beyond the Home Campus

The decision to begin marking programs beyond the home campus, that is to become a program provider, should not be taken lightly. Before the Web site is put up or brochures can be sent out, there are several issues that must be addressed. First, it is very important to secure the support of the university's senior administration before proceeding with an external marketing plan. Having students from other colleges enroll in the institution's programs abroad can have significant legal, risk management, personnel, and financial aid ramifications. Second, the education abroad office must be sure it has the capacity on-campus to accommodate these students within the scope of office procedures, as well as capacity overseas. Unlike the institution's own students, outside students may never be seen by a member of the institution's education abroad office staff until they arrive at the program site. All contact with them may well take place over the phone or through e-mail or regular mail. Predeparture orientation sessions will have to be provided as "distance learning." Not only does this mean an increased demand on staff time, but also an increase in mailing and other costs. Moreover, the education abroad office will need to have the cooperation of a number of offices on campus: for example, the admissions office (to enter the students into the administrative computer system), the business office (to handle the tuition payments), the registrar's office (for transcripts at the conclusion of the program), and so forth. The education abroad office will also need to work with the financial aid office to clarify responsibilities under federal aid regulations. Offering an outside student a "scholarship" to attend another institution's program may have long-term consequences for the institution's financial aid office. Finally, it is most important to note that opening programs to other students may not bring in the thousands of additional dollars that some university administrations anticipate.

To successfully market programs outside the home campus, the education abroad office (in its role as program provider) should be sure that either it has the permission of the sending institution to enroll their students or that the students have been granted individual permission to enroll in the programs. For any number of reasons from financial aid to risk management it is important that students on the program receive academic credit for the experience abroad. They are, thus, more likely to take the program seriously. Permission to enroll from the home institution is also important for transferability of federal, state, third-party and institutional financial aid to the program. Under U.S. Department of Education financial aid regulations, a "consortium agreement" is required in order for the home campus to transfer a student's federal aid to the program (see: 34 CFR 668.5 and the *Federal Student Aid Handbook* on the Department of Education Web site). Typically, the financial aid office on the sending campus prepares the consortium agreement according to its own requirements. There is no one standard for institutional approval of outside programs, and each sending campus may have a different procedure.

Understanding the complexities of federal financial aid is only a small part of marketing programs beyond the home campus. The resources needed to be successful in recruiting and retaining outside students will, in large part, be determined by the scope of the outreach effort and the target number of students to recruit. As with on-campus recruiting, carefully targeting the marketing effort to specific constituencies is crucial to its success.

Developing a Marketing Plan

The first step in any marketing effort should be the development of a marketing plan. Keep in mind that a marketing plan implies a broader view of one's efforts than simply promotion and publicity. Program design, cost, target audience, and a survey of the programs already open to other students are all elements of a comprehensive marketing plan. Regardless of whether the goal is to design a program targeting only external students or supplement enrollment in a program developed for the university, the assessments required in creating a marketing plan can help education abroad professionals successfully direct their efforts and maximize their use of resources. Although program design and planning can be important elements of a comprehensive marketing plan, this section will focus on the program promotion aspects of developing a marketing plan.

Before they develop a marketing plan, it is advisable for education abroad professionals to conduct a market survey of all of the other programs similar to the one being marketed. Sources such as the Institute for International Education's *Academic Year Abroad* and *Short-Term Study Abroad,* the Petersons academic guides, or *The Princeton Review*, as well as Web sites such as studyabroad.com, goabroad.com, iiepassport.org, etc. college, and many more, will provide you with descriptions of what the other programs offer and what is included in their prices. While conducting the market survey, education abroad professionals will want to plot their data on a chart for easy program comparison. Some programs do not include airfare; others do not include meals. Once the data have been collected and the program being marketed has been added to the chart, it should be clear where the program stands in relation to the others, as well as what distinguishes it from the others. This information will be very useful in developing a marketing plan. The education abroad professional's choice of marketing strategies, as well as the institutions and majors to target, will depend on what he or she knows about the "competition."

While surveying the other programs on the market, education abroad professionals will also want to undertake an organizational assessment to identify their staffing and funding resources. The more limited the resources, the more targeted the approach will need to be. Professionals should consider the strengths of the organization, such as reputation, network and contacts, and administrative and faculty support. They should also consider whether there are any external opportunities that might impact their ability to market the program, such as increasing interest in a geographic region, a specific discipline, or a particular language, or hiring priorities for graduates with international experience in specific areas. Finally, are there external challenges, such as political unrest, safety concerns, economic issues, that might limit interest in the program? It is also helpful to consider current trends in education abroad in the location, field, and type of program being considered.

It's helpful to think of the timeline and stages of recruitment while developing a plan. At each stage, there will be a variety of strategies available to achieve the desired outcome. The first goal is to increase awareness of the program. Then, once students have become aware, the education abroad office will want to provide students with more detailed information to help them make a decision about whether to apply. As students move toward application and selection, the education abroad office will want faculty members to encourage and support the students. Finally, the office will need to provide detailed information to each selected student. Each of these steps can be implemented using a variety of approaches, from advertising to posters to brochures to Web-based information.

Next steps include determining who the target audience is, where they are located, how to reach them, and who influences their decisions. And, as mentioned earlier, it is highly beneficial to research the campus philosophies of the various institutions where recruiting efforts will be made. It is also important to assess the competition for the program being marketed. Who offers competing programs? How does the program being marketed compare in terms of location and features? Is the pricing competitive? Analyzing this information will help the education abroad office determine how to position its program, and where and how to direct its recruiting efforts.

Effective targeting is a key element of successful recruiting. Promoting a $14,000-per-semester program focusing on art history in Florence to a campus where student expenses average less than $6,000 a semester, to a school that has its own art history program in Florence, or to an institution that provides only minimal support to outside programs, may not be the most effective use of the education abroad office's marketing resources.

Budgeting

Recruiting costs can vary dramatically, ranging from practically nothing to relatively expensive, depending on the strategies chosen. Education abroad professionals should know how much they can afford to spend on recruiting, based on anticipated program revenue and expenses. The effectiveness of particular strategies should be considered in relation to their cost. A newspaper ad gives broad exposure but may be quite expensive and may not be well targeted. Promotional costs should be factored into the overall program budget, and marketing factors, including competitive pricing, should be considered when program fees are set. The education abroad office should realistically analyze the number of students who must be enrolled to enable the program to break even financially, and honestly assess whether this number is attainable, given the office's or institution's resources and market position. For example, external marketing of a short-term, faculty-led spring break program might make sense if relatively inexpensive strategies such as personal faculty networks or e-mail discussion lists can be used. If, on the other hand, expensive promotional materials need to be developed, or a series of campus visits are required to promote the program, the costs versus the potential net revenue should be carefully analyzed.

The materials and effort required for off-campus recruiting differ qualitatively and quantitatively from those used on campus. For example, the information that can be distributed by word of mouth or through an on-campus meeting will need to be organized and disseminated in a more formal manner off campus. Distribution channels, which might include mailings to advisers, faculty, and students, e-mails to the same groups, as well as fliers, posters, advertising in publications, printed directories, or online directories, will need to be developed. In addition, face-to-face marketing efforts, such as conducting campus visits and attending study abroad fairs and conferences, should be considered. The challenge to program providers is to identify the most appropriate and effective means within their budget to successfully appeal to the target audience as well as to those who influence their decisions.

Producing Materials

When recruiting external students, program providers should expect to provide substantive, well-documented materials describing the program and the sponsoring organization. These materials can be either in print, on CD-ROM, or online, or even in video format on tape or DVD. They do not need to be expensive, professionally produced, multicolor, graphically complex pieces. Clean, simple, and straightforward can be most effective. New graphic and video editing software packages have enabled many organizations to produce very attractive and cost-effective presentations in-house.

As the education abroad office develops its materials, it should remember the varied audiences who may view its materials (i.e., education abroad advisers, deans and faculty, registrars, parents, students). Consideration should be given to what their interests and concerns are and what media they prefer. Students may prefer to access information online or via CD-ROM or DVD, whereas parents, deans, and faculty may prefer print. The particular information that supports and defines the program, as contrasted with other programs, should be defined. Consideration should also be given to how specific materials are intended to be used. Faculty and advisers may want more detailed information upfront, without additional steps and mailings. If broad distribution to a more general audience is anticipated, such as at a study abroad fair, it may be logical to develop a brief overview piece that tells the reader how to get access to additional information. If the materials are for an education abroad office, consideration should be given to how the libraries in that office are arranged (such as topically or geographically) and how materials are displayed.

It is critical that all materials be accurate. The education abroad office and the institution will be expected to deliver the program and services they describe. The program or any element of it should not be oversold, and any possible risks should not be downplayed. The program's sponsoring organization may be held legally accountable for any promises, and, so too, may the institutions that actively support the program. Carefully consider the accuracy of the message implied by photos and other materials. If the program is based in Xian with no planned excursions to Beijing, using a picture of the Forbidden City is hardly an accurate representation of the program. It is always wise to have the publications and other materials reviewed by external parties, including representatives of the target audience and the institution's legal counsel. Remember, if one of the goals of the marketing effort is to receive active support and approval from other institutions of higher education, the marketing materials may be reviewed by their legal advisers as well. The education abroad office's marketing materials also begin the process of setting expectations, and send a message about what kind of program it operates, what the program offers, and, perhaps most importantly, what it does not.

Program Brochure

Most programs have a publicity piece that contains basic program information and gives students sufficient detail to allow them to make a preliminary decision about applying and participating. The main program promotion piece should cover

- history of the program and the sponsoring organization;

- description of any academic affiliations, including host country sponsors;

- information on accreditation, including who issues the transcript;

- a detailed explanation of the program's objectives;

- complete descriptions of all courses, including content, required course or field work, program hours and credit, and how student performance is evaluated and documented;

- profiles of faculty and administration, including degrees and affiliations;

- details on academic facilities, housing arrangements, and meal options, as well as lifestyle expectations;

- a detailed breakdown of costs, including program fees, room and board, travel expenses, insurance or other required coverage, living expenses, and any other expenses students might expect to incur;

- a list of requirements for admission, including prerequisites and other eligibility standards;

- policies for issues such as payment, refund and cancellation, nondiscrimination statement, conditions of participation, etc.; and

- a list of names and addresses, phone and fax numbers, e-mail addresses, and Web sites where more information can be obtained.

Posters

Posters can be especially effective in reaching audiences that might not initially know there are programs appropriate to their interests and financial circumstances (and therefore do not use the education abroad office or directories), or if a program is being introduced in an unusual location or discipline.

Designing posters involves a number of important considerations, including size, message, and response mechanism. Some posters direct the viewer to a Web site or phone number for additional information; others provide response cards. A postage-paid response card may generate higher initial inquiry rates, but a card that requires a stamp or an envelope may narrow the respondents to those who have a higher level of interest, and may therefore lead to higher enrollment rates.

Understanding the level of competition for the program and how large a pool of inquiries and eventual participants is being sought is one key to designing an effective poster campaign. A second is ensuring that the posters actually get posted. One approach is to use alumni to put up posters on their home campuses. Some organizations have their own staff put up posters during campus visits. There are also individuals and companies who place posters on campuses and provide assurance that the posters are in place. In all cases, both the program provider and the individual doing the actual posting must understand and adhere to the specific regulations regarding posting on individual campuses.

Fliers

A flier is a brief promotional piece. It is usually eye-catching, has large print, and focuses on a few key points. Fliers can be especially helpful in promoting a program to a specific audience, or as an inexpensive alternative to the main publicity piece when widespread distribution is called for in a high traffic setting, such as at a fair, campus event, or orientation.

Predeparture Orientation Materials

Although predeparture orientation materials may not be thought of initially as a part of the promotional campaign, they are a crucial part of the interaction with students. After having gone through the process of application and selection, students are likely to withdraw if the education abroad office is not able to provide appropriate materials after acceptance—and all of the marketing effort and expense will have been wasted. Students have not been fully recruited until they have begun the program abroad.

Disseminating Materials

Once the program has been designed and the supporting materials developed, there needs to be a means to disseminate the information to potential participants and to advisers, faculty, and others who can play a key role in referring or approving the program. The next sections cover a variety of means, suitable for a range of budgets, to get the word out.

Mailing Lists

Some program providers are able to develop their own very complete mailing lists over the course of a number of years of operation. Maintaining a mailing or contact list is an ongoing project requiring regular updating, confirming, and purging. But what if the education abroad office is developing a program in a new curricular area or is just beginning to market its programs externally? To whom does it send its materials and how does it find those people? Many professional organizations, including NAFSA and discipline-focused groups of faculty, rent their member lists to qualified organizations. Purchasers should be prepared to provide a sample of the materials they intend to distribute in order to qualify to purchase names from most associations. In addition, there are a number of list brokers who compile and sell faculty and administrator names and addresses based on numerous qualifying characteristics. Increasingly, one can also purchase e-mail addresses. If, for example, the education abroad office has developed a new program targeted at engineering students, purchasing a list of names of engineering faculty or program directors might be a cost-effective means of getting program materials to a targeted group that has direct and credible access to the target audience. Also, by including a space on the program application that requests the name and contact information of the study abroad adviser, and, perhaps, a faculty adviser at the student's campus, the education abroad office can insure an ongoing source of accurate and up-to-date contact information that can be added to its mailing lists.

Print Advertising

Directories, conference programs, journals, magazines, and campus newspapers all offer options for advertising programs. Print advertising can be expensive but also effective, if the education abroad office carefully selects the locations in which it advertises. An advertising evaluation should be based on the target audience, the circulation of the printed piece, the longevity of the publication (some "coffee table" journals are kept for months or longer, whereas newspapers have a much shorter "shelf life"), price, and where the advertisement will be placed (e.g., in a highly visible cover spot, accompanying a relevant article, or in a special advertising section). It is often possible to secure free listings for relevant program options in professional journals. Advertising a campus visit in a university newsletter can also be very effective. When arranging a campus visit, it is important to keep the staff in the education abroad office from that institution informed about details, regardless of who is sponsoring the visit, as no doubt they will receive questions about the time and place, etc. having to do with the visit.

Web Advertising

The internet has dramatically changed student recruiting. Prior to the mid-1990s, typically only larger program providers had the resources to mount large-scale national recruiting efforts. The most viable recruiting strategies of that time required extensive printing, mailing, and travel budgets. The internet has served as a great leveler, providing low-cost options for small programs to reach large, national audiences. Not all Web-based recruiting is inexpensive, but there are good options available for every budget.

There are two key components to Web advertising. One is to have a clear, informative, easily navigable, and attractive Web site. The second is to use online directories, search engines, e-mail, e-mail discussion lists, and links appropriately to promote the program and direct users to its Web site.

There are a growing number of online directories listing education and work abroad options and international university offerings. A list can be found by using search engines, checking the Education Abroad Knowledge Community area of the NAFSA Web site, and by visiting exhibitors at NAFSA conferences. Many education abroad directories offer free or low-cost listings or online links to an institution's Web site. For an additional cost, the directory listing for the institution can include direct links, a detailed program description, or banner ads or buttons that bring users to the institution's Web site. As the number of directory vendors grows, it is important to research and understand which directories are best suited for reaching the target audience. As in all marketing efforts, results should be tracked so that the marketing plan can be refined and resources are sure to be used on the most effective recruiting options.

There are other low-cost and even free options to market programs on the Web. One way is to ensure that keywords that are recognized by search engines are coded into the headlines of the Web site program description. Many e-mail discussion lists used by advisers and faculty, including SECUSS-L, offer free announcements of programs that are of interest to their participants. These can be effective and affordable options, but it is important to understand the etiquette of each e-mail discussion list; some do not allow marketing of any kind whereas others allow it under prescribed circumstances, usually in the interest of information sharing. Education abroad professionals should be sure to also consider related Web sites that might be willing to provide a link to the program's or sponsoring institution's Web site if that site does the same for them.

Determining how to effectively use the information provided by visitors to the program Web site can be an interesting challenge. When students have willingly provided their contact information, following up with an e-mail message providing new information can be an effective and inexpensive tactic, as long as there is an opportunity for recipients to indicate they wish to be removed from the future contact list. To repeat, unsolicited messages are considered to be spam.

Personalized Marketing

Meeting face to face to explain a program to students, advisers, and faculty is one of the most effective recruiting techniques. It can also be expensive, time and staff intensive, and challenging to set up. Many program representatives underestimate the length of time necessary to build the relationships that will generate external students for programs, both on a first-time and on an ongoing basis. At the same time, winning allies on a particular campus to assist in that institution's goal of recruiting qualified students is a highly effective way to promote programs.

Program representatives should always keep in mind that campus-based education abroad staff devote long hours to their professions, often with limited appreciation and understanding of their work and goals by others on campus or in society at large. Successful personalized marketing is nothing more than building productive, rewarding, and mutually beneficial professional relationships with colleagues on campuses. Making the effort to build and maintain professional and personal relationships will enable program providers and their representatives to gain on-campus recruiting support and enable institutions to increase education abroad enrollments, scholarships, and other support. Examples of personalized recruiting include campus visits, study abroad fairs, conferences, and program visitations.

Campus Visits. Laying the groundwork for a successful relationship will require several visits to a campus. The first visit might be a short meeting between the program representative and the campus-based education abroad adviser. This will certainly provide an opportunity to gain further insight and information as to whether there is potential to work with this institution, and how to interact and expand on these possibilities. A second meeting, if appropriate and encouraged, might include relevant faculty or deans, before a representative has an invitation to meet with students or participate in a study abroad fair.

For program representatives, the goals of a campus visit include

- creating an awareness of a program;
- developing relationships with the education abroad office staff, as well as with key faculty and advisers; and
- meeting potential students for a program.

All of these are reasonable objectives, especially if representatives have appropriate expectations and are strategic in their choice of visits and advisers with whom they meet.

Select campuses based on target audiences, keeping demographics, curricula, program price and focus, and competition in mind.

Check with the education abroad office on that campus for the appropriate procedures and contacts to set up a visit. Ask with whom a representative should meet. Understand that not everyone, especially faculty and students may be available, during a first visit. Building relationships takes time. Access to an institution, and its community, may be limited initially. Always keep the study abroad office informed of any subsequent contacts with campus faculty and administration.

If denied a visit, do not take it personally. Understand that study abroad advisers have literally hundreds of program providers requesting meetings, and they have to limit visits to programs they believe are strategic matches for their students, or which fit their institutional philosophy. At the same time, if the advisers are willing to explain why an invitation to visit is not being extended, the program representative has an opportunity to address areas of concern that are within the provider's purview. (See "Marketing Etiquette for Program Providers and Campuses" earlier in this chapter.)

Research each school's policies and programs before requesting a visit. This will save time and resources if they do not mesh with program.

If appropriate, ask how to publicize the visit. If a campus and its study abroad office are amenable, work with them to schedule a student meeting with interested and qualified students.

Schedule the visit well in advance. Be prompt and well prepared. Know when it's time to leave. Send a thank you note following the visit.

Exhibiting at Study Abroad Fairs. A growing number of campuses are hosting study abroad fairs as a means of introducing their students to a variety of program options. Participating in a study abroad fair can help a program representative with a number of goals including

- meeting large numbers of students, often early in their university years, to share information about program(s);
- strengthening relationship between the program and key advisers and faculty; and
- demonstrating the program's support for international education and the international education office at that campus.

Many study abroad fairs are by invitation only, while others are open to all interested programs. For an updated national calendar of education abroad fairs visit the SECUSSA National Education Abroad Fair Calendar page on the educationabroadfairs.info Web site, or search on "education abroad fair." An invitation to participate in a study abroad fair is usually not the first step in establishing a relationship with a particular school, but rather, may follow after a successful campus visit or the successful participation of a student from that

Part III: Program Development, Campus Management, Marketing, and Evaluation

school in the program. On the other hand, some institutions allow independent vendors to have direct access to their students *only* at study abroad fairs, using the fairs to provide a blanket disclaimer of sponsorship of any particular program, while assisting all outside vendors in a fair and equitable manner.

The same recommendations apply to attending fairs as to campus visits. Issues program providers and their representatives should consider include

- being familiar with the school's specific processes and policies, including transfer of financial aid and credit, program requirements and approvals, and deadlines, so that students can receive accurate advice;

- understanding any requirements regarding who can represent the program at the fair (e.g., alumni, or only professional staff);

- advising students accurately and professionally, and, when possible, referring students who can't be assisted to other programs appropriate to their requirements;

- respecting the campus's decision on invitations, and attending only if invited;

- being strategic in the choice of fairs;

- arriving early to set up and staying for the entire fair (leaving early is the best way to never get another invitation);

- cooperating with specific requests or instructions from the hosts of the fair ("Please return your sign," "Do not leave excess promotional materials behind," "Dispose of your lunch trash in nearby receptacles," etc.), and observing parking regulations (neglect of which can be a costly miscalculation);

- being sensitive about not using the fair as an opportunity to provide extensive briefings to the study abroad office about particular programs (the office staff is focused on the myriad details of hosting a successful study abroad fair, and they may resent the distraction); and

- if costs allow, developing a special information piece for fairs that gives an overview of the program, with contact information for students seeking more detailed information.

Exhibiting at Conferences. Professional conferences can offer a valuable opportunity to connect with a large number of contacts from the target group in a single setting. A conference can be an excellent forum in which to introduce a new program and make new contacts, as well as reconnect with old contacts and strengthen existing relationships. Conferences also provide an opportunity to gauge current trends and opportunities, and size up the competition. Exhibiting at conferences can be expensive when one adds up travel, hotel, meals, registration, materials, shipping, and exhibit fees. On the other hand, it can be worthwhile if one is strategic in the choice of conferences and the activities.. Once again, a little preparation pays off. Send a note to those who will be at the conference and invite them to stop by the exhibit or schedule a meeting with them. This can be a great opportunity to meet with an adviser from a campus where there is a good fit for your program, by taking him or her to lunch. Some program providers use the occasion to host cocktail receptions or breakfasts that generate useful goodwill (even if all of the guests do not attend, the program will have accrued some status and reputation for generosity and hospitality). Review the conference schedule and identify any presentations or speakers that might be relevant to the program. Conferences can be both a recruiting and learning opportunity.

Program Visits. Another often effective, albeit expensive, form of personalized marketing involves inviting faculty and study abroad advisers to visit the overseas program or U.S. base of operations. Meetings and mini-conferences that bring groups of faculty or advisers together at headquarters to address specific topics, or for program updates, can be an excellent way for them to meet the program's staff (especially if overseas program staff are included) and see the operation in a setting that combines professional development, relationship building, and social interaction. There are few more effective means of building an appreciation of the specifics of a program than inviting faculty or advisers to visit it abroad. Faculty and advisers who have actually seen a program site and operation first hand usually feel much more confident in advising their students about these opportunities. For program providers, these visits present an unparalleled opportunity to showcase the program's strengths, as well as to glean constructive feedback and market research from the visitors. Because of the high value of these on-site professional development opportunities, many programs are able to subsidize visits by faculty or advisers, and some study abroad offices have funds to help support program visits by their campus staff.

Faculty Networks. One very inexpensive and often overlooked recruiting tactic involves drawing on the personal networks of the institution's faculty. This approach can be very effective in the case of faculty-led, short-term courses that are open to outside students and for which there are very limited resources. Asking the participating faculty to send their colleagues an e-mail or mailing describing the program can be a very low-cost way to fill those last few spaces. Faculty members have considerable influence on their students' selection of a study abroad program. Again, as a courtesy, always keep the study abroad staff at the targeted institution informed of these communications and activities with their faculty.

Staffing

Of course, none of the most carefully thought out elements of a marketing plan will succeed without someone to actually implement the plan. Thus, one of the most important components of a marketing plan is the careful selection of the individual or individuals who will represent the program. Staffing comprises a significant portion of many marketing budgets, and is absolutely essential to establishing effective recruiting relationships.

Because it is the education abroad staff who convey the image that the field will have of the program and the organization, these individuals must embody the characteristics the office wishes to have associated with the program. Personal credibility, integrity, and approachability will go a long way with the target audience and with those who influence their decisions. Because programs are accountable for the information provided by their representatives, the education abroad office or provider will want to insure that the individuals representing the program know the program thoroughly, understand the field and expectations of education abroad, appreciate the need to research the schools they are visiting, and are as good at listening as they are at dispensing information. There are also those intangible elements of charisma and charm, which may be required, particularly if the program is hoping to personalize its relationships and win over allies through personal contacts. The expectations and professional competencies of NAFSA members and the NAFSA Code of Ethics can be found on the NAFSA Web site.

Summary

In addition to creating good programs overseas and advising students about the plethora of opportunities that exist in education abroad, the education abroad office will likely also be responsible for using its imagination and persuasion to publicize and promote these opportunities to students, faculty, the administration, and the local community. Employing some of the methods of sound marketing and advertising can work to the office's advantage. This is not a matter of simple public relations hype or slick promotional gimmicks. Good and effective promotion involves knowing the target market and knowing the best range of programs for that market, then using a variety of convincing strategies to sell the programs and services. And as international educators and their institutions and organizations offer an increased menu of quality education abroad options, they are strengthening the field of international education and better serving the students, especially by offering new topics in less visited locations or for underserved groups. Advisers and program providers, working with shared expectations regarding appropriate and effective recruiting, can help the field reach its goals of increased international opportunities for its students.

CHAPTER 5

Program Assessment and Evaluation

Contributors: Stacia Zukroff, Stephen Ferst, Jennifer Hirsch, Carla Slawson, Margaret Wiedenhoeft

The evaluation of education abroad programs and the assessment of activities and student learning are vital, ongoing tasks for every program sponsor and for every sending institution. The results of a program evaluation should influence all aspects of the program, from its direction and goals to the scope and content of its day-to-day activities. A person who asks, "How good is this program?" really means, "Is the program good enough to meet the [academic, intercultural, revenue, experiential, financial, geographic] expectations of the [faculty, students, administration, parents, departments]?" By collecting information about the program and the student experience, education abroad administrators can begin to answer this and a host of other questions.

Over the years, education abroad administrators have found that the task of assessing education abroad programs is probably no more complex than the task of designing, implementing, and running such programs—which is to say, overwhelming. It is therefore no wonder that, when asked how a particular program is doing, education abroad administrators really just want to reply, "Fine." The problem of how to answer is further exacerbated when the inquiry comes from the president, provost, or dean. The future of the program or the program staff (including the education abroad administrator) could well hang on the response. But "Fine" is not usually an acceptable or useful outcome of any evaluation. In order to garner useful information from program evaluation, education abroad administrators must pay careful attention to the collection of the data, the questions asked of the data, and the interpretations of the results.

A "Culture of Assessment" Within U.S. Higher Education

The movement of U.S. higher education toward a "culture of assessment" that marked the 1990s has continued unabated into the new century. Regional accrediting agencies, federal programs, and foundations require colleges and universities not only to have well-developed assessment plans, but also to actually do the assessment activities and use the information to improve the quality of programs, and guide future plans. In 1995, Thomas Angelo, then director of the Assessment Forum of the

American Association for Higher Education (AAHE), proposed the following definition of assessment:

> Assessment is an ongoing process aimed at understanding and improving student learning. It involves making our expectations explicit and public; setting appropriate criteria and high standards for learning quality; systematically gathering, analyzing, and interpreting evidence to determine how well performance matches those expectations and standards; and using the resulting information to document, explain, and improve performance. When it is embedded effectively within larger institutional systems, assessment can help us focus our collective attention, examine our assumptions, and create a shared academic culture dedicated to assuring and improving the quality of higher education (Angelo 1995).

As university faculty and administrators change their perception of assessment from an externally mandated requirement of visits every ten years by a regional accreditation team to a desire to satisfy their own "intellectual curiosity about how students learn in the disciplines, how students integrate their liberal learning into their majors, or how Web-based technology, for example, develops or transforms thinking" (Maki 2002), the institution is poised to develop its own culture of assessment.

The U.S. higher education assessment community often refers to three basic types of assessment activities: assessment for improvement, for accountability, and for accreditation. As the terms imply, assessment for improvement channels the information learned back into the program's design and development, so that it becomes part of an ongoing quality improvement process, answering the question, "How can we make the program better?" Assessment for accountability looks at the overall success or failure of the program or project, and answers the question, "Did it do what it was designed to do?" Finally, assessment for accreditation measures the program against a set of standards developed by the accrediting agency. The ongoing assessment of a project, program, or activity is known as formative, and assessment at the end, summative. As Robert Stakes has put it, "When the cook tastes the soup, that's formative; when the guests taste the soup, that's summative" (quoted in Scriven 1991).

The terms—improvement, accountability, and accreditation—refer to the use made of the data collected. Formative and summative refer to the point (or points) in time of collection. In addition to working through these distinctions, the assessment community has also had a great deal of conversation in an effort to understand and define the difference between assessment and evaluation. The Evaluation Center (2003) considers evaluation to be the "systematic investigation of the worth or merit of an object; e.g., a program project, or instructional material," and assessment, "the act of determining the standing of an object on some variable of interest, for example, testing students, and reporting scores." Kizlik (2003) expands on these definitions, noting, "Assessment is a process by which information is obtained relative to some known objective or goal." On the other hand, evaluation is "perhaps the most complex and least understood of the terms. Inherent in the idea of evaluation is *value*. When we evaluate, what we are doing is engaging in some process that is designed to provide information that will help us make a judgment about a given situation" (Kizlik 2003). Huitt et al. (2001) summarize the distinction by saying that assessment refers to "the collection of data to describe or better understand an issue," while evaluation refers to "the comparison of data to a standard for the purpose of judging worth or quality." Thus, assessment collects measurement data on individual performance or from individual activities; evaluation is the interpretation of scores, statistics, along with other types of information, to formulate a judgment or conclusion about the value, quality, merit, etc. of whatever is being evaluated.

This distinction between assessment as measurement and evaluation as interpretation or judgment tends to be far more prevalent in the abstract than in application. In both the literature as well as the practice of gauging student progress or program effectiveness one finds that the two terms are often conflated. Or else they are used as synonyms, leaving the reader to sort out whether the author is referring to measurement or judgment/interpretation. Because this chapter focuses on ways of determining how well (or to what extent) a program is meeting its own or someone else's goals, rather than individual student learning, the general aim will be toward evaluation.

This distinction raises the question of what to call the feedback received from students at the end of the program abroad, typically referred to as "student evaluations." If the purpose of these surveys is to measure student satisfaction, then they are certainly evaluations. If the purpose is to measure individual student learning, then they ought to be called assessments. However, these surveys often contain both types of questions. Thus, this chapter refers to student feedback forms as "student questionnaires."

The term, "program evaluation," can give rise to a similar dilemma. Typically, the term is used to describe both the periodic review of an education abroad program, as a type of quality control exercise, and the process by which a program is certified for credit transfer—either for an individual or on an ongoing basis (so-called "program approval"). As a judgment of the quality, merit, or value of an education abroad program, either in a periodic basis or with regard to the transfer of credit from the program abroad to the home institution, program evaluation would seem appropriate. And from a risk management standpoint, "evaluation" is a better term than "approval." Unless the term, "approval," is limited by additional descriptors such as "preapproval for transfer of credit," a plaintiff's lawyer might argue that university "approval" means approval of all aspects, personnel, activities, and facilities of the program, thereby greatly increasing the university's liability exposure.

With more and more U.S. undergraduates participating in more and more education abroad programs, it is time for education abroad to be fully integrated into the growing culture of assessment in higher education. At those institutions where assessment activities are in full bloom, education abroad should join and do all it can to support this effort; at all other institutions, education abroad professionals must lead by example. This holds both for campus-sponsored programs as well as provider-sponsored ones. In fact, several of the larger provider organizations have led the way for the profession not only by publishing the assessment and evaluation criteria for their programs, but also by publishing summaries of the results (e.g., the Council on International Educational Exchange and the IES MAP). The Forum on Education Abroad has made outcomes assessment one of its goal areas. The Forum has also developed a set of *Standards of Good Practice,* which will no doubt find their way into program assessments and evaluations (Forum 2004). Certainly *Responsible Study Abroad: Good Practices for Health and Safety,* (hereafter referred to as *Good Practices*); can form the basis of a risk assessment of a program. Finally, the topic of standards is the subject of the second of CIEE's "Our View" series. Meant to "stimulate discourse in furtherance of the study abroad enterprise," the piece aims to begin a discussion of the kinds of standards education abroad needs, concluding that:

> there is an implicit assumption in study abroad that we all know where we're going—that we all agree on what good quality is, and that we all are seeking to do the best job possible in the context of shared assumptions. We're not sure this is always the case. We believe that some added attention to the desired outcomes will be of great benefit to the task of crafting standards, and that standards tailored to specific program goals, is the right approach. (2005)

Developing Assessment and Evaluation Models for Education Abroad Programs

The Quality Trap

The field of education abroad has always tackled the question of program or faculty quality cautiously. It is an important—and often controversial—topic, sparking lively public and private debate among colleagues. There is no simple determination of good or bad with regard to quality. Anecdotally, colleagues can provide opinions based on their experiences, but their judgments will be affected by how the program met their own students' expectations and the institution's needs. Likewise, former student participants can weigh in through written questionnaires or focus groups, but each participant is likely to have different criteria for judging the value of his or her experience. While their opinions, expectations, and judgments are important, the task of evaluation begins and ends with the home institution and its own assessment and evaluation process.

To be effective, that process must do more than ask for opinions and make a few superficial comparisons. As Marilee J. Bresciani (2002) notes, "student satisfaction studies rarely help us understand how our services impact student development and learning" Such assessment short-sightedness is especially deplorable in the current economic climate, when international educators know that assessment and evaluation results will be used to set program budgets, determine program and department staffing levels, make changes in direction and goals, and decide whether to add or close programs. By going beyond satisfaction surveys, and especially by folding the assessment of education abroad programs into a larger institutional culture of assessment, educators are able to find answers to the larger questions (Bresciani 2002).

A judgment of the quality of an education abroad program should be made on more evidence than student questionnaires or the similarity of the course descriptions abroad to those on the home campus. While education abroad advisers and administrators have plenty of personal opinions about the basis on which programs abroad should be evaluated, the results of the initiatives such as the standards development and outcomes assessment projects of the Forum on Education Abroad are needed to be sure that, as a profession, education abroad professionals are using a common scale of measurement and a common vocabulary of assessment.

Chapter 5: Program Assessment and Evaluation

Assessing Education Abroad

In many respects, an education abroad program mirrors the activities found on a typical U.S. campus. There is an admissions office that provides everything from brochures to Web pages, as well as admissions counselors. From admissions, the organization continues to the registrar; to academic courses; to student life, activities, and housing; to a complete co-curricular program; to internships and service learning; to libraries and information technology; to certificates and transcripts; to financial services; to housing. All pieces are necessary for a program abroad to work successfully. Thus, the assessment of education abroad could easily become as complex as the process preceding the visit of the reaccreditation team at its ten-year intervals. It is precisely because of the complexity involved in delivering postsecondary education that a comprehensive assessment of an institution's activities occurs just once a decade. However, the ten-year scheme assumes that in the intervening years assessment activities will continue in the various colleges, faculties, departments, offices, and programs of the university, not only because eventually the reaccreditation team will show up again, but more importantly because all who are involved with the delivery of educational services want to provide a better experience for the students and themselves. In order to manage a continuous flow of assessment activities, institutions need an assessment plan—one that will be a time line, as well as a reminder and checklist that, when completed, will be an indication that the assessment has been comprehensive.

In developing and carrying out an assessment plan for education abroad, education abroad professionals can use Brescianni's outcomes questions to sketch out the process in broad strokes:

What are we trying to do and why are we doing it? What is the goal, the purpose, the mission, the larger outcomes that we are trying to achieve with this program? Where does this program fit in with the other programs in the department or the institution?

What do we expect the student to know or do as a result of our program? What student learning do we want to see occurring? As a part of undergraduate education (and as the term itself suggests), education abroad is about a student learning something. As will be discussed later in this section, a number of education abroad professionals—universities as well as associations such as the Forum on Education Abroad or American Council on Education (ACE)—are looking at sets of possible student outcomes from education abroad in order to develop for all of U.S. higher education a coherent and achievable set of student learning goals as well as sets of tested and standardized tools with which to assess student learning for each goal. (See, for example, the International Initiatives projects of ACE and the Forum on Education Abroad; and, while not directly related to education abroad, the *Greater Expectations* (2003) project of the Association of American Colleges and Universities (AAC&U), which includes intercultural outcomes among its learning objectives.) As U.S. higher education continues to work toward a national set of student learning outcomes for education abroad, individual programs can and should be as specific as possible about what they want participants to learn. Without a clearly stated and measurable outcome, there can be no assessment.

How well are we doing it? By comparing the progress made with the program's goals and objectives, what judgments can we make, and what conclusions can we draw from the various assessments and other information we have collected?

How do we know? What specific assessment data leads us to our conclusions?

Finally, an assessment plan for a program should distinguish among

- the areas to be examined (e.g., foreign language acquisition),

- the sources of information (e.g., students, instructors, home-stay families, etc.),

- the modes of its collection (e.g., pre- and posttests, oral proficiency interviews, role playing, placement tests, achievement tests, listening comprehension tests, students' test scores, instructors' assessments, home-stay families' assessments, etc.), and the goals and objectives against which progress in each area is to be measured (e.g., the oral proficiency scale of the American Council on the Teaching of Foreign Languages 2003).

How the areas that will be assessed are organized is entirely up to the education abroad professional and his or her institution. It may be useful to look at the students' experience in the program abroad on a chronological basis, from first information contact through advising, application, selection, and enrollment; followed by the various facets of the program overseas; and concluding with return and reentry. The assessment can easily be structured from the resident director's point of view, or that of the study abroad office, or parent, and so on. The important point is for the education abroad professional to get the information needed to complete the assessment he or she has set out to accomplish. (See Maki 2002.)

There are numerous resources on the Web about assessment in general and assessment plans in particular, including plans and instruments from individual programs, campuses, and providers. The assessment area of the American Association for Higher Education (AAHE) Web site is particularly useful in this respect. Education abroad professionals should use the resources to stimulate their thinking, and they will serve as examples of what other people look at when they assess their education abroad programs. Although the number and complexity of areas to assess in a program abroad have grown considerably since the first publication of *Study Abroad Programs: An Evaluation Guide* (1979) by the Task Force on Study Abroad of the American Association of Collegiate Registrars and Admissions Officers (AACRAO) and NAFSA, the general areas remain part of every assessment:

- *Basic information:* What does the program say about itself and its objectives?

- *Academic aspects:* What is the nature of the courses offered, of the instructor teaching, and of the academic infrastructure supporting the instruction?

- *Interaction with the host culture:* How and on whose terms do participants interact with the host culture? What are the provisions for meals and accommodation? What student support structures are available? What is the administrative structure of the program? (AACRAO and NAFSA 1979)

Today, the areas indicated in *Good Practices* could certainly be added to these general areas. In addition, it may be useful to look more closely at particular experiential aspects of the program such as internships, field study, or service learning

Chapter 5: Program Assessment and Evaluation

opportunities; at academic resources such as library or connectivity; or at predeparture and reentry programming. Moreover, the sources of information for each of these areas can vary considerably across programs, as well as across institutions.

Many assessments, and the resulting evaluations, are aided by using questions to guide the examination. The questions must be general enough to allow for flexibility, but specific enough to give the process a concrete direction and focus. Some typical questions include the following:

- Does the program help to fulfill the institution's overall mission, general goals, and strategic plan—that is, does it do what it promises?

- What distinctive academic features or characteristics does the program have?

- How does the program's design and pedagogy help it achieve its defined goals?

- How does the academic program abroad compare with the home institution's on-campus courses, regarding course assignments, reading, test score distribution, etc.?

- To what extent does the program complement or supplement (rather than merely duplicate) course work available at the home institution?

- What distinct advantages come from offering the program abroad?

- What rationale is offered for the program's particular location?

- How does the program aid the institution in fulfilling its own academic and cross-cultural education mission?

- How does this particular program fit in to the overall array of overseas study programs offered by the institution (e.g., for a given geographic area, or in regard to language study options or available academic subjects in general)?

- How effective is the program design in meeting the stated objectives of the program?

- To what extent does the program take advantage of the features and resources unique to education abroad, such as the level of integration into the host institution's academic and student life, the length of time spent abroad, and the nature and degree of exposure to the host culture and language?

- How available and adequate are the academic resources and support services abroad?

- What are the levels of student and faculty interest and commitment in maintaining this particular kind of program and this program in particular?

Assessing Programs and Evaluating Their Effectiveness

The following sections will look more closely at issues associated with information sources that can be used when evaluating programs sponsored by an institution. The discussion will then turn to issues that stem from the selection of the program areas to be assessed when evaluating programs external to the institution. Next, the chapter will discuss some of the special assessment and evaluation problems that direct enrollment and exchange programs present. And finally, the issue of how to use the results of the assessment efforts will be examined.

Internal Programs

An institution's own study abroad programs (its internal programs) represent not only the investment of considerable campus resources and staff in program design, creation, and management, but also a considerable source of institutional pride, often evidenced in many marketing strategies and stories in the alumni magazine. For these and many other reasons, the assessment of an institution's own education abroad programs must be firmly situated in the institution's overall assessment plan. Among the many challenges education abroad professionals face when assessing the education abroad programs sponsored by their campus or organization, is being certain all of the stakeholders have been provided with ample opportunities to give their input. The stakeholders are those individuals who have some interest in the program, such as students (especially returnees), faculty (especially from departments with a stake in the program), resident directors (if these are different than faculty), parents, study abroad office staff, and staff from other campus offices (e.g., financial aid, business office, student affairs). The following discussion looks at typical stakeholder groups and the types of assessment questions that are often addressed to each.

Student Input

Institutions solicit information from students to assess programs abroad, particularly with an eye toward getting their input on academic work, housing, extracurricular activities, program staff, on-site orientation, and reentry activities. In addition, institutions ask students about the home institution's predeparture orientation, as well as the advising, application, and enrollment processes, and other areas suggested by staff in the education abroad office. The aim is to determine whether the expectations relayed by program materials and by the sending and receiving institutions correlate with the day-to-day reality of the program, and if not, how they differ and why. As they would for on-campus courses, students can also provide comments about the instructor, course content, and relevance of course materials and activities.

If the education abroad office collects student surveys of the program overseas, that program may ask for copies or summaries of the student responses. Decide what the education abroad office will furnish to its foreign partner as the questions are being designed. It may be more polite to wait until the students return to the home campus to have them fill out the questionnaire.

As the "real" experts on the program (that is, as the ones who lived through the program), students can furnish more than just "satisfaction" information. They can be an important source of firsthand information for the education abroad office about the program. Many colleges keep files of student questionnaires and make these (or summaries of the information collected) available to other students interested in the same program. A typical list of questions for students includes the following:

- Did the predeparture orientation provide accurate information for student participants? Did the students feel they had reasonable access to orientation resources?

- Was the advising process informative? Did the students have adequate access to information about the program prior to application?

- Did students have access to former participants and other resources to help answer questions about the program and the site?

- In retrospect, what other information do students wish they had received earlier?

- Were the courses offered by the program the same ones that were advertised in program's brochure or on its Web site? Were the course prerequisites and course descriptions adequate? Did students feel they had sufficient preparation for on-site academic expectations? How did the courses abroad compare with similar ones on the home campus?

- What were the students' opinions of instructors, their course preparation and delivery, the syllabus, the reasonableness of reading assignments, assessment methods, etc.?

- Were the resident director and other on-site staff available to students on a reasonable basis?

- Were on-site meetings, orientations, and other activities held during the program informative and useful? What kind of information did the program provide about the local academic culture, typical teaching methods, classroom behavior, approachability of professors, etc.?

- How much effort did the students contribute to the study abroad experience, compared with going to class on the home campus?

- Did students feel they had sufficient opportunities to interact with the local students and home-stay families, and partake in other aspects of local everyday life?

- Were the academic, intercultural, medical, psychological, and other support services available at or through the program adequate for the needs of the students?

Other areas for student questions include foreign language preparation before the program, language proficiency following the program, amount of spending money, amount of time spent in independent travel, program excursions, program cultural events, and internships or service learning.

One common approach to obtaining student feedback is to distribute questionnaires at the end of the program. These may include both closed and open-ended questions, use of Likert scales of agreement or disagreement with a statement about an aspect of the program or experience abroad, open comment spaces, etc. The questionnaires can be distributed in paper form or as an online survey. If the education abroad office has the technical expertise to develop, debug, and support Web-based surveys, it should consider using an electronic document, because such a tool will probably garner a higher percentage of student responses. As another way to achieve a high response rate, some colleges require that students turn in a completed assessment before their off-campus grades are posted on the student's on-campus transcript. However, this policy risks producing useless data, because students will be tempted to complete hastily (and grumpily) yet another form for the education abroad office.

Institutions typically distribute questionnaires to students after they arrive back on campus, sometimes as part of a "welcome back" packet or workshop. This makes sense for shorter programs. For semester or academic year programs, education abroad professionals may want to consider distributing a questionnaire after each segment of the study abroad program, that is, after predeparture orientation, after on-site orientation, during the reentry process on-site, and after the return to campus. This approach shortens the length of the individual questionnaires (because each section would be distributed separately) and may lead to more accurate feedback.

Once surveys or questionnaires have been returned, the most important phase begins. The information collected from the students must be compiled (very easy with a Web-based survey, somewhat more tedious with paper) and analyzed. When program administrators review the student responses, they should keep in mind that many factors influence what the students write on surveys, and they should also look at the amount of elapsed time between the experience and the survey when considering overall response rates. It is also important to remember that students "return" from their experiences abroad at different rates. Because of the processing time students need following their return from their international experiences, the information they can supply at one particular time will be different from what they can supply at another time. That is why continuing studies of the same cohort of groups should to be done, so as to measure the students' awareness of the learning achieved, as a function of "returned time."

Surveys and questionnaires are not the only methods available to the education abroad administrator to hear from students. Advisers can convene focus groups on a specific component of a study abroad program. Although focus group conversations do not typically result in quantifiable data, they can provide valuable qualitative feedback on a specific program aspect. Focus groups often have two or more facilitators (one to keep the discussion moving and one to make notes) and are recorded for accuracy. Establishing some ground rules with regard to the boundaries (politeness and otherwise) will also help the conversation stay on track. An office form to capture notes from staff and advising conversations with students is another information collector. Finally, don't forget informal sources, such as a comment tool on the department's Web site, or student essays and journal excerpts in a study abroad magazine, as yet more ways to hear from students.

Faculty Input

The types of information education abroad professionals can receive from faculty depends on the roles that faculty play in education abroad on the home campus: Do faculty lead programs abroad or do they prepare the students for the experience abroad and then receive them following, or both? If faculty lead programs, how much autonomy and authority do they have for their programs? Is there a faculty committee with oversight responsibility for all of the programs abroad? Are some programs administered from a centralized education abroad office and others from departments, while still others are handled by individual faculty members? Are summer faculty-led programs run from the summer programs office instead of the education abroad office? Once education abroad professionals have clarified who is responsible for what, they will be better able to formulate their questions. Typical questions for faculty include the following:

- How do the off-campus courses fit with students' on-campus course work, particularly for majors, minors, and other special programs?

- Do the courses offered complement the home-campus offerings, or are they a repetition of already-existing, on-campus courses?

- Are students able to earn appropriate credit? Is the credit transferable to the home campus?

- Is the language level of incoming students appropriate for language courses and language programs?

Again, since the object is to assess the program abroad according to the university's stated international education goals, engaging faculty in the assessment process is a useful way to familiarize them with the program, and also, for them to become well-informed advocates and advisers. For those institutions with faculty- and department-led programs, comments from faculty members not associated with the program will also be important.

When arranging faculty visits to one of the institution's own programs is important that both the faculty members and the education abroad office have a clear understanding of the goals for the visit and the type of report that is expected upon their return. Predeparture and return meetings are just as important for faculty as they are for students. During a typical program visit, faculty have meetings with instructors, observe some classes, talk informally with students, meet program staff, and whenever possible, meet and get to know their colleagues from the host institution who are teaching their students. Reports can be in the form of a meeting with appropriate staff in the education abroad office with a "memo for the file" as a follow up or a more formal written report.

Unfortunately, no education abroad office will ever have enough money to send all of the key faculty members to the many programs abroad where the university has vested interests. If there is only limited funding available for faculty site visits, education abroad professionals will have to be creative with the resources at their disposal. This can include making sure that when colleagues from the university's international partners visit the campus, they meet with key faculty and departments. Having faculty review relevant course syllabi and reading lists, as well as sample examination questions is another way for faculty to gain a sense of the program. Keeping a file of course syllabi in the education abroad office for faculty and students to consult (or knowing where to find these on the Web) can establish the office as a trusted information source (Van de Water 2000). The foreign language department may want to do pre- and post-study abroad proficiency testing. Finally, education abroad professionals should encourage faculty to send them salient comments heard from students, regardless of whether these are positive or negative. Being open to criticism as well as praise is a necessary part of assessment for improvement.

Resident Director and On-Site Staff Input

On-site resident directors and program staff play a key role in the assessment of internal programs, because they can provide valuable insights into how program realities matched participants' expectations, and how the students reacted when they didn't. Host country staff can provide information to the home institution on certain program aspects, and can review program materials from a local point of view. However, education abroad professionals must consider local and intercultural sensitivities when asking host country staff to submit their assessments of other staff, students, or the U.S. faculty director.

At some foreign universities, there are several U.S. programs, each represented by a local resident director, while at others there is one individual or office that handles the students from several U.S. institutions. Either arrangement offers the opportunity to ask for feedback about your students in comparison to those from other institutions. Resident directors should also be able to assess the program's fiscal model, and advise the program administrator on whether budget and expenses are appropriate to the site. In addition, on-site staff should provide feedback on program activities like excursions and field visits, explaining how these trips complement the program as a whole and whether it makes sense to continue to offer them.

Related matters directors and staff may address include the following:

- Arrival and orientation programs.

- Home-stay and other housing arrangements, including whether certain families or residences continue to be recommended, including documented reasons.

- Academic content as well as academic logistical issues, such as how successful the students are at navigating the host institution's system of registration and lectures, course and grade equivalencies, and available new courses.

- Excursions and field visits, including the extent to which they fit within the program's stated goals and mission.

- Participant selection, including the extent to which the home institution's application and selection process is successful in selecting students who do well on the program.

- The host institution's student services, or description of equivalent arrangements (English-speaking medical personnel, counseling, or rehabilitation services).

- Health and safety issues and their impact on U.S. students, including a report of any incidents occurring over the course of the program (to be updated as necessary over the academic year).

- Budgets, costs, and expenditures, including suggestions on any changes the sending institution should consider for the next fiscal year).

- General comments and recommendations.

The easiest method of collecting assessment information from the resident director is through a resident director's report submitted at the program's conclusion. Site visit reports of faculty site visits and their notes from conversations with resident directors and local staff are another information source.

Parent Input

Given the increasing contact that institutions abroad and education abroad offices have with parents, any program assessment should also include their feedback. Parents' comments may relate to a specific program abroad, the sending institution's education abroad office or to that institution's study abroad program as a whole. Although not direct participants, parents may have opinions on many program aspects, including the availability and accuracy of information about the program, the availability of support services, and, if the program or the student has experienced an emergency, the quality of communication from the education abroad office and the accessibility of home institution staff.

Some institutions provide a separate orientation session for parents prior to their student's departure. A parent's orientation provides an opportunity for parents to meet the education abroad staff and also to receive first-hand information about the program abroad. At the conclusion of that session, a parental questionnaire collects feedback on topics and information covered. Most education abroad offices will find that a lot of parental feedback occurs on an informal and often irregular basis, typically in the form of phone calls or emails from often distraught parents. A more formal process of gathering comments from parents, not only makes them feel that their concerns are being heard, but also gives the education abroad office a basis from which it can consider possible changes in the design of program materials, as well as in the ways in which it communicates with parents and students.

The Role of the Education Abroad Office

The education abroad on-campus program manager is central to the process of evaluating internal programs. The program manger, that person in the office who has oversight responsibility for that program, is often the one who is asked to undertake (or provide administrative support for) the program review and, thus, would receive the feedback from the stakeholders. The internal review process should be transparent, consistent, and, to the extent possible, set down in a formal procedural document, so that stakeholders are aware of their various responsibilities in the process. At some institutions. the education abroad office staff compiles the information received from each stakeholder. At others, this is handled by a faculty committee.

Within the administrative and faculty governance structure of the university, the education abroad office can be responsible for answering all or some of the following remaining questions: How often should individual programs have a comprehensive assessment? How often should the entire education abroad program and office have a comprehensive assessment? What should the program and the office do in between assessments? This last question needs to be answered in the context of institutional policy and procedures. Colleges and universities must undergo an accreditation review every ten years (although some reviewers want to see an interim progress reports in the mean time). Many postsecondary institutions review academic departments and programs every five years. The frequency of an institution's assessment of its internal programs is typically a function of the allocation of resources (both human and financial) and the perceived need. Many institutions try to review each of their education abroad programs comprehensively every five years. This is a matter to be worked out with senior administration and also with the faculty education abroad committee.

External Programs

When a university sends its students to study abroad on their own programs, the university has significant control over most, if not all, aspects of the program. Thus, the university could be reasonably confident (because of the culture of assessment within the program, the education abroad office, and the institution) that, at a minimum, the program and its component parts meet the academic standards of the institution. Ideally the program design and implementation will have included all those elements discussed in the earlier chapters of Part III. Thus, if there are problems with a particular program, the university, as the program's sponsor, has the ability, and indeed as the chapter on "Legal Issues and Education Abroad," (Part III, Chapter 7) will discuss, the duty to make all appropriate changes, or, if necessary, close the program down. Assessing someone else's program presents a different range of challenges, particularly given the large number and variety of programs available to students and universities, as well as issues of collegiality and politeness, not to mention confidentiality and the proprietary nature of some information. However, once an education abroad office has established an appropriate set of program assessment guidelines, the process can proceed smoothly and be accomplished within a reasonable timeframe.

A common reason for undertaking the assessment of an external program (i.e., a program operated by another institution or organization) is the desire to propose the program for formal approval of the transfer of credit from it to the institution doing the assessment. Ideally, education abroad professionals will conduct this type of review before any students are permitted to participate in the program. Every U.S. college has a process for the adoption of new courses into the curriculum. Similarly, many colleges have an analogous procedure for the recognition of the creditworthiness of off-campus programs, including education abroad programs. At some colleges, the process is handled within the education abroad office (often in collaboration with a faculty committee); at others, it is the prerogative of the academic dean or registrar or a combination of these three groups. In these very litigious times, it may be wise to have a conversation with the college's legal counsel about the use of the term "approved" in conjunction with education abroad programs. Because "approved" is so broad a term, it may be difficult to reduce its scope in a lawsuit. "Preapproved for credit transfer," although awkward, does capture what an approved program means, without increasing the risk. (See Part II, Chapter 7, "Predeparture Orientation and Reentry Programming;" Part III, Chapter 1, "Program Designs and Strategies;" and Part III, Chapter 7, "Legal Issues and Education Abroad.")

There are a variety of reasons for a college to wish to add an external program to its education abroad options. The college may not have the staff, budget, or perhaps the desire to run its own education abroad programs. Or it may want to expand the number of programs and locations available to its students with external programs for the short term, while it considers other long-term options. At some colleges, the majority of students participate in externally sponsored programs, whereas at others external programs serve fewer students, but provide geographic and academic diversity. For example, a college may offer Korean in its less commonly taught foreign language program but not want to establish its own program in Korea for two students per year. A visiting professor in biology may stimulate student interest in tropical ecology. By using a program sponsored by another institution, the college can furnish these students with a discipline-specific study abroad program while it determines whether there will be sufficient continuing interest to justify starting its own program. Colleges also consider external programs when they want to explore new options, because a program (or provider) they currently use no longer meets their needs, or because of a sudden upsurge in enrollments. External programs can have any of the program designs discussed earlier, ranging from faculty-led study tour, to branch campus, to direct enrollment, to independent study. (See Part III, Chapter 1, "Program Designs and Strategies.")

Clarifying Selection and Evaluation Criteria

Before opening any brochures or looking at any Web sites, education abroad professionals considering the addition of a new program must be able to give at least a tentative answer to the "why" and "what" questions: Why do we need a new program in this academic area at this location? What academic and intercultural needs of our students remain unmet with the current array of program choices? This very self-reflective first question will take international educators back to the mission of the university and a reconsideration of the purpose and place of education abroad within that mission. Program assessment for the purpose of selecting a new program addition requires as much current knowledge of the home institution as of the program under consideration. Unless the institution and the education abroad office know what they want out of the program, they will have a very difficult time finding one that meets their expectations.

As noted earlier, the education abroad profession does not yet have a uniformly recognized or adopted set of program standards or learning outcomes, although we are moving closer to this. Thus, an institution's mission and educational goals, those of the education abroad office and the relevant academic departments, the standards outlined in *Good Practices* for health and safety in study abroad, the *Standards of Good Practice* (Forum 2004), NAFSA's *Code of Ethics,* and other professional standards can serve as the guiding principles when assessing a new external program.

The broad outlines for specific review questions and criteria can be taken from the lists discussed earlier in this chapter. A fairly standard list of areas to assess includes program logistics, student services, academics, housing, and opportunities for learning outside of the classroom. What is not noted in this type of list are the criteria against which the program under review is being measured. This ought to be resolved at the outset of the assessment process. What is an acceptable level of compliance with the various 'good practices' for an external program? Should there be complete congruity between the program overseas and the the home institution? Is something close to that acceptable? If so, how close is close enough and why? What is the institution's policy or practice with regard to instruction in the target language, and its policy about instruction in English in non-English speaking countries? Will students have to get transfer credit preapproval for each course taken abroad *before* they enroll in the program overseas? What qualifications are required of the instructional staff? What accreditation is required of the program or the agency that issues the transcripts? Does the institution require an official transcript from an accredited postsecondary institution? Most importantly, before beginning the program review, those involved should know who makes the final decision with regard to selection of the program.

Identifying Program Options

Once the criteria for selecting a new program have been decided, the first challenge is to identify possible program options. There are many resources available to help advisers find programs that will meet their general needs. The most obvious include the education abroad program resource guides, *Short-Term Study Abroad* and *Academic Year Abroad*, published by the Institute of International Education (available on the IIE Web site), and *Study Abroad* and *Summer Study Abroad*, published by Peterson's Education Center (available on the Peterson's Web site). These guides are updated annually and organized by location. Both the paper and the Web versions have cross-references to find programs using other criteria, such as sponsoring organization, cost, field of study, and special options. Although the program summaries are furnished by sponsors, and may not be absolutely accurate, the guides do their best to keep them current, to define carefully what their terms mean, and to be impartial. Because the listings are very brief, even terse, they will not provide detailed answers to probing questions, but do offer a convenient place to begin a program search.

Even handier (and less costly) than these guides are the study abroad program search engines on the World Wide Web. In addition to the ones offered by the Institute of International Education, and Peterson's Education Center, studyabroad.com, goabroad.com, and the University of Minnesota's Learning Abroad Center (www.umabroad.umn.edu), among very many others, allow users to search for programs according to specific criteria, such as location, language, subject, and program length. Some even allow for more advanced searches. As in the printed guides, the program descriptions in these search engines give short summaries of the thousands of study abroad programs throughout the world. While they do not provide much detail about the programs, they cover enough information to help advisers begin to narrow down their early search options.

Another method for identifying program options is to ask on-campus faculty members about programs related to their field that they would recommend. However, unless the institution has a very decentralized education abroad model, most faculty (including language faculty) may not be very familiar with programs outside of those sponsored by the institution. However, they can be asked which U.S. universities and colleges they consider to be peer institutions in terms of their particular department. Then the education abroad professional can find out which study abroad programs those institutions use for their students. Often this can be done by simply looking at other institutions' Web sites. If a list of education abroad programs is not available on the Web site, call that institution's education abroad office and find out which programs are used in a particular region or subject. One final note on working with faculty: involving faculty throughout the program assessment, establishes their position as stakeholders in the program. This is certainly helpful not only in the approval for transfer of credit process, but also in marketing the programs once they have been endorsed by the institution. In addition, faculty who buy into a program from the beginning can be very useful in working with other faculty who may be wary of the creditworthiness of a particular program abroad or of study abroad in general.

Conducting the Assessment of External Programs

After identifying three to five possible program options, each one should be examined in detail. The assessment aspect of the evaluation process is quite time-consuming because it involves intensive research of program details. However, much initial data gathering can be done by student workers, rather than by advisers, since most of the information is easy to find. Once all the basic information is collected, the adviser can then reenter the process to complete the final assessment and evaluation.

In order both to streamline the assessment process and to provide for uniformity, education abroad professionals will find it helpful to put together an assessment worksheet consisting of all the questions the university asks of all outside programs, grouping them according to the categories. A worksheet ensures that whoever gathers information will know which questions to ask; it also makes it easier to assign the project to student workers. Of course, each institution must develop its own set of worksheet questions and

Chapter 5: Program Assessment and Evaluation

criteria, consisting of issues made important by its institutional philosophies about education abroad and experiential learning. The general categories and specific issues outlined below are intended as guidelines for creating a customized set of standard assessment questions.

The overall goal of this type of assessment is to collect the information that will allow the education abroad office or the appropriate committee or senior administrator to determine whether the prospective program abroad will provide an appropriate educational and experiential opportunity for the institution's students. In other words, you are looking for "fit." How do the program's academic, intercultural, and experiential learning outcomes fit with those of the university? How do the program's administrative and communication models fit with those of the education abroad office and the university? How does the cost of the program abroad fit with what students are accustomed to paying for a semester or year? How do the program's standards of care and nurture of the students, and its attention to health, safety, and security issues fit with those of the institution and with the standards outlined in *Good Practices*? Will working with this program provide international or intercultural opportunities for faculty or staff? How can this relationship be or become mutually beneficial, and how easily can it be sustained over time? All of these and similar questions lead to one final question: Will the institution be able to defend both the process of selection and the program selected in a lawsuit? (See Part III, Chapter 6, "Maximizing Safety and Security and Minimizing Risk in Education Abroad Programs.").

Collecting Information for the Assessment

Most U.S. education abroad program-provider organizations conduct regular internal program reviews in order to assess how a program is meeting its goals. When the sponsoring organizations are independent of universities, a team from the provider's academic council or advisory board generally conducts these reviews. If the program is run by a university or college, reviews are usually conducted by a team comprised of home-campus faculty and administrators, sometimes augmented by outside education abroad administrators. Ideally, either the entire review or a summary of it is made available to advisers. Some providers automatically send these reports to their sending schools; others publish executive summaries or edited versions without personal information of these reports on their Web sites. Resident directors at the programs abroad also typically submit annual reports to their central offices. Education abroad professionals can check with the program's sponsor to see if these reports, or a summary, can be made available to them. Of course, advisers need to keep in mind that these reports, especially if they are widely distributed, may be as much marketing tools as they are assessments. Nonetheless, these review reports can significantly help advisers become more familiar with programs, and can enable them to track their development over time. They often mention the challenges the program has faced, even if not in full detail.

Much of the detailed assessment information advisers will want to explore may not mentioned in program materials. Typically, the staff at the program's sponsor are happy to answer questions by either e-mail or phone. Advisers should also feel free to request particular information; for example, questionnaires from past participants, course syllabi, curriculum vitae of instructors and staff, examples of final reports from internship courses, etc.

Finally, it is certainly appropriate to ask the program's sponsor to send a staff person to meet

Part III: Program Development, Campus Management, Marketing, and Evaluation

with education abroad advisers, faculty members, and other administrators. Make sure that both the program representative and the faculty and administrators at your university understand that this visit is part of the program evaluation and approval process, and is not for recruiting. This visit should focus on detailed discussions about the program and what it can offer. Meetings with potential student participants would not be appropriate at this time.

One review method is to follow a program more or less chronologically, from the first information card, to application and admission, to enrollment, to participation and return. This allows the education abroad professionals to put themselves in the student's place. It should also give the education abroad professionals an opportunity to compare the proposed program to one of their own, or one with which they are familiar. The following questions offer some suggestions of information to collect about the program.

Predeparture Information and Admissions Processes.

- How clear are the program's objectives? How does the program and its location and resources contribute to the fulfillment of these objectives?

- How long has the program operated? How financially sound is the sponsoring organization?

- How adequate and accurate are printed and electronic materials describing the program?

- What are the admission requirements? How do they relate to the program's objectives? How are admission requirements enforced?

- What is the advising process? What are the application and selection processes? What are the eligibility and selection criteria? How are accepted students notified?

- What information is furnished to students at the various stages of the application/selection/acceptance process about academics; costs and financial assistance; health, safety, and security issues; program policies and regulations?

- How much does the program cost? What is included in the cost? How accurate is the cost information provided to students? How often is cost information updated in the application and enrollment process?

- Will this program be eligible for the transfer of state, federal, institutional, and third-party financial aid? How will this be managed? If the program offers scholarships, what impact will this have on students' financial aid packages?

- How does the program handle billing? Does the program require a financial guarantee or bank statements?

- What is the nature of the predeparture orientation and other materials?

- What are the travel arrangements? Who makes and pays for travel? Who meets the students upon arrival?

- What are the academic calendar and the length of the terms?

- How many students can the program accommodate? What is the average class size?

- What majors are most common? Which other U.S. universities send students?

- What type of transcript is issued? What does it include? Can the U.S. institution's registrar's office interpret it?

Location in the Host Country.

- Why operate this particular program in this particular location?

- Are the program's facilities appropriate for its instructional purposes? How will students access library and other materials? Are computers available for student use?

- What advantages does the location of the program bring to it? What barriers does the location present?

- Where is the program located in relation to where the students will live?

- How does the location affect the health, safety, and security of the participants and staff? What protocols and plans are in place for emergency preparedness and response?

Academic Aspects. Assessing the academic quality of a course or program taught by the local faculty of the host country and offered within that country's academic culture is not an easy undertaking. It is equally difficult to assess the quality of the faculty themselves. Often, the assessment of the quality of a course or program or faculty member is made primarily on the basis of its similarity to the home institution. While that is certainly one measure of quality, education abroad professionals might also want to ask some different questions, such as:

- How does this course fit into the educational program of the host country?

- How is knowledge created and transmitted within this culture?

- How is learning defined, and how are students supposed to learn the material?

- What are the typical qualifications of the students who take this course?

- After obtaining answers to these questions, education abroad professionals should then ask whether this is an appropriate course for their students at this time in the students' academic careers.

Many education abroad programs try to address concerns about academic quality by offering special courses geared to foreign students or by offering U.S. courses taught by local faculty. Some others avoid the issue by importing U.S. faculty to teach a U.S. course in the foreign location. However, some inherent tensions usually exist between U.S. and foreign academic cultures: (1) U.S. students usually prefer classes with lots of discussion and student participation, whereas courses taught abroad—unless they are specifically for study abroad students—generally revolve around large lectures; (2) U.S. students like to have regular access to faculty members—for example, through regularly held office hours—but faculty abroad often have little or no communication with students outside the classroom; and (3) U.S. students are used to structured assignments and being evaluated a number of times during the term, whereas faculty abroad often expect students to learn more independently, and so give unstructured assignments; for example, they may distribute a long reading list that is relevant to the class subject, advise students to read what interests them, and then evaluate students only once at the end of the course.

Naturally, most international educators see these tensions as positive, since one of the most commonly expressed goals of study abroad is to expose students to cultural differences—and education is a part of culture. (An interesting resource on the relationship between culture and education is Linda Chisholm and Howard Berry's book, *Understanding the Education—and Through It the Culture—in Education Abroad* [2002].) However, these tensions do complicate the assessment process, especially when faculty from the home campus are part of the process, and their support is needed for program approval. It's also challenging to accurately interpret comments that returning students write in their returnee questionnaires, because they often judge a program based on their own culturally biased expectations.

The assessment of the academic aspects of a program abroad is further complicated by the variety of available course settings; for example, courses organized for only U.S. students (which may be taught by local faculty or by faculty from the home campus), courses organized for visiting students from all countries, and regular university courses (which can be part of a foreign university program or part of a U.S. university program offered in a foreign country). Determining the course setting or settings under review may help bring some clarity to this part of the assessment.

For program courses taught outside the local postsecondary education structure, education abroad professionals may wish to use such questions as the following:

- How does the curriculum contribute to fulfilling the program objectives? How does it benefit from the host environment? How does it compare with the home curriculum in terms of level and degree of difficulty?

- How does the curriculum abroad relate to and mesh with the on-campus curriculum?

- Who is responsible for supervising the curriculum abroad?

- How supportive is the home campus of the program abroad?

- What are the qualifications and attitudes of the faculty teaching the courses abroad?

- What are the academic resources available at the program location (e.g., library and laboratory facilities, language labs)? How do those resources support the program's curriculum?

- What is the language of instruction at the program? If the courses are taught in the target or local language, does the program have tutorial assistance available? Is there a preterm intensive language course offered? What is its cost?

- How are course credits calculated? How many courses make up a full load?

- Does the program offer a preterm course that teaches intensive language and educates students about the host country's university system and other

Chapter 5: Program Assessment and Evaluation

cultural issues? Are students granted credit for this course?

- Does the program, or do some of the courses, have field study components?

- If the program offers internship or service-learning courses for credit, how are these structured and how much credit can be earned? Are they mandatory or optional? Who teaches the course? How many hours do students spend in the placement per week? What kinds of assignments and assessments are typical for these courses?

- Are the courses open to local students? What is the mix of U.S. students to local students?

For courses offered at a local university, consider these questions:

- Which departments or courses are open to U.S. students? Are they available in all terms or semesters? Do qualified U.S. students have access to upper-level or honors courses?

- What is the typical class size? What is the instructional format (e.g., lecture, discussion)?

- How accessible are faculty to U.S. students?

- What modes of assessment are used in the course? Do U.S. students have the same assessments as regular degree students? Do they take them at the same times? (This is often an issue because of differences in academic calendars between the U.S. and other countries,

and may be of special concern to home-campus faculty.)

- If the local university offers special courses for foreign students, do U.S. students have access to these courses? What is the language of instruction? What other U.S. programs allow their students to enroll in these? What credit do U.S. students receive for these courses?

- What academic support services, such as academic advising or tutorial help, does the program offer?

Opportunities for Learning Outside of the Classroom. It is a fact that more than 75 percent of a student's time on any campus (not including sleep time) is spent outside of the classroom. International educators have long held that a significant portion of students' intercultural and personal growth occurs outside the classroom. Education abroad professionals should therefore consider how the program being assessed will provide opportunities for students to engage in the local culture, keeping in mind the criticism of John Engle and Lilli Engle that, with rare exceptions, the "foreign landscape [is] increasingly strewn with on-site foreign study programs facilitating an international education which is neither significantly international nor truly educative" (Engle and Engle 2002).

When looking at the opportunities for interaction between the students and the host culture, education abroad professionals could consider the following:

- What is covered in the arrival and the on-site orientation sessions?

Part III: Program Development, Campus Management, Marketing, and Evaluation

- To what degree, and how, does the program promote and facilitate student interaction with the host culture? How successful is the program with these activities?

- What experiential learning activities are available or required as part of the program? What social activities, language partners, or sports opportunities does the program offer?

- Does the program help students find jobs, internships, or volunteer placements? Can the program help the students make connections to nongovernmental organizations or service clubs and organizations?

- What university clubs or other organizations are available, and do many students get involved in these?

- Does the program offer a language partner program?

- How are local and national cultural events celebrated during the year? How many of these celebrations involve host nationals?

- Does the program provide or facilitate placement with a local home-stay or weekend family?

A program may offer opportunities other than those listed here. It's a good idea to look into these alternative learning experiences when reviewing a program.

Student Life Aspects. U.S. students typically come from universities with highly structured residential and campus life programs. Typically, residential life is not part of the array of programs available overseas. These questions will help education abroad professionals gauge how successful the program is in moving students from their U.S. campus lives to living in the host culture:

- How do the students spend their free time? What social and recreational activities are available?

- Are there sufficient support services (e.g., personal, intercultural, academic advising, and medical and psychological health services)? Do the physical and mental health services staff have experience working with U.S. patients?

- What disciplinary problems are most prevalent at the program? How are they handled? When do the students learn about the consequences of violating the program's conduct code? How strictly is the conduct code enforced?

- What reentry activities does the program offer participants?

- What follow-up activities are there once the participants have returned to the United States?

Student housing is chief among the issues in the student life area of a program, and after academics, the second most important aspect overall for many advisers. Certainly U.S. students (and their parents) are very concerned with where they will live while abroad. Until that issue is settled, they are often unable to concentrate on anything else. Housing can also have an instructional purpose, if, for example, the U.S. students live with host nationals and are committed to speaking the local language. It is also worth noting that in housing, as in other aspects of programs overseas, a similar-sounding option can actually be very different. A dormitory at a foreign

Chapter 5: Program Assessment and Evaluation

university is a very different place than one at a U.S. college; the former is where students sleep, the latter is often the center of the students' social life.

- Does the program have a staff person dedicated to housing arrangements? How does the program handle housing problems (especially if a student needs or requests to be removed from a housing arrangement immediately)?

- Where is the housing located in relation to the program's academic component?

- Do students have housing options, or do all students have the same living arrangement? If they have options, do they tend to choose one option over another? Do all options cost the same?

- Do students have the option live with host nationals? If so, how much contact will they have with them on a regular basis? Do they share a room, a suite, a bathroom, or a kitchen, or are they just in the same building?

- How new are the facilities?

- How social are the dormitories or residential colleges?

- Do students cook for themselves? Do they have the option of enrolling in a meal plan?

- If students will be living in apartments, are the apartments furnished?

- If the students have a home-stay option, who selects the families and monitors the placements? With what types of families are students placed? What kind of orientation for home-stay families

does the program offer? How much are the families paid? How are the families paid? (Using the students to deliver payment to the families raises a number of professional and ethical issues.) What is included in the home-stay? How are the home-stays evaluated after a student leaves? What percentage of the families is new and what percentage has been hosting students for many years? How much contact do students typically have with the host families? How many students live in each home-stay?

- How many meals in are included in the home-stay arrangement? Does the program have families that can accommodate students with special dietary needs? Are students allowed to use the kitchen?

- Are students allowed to use the home-stay family's phone to receive and make calls? Are they allowed to use laundry facilities?

- Will the students have their own rooms at the home-stay location? Who in the host family will be displaced for the student to have a single room? Will the students have their own beds? Is there a closet or other secure place for the students to lock up passports and other valuables?

- If students live off campus, how long is the typical commute to school, and what mode of transportation do they use? In what kinds of neighborhoods do they live? Are they safe according to local standards and a local assessment? How safe is the neighborhood according to U.S. standards? (Note: It is often difficult to judge whether a neighborhood is "safe." Some neighborhoods abroad that may look unsafe to Americans may actually be safe, and vice versa. Trustworthy on-site staff are the best judges of a neighborhood's safety.)

Administrative and Financial Aspects. No program can survive over time without adequate administrative and financial structures. Education abroad professionals may find that some of the following information is confidential, but they should keep asking questions until they learn what they need to know about the program.

- What is the level and extent of the financial support of the sponsoring agency or institution for the program abroad?

- How supportive is the sponsor's senior administration of the program abroad?

- How effective is the program's on-site support structure, including the resident director and administrative support staff?

- How is the program affiliated with the host institution?

- What training is or has been available to program staff? How much and what kind of contact do they have with the sponsoring institution?

- What is status of the program's emergency procedures? How do they compare with the health and safety standards outlined *Good Practices*? When were they last drilled as a practice exercise?

- What is the relationship of the program and the program staff to other study abroad programs in the host city and country?

- What is the relationship of the program to the responsible U.S. embassy or consulate?

- Does the program have adequate financial resources available for day-to-day operation, and a sufficient reserve in case of emergency?

- Is there a regular budget development and expenditure review process? How are expenditures tracked and audited? Does the program have an audited financial statement, and will the administrators share that statement?

- How does the program assess and evaluate its own activities? What happens with these evaluations? Will the program administrators share the assessments and evaluations or summaries?

Other Sources of Assessment Information. Questionnaires, surveys, and other information from student alumni: In addition to obtaining program assessments and evaluations from the sponsoring organization, education abroad professionals should request the names and e-mail addresses of past participants, preferably those who attended the program within the past two years. Ideally, the list should include students from peer institutions and students who are similar to the sending institution's potential students in terms of majors and other factors. (Because of privacy restrictions, education abroad professionals should understand that a responsible provider will not send a list of students without the students' permission and education abroad professionals should not use such a list unless they have proof of those permissions.) Education abroad professionals can then contact the students by phone, or e-mail them some questions about their perspective of the program abroad. In addition to demographic questions (year in college, gender, major), professionals may wish to consider asking questions such as the following:

- When did you attend the program?

- How would you describe your overall experience?

- What courses did you take on the program, and where?

- In what language were you taught?

- Did the program take advantage of the local surroundings?

- How challenging did you find the courses as compared with those offered at your home college?

- Did you find the courses intellectually stimulating? Academically challenging? Why, or why not?

- How much do you feel you learned? What contributed to this?

- Where did you live? With whom?

- How did you like your housing situation?

- What kind of interaction did you have with host nationals?

- Would you recommend this program to others? If so, to which kinds of students? If not, why not?

While student feedback can be invaluable in program assessment, student responses should be read with caution. Students are likely to use criteria for judging the value of their experience that are quite different from those used by faculty to determine academic creditworthiness. Sometimes student criteria are quite visceral (e.g., how much "fun" they had, or how many new places they visited). More often, students are eager to reflect on their personal growth. Whatever a student's immediate conclusions about the experience abroad, they are quite likely to change over time. The final reason for caution has to do with the differences in academic cultures, discussed above. Students may rate courses negatively because they were taught in the style of the host country rather than in the style of their home university. For example, students may perceive their overseas courses as having been easier, simply because they did not include ongoing assessment (e.g., papers, quizzes, midterms).

Three suggestions for structuring the e-mail questionnaires to get helpful student feedback include the following: (1) ask specific, as well as general, questions; (2) focus on what students feel they learned abroad through their courses—including things they could not have learned at home—rather than on workload or whether the classes were "easy;" and (3) if students' responses are unclear, or if they seem to contradict themselves—for example, if they describe the overall program as weak but have all positive reactions anyway—try to contact them by telephone to get clarification. Good resources for student questionnaire templates are the NAFSA publications *Abroad by Design* (Lamet 2002) and *Forms of Travel* (Carr and Summerfield 1994).

Colleagues in Study Abroad Offices of Major Sending Schools. In addition to requesting the names and contact information for students who participated in the program, education abroad professionals should ask the program's sponsor to send them the names of the universities that have sent the most students on the program. Then they should contact the education abroad offices and talk to them about their experiences with the program. Hopefully, both the education abroad office and the students will have had equally good experiences. The study abroad field is very open, and most advisers are happy to share their experiences with a particular program. It is important to note, however, that these discussions are best conducted over the phone rather than by e-mail, since written assessments shared among colleagues in the field can lead to legal complications. (See Part III, Chapter 7, "Legal Issues and Education Abroad.") The NAFSA study abroad e-mail discussion list, SECUSS-L, has specific "netiquette" for these kinds of questions. (Beginning in late 2005 this will be moving to the Professional Resources and Networks section of the NAFSA Web site).

Site Visits. Making a two- to three-day program site visit is an excellent way to conclude an assessment. Even if the education abroad office has only limited travel funds, the cost of a visit can be offset in a variety of ways. For example, determine if the sponsoring organization offers familiarization trips—or perhaps a visit to this program can be combined with other professional travel. Education abroad professionals might also ask the program's sponsor if it offers travel grants for site visits. A visit to the program abroad should be a final step in the assessment process, not a beginning. Time spent on site should not be used to gather information that could have been gathered in the United States. Site visits provide an opportunity both to see the program in action and to meet with administrators, faculty, staff at affiliated institutions, and with students. In this way, education abroad professionals can learn program details in context, gain multiple perspectives, and develop an overall, well-rounded impression of the program goals and how the program actually works on the ground. *Abroad by Design* has a template for a site visit form. Others are available in the SECUSS-L archives.

When possible and relevant, it is highly advisable for education abroad professionals to visit overseas programs together with a faculty member from the department most related to the programs under evaluation. For example, a faculty member from the Spanish department might accompany a study abroad adviser on site visits to programs in Spain or Latin America. Similarly, a faculty member from the English department or theatre department might accompany the adviser on site visits to programs in London. Bringing faculty along generally improves the quality of the site visit, because they will be able to evaluate certain academic aspects of the programs, including their fit with the home institution, that the administrator might not be qualified to evaluate. In addition, this is a good way to better educate academic departments about study abroad opportunities for their students, as well as to get more buy in from the departments regarding study abroad in general.

Direct Enrollment Programs

The assessment process is more difficult when students enroll directly into overseas institutions either through an exchange agreement or through the foreign university's international office. Both the U.S. and overseas institution take pains to ensure the quality of services and the educational programs offered, but structures, goals, and aims can be so different that employing the usual assessment strategies and criteria may be difficult. Therefore, a different set of criteria should be considered when the focus is an overseas school.

A direct enrollment program gives U.S. students an extraordinary chance to examine their own values and cultural upbringing. Such a program also gives them the opportunity to experience an educational system different from their own, on the same terms as the local students. But an assessment of this type of program may amount essentially to an assessment of the entire institution.

When considering a foreign university for a direct enrollment experience, education abroad professionals will want to consider the same questions discussed above, keeping in mind that in a direct enrollment situation, the student will be one of many international students at the university. While the university will certainly have some mechanism or office for dealing with international students, U.S. students will find that this is a much different experience than being in a study program, where there is a much more visible academic and intercultural support system and safety net in place. Thus, it may be wise to pay particular attention to the following concerns:

- The foreign university's level of commitment to and support for foreign students.
- The institutional structure and academic culture of the university. (The institutional governance, assessment procedures, and the academic culture may be radically different abroad. One may find schools or departments that operate in a fairly autonomous fashion, setting independent curriculum, calendars, and tuition costs. Rules applying to one division may not apply to another. Furthermore, the academic culture of a particular school may limit access to professors by undergraduates. Advance access to course schedules, reading lists, syllabi, and descriptions may be slow or even impossible.)

- The language of instruction (As students venture farther from the more traditional places to study abroad, and the course and language offerings expand, it may be difficult to evaluate locations where the language of instruction is not taught or spoken on the home campus.)

- Grade reports and transcripts. (Be certain that the home institution's education abroad and registrar's offices have come to an agreement about what is required in order for the student's work abroad to be posted on the home-campus transcript.)

- Effort versus benefit. (In any undertaking, a variety of resources is devoted to completing the process. It is prudent to maintain an understanding of the required assessment efforts and potential benefits. A long assessment that includes a site visit and exploration is not a wise investment for a single enrollment.)

Sources of Information for Assessing Direct Enrollment Programs

Home-campus Faculty. Often, faculty at the home institution are aware of the reputation and expertise of an overseas school or department. Consulting the home faculty makes it possible to gain a better assessment of the strengths and weaknesses of an overseas school.

The Office of Foreign Student Affairs at the Host Institution. Fortunately, an increasing number of foreign institutions have set up international program offices to deal with overseas students. Many have also produced catalogues and other literature. At times, these universities send representatives to the U.S. for campus visits that are particularly helpful in determining the quality of the academic programs and the student services.

The International Admissions Office at the Home Campus. If the home university offers graduate programs, its international admissions office may have dealt with students from the potential host institution. The admissions office will also have access to various handbooks on international transfer credit and degree programs around the world.

International Education Organizations Overseas. Valuable information about contacting overseas institutions during the process of assessing direct enrollment systems is obtainable from groups such as the following:

- Japanese Association for Foreign Student Affairs (JAFSA)

- European Association for International Education (EAIE)

- Australian Association for International Education (AAIE),

- Overseas Educational Advisers (OSEAS),

- British Universities Transatlantic Exchange Association (BUTEX)

- Korean Association for Foreign Student Affairs (KAFSA)

- Trans Regional Academic Mobility and Credential Assessment Information Network (TRACE)

The American Association of Collegiate Registrars and Admissions Officers (AACRAO). An organization such as AACRAO provides information about the transferability of work (i.e., credit and transcript assessment) undertaken through direct enrollment at foreign institutions. Colleagues in the admissions and registrar's offices might also provide assistance. There are also many private organizations and consultants specializing in evaluating transcripts from foreign institutions. While this sort of credential evaluation is usually for foreign students, it can be applied to grades earned by U.S. students in a foreign university.

Contact with Colleagues. The regional and the annual conferences of NAFSA and other international education organizations can provide excellent settings for discussing program evaluation in connection with direct enrollment. The required evaluation information can be obtained by speaking with colleagues from U.S. institutions that have a program at or otherwise send students to the overseas institution.

Other Agencies. Another approach—although more time consuming and cumbersome—is to check with the country's accrediting agencies (e.g., the ministry of education), the local U.S. embassies and consulates, or the U.S. Department of Education, or to read the many handbooks on evaluating overseas institutions.

Although it may seem obvious, it's worth noting here that when reviewing a foreign university for a direct enrollment program, the reviewer must be mindful of using standards set by the other country. Simply, it is important for education abroad advisers to practice what they preach, and not impose U.S. culturally specific quality standards on a foreign institution. However, efforts to use local standards may fail in the face of pressure from the home institution. As U.S. institutional responsibility for quality and safety in programs abroad increases, so this pressure will also be felt in direct enrollment programs. Beyond simply assessing the academic standards of an overseas institution, the U.S. university may soon become responsible for ensuring that the host institution meets the standards for safety, health, and support set by U.S. institutions, as well.

Assessing Programs on an Ongoing Basis

While the most common external program assessment involves institutional approval for transfer of credit, ongoing assessments of all programs approved for transfer of credit are equally important. As part of the university's culture of assessment, the education abroad office must be able to show that the programs to which the university regularly sends its students continue to meet the university's academic standards and other criteria. The extent to which an institution conducts ongoing assessments of its education abroad programs depends chiefly on office staffing and budget. Unfortunately, most education abroad offices do not have the staff, time, or money to conduct a thorough yearly assessment of all of the programs abroad their students attend. However, just as academic departments are reviewed at regular intervals (often every five years), education abroad offices should establish a timetable that will result in a thorough review of all programs over a specified period. By reviewing a few each year, the education abroad office can make the work more manageable. In the meantime, all offices should make it a priority to remain up-to-date on details of the programs to which they send students.

Read Every Student Returnee Questionnaire

At least one adviser in the office should read every student questionnaire to get a sense of the types of experiences students have had, and to identify any program problems. If students consistently give a program bad reviews—or even if they just consistently mention aspects about which the adviser is not well informed—it is important to follow up and learn more, perhaps through a focus group of returnees. Then use the information for improvement or changes. Asking students for their assessment of the program and then ignoring their responses can be seen as a breach of duty and will be very difficult to defend in a lawsuit. (See Part III, Chapter 7, "Legal Issues and Education Abroad.")

Maintain Close Relationships with the Program's Sponsors

It is very easy to maintain close relationships with sponsoring organizations if they are based in the United States. Most organizations have program representatives who are happy to visit their sending schools to meet with international educators, administrators, faculty, and students. Sometimes organizations will even send resident directors from the overseas programs to visit top sending schools or schools that might become top senders. Also, if an institution sends a large number of students on a study abroad organization's programs, the organization might even be willing to pay for the school's advisers to attend its annual conference or to visit its headquarters to learn more. It may even provide some travel funding for a site visit.

Conferences typically feature an exhibit area. An especially extensive and diversified exhibit area can be found at the NAFSA annual conference. Many of the major U.S. and foreign-based education abroad sponsors have booths at the NAFSA conference and other conferences. Education abroad professionals who are attending a conference and would like to meet with someone from the program's sponsor, should contact the program and set up an appointment in advance. In addition to educating themselves about the sponsor's programs, sending institutions should also share with the sponsoring organization important program feedback from students and others. If a sponsoring organization strives for continual improvement—which all good organizations should—it will welcome the information and may even use it to initiate changes.

Conduct Site Visits When Possible

As discussed earlier, site visits are a wonderful tool for learning about the program. In some respects, they may be even more valuable if made after students begin attending an approved program, rather than during the initial assessment and evaluation process, because they could contribute to the ongoing review. The more experience advisers have with a program, the more they will know what to look for during a site visit. If feasible, it is helpful for a relevant faculty member to make the visit with the adviser, not only to investigate the program's academic aspects further, but also to help promote it later among colleagues and students.

When planning a site visit, it is very important to talk with the sponsoring organization in advance about the goals for the visit. First, the more the organization knows about what the education abroad professional wants to gain from the visit, the easier it will be to arrange the schedule. Second, if the purpose of the visit is to assess and evaluate the program, rather than just get a general feel for it, the education abroad professional should make the sponsoring organization and on-site staff aware of this. If the professional plans to write a site visit report based on the visit and to share feedback with the organization, it is also a good idea to discuss this with the sponsoring organization before visiting the program. First, however, the education abroad professional should make certain that his or her institution will permit the professional to share the feedback. Also, while most organizations say they welcome feedback, sharing site visit reports that contain criticism has not been a common practice in the field to date. So before offering to share a report, education abroad professionals should determine the extent to which the sponsoring organization is eager to receive feedback on its programs from its sending schools. He or she should also find out all the persons or offices the sponsor would like to have the report sent to (e.g., the U.S. office, on-site staff), and who will respond to it. Discussing all these issues will help to avoid tension that could arise at a later point if the organization or program did not realize the extent to which they were being evaluated.

The Evaluation: Making Decisions About a Program

When it comes to making a final decision about the suitability of a program abroad for an institution and its students, education abroad professionals may find themselves in an awkward situation. On the one hand, faculty members involved in the assessment process typically want to spend a great deal of time looking at all of the alternatives and considering all of the issues in great detail. On the other hand, senior administrators at the college might want an answer (especially concerning financial ramifications) 'yesterday.' Students will also be eager to know if the program will be available to them next semester or next year. Establishing a timeline and a set of decision criteria for the entire approval process at the outset will certainly help alleviate the tension among these groups of stakeholders. It is also very important to have all parties understand who has the final authority to make the decision. If the faculty's role in the process is advisory, then it is absolutely essential that this be made clear from the very beginning. Lastly, when a new program is added to a university's list of programs approved for transfer of credit, it is very useful to have a mechanism to indicate that this is new and developing relationship. Marking the new program as being 'under development' is one way to indicate to all stakeholders that, even though the education abroad office and the institution feel the program is appropriate for its students, there may be some surprises along the way.

Assessing the Long-Term Impact of Education Abroad

The benefits of education abroad have long been discussed and praised by those who have studied abroad, their professors, their employers, and by professionals working in the field of education abroad. However, any conclusions drawn from their discussions and praise have been based largely on anecdotal evidence. Demonstrating that studying abroad influences future behavior in such areas as career path, foreign language use, post-undergraduate academic choices, international activity, and personal attitudes is, of course, no small task. The inherent challenges of designing and carrying out formal studies may explain why there has been comparatively relatively little research on student learning in the field (but see, for example, Carlson et al. 1990, Opper et al. 1990, Burn 1991, Laubscher 1994, Kauffmann et al. 1992, Engel and Engel 2002, Rinehart 2002, Chieffo and Griffiths 2004, and several articles in the Fall 2003 and the entire Fall 2004 issue of *Frontiers: the Interdisciplinary Journal of Study Abroad*).

There are some encouraging signs on the horizon, indicating that education abroad is devoting more time to research and outcomes assessment, and more importantly, more funding. At the 2003 NAFSA annual conference in Salt Lake City, Utah, SECUSSA (Section on U.S. Students Abroad—recently reorganized as NAFSA's Education Abroad Knowledge Community) created a research committee. Research into outcomes in education abroad and other international education programs has also been supported by the Association of International Education Administrators (AIEA) for years. The Forum on Education Abroad has set outcomes assessment and other research as one of its five main task areas (Forum 2003). In addition to the committee work on research and outcomes assessment, the Forum has posted a position paper on outcomes assessment (Whalen 2003), and a listing of twenty current research projects on aspects of education abroad, including an investigation of the impact of an education abroad experience on the psychosocial development of undergraduates, several other impact studies, several language proficiency studies, and changes in personal perspective, among others (Forum 2003).

One of the more ambitious efforts in the area of assessing international learning outcomes is the project led by the American Council on Education (ACE). Supported by a grant from the U.S. Department of Education's Fund for the Improvement of Postsecondary Education (FIPSE), the project has brought together six colleges and universities representing a cross-section of U.S. higher education (Dickinson College, James Madison University, Kapi'olani Community College, Michigan State University, Kalamazoo

College, and Palo Alto College) to develop a set of common international education learning outcomes and assessment measures that are applicable across all types of institutions. Information on the project is available on the "International Initiatives" area of the ACE Web site.

However, if the field of education abroad is going to compete effectively for increasingly scarce campus and government resources, education abroad professionals must do a better job of collecting data, as well as of quantifying and measuring the impact of study abroad on participating students. As one senior analyst for the U.S. Department of State was heard to remark at a 2003 NAFSA workshop on campus internationalization, data is not the plural of anecdote.

Uses of Longitudinal Research

There are many reasons to conduct longitudinal research in education abroad besides strengthening the field's position within the higher education hierarchy. If effectively implemented, this kind of research can help study abroad program developers assess the relative impact of key program elements on students' study abroad experience. How important is housing choice on future use of and proficiency in foreign language? Will an internship abroad influence one's career path toward an international position? Does second-language proficiency acquired or enhanced during a study abroad sojourn enhance career prospects and satisfaction? Does the length of the participant's study abroad experience influence the type of change that occurs in personal attitudes? Does study abroad correlate with earning an advanced degree? Do students who study abroad earn higher incomes than students who do not? Does study abroad have long-lasting effects on participants' political and cultural viewpoints? Effective research can answer these and other questions, and help program developers improve the quality of programming before, during, and after study abroad. Such research can also help education abroad advisers provide better counsel to prospective students (and their parents) in order to help maximize the experience. Another possible use of longitudinal research is to contrast responses from former participants long after their sojourns abroad with student questionnaire responses given immediately after their return from the experience. Such comparisons can illuminate changes in attitude, as well as provide insights into differences between the immediate and the long-term impact of study abroad.

Finally, longitudinal research can be shared with the general public and funding agencies, including the federal government, to create a wider understanding and appreciation of the benefits of studying abroad, based on scientifically reliable data rather than collections of anecdotes. Although education abroad participation has experienced significant growth over the ten years from 1993 to 2003, less than 10 percent of college students study abroad during undergraduate years. Yet recent ACE surveys indicating that more than 50 percent of U.S. high school seniors say they would like to have an international experience as an undergraduate (Hayward and Siaya 2001). There is clearly great potential for more students to share in the benefits and outcomes of study abroad, all of which need to be measured and the results widely shared.

Challenges to Launching Longitudinal Research

Two key challenges to launching effective longitudinal research are (1) the direct costs of managing a research project (collecting the data), and (2) the cost of staff resources and professional researchers to interpret the data. Specific direct costs include the costs of developing a reliable database of potential respondents, of creating an effective and concise survey instrument, and of paying for survey postage. Staff or professional resources, needed to tabulate, evaluate, write up, distribute, or publish the results, are an additional cost.

Related to the costs are the sample size and response rate. The larger the sample size, the larger the direct costs will be. A larger sample size makes it more expensive to increase the response rate, because multiple mailings are usually needed to maximize return. The response rate affects the estimation of the results' validity (or the probability that the sample accurately reflects the population) and reliability (or the interval around which the results are accurate).

Another way to delineate sample representation is to define and survey key measurable demographics and then compare them among respondents and nonrespondents. The degree to which respondents are representative of a surveyed population is illustrated by examining the response variation rates between respondents and nonrespondents across the previously defined demographic variables. Examples of relevant demographic variables collected and compared by response rates are year of study abroad participation, location of study abroad experience, duration of study abroad experience, program type, and undergraduate institution attended.

Finally, defining the control group is a challenging issue in this kind of research. A question that is often raised concerns the makeup of a viable control group. Should the control group consist of students who do not study abroad? Or should the control group be students who were planning to study abroad but then ended up not participating?

Furthermore, the additional cost of including a control group in research can be quite daunting. There is some debate about whether it is even necessary to include a control group. Much educational research does not include control groups, but instead focuses on impacts and outcomes for their own sake, regardless of control group. Each research project will have to assess the benefits and costs of using a control group, and the research results should indicate how the control group issue was managed.

Getting a Longitudinal Study Off the Ground

Institutions or organizations interested in designing and implementing a longitudinal study of student learning will proceed in one of two ways. Those fortunate enough to have access to reasonably complete alumni records that identify students who studied abroad (and where and when they studied) will be able to carry out a retrospective longitudinal study. A retrospective study involves surveying former participants about a variety of things, such as the nature and memories of experiences, and how those experiences impacted lives and careers. Institutions or organizations that cannot rely on having accurate alumni data, or who are, for whatever reason, interested in assessing the impact of study abroad on future participants, will carry out a future-focused longitudinal study. A future-focused study involves collecting participant data over many years, relative to the nature of the research questions.

Institutions deciding to pursue either type of longitudinal research are well advised to collaborate with experienced, qualified researchers. Some of the current studies have been undertaken as masters or doctoral theses, or have become a faculty member's ongoing research interest. The validity of any study's results depends on, among other things, sound methodology and research design. Institutions carrying out any research on student learning abroad may also wish seek external funding. As noted, the cost of carrying out a well-designed study can be considerable. Finally, institutions researching student learning abroad will ideally also seek out a research partner. Collaboration among two or more institutions creates economies of scale and provides for cost sharing. Collaboration can also lend legitimacy to the eventual research results; studies focused on students' experiences in a single institution can too easily be discounted, if not dismissed entirely, by faculty and administrators from other schools, who will assert that the subjects of single-school studies 'are not like the students at my institution.'

Summary

The regular assessment of student learning and student satisfaction in education abroad programs is an essential task for every program and sponsor. Like all other units of the university, education abroad programs should develop their own culture of assessment. An assessment plan typically begins with the definition of the area to be assessed, the sources of information, the modes of collecting the information, and the goal and objectives against which progress (or the lack thereof) will be measured. The information gained from a program review is typically used to show which aspects of the program (academic, student life, intercultural, health and safety, etc.) are meeting the performance objectives, and to suggest improvements for those that are not. When reviewing their own programs, sponsors need to provide stakeholders with opportunities to give their input, and also need to be sure that they have clearly established the assessment criteria. Universities evaluating the external programs in which their students participate face a different range of challenges, but the same goal: assuring themselves that the programs will provide their students with appropriate academic and intercultural experiences. As the profession works towards agreement on national standards for education abroad programs, there is a need for studies on the long-term impacts and student-learning outcomes of the experiences abroad.

CHAPTER 6

Maximizing Safety and Security and Minimizing Risk in Education Abroad Programs

Contributors: Barbara Lindeman, Natalie Mello, Joseph Brockington, Margit Johnson, Les McCabe

The health, safety, and security of education abroad participants have always been primary concerns for education abroad administrators, resident directors, and program sponsors when designing, monitoring, and evaluating overseas studies programs. During the past decade, however, the field has strengthened its efforts to provide guidance, resources, and training to education abroad professionals about health, safety, and security issues involved in study abroad programming. This increased emphasis has come about in part as a response to the significant growth in the number of students participating in education abroad during the 1990s and the concomitant growth in the number of programs, sponsors, and providers. The growth in study abroad participation has been met by a growing interest on the part of the media and some members of the U.S. Congress in issues of safety and security, especially following rare reports of serious injury to or death of U.S. students abroad.

By 1997, the field of education abroad had developed several responses to the challenge of providing resources and training in the areas of health, safety, and security. The University of Southern California received a U.S. Department of Education Fund for the Improvement of Post-Secondary Education (FIPSE) grant to establish a Web-based clearinghouse of information related to safety in education abroad, known as Safety Abroad First Educational Travel Information (SAFETI). The SAFETI project, now located at Loyola Marymount University, has brought together numerous electronic resources on health and safety abroad, including resources developed by the U.S. Peace Corps for use in training Peace Corps volunteers. The SAFETI site also hosts an annotated, searchable, bibliographic database of publications in education abroad, and has sponsored a number of workshops around the country.

NAFSA's Section on U.S. Students Abroad's (SECUSSA—which has recently been reorganized as the Education Abroad Knowledge Community) Health and Safety Committee expanded its role by developing a Professional Practice Workshop (PPW) entitled, "Safety and Responsibility in Education Abroad," which is offered annually at the NAFSA national conference. This workshop brings together a variety of experienced practitioners in the field, who provide guidance to the profession based on best practices, and address relevant legal issues and world events. The Health and Safety Committee provides ongoing guidance to the profession in responding to global events that impact study abroad programs, through postings on its e-mail discussion list, SECUSS-L, and by making resources available on the NAFSA Web site.

Perhaps the most significant contribution to the profession was the effort to establish agreement on a set of good practices that would guide stakeholders (education abroad administrators, home institutions, programs abroad, participants, and families) in thinking about and responding to health, safety, and security issues. In 1997, an Interorganizational Task Force on Safety and Responsibility in Study Abroad (now known as the Interassociational Advisory Committee) was formed by the Council on International Education Exchange (CIEE), NAFSA, the Association of International Education Administrators (AIEA), and the National Association of Student Personnel Administrators (NASPA), and included representatives from other international education organizations and program providers. Members of this task force and their successors produced *Responsible Study Abroad: Good Practices for Health and Safety* (hereafter referred to as *Good Practices*; 2003). While "aspirational in nature" and voluntary in adoption, the *Good Practices* have been broadly disseminated and discussed among education abroad administrators around the world, and provide a framework with regard to health and safety for the design, development, and administration of education abroad programs. The *Good Practices* also provide guidance for ongoing professional development efforts for the field of education abroad, including the NAFSA PPW, "Safety and Responsibility in Education Abroad."

THE NATURE AND MANAGEMENT OF RISK IN EDUCATION ABROAD

What is Risk?

Any discussion of safety, security, or risk must begin with some definitions. As it is used in this chapter, "safety" has reference to an individual person or to groups of persons. The companion term "security," on the other hand, has reference to the range of conditions in a locale or region. "Health" refers to the physical, psychological, and spiritual condition of an individual. When issues of health, safety, and security are discussed, the inner and outer conditions affecting a person are examined within the context of a particular location. The various risks associated with each can then be discussed, so there can be health risks, safety risks, or security risks, remembering that "risk" is a statement about the possibility that exposure to a hazard will result in a negative consequence (Ropeik and Gray 2002; International Organization for Standardization [ISO] 2002).

In the introduction to their book, *RISK! A Practical Guide for Deciding What's Really Safe and What's Dangerous in the World Around You*, Harvard researchers David Ropeik and George Gray move from a quote by Epictetus, "People are disturbed, not by things, but by the view they take of them," to the comment that, "the facts about risk are only part of the matter. Ultimately we react to risk with more emotion than reason. We take the information about a risk, combine it with the general information we have about the world, and then filter those facts through the psychological prism of risk perception. What often results are judgments of risk far more informed by fear than fact" (Ropeik and Gray 2002). Noting that behavioral scientists "have discovered psychological patterns in the subconscious ways we

Chapter 6: Maximizing Safety and Security and Minimizing Risk in Education Abroad Programs

'decide' what to be afraid of and how afraid we should be," they go on to list a number of "risk perception factors."

- Most people are more afraid of risks that are new than those they've lived with for a while.

- Most people are less afraid of risks that are natural than those that are human made.

- Most people are less afraid of a risk they choose to take than of a risk imposed on them.

- Most people are less afraid of risks if the risk also confers some benefit they want.

- Most people are more afraid of risks that can kill them in particularly awful ways.

- Most people are less afraid of a risk that they feel they have some control over (e.g., driving), and more afraid of a risk they don't control (e.g., riding or flying).

- Most people are less afraid of risks that come from places, people, corporations, or governments they trust, and more afraid if the risk comes from a source they don't trust.

- People are more afraid of risks that they are more aware of and less of afraid of risks that they are less aware of.

- People are more afraid of risks when uncertainty is high, and less afraid when they know more.

- Adults are much more afraid of risks to their children than risks to themselves.

- People will generally be more afraid of a risk that could directly affect them than a risk that threatens others. When the risk becomes personal fear goes up, even though the statistical reality of the risk may still be very low. (Ropeik and Gray 2002)

Ropeik and Gray further note that these patterns of risk perception and risk response "can be dangerous. What *feels* safe might actually be dangerous" (2002). In order to deal effectively with health, safety, and security concerns associated with administering study abroad programs, it is then incumbent upon all education abroad administrators to learn to differentiate between *perceived* risks and *actual* risks. This distinction does not imply that education abroad professionals can ignore what is perceived; only that actual risks and emergencies may require a different response than perceived ones. Moreover, a careful examination of perceptions and a statement of whose perceptions are being reported are very useful when collecting information about an incident. Is the report of risk or emergency coming from a student who has been in the country for fewer than twenty-four hours? From an anxious parent? From that country's ministry of internal affairs? From the U.S. Department of State? From the foreign ministry of another country? From CNN, Fox News, or the local television station? Learning to separate perceived risks and emergencies from actual ones takes time and practice, but is absolutely essential in designing and implementing an effective response plan.

Managing Risk

Given Ropeik and Gray's definition of risk as a statement about the possibility that exposure to a hazard will result in a negative consequence, risk management becomes the process of reducing the potential exposure to hazards to an acceptable level, and minimizing the negative consequences (Priest 2000). When investigating accidents, risk managers typically group the causal factors of the accident into one of two general categories: environmental or objective factors, and human or subjective factors (Leemon and Erickson 2000). Thus, a "hazard" can be considered the factor (action, event, object, situation, individual, etc.) that causes (or at least has the potential to cause) harm, loss, or injury. Effective risk management requires the combination of two methodologies: the design approach, which focuses on identifying and analyzing hazards for each program or activity, and then managing risks in advance of the program's operation; and an operations approach, which implements specific risk management strategies for each component, segment, and activity in the program abroad. The ultimate goal of this combination approach is to protect the participants, the staff, the program, and the institution.

Each institution must begin the risk management process by defining what is an acceptable level of risk for a program abroad, and especially for the individual components and activities of that program. This is a potentially intense conversation that must involve all key policymakers, and should be held in an atmosphere of honesty and trust. When talking about acceptable levels of risk, the discussion is really about what kind of injury or loss the program and the university are willing to assume in order to provide the type of opportunities for students that will contribute to the desired outcomes for the study abroad programs, given the institution's particular set of financial circumstances. International educators must acknowledge that in any activity or component there may well be negative consequences for individual participants or staff. Consider, for example, a program abroad that uses home-stays. Education abroad professionals generally agree that having students live with host families is an excellent way to facilitate cultural integration, and, where applicable, language acquisition. However, assigning students to live in a home-stay is not without risks. Table 1 illustrates the factors in a home-stay program that contribute to the risk involved with such a program.

For each of the potential hazards listed in Table 1, education abroad professionals can consider both the exposure to the hazard and the range of consequences that might follow from the exposure. It is even possible to put together a simple calculation to determine risk (Priest 2000). The combination of high exposure to a hazard with severe consequences (placing a student in a home-stay where previous students have reported domestic problems) would certainly increase the probability of

Table 1. Potential hazards of a home-stay program.

OBJECTIVE FACTORS	SUBJECTIVE FACTORS
3 Food poisoning	3 Carelessness of participant
3 Slip-and-fall type of accident	3 Illness of participant
3 Earthquake	3 Alcohol abuse
3 Fire in house	3 Drug use
3 Robbery or break in	3 Unfamiliarity with household appliances
3 Physical or sexual assault	
3 Civil unrest	3 Unfamiliarity with telephone to call for help
	3 Inability to speak the local language sufficiently well to hear or understand warnings

an incident, and thus the risk. On the other hand, a hazard with a normally insignificant consequence, such as not being able to speak the local language well enough to use the phone, is low risk, unless something happens, such as a fire. When program administrators speak of managing risks, what they really mean is reducing the likelihood that an incident will occur; reducing the severity of the consequence (to the participant or program) that will result from the incident; reducing (or removing) the exposure to the hazard; reducing (or removing) the hazard; deciding how much injury or loss they can live with and still stay in business, and then insuring against possible loss, as well as using "hold harmless" agreements or releases and waivers to transfer the inherent risks of participation in the program to the individual participants (Kaplin and Lee 1997); or all of the preceding pre-emptive steps.

In order to make the risk management process function smoothly, the risk manager (or risk management team) should identify the various hazards present, the potential exposures to the hazards, the potential negative consequences arising from exposure to the hazard, and then, after determining the program's or institution's ability and willingness to withstand these potential losses, decide how to handle the risk. Does the program or institution want to take out insurance against the risk? Have the participant assume the risk? Modify the program appropriately? Educate participants and staff as to how to handle the risk? These decisions then become the basis of the program's operating policies and procedures. However, for these policies and procedures to be effective (and to fulfill legal duty and responsibility), everyone associated with the program must be required to follow them. It will be extremely difficult to defend a deliberate violation of operating policies and procedures if a lawsuit is filed against the program.

Collecting and Tracking Incident and Near-Miss Reports

Ideally, every incident, accident, and injury, as well as all near misses (an accident or injury that almost happened), will be investigated by the program staff at the program locale and then reported back to the sponsor. In addition to looking into the factors that led to the incident or near miss, the investigation should also include a review of the program's policies and procedures to ensure that they were followed, that they did not contribute to the incident, and that they are still appropriate in light of the incident (Leemon and Erickson 2000). The investigation of incidents and near misses should not be focused on finding fault or placing blame, but rather on the fundamental question of how to improve the health, safety, and security conditions under which the program operates, and thus reduce the students' exposure to potential harm. Incident investigation, however, does carry certain responsibilities. By agreeing to investigate accidents and injuries, program administrators commit themselves to making changes and improvements to the program. There is no defense against a program's choice to ignore the recommendations of its own investigation.

Although many programs and sponsoring institutions have their own informal incident investigation criteria and checklists, educators within the field of education abroad have not yet formally agreed on what should be looked into during an incident investigation, or how the results of that investigation should be reported—or whether the results even should be reported. An agreement on a common investigatory and reporting rubric for incidents and near misses for program participants, directors, and faculty would be an excellent first step.

Reporting the results of incident investigations beyond the program and its sponsor will certainly be more complicated than keeping the reports in-house. Incident reporting itself will also be problematic on several levels. The first of these problems is what to report, to whom, about what? Does a twisted ankle as a result of hurriedly stepping off the curb in Argentina count as an incident? Is an auto accident without injuries an incident or a near miss? These are questions for the profession to decide, perhaps through the interassociational process. Incident reporting is also problematic on the level of comparison data for similar incidents. When talking about the number U.S. students injured in auto accidents in Kenya, should that number be compared to the number of accidents on the home campus? To the number of foreign students in Kenya? To the total number of U.S. citizens in Kenya? To the total number of foreigners in the village, city, or country?

Among the many current impediments to comprehensive risk assessment in education abroad is the almost complete lack of comprehensive data on accidents, injuries, losses, and fatalities among participants and staff. An incident reporting project will allow the profession to respond to media reposts with facts, rather than conjecture and anecdotes. Reporting incidents may raise issues with campus risk managers. However, if the ongoing incident data collection project in outdoor and adventure education is any guide, the results will be well worth it (Leemon and Merrill 2002; Leemon 2003).

Annual Risk Management Policy and Procedure Review

Effective risk management further requires that all policies and procedures be reviewed on a regular (i.e., annual) basis. Ideally, this review will not be simply an annual exercise. Institutions should carry out an ongoing assessment of conditions at each program location. The assessment should solicit information from students (through questionnaires and returnee surveys), local coordinators and resident directors, housing and home-stay coordinators, local university officials, and any others involved with the program.

Managing the Risk Presented by Specific Hazards

This material has been prepared for educational and information purposes only. It does not constitute legal advice. In order to address specific legal issues that arise, readers should consult appropriate legal counsel.

Students

Education abroad program administrators are accustomed to viewing those who take part in the programs abroad as students, or perhaps more generically, as participants. Risk mangers view students participating in the program as the greatest risk factor present in any program. Accidents and unfortunate incidents occur through a combination of human and environmental factors, and ultimately, the health, safety, and often security, of an individual participant rests in the decision making power of a 20-year old—something that, as anyone who has worked with college-age young people knows, can vary greatly from student to student. Students who choose to behave in a manner that acknowledges and respects their locale and the social and intercultural conditions around them, and that is appropriate for their abilities, are far less likely to

Using Waivers, Releases, and "Hold Harmless" Agreements

While using waivers, releases, and "hold harmless" agreements will not prevent accidents or injuries, their use can be an excellent risk management strategy. Waivers and releases are used to transfer the inherent risk from the program to the participant. By executing these types of agreements, participants agree to release the program from any liability for injuries or losses that they might suffer (Kaplin and Lee 1997). "Although some people believe that releases will not hold up in court, the truth is a well-written release that is presented properly can be and has been used as a powerful legal document" (Hicks 2000). To be effective, a release must be drafted with the assistance of an attorney. Taking someone else's release (especially a release from another state) can prove to be ineffective in the event of a lawsuit. There are also a number of rights (such as one's basic civil rights) that cannot be waived. Finally, "a perfectly drafted release is worthless without the *informed consent* of the signer" (Hicks 2000); that is, participants should not be requested to sign a release without being given an opportunity to study the document and fully inform themselves about the inherent risks of the program. Many releases and waivers enumerate the risks and possible negative consequences (including death) that may befall a participant. The program sponsor may choose to use a video or a script (reviewed by legal counsel) to educate participants about these risks prior to having them sign a waiver, release, or hold harmless agreement. If a study abroad program is provided by a third-party program provider, ideally the program's sponsor will have begun the process of educating potential participants about both the benefits and the inherent risks of the program through its marketing material. Likewise, the home-campus education abroad adviser must take care to present a balanced description when advising students about appropriate program choices. Discussions of risks and potential negative consequences, as well as the benefits of education abroad, should be included with discussions of other facts about a program.

Staff

No less than the student participants, program staff can also be the source of increased risk, particularly if their actions do not conform to program policy and procedures. On the other hand, properly trained staff are an essential part of an effective risk management strategy.

Campus-based faculty and staff are often chosen to participate as directors or residential advisers at overseas sites. Training overseas academic directors, resident directors, and program staff is as important in the program planning process as preparing students and their families for participation in an education abroad experience. The standard training for on-campus student support staff can serve as an excellent model for training academic directors and program staff who must serve overseas as dean of students, bursar, counselor, registrar, and nurse.

Program staff are responsible not only for the typical issues that arise on the home university campus but also for all risks that arise due to living in a foreign country and an unfamiliar locale. The *Good Practices* recommends that health and safety training be provided "for program directors and staff, including guidelines with respect to intervention and referral that take into account the nature and location of the education abroad program" (2003). Training should address the basics of first aid, first response in an emergency, standard warning signals for physical or mental stress, current best practices in student support services, and emergency protocol and resources appropriate to the program site. Areas of concern that should be addressed during staff training include sexual harassment, drugs and alcohol, recognizing and responding to students at risk, health and safety issues, transportation, housing concerns, students' behavior, social and personal growth, and helping students get the most out of the cultural experience. Education abroad administrators should plan these training programs well in advance and should consult with and involve those who offer services addressing these issues elsewhere on campus (e.g., counseling center, student life office, diversity office, academic advising, health services, etc.). Include them in the design and facilitation of the training sessions to offer expert advice about how to deal with the issues off-campus. Finally, all the information presented in the training should be collected in a handbook and given to program staff. The training should be "refreshed" at staff meetings, and knowledge of and compliance with program policies should be made part of every program evaluation.

Locale

Managing the risks present in the program location is an enormously complex undertaking. Many of the risk factors are environmental, including typical issues of modern life such as crime, socioeconomic conditions, air and water quality, and the political and national security situation. There are also issues related to the program's academic and residential facilities, such as the condition of the buildings and classrooms, the neighborhoods where the students live, and the transportation the students use to get from their accommodations to classes. Finally, there are conditions present on excursions and during activities, as well as a host of other factors.

Perhaps the most important starting point to consider when conducting risk assessments and preparing a risk management strategy for a locale is consistency in the sources of information and procedures used to develop a set of standardized internal procedures. In this regard, education abroad administrators may want to consider the process as a three-tiered approach to information gathering and decision making. The starting point is general information about countries to which the institution is sending students, to provide a solid set of background information about each destination. Sources typically include periodicals, subscription services, guidebooks, general media, and other information that is generally available to the public. Second, the information gathered can be narrowed and refined by using specialized country-specific risk assessment resources. These include private risk assessment companies, nongovernmental organizations with working knowledge of the specific country (e.g., Peace Corps, humanitarian organizations), nonprofit organizations dedicated to health and safety in international travel, and colleagues in the field of education abroad, both in the United States and overseas. Information on many of these sources of information can be found in the Education Abroad Knowledge Community area of the NAFSA Web site. A third tier of risk assessment information includes those sources on which the program will rely for making decisions about whether to continue study abroad programming in a particular country and/or whether to continue certain program activities. Among the sources of information employed by many education abroad programs are information sheets, public announcements, and travel warnings provided by the U.S. Department of State. Additional sources from the U.S. Department of State include the Overseas Security Advisory Council (OSAC), as well as in-country resources such as the Regional Security Officers (RSOs), located in U.S. consulates and embassies abroad.

Once an education abroad program has determined what sources of information are most pertinent to its type of program, and the order in which those resources are assigned priority in relation to decisionmaking, the program can then proceed to develop appropriate risk management strategies. These might include additional training and information for participants about environmental hazards present; transportation protocols that limit students to particular modes or vehicle types; protocols regarding independent travel, and the like.

Program

The greatest risk lies in approaching an overseas program—its activities and components, academic and residential facilities, the local staff, the neighborhood, city, and region where it is located—as though it were taking place on the on the home campus. In other words, students participating on study abroad programs often get into trouble when they perceive and try to understand events occurring in an unfamiliar cultural context from a perceptual framework that does not apply. A case in point is student, the newly arrived in the United Kingdom, who looks only to her left before stepping off the curb when crossing the street. Such inattention (such "ignorance") could lead to her death in a country where traffic drives on the left; and indeed, it is sad to say, U.S. students have died as a result of making this mistake. The problem of applying the "wrong" (or better, "inappropriate") point of view to an intercultural setting is often exacerbated when both the program and the host country use English. It seems to take students longer to accept the fact that they are in a foreign country when they can read all of the signs and understand (most of) the conversation around them.

From the risk manager's point of view, training, in the form of ongoing orientation and familiarization exercises, is generally considered to be the best way to address this risk of the foreign appearing familiar. It is important to confront the students with "real life" experiences that stress the foreignness of their study abroad site and call on them to employ the cross-cultural skills they have been building. Pairing the U.S. students up with local "buddies" for the initial period after arrival has proven successful in helping students make a safe and healthy adjustment to a new cultural context. Being told to look the other way when crossing the street may be more palatable if it comes from a peer rather than a senior program staff member.

Conducting a thorough risk assessment of the program will no doubt lead to the identification of a multitude of hazards, ranging from marble stairways, to no smoke alarms, to the local staff themselves. Excursions and nonacademic activities built into the program present additional risk management issues. When assessing the inherent risks present in these activities, risk managers should be mindful of several things:

If participation in the activity is mandatory or even merely included as part of the program's costs, how does it relate to the program's stated mission and learning outcomes? It would be very difficult to defend against an injury suffered during a whitewater rafting trip offered as part of a language and culture program in Spain.

Part III: Program Development, Campus Management, Marketing, and Evaluation

If participation in the activity is voluntary and optional, it should be presented as such to the students. If the activity requires certain skills (e.g., the ability to swim), this requirement should be included in the release that participants sign.

How will the participants be transported from the program or their accommodations to the activity? Statistics collected by organizations such as the Association for Safe International Road Travel (ASIRT) and the U.S. Department of State show that road travel is more dangerous almost everywhere in the world than in the United States. Program administrators should carefully consider how they wish to manage the risks presented by various transportation options. Some programs will use only licensed common carriers, municipal, or state-run public transportation to transport students. Others require transportation companies to furnish insurance certificates. Strategies to manage the risks present when transporting students in private, or even program-owned, vehicles might include driver training, extra insurance, special waivers and releases signed by the students, the implementation of strict transportation policies and protocols, or all of the above.

Every program should decide how it will handle the issue of alcohol use among students, whether it is serving alcohol to students at program events, allowing students to bring alcohol on a bus or on excursions, or limiting staff consumption of alcohol. Because the alcohol issue is fraught with legal, cultural, and intercultural issues, including home-campus student- and staff-conduct issues, it should be discussed by all stakeholders (including university legal counsel), and appropriate policies and protocols should be developed and communicated clearly to all concerned.

SAFETY AND SECURITY ISSUES

Virtually all senior university administrators and education abroad professionals, when asked about safety and security, will respond that the safety and security of their students is paramount. And certainly, safety is a chief concern of all involved in study abroad endeavors—participants, their families, advisers, institutions that send students abroad, institutions and programs that host them, and staff that operate the programs. While meaningful comparative statistics are hard to come by, most education abroad professionals believe that study in a foreign country is less perilous than study in the United States. This perception is underscored by the yearly reports of campus crime statistics in the *Chronicle of Higher Education*. (See, for example, the May 28, 2004 issue of the *Chronicle*. This information is also available through the Office of Postsecondary Education pages on the U.S. Department of Education Web site.) Yet there are inherent safety and security risks present in any off-campus setting, some of which are intensified in education abroad programs. When incidents and accidents happen, the effect on participants and their families is often more extreme because of the unfamiliar context and the distance that separates participants from their usual sources of consolation and support, especially their families.

When talking about safety and security (as well as health) in education abroad programming, what is really being discussed is establishing a relationship between how safe an individual would be at the overseas program site as compared with how safe he or she would be at home or on the home campus; that is, an implied comparison between the foreign and the domestic always underlies the discussion of these topics. Within the question, "Is it safe for students to study abroad in a particular location?" are two unstated questions. The first is, "Will the students be as safe there as they would be here?" The honest answer to this first question is, "It depends." As shown below, a student's safety anywhere depends on a number of factors, coupled with his or her ability to make good decisions. The second question is more troublesome: "Is there a guarantee that the students will be safe?" Here, the answer can only be an unqualified, unambiguous, "No." Certainly, real life offers no guarantees, and responsible program administrators do not offer them. But as shown in the preceding section, part of any risk management strategy must be the management of participant and family expectations. If there is an expectation of absolute safety and security for the participants on the part of anyone, the program must work to bring this expectation in line with reality—by conducting thorough predeparture and arrival orientations, obtaining informed consent, and collecting appropriate releases, waivers, and hold harmless agreements. Frustrated expectations can lead to lawsuits.

When considering safety abroad, program sponsors and staff should remember that different stakeholders have different approaches to safety issues. Education abroad professionals endeavor to practice safety in every aspect of program administration; senior university administrators discuss it; parents demand it; the media report on it (or on their perception of the lack of safety); and Congress investigates it. Students, however, are too often very ambivalent about safety. *Good Practices* provides an excellent starting point from which programs can examine their safety policies and procedures. The fifteen good practice statements directed to programs can be grouped into four broad categories: the assessment of various aspects of the program, student issues, orientation and training, and information and communication

Assessment

Good Practices calls for program sponsors to conduct periodic assessments of the health and safety conditions of their programs. Program sponsors are to assess the health and safety risks inherent to the program and its locale, assess the availability of medical and other professional services, and assess the suitability and reliability of vendors and contractors who provide services to the program (such as travel and transportation). In addition to the program's periodic assessment, *Good Practices* also calls on sponsors to communicate the results of their assessments and inquiries to program participants and their parents. This information sharing is particularly important when there have been changes in the inherent risks presented by the program's location, or in the availability of certain medical and other professional services Sponsors must avoid the tendency to gloss over anything negative about either the program or the availability of services. Participants, families, and university administrators deserve to receive an honest and straightforward appraisal of what is present in the program and its location. This will serve both to help set realistic expectations on the parts of all stakeholders and to help potential participants make truly informed choices about the program's suitability for them.

In developing these kinds of health and safety assessments, program sponsors should consider questions such as the following:

- Does the sponsor have the most current information about the health, safety, and security situation and local resources at the program's location? How reliable are the information sources? How often is this information updated?

- Do the on-site resident directors and other program staff have sufficient expertise and experience to operate the program in this location? Are the resources available to the field staff through the main office adequate in case of emergency?

- Does the sponsor possess general and any necessary specific liability insurance coverage needed? When was this insurance policy last reviewed? What is covered and what specifically is excluded from the coverage? Are the amounts of the policy in line with recent costs and jury awards?

- Does the sponsor have a written risk assessment and emergency response plan?

Student Issues

Good Practices addresses a number of student issues, including establishing specific health, safety, and behavior criteria for selection of student participants, developing student conduct codes and criteria for dismissal from the program, and requiring all participants to have appropriate insurance.

Participant Screening

Disciplinary and Behavioral Issues. Programs abroad regularly try to screen potential participants for past behaviors that indicate an unwillingness to follow rules and social norms. Disciplinary problems that have surfaced on the home campus often intensify overseas. Campus-based program sponsors are generally able to work with the campus office of judicial affairs to obtain information about a student's disciplinary status. Permission to access a student's academic and campus judicial records can also be given by the student as part of the written application to the institution's program. Typically, institutions require that students be in good academic and disciplinary standing in order to participate in study abroad programs. For example, an institution could have a policy that sets minimum academic and disciplinary eligibility requirements, and states that students who, in the judgment of the director of education abroad or dean of international education, do not meet these minimums will not be allowed to participate. The program or the on-campus education abroad office should continue to monitor each applicant's academic and disciplinary record up to the time the students depart. The person doing the monitoring should be aware that students who have committed disciplinary violations, depending on the nature of the offense, often have had very successful education abroad experiences under the auspices of "behavioral contracts." Behavioral contracts stipulate behaviors to which a student must adhere while abroad in order to remain on the program.

Health Issues. Reports in the *Chronicle of Higher Education* and elsewhere note that U.S. undergraduates are arriving at college with more medications and diagnoses, especially for mental health issues, than ever before (Kadison and DiGeronimo 2004, Duenwald 2004; a search of back issues of the *Chronicle* for 'student health' and 'mental health' yielded over 60 stories from January 2002 to January 2005). Education abroad administrators must consider students' health issues when discussing program options with potential applicants. Whether these health issues can be part of an admissions decision to a particular study abroad program is a matter to be discussed with campus legal counsel and the campus Americans with Disabilities Act (ADA) compliance officer. The program wants to be reasonably assured that students are physically and psychologically able to fully participate in the chosen study abroad program; however, that determination must be made within the boundaries of U.S. higher education law.

One way for programs and institutions to be able to make use of a student's health information without violating a student's legal rights is to have a two-part admissions process. In part one, the student is admitted to study abroad but not placed in a particular program abroad. Part two, placement, follows after the program has received a health information form that provides a full account of the student's physical and mental health and concludes with a declaration of appropriate health, signed by the student. If a student has medical conditions, disabilities, or other limitations that may affect full participation in a study abroad program, the student should certainly disclose this information in advance of program participation. The program administrator then can work with on-campus and overseas contacts to further define what the student's needs are, and can arrange, to the extent possible, for reasonable accommodation at the study abroad site, if the student so requests.

Unfortunately, there will be some students who for any number of reasons will not report their physical or mental conditions accurately or honestly on their health questionnaires, and who will still sign certifying that they are in good health and can handle the physical and mental demands of the overseas experience. This presents a dilemma that will need to be addressed through policies discussed and developed by the relevant campus offices, including education abroad, student services, health services, counseling services, and university legal counsel. At issue here is the question of who has the responsibility and the authority to decide that a student has the mental and physical health required to participate in the program—the student or the program's sponsor or a physician? In order to avoid having to make medical decisions without a medical license, some programs require the student to have a physical examination by a physician. Others have contracted with physicians to review medical and health information that students self-disclose and then make recommendations to the program's sponsor about the suitability of individual participants. In cases where it is still not clear whether a student's health or medical condition will affect his or her participation in the program, the program can always ask the student for permission to contact the physician or therapist, or with appropriate advice from legal counsel, require the student to obtain a release from a physician.

Student Conduct Codes and Participation Agreements

To a large degree, the considerable nonacademic benefits of a period of education abroad are related to students' personal growth and development into thoughtful, responsible adults. For many participants, the education abroad experience is their first opportunity to function as independent persons—away (indeed, often far away) from family and, often, from lifelong friends. For these reasons, education abroad can be intimidating. At the same time, the existential challenge of living alone in the world, the responsibility of making scores of daily decisions which have, until now, been made on one's behalf by others, the liberation of leaving behind people and institutions who know who one is, what one has done, and what's good for one all contribute to the thrill and excitement of being on one's own.

For most undergraduates, the freedom of the education abroad experience—the challenge to make independent decisions about their schedules, their diets, their dress, and their behavior—reaffirms the years of training and education about life that they have previously experienced. A few students, though, break with their prior lives and experiment with becoming someone entirely different. Neither extreme is wrong. Having the opportunity to test oneself in the atmosphere of independence that surrounds education abroad is usually a very positive experience. Experienced program administrators are alert to the external and internal forces that influence student behavior, and are prepared to address difficulties or manifestations of extreme experimentation as they arise. Programs abroad function most successfully when participants, their families, their home institutions, and the program sponsors understand and accept, as suggested in *Good Practices*, responsibility for their respective roles.

Students need to informed, and then reminded, in writing, of the level of personal responsibility each of them must assume for their individual safety and security and for that of the others in the education abroad group. No matter whether the program spans only a few days, a few weeks, or an entire year, its effective operation depends on the participants' understanding, acceptance, and exercise of personal responsibility. The opportunity to help students understand the interaction between their acceptance of responsibility for their individual decisions and the program's (or the host institution's) policies and regulations is one of those important "teachable" moments in students' lives. Having voluntarily placed themselves outside their normal environment, they now have an opportunity to examine the relationship between their individual impulses and desires, and local cultural and social norms.

Students participating in education abroad programs should each receive a copy of the program's code of conduct, which they should be required to date and sign, certifying that they have read, understood, and agreed to it. This document is often part of a handbook which includes policy statements sanctions, and procedures regarding such issues as sexual harassment, alcohol abuse, illegal drug use, technology abuse, motor vehicle use, residence life, and academic responsibility. The constitution of review panels, hearing boards, and judicial authority should be clearly delineated. The code should also contain language that gives the program the right to dismiss students if, in the judgment of program administrators, the students' behaviors present a danger to themselves or others, or will sully the image of the program, or if they are unable to fulfill the essential duties of a student (such as going to class). (Examples of conduct codes and participation agreements can be found in *Abroad by Design* (Lamet 2002) and in the Education Abroad Knowledge Community area on the NAFSA Web site).

Verifying Health Insurance Coverage

Insurance is an excellent way to manage risk by ensuring that, in the event of an injury or illness, the participant will have the financial means to obtain proper medical care. It is worth noting, however, that the risks associated with many health issues and diseases are better managed by changing behavior than by insurance. While health insurance will help a student obtain the means to recover from malaria; a good mosquito repellent and the appropriate medicine may well prevent a student from contracting the disease.

Prior to departure, the program (or program's sponsor) should verify that each student has comprehensive health insurance that is valid overseas. Program sponsors may wish to establish minimum coverage amounts, and also determine whether participants (and staff) should be required to have additional insurance for medical evacuation and for repatriation of their remains. Many education abroad insurance plans currently available include all three. Recently, a number of education abroad program providers, and some U.S. colleges and universities, have made it mandatory that participating students purchase an insurance policy that the program has selected. This practice eliminates the need to verify student insurance coverage and ensures that all students are adequately insured while abroad. However, it may require students who are already insured to purchase duplicate coverage. Program sponsors should discuss with legal counsel the advisability of identifying or requiring a specific policy or coverage.

Everyone should pay particular attention to the exclusions of their particular policies (i.e., things not covered under the insurance policy) prior to planning and participating in an education abroad program. Some program activities (e.g., participation in water-related activities) are often excluded from insurance coverage. Even if the country where students will be studying offers or requires participation in the national health care plan, it is still important for students to maintain health insurance coverage that will cover them outside of the host country in case they are injured while traveling or while in transit. In addition, students should be advised to carry or maintain insurance that will cover them in their home country in the unlikely event that they may need to return for long-term care or convalescence.

Recently, some program sponsors have discussed the advisability of identifying and vetting on-site care providers of physical and mental health care. At the very least, however, programs should provide participants with a list of local physicians, clinics, and hospitals that will treat foreign students. Overseas colleagues can offer valuable advice regarding reputable health care providers in the host country. However, program administrators should consult with their institution's legal counsel to determine which approach to health insurance coverage and identification of health care providers abroad corresponds to their interpretation of the institution's responsibilities.

Orientation and Training

Comprehensive Predeparture Orientation

Providing students with a comprehensive orientation before they leave the home campus is one of the most important means of avoiding potential crises. In addition to whatever academic preparation students participate in, they also need preparation for the cultural, religious, and ethnic differences they should expect to encounter off campus, and some discussion of appropriate ways of interacting with local people and their culture. At a minimum, predeparture orientation programs should cover personal safety and security issues, health and medical issues (including medical insurance), and cross-cultural communication and adjustment. Information specific to the host country culture and academic system should also be provided. Every orientation program should also address issues such as alcohol and drug use, which are governed by specific home-campus policies. It is particularly important to review the home-campus and program policies, their enforcement while off campus, and the range of consequences and sanctions that will follow a violation. Showing the students a video can reinforce the seriousness of the issues discussed. Both Big World, Inc., and the Institute for Shipboard Education have produced videos with the title, *Safety and Study Abroad* (Darrah 1999, Institute for Shipboard Education 2003), specifically to cover these issues for students participating in education abroad.

Part III: Program Development, Campus Management, Marketing, and Evaluation

Students should be informed ahead of time about how they can access support resources on the home campus while overseas. Programs should consider providing students and families with a laminated wallet card with the contact numbers (office, home, cellular, fax, e-mail) of the home-campus education abroad office, as well as those of the leadership team of the program overseas, for use in case of an emergency. In addition to discussing these topics in an orientation program, the program should give every participant written copies of the material in a predeparture packet, in an effort to assure that all participants are as thoroughly prepared as possible before they leave campus. It is also a good idea to provide the students' families with copies of all of the essential materials given to the students. (See Part II, Chapter 7, "Predeparture Orientation and Reentry Programming," for a more thorough discussion of predeparture preparation.)

Arrival Orientation

The value of holding an orientation at the education abroad program site is tremendous. Here, the students have an immediate context in which to apply the information they have been given about the host country and culture. Before they arrive at the program and can see things for themselves, students who have never traveled out of their home state may not be able to fully appreciate issues of safety and security in a foreign country. (And sometimes it is even more difficult to talk about these issues with students who have considerable international experience as tourists.) Arrival orientations can provide a review of all program policies, practices, and procedures, as well as information that may be common knowledge to local residents but may not be immediately apparent to students, such as host country laws that differ from those in the United States (particularly in relation to drug and alcohol use), and how to develop street smarts in the new country and city. When the participants are physically in the foreign context, it is much easier to discuss with them specifics about what neighborhoods to avoid, where to go to fill prescriptions, the closest medical facilities, interacting with local police, etc. The best person to facilitate this on-site orientation is someone with local knowledge and expertise. Distribution of local emergency contact information, in a form such as wallet cards, should be done at this time. These cards should provide information about how to contact local advisers, site directors, and the equivalent of the '911' emergency number.

Information and Expectations

As part of the management of student and family expectations, program sponsors need to be very clear about what the program abroad can provide and what it cannot. Programs that are located in large metropolitan areas will be able to refer students to more resources than a program that spends most of its time traveling through the rural areas. Although one might think that which services can and cannot be provided would be evident from the description of the program, it is better not to leave this to chance. A clear statement of what students can expect and what they will have to do without will go a long way to ensuring that students will make truly informed decisions about their participation, as well as guard against the "you never told me" syndrome. Clarity is even more vital when it comes to informing students, families, and other stakeholders about those things over which the program has absolutely no control. Again, it might seem self evident that an education abroad program would have no control over an airline; but if the program includes air travel (or even requires that the students travel by air to join the program), someone may assert that the program has

Chapter 6: Maximizing Safety and Security and Minimizing Risk in Education Abroad Programs

a certain responsibility in that area. A clear and unambiguous statement in the program's materials or participation agreement stating where the program's responsibility ends and where the responsibility of others, including the student participants and their families, begins can save the program a lot of trouble in the long run. Sponsors should consult legal counsel in drafting such a statement.

Communication

Communication takes two forms. On the one hand (as discussed earlier), program sponsors need to stay in regular communication with all stakeholders, but especially with participants and families, with regard to health, safety, and security issues at the program location. On the other hand, programs should develop a communications plan to be used in case of emergencies or a sudden change in circumstances at the program site. The issue of when to notify parents that their child has been injured or hospitalized is a case in point. Because most student participants in education abroad are at least eighteen years old, and thus adults in the eyes of the law, the Family Education Rights and Privacy Act prohibits the program from disclosing certain information to anyone without the student's written permission. While full extent to which universities will be affected by the Health Insurance Portability and Accountability Act [HIPAA] is still being assessed, the American Council on Education (ACE), the National Association of College and University Attorneys, and the American College Health Association, to name only three associations, all have HIPAA related information available. Because program administrators never want to be in the position of saying to parents that they cannot tell them anything about the health of their child while she is overseas, sponsors may wish to include language in the participation agreement, or draft a specific release, that gives the sponsor or program permission to release health information to parents, or other designated individuals, if the participants are not able to do this themselves. The release can also set a threshold for the circumstances under which information would be shared, such as in the case of hospitalization, serious or life threatening injury, or any other situation that, in the program sponsor's judgment, requires the release of health information.

In addition to establishing a communication plan, program sponsors should consider how they would use the newest communication tools. Recent technological developments have made planning and communication much easier than in the past. Students and families are used to having instant contact with each other and with their home institutions through the use of the internet, cell phones, e-mail, and other communication tools. Education abroad professionals can use these tools to their advantage when maintaining emergency contact lists, records of itineraries, and medical files, and in meeting basic communication needs.

Staying in Touch with Participants

Some institutions have chosen to provide cell phones to their off-campus program participants. This is a relatively inexpensive and reliable means of communication, and it assures that all students at least begin the program with the ability to keep in touch. If a program employs on-site advisers or directors, implementing the use of local cell phones should be relatively easy. In many areas of the world, it is common for locals to use cell phones. The purchase of calling cards or SIM cards (subscriber identity module) for international standard GSM phones is straightforward and inexpensive. Requiring students to carry cell phones allows families and administrators can contact participants in the event of an emergency. It also provides students and advisers with a ready way to access local authorities, institutional resources, and families, in the case of an emergency. The disadvantages of having the students purchase cell phones locally after arrival include the cost to the student and the fact that the program will not have the students' phone numbers ahead of time. However, there is no question of whose phone it is and who is responsible for the charges.

When the program's sponsor provides cell phones, the sponsor may be able to take advantage of volume purchasing to guarantee affordable rates. Program administrators will have the phone numbers before the students leave campus (or in the case of an overseas program providing phones, when the students arrive). These numbers can be entered into various emergency lists and shared with those who may need to contact the students in an emergency. Students are accessible during travel before and perhaps after their program begins, and they will have a way to make emergency calls during any extracurricular travel as well. (Worchester Polytechnic Institute is an example of one institution that has successfully instituted a cell phone policy for its programs abroad.) Cell phones are not a panacea, however. While they can be a communication lifeline in the case of an emergency (and true emergencies are rare), such an easy link to home can also become an impediment to intercultural communication and, thus, to cultural integration.

The advent of reliable Web-based programs and off-the-shelf database products has made recordkeeping much easier for the education abroad administrator. Having a single repository of information that is accessible on the Web from the office, from home, and from abroad eliminates the need to duplicate paper records. At some institutions, students, staff, and faculty can complete a single online form to inform the institution of their international travel plans. (The University of Michigan employs this type of Web site.) Data for each participant, including travel itineraries, health records, scanned copies of passports, on-site addresses and local phone numbers, cell phone numbers, and emergency contact information is kept in a secure database, permitting access only to those people who need this confidential information. Other education abroad programs have staff enter the data, which is then available on a private network or a password protected Web site. When considering this type of communication tool, education abroad administrators should talk with university legal counsel about the consent forms that will be needed from the participants. They will then need to develop a policy that specifies who has access to what information, in order to protect everyone's privacy and yet guarantee that those who need the information in an emergency will have access to it. A determination is also needed on how the program sponsor would access this information in the event of an emergency that precluded access to the computers and databases that are normally used. There should always be a backup system.

A further advantage of a database of participant information is that these can be easily downloaded to a laptop computer, PalmPilot or other personal digital assistant (PDA). A handheld device is easier to carry around than several folders of paper records. Emergencies rarely occur during business hours. Having student records and databases reliably available at all times is key to responsible program administration. With a battery operated handheld device, one does not have to rely on having electric power, working phone lines, or access to a computer or the internet.

Interaction with Campus Security

As indicated earlier in this chapter, education abroad administrators should take advantage of the professional expertise, training, and experience available on their campuses by collaborating with other offices and departments that share their concern for student welfare. Since 1990, federal law in the United States has required that this collaboration take place in the area of safety and security reporting. The Jeanne Clery Disclosure of Campus Security Policy and Campus Crime Statistics Act (2003), known as the "Clery Act", was named in memory of Jeanne Clery, a student who was murdered on her university campus in 1986 (Security on Campus, Inc. 2003). The U.S. Department of Education's statement on this requirement says, in part, "Campus security and safety is an important feature of postsecondary education. The Department of Education is committed to assisting schools in providing students nationwide a safe environment in which to learn and to keep students, parent and employees well informed about campus security. The Department is committed to ensuring that postsecondary institutions are in full compliance with that Act, and enforcement of the Act is a priority of the Department" (Code of Federal Regulations 34 CFR 668.41-48).

While the Clery Act requires that an institution's annual report to the Department of Education includes information and statistics about crime occurring on property that they own abroad (e.g., a branch campus), the Department of Education has not issued a definitive ruling about reporting of incidents on other properties abroad leased, rented, or otherwise controlled by U.S. universities. Some U.S. institutions include statistics for these properties in their reports; others do not. Education abroad administrators will want to check with their campus security department and university legal counsel regarding their campus policies.

Even if a campus chooses not to include overseas statistics in its report, the campus may be willing to track crimes, accidents, and injuries that occur during the program abroad. These data are not only useful in the compiling the yearly safety and security assessment of the program, but they also provide education abroad professionals an opportunity to work with the office responsible for Clery Act reporting, typically the security office. In the course of such interaction, numerous areas of common concern and potential collaboration may well be discovered. The expertise and resources available to security offices can often be usefully applied to the conduct of safety and security reviews at overseas sites. Some U.S. campuses actively involve their security directors or private security firms in inspections and reviews of the education abroad sites for which they are responsible. Both U.S. and overseas offices benefit from this type of collaboration. The overseas staff gain from having an objective and trained professional review their activities and environs and make recommendations, and campus-based education abroad staff benefit from the increased understanding of their objectives and activities that comes from the firsthand involvement of security officials. The Security on Campus, Inc. Web site has a number of materials related to campus safety, as well as a useful campus safety and security "tips and evaluation" brochure.

EMERGENCY PREPAREDNESS AND RESPONSE

Responsible education abroad program administration requires that offices and individual administrators think through the types of emergencies that can arise when people are put in

Part III: Program Development, Campus Management, Marketing, and Evaluation

unfamiliar situations in locations where they most likely cannot communicate well with those around them. Many of the emergency response protocols used by education abroad program providers are rooted in work done in the field of college student affairs. Added to the work of education abroad professionals' on-campus colleagues, however, are numerous elements unique to the overseas context.

Before taking a closer look at emergency preparedness and response, the terms used in such a discussion must first be defined. For the purposes of this discussion, "emergency" is used to refer to an event that threatens the health, safety, or security of someone associated with the education abroad program. Emergencies are typically divided into two types: perceived emergencies are situations where there is no direct threat or harm to anyone associated with the program; actual emergencies are situations where there is a real, credible, direct threat to someone associated with the program. Three additional terms are also used here: "incident," "emergency response plan," and "crisis." An incident is the event or action that triggers the emergency. An incident can be an injury (i.e., an accident, defined here as an undesired or unexpected event that results in injury or loss) or a near miss (defined here as an accident or injury that almost happened). All emergencies (both perceived and actual) require a response, and thus should be the subject of an emergency response plan. A crisis, on the other hand, is an emergency for which there is no plan.

Emergency response plans and protocols must be specific enough to provide real guidance to whomever is working through the cover all of the possible types of emergencies that may befall students: serious accident or injury, epidemics, psychiatric emergencies, suicide attempts, emotional health problems, disruptive behavior, psychotic behavior, eating disorders, crimes against a student not including sexual assault, sexual assault, crimes committed by a student, report of a missing student, and death of a student. Then there are those emergency situations that may affect all of the education abroad programs in a country or region, or perhaps all those sponsored by a specific institution, such as political, economic, and social crises, terrorism, toxic spills, fires, natural disasters, coups, or injury or death of a program abroad leader. Throughout the development of emergency response protocols, consideration must be given to how best to respond to the immediate needs of the student or students directly affected, the needs of other program participants, the needs of families and friends, the needs of the program staff abroad and at home, the needs of the sponsoring institution, and possibly, the needs of the media and the needs of the sponsor's defense attorney. In addition, the emergency plan should have a section that deals with serious violations of institutional policies (e.g., alcohol and drug abuse, sexual harassment, academic dishonesty). The program emergency response plan for campus-based program providers needs to be tied into the general emergency response plans and the emergency response team on the home campus. The overall goal of emergency preparedness and response protocol is to provide an effective plan of action that has been thought through and practiced. Every program staff member should be prepared to respond to all emergencies that can occur in the context of an education abroad program. Ideally, the emergency response plan will serve to remove or minimize harm to program participants, their families, the sponsor, the staff, and the program.

Three excellent resources should be consulted when designing an emergency response plan: *Good Practices* (noted earlier in this chapter), the Health and Safety Resources maintained in the Education

Abroad Knowledge Community area of the NAFSA Web site, and the NAFSA publication *Crisis Management in a Cross-Cultural Setting* (Burak and Hoffa 2001).

Emergency Preparedness Planning

Most U.S. institutions of higher education have a protocol or set of procedures to deal with emergencies on campus. Before an education abroad program is launched, specific contingency plans must be developed that tailor the institution's emergency preparedness plan to the program site abroad. The academic director or program sponsor should compile contact information for the U.S. consulate or embassy, other program sponsors in country, local resource people, medical providers, and other emergency response information specific to that country. In addition, the academic director or program sponsor should identify one or more adults who can take charge of the students in the event the program or academic director is incapacitated or "incommunicado." Campus-based administrators should receive copies of all on-site resources. Likewise, the campus-based administrators should share with their academic directors a list of campus resources and support services. The exchange of on-campus and program site phone numbers for work and home, e-mail addresses, and Web site information should facilitate communication twenty-four hours a day and seven days a week.

The established communication network must accommodate the distances, time zones, and complexities of international communication. The campus-based education abroad administrator and members of the campus emergency response team may find themselves on call during the middle of the night in the United States, and should anticipate ways to contact one another or other key decisionmakers in the event of an emergency during nonworking hours. It may be necessary to develop alternative methods of communication in the event that phones and electricity (and therefore computers) are unavailable or not working during a crisis at a program site. For example, the School for International Training in Vermont encourages its academic directors to use cell phones, satellite phones, preorganized land/water transport of messages, and/or local colleagues as communication partners as part of its emergency planning.

Planning for emergencies that may occur on an overseas studies program includes preparing and training program participants. As discussed previously in this chapter, site-specific health, safety, and security issues should be thoroughly discussed during predeparture orientation meetings and on-site orientation sessions. Students should be aware of host country laws, customs, and resources prior to their departure, and should review them again on site. Known risks and hazards must be shared with students upon arrival at the program site. A communication tree among students and the academic director or program staff should be established, using land phones, cell phones, e-mail, and/or a common meeting place for rapid exchange of emergency messages. Students should provide to the program sponsor or academic director emergency contact information and itineraries and dates of their independent travel during the program.

Parents and guardians should be aware of the possible risks of study abroad, and the safety measures in place in the event of a crisis. They should be fully informed about the student's program choice so that they can determine if it lies within the family's threshold for risk. Parents and guardians should discuss their student's travel plans that may be independent of the program. Ideally, at least one parent or guardian should have a current passport, in the event of an emergency when it may be necessary for a parent or guardian to travel to the program site on short notice. Parents and guardians and students must confirm that their health insurance covers services rendered to students while overseas. Parents and guardians may want to purchase medical evacuation insurance for the duration of the student's travel, if it is not provided by the program. They may also want to check on their property insurance policy to determine if it covers valuables such cameras and computers that may be lost or stolen overseas. Parents and guardians must exchange contact information with their child prior to departure, so that they can get in touch with one another in the event of an emergency at home or abroad. The same information may be shared with the student's home institution as part of the institutional preparedness protocol.

Developing an Emergency Response Plan

In preparing for off-campus emergencies, education abroad administrators who are campus based should first work with their home campus colleagues to learn more about the emergency procedures employed on campus. These procedures can provide the foundation for education abroad emergency preparedness protocol. Information about key decisionmakers, legal standards adopted by the institution, criteria used to differentiate between real and perceived emergencies, communication networks on campus and with students and parents, and offices that provide support to those dealing with an emergency needs to be collected. (See also Grey 2003.)

The education abroad emergency protocols should be a logical and appropriate extension of the institution's on-campus procedures. The decisionmakers for on-campus emergencies often include the academic dean or provost, the dean of students and other student affairs staff, health care providers, counselors, education abroad administrators, and in some cases, the president of the institution. They will be instrumental in working with program sponsors and academic directors to make decisions pertaining to off-campus and education abroad emergencies. The response to an emergency typically begins with an initial contact. Following this contact, a small group of people on campus, sometimes referred to as the "first response team" or the "core crisis management team," work through the various steps in the emergency response plan. The first response team may consult other campus staff as needed—counselors or medical providers for health advice, campus counsel for legal advice, or the provost or president for decisions affecting the entire college or university.

Elements of the Plan

While the specifics of an emergency response plan will vary according to the nature of the program abroad and the type of institution or organization that sponsors it, these plans typically contain the elements depicted in Figure 1.

Emergency Response Team

Emergency response teams typically consist of a leader, who serves as point person, and a first response or core crisis management team on campus or at the program provider's office. The leader can be someone in the education abroad office or provost's office, the dean of the college, or another senior administrator. The first response team should include decisionmakers such as representatives from academic affairs, the business office, student services health services, counseling services, facilities

Chapter 6: Maximizing Safety and Security and Minimizing Risk in Education Abroad Programs

management, the chaplain's office, campus security, and the office of communications. The structure of the team should make it very clear who has the final authority and responsibility for decisions made in the course of working through the plan.

When the education abroad office or the program director is notified that an incident has occurred, whoever receives the call informs the team leader, who then makes the initial decision of whether this incident should be designated an emergency (either real or perceived), and whether to put the emergency response plan in effect. The team leader designates a monitor and also briefs the other members of the first response team on the incident. As they work their way through the steps of the emergency response plan, the team considers all aspects of the incident and calls upon other on- and off-campus colleagues for information and advice as they make decisions. Campus resources include university legal counsel, public relations and security staff, a medical officer, the insurance specialist, and international deans or staff. Other resources available in the United States are the U.S. Department of State, the U.S. Centers for Disease Control and Prevention, reliable travel agencies, and legislative offices.

Depending on the degree of autonomy of the program abroad, program sponsors may want to consider assembling an emergency response team at the program site. Like their on-campus counterparts, the team could call on local resources, medical providers, consulate or embassy offices, and other

---

Figure 1. Typical Emergency Response Plan
Statement of guiding or operating principles
- Introduction
- Definitions and distinctions (e.g., real versus perceived emergency)
- Procedures

A. Emergency Reporting	B. Emergency Response
Determine real or perceived	If a perceived emergency
☐ Gather information	☐ Non-acute emergency response
☐ List of general questions to ask during information gathering phase	If a real emergency
Make chronology of events	☐ Acute emergency response
☐ Assess specific situation	Special case: death of participant or staff
List of specific questions for	
Serious illness — Arrest	
Serious injury or accident — Hostage situation	
Physical and sexual assault — Political emergency	
Robbery or break-in — Natural or man-made disaster	
Missing person	

- Composition and duties of the emergency response team
- Communication plan
- Appendixes
  Staff and home-campus contact information
  Program's contact information
  U.S. Department of State telephone numbers and pertinent Web sites
  U.S. embassies and consulates telephone numbers and addresses
  Decision tree

education abroad organizations in the host country when responding to an emergency. However, for liability reasons, U.S.-based program sponsors may prefer to have only one emergency response team, located at the program's main office. Regardless of the whether or not the program decides to form a response team at the program site, resident directors and staff abroad should be included in the development of and training for implementation of the emergency plan.

Emergency Reporting

The most critical aspect of any emergency response plan is the obligation to write everything down at the time it is said or done. This contemporaneous reporting can prove crucial to an investigation of the incident and can also be used in court to show that the education abroad administrator did indeed follow his or her organization's established emergency procedures. It is also very important that a member of the emergency response team be designated in the plan as an emergency response plan monitor. The monitor's role is the check off the steps of the plan as they are accomplished, and to remind the emergency response team about what is next. The monitor should be someone other than the team leader, as the leader will be busy carrying out the required steps of the plan.

Guidelines for Media Inquiries

If the emergency catches the attention of the media, education abroad administrators can expect to have cameras and reporters in their offices in no time. Therefore, it is very important to plan how to work with the media *before* an emergency occurs. Ideally, the existing campus or institutional emergency plan will have a media plan. If not, then it is the education abroad administrator's responsibility to develop a plan for working with members of the press and other media representatives. At a minimum, program administrators should identify a spokesperson for the program, and assemble a press kit that contains background information on the program and the sponsoring institution, a map showing where the program is located in relation to other major landmarks and cities, the program's goals, and additional relevant information on the program's location. A program administrator's approach to dealing with the media and releasing information should be worked out with senior administrators and university legal counsel long before an incident occurs. "No comment" does not play well with the media, and can lead to suspicion of a cover up (Hardt 2000). See the sidebar in this chapter, titled "When a Reporter Calls."

Decision Trees

A decision tree is a useful tool in emergency response planning, in that it provides a "highly effective structure within which you can lay out options and investigate the possible outcomes of choosing those options." A decision tree starts from the decision to be made and then looks at possible outcomes of that decision. Because it clearly lays out the problem so that all options can be challenged, a decision tree can help education abroad administrators fully analyze the consequences of a decision, including guesstimates of the costs involved (Mindtools 2004). Combined with a list of information sources, a decision tree can help program administrators make informed decisions under extremely trying circumstances. However, to be used effectively, this strategy, like all parts of the emergency response plan, must be considered and practiced in advance.

Chapter 6: Maximizing Safety and Security and Minimizing Risk in Education Abroad Programs

Practicing the Plan

A well-trained staff is key to the successful implementation of any emergency response plan. Both on-campus staff and program staff abroad should be trained on a variety of scenarios, ranging from innocuous perceived emergencies to worst cases with multiple fatalities. Everyone involved should be clear about his or her responsibilities under the plan. Institutions that organize their own overseas programs, and staff them with their own faculty, should provide a comprehensive handbook to all resident directors who are abroad with the students. Programs may want to consider developing a companion Web site, or putting the handbook and emergency materials in a personal digital assistant, or other handheld tool, to provide faculty directors quick access to information they may need while abroad. It is also important to continue with regular meetings with faculty directors before departure in order to review health, safety, and emergency information and address other issues of concern.

If the campus is drilling the larger emergency response plan, ask to have the education abroad emergency response plan included. Other opportunities to practice emergency response can be taken from news reports of world events, which can be developed into critical incidents. Apply the emergency response plan to the critical incident and determine which aspects work and which need to be improved. By using an actual situation to practice the plan, program administrators can access all of the information sources required by the plan, and use real information to formulate their responses.

Finally, all training should emphasize the fact that program directors and staff are not alone in the field, if and when an emergency arises. The numerous resources, both on campus and overseas, are but a phone call or e-mail away, and stand ready to assist the program director during an emergency.

Former SECUSSA chair Mickey Slind, Institute for Study Abroad, Butler University, offers a number of useful suggestions for how to handle media queries in her tip sheet, "When a Reporter Calls" (1997), reprinted here with permission.

When a Reporter Calls

- Take control; don't answer questions until you're ready
- Note the reporter's name, affiliation, and phone number
- Ask what the story is about
- Find out the reporter's deadline
- Define the role you'll play in the story
- Suggest other sources
- Set ground rules for the interview: subject area, time, place, duration
- Pick an interview site that is convenient and comfortable for you
- Call your university news service for assistance
- Regard the interview as an opportunity to tell your story or to make your points
- Remember your audience is the public, not the reporter
- Decide what you want the public to understand about the subject
- Pick one or two points you want to make
- Keep your language simple, as though you were explaining to a neighbor
- Avoid jargon
- Prepare relevant examples and analogies
- Make notes for easy reference
- Prepare a list of probable questions and short, concise answers
- Collect material that will help the reporter understand the story

Continued...

Part III: Program Development, Campus Management, Marketing, and Evaluation

Implementing an Emergency Response Plan

Once an emergency preparedness plan has been developed, tested, and drilled, it is ready for implementation in the event of an emergency. In order to effectively implement an emergency response plan, program administrators need to take the following actions:

- Ascertain the nature and extent of the emergency. Reliable and accurate information regarding who and what is involved in the incident is essential for an effective response.

- Address the immediate needs of those involved. Instructions to all program staff should include taking the steps necessary to separate the affected individual or individuals from the situation, with particular emphasis on responding first to those who might be in life-threatening situations. To address those needs, program administrators need to have identified their resources in advance of the crisis so that they can use the resources as necessary. Minimally, these resources should include a list of overseas medical facilities, health contacts in the United States, contact information for country-specific U.S. embassies and consulates, emergency medical and repatriation services, and a list of U.S. and overseas legal counsel.

- Establish an emergency communication center and a reliable means of communication. Information about whom to call at which numbers should be part of the plan.

- Rehearse with someone you trust
- If possible, tape the interview so you can catch your own errors before they're part of the permanent print or broadcast record
- If a reporter asks you to comment off the record, decline. Assume everything you say in an interview will appear in the story
- Don't wait for the reporter to ask the "right question." Make your main point early and often
- Be concise; you will be less likely to be quoted out of context if you are clear and concise
- Make sure you understand each question
- If a question contains erroneous information, don't let it slide. Correct it
- Don't evade questions. If you don't know the answer, say no
- Never lie
- Beware of hypothetical questions; don't be pressured into speculating
- Don't ask or expect to approve the story before it is printed or broadcast
- Review your tape; if you misspoke, call the reporter with corrections or clarifications
- Be available for follow up; encourage the reporter to call back with other questions or for clarifications
- Ask others what they thought of the story
- If the story has major errors, don't let anger or embarrassment rule your response
- Call the reporter to correct errors in the story; uncorrected errors get repeated as fact in follow up stories
- If other reporters call you, use the new contact as an opportunity to correct any errors or misperceptions.

Chapter 6: Maximizing Safety and Security and Minimizing Risk in Education Abroad Programs

- Call the emergency response team together.

- Maintain good documentation throughout the emergency. Detailed and accurate written information is needed from the moment of first notification of the emergency through its resolution (see "Emergency Reporting"). Gather and document all facts, decisions, and actions, indicating who, what, where, when, why, and how. Note the time and date of everything, especially communications, phone calls, meetings, and instructions given to staff. Memory is not sufficient to retain this information. Contemporaneous written records will be needed in case of a review and investigation of the incident, and also if there is a lawsuit.

- Notify relevant parties. During the confusion and chaos of an emergency, it is easy to forget people not directly affected by the incident. Ideally, the emergency response plan will identify who should be contacted when, and what they should be told. The family of the student or staff member, and a contact person on the student's home campus, should be on the list. Staying in close and regular contact with families during an emergency may alleviate the kinds of frustration that often lead to lawsuits. Likewise, it is important to communicate with the other student participants on the program. The details of a briefing schedule for participants should be part of an emergency response plan. Depending on the nature of the emergency, it may be appropriate to provide students access to telephones, assist in arranging for transportation home as necessary or requested, offer counseling as needed, and conducting postcrisis follow-up.

- Create a media response plan as part of the emergency plan (see "Guidelines for Media Inquiries"). The media are quick to develop interest in any situation involving a crisis abroad. Therefore, programs can expect to get calls from reporters and others shortly after an incident occurs. A well-planned media response should include a press kit, fact-based statements; simple but not vague statements; a request for confidentiality when applicable (but do not ever expect that the media will keep things off the record); a designated spokesperson; avoidance of legalistic language and "no comment" responses; discussion of what is known; prompt replies to media inquiries; and a proactive stance with information (Hardt 2000).

- Program administrators should remember to take care of themselves and their program staff. Be sure that everyone gets sufficient rest and regular meals and lots of fluids.

- Conduct a postemergency follow up and re-evaluation. At the conclusion of a crisis, a sense of relief can lead to complacency. However, follow-up and evaluation are critical to ensure that the information learned from this particular situation can be used to make improvements to the program and also to the emergency plan.

The postemergency follow up may need to address posttraumatic stress in both program participants and program staff. Even though a person's physical well being may be secure and the events have passed, students, and also those indirectly involved in a crisis, can experience posttraumatic stress syndrome. The emergency response plan should include provisions for participants or staff to consult mental health professionals or counselors during and following the emergency. Maintaining contact between the program sponsor and affected students, family members, relevant institutions, the media, and constituents can aid in the crisis recovery process. Program sponsors may also want to consider a program of Critical Incident Stress Management (CISM), which includes critical incident stress debriefing (for more information contact the campus health services office or Web site of the International Critical Incident Stress Foundation). Following the resolution of a crisis, the emergency response team should gather all of the information related to events leading up to the emergency, the incident itself, the actions of all involved, and the resolution of the emergency. It is always useful to go back and examine the causes to determine what, if any, changes should be implemented to prevent a similar situation from occurring. In some cases (e.g., natural disasters), prevention measures are limited, but there may be improvements to be made in the response. In addition, the team should assess the effectiveness of its response and discuss the various aspects of the emergency response that did or did not work. Soliciting feedback from those affected by the crisis, both directly and indirectly, will help in the ability to plan the most effective emergency response plan in the future.

Paying for Emergencies and Response

Ideally, money should not be a factor in either the response to or resolution of an emergency. However, there are always financial costs, including medical care, transportation, hotels, meals, phone bills, staff overtime, and more. Obtaining adequate insurance coverage for both the program sponsor and participants in advance of the education abroad program is very important. Decisions about finances and financial limitations for responding to emergencies should be made as part of developing the emergency plan. Ideally, either the program or the program's sponsor will have established an emergency or reserve fund. In calculating the amount of money that should be in such a fund, one should estimate the cost of a worse case scenario (e.g., an incident that requires that the program abroad be terminated before the students have completed any academic work, but too late for them to enroll in courses on the home campus; there can be no recovery of any money spent abroad and the program will have to purchase new one-way return air tickets for the group) and then double that amount (Brockington 2000).

Suspending or Canceling a Program Abroad

It is an unfortunate fact of modern life that few education abroad professionals will escape having to wrestle with the question of whether to suspend or cancel a program abroad, or just wait and see if things get better. Because of modern news reporting and the availability of these reports around the clock on television and on the internet, anxious family members may be the first people to contact the program or the program's sponsor within minutes of the report of a serious incident near the program site. The decision to cancel or suspend a program

Chapter 6: Maximizing Safety and Security and Minimizing Risk in Education Abroad Programs

should not be made lightly, but should remain one of the options available in every emergency response plan. In this context, "cancel" means to close down the operation of the program for an unspecified period; "suspend" means to halt the operation of the program temporarily, for a specified duration. The emergency plan should also include a list of events and actions that would trigger a discussion of possible cancellation or suspension of the program, as well as the information sources that will inform the decisionmaking process. The list might include such things as the following:

Information sources

- Program staff in the host city and country
- University officials at the partner university
- U.S. embassy or consulate officials in the host country
- Other officials from U.S. agencies and nongovernmental organizations
- The appropriate U.S. Department of State country desk officer
- The foreign ministries of other countries that have a number of their citizens in the host country
- The education abroad office's own assessment of the events in the host country

Presenting events

- Declaration of war by the United States against the host country or an adjacent neighbor
- Declaration of war by a third country against the country of the program's location
- Significant terrorist activity in the program city
- Protracted or indefinite closure of the university
- Inability of the local staff to organize and carry out an academic program outside of the university
- Disruption of public utilities and/or services
- Widespread civil unrest, violence, or rioting
- A declaration of martial law in the program city
- Recommendation of suspension or cancellation by the local program staff in the host country
- A travel warning or specific directive by the U.S. Department of State, or the local U.S. embassy or consulate

Program sponsors will have to decide whether any of these events and actions is sufficient by itself to cause the cancellation or suspension of the program abroad. Some university risk managers, university legal counsel, and insurance providers apply a very strict interpretation of announcements and warnings issued by the U.S. Department of State. The U.S. Department of State provides an explanation of its materials (i.e., travel warnings, announcements, and consular information sheets) on the Bureau of Consular Affairs Web site.

Using a decision tree when considering the implications of a decision to cancel a program abroad can help education abroad professionals identify all of the potential financial consequences (e.g. the loss of credit for the students; the need to either refund the program fee or provide alternative courses; the cost of transportation from the program's location; and the cost of housing, tuition, and staff salaries at the program) as well as the potential nonfinancial ones, (e.g., loss of face with the host institution and with peer institutions in the United States; damage to long-term personal, professional, and institutional relationships in the host country; damage to relationships with the U.S. consulate or embassy abroad; damage to relationships with program and university alumni; and loss of income to local vendors and staff whose livelihood may depend solely on the program).

The emergency response plan should also include provisions for students who wish to withdraw from the program because they are upset by emergency circumstances at the program location. By offering students and their families a well-thought-out plan, with a clear description of the financial cost and academic consequences of an early departure, program sponsors can avoid creating a potentially hostile and frustrated relationship with the student and the student's family, which all too often can end in a lawsuit.

Finally, no matter what the circumstances are for the visiting U.S. students during the time of an emergency abroad, program sponsors and home-campus education abroad professionals must remember that things are generally much worse for the local people who will continue to live in the country after the emergency has passed. They will appreciate the understanding, kindness, and consideration of the program administrator as he or she works through the emergency plan.

Resources Related to Safety, Security, and Emergency Preparedness

Education abroad professionals have access to many resources to aid them when working on safety and security issues, assessing risks, designing risk management strategies, and developing emergency response procedures. Resources provided through NAFSA: Association of International Educators include professional practical workshops and sessions on health, safety, and security in education abroad programming, held at regional and national conferences. The NAFSA *Code of Ethics* provides a benchmark for education abroad professionals to measure their actions (NAFSA 2003). The Education Abroad Knowledge Community Health and Safety Committee of provides direction to the education abroad community regarding best practices for dealing with events that may impact the health, safety, and security of U.S. students abroad, through their collection of resources on the NAFSA Web site and the education abroad e-mail discussion list, SECUSS-L. When world or regional events affect the health, safety, or security of U.S. students abroad, both the Health and Safety Committee and the Interassociational Advisory Committee offer counsel and practical suggestions to the profession, through the Education Abroad Knowledge Community area of the NAFSA Web site and over SECUSS-L. Among the many other books and Web-based resources available, the NAFSA publication, *Crisis Management in a Cross-Cultural Setting* (Burak and Hoffa 2001), is particularly useful to education abroad administrators.

Education abroad professionals who work on college or university campuses should also contact their colleagues with expertise in handling a wide variety of student emergencies. Student affairs administrators are experts in dealing with emergencies affecting individual students and entire residence halls. Counseling and health service staff may be willing to put on a workshop for education abroad staff and study abroad participants (both prior to their departure and after their return from study abroad). And education abroad professionals should not forget the campus risk management office and university legal counsel, as well as the media relations office. The list of people on campus who can assist the education abroad office and its staff in crisis prevention and crisis management is as long as the university's phone directory. Remember, in an emergency, the education abroad staff are not alone.

Summary

This chapter offers guidance on risk management, safety and security issues, and emergency response. It discusses how education abroad administrators can use *Good Practices* in administering education abroad programs. Program sponsors should take into account the unique nature of their programs, the location abroad, and the context of their particular institution when assessing risk and developing emergency response plans. It is important to approach crisis management and emergency preparedness from the standpoint that one size does not fit all. Once program protocols and procedures have been established, they should vetted by university legal counsel and then drilled on a regular basis. Finally, education abroad professionals do not need to operate alone in developing crisis management and emergency response protocols. During the last several years, the education abroad field has developed a significant number of resources that enable program professionals to construct plans that suit the needs of their particular institution or organization. These resources represent information and professional expertise that allow education abroad administrators to construct, deploy, and evaluate an effective crisis management and emergency response plan.

CHAPTER 7

Legal Issues and Education Abroad

Contributors: Gary Rhodes, Robert Aalberts, William Hoye, Joseph Brockington

Editor's note: This material has been prepared for educational and information purposes only. It does not constitute legal advice. In order to address specific legal issues that arise, readers should consult legal counsel.

Among the many paradoxes of modern life is the perception (especially in the United States) that we are surrounded by great risks and threats, even though the world is far safer in many ways than it has ever been (Ropeik and Gray 2002). Advances in medicine, disease control and prevention, public health, and communication technologies; revolutions in technology (particularly in computing and communications); and improvements in product safety and reliability have greatly increased both life expectancy and the quality of life for many United States residents. However, these advances and improvements have also led to an increased perception of danger and risk. New political threats in the form of regional conflicts and international terrorism have replaced those of the Cold War. New diseases such as SARS and AIDS have likewise taken the place of old ones; new technologies and products have created new dangers and risks. Moreover, despite the myth that institutions of higher education are ivy-covered sanctuaries of learning, where students, professors, administrators, and staff are united as an academic community in their quest for knowledge and truth, "college education is filled with potential safety risks for students" (Bickel and Lake 1999), as well as for faculty and staff.

We live in litigious times. U.S. citizens tend to react to risks and the negative consequences that too often result from them by filing lawsuits. We want to fix blame and assign responsibility; we want someone to pay for the losses we have suffered. When we combine the many, varied, and complex risks typically present on a college campus, with a foreign location, and then mix in 20-something-year-old students, we have a situation that, from a legal standpoint, could cause sleepless nights, if not worse. Fortunately, there have been relatively few reported court decisions involving higher education institutions and their abroad programs over the years (Hoye and Rhodes 2000). This does not mean that there have been no problems, but rather, for a variety of reasons, that they have not been publicized or have not otherwise caught the attention of the media. In addition, a number of cases have been quietly settled out of court. But where trouble can exist, sooner or later, it will be found. As a result, it behooves education abroad advisers and administrators to become ever more aware of potential legal liability and risk, and, through prudence and planning, to take proactive steps to help minimize institutional risk while reasonably protecting students from foreseeable harm.

Whether the potential injury or loss comes from an accident, an act of nature, a political crisis, social chaos, or other forces, students who participate in education abroad programs face a number of inherent risks and dangers (real and potential) to their health, safety, security, and general welfare. (See Part III, Chapter 6, "Maximizing Safety and Security and Minimizing Risk in Education Abroad Programs.") But natural catastrophes or political strife are not the only problems that can result in legal action. In point of fact, the litigation that has recently been bedeviling colleges and universities has centered less on physical injury or death than on a host of contractual matters: disability discrimination, sexual harassment, admissions standards and criteria, student misbehavior and appropriate discipline, misunderstandings over the nature of the academic program, disagreements over what is included in the program fee, and other more mundane (but to students and parents, essential) details. It may be easy to dismiss such risks by noting that, according to statistical data, equally grave risks can be found on any university campus (or in any city or town) in the United States. Unfortunately, however, relying on statistics alone for protection not only can put lives at risk but can also expose the institution to the considerable time, expense, and damage to its reputation that litigation involving an international program can engender.

SOME BACKGROUND ON U.S. HIGHER EDUCATION LAW AND ITS IMPACT ON EDUCATION ABROAD

Education abroad does not exist separately or apart from the legal context in which all of U.S. higher education operates. U.S.-based colleges and universities are subject not only to a wide variety of U.S. laws from local, state, and federal jurisdictions but also to regulations issued by a myriad of state and federal agencies. Moreover, there can also be a great difference in how various laws and regulations apply to public, as opposed to private, institutions. When one adds to these domestic laws those of the foreign governments in the locations where a university operates education abroad programs (or even has students participating in a program sponsored by another institution), the legal situation is enormously complex. While a comprehensive treatment of the laws and regulations of the many foreign locations of U.S. education abroad programs and students is beyond the scope of this chapter, the chapter can offer a general overview of the application of some key U.S. laws and regulations to education abroad.

Few if any of the laws and regulations under which education abroad programs operate were developed specifically with overseas study in mind. Thus, it is important for education abroad professionals to get to know and develop a collaborative working arrangement with other offices on and off campus. In addition to employing an institutional risk manager or having an office of risk management, virtually all postsecondary institutions now employ legal counsel (either in-house or from outside law firms) who advise them on how to comply with applicable law. These professionals also can help identify, manage, and reduce risk and potential liability.

By becoming familiar with a few general principles of law as they apply to U.S. higher education, and with some of the nuances of what compliance entails, study abroad administrators can be better positioned to make recommendations to university policy- and decisionmakers on issues that affect education abroad students and programs. In addition, administrators can obtain a great deal of knowledge, information, and expertise concerning the issues raised in this chapter from student affairs, academic affairs, and the human resources office. Some colleges and universities also have special offices on campus dedicated to handling issues and questions regarding the Americans with Disabilities Act (ADA) and similar laws and regulations. Remember, even if an institution's students are living and studying a long way away from the campus, they are still students of that institution, and therefore, the institution may retain certain legal duties and responsibilities toward them, and they are still entitled to receive the benefits of the education abroad professional's own professional and ethical duties. While nothing can prevent someone from filing a lawsuit against an institution (or, in some circumstances, against the education abroad professional personally), being prepared for the worst-case scenarios, using proactive risk assessment and preventive law, and doing everything possible to reasonably manage the foreseeable risks of harm, can make an important difference when the case is heard and adjudicated.

Contract Law and Education Abroad

Contracts often regulate the myriad relationships in postsecondary education, from the mundane to the most consequential. Properly constructed, contracts establish, define, and help regulate the legal relationships between the contracting parties, thereby mitigating most problems that might subsequently arise. A contract may involve goods, services, real estate, or a combination of these, and can be written or oral. "University and education abroad administrators should pay careful attention to the negotiation of contracts and the delegation and exercise of authority to enter into them, as well as the faithful and responsible fulfillment of the contract's terms" (Kaplin and Lee 1997).

Some of the complex relationships and issues in education abroad are regulated by contracts, which are often called agreements or memoranda of understanding. Historically, these types of agreements have included few legal terms and have not clearly set forth the specific rights, duties, and obligations of the parties. The university's attorney should be involved in the negotiation of all contracts. When the education abroad office receives draft agreements written by others, it should (1) work with the institution's legal counsel to develop any documents, and then send copies to the university counsel's office for review and approval before they are signed; (2) be absolutely certain that the education abroad office representative has the authority to enter into the contract on behalf of the institution, and that the delegation of authority to the representative is clear.

Enforcement of Authority and Responsibility

Typically, the institution's board of trustees delegates authority for administration of the university to the president. The president, in turn, often delegates to the faculty the authority to set the curriculum of the university, as well as the academic processes, policies, and regulations that define the academic structure. The president delegates administrative responsibility for particular programs, activities, and processes to the administrative officers of those programs. Moreover, administrative procedures, policies, and regulations are under the jurisdiction of specific program directors and administrative officers; and they sometimes specify that these directors and officers have the authority to address violations and impose a range of identified sanctions.

By clearly laying out the delegation of authority and the permitted range of sanctions that can be imposed for a student's violation of an administrative policy or procedure, an institution can avoid having to ratify an administrator's action after the fact (if it chooses to), and administrators know exactly how much latitude they have to operate. Education abroad administrators can use similar language in program handbooks to clearly lay out both their authority to administer the program and their expectations of faculty members, staff members, and student participants in the program.

Contract law also applies to program documents, catalogues, handbooks, and oral statements. Thus, institutions and program administrators should be very careful when making written or verbal claims or assertions about their programs. Promotional language used to describe a program may create an implied contractual relationship. In addition, misrepresentations can lead to potential tort and statutory claims. Programs should avoid promising more than they can deliver, or even appearing to make such an offer, particularly with regard to safety at the program site or at destination during the program. A breach of contract suit can easily result from a student's (or parent's) frustrated expectations. Adding a "disclaimer" to all publications (including Web pages) could sometimes help to reduce the institution's potential contractual, statutory, or tort liability stemming from frustrated or unmet expectations.

A well-settled principle of contract law is that ambiguous or misleading language is construed against the party who wrote it. Materials describing a program should be honest, forthright, and specific in describing accommodations and support services. One way to be clear about potential hidden costs is to include a question about costs in the program evaluation and then listen to what students say, incorporating it into the program's subsequent materials. Cost is often a decisive factor when students choose a program, so all program expenses should be clearly stated, including, for example, side excursions, entertainment, events, and so forth, that require extra on-site money. The waivers and assumption of risk agreements discussed in Part III, Chapter 6, "Maximizing Safety and Security and Minimizing Risk in Education Abroad Programs," are another form of contract. Under the law of most states, informed consent requires that if a program includes high-risk activities such as scuba diving or mountain climbing, the program literature available to students must fully describe the inherent dangers involved. Before asking students to participate in high-risk activities in a study abroad program, the program administrator must carefully evaluate these activities in terms of their contribution to the mission and outcomes of the program. In addition, participants and staff must be appropriately trained and their skill levels assessed, and the risks these activities present must be effectively managed, including giving all participants an opportunity to choose not to participate in that particular activity.

Another contract law issue concerns the relationships with the various parties that supply the program's goods and services. An education abroad program may, for example, contract with a local institution to use its facilities; with local transportation companies for bus or car service for program excursions; with local colleges, universities, and organizations for instruction; and also with travel agencies. The contracts used should state each party's rights and obligations, the schedule and the terms and amount of payment, as well as what will happen in the case of a dispute arising out of the contract. Many contracts also include provisions for early termination.

In the case of a dispute, a contract can be used to clarify each party's responsibilities. For example, a university contracts with a U.S. travel agency for services, and the agency does not provide the agreed upon services. Often, the university itself will be sued first by an aggrieved student plaintiff. If the university must later pay the court's judgment or a portion of it, having a contract clause that states that the travel agency will reimburse or indemnify the university can greatly facilitate the university's ability to recapture the lost monies from the travel agency. Contracts that clearly state which party bears what risks and responsibilities are generally preferable and much more efficient than relying on the outcome of protracted and expensive litigation with an unknown result. It is always a good idea for education abroad programs to have their contracts reviewed and approved in advance by university counsel.

The legal status of a program in its host country can also influence an institution's legal exposure. An education abroad program can take many forms; it may be a joint venture, a reciprocal exchange with a foreign university, incorporated as a foreign corporation under the laws of the host country, or a unit of a U.S. college situated in a foreign locale. Each type of legal status has different potential vulnerabilities and liability exposure for the U.S.-based institution. Investigate various corporate governance models and structures thoroughly before contracts are signed or programs are established. The corporate governance structure of existing programs should be revisited from time-to-time for each of the institution's programs, in consultation with the institution's counsel in the United States, as well as foreign counsel in the host country.

Additional Clauses Used in Contract Law

Among the other legal provisions available in U.S. contract law, three may provide some additional protection to the postsecondary institution forming or establishing an education abroad program (Aalberts and Evans 1995).

Forum Selection

This type of clause in an agreement specifies the legal jurisdiction (usually a state or country) that will provide the setting where any lawsuits arising out of or relating to the agreement must be litigated. For example, for a program in Senegal sponsored by a university in Colorado, a U.S.-based attorney may choose the state of Colorado as the forum where all lawsuits must be brought. This would be specified in the parties' agreement for the conduct or sponsorship of the program. In addition, the waiver forms signed by each student might specify that any dispute must be litigated in the Colorado courts. Without a "choice of forum" clause, the plaintiff might be legally able to sue the Colorado university in Senegal, in the student's home state, or elsewhere. Any venue other than the university's home state can create additional expense for the institution and strategic or procedural disadvantages for the institution in defending itself. In order to be considered a reasonable choice, the venue named in the forum selection clause must be designed to create predictability and efficiency in prosecuting a case. A university's home state will most often satisfy the legal demands of reasonableness.

Choice of Law

A choice of law provision in a contract specifies which jurisdiction's substantive law will apply in any litigation. Using the foregoing example, a university in Colorado would most likely prefer to have Colorado law apply to any dispute. The familiarity and predictability of its own law may be a benefit to the university and its legal interests in defending or prosecuting a case. Without a "choice of law" clause in an agreement between parties in diverse states or countries, very complicated (and expensive to resolve) procedural issues can arise with respect to the law that will be applied by a court to resolve a dispute between the parties.

Alternative Dispute Resolution

Finally, a program may wish to insert into the agreement for an international study abroad program a clause requiring a predetermined alternative dispute resolution (ADR) method to be used to resolve a legal conflict. The most common ADR methods used as alternatives to litigation are mediation (where a neutral third party attempts to facilitate a settlement between the parties) and arbitration. In arbitration, an individual or a panel of arbitrators listen to the parties and make a decision (which can be binding or nonbinding, depending on the terms of the parties' original agreement), and apply the laws of a specified country to decide any contractual disputes. Arbitration clauses generally require the decisions of the arbitrator to be binding on both parties, with very little opportunity for appeal. Arbitration typically brings closure more quickly than does mediation, and provides an opportunity for nonpublic proceedings and for the use of experts as decisionmakers. While the application of a specific state's or country's substantive law is not a necessary condition of ADR, it can be specified in the parties' agreement. ADR is generally quicker, cheaper, and more efficient than litigation. It is becoming the preferred method of resolving disputes in many areas of the law, including securities law, labor and employment law, construction law, and many other areas. There is no reason why it cannot be similarly used to resolve disputes between students and an education abroad program or the program's sponsor.

TORT LAW AND EDUCATION ABROAD

Although contract law is critically important for education abroad programs and their sponsors, issues relating to tort law can have an even greater potential impact on students, faculty members, administrators, and higher education institutions. Simply stated, a tort is a civil wrong—other than a breach of a contract—that results in injury, loss, or damage. Judgments in tort law can bring significantly greater damages than judgments in contract law (which are measured in terms of actual economic or out-of-pocket losses). "A postsecondary institution is not subject to liability for every tortious act of its trustees, administrators, or other agents. But the institution will generally be liable, lacking immunity or some other recognized defense, for tortious acts committed within the scope of the actor's employment or otherwise authorized by the institution or subject to its control" (Kaplin and Lee 1997). Although the university generally will not be held liable for torts (injury or loss) caused by students, in certain instances the institution can be found liable for the actions of volunteers and other nonemployees, under the concept of "gratuitous employee." Moreover, the university's status as landowner and landlord (e.g., of the residence halls) creates an additional source of potential liability.

The following examples illustrate one of the differences between a university's liability under contract law and its liability under tort law. If a court finds that ambiguous language in a program brochure led a student to believe that the program fee included an excursion to Bangkok (when, in fact, after arriving at the program's location, the student learned that there was an extra charge for this trip), the court's judgment in a breach of contract action might award her damages for the dollar value of the trip. On the other hand, if the same student went trekking in the Himalayas as part of the program abroad, got lost, suffered hypothermia and died, and the court rules, under tort law, that the program was negligent (by, for example, not sufficiently warning the student about the foreseeable dangers and inherent risks unique to the mountains in which she was trekking), the court's judgment might award the student's heirs damages running into the millions of dollars. In short, under tort law damages are awarded not only for actual economic losses (such as medical expenses and loss of income) but also for pain and suffering (general compensatory damages). A jury often determines the amount of damages in a tort case; and in many jurisdictions there are no set limits on the verdict a jury may return. Generally speaking, so long as the verdict does not "shock the conscience" of the court, a jury verdict in most jurisdictions will not be set aside as excessive, on appeal.

As with contract law, "public institutions can sometimes escape tort liability by asserting sovereign or governmental immunity" (Kaplin and Lee 1997) as a defense if it is available in the state where they are located and if the court determines that the university is "an arm of the state" rather than a "separate entity." Private institutions cannot claim sovereign immunity, although in certain states "non-profit schools may sometimes be able to assert a limited 'charitable' immunity defense to certain tort actions" (Kaplin and Lee 1997).

Torts of Negligence

While there are many kinds of recognized torts, simple negligence is the source of an increasing number of lawsuits against postsecondary institutions. In a negligence suit, the plaintiff must allege that the injury or loss occurred because the postsecondary institution (or its employees or agents) was negligent in its acts or omissions. In one of the very few reported education abroad cases alleging an intentional tort by a university agent, *Furrh v. Arizona Board of Regents*, 676 P.2d 1141 (Ariz. App. 1983), the University of Arizona and one of its professors were sued (and later exonerated) for the tort of false imprisonment. In that case, the professor of a biology field school had tied up a chronically mentally ill student who risked great physical harm to himself by repeatedly running away from the program's location in the Mexican desert.

The tort of negligence consists of four elements—duty, breach of the duty, proximate cause, and injury—all of which the plaintiff must prove to be successful in the suit. Torts of negligence often turn on the concept of "duty," which, in their book *The Rights and Responsibilities of the Modern University*, Bickel and Lake acknowledge, "can be an elusive legal concept" (1999). A duty is said to exist when the risk in question is deemed to be reasonably foreseeable through the objective eyes of a reasonably prudent person. "In determining whether a legal duty exists, the court may consider whether the harm that befell the individual was foreseeable . . . . the specific event need not be foreseeable, but . . . the risk of harm must be both foreseeable and unreasonable" (Kaplin and Lee 1997).

Bickel and Lake go on to note that the case law of the last two decades of the twentieth century supported the idea that for colleges and universities

> a duty to use reasonable care exists to manage and supervise curricular and co-curricular activities, including internships, externships, field trips, and study abroad. ... Students assume the ordinary and obvious risks of such activities. There is no duty to protect against inherent, obvious, and primary risks of such activities. But students do not assume the risks of (1) reckless or deliberate and intentional behavior compromising safety, (2) hidden (or non-obvious to them) or non-ordinary dangers and (3) that an institution will take a student to a level of risk that the student is not capable of handling without proper instruction and guidance. (Bickel and Lake 1999)

Whether a court holds a university liable for an injury or loss to a student or not in a particular case depends on the facts of that case; however, "courts largely agree on the relevant factors to consider regarding duty and liability: foreseeability of harm; nature of risk; closeness of the connection between the college's act or omission and student injury; moral blame and responsibility; the social policy of preventing future harm (whether finding duty will tend to prevent future harm; the burden on the university and the larger community if duty is recognized; the availability of insurance" (Bickel and Lake 1999).

Many lawsuits by students or others against universities stem from injuries received on campus or at off-campus events. "Although most college students have reached the age of majority and, theoretically, are responsible for their own behavior, injured students and their parents are increasingly asserting that the institution has a duty of supervision or a duty based on its 'special relationship' with the student that goes beyond the institution's ordinary duty to invitees, tenants, or trespassers" (Kaplin and Lee 1999). This relatively new and distinctive duty is particularly relevant in residentially based higher education, and is often viewed by the courts as different from what landlords traditionally owe their tenants. This special relationship duty (based as it is on the foreseeability of harm) might oblige an institution to take some additional steps to limit potential harm to its students, such as increasing security staff and adding lighting and other safety features. Because education abroad programs can be seen as transplanted versions of what happens in the United States, some observers believe the special relationship duty could be viewed by the courts as having an even greater impact on programs abroad, owing to the unique milieu and to student expectations that the participants will be provided a safe environment (Evans 1991).

Arguably, institutional duty–related liability can apply to university-arranged transportation (e.g., if it is negligently selected, even if neither the driver nor the vehicle is part of the university); athletic events; maintenance of buildings, grounds, and equipment; and the failure to prevent the criminal acts of others (including outsiders). With regard to education abroad programs, negligence can take many forms, including problems with program design and support services, lack of preparation for responding to accidents and injuries abroad, and insufficient warnings being given to participants about the natural, social, political, cultural, legal, and other known risks inherent in the foreign environment where the program is located.

From a risk management standpoint, education abroad administrators would be wise to review the safety record and insurance documents of any transportation company the program plans to use, and should obtain and keep copies of those documents for the program's records. Program administrators should also identify and address health, safety, and security problems in academic and residential facilities the program intends to use. A comprehensive risk assessment audit of each university-owned or -operated program is recommended (Hoye and Rhodes 2000). Such an audit will address a plethora of questions, such as whether or not there are smoke alarms and fire extinguishers present and in working order; what the condition of the stairs and windows is; whether the doors lock; and whether the lighting is sufficient. Operating a program in a foreign country often increases the perception or the reality that there are security concerns, ranging from petty crime to serious crime, civil unrest, or terrorism, which must be appropriately addressed. On-site staff should be vigilant in watching for suspicious outsiders. Some programs hire security personnel to guard their premises, as appropriate. Because of the many U.S. Department of State announcements and warnings concerning recent terrorist activities, all students should be encouraged to stay away from known U.S. hangouts, to dress more like locals, and not to advertise their activities. Universities and programs must take care that their program brochures and materials do not paint an overly safe picture of life in the program and at the locale. Their materials need not paint an overly negative picture either, of course. The goal is to be forthright and truthful, and to warn of known dangers. When the program is not in a position to attend to all of the problems identified, then this information should be communicated to the participants and staff, and can become part of the "informed consent" portion of the participation agreement.

Some the writers of legal commentaries, and certainly the parents of students injured or killed while engaged in educational programs on- or off-campus, would like to see a change from the concept of a special relationship duty in the higher education setting, and a return to the much older notion of *in loco parentis* (Kast 1998). In a late eighteenth century commentary on English law, Sir William Blackstone notes that a father "may also delegate part of his parental authority, during his life to the tutor or schoolmaster of his child; who is then *in loco parentis,* and has such a portion of the power of the parent committed to his charge, *viz.* that of restraint and correction, as may be necessary to answer the purposes for which he is employed... *In loco parentis* was thus, in sum, the *delegation* of a *father's* right to *discipline*" (Blackstone 1765). When first applied to U.S. higher education, "*in loco parentis* was not about university *duties* towards student but about university rights and *powers* over students" (Bickel and Lake 1999). Kaplin and Lee note that since the early 1960s, a number of court decisions have either "implicitly rejected *in loco parentis* or stated, quoting the court in the 1993 case of *Nero v. Kansas State University,* 'the *in loco parentis* doctrine is outmoded and inconsistent with the reality of contemporary college life.' The court continued, however, by stating that a 'university has a duty of reasonable care to protect a student against certain dangers' including criminal acts, if these are 'reasonably foreseeable and within the university's control'" (Kaplin and Lee 1997).

Many students (and parents) understandably expect that a program sending students to a location abroad has a unique obligation to protect the participants, who may not have sufficient cultural or general knowledge of the locale to (at least initially) act as independently as local students, who have lived there for years. On the other hand, education abroad is designed to provide students, who are adults, opportunities that do not exist on campus.

Moreover, among the many outcomes of participation in a program abroad is the development of greater personal and intellectual maturity in the program participants. Thus, being overprotective while students are abroad defeats one of the main goals of the program. It is possible, however, to balance these seemingly competing interests. For example, program sponsors can provide information and training in the form of predeparture and arrival orientation sessions, a detailed program handbook, a set of clearly defined rules and behavioral expectations, and a listing of known hazards, dangers, and inherent risks (which might be contained in program materials and in the participation agreement). Having participants acknowledge these risks by giving their informed consent in waivers, releases, and participation agreements is advisable. Comprehensive and careful program planning and operation, as well as admissions screening, can also help.

Breach of Duty and Proximate Cause

Whether or not a legal duty exists is a matter of state common law. "Once a legal duty is found to exist…a court must determine to what standard of care the defendant will be held under the circumstances" (Kaplin and Lee 1997). A typical standard of care for a postsecondary institution would be "reasonable care under all the circumstances" (Kaplin and Lee 1997). If an institution breaches a legal duty, the plaintiff still must prove that the breach of duty was the proximate cause of the plaintiff's injury or damage. For example, when even after several reports to university maintenance, a light in a dorm parking lot is not still not repaired, and a student is subsequently attacked in the dark parking lot, a court is very likely to find that the university had a legal duty to replace the light, in that a reasonably prudent person should have foreseen an attack on a student due to the lack of lighting. The next question for the finder of fact will be whether the breach of the legal duty proximately caused the plaintiff's resulting injury or damage. If the court concludes that the student would not have been injured if the light had been repaired, then the element of proximate cause will have been satisfied. If, however, the fact finder was to conclude that the unforeseeable criminal conduct of a third party (the attacker) proximately caused the student's injury, then the university would likely not be held liable. At home or abroad, the prudent course is a combination of planning and preparation, choice of appropriate locations for program activities, choice of appropriate program providers and partners, notification of inherent risks and dangers, orientation training conducted by the program, and informed consent provided by the participant in the form of a waiver and release.

Assumed Duty

With regard to an institution's duty to its students, it is also important to point out that some actions that the university might take to control or prohibit inherently dangerous behavior and activities of its students can actually increase the level of duty the university owes to them. With regard to a hazing case (*Furek v. University of Delaware*, 594 A.2d 506 (Del. 1991)), the "court determined that the university's own policy against hazing, and its repeated warnings to students against the hazards of hazing, 'constituted an assumed duty'" (Kaplin and Lee 1997). Thus, a university's pervasive regulation of a dangerous activity can create a legal duty. For education abroad programs, this underscores Butcher's maxim of "don't adopt policies, procedures, or practices that you can't or won't enforce" (1999).

The concept of assumed duty is particularly apropos when programs and universities deal with student alcohol consumption. "Surveys have found that alcohol is a factor in most incidents leading to injury or death of students or campus visitors. For example a survey of claims by an insurer of a national fraternity between 1987 and 1991 showed that 86 percent of all fatalities, 86 percent of injuries resulting in paralysis, 72 percent of the serious injuries reported, 88 percent of psychological injuries, and 97 percent of reported cases of sexual abuse involved alcohol use" (Kaplin and Lee 1997). The court's ruling in a 1981 case from Pennsylvania, *Bradshaw v. Rawlings,* 612 F.2d 135 (3rd Cir. 1979) determined "practicality prevented the imposition of a legal duty on the college to control student drinking. The prevalence of alcohol consumption on the modern college campus would make compliance with such a duty almost impossible, and the use of alcohol by college students is not so harshly judged by contemporary standards as to require special efforts to eradicate it" (Kaplin and Lee 1997). Despite this ruling, many states have "social host" laws that may hold the institution or its agents liable for loss or injury stemming from student drinking. Because U.S. students have an all-too-well-deserved reputation for consuming excessive amounts of alcohol while abroad, the issue of alcohol merits serious conversation among education abroad administrators, program directors, university counsel, risk management, and senior decisionmakers. Another challenge when it comes to alcohol policy is that most undergraduate students participating in study abroad are under 21 and thus cannot legally drink alcohol in the United States. When they are abroad, however, they are suddenly of legal age. This can result in problems with alcohol abuse as well as conflicts between local laws and the program's policies.

Duty and Standard of Care in the Context of *Good Practices* and NAFSA's *Code of Ethics* and the Statement of Professional Competencies for International Educators

In addition to providing guidance for the practice of the profession in education abroad, *Responsible Study Abroad: Good Practices for Health and Safety* (hereafter referred to as *Good Practices*; 2003) the *Code of Ethics* (NAFSA 2003), and the Statement of Professional Competencies for International Educators (NAFSA 1996) could also be viewed as setting a standard of care that education abroad professionals owe to their students, program staff, colleagues (at home and abroad), and institutions. While the *Code of Ethics* and the Professional Competencies are directed at all international educators (although the Professional Competencies also lists qualifications by area of specialization), *Good Practices* applies solely to education abroad.

First published in 1998 and revised in 2002, *Good Practices* is the product of the Interassociational Advisory Committee, made up of representatives from the Council on International Education Exchange (CIEE), NAFSA, the Association of International Education Administrators (AIEA), and the National Association of Student Personnel Administrators (NASPA), and includes representatives from other groups in international education. In addition to describing responsibilities of students and their parents, *Good Practices* also describes what steps program sponsors and providers should undertake with regard to their role in the education abroad experience. The operative term in relation to individual or institutional duty is the word "should." (Similarly, the *Code of Ethics* says that NAFSA members "shall" or "have the responsibility to" act in an ethical manner.) As this volume goes to press, neither the contributors nor the editors of this guide know of any published case in the United States that cites *Good Practices*, the *Code of Ethics*, or the *Professional Competencies*. One could reasonably expect, however, that some attorneys might attempt to use them as examples of a standard of care applicable to an institution or program sponsor.

Programs Sponsored by Others

Typically, U.S. universities allow their students to participate in education abroad programs sponsored by other U.S. institutions, foreign universities, consortia, and other independent operators based in the United States or abroad. In these cases, the university's education abroad office generally serves as a resource center for information about these programs, which raises the question of the extent to which (if at all) an institution has a duty with regard to these programs. Although this is an admittedly undeveloped area of the law, aggrieved parties are frequently encouraged to go after any and all parties whose actions they believe may have contributed to their injury or loss. To manage this potential risk, the institution and the education abroad office need to have a clear policy concerning how education programs are approved for transfer of credit, the criteria by which this decision is made, clarification of who has the authority to make the decision, a statement of the limits of liability that the university is willing to assume, and finally an agreement with the student in which the student (after informed consent) assumes all remaining risks. Some institutions place a disclaimer on program materials and other publications from third parties, clearly stating that the student's home institution does not sponsor these programs. Because of the great variation among U.S. universities in the policies and procedures that govern how their students can participate in these programs, this is a matter that should be taken up with university counsel on each campus.

Federal Laws and Regulations and Education Abroad

Since the mid-twentieth century, the U.S. government has used its constitutional powers extensively to regulate and fund higher education, creating many new legal requirements and new forums for raising legal challenges. Students, faculty, staff, and third parties have become more willing and more able to sue postsecondary institutions and their officials. Courts have become more willing to entertain such suits on their merits and to offer relief from certain institutional actions (Kaplin and Lee 1997). What is less clear is the extent to which U.S. postsecondary institutions can be held accountable for violations of federal laws that occur outside the borders of the United States in connection with study abroad programs sponsored in whole or in part by U.S.-based higher education institutions.

Among the many federal laws and regulations that might have an impact on the operation of an education abroad program are the ADA, Section 504 of the Rehabilitation Act of 1973 as amended, Title IX of the Education Amendments of 1972 (Title IX; governing gender-based discrimination), and the Family Educational Rights and Privacy Act of 1974 (U.S.C. §1232g) (FERPA). While a full treatment of the implications that these and other federal laws and regulations have for education abroad is beyond the scope of this chapter, several issues do warrant mention in this context.

The ADA and Section 504 prohibit discrimination on the basis of disability in admissions and recruitment. The ADA and Section 504 statutes and enabling regulations define disability as "a physical or mental impairment that substantially limits one or more major life activities" (42 U.S.C. §12102) of an individual; and the definition of impairment includes "contagious diseases, learning disabilities, HIV (whether symptomatic or asymptomatic), drug addiction, and alcoholism" (36 C.F.R. §104). "The ADA specifies ten areas in which colleges and universities may not discriminate against a qualified individual with a disability: eligibility criteria; modifications of policies, practices, and procedures; auxiliary aids and services; examinations and courses; removal of barriers in existing facilities; alternatives to barriers in existing facilities; personal devices and services; assistive technologies; seating in assembly areas; and transportation services. And also accessibility issues for new construction or renovation of existing facilities" (Kaplin and Lee 1997). A central provision of ADA and Section 504 prohibits discriminating against otherwise-qualified disabled students in admissions decisions. (A 1979 Supreme Court Decision, *Southeastern Community College v. Davis*, 442 U.S. 397 (1997) ruled that an "otherwise qualified" individual is one who is qualified in spite of (rather than except for) the disability (Kaplin and Lee 1997). In the workplace, this is often taken to mean that the disabled individual is able to perform the "essential function" of the position (National Center for Educational Statistics (NCES) 2003), and some universities have carried this over to define an otherwise-qualified student as one who is able to perform the essential function of a student. Moreover, colleges are not required to admit disabled students if to do so would require a substantial modification of standards or fundamental alterations in the nature of the program, although they may be required to make reasonable accommodation. The effect of ADA and Section 504 on education abroad programs is very much in flux.

Nearly every U.S. postsecondary institution most likely has an administrator who is responsible for monitoring the university's compliance with ADA and Section 504 laws and regulations. It is important for education abroad administrators to consult with the ADA officer or the institution's legal counsel on a regular basis, and especially when designing or considering new education abroad programs.

The antidiscrimination requirements of Title IX likewise should be of special interest to education abroad program administrators. Title IX is probably best known as the statute designed to remedy gender discrimination in both academic and athletic programs in higher education. Title IX also protects students from sexual harassment (another form of gender discrimination), whether it is perpetrated by a faculty member, a staff member, or another student. Most U.S. postsecondary institutions that receive federal funds have a designated Title IX compliance officer.

In a 2002 case, *King v. Board of Control of Eastern Michigan University*, the U.S. District Court for the Eastern District of Michigan, Southern Division directly answered the important question of whether Title IX applies outside of the United States (221 F.Supp.2d 783 [2002]). The setting of the *King* case was a program in the Republic of South Africa, sponsored by Eastern Michigan University. Fifteen students, nine women and seven men, were enrolled in the program initially. Eventually, however, nine students left the program early, including six of the women. They subsequently filed a lawsuit alleging that three male students, one of whom was the assistant to the program's director, sexually harassed them. The issue of whether or not the women were in fact sexually harassed was not ultimately resolved, because the case was settled shortly after the court ruled that Title IX does apply extraterritorially to the programs of a college or university. The narrow issue addressed by the court in its decision in *King* was whether a federal district court could exercise subject matter jurisdiction over a case in which the purported violations of Title IX occurred in a foreign country.

The university's argument was that federal statutes are presumed to apply only within the territorial borders of the United States. To overcome this presumption, the university contended, the plaintiffs were required to present evidence that Congress intended otherwise. (The relevant provision of Title IX to this case provides that, with only limited exceptions such as in the case of single sex institutions, "No person in the United States shall, on the basis of sex, be excluded from the participation in, be denied the benefits of, or be subjected to discrimination under any education program or activity receiving Federal financial assistance..."(20 U.S.C. §1681 *et. seq.*). Not surprisingly, the university defended itself by arguing that the words, "No person in the United States," meant the incident must arise within the United States, while the six plaintiffs focused their attention on the words, "under any education program," which they asserted meant that Title IX protected them in this or any other program sponsored by Eastern Michigan University. In the end, the court sided with the plaintiffs, relying on two important characteristics of Title IX. The first was that Title IX does not expressly exempt study abroad programs and in fact is very broadly worded so as to avoid exempting any educational programs. Second, the court concluded that Title IX was created to be remedial in nature, and remedial statutes are to be read broadly in order to advance the statute's purpose. The court found that the legislative history of Title IX indicated a strong desire by its chief sponsor for the law to be "broad" and "far-reaching" as well as to be a "strong and comprehensive measure." (221 F.Supp.2d 783 [2002]).

Indeed, in the end, the court made it very clear that Title IX is intended to be a strong measure for remediating gender discrimination in connection with educational programs and activities, wherever it may occur. Moreover, in a strong endorsement of protecting students participating in foreign studies, the court explained that "[S]tudy abroad programs are an integral part of college education today," and a "denial of equal opportunity in those programs has ramifications on students' education as a whole and detracts from their overall education" (221 F.Supp.2d 783 [2002]). According to the court, if a university's students are protected in their on-campus or domestic off-campus programs from gender discrimination and sexual harassment, the same protections should apply to a university's students studying for credit or participating in an endorsed program abroad. Note, the *King* case is only legally binding in the Eastern Federal District of Michigan. However, these issues are certain to arise again, and the *King* case provides useful guidance to colleges and universities.

With regard to issues of sexual harassment, the *King* case offers university and education abroad administrators an opportunity to consider taking a number of proactive steps, including the following:

- The education abroad office should be familiar with the university's own policies and procedures regarding handing sexual harassment allegations.

- When the education abroad office or its representative receives a complaint of sexual harassment, even if it comes from someone other than the alleged victim, the office should notify the proper university office and be prepared to investigate it promptly and as discreetly as possible. Education abroad administrators must also be prepared to take swift appropriate action to protect the rights of both the victim and the accused.

- Faculty and staff taking students abroad must be oriented to the institution's sexual harassment policy. The participants should know that the program administrator will investigate every complaint and that he or she will try to preserve confidentiality. The program staff must be informed about how and to whom complaints should be reported under the policy and how quickly they must be reported.

- As part of the university's and the program's emergency response plan, a separate plan for dealing with a reported case of sexual harassment abroad should be included.

- Program administrators should review institutional sexual harassment policies to make sure they can reasonably be applied in a foreign setting. For example, does the policy specify who will investigate complaints of sexual harassment at off-campus locations? Does the policy provide for what happens if the alleged harasser is the only university employee on the trip?

- Ideally, the university's sexual harassment policy will designate which office or administrator is responsible for investigating complaints or who has the authority to make that decision. If this is not the case, education abroad administrators should clarify this point before the beginning of the program abroad.

- Students should be provided with the institution's and the program's policies in advance of their arrival at the program abroad, and informed about how and to whom complaints should be reported, both abroad and on the home campus.

- Program administrators should consider developing a policy and procedure for those students leaving the program early due to actual or alleged sexual harassment, which addresses such matters as refunds, credit, and grades, and enrollment issues.

- Programs should consider including in their participation agreements language, that allows students to be dismissed from the program and sent home, if, in the judgment of the program's leader or other designated institutional administrator, the students have violated institutional rules or policies, pose a danger to themselves or others, or behave in a manner that disrupts the academic program or causes harm to the institution's reputation. The policy should also address matters such as the procedure for such an action, appeal, refunds, credit, grades, and enrollment issues (i.e., does dismissal from the program mean dismissal from the university).

FERPA, or the Buckley Amendment, and its enabling regulations establish requirements pertaining to "(1) students' right of access to their education records…; (2) students' right to challenge the content of their records…; (3) disclosure of 'personally identifiable' information to personnel of the institution or to outsiders…; (4) the institution's obligation to notify students of their rights under the Act and regulations …; and (5) recourse for students and the federal government when an institution may have violated the Act or regulations" (Kaplin and Lee 1997). FERPA covers all current and former students at U.S. postsecondary education institutions, regardless of their age and their status as dependents. Given the extensive breadth of FERPA coverage of students' education records, defined as "documents containing information related to a student that are maintained by an educational agency" (20 U.S.C. §1232g(a)(4)(A)), education abroad administrators should take advantage of FERPA expertise on their campuses when creating or reviewing policies and procedures that make use of the information in student records, and should also have a copy of both the campus FERPA policy and the regulations themselves close at hand.

The FERPA definition of education records includes letters of recommendation that are typically part of an application packet. Many programs have added a FERPA release to their recommendation forms, which gives students the opportunity to either waive their FERPA rights for this one document, or not. This also signals to those providing such letters whether their comments will be completely confidential between themselves and the program, or whether the student will also have access.

Student disciplinary records raise other FERPA issues. On some campuses, FERPA is interpreted so narrowly that these records cannot be shared with other campus offices without a specific release from the student, while on other campuses, program directors are allowed access to disciplinary records. Without access to an applicant's campus disciplinary records, the education abroad office runs the risk of sending a student to a program abroad whose on-campus behavior is deplorable. If this same student were to cause an injury to another program participant while abroad, the home campus would be in an untenable position, having allowed one office to permit a student to enroll in a program because it was prohibited access to information that another office on the same campus had in its files. Including a release of records as part of the student's application for education abroad is one way for the education abroad office to assure that it has access to the records it needs to make admissions decisions. Adding another release to the student participation agreement, one that allows the program to share information on disciplinary infractions (especially those involving alcohol) with parents and appropriate on-campus offices, will ensure that the program remains in compliance with FERPA. (Although recent FERPA rulings do allow colleges to contact parents when their students have violated campus alcohol policy, having a signed release removes all doubt from this action.) Lastly, departing students should be advised that FERPA requires the college's registrar to have a signed release on file in order to be able to send out transcripts to accompany the student's application to summer internships and jobs, scholarships, graduate schools, and so on.

Finally, although there are certainly many other federal requirements that in one way or another affect education abroad programs, there is currently an ongoing discussion among education abroad professionals, senior higher education administrators, staff at the U.S. Department of

Education, and other interested parties with regard to the applicability of the Jeanne Clery Disclosure of Campus Security Policy and Campus Crime Statistics Act (20 U.S.C. 1092(f)) to education abroad and other international programs sponsored by U.S. educational institutions. Named in honor of Jeanne Clery, a student who was murdered on her home campus in 1986 (Security on Campus Inc., 2003), the Clery Act requires all U.S. colleges and universities to collect and publish campus crime statistics and the institution's security policies annually. As with other federal requirements, each campus has designated an individual or office to monitor that campus's compliance. For the Clery Act, this is typically the campus police or campus security office.

At issue for education abroad programs are the definitions of "campus," "non-campus building or property," and "branch campus" under the Clery Act, and whether any or all of these terms apply to facilities U.S. colleges own, lease, or rent overseas, either for program activities or as accommodations for students participating in the program. In September 2000, several members of NAFSA's Section on U.S. Students Abroad (SECUSSA, as the Education Abroad Knowledge Community was then known) national team talked with representatives of the U.S. Department of Education about how Clery Act reporting requirements apply to U.S. postsecondary institutions that sponsor education abroad programs and to universities that have students studying abroad on programs sponsored by other U.S. and non-U.S. institutions. Both parties came away from the meeting with a better understanding of the issues and the knowledge that this was only the first of many meetings before the reporting requirement for education abroad is completely clarified.

In the meantime, however, some universities and program providers are collecting and reporting crime data for their programs abroad using the Clery Act rubric. Others are collecting the information, but have decided not to make it public. As noted in Part III, Chapter 6, "Maximizing Safety and Security and Minimizing Risk in Education Abroad Programs," it is time for education abroad administrators, sponsoring institutions, and program providers to consider how to collect not only crime statistics, but also information on injuries, accidents, and near misses, so that as a profession and educational enterprise we have a more accurate picture of the risks involved for U.S. students, professors, and staff when participating in programs overseas. This will not be an easy task. Any statistics collected will need to have comparison data on the incidence of similar crimes, injuries, accidents, etc. in the program's foreign locale, in order for this information to be useful. It will not be very helpful to compare the incidence of crimes against program students in London with that of the students' home college location in a small town in the United States. Despite these difficulties, it is time to begin working on the development of a consistent and coordinated approach.

THE POTENTIAL PERSONAL LIABILITY OF EDUCATION ABROAD ADVISERS AND ADMINISTRATORS

The personal liability of postsecondary education administrators, faculty, and staff falls into the same categories as institutional liability. Of particular interest to education abroad professionals, program directors, and faculty is the potential personal liability that may come from contracts, torts, and federal statutes. There is really no protection against being named in a lawsuit. Anyone whom a plaintiff believes is even partially responsible for an injury, loss, or damage can be sued. That does not mean, however, that a court will find the individual defendant liable. In order for liability to be found, the individual named as a defendant must have acted unlawfully or tortiously, or breached the contract. Many colleges and universities will provide a defense to their employees and pay resulting damages, as long as the individual employee was acting within the scope of his or her employment. This is a matter of each college's or university's policy, and there are often important differences in this regard between public and private institutions. Proper planning and following institutional procedures are key to mounting a legal defense if an education abroad professional is personally named in a suit.

Personal Contract Liability

In the course of their duties, education abroad professionals will sign any number of contracts, admission letters, agreements, memoranda of understanding, and the like that bind their institution or program to a certain course of action. "The extent of personal liability depends on whether the agent's participation on behalf of the institution was authorized—either by a grant of express authority or by an implied authority, an apparent authority, or a subsequent ratification by the institution" (Kaplin and Lee 1997). As with institutional contract liability, the delegation of authority to act on behalf of the institution is central to an individual's defense against personal contract liability. "If the individual's participation was properly authorized, and if that individual signed the contract only in the capacity of an institutional agent, he or she will not be personally liable for the performance of the contract" (Kaplin and Lee 1997). Without proper authorization, however, there may well be personal liability under some circumstances. For this reason, it is always important to verify one's authority to sign or enter into agreements on behalf of the institution, and to make sure that the institution's legal counsel drafts or reviews and approves all agreements in advance of signing.

Personal Tort Liability

In some circumstances, an individual faculty or staff member whose actions cause injury, loss, or damage under tort law may be named as a defendant in a lawsuit, or even held personally liable, even if the tort was committed while acting as a duly authorized agent of an institution. However, "the individual must actually have committed the tortious act, directed it, or otherwise participated in its commission, before personal liability will attach" (Kaplin and Lee 1997). Moreover, as noted above, many colleges and universities insure and defend their employees, at the institution's expense, for activities undertaken within the scope of their employment, as long as the employee did not engage in intentional, willful, wanton, grossly negligent, or reckless conduct. One employee cannot be held personally liable for the torts of another, merely because they are both agents of the same institution. However, an institution's potential liability does not provide relief for an individual's liability. As noted above, the authority that has been granted to the employee to act on behalf of the institution is often one of the central elements of a defense against a personal claim.

Thus, it is vital that campus-based education abroad administrators and advisers, as well as faculty program leaders and staff members, clearly understand the source and scope of their authority to act on the institution's behalf. Moreover, it is also very important for everyone involved in education abroad to understand exactly what constitutes appropriate and inappropriate conduct or behavior on campus (often formally stated in campus handbooks) and overseas. The NAFSA *Code of Ethics* (2003) and Statement of Professional Competencies for International Educators (1996) also provide guidance, setting forth an appropriate standard of care for education abroad advisers and administrators.

It is important for education abroad professionals to be familiar with their institutions' support mechanisms in the event of legal action. Many institutions purchase insurance policies that cover administrators acting as authorized agents of the institution. The institution's risk manager and counsel are important resources with respect to these issues and with respect to what conduct is and is not covered by the university's insurance and by its internal policies. Whether an employee should have the further protection of a personal liability insurance policy is a personal decision in each individual case and on each campus. Often it is not necessary. However, this question must be addressed in consultation with each particular institution's counsel and risk manager, as well as the individual employee's counsel. The answer often will depend on the employee's position in the institution, whether the institution is public or private, and what the applicable state law and the university policy provide with respect to individual employees' legal liability.

No institution or individual wants to have to go to court, but in the event of litigation, doing so will be far more pleasurable if the employees and agents have followed applicable institutional polices and procedures, and acted in accordance with recognized professional standards.

Other Instances of Potential Personal Liability

Individuals can also be sued for torts such as defamation and libel, as well as violations of federal statutes and regulations (e.g., ADA and Section 504, Title IX, and FERPA, in addition to a host of other possibilities). They are subject to federal laws and regulations in much the same ways as institutions. As institutions seek to comply with the demands placed on them by ADA and Section 504, Title IX, FERPA, and other federal statutes, individuals are the ones who carry out the compliance measures. Thus, even if the alleged unlawful conduct occurs in the exercise of a duly authorized and delegated task, individual administrators, faculty, or staff may not be insulated from a lawsuit or potential legal liability with respect to these or any number of other issues. The best way to manage this risk is to have a clear institutional policy and set of procedures for issues related to these statutes, to adhere to the stated policies and procedures, to document everything, as appropriate, and to have institutional insurance that will cover the cost of most litigation.

Defamation and Libel

Both slander and libel are forms of defamation. They are torts where the injury to one's reputation (which includes not only individuals but also entities such as corporations and academic institutions) results from the publication (i.e., communication) to a third party, in either oral or written form, of false and defamatory information. (See Kaplin and Lee 1997.) In the education abroad field, defamation might become an issue in a number of contexts. When programs sponsored by other institutions (or individuals associated with the program's sponsor) are discussed with students, parents, or colleagues, care must be taken to portray them in a manner that is truthful and accurate, in order to avoid allegations of defamation. The same applies when responding to queries about a program via online or e-mail communication. Thus, when replying to an e-mail query sent to the Education Abroad Knowledge Community e-mail discussion list, SECUSS-L, or elsewhere, education abroad professionals should avoid replying to the entire list if they are voicing a personal opinion about a program or colleague. A factual, truthful, accurate, and considered response only to the person who sent the inquiry or made the telephone call is often a more prudent way in which to communicate negative information. Defamation has also been alleged on the basis of letters of recommendation. This does not mean that education abroad professionals cannot discuss what seem to them to be negative features of programs (including their own) or negative opinions of students or colleagues, but rather that professionals should make sure that before they voice their concerns, their comments are true and accurate, as well as relevant to advising students and in a manner consistent with the NAFSA *Code of Ethics* (2003) and Statement of Professional Competencies for International Educators (1996).

Preventive Law: Risk Management Strategies for Legal Issues

The Legal Audit

The overall risk of potential legal liability, at home and abroad, cannot be managed effectively until individual risks are identified and assessed. The idea behind a legal audit comes out of preventive law, which emphasizes limiting liability and avoiding legal action by taking appropriate prior actions. Simply put, like a financial audit, which determines the financial status of the institution, in a legal audit university counsel and an attorney who practices in the program venue country, along with a risk manager and a local insurance representative in the program venue, carry out a comprehensive health, safety, security and legal compliance review of all education abroad programs currently owned, operated, or sponsored by the university (i.e., those where it leases or owns facilities or employs individuals). The legal audit is a tool to determine what parts of an institution's programs are following a "reasonable and prudent" standard of care, and which areas need to be upgraded to a better standard of care (Hoye and Rhodes 2000).

Brown and Kandel focus on the process as an analysis: "Analysis should be made to detect, within reasonable limits, compliance with the law in the operations of the enterprise including all record keeping and recording requirements. Legal risks are minimized whenever some legal noncompliance is identified and corrected" (1991). The audit basically examines each program against a checklist based on legal compliance and indemnification. It typically includes such items as accreditation, insurance policies, contracts and linkage agreements, advertising and promotion, admissions standards and procedures, emergency response planning, cancellation, student behavior policies and grounds for dismissal, personnel policies, budgets, cash transfers, accounting procedures, student records, consent and disclaimer forms, orientation and predeparture information, and program evaluation procedures.

When completed, the legal audit provides an impetus and rationale for taking corrective and preventive action. A further outcome of the legal audit is a priority list of areas that need immediate, short-term, and long-term action. An example of a study abroad legal audit developed by Gary Rhodes (1994) is available on the SAFETI Web site.

The Risk Assessment Audit

Like the legal audit, a risk assessment audit is a confidential, comprehensive review of key health, safety, and liability issues and conditions of an education abroad program. It involves seven discrete steps (Hoye and Rhodes 2000):

1. A comprehensive review by in-house counsel of policies and procedures from the home campus;

2. A visit to the program's location abroad by a small review team, (e.g. the institutional risk manager, one of the local program staff, in-house counsel, a local insurance representative, and someone from the education abroad office) which includes a walk-through of facilities used by the program to look at local fire, safety and building codes in the venue, as well as applicable zoning laws, ordinances, and overall safety and security issues and problems;

3. Having in-house counsel and the risk manager conduct interviews of program faculty and staff abroad, as well as of randomly selected student participants in the program;

4. A comprehensive review by in-house counsel of local program policies and procedures, with regard to their consistency with policies and procedures on the home campus, their compliance with applicable U.S. law, and, if relevant, with policies, procedures and protocols in place at other programs abroad sponsored by the institution;

5. Review by in-house counsel of orientation, promotional and marketing materials for the program, all forms and program materials provided to participants by the U.S. sponsoring institution or the program abroad, as well as all agreements and contracts the sponsor or program has entered into.

6. Review by local counsel, familiar with higher education in the host country, of the corporate structure, status, governance structure, and operation of the program under the law of the host country, as well as any agreements relating to the program. The review should include a meeting between the local attorney and in-house counsel to discuss these issues is recommended during the site visit.

7. When the review is complete, the review team and in-house counsel should prepare a confidential report for the sponsoring institution's education abroad administrators and other appropriate policy makers. As a confidential document prepared by in-house counsel and only circulated to employees of the institution, it is protected from disclosure by the attorney-client privilege. The report should include an action plan identifying the specific steps that need to be undertaken to achieve identified objectives.

Ideally, the report should also include a follow-up visit to the program abroad by an appropriate administrator from the sponsoring institution, to ensure that the recommendations, the review visit, and the report have been considered and implemented as deemed appropriate and necessary.

While risk assessment audits can be very helpful to an institutional education abroad program, they are not a panacea. They can help identify, analyze, assess, and reduce institutional legal liability but they cannot prevent it entirely. They can enhance program safety but they cannot guarantee the protection of the institution's students, faculty, and staff from harm. They can improve institutional legal compliance with U.S. and local laws, but they cannot prevent an institution from being sued, or stop claims from being filed. In fact, even with a comprehensive risk assessment audit program in place, accidents and injuries will still occur on occasion. One would hope, however, that the proactive steps taken by the institution to improve health, safety, security, and legal compliance as a result of a comprehensive legal and risk assessments will ultimately help a program sponsor to prove that it discharged its duty to exercise reasonable care in the operation of its programs abroad.

> *Thomas Butcher's "Top Ten Tips for Study Abroad Administrators" (1999) offers another succinct summary of the legal issues in education abroad.*
>
> **Top Ten Tips for Study Abroad Administrators**
>
> - Do the right thing.
> - Do something, rather than nothing
> - Consider what a reasonable prudent person would do, and carry it out.
> - Consider what can go wrong before a program departs.
> - Disclose the dangers of a given program or destination.
> - Obtain signed waivers (informed consent).
> - Don't adopt policies, procedures, or practices that you can't or won't enforce.
> - Inform students of the risks, laws, penalties, and responsibilities related to the consumption of alcohol.
> - Prepare program directors and participants.
> - Involve and educate your campus president, provost, legal counsel, risk manager, public affairs staff, business office, office, health services staff, counseling office and any other office associated with your study abroad program.

DEALING WITH EMERGENCIES

Education abroad professionals must be prepared for the worst. It is therefore important to have an emergency response plan in place, detailing all that needs to be done overseas and on campus. This will include establishing lines of communications with all students, with parents, with legal counsel, with investigative authorities, and with other appropriate campus personnel. Once the incident is past the emergency stage, it is crucial to investigate what happened on site as thoroughly and quickly as possible, so as to establish a contemporaneous record with all the facts of the incident. Memories of events and conversations fade very quickly—so accurate, and, if possible, contemporaneous notes can ensure an important degree of credibility. Disclosing and discussing inherent risks known to be present in the program or in the program's locale are important risk management strategies for legal liability.

Summary

Education abroad advising and program administration do not exist in a vacuum, removed from the legal strictures and issues present in U.S. higher education. Sponsoring institutions must acknowledge that education abroad programs and staff have a legal and ethical duty to provide a reasonable standard of care to their program participants, program staff, colleagues (at home and abroad), and their own and any cooperating institutions. Moreover, education abroad administrators and programs are subject to many of the same statutes and regulations that regulate U.S. higher education domestically, as well as a number of foreign statutes and regulations. International educators should take proactive steps to reduce actual risks to participants and legal risks to the institution. By seeking the guidance and assistance of campus legal counsel, risk managers, institutional federal compliance officers, student affairs and financial aid administrators, among many others, education abroad administrators will be better prepared to assess the legal exposure presented by programs, activities, staff, etc., and take appropriate measures to address problem areas.

Part IV
OVERSEAS PROGRAM DIRECTION

IV-1
The Program Director and the Program
Skye Stephenson

IV-2
The Overseas Program Cycle and Critical Components
Skye Stephenson, Anthony Ogden, Karen Rodriguez, Melissa Smith-Simonet

IV-3
Managing Students and Issues On-Site
Skye Stephenson, Mary Lou Forward

Introduction
William Hoffa

Although U.S. education abroad begins and ends on the campuses of U.S. colleges and universities, it takes place, by definition, in a foreign institutional and cultural setting, and is overseen by on-site staff operating far from U.S. shores. The professional advice contained in Part IV, "Overseas Program Direction," complements discussions about the role U.S. based faculty and staff leading overseas programs, found in Part I, Chapter 2, "The Profession of Education Abroad," and Chapter 5, "Faculty Roles," as well as all chapters in Part III, "Program Development, Campus Management, Marketing, and Evaluation." Part IV looks at issues related to sound program management from the perspective of those who direct programs on-site.

Chapter 1, "The Program Director and the Program," describes the personal and professional qualifications needed by anyone who aspires to be successful in leading overseas programs. It outlines the basic responsibilities of the job of program director, and surveys the various links the program director must establish with local constituencies for the benefit of the students and the program.

Chapter 2, "The Overseas Program Cycle and Critical Components," discusses the basic phases of any education abroad program. The cycle of activity begins even before students arrive in the host country and does not end until after they return to their home campuses. Chapter 2 discusses orientation programming, accommodations, classroom and extracurricular learning, enrichment activities, and strategies for encouraging cross-cultural learning.

Chapter 3, "Managing Issues and Students On-Site," highlights the issues, questions, and problems that may occasionally confront overseas programs, including students' physical and emotional health and misbehavior. It also examines problems that can affect an entire program, such as geo-political disruptions and natural catastrophes. Seasoned wisdom suggests that there is great value in being prepared for these and other challenges.

CHAPTER 1

The Program Director and the Program

Contributor: Skye Stephenson

Study abroad programs function successfully in great part due to the dedicated work of on-site staff and the support of key members of the host community. Whatever may be offered to students domestically before departure or after return, what occurs during the actual living and learning experience abroad makes or breaks a program. Successful program outcome is essentially linked with the work of the program directors and staff, and the cooperation of many members of the host community.

THE PROGRAM DIRECTOR

The program director (PD) is the individual who leads any on-site program that receives students studying abroad. The PD's position embodies concrete responsibilities and authority, as well as symbolic importance. Often, the program and the PD become synonymous in the eyes of many host nationals, especially in cases where the PD has a relatively long tenure. In any case, PDs are always the key individuals on site and are important facilitators of home-host interrelations. As study abroad programs have proliferated in recent years, the number of PDs has grown concomitantly; these days, there are literally thousands of PDs scattered around the world, serving in locales from Paris, France, to Timbuktu, Mali. As such, they represent an important group within the international education field.

While the tasks and responsibilities of PDs can and do vary considerably depending on program type, location, and size, there are, nonetheless, certain common denominators shared by all such professionals. Although there are, at present, no standard minimum requirements to be a PD, as there are for more established professions (Reid, Joy 1988), PDs tend to fit a certain professional profile. The profile includes all, or at least a majority, of the following qualifications:

- a solid academic background, usually with an advanced degree in a relevant discipline;

- firsthand experience with situations of intercultural dialogue and interchange;

- the ability to effectively multitask;

- strong interpersonal skills;

Part IV: Overseas Program Direction

- the capacity to work in situations of ambiguity;
- the ability to exercise both leadership and team-building skills;
- an agreement with the mission and goals of international education exchange;
- a dedication to working with young adults; and
- a basic, instinctive, vocation for the job.

Perhaps the factor that most unites PDs everywhere is the nature of their trade, which is even harder to define and categorize than the PD position itself. Such definition has real importance beyond mere classification, because the way that the job is viewed has important implications for job benefits and conditions, and treatment of the PD. Consequently, how to best categorize what directors of study abroad programs actually do has become an increasingly heated topic in some study abroad organizations of late. The author has personally been witness to two such debates. In one instance, the leader of an international education organization likened PDs to hospital administrators, claiming that although many were academics by training, the PD position was primarily an administrative one whose main function was more akin to "keeping a hospital running" than "operating on patients." Conversely, at a different organization, a group of PDs told their supervisors that they considered their work comparable to that of a faculty chair.

Considering the PD role as objectively as possible, it seems clear that most PDs are neither faculty heads nor hospital administrators. In fact, it can be cogently posited that the position is so sui generis that it really cannot be compared to any other, even those in international education. This implies that the PD job needs to be conceptualized according to its own task parameters. What might those parameters be?

Several individuals over the years have tackled this thorny issue (Allaway, 1965, O'Neal 1995). One of them likened the job to that of wearing many different hats (O'Neal 1995). Among the wide variety of roles PDs may be called on to perform as integral aspects of their jobs are teacher, mentor, administrator, academic adviser, facilitator, counselor, judge, disciplinary officer, banker, legal assistant, tour operator, travel agent, local expert, intercultural facilitator and communicator, troubleshooter, safety and health adviser, crisis manager, office manager, purchasing agent, public relations point person, editor, host or hostess, financial coordinator, insurance adviser, and more. Not only must PDs don these numerous "hats"—often simultaneously—but they also are oftentimes called on to juggle several of the hats simultaneously when circumstances warrant.

When a study abroad program is in session, a PD is never really off duty: day or night, weekday or weekend. Indeed, PDs are truly jacks-of-all-trades in the real sense of the term, as cogently expressed in a jingle written by Will Migniuolo, a longtime PD in London for Arcadia University, which recasts the old fortune-telling rhyme "Tinker, Tailor, Soldier, Sailor:"

Dean and Jailor, Priest and Player
Realtor, Recruiter, Counsellor, Computer
Academic, Para-medic,
Transporter, Translator, Banker and Book-orderer,
Manager of crises, currency, faculty, facilities,
and of disabilities,
Bursar, Registrar, Chauffeur for the faculty car,
Janitor, Adjudicator, Grade Evaluator,
Secretary, Dictionary, always Functionary,
Health and safety Protector, quality Inspector
You're the Resident Director.

Chapter 1: The Program Director and the Program

Due to the rigors and challenges of their jobs, PDs seem to naturally gravitate to one another when they meet, usually swapping information and sharing work-related tales. At several program destinations, this type of spontaneous interchange has led to more formalized links, including the creation of "director associations" in several countries. An ancillary phenomenon has taken place at recent NAFSA conferences, with a group of veteran PDs leading presession workshops to train new program directors. In fact, several of the contributors to Part IV, Chapter 2, "The Overseas Program Cycle and Critical Components," developed their material from these NAFSA workshops.

Types of PDs

There are notable differences among PDs on several levels; it can be argued that PDs are perhaps the most diverse group of individuals in any sector in international education. This is manifested in numerous ways. PDs vary according to national and cultural origins, professional background, job demands (e.g., some work more in the academic ambit, whereas others play a more administrative or managerial role), program location, and program pedagogy (e.g., overseeing a direct enrollment program can be quite different from leading an experiential field-based program). This diversity is augmented by the fact that PDs are literally scattered around the globe. Whereas some PDs are concentrated in certain popular study abroad sites (e.g., London, Paris, Madrid), others may be the sole PD in their town, region, or even country.

One of the most notable distinctions among PDs is related to employment status. PDs can be divided into three distinct groups based on whom they work for the anticipated duration of their employment as PD, and the exclusivity of their work with a single U.S.-based study abroad group. The three groups are faculty program directors, host-national institution program directors, and professional program directors.

Faculty Program Directors

Faculty program directors (FPDs) are discussed quite extensively elsewhere in this volume. (See Part I, Chapter 5, "Faculty Roles.") FPDs are faculty members (or, in some cases, individuals who are employed in other university positions) who are appointed to lead a program for a limited period of time, usually one or two years. In some instances, the individual will never have done the work of a PD before; in others, the individual will be part of a departmental (usually language) team that rotates responsibilities annually.

Host-National Institution Program Directors

Host-national institution program directors (HNIPD) are employed by the receiving institution at the program site, and are usually in charge of several different international student groups with a variety of national origins. The position of HNIPD is similar to that of the foreign student adviser, which can be found at any U.S. college or university. For our purposes, an individual will be considered an HNIPD if and only if he or she is the ultimate on-site authority for a particular group of study abroad program students. In some cases, an individual may serve as an HNIPD for one group of study abroad students, whereas for another group that has a PD on site, he or she may serve as a host institution adviser.

Part IV: Overseas Program Direction

Professional Program Directors

Professional program directors (PPDs), for want of a better term, will be the term used to designate the third type of PD. PPDs can be distinguished from the other two types of PDs in that their primary job is to direct a single study abroad program on site over a sustained period of years. In contrast to many FPDs, PPDs are based at the program locale in a permanent or semi-permanent manner, and are hired to carry out study abroad work. In contrast to HNIPDs, PPDs are employed, usually with an exclusive contract, by the study abroad providers.

Because PPDs make study abroad program leadership their profession, at least during the period of employment, certain considerations arise related to their hiring, retention, and professional development that are not as salient among the other two types of PDs. Due to the nature of the job, the diversity of individuals who may become PPDs, the differing national and legal contexts in which PPDs operate, and the fact that PPDs are "long-distance" employees whose supervisors are typically located thousands of miles away, hiring and retaining PPDs incorporates a host of considerations that can be markedly different and, oftentimes, more complex, than what is involved with hiring someone stateside. Some of the most critical variables are outlined in the following paragraphs.

Nationality. The nationality of a PPD can affect a variety of legal and nonlegal employment issues, and brings to the fore concerns regarding the nature of home-host relations, the symbolic and real implications of expatriate versus local hiring, the dynamics of working with a multicultural team, and other concerns. On the legal side, whatever the PPD's nationality may be, the employer should ensure that the hire is fully legal under local laws. If the PPD is not a host national, a work visa usually needs to be obtained, which in some countries can be a complicated, time-consuming, and/or expensive procedure. If the PPD is a host national, attention should be given to determining the legal requirements and implications, including tax and benefit obligations, of both the employer and employee, under host-country rulings. The nationality of a PPD may also need to be taken into consideration in some cases for training, managerial, and evaluation purposes.

Salary. The criteria employed for PPD salary determination is important not just because the criteria impact employees' remunerations, but also because they illustrate the values of the employing organization. The key question is whether PPD salaries should be based on a standardized scale, ad hoc negotiations between employer and potential employee, or a combination of the two. Particularly controversial and ethically challenging is whether host-national and expatriate PPDs should always be remunerated at the same rate for carrying out the same job at the same locale. At program locales that have considerably lower pay scales than the U.S. home campus, what may be considered a moderate salary by U.S. standards may represent a real windfall for a host-national PPD. Conversely, at other sites, the opposite situation may be true, and employers may have to do some "creative financing" to come up with a strong enough salary and benefits package to be acceptable and competitive under local conditions. Under these very different scenarios, what is a "fair" salary?

Contract. Contract type and stipulations are important considerations for both employer and employee, and all PPDs should have a signed contract before beginning their jobs. The two principal types of PPD contracts currently in use are at-will and term contracts, each of which has its own advantages and disadvantages. Other contractual issues may be PPD job duties, the time frame for

Chapter 1: The Program Director and the Program

PPD employment, and clarification of the nature and extent of outside work that a PPD may engage in while under contract.

Benefits. The benefits package, which can include both mandatory and optional benefits, is closely linked with contract and salary concerns. In some situations, figuring out what benefits are legally required in the host country can be complicated. Consulting with a competent local consul may be advisable to avoid unwittingly violating host-country employment laws. Optional benefits can vary widely and are, for the most part, up to the discretion of the employer. Some employers offer few, if any, benefits beyond what is required, whereas other employers may provide such benefits as a moving allowance, housing and utilities coverage, a home leave policy, a sabbatical option, and professional development support, and others.

Evaluation Procedures and Criteria. The method and frequency of the PPD's evaluation should be clearly stipulated from the start of employment and conducted periodically whether linked to salary adjustment or not. Because much of the PPD job is conducted far away from supervisors and in settings quite different from the employer's home country, providing a fair PPD job evaluation can sometimes be a challenge. A host of criteria should be taken into consideration, including the PPD's relations with the host university and members of the local community, efficiency in performing administrative tasks, financial capability, communication with the home office, academic knowledge and skills.

Frequently, student evaluations are the principal means of a PPD's evaluation. While student evaluations are obviously an important source of feedback regarding PPD performance, some PPDs (and others) believe that student evaluations may be given undue weight in performance assessment, due to the "student as consumer" orientation of U.S. higher education as well as the fact that student evaluations are an "easy" means for assessment because they are readily available. Additionally, at most program sites, students evaluate the PD but the PD does not have a chance to evaluate the student beyond assigning an academic grade.

Professional Development Needs. Two final variables affecting PPD recruitment and retention are professional development trajectories and future career possibilities. Typically considered "not as academic" as their full-time university-based peers, yet "not as managerial" as those who run international education offices, many PPDs find it challenging to carve out a career path that allows for both professional growth as PPDs and viable employment options should they leave the PPD position. This situation is compounded by the fact that most employers do not dedicate many resources or much attention to PPD professional development. Additionally, the all-consuming nature of their jobs can make it difficult for PPDs to find the time and tranquility to keep up with their professional interests. Consequently, some PPDs find their employment options are limited after they leave their posts. Even for those PPDs employed by institutions that promote interorganizational career advancement, in most cases the only "move up" is to the U.S. office, which may not be the PPD's preference or, in the case of some host-country nationals, even a possibility.

Program Set-Up and Coordination

Program Legalization and Liability

A program's on-site legal status can have major implications for PDs, and indeed for the entire program structure. Study abroad programs have always needed to legally "fit in" within the host country, but what this specifically means differs from site to site and time period to time period. In the past, many programs seemed to function primarily with the tacit support of local institutions, but recent changes in the international arena have placed international education programs under greater legal and financial scrutiny than ever before. One consequence has been the need to insure that study abroad programs are officially legal in the host country. In some cases, programs have been compliant for years, whereas in many other situations, both local and stateside program staff are scrambling to become compliant—not always an easy task.

Whatever the study abroad program's on-site legal status may be, it has major implications for the PD. If the program is not yet fully compliant, the repercussions can fall on PDs in numerous ways, including legal accountability on site. In some countries, the situation can even lead to possible lawsuits or criminal procedures. If the program is in the process of becoming compliant, oftentimes the U.S. office will ask for PD support in shepherding the program through the process. Whether PDs should receive extra compensation for these efforts is worthy of consideration. In some cases, the PD is named titular head or one of the titular heads of the host country legal entity; when this occurs, the PD should be made fully aware of the legal responsibilities and liabilities that may be involved as well as recognized in some way (financial or otherwise) for the extra responsibility that this entails.

PDs' views regarding the need for and importance of on-site compliance can run the gamut from avid advocacy to uneasy acquiescence, depending on locale, PD attitude, and other factors. At some sites, PDs have pressed the U.S. office for compliance. In other situations, the opposite has occurred and PDs have been reticent because full compliance may mean greater oversight responsibilities for program affairs and, in some cases, additional personal tax liabilities in country.

Whatever the program's legal status in the host country, its legal situation in the United States, especially in regard to liability issues, is another ponderous concern for all individuals related to program oversight. The increasingly litigious environment in the United States can include within its purview happenstances that occur at study abroad program locations, and there have already been several high-profile and many lesser-known lawsuits brought against study abroad providers because of events or accidents that occurred at the program site.

Although nearly all PDs are only too aware of this reality, many, especially those who are not very familiar with the U.S. legal system, do not fully understand either the legal parameters commonly employed in liability cases or the extent to which they may be held personally and legally accountable. Well-informed guidance on these issues should be a paramount component of PD training. Such training should incorporate both general information as well as practical suggestions on how to best handle potentially litigious situations. Additionally, all PDs, and perhaps even other local program staff, should be included in employer liability policies and be fully informed of the terms and conditions of this coverage.

Working With U.S. Sponsoring Institutions

Due both to power disparities (employer/employee) as well as task differentiation, it is quite common that some degree of an "us" versus "them" mentality arises between the PD, located in the field, and his or her employer, located far away in the U.S. office or within the administrative structures of a foreign institution. Typically, issues of control and proprietorship come to the fore in these interactions, and although this rarely leads to an adversarial relationship, PD–U.S. office relations can, nonetheless, manifest elements of understated apprehension or sporadic episodes of frustration.

On the one hand, PDs may sometimes feel that folks at the U.S. office simply don't completely understand their work dynamics and cultural realities, and that the U.S. office can, consequently, enact policies and demand responses that may be ill advised, difficult to implement, or culturally inappropriate. Exacerbating this perception may be situations in which PDs' advice and suggestions appear to be ignored or not followed through on by people at the U.S. office, making PDs feel that they are not being taken seriously. On the other hand, staff in the U.S. office may feel that many PDs are excessively single-minded in their focus on their own programs, and that they don't take into consideration the bigger picture.

Expectations and structures regarding home base–PD interactions do vary significantly among organizations, adding yet another element that can influence the nature of PD–employer interactions. While some institutions and organizations maintain a firm and clear separation between program site and home office, others are more inclusive of PDs and try to incorporate them to some degree within their management and policymaking apparatus through such means as regional management appointments and governance structures. Whatever the balance, managing U.S. office–PD interactions can present challenges that call for clarity in communication, cross-positional empathy, and creative responses.

For those study abroad programs that draw participants from various universities and colleges, the interaction between the PD and the sending institution is another relationship to take into consideration, although it is typically more limited than PD-employer interface, oftentimes due in part to employer policies and procedures. Nonetheless, it can raise a separate set of challenges and issues. This is especially true when sending institution expectations or demands do not easily mesh with host-country realities. Among the most salient issues are academic quality and content concerns, grading and evaluation policies, language instruction and support methods (where relevant), disciplinary actions and outcomes, student medical situations, and coordination and dialogue during emergencies of various sorts.

Academic affairs are frequently among the most challenging issues to manage, usually due in large part to intercultural differences regarding educational structures, pedagogy, and grading. While many sending institutions may initially request that their students be treated the same as host nationals, especially in direct enrollment situations, their requests can sometimes be set aside when particular students encounter academic problems of various sorts and request special assistance or accommodation. Navigating through such situations and enacting the most equitable policies for all concerned is not always an easy task for PDs and other involved parties.

On a different note, ties between PDs and sending institution representatives often develop through a variety of means, and may serve as an important factor for specific, job-related communication and broader professional considerations. One of the most important ways that such relationships develop is through site visits, where PDs and sending institution representatives have the chance to meet face to face. Another important forum for interface at some study abroad provider sites is through participation in program evaluation visits. While most program evaluators are well-informed professionals who carry out their tasks in an exemplary manner, there have been instances where this was not the case. For example, in an evaluation visit to a program in Japan, one U.S. team member commented, after attending a popular Japanese professor's class (taught in English), that he considered the professor a poor instructor because he had a very circular way of presenting material, which would be hard for most U.S. students to follow!

Working with Program Staff

At most U.S. study abroad program offices overseas, the PD has a local staff to provide support and assistance with program implementation. Although the number and position of these program staff can and do vary considerably, from a single assistant or secretary at smaller operations to a sizable and diverse staff at some of the larger sites, these local staff members are important contributors to program success. While they are usually almost "invisible" from the stateside perspective, which is not necessarily a problem per se, their importance within the international education community should at least be acknowledged.

The PD is usually the individual responsible for overseeing the local program staff; indeed, this is one of the most important aspects of the PD job. Thus, while the PD is being overseen by his or her employer stateside, the PD is overseeing and interacting on a daily basis with the local staff at the program office abroad. The intensity of the relationship between the PD and other program staff is frequently among the strongest of all PD professional relationships. Whatever individual and program differences there may be in these work-based relationships, the relationships nearly always incorporate a significant degree of what can be termed "dual culture blending," meaning that aspects of both the host and U.S. cultures become relevant and actively incorporated into office dynamics.

At its most concrete manifestation, a combination of norms and policies from both locales are usually followed. On the one hand, host country rules and regulations regarding employment and benefits should be adhered to if the program staff are host nationals (in some sites this is not easy to do if the program is not fully compliant). Since most PDs are not well versed in human resource issues, it is usually a good practice to consult with a local lawyer or human resource specialist when hiring local professionals. This can help the program avoid potential labor disputes, which can be time consuming, expensive, or, at a minimum, just plain frustrating.

As important as following local labor practices is making sure that local staff members are familiar and comply with program rules and regulations, many of which stem from U.S. cultural norms and practices. Examples of such regulations are those concerning expectations regarding staff and participant interaction, sexual harassment, and alcohol use. Some of these rules may be explicitly written down in program manuals and materials, whereas others may be based on educational or social practices that are understood and accepted stateside, but that are not written down anywhere. Embedded in many of these norms and rules is the implicit "student as paying consumer" attitude, so emblematic of the U.S. educational approach and so different from the treatment accorded university-level students in most other countries.

An ancillary issue of working with program staff is program liability. Although the PD is the individual ultimately accountable for any potentially litigious situation that happens on site, the actions of the on-site staff may contribute to such situations. Additionally, local staff are typically aware of the very litigious nature of U.S. society, and they may be concerned about how it may impinge on them. The PD can help assuage such concerns by explaining about liability insurance as well as providing guidance and training on how staff can function in a manner that will minimize the likelihood that a potentially litigious situation will transpire. Such training is a crucial component of on-site staff program preparation.

A quite different aspect of dual culture blending is the development of an office dynamic that is an amalgam of host-country and U.S. cultural configurations and manifestations. This blending can be seen in staff language use, greeting patterns, managerial styles, communication modes, and other ways. Many program staff consider this cultural blending to be one of the most interesting and invigorating aspects of their jobs, and often contend that the best of both worlds is enacted in their workplace. A staff member at a Latin American program office once commented, "My favorite part of my job is how we relate to each other in the office. I can't imagine ever going back to working in a standard Latin American office again because I am not sure I could adjust to that top-down management style."

This quote not only highlights the positive aspects of dual culture blending but also raises a concern regarding local staff professional trajectories and postprogram employment possibilities. It is worthwhile for supervisors to thoughtfully consider both the nature and kind of responsibility embedded in using local professionals in the unique environment and context that most study abroad offices represent within the host culture.

Host Nationals as Key Study Abroad Program Supporters

Of all the on-site parties responsible for study abroad program success, the host nationals are, in the deepest of meanings, the most significant. Truly, any study abroad program owes its existence and maintenance to its hosts, for several reasons. At the broadest, it is, in large part, those qualities and characteristics embodied in the host country's natural and cultural environments that serve to make a particular locale an attractive program site. Additionally, considerations such as host country safety and security, health conditions, and how foreigners (especially people from the United States) are received, serve to influence program location decisions. Although the host culture or nation provides the backdrop for study abroad programs, key individuals and institutions in the host culture can and do play a significant role in sponsoring, receiving, and supporting study abroad programs.

In fact, without the host's willingness to accept and support the study abroad endeavor on site, no program could function. Although the vast majority of host nationals will have little, if any, interface with study abroad program participants, at any program site there are always certain key groups and individuals that have significant linkages with study abroad program employees and participants—linkages that can, and usually do, involve financial, practical, intellectual, and emotional components. Consequently, consideration of the host-national element not as a passive backdrop to study abroad programs but as an active and contributing actor is crucial to any serious study regarding international education. It is also an exceedingly complex and multifaceted topic, the purview of which extends far beyond the few pages allotted here. Within these constraints, this section is designed to give a brief overview of some of the most salient considerations and actors within the host-national context, and to provide a forum for several host nationals to speak out regarding their views about hosting U.S. study abroad students.

Making any sweeping generalizations regarding host-national perspectives of U.S. study abroad is complicated by the great diversity of program sites, the multitude of host nationals who interface with the program, and the host nationals' various motivations for working with study abroad students and staff. Despite these differences, host nationals are linked by one commonality, which is trying to figure out why U.S. university students would want to come to their society to study and live, and what they think about the phenomenon. These questions are not as transparent as they may seem; and although the general supposition has been that study abroad programs are naturally a win-win proposition that benefits program providers, participants, and host nationals, this tenet is being questioned on several fronts.

Host-national educators at many institutions around the world are desirous of gaining more than financial compensation for receiving program participants, and are pressing for greater opportunities for reciprocity and exchange so that their own students can have similar international educational experiences. Some host communities are realizing that bringing program participants into their homes and lives may have deleterious effects, especially in regards to behavioral norms and displays of economic prowess. And some academics who support participant research projects are questioning what the host society receives in return from such studies.

Such questioning does not imply that host nationals are an unsatisfied or disgruntled lot; in fact, quite the opposite is true at most program sites. Such questioning does, however, bring to the forefront the increasing importance for study abroad program leaders both on site and in the U.S. office to seriously consider the impact of their program in the host community, and what concrete actions they may take to give back to the hosts even some small measure of what the program and its participants receive from them. Facilitating this dynamic intercultural dialogue is among the most important of all the hats that a PD dons, because it embodies the deepest mission of study abroad.

Working with Local Government Officials

Although the role and importance of government officials and bureaucrats in facilitating study abroad endeavors are not usually discussed, as any one who has worked in the education abroad field knows only too well, both the formal procedures and the informal facilitation of program participants' and employees' paperwork, visas, identification cards, and more can change the dynamics of a study abroad program. If obtaining and registering student visas is required and the process is complicated, much program attention may need to be devoted to these activities early on. This may serve as an ultimately useful but also frustrating exercise in host-culture bureaucracy and procedures. PDs would do well to keep in mind that similar, or perhaps even more complicated, procedures await foreign national students in the United States.

Chapter 1: The Program Director and the Program

The importance of local government officials can, in some countries, extend far beyond the facilitation of student and staff paperwork. Depending on the political system in the host country, it may be government officials, sometimes at the highest levels, who outline the nation's approach to international educational exchange, and who encourage (or not) local academic institutions to sponsor such groups. It has been rumored that even the top leaders in some countries have been actively involved in approving (or disapproving) international educational exchange. For instance, Fidel Castro's behind-the-scenes support for several study abroad programs has been perhaps the most important factor influencing their reception and acceptance in Cuba.

Although a country's top executive usually is not directly involved in study abroad, Ministry of Education officials and other high-level officials may be, and their interest (or lack of it) in facilitating study abroad programs can go far in making a particular site an attractive program location. As one example, the Chilean government's internationalization thrust, manifested in part through Ministry of Education policies that facilitate the arrival and support of various types of international educational exchange, has had a large role to play in making the mid-sized Andean nation among the top receivers of study abroad students in South America. The Chilean experience contrasts with the other two educational leaders in South America—Argentina and Brazil—whose governments to date have been much less interested in actively supporting internationalization of their higher education systems. As another example, across the Pacific, the Australian government's assertive and well-financed campaign for international exchange students has brought increasing flows of study abroad students to that country. Other examples can be noted from other regions as well.

Working with Host Academic Institutions

The nature and degree of the linkage between study abroad programs and host country academic institutions can vary widely from cursory to intermeshed—but it is indeed a rare program that does not have some kind of affiliation. Even most "island" study abroad programs rely to some degree on lecturers, facility use, or other services provided by local universities, colleges, or research centers. Since a primary justification of all credit-bearing study abroad programs is their academic content and quality, the importance of working with host country institutions cannot be overstated.

In many cases, the importance of program linkages with host country academic institutions extends far beyond the academic. Oftentimes, these institutions and key individuals within them provide "local legitimacy" for the program, facilitate contacts with other members of the host society, and give advice and support, especially during various types of emergencies. Feelings of warmth and affection frequently underlie interactions between the program representatives and the host university, and many PDs' closest on-site colleagues are folks from the host institution. Nonetheless, there may also be tension, especially when negotiating the details of accords, pricing, and service issues. Other potentially contentious issues may arise as well, especially around areas of visa issuance, facility use, and so on. In some cases, local circumstances at the university or in the host country can severely impact the study abroad program. One of the most dramatic examples is when university staff or students go on strike, sometimes profoundly upsetting an entire semester of a study abroad program.

While the benefits of sponsored study abroad to the home institution are clear, it may be less obvious why host institutions are willing to go through the extra trouble and challenge of hosting study abroad programs. In most situations, the actual rationale behind any institution's approach to receiving study abroad program students is composed of a combination of factors based on national priorities and realities, institutional goals and perceived needs, and individual initiative and interface. In addition to the obvious financial benefits that accrue to host institutions from providing educational services to study abroad program providers, there are other important considerations as well. Nuria Alsina, director of the international programs office at Pontifica Universidad Católica in Santiago, Chile, notes that many of the same factors that motivate U.S. colleges and universities to internationalize also motivate many receiving institutions. Such motivations include an increased international knowledge base and competence for the professors, support for culture and intercultural dialogue, and greater internationalization of the campus. Sites that do not have a long tradition of receiving a significant number of foreign students may be especially motivated to host a study abroad program.

PDs in other parts of the world express additional reasons for hosting students from other countries. Tomadar Rifat of the American University of Cairo, for instance, highlights a more mission-based and international-understanding rationale for her institution to host foreign students. In her words, the main reason that American University of Cairo receives study abroad students "is to promote understanding and knowledge of Egypt, the Arab World, and the Middle East in the West and knowledge of the West for our Egyptian students, and other Arab students in order to create a bridge of mutual understanding." Laars Franson of UppsalaUniversity of Sweden points out that, in some cases, receiving foreign exchange students, especially from prestigious sending universities, can serve to enhance a host institution's prestige. In this case, university-based study abroad programs are at a distinct advantage, since they may have greater international name recognition than many third-party providers.

Additionally, such connections can lead to greater communication and even, in some cases, collaboration among faculty from the two institutions. Sometimes, joint research work has grown out of initial student exchanges. An additional benefit for some departments, especially those with a declining number of native students, is an increase in student numbers. Some universities also provide financial or other types of departmental benefits based on study abroad student enrollments in departmental classes.

Faculty

Many professors at receiving institutions find that having foreign students in their classrooms contributes to a diversity of viewpoints and stimulates local students' learning. At some sites, professors have even contended that the punctuality of U.S. students and their concern with grades and work completion have served as good models of behavior for the host country students. Of course, at some sites, just the opposite may be true. Local professors have sometimes had to learn, often through trial and error, how to better meet the expectations of U.S. students, particularly regarding classroom discussion, syllabi production, assignment clarity, and grading norms.

Local Students

At campuses that do not have a long history of foreign student presence, the arrival and settling-in of U.S. study abroad participants can have repercussions that extend far beyond academics and financial inflows. Differences in dress, attitude, relations with members of the opposite sex, views regarding diversity, and so on begin to influence campus life on many levels, just as the study abroad students come to be influenced by life on the host campus. In one case, the author was told how, a decade ago, the habit female U.S. students had of wearing shorts to class eventually led host country students to wear shorts to class about a year later. This phenomenon seemed to be repeated several years later, with tattoos, piercings, and the like.

It must be kept in mind that U.S.-based study abroad students represent just one type of exchange student within the international context, and a unique one at that. In fact, the overseas study abroad program office with a full-time PD and other on-site staff is pretty much a U.S. phenomenon, and contrasts sharply with how most other foreign students are hosted during their academic sojourns. For most receiving institutions, this reality strongly shapes their dealings with U.S.-based study abroad programs and students, whom they find to be, in general, quite demanding.

Host university staff at many sites around the world feel that U.S. students, compared to other international students, require considerably more service and assistance. While this may or may not be true, some reasons suggested to explain this feeling are that universities in the United States are more service-oriented than universities in other countries, that U.S. students often are slightly younger than their host university counterparts, and that U.S. students usually have not traveled as much internationally as most Europeans, and thus naturally lack some confidence in the international arena. (Paraphrased from Lars Franson correspondence with chapter author [2003].)

With the changes that have taken place both within the United States and internationally since the events of September 11, 2001, U.S.-based study abroad students now seem to require even greater support than they did previously at many sites due to additional security concerns and rising anti-U.S. sentiments While one can cogently contend that, given recent world events, it is more crucial than ever that U.S. students have the opportunity to "go global" and partake of life and study in other nations and cultures, an equally strong argument can be made that students at the receiving institution should be accorded the same opportunity when feasible. In fact, the issue of reciprocity is often being raised by individuals at many receiving institutions, who are asking, 'where is the "exchange" aspect of U.S.-based study abroad?' As a European international PD put it, "Exchange has a distinct advantage over study abroad or one-way mobility because it promotes collaboration and a sense of natural relationship between home students and international students."

In general, U.S.-based study abroad providers have been slow to respond to the increasing clamor for greater bilaterality, despite some notable exceptions. Because of the high cost of a U.S. education, many foreign students cannot afford the airfare, living expenses, and other costs associated with spending a semester or year in the United States, even if tuition waivers are arranged. Some foreign universities have devised creative ways to financially support their nominated study abroad students (e.g., by arranging loans, setting up scholarships, and so on), but at many locales it is quite common that students simply cannot take advantage of offered opportunities because of personal financial constraints. In Europe, however, with its increasing movement toward harmonization of university-level degrees and provision of opportunities across national borders, many Europeans are finding it easier and cheaper to study within European borders than in non-European countries. In a more limited context, if actual exchange options are not possible, at the least good faith efforts to incorporate host country students within some of the study abroad program academic classes and activities, when feasible and productive, can be fruitful and empowering for all involved.

Working with Host Families

Many other host nationals besides those within the academic context are affected by and can affect study abroad students during their sojourn in the host country. Among the most significant of these host-national influences are host families (when used), with whom program participants live and interact on a daily basis. In fact, it is often the host family–student relationship within which the strongest bonds of emotional connection are formed and the greatest intercultural learning takes place. Although this relationship is often not given its due attention as a transmitter of cultural knowledge, some recent research studies (Stephenson 1999; Levy) acknowledge the key role played by host families not only as service providers but, more significantly, as purveyors—both wittingly and unwittingly—of host culture norms, behavior, and knowledge. These studies raise the implications of this complex interrelationship for the international education field as a whole. Other host nationals who may be connected with study abroad program participants are providers of services, such as hotel operators, bus companies, and banks; friends and other peers; and individuals at internship or work sites, among others.

SUMMARY

Program directors, program staff, host-national supporters, and collaborators are crucial to study abroad programs; without their sustained work and creative solutions to the wide host of issues and situations that can and do occur during program set up and implementation, study abroad programs would not be possible. Because much of this work is done overseas, beyond the daily purview of the U.S. educational establishment, the work of these contributors to study abroad programming has not been accorded the amount of attention that has been dedicated to other actors and institutions involved in study abroad. However, changing circumstances, including the increasing number and the professionalization of PDs, more stringent legal and financial regulations, the proliferation and deepening of international educational exchange agreements and programs in many geographic areas of the world, the changing position of the United States in the world community, and growing calls by host countries for greater reciprocity and return from study abroad, indicate that in the near future voices from the field will become an increasingly critical factor in U.S.-based study abroad programming.

Chapter 2

The Overseas Program Cycle and Critical Components

Contributors: Skye Stephenson, Anthony Ogden, Karen Rodriguez, Melissa Smith-Simonet

Successful on-site study abroad programming is characterized by a smooth and progressive program-cycle flow, interfaced with soundly conceptualized and carefully implemented critical program components. Like nimble dancers, program directors and staff must know the program's choreography, beat, and style, while simultaneously moving and adjusting program dynamics if and when extenuating circumstances arise. It is this combination of program component design, structure, and timing that make a study abroad program successful for student participants and their home institutions.

The Basic Cycle

Whatever their differences may be, all study abroad programs share a common cycle of activities that begins prior to participant arrival and continues even after their departure. For our purposes, this cycle has been broken into six distinct phases: prearrival, arrival, settling in, fitting in, preparing to leave, and follow-up.

Prearrival: Preparation and Planning

The work put into program planning and organizing before the participants arrive is without a doubt some of the most crucial work necessary for the successful execution of the program, and will save time, energy, and scrambling for information once the program is underway.

Suggested activities during this period include

- reviewing the previous program and considering modifications to the upcoming one;
- evaluating or undertaking local staff training;
- reviewing the new program budget;
- touching base with the local bank to assure that all program funds are in order;
- arranging student housing;
- organizing the program office, including ordering supplies;
- setting up the new program schedule;

Part IV: Overseas Program Direction

- planning the orientation period and contacting involved individuals;
- obtaining the materials needed for student orientation and the program term;
- updating safety, security, and medical information;
- revisiting risk-management analysis, and modifying it if necessary;
- making student emergency contact cards;
- organizing student files;
- contacting academic and other supporting institutions to discuss the new group of students;
- providing the host institution (if applicable) with required student documentation;
- checking with the closest U.S. embassy or consulate regarding passport or U.S. citizen registration;
- setting up lecturers, volunteer work sites, internship sites, language exchange, and so on;
- coordinating any new policies or procedures with the home office; and
- checking and rechecking participant arrival plans and information.

Arrival: Program Initiation and Orientation

The participant arrival and orientation period is without a doubt one of the most significant times of the study abroad cycle. During this exciting, yet demanding, period, students are welcomed to the program site and intensively prepared by program staff for their upcoming cultural and academic immersion experience. A successful orientation can help set the stage and outline the parameters for a dynamic and productive study abroad experience.

Suggested activities during this period include

- welcoming students and settling them in;
- discussing safety and security issues;
- informing participants about how to communicate with friends and family back home;
- notifying the home office and the sending institutions of the participants' safe arrival;
- orienting participants to the program site via discussion and experiential activities;
- providing information regarding how to get around in the program locale;
- establishing rules of conduct and informing participants of the consequences of misbehavior;
- notifying participants of host culture laws and norms, in particular those related to drug and alcohol use;
- distributing emergency contact cards;
- discussing policies and procedures related to group and individual travel;
- establishing emergency procedures;
- bringing in host culture peers, discussing patterns of dating behavior, views towards sexuality and sexual orientation issues;

Chapter 2: The Overseas Program Cycle and Critical Components

- allaying any worries and concerns;
- undertaking ice-breaker activities, drop-offs, and other types of orientation activities;
- finding ways to integrate members of the host community into the orientation activities;
- following-up with any pending information issues (e.g., housing, academics, health, etc.);
- fomenting positive group dynamics and reassessing, on an as-needed basis, housing arrangements;
- orienting students to their on-site lodging situation and establishing any rules related to the housing situation;
- overseeing participants' exit from the orientation site and their settling in at the housing location;
- assessing participants' language levels (if relevant);
- conducting initial intercultural exercises and discussions;
- checking on passports and visas, and undertaking any necessary paperwork to ensure participant legality on site;
- registering participants with the U.S. embassy or consulate;
- carrying out medical and health orientation, preferably with host culture experts when feasible;
- providing students with unscheduled time to process their initial experiences;
- organizing activities to engage and excite students regarding their upcoming experience;
- informing and guiding students regarding program academics;
- undertaking course selection, depending on program content;
- instructing students regarding the host country's educational system and pedagogical style, if host-national instructors and course work will be undertaken;
- providing background information about host country realities and dynamics, through lectures, discussions, or readings;
- being available for individual appointments with participants on an as-needed basis;
- working with participants to set goals and expectations for their experience;
- troubleshooting, as needed;
- working with the group to establish specific codes of conduct for the program duration ;
- providing an opportunity for student representatives to be designated to work with program staff regarding activities planning; and
- evaluating the orientation period.

Part IV: Overseas Program Direction

Settling In: Adjustment and Accommodation

The immediate postorientation period, up until the time when participants begin to feel settled into the host culture, is a key period in the study abroad experience. During this time, the initial "honeymoon" phase abates, and the reality and dynamics of the students' new living situation begins to emerge and be dealt with. The way that this period is navigated by the participants and supported by the program staff sets the stage for how the remainder of the study abroad experience transpires.

Suggested activities during this period include

- deepening academic support, including course selection if relevant;

- monitoring initial classes and making adjustments as needed;

- sending student class information to the head office or the sending institutions, as appropriate;

- sending a program update to the sending institutions;

- checking with the host institution or institutions to ensure adequacy of submitted paperwork;

- providing extra emotional support to students in need of such support during this period;

- checking up on housing situations, and making changes if necessary;

- continuing with intercultural support on an individual or group basis;

- finding ways to encourage participants to reach out to host culture members; and

- executing activities to inform and excite students about the host culture.

Fitting In: Creating Routines and "Bridging"

Whatever its duration, the chronological bulk of a study abroad program occurs during the fitting-in phase, when participants are installed in their academic and living situations and begin to be more comfortable navigating their way around the host culture. Despite differences among students in their levels of cultural adjustment, and among programs regarding the actual amount of program-directed activities (both academic and nonacademic), careful monitoring and possible program adjustment need to take place to ensure a successful outcome for all participants.

Suggested activities during this period include

- checking that all student academic and course information is correct;

- monitoring student academic progress and supporting students who are academically challenged;

- monitoring students' personal progress, and supporting students experiencing social and/or cultural adjustment issues;

- arranging complementary experiential activities;

- following up with internships, volunteer activities, and language exchanges, if relevant;

- dealing with "difficult" students as situations arise;

- providing continued intercultural learning support in a variety of ways;

Chapter 2: The Overseas Program Cycle and Critical Components

- suggesting activities to students to promote greater intercultural learning;
- adjusting academic programming as needed;
- ensuring the participants' continued satisfaction with their living arrangements; and
- updating the home office and the sending institutions about students' progress or program changes, on a need-to-know basis.

Preparing to Leave: Parting and Reentry Concerns

The period at the end of a program is an emotionally charged and bittersweet time for most participants and staff, and it is typically a very busy and intense period. There are practical matters to take care of, as well as intellectual and emotional concerns to address and explore in this phase. It is imperative that on-site staff provide adequate support and opportunities for participants to bring some degree of closure to their study abroad experience.

Suggested activities during this period include

- ensuring completion of participants' academic responsibilities, and supporting students with academic difficulties or special circumstances;
- interfacing with internship sites, volunteer groups, and others (if relevant) to assess participant experiences;
- carrying out reentry activities;
- making sure participants return any borrowed items to the program office;
- being available to support participants emotionally as they prepare to say goodbye;
- hosting an end-of-program activity, usually a dinner or ceremony;
- thanking host families and other host nationals who were engaged with the participants during the program duration;
- conducting exit interviews with participants; and
- conducting student and staff program evaluations.

Follow-up: Completion and Closure

A strong postparticipant finish to a program is just as important as the other phases of the study abroad cycle, and necessary for successful program closure as well as for generating effective feedback for the future.

Suggested activities during this period include

- following up with any pending grade or academic issues;
- obtaining final grades and sending them to the home office;
- assessing any outstanding student loans, debts, or other issues that require follow-up;
- writing an end-of-program report;
- settling final bills and accounts;
- closing the semester budget and informing the home office of the program's final financial situation;

- supporting returned students regarding reentry and other issues;
- thanking office staff and host nationals who supported the program and the students; and
- catching one's breath!

CRITICAL PROGRAM COMPONENTS

Despite the vast differences among study abroad programs, they all share certain program components that are essential to the nature of the study abroad experience. The most critical of these are orientation, housing, academic issues and advising, program enrichment activities, intercultural learning, and reentry. Although each of these components may be conceptualized and implemented quite differently, depending on program content and purpose as well as program director and staff inclination, each component is a crucial element of the entire program package; in fact, it is in large part how these components are carried out that serves to shape and characterize the aspects of a program that make each one unique. Thus, program leaders both on site and stateside should give concerted and thoughtful attention to each and every program component, taking into consideration the ways in which the design and implementation of a particular component can serve to enhance the program's mission and goals. What follows is just a brief overview, a brush stroke, of each of these critical components; those who desire additional information on any of these topics should consult supplementary sources.

Orientation: An Ongoing Activity

Orientation is necessary at all points in the study abroad process, and should be viewed as an ongoing process rather than just a series of activities at the start and termination of a program. Whatever the nature of the program, the primary objectives of on-site orientation should be to

- meet a broad range of pre-existing needs for students with diverse predeparture preparations;
- provide immediate and continual logistical needs (e.g., housing information, academic expectations, language development, internships, etc.);
- inform students of program guidelines, expectations, and regulations;
- facilitate cultural adjustment and intercultural understanding;
- promote the personal, physical, and mental well-being of each individual; and
- foster a positive impact of the study abroad experience on students' lives and future careers.

Generally, on-site orientation can be divided into three distinct periods, each with its own dynamics; these are the welcome orientation, ongoing orientation, and reentry (the latter will be discussed later on in this chapter).

The Welcome Orientation

The initial orientation period sets the tone for the entire program; therefore, it is crucial for program staff to plan the welcome orientation carefully, taking into consideration the many factors that can influence its success, such as scheduling, style, content, location, venue, length, entertainment, and accommodation. While topics addressed during the initial orientation vary with destination and program design, most welcome orientations include presentations on the academic program and semester overview, housing options, regional geography and transportation systems, health services, safety measures, rules of conduct and host culture laws, and general issues on getting started and living in the new country. Students can also be encouraged to hold individual meetings with the program director or other program staff to discuss individual concerns, goals, and expectations.

Involving Local Students and Members of the Community. A strong student and community volunteer network will allow the study abroad program to provide students with a meaningful level of interaction with host nationals and, in turn, help prevent program participants from "hanging out" to a significant degree with co-nationals, an ubiquitous phenomenon at many program sites around the world. Including local students and members of the community in orientation activities will not only encourage the students to seek relationships outside of the program participant population, but will allow the program to extend campus and community networks. Some study abroad programs are now developing "ePal" programs, in which program participants are assigned to local students as ePals. Introductions are made via e-mail as early as two months prior to arrival in the host country, so that students may carry on "conversations" with their host country ePals. The local student meets the U.S. student upon his or her arrival in the host country, and participates in the welcome orientation. Such programs can better prepare students prior to departure, and jump-start the cultural integration challenge of meeting local people. In some cases, an ePal can also serve as an on-site language partner and cultural informant.

Addressing Issues of Multicultural Diversity. Orientation provides an excellent opportunity to encourage students to reflect on and question their culturally based ideas and definitions of multicultural diversity, and to explore their identity development within a new cultural context. Students will encounter a significant range of attitudes regarding diversity, and they need to understand that these cultural differences may influence how others perceive them.

Including Issues of Safety and Security. As the semester begins, the welcome orientation provides a key opportunity to review the program's contingency plan for crisis management and evacuation. This is also the time to review any additional measures the program takes to ensure student safety and security. For example, are students required to leave itineraries with the program during independent travel? Does the program have a rapid communication system in place to contact all students in the event of an emergency? Do staff members carry emergency contingency folders that include contact information for each student? Distribute student identification cards and review emergency protocol, and if applicable, include this information in the student handbook. Culture- and region-specific information should also be addressed and, if possible, a representative of the local police should be invited to speak with the students. If students are to be registered with their respective embassies, this might also be a good time to collect and photocopy their passports.

Discussing Differences in Academic Expectations and Learning Styles. Orientation should address the academic expectations of the students, but within the framework of the host culture. Offering an overview of the local educational system can go a long way in helping students fully appreciate their academic studies. Topics might include classroom format and style, the approach to discussion and interaction with the professor, the degree to which feedback is given, and independent versus dependent learning. Also, the academic orientation should include the practical issues of course registration, the attendance policy, course add/drop and withdrawal periods, and the purchase of textbooks. If time permits, administering a learning style inventory during the welcome orientation is a good way to generate discussion of individual academic needs. Individual meetings with an academic adviser during this period can also be very helpful.

Incorporating Language Development Opportunities. For programs that integrate language study, the orientation can offer an overview of the language program structure and also work to foster an environment within the student body that is mutually supportive of language learning and risk taking. Building in optional language tutorials during the orientation allows beginners to get a head start on language learning. Offering a learning strategies seminar is useful too, especially if it can be linked to the language pedagogy of the program.

Providing Exploration Time and Optional Activities. When planning orientation, it is crucial to allow students time for recuperation from jet lag, individual exploration, and entertainment. Many students will also want time to contact their families shortly after arrival in the host country. Scheduling theme-based outings such as city tours and scavenger hunts are entertaining, educational, and encourage students to begin exploring their new environment.

Explaining Rules and Codes for Student Behavior and Responsibility. Students participating in study abroad are expected to take responsibility for their own actions or failure to act, and program staff and faculty must hold students accountable. Students are expected to abide by a code of student responsibility as well as the laws and customs that govern the host country and any other laws that are applicable to foreign citizens in the host country. The orientation is the time to clearly explain the student code of conduct (including issues of alcohol and drug use), academic honor code, and the sexual harassment policy. Judicial procedures and appropriate sanctions for students must also be explained and, as possible, distributed in writing.

Ongoing Orientation

Since students encounter different challenges at varying stages of their intercultural adjustment, the welcome orientation should be considered phase one of an ongoing orientation program designed to guide students through the study abroad experience. Ongoing orientation can help students successfully navigate difficult situations and prepare them to incorporate their experiences in ways that will lead to immediate and future personal and career development.

Depending on program structure and outlook, ongoing orientation may include follow-up workshops on housing, cultural adjustment, writing across culture, contrast-culture, career preparation, and pre-reentry. Ideally, these themes should be timed to address students' needs at a specific stage in their cultural adjustment and be scheduled as a regular part of the curriculum. For example, at about week five, when students leave the initial honeymoon stage and cultural realities start to set in, it is helpful to offer a workshop on cultural adjustment. Midway through the program—as students delve into a more subjective understanding of the host culture, forcing them to question their own deep-rooted cultural values and assumptions—workshops encouraging self-awareness and exploration would be helpful.

Housing

All too often, housing is viewed as a minor component of a study abroad program. Because housing can be (and often is) one of the most important venues through which participants learn about the host culture, and thus is a key aspect of all study abroad experiences, viewing housing in this manner is a grave mistake. In many cases, participants will, at the end of the program, conclude that their greatest intercultural learning took place as a valuable byproduct of their housing, whatever of the many varieties this might have been. Given this, the program director and other study abroad staff play a crucial role in helping students choose appropriate housing and placement, facilitating participant learning in their lodging experience, and dealing with housing issues in a proactive manner, if and when they arise.

A wide variety of housing options exist, depending on the location, economy, and a host of other variables. Standard options include home-stays, student residences, shared apartments, and pensions or hotels. The exact offering or offerings available to students will be defined by many local realities, program priorities, and of course, student demand. As suggested, a student's housing situation impacts much more than where she or he sleeps at night, and shapes in innumerable ways the nature and development of the intercultural experience. Being the sole program member in a home-stay will be quite a different experience from being one of many program participants living in a shared apartment. Thus, housing choices need to be carefully considered and weighed by all those invested in the program structure and mission.

Whatever the program director's role in making housing options available or in the selection process, she or he is the person who usually has the ultimate responsibility for dealing with any problems that arise. This is often true even if the program has a designated housing coordinator. All housing decisions should incorporate not only student comfort and desires, but also safety, security, and financial considerations. At some sites, payments for housing may even have legal and tax implications that need to be taken into account. Sometimes, program directors for different programs in the same locale will contact each other to share information regarding housing pricing and quality, and to share lists of inappropriate or substandard housing providers and housing units.

Participants are usually assigned a tentative housing placement before their arrival in the host country, so the pre-program housing questionnaire plays a key role and should be carefully constructed, and the students' answers followed-up on, to be useful. At a minimum, questions regarding participants' interests, family background, views regarding living with children and pets, allergies to food, attitudes to smoking, and the amount of interaction expected or desired with local hosts should be included. It may be useful to include an optional section that asks students more personal questions that could be important in housing placement, such as their sexual orientation, religious beliefs, health concerns, and other issues. If host families are used for housing placements, it is a nice idea to have participants write a personal statement for their prospective host families, and include a photograph.

Time spent carefully reading housing request forms and considering what housing option will be best for a program participant is never time wasted. It is always better to get a student's placement right the first time than to have to deal with housing issues, which can be upsetting for the student, stressful for the program director and program staff, and sometimes expensive for the program. Some program staff try to arrange definite student placements long before the program starts and encourage pre-arrival communication between the participant and his or her host family, whereas other program staff prefer to make final placement decisions after student arrival, so they can assess the participants firsthand.

Whichever method is preferred, initial host placement is just the start of the program support necessary for a positive housing experience. Program support is especially important in the case of host family placements, which need to be monitored and nurtured throughout the program period. There are many venues that can help facilitate the participant–host family relationship, including initial receptions, program-sponsored activities of various sorts throughout the semester, and end-of-program receptions. It is just as important to provide ways for students to process their living experiences throughout the semester, both individually and as a group. Sometimes, just realizing that other participants are feeling the same frustrations and anxieties that they are can go far in reassuring students and giving them additional energy and strategies to deal constructively and productively with their own challenging intercultural experiences.

Some programs have successfully used a follow-up housing orientation to complement the initial housing workshop held during the welcome orientation. If it is offered approximately two weeks after the students enter their housing placements, such a workshop can provide students with an opportunity to discuss their first housing experiences with other members of the group, and to ask lingering questions about living with local families or interacting with local students in dormitories. Students may wish to discuss issues related to family life, communication styles, intercultural conflict resolution, private/public behavior, and relationships with family members and local students.

Increasing recognition is being given to the key role that host families play at many study abroad programs, not just as providers of logistical support but, more importantly, as cultural producers, as discussed in Part IV, Chapter 1, "The Overseas Program Director and the Program." Such recognition implies that programs should consider the unique contributions of host families, and the families' potential needs as well, and find creative and empowering ways to incorporate the families into program support and structure, when feasible.

Depending on the nature of the housing options as well as host culture norms, it may be advisable to use housing contracts that spell out the nature of the arrangement, both financial and otherwise, as well as the expected rights and responsibilities of all parties involved. This may include a wide range of issues, such as provision of keys, curfews, use of the telephone and other utilities, meals and kitchen privileges, laundry facilities, the guest policy, use of alcohol, provision of furniture, liability concerns, and more. The housing contract should clearly state the procedures to be followed if a student wishes to move out before the end of the contracted period, and what penalties, if any, would be incurred in such a situation. The contract, whether legally binding or not, should be signed by all parties involved and gone over point by point with the students. A signed copy should be kept in the student's file.

No matter how well done the housing arrangements may have been, some problems always arise during the course of the program that need to be effectively and carefully handled. From the start of the program, participants should be informed about what program staff they should contact in the event of a housing problem, and they should be encouraged to do so. Sometimes, a proactive approach may need to be taken in instances where participants seem to be unhappy in their housing arrangement but do not want to bother anyone about it.

Whatever the situation, the key elements in dealing with housing troubles are hearing the student out, acting quickly through the appropriate venues, and resolving the issues both creatively and efficiently. Sometimes, this may mean simply listening and providing support to the student, whereas at other times it can mean the rapid removal of the participant from an inappropriate or possibly even dangerous situation. Not infrequently, a housing dispute may involve a component of intercultural misunderstanding, and the successful resolution of the crisis (whether through adjustment and accommodation or through confrontation and change) may actually facilitate important personal and cross-cultural insights for the involved parties.

Academic Advising and Support

Academic issues loom large in the job purview of all program directors, whatever the program type and locale. While much of what program directors undertake in this arena is part and parcel with study abroad academic programming and requirements stateside and has been addressed earlier in this book, nonetheless there are several ways in which academic advising and support at the program site is truly sui generis. Among the most significant are the multitasking quality of the work, the intercultural aspects that add an additional, and very important, dimension to study abroad academic advising and support on site, and the opportunities and challenges offered by the program setting.

All program directors are necessarily involved in oversight of the program's academic dimensions and, in fact, this is one of the key elements of their jobs. Whereas stateside there are numerous individuals within the home educational setting who assist and support students with their academic needs (e.g., professors, academic advisers, registrars, international education office staff, etc.), at the program site the program director typically assumes much of the advising and support role, although sometimes he or she may receive assistance from other program staff or people from the host institution. Nonetheless, the ultimate responsibility falls on the program director's shoulders. As such, program directors often have to function as mini-deans, registrars, academic counselors, and more. In cases where the program director teaches classes, they are also teachers or tutors (See Part I, Chapter 5, "Faculty Roles.") Some common academic tasks required of all program directors and on-site program staff include

- providing host institutions with student transcripts and applications;
- advising students regarding course choices and requirements;
- making sure that course selection material is available and up to date;
- providing clear and approved credit and grade transference guidelines;
- maintaining the course syllabi and other course information;
- evaluating courses and providing feedback to home and hosting institutions;

Part IV: Overseas Program Direction

- explaining academic policies and procedures;

- generating participant course registration forms and transcripts;

- establishing and enforcing add/drop policies and other academic norms;

- monitoring student academic progress and providing assistance if needed;

- liaising with host professors and staff and discussing academic situations;

- responding to grade appeals and other academic concerns;

- informing students and their sending institutions in the case of academic difficulties, including attendance problems;

- keeping abreast of local academic changes;

- educating individuals who are involved with the program back in the United States regarding host country educational realities and dynamics; and

- hosting visiting academics and international office staff.

Almost all of the aforementioned on-site academic responsibilities include a strong intercultural component. To be successful, the program director must serve as a liaison between the host country institutions and academics and the program participants and sending institutions; these individuals and groups may have quite different academic expectations, realities, pedagogical approaches, and grading policies. It is up to the program director to not only maneuver through these differences, but to clarify them for all parties involved so that the academic component of the program can be understood and validated, and full credit can be ensured back in the United States.

Such work is crucial because the supposed academic quality and reputation of a program has a large role to play in participant and institutional satisfaction, and can literally "make or break" a program. Increasing scrutiny of program quality, credit, and grading means that program directors need to be sharper than ever in making sure that their programs meet the requisites and standards of the sponsoring organization, evaluation committees, and sending institutions.

Additionally, many program participants find it challenging and stressful to live and learn in a setting different from the one they are accustomed to, which is a natural and perhaps even necessary aspect of the study abroad experience. That said, it is incumbent on the program director to help program participants navigate the international, intercultural academic experience as smoothly as possible, by assisting them at the start with solid information about the host country's educational system, pedagogical style, and academic standards, and then monitoring their academic progress throughout the program period. This is especially true in the case of direct enrollment programs, where participants take classes at host country institutions that are typically quite different from their home schools. In countries where English is not the language of instruction, the added element of language learning can be another factor that contributes to students' stress.

Almost all program directors will be called on at some point in their careers to support nervous and sometimes crying students who are upset about some aspect of their academic work. Assessing the reasons for this stress, and then finding the best means to help the student, takes calm thinking, knowledge of the home and host country educational systems and realities, and a good deal of insight into human nature. Some veteran PDs contend that this phenomenon seems to be on the rise among many program participants, probably due to both the increasing prevalence of the "student as customer" mentality in U.S. higher education and the creeping grade inflation evident at many universities and colleges in the United States. In some cases, student stress regarding academic performance can lead some participants to push to modify their initial academic programs in order to ensure better grades; in other situations, participants may contest the grades they receive and even submit grade appeals after returning to the home campus. Keeping accurate academic records and clearly spelling out academic rules and policies is an important key for successfully resolving grade and other academic disputes.

In addition to serving as academic advisors and support, many PDs have a key role to play in course content through how they design and deliver the academic program on site; this is particularly true in so-called "island" programs. This occurs via various means, including the professors and other speakers selected, the incorporation or exclusion of certain topics and issues in the program design, and/or the actual teaching of classes. Being aware of the power of this role, and considering carefully the design and delivery of the academic portion of the program is one of the most exciting and challenging aspects of running a study abroad program.

A final and very important consideration for all program directors is how to take fullest advantage of the host culture as a key element of the academic experience. After all, many of the courses offered at study abroad programs are also offered at the students' sending schools; it is the setting and, in some cases, the host-national professors, that set the program course work apart. A wide variety of methods and techniques can be employed to take advantage of the program setting, depending on program type and orientation. Some programs use experiential learning techniques, field-based course work, educational excursions, independent student learning with reports from the students, periodic debriefings on the nature of students' academic experiences, and student assignments such as journaling to encourage deeper probing into the intercultural learning and interface. Program directors and programs have their own preferred methods.

Program Enrichment Activities

Of course, not all host-culture learning activities need to be linked to academic course work. The learning that takes place outside the classroom can be among the most rewarding and empowering experiences for many study abroad students. It is up to the overseas program staff to foster an environment and arrange opportunities for participants to take advantage of experiences that can propel them toward a deeper appreciation and adaptation to the host culture as well as a better understanding and acceptance of their own values and capacities. While the academics of overseas study must pass U.S. academic muster, it is what students learn outside the classroom that gives study abroad its uniqueness and makes it such a tranformative experience for many. Much of students' experiential education comes simply from the beneficial shocks and pleasures of living outside of the rhythms and values of the home culture. However, programmed activities are a useful supplement to classroom learning. Examples of such activities are field trips, volunteer work and community service, language exchange, involvement in host campus–based extracurricular activities, and outreach to the local community.

Field Trips and Excursions

Programs vary regarding the type of field trips used and the degree to which they are offered, but, generally, the purposes of such activities are to further students' academic development, promote intercultural competence, and offer students cultural opportunities that are not readily available to them. Timing, location, theme, cost, and duration are just some of the many variables that will influence the success of field trips. In some cases, incorporating student input into the field trip destination decision can prove empowering to all parties involved.

Field trips are usually planned and facilitated by the program staff, but this does not always need to be the case. In fact, using local students and community volunteers in the process, when feasible, can increase student integration into the local community and provide an opportunity for language and intercultural exchange. For example, some programs periodically offer "art and culture" activities to give students a taste of the traditional arts and crafts of the host country. Members of the community who regularly offer formal instruction in the local community can lead these activities, preferably as volunteers. If they are interested, students would have the option of pursuing private instruction outside of the program with the featured instructors. Another strategy for promoting extracurricular learning is to establish a student council each semester. The elected individuals would represent the program's students in the planning and implementation of field trips and in other programming decisions. The student council can even be allocated a budget to fund programs that are entirely student led.

Volunteer and Community Service

Service work engages students with members of the local community they might not otherwise meet on a daily basis, providing students with expanded insight into the host culture, and an opportunity to contribute to the local community. Volunteer work can be organized for individual or group participation and structured as a one-time or ongoing experience. Program staff play a key role, in most cases, in carefully designating and monitoring potential sites in a way that is sensitive both to local realities and participant interests. Ideally, volunteer opportunities should be highlighted from the start of the program, and the ways to participate made clear and accessible to all students, even those who may be reticent due to cultural or linguistic adjustment concerns.

Language Exchange

Language exchanges are partnerships in which a program participant is paired with a host national who wants to practice his or her English-language skills; the pair agrees to jointly practice the host national and English languages. Language exchanges are a relatively simple way to provide participants with a chance to develop their language skills and meet members of the host community. Care should be exercised in the selection of the language partners and orientation of program participants to insure that all involved are responsible and reliable partners.

Campus-Based Involvement

Study abroad programs that are campus-based or that have affiliations with a local university can often take advantage of the campus facilities and other campus-based opportunities to engage students in cultural and social activities. Meaningful integration with the local student population can effectively break down the perception of the program participants as a "U.S. flock," and also encourage the development of language and communication skills. Students may naturally gather in university-based facilities such as a campus computer center, library, or cafeteria, but in other instances the study abroad program may need to provide additional support and assistance. For example, are students invited to participate in campus clubs or athletic teams? Can the students audition for musical or theatrical performances? Does the campus have an employment center that would be willing to introduce students to companies offering internships? Is there potential for joint programming, such as with guest lecturers, or for field study opportunities? Reciprocally, does the study abroad program regularly invite the participation of local students in its activities and programs? These are all potential avenues for learning, engagement, and pleasure.

Experiential Projects and Field Work

Experiential projects, which may or may not be credit bearing, enable students to deepen their understanding of the host culture by working for a period of time, usually in an internship, extended volunteer work, or field placement capacity. Usually considered a positive addition to programmatic content, such experiential opportunities often require a huge commitment of time, energy, and dedication on the part of any overseas program. This is especially true in host cultures that do not have a strong familiarity with internship placements. When experiential activities need to be integrated with academic course work, even more work is added for on-site staff.

Many factors need to be taken into consideration in setting up experiential programs of whatever type, including program design, cost, feasibility, student expectations, and academics, to list but a few. Answering the following questions will help clarify the processes and procedures needed to facilitate an experiential program:

- Does the program have clear goals and objectives that are well articulated to students, staff, and home institutions?

- Does the overseas program design support an experiential component (e.g., practicality, curriculum design, local business culture, etc.)?

- Is the experiential program feasible (e.g., duration, admission requirements, interview and selection process, etc.)?

- What will the program cost (e.g., staffing, student transportation reimbursements, costs to hosting organizations, insurance, etc.)?

- How will the program secure placements (e.g., screening host organizations, using community networks, marketing and promotion, maximum enrollment, etc.)?

- How will the program manage student expectations (e.g., predeparture information, on-site orientation, troubleshooting, ongoing evaluation, etc.)?

- How will the program develop the academic component (e.g., awarding academic credit, curriculum design, assessment, resources, etc.)?

Part IV: Overseas Program Direction

Intercultural Learning

Intercultural learning, although defined differently by different programs, is one of the most common desired outcomes for study abroad. While it is hoped that students learn content information, improve language skills, and become experts at logistical manoeuvring (all of which can be enlightening and empowering), the intercultural gains that students make, be they humble or awe-inspiring, are among the most meaningful, and even thrilling, aspects of study abroad facilitation. However, trying to create experiences that lead to this sort of learning can be enormously challenging, and most study abroad programs are still far from living up to their full intercultural learning potential.

Intercultural learning should not be reduced to isolated workshops or the occasional critical incident activity; rather, it should infuse all parts of programming abroad, from curriculum design and facilitation to policymaking, local relationship development, and so on. This conceptualisation of intercultural learning stands in contrast to the more traditional view, in which much of intercultural learning was relegated to predeparture or quick-and-dirty on-site orientations, sometimes with a re-entry counterpart, before leaving the program site or after the return home.

At its broadest level, planning for intercultural learning should involve

- articulating what intercultural learning means for a particular program, and what each person's role in the process should be;
- creating an environment that reinforces that intercultural learning is both important and challenging;
- attempting to consciously model the sort of learning and values espoused by the program; and
- defining indicators of success, and critically evaluating (from within and without) how well each aspect of the program is working, in order to continually refine knowledge and practice.

Although there is no single way to catalyse intercultural learning—methods and strategies can and should vary with program type, size, location, academic emphasis, and on-site staff identity as educators—an overall learning plan should take into consideration several key aspects, as defined in the paragraphs below.

The Program's Most Urgent Ideas

The absolute bottom-line ideas that the particular program needs to get across to achieve its own definition of success should be clearly defined, and then recycled and pulled forward in new formats, in increasing depth and degree of challenge, throughout the program. For some programs, these ideas might relate to service and social justice, for others the ideas will foster an appreciation of the link between language and culture, or the development of empathy and tolerance, and so on, depending on the program's individual and institutional mission.

Timing, or the Phases Within the Program

Whether short- or long-term, programs tend to take a particular shape as they play out. The timing of intercultural activities, messages, and workshops is crucial since there are key moments when students are particularly receptive to certain ideas. Orientation is clearly a prime manoeuvring period, but certain ideas or concepts might not be acceptable until later in the program after the students have had a certain experience, interacted with a wide range of local people, or developed a keener sense of who they are within the host culture.

The Balance Between Self and Other

Programs need to create ways for students to relate their increasing knowledge of themselves with growing their knowledge of the other culture in ways that will directly lead students closer to achieving empathy and dialogue within difference.

Methods Balance

While no one learning method is inherently better than another, most educators would probably argue that using a range of tactics will increase the chance of successful learning. Common strategies that foment intercultural learning by either sending students out to elicit knowledge and experience or providing them with a structure in which to analyze (and the two should be balanced) include personal journals, observations, group discussions, critical incidents, research projects, small group activities, interviews, writing exercises, oral presentations, one-on-one counseling, and creative expression (story-writing, art-making), to mention just a few.

Perhaps the most important ingredient in a creative and fruitful imparting of intercultural learning on-site is a willingness on the part of program staff to try myriad combinations, not only to find a design that works, but also to augment their own learning along the way. Unfortunately, there is still a noticeable paucity of literature about actual on-site intercultural learning, a clear indicator that the field needs more sophisticated accounts of on-site practice as well as more intense work on theory-building and intercultural learning pedagogy specific to overseas programs. Currently, the literature that is easily available in the United States can be categorized to resources aimed at students and other sojourners and resources aimed at program directors and other facilitators. See, for example, *Maximizing Study Abroad* (Paige et al. 2004), *The Art of Crossing Cultures* (Storti 2001), and *Whole World Guide to Culture Learning* (Hess 1994), *Figuring Foreigners Out* (Storti, Craig 1999), all of which include some good activities and helpful introductory information, although the text can seem fairly rudimentary to many PDs.

Literature written specifically for the overseas program director is still tremendously scarce, although such works as *Beyond Experience* (Gochenour 1993) and *Education for the Intercultural Experience* (Paige 1993) are excellent starting points for looking at on-site issues in depth. General reading in *Frontiers: The Interdisciplinary Journal of Study Abroad*, NAFSA's *International Educator*, and other magazines and journals will also keep international educators up-to-date with scholarly work and current concerns in the field. These and other resources are increasingly being made available online, a key consideration for educators working outside the United States.

More in-depth work about different aspects of teaching and learning, cross-cultural interactions, and other issues can be found by borrowing resources from other fields and disciplines, and examining them for both theory and examples of practice. Existing work in areas such as service learning, experiential learning, intercultural communication, critical studies, anthropology, and second-language learning provide a wealth of ideas; a general knowledge of the basic tenets of these fields is recommended. Many vital values-oriented issues such as relationship building and reciprocity within the community, ethical decisionmaking, and conflict resolution, as well as postprogram applications, can also be found in literature from these and other areas, and they can frequently be reframed to fit the foreign culture and study abroad context.

Values and Ethical Considerations

Intercultural learning is intrinsically tied to values and ethical concerns for several reasons. First, it is hoped that intercultural learning will promote the development of specific values, such as respect, tolerance, and open-mindedness. Intercultural learning is also embedded in ethical issues, since there are a range of stakeholders in the study abroad process (e.g., students, sending institutions, members of the local community), who all deserve that these cross-cultural encounters be managed and experienced in such a way that everyone is valued as an actor, learner, and potential beneficiary of the changes international educators hope to engender.

The ethical issues raised by study abroad are numerous and complex, and do not lend themselves to quick analysis. Whether the work of study abroad is undertaken in big cities or small communities, there is an immense number of questions related to power, politics, money, privacy, and so on that need to be closely examined. At the very least, on-site directors must carefully think through the potential ramifications of all intercultural interactions, and share their concerns with students as part of the learning process.

Reentry

Although students usually anticipate that they will encounter different ways of thinking and living in the host culture, they are often unaware that they may encounter similar difficulties in preparing for and returning home. Overseas programs can serve students well by providing pre-reentry workshops that address the potential challenges participants may face after completion of the program. These workshops could also allow students an opportunity to reflect on their overall study abroad experience. Such pre-reentry training has become a regular and often required component of study abroad programming, and is best held within a few weeks of departure.

The most commonly expressed goals of pre-reentry workshops are to

- encourage students to identify and examine issues common among students returning home;

- provide guidance and encouragement on appropriate ways to say goodbye in the host culture;

- create an environment in which students feel comfortable considering their personal changes as well as changes that might have taken place at home while they were away;

- solve potential reentry problems by identifying the skills students have developed through their entrance into a new culture;

- encourage students to reflect on the semester as a whole and the individual goals they set during the welcome orientation;

- encourage students to set new goals for their return home;

- show students how to apply the skills they learned abroad to their return home; and
- begin logistical preparations for the students' departure.

As at the beginning of the program, students should be provided with time during the workshop to meet individually with the program director and other staff. Exit interviews are an ideal opportunity to assess students' satisfaction with the program, language learning, intercultural competency development, and academic achievement, as well as give the students some closure to their abroad experiences.

SUMMARY

Running a successful study abroad program necessitates a combination of strong organizational skills, good planning, proactive thinking, extensive networking, careful coordination among interested parties and, most importantly, a tremendous amount of interpersonal and intercultural understanding and empathy. While study abroad programs should seem to flow seamlessly from start to finish as an integrated whole, in fact they are comprised of several distinct, yet interrelated, components and follow a cycle of planning and implementation, whatever their differences may be.

CHAPTER 3

Managing Students and Issues On-Site

Contributors: Skye Stephenson, Mary Lou Forward

The on-site program cycle and critical program components discussed in the previous chapter describe the major aspects of study abroad program planning and implementation, but anyone who has ever run a program knows all too well that things do not always go according to plan. Events, personalities, and issues can and often do deviate from what is anticipated, challenging even the most experienced overseas program staff. Issues can range from the humorous to the tragic, and can involve a single student or the entire group. In all cases, they test the mettle of those involved. The successful resolution of unanticipated issues and challenges is one of the key indicators of a well-functioning study abroad program. Although each case is truly *sui generis*, most situations nevertheless usually fall into one or more of the following areas:

- Personal and intercultural adjustment issues
- Nonacademic counseling and disciplinary issues
- Medical and psychiatric problems
- Social disturbances
- Geo-political problems

ON-SITE PROGRAM STAFF AS ADVISERS AND EMERGENCY RESPONDERS

Being available for participants in need of personal assistance, guidance, or discipline is one of the most important, yet often least visible, aspects of the program director's and on-site staff's responsibilities. Given the intense and often dislocating nature of study abroad for student participants, it is crucial that program staff be ready to provide support for the range of issues that can arise. Preparedness is also what sending institutions and participant parents expect, trusting overseas staff to ensure the safety and well-being of these young adults. Due to changing world circumstances and the changing nature of the student pool, (which as Kadison and DiGeronimo note in *College of the Overwhelmed* (2004) is characterized by an increasing number of students who arrive on campus with significant medical, psychological, even psychiatric conditions many of which become acute during the student's undergraduate experience) the demand on program directors to function as student advisers, counselors, crisis managers, and emergency responders seems greater than ever.

Carrying out the support function effectively and empathetically is one of the most challenging aspects of the program director's job. Most program directors do not come to their positions with extensive advising, counseling, or emergency management experience. Once hired, however, they often find that a significant amount of their time and energy must be devoted to helping a minority of students who are in need, and dealing with unanticipated problems that are usually a far cry from anything they have previously encountered in their professional lives.

Most employer-provided training and preparation for these crucial aspects of the program director job tend to be less thorough than that provided for other job responsibilities—such as academics, reporting, and budgeting—and sometimes the training is even perfunctory. This may be because dealing with student issues such as behavioral issues, psychiatric problems, health problems, adjustment difficulties and the like are so complex to deal with, for staff, students, professors, and even parents alike. Greater attention will have to be devoted to expanding the scope of staff training to include these and other emerging areas. Dealing with the complex, often contradictory issues students present is a challenge for the profession as a whole, of course, not just for overseas staff and program directors. Staff training at home and overseas should include clear statements of the responsibilities of each staff member, a discussion of obligations of the role of each within the team and the program and finally an extensive consideration of the 'duty' (that is the extent of reasonable care) owed to the students and to each other. These are especially important with regard to job performance and in reducing the programs exposure to risk.

Personal and Intercultural Adjustment Support

During the study abroad sojourn, students' personal growth and learning is intrinsically intertwined with the intercultural interface. In fact, learning firsthand about "the other," and, in the process, learning more about oneself and one's own culture, may be the most essential component of education abroad and what distinguishes it from study on the home campus. Much was discussed in the previous chapter about planned intercultural adjustment activities and the centrality of these exercises in study abroad programming. While such activities can indeed go far in promoting and supporting participants' intercultural learning and adjustment—as anyone who has ever lived overseas knows all too well—it is never easy living in a culture different than one's own. Culture shock, as we know, affects just about every student in some way. In fact, students who do not experience some degree of culture shock might be worrisome, since an absence of culture shock could indicate they are not fully involved in the new culture that surrounds them. In the majority of cases, with proper preparation and orientation, students become able to navigate themselves through the intercultural learning process without a need for undue or excessive support from program staff.

On the other hand, it is important to remember that nearly all participants will experience a challenging period during their overseas stay. During such times, support from program staff can go far in allaying some of the students' temporary distresses, prodding them along the path of further intercultural growth. Some individuals, however, may experience more severe and long-term signs of distress and disorientation. In some cases, the manifestations may be primarily ideational, whereas in other cases there can be concrete, observable physical symptoms too. It takes a savvy program leader to spot the students who are experiencing excessive adjustment issues, and initiate whatever additional advising is necessary to guide them through the adjustment period as smoothly as possible. Such help is sometimes crucial. Because the program aim is to encourage and support cross-cultural experiences that allow all participants to learn as much as they can during their sojourns, severe and unresolved intercultural adjustment can lead to behavioral, academic, and even medical or psychiatric problems.

Although no one technique works in all cases, probably the most useful approach is empathetic listening and guided reflection, which encompasses three discrete stages. The first stage embodies deep and concerned listening on the part of the support person, hearing what the individual spews out and taking it all in; such listening requires patience and restraint, and can take hours and even days. In the second stage, the support person assists the participant in contextualizing his or her feelings and experiences, guiding the individual to consider current experiences within the context of his or her life and in connection with others. Not infrequently, what may seem to the individual experiencing intercultural stress to be an issue or problem unique to him or her is proven to be common for other program participants as well. This realization can help alleviate a student's other concerns. If another, third stage of counseling is needed, the support person should gently but firmly guide the participant to focus on the near future and the remainder of the program experience. The support person can help the participant set concrete goals, towards which the participant's energies can be devoted, and his or her new personal and intercultural skills and resources can be used. Many other methods can be employed to help participants ease intercultural adjustment "bumps," and some methods do not involve intensive work on the part of program staff. Participants can be encouraged to keep journals or carry out other reflective practices. Group-dynamic work, such as periodic debriefings, peer exchange, or intercultural thematic dialogues with host nationals, can also be very effective adjustment tools. In some cases, it can be helpful for students to maintain ties and communication flows with family and friends from home, but excessive contact with people back home can actually inhibit adjustment to the host culture and increase intercultural angst. Recently, some program leaders have begun to use less conventional techniques to ease students' adjustment period stress. For example, in some cases dreams serve to incubate intercultural issues. Discussing dreams can be a way to uncover the areas of greatest concern and stress to a participant, and those areas can be worked on through other venues (Stephenson 2003). Needless to say, this is not an approach that works for everyone, and special degrees of trust on the part of the student, and sensitivity on the part of the facilitator, are required.

Another way that personal and intercultural issues may surface is through students testing the limits of appropriate behavior or trying on new roles and behaviors. In a new and quite different setting than their home base, with people they have never met before and might never see again, some participants will act in ways they never would back home. Within limits, taking on new roles or behaviors can be a very positive aspect of study abroad, and can foster personal growth and maturity. In some cases, however, if taken to extremes, such change can be worrisome and even potentially dangerous to the participant or other people with whom the participant is interacting. Examples of such behaviors include increased partying, lessened concern for personal safety and security, changing patterns in alcohol use, and different interactions with possible sexual partners. If and when these types of behavior occur, program staff need to monitor situations and deal with them sensitively but proactively, to avoid potential problems later on. In some cases, program staff may have to reprimand or take disciplinary action against the involved participant.

DISCIPLINARY ISSUES

One of the most difficult tasks of the program director can be dealing with students who violate the standards of acceptable behavior. On-site staff have to handle the types of issues faced at home by a host of U.S. campus staff, but with additional dimensions of complexity from intercultural and distance factors. While some program participants may behave in a way that is not any different abroad than it is at home, others use the study abroad experience to try out new ways of thinking and being. Students who have no previous record of behavioral problems may "act out" during a study abroad program, while other students who have problematic behavior at home may "pull it together" on site, surprising everyone involved.

Such a variety of participant responses to the study abroad experience underscores the uniqueness of each participant's experience on site. Program staff can and should employ a variety of means to encourage positive participant behavior and sanction inappropriate behavior. Four principal means of doing this are

- norm establishment,
- activity scheduling,
- monitoring student behavior, and
- intervening appropriately.

Norm Establishment

From the outset, program rules and norms should be clearly articulated to participants and thoroughly discussed. Many sending institutions have rules of student conduct that participants are expected to understand and comply with while abroad, and nearly all study abroad organizations do as well. Thus, most program participants have already signed some sort of code of conduct prior to arriving at the program location. Additionally, many programs have developed their own rules of conduct, which should mesh with any rules in use at the home institution. At a minimum, these policies should include the program's positions on alcohol and drug use, sexual harassment, and appropriate and inappropriate behavior; guidelines for using services offered by the program and host university (when applicable); and disciplinary measures used in cases of program-rule violation. Some program directors find it helpful to require students to sign the rules, and some even engage the students in tests or discussions about the rules. When feasible, it is important to explain the reasons for the rules, and link them, as appropriate, to intercultural differences and realities.

Some program directors have found it useful to move beyond imposing already established rules to working with the newly arrived group to establish its own code of conduct. Those who support this approach find it invaluable in fomenting active group dynamics because the participants become invested in respecting the rules and guidelines they develop. Such contracts seem to be especially useful in issues related to language use (at sites where this is a relevant issue), behavior on field trips, engagement with the host community, and the like. These guidelines can sometimes be developed along with personal and group goal setting at the beginning of the semester, and periodically returned to throughout the program for assessment and reevaluation.

Activity Scheduling

Complementary to the establishment of behavioral rules and guidelines is the scheduling of activities designed to provide emotional and personal support to the students. During the early stages of a program, it is advisable for program staff to hold discussions or plan relaxing activities that can help reduce students' emotional stress. Periodically scheduling events such as group meals, informal discussions concerning students' experiences, or carrying out debriefings designed to assess the current group dynamics and concerns can provide invaluable support to participants and help staff get a better sense of the salient issues and concerns that participants may be dealing with.

Additionally, students should be informed at the beginning of the program of staff availability and guidelines for seeking assistance. It is also important that students know that there are other resources available to them beyond the program structure, and that they will be referred to the extra resources as appropriate. Reasonable use of staff time for counseling and support should be encouraged, but if a student is using excessive amounts of staff time for personal support, other options for supporting that student should be investigated. Host family members or members of the host institution community often prove to be invaluable sources of support for participants, and are usually willing to work closely with program staff in this regard.

Monitoring Student Behavior

The third component of nonacademic program assistance is monitoring student behavior. It can sometimes be hard for program staff to evaluate if a participant's inappropriate or seemingly abnormal behavior is a result of cultural stress, peer pressure, a difficult event in the student's life, or if it is a regular feature of the student's behavioral repertoire. If a student seems to be acting "off," or is reacting in an unexpected way, intervening to offer the student support is usually the most appropriate response. Often, it is enough for students to have the opportunity to talk their situation over with someone, and little follow-up is required. However, staff should be on the lookout for symptoms of more serious issues, which might necessitate referral to a counselor, advising appropriate individuals on the home campus, or more aggressive intervention techniques. In no case should staff try to counsel students on an ongoing basis or deal with issues that they do not feel qualified to address.

Intervening Appropriately

In cases where the student's behavior violates the rules of the program or is offensive to members of the host culture, other students, or staff, disciplinary measures should be taken. Options for disciplinary action include verbal or written warnings, probation, removal of the student from one or more aspects of the program, and dismissal from the program. Generally speaking, verbal and written warnings are used for a first-time, relatively minor offense, such as rude or inappropriate behavior, while probation is used to address repeated offenses or a more serious violation of program rules. Usually, the student is given a letter of probation, which should clearly spell out the problem, the expectations for the student's behavior or responsibilities from that point forward, any sanctions given to the student, and the consequences of breaking the terms of probation. The appropriate program staff member and the student should sign such a letter; one copy should be kept on file in the program office, one copy given to the student, and one copy given to the home office.

A student's removal from the program can be warranted in extreme situations or when the terms of a student's probation are not met. If dismissal is recommended, the appropriate administrator (who could be located at the program site or at the sponsoring institution, depending on the structure of the program) must approve the decision. It is important not to tell the student that he or she will be dismissed until after the approval has been secured, because if approval is not given the credibility of program staff will be in serious question. Dismissal can be quite complicated, and involves notification of the host university and the home university, the student's removal from program housing, consideration of how and what other students will be told about the dismissal, and dealing with follow-up issues.

It is important to keep in mine that in some cases program dismissal does not always mean that the dismissed student will go home, or even that the student will leave the program site. There have been situations in which the dismissed student had decided to remain at the locale, either taking classes at some other institute on their own, working or "just hanging out." When this occurs, the negative impact of a dismissed student remaining in the vicinity of the program can be great, particularly if the student has the sympathy of one or more students or staff. On the other hand, the negative impact of a student who has flagrantly violated program rules remaining on the program can be even greater.

MEDICAL AND PSYCHIATRIC ISSUES

All on-site program leaders need to be prepared for the moment when a serious medical or psychiatric problem suddenly emerges, bringing into play a plethora of different issues and responsibilities. (Health and safety issues are treated in Part II, Chapter 5, "Health Issues and Advising Responsibilities," and Part II, Chapter 6, "Advising Students on Safety and Security Issues," and Part III, Chapter 6, "Maximizing Safety and Security and Minimizing Risk in Education Abroad Programs") Unless program directors and local staff are fully trained and certified in advanced first aid or licensed medical specialists, they should not provide medical services during a program except under the gravest and most critical emergency circumstances. All participation agreements should include language allowing program staff to apply first aid as a last resort before the arrival of emergency medical personnel. In all cases, it is crucial that study abroad program staff have an updated listing of local doctors, psychiatrists, and medical facilities, and that they know when it is appropriate to refer participants to those resources. That said, it is advisable for program directors and other staff to receive some type of emergency first aid training when feasible, especially for staff working on programs that have incorporated educational excursions to areas not rapidly accessible to medical facilities, as can be the case in many rural program locales.

An important responsibility of local program staff is to stay abreast of and keep stateside collaborators and program participants informed of major health concerns and developments in the program locale. While it is not possible to provide comprehensive information about every potential on-site health risk, particular attention should be given to two areas: (1) emerging or rapidly increasing health problems in the program locale, especially those that might not be readily known back in the United States; and (2) potential health risks that may be quite different from those in the United States, such as health issues related to pollution, use of heating devices, traffic patterns, certain foods or beverages, and others. All of this information should be imparted during student orientation and provided in a written format when possible, both for student reference as well as for legal reasons. It is often very useful to invite a program doctor, public health worker, or other host-national health specialist to address the group about some of these issues. Participants tend to take the comments of a local expert more seriously than those of the program staff.

It is also very important that program participants be informed early on regarding how to proceed in the case of a routine or emergency medical problem, and that they are reminded about their insurance coverage and their own liability. At some programs, for example, students do not receive any insurance coverage if they engage in certain activities such as skydiving, scuba diving, or horseback riding, or if they fly on aircraft that are not part of the International Air Transport Association system. Other types of insurance coverage may require participants to make a copayment for doctor visits and the like.

Especially at program sites where the host culture language is not English, students may have anxiety about going to a doctor or medical specialist who might not speak English very well or at all, and some participants may request that a member of the program staff go with them. Whether and in what situations a member of the program staff should accompany participants to routine doctors' visits raises a whole host of issues. It is not uncommon for some participants to feel hesitant to use the health care system in an unfamiliar environment, and their feelings are totally understandable, but at some program sites, staff can be overwhelmed with requests for accompaniment to doctors' visits, leaving the staff with little time for other program activities. Obviously, some middle ground needs to be reached.

Whenever a participant is experiencing a medical situation serious enough to keep him or her out of class for more than 24 to 48 hours, the U.S. program staff should be informed. In some cases, the sending institution may also request to be informed of this type of situation. Needless to say, anytime a participant is hospitalized, for whatever reason, the home office should be informed and kept updated regarding the student's progress. In some cases, such as when a student contracts malaria in certain program locales in the tropics, hospital visits may be routine, but information about the student and his or her progress should be transmitted to the folks back in the United States to allay excessive worries.

While participant medical problems are obviously an area of serious attention and concern for program staff, psychiatric issues typically prove to be even more challenging to deal with. Given the variety of possible psychiatric issues such as eating disorders, depression, and bipolar disorder, among others some participants may have and the expansion of student participation in study abroad programs,, it is not surprising that many program directors number dealing with psychiatric issues of the participants among their most challenging experiences on the job. In some cases, a student's application clearly indicates the student's psychiatric situation and staff are informed prior to the participant's arrival; in other cases, staff have no idea of a student's psychiatric issues and can only surmise based on observation, and sometimes the participant's comments, throughout the course of the program.

Whatever the situation, dealing with students who have psychiatric issues is never easy. Not infrequently, especially at smaller, more integrated programs, even having one or two such participants can alter the entire group dynamic, and in some cases the afflicted participant may need large amount of time and energy of the from the staff and others. Finding host-national psychiatrists to guide and support such individuals can be even more difficult at many program sites than locating other competent medical professionals, due to language issues and, even more significantly, marked cross-cultural differences regarding definitions of psychiatric wellness and techniques for dealing with psychiatric disturbances. For instance, views of family and a student's ties with his or her family are usually quite different in the United States than in many other cultures around the world. The United States typically differs, too, in its views regarding adolescence, male and female behaviors, and sexuality, among others.

This information is not meant to dissuade potential participants with a psychiatric history and their proponents among family and sending institutions from participating in study abroad; in fact, in some cases there have been clearly marked improvements for such individuals as a result of their study abroad experiences. It is intended, however, to raise some of the important issues and concerns that may be involved when dealing with such participants, especially from the perspective of overseas program staff.

The questions of when and under what conditions on-site staff should inform parents or guardians in the case of a medical or psychiatric emergency, especially when the student requests confidentiality, raise profound ethical and legal concerns. Whenever possible, the home office should be consulted in such cases. In the event that consultation cannot take place, the program director may have to unilaterally choose how to proceed, guided by the severity of the situation, the guidelines of the program and any signed medical release forms, and liability concerns.

Geo-Political Issues

A quite different area of concern and attention for program staff concerns the possible impact of social disturbances or geo-political issues on the participants of a study abroad program. Such concerns have always been part of any international educational enterprise, especially at certain locales, but with the changes that have taken place both within the United States and internationally since September 11, 2001, U.S. students abroad now seem to require greater support than ever before. While one of the most important aspects of the study abroad experience is providing participants the chance to view the United States from abroad, recent events worldwide have given rise at many sites to an increase in anti-U.S. sentiment. This sentiment

Chapter 3: Managing Students and Issues On-Site

may be manifested in a variety of ways, including individual comments, academic dialogue, media commentaries, demonstrations or political events, and other, more extreme situations.

Whatever the geo-political situation is at the program site, program staff should take a proactive role in informing and guiding students on the reasons that some host nationals may harbor anti-U.S. sentiment. In addition, such commentaries must be empathetic and politically neutral, validating the perspectives of both the participants and host nationals, and recognizing the diversity of opinions within both groups. Care must be taken to permit participants their own views regarding the United States and its foreign policy, and provide a safe space for intragroup differences.

In addition to encouraging intragroup discussion regarding views of the United States in the host society, other techniques are useful. Sometimes, asking qualified host nationals to discuss their views regarding the United States and its foreign policy with the group can be an enlightening experience for many participants. So too can a visit to the nearest U.S. embassy or consulate, when feasible.. In some locations, host country institutions have been very helpful and supportive of their U.S.-based visiting students. One such example is the American University in Cairo (AUC). Tomadar Rifat, director of the international office, explains some of the ways her institution has attempted to support U.S. students during trying times:

> With the political tension that surfaced in the aftermath of Sep 11 and increased with the Iraqi war, a special challenge had to be confronted by AUC. In order to relieve U.S. student stress, reduce their anxiety level, discuss their worries and concerns, and help them not to be intimidated by threats of political violence (sometimes inflated by the media etc.), several debriefing sessions were held between the different constituencies of international students and senior administrators and counselors. Some American students even got involved in the Model United Nations (MUN) and the Model Arab League (MAL) as delegates representing Arab countries. By being involved in political, economic, and cultural discussions in a healthy atmosphere and doing the needed research, these students reached a higher level of understanding of the issues taking place in the Middle East and learnt that there is no one sided view. This understanding makes the student gain a clear vision of what is going on, feel more comfortable and definitely less threatened by any alarming tone of the news.

Yet another way to help allay some of the feeling of increasing U.S. "particularism" in the world is by providing more opportunities for true reciprocity and exchange with program partners in the host culture. While one can cogently contend that it is more crucial than ever that U.S. students have the opportunity to "go global" and partake of life and study in other nations and cultures, an equally strong argument can be made that students from the international receiving institutions or other members of the host society should be accorded the same opportunity when feasible. The issue of reciprocity is being raised more often by many receiving institutions, which are asking, Where is the "exchange" aspect of U.S.-based study abroad? As Lars Fransen from Uppsala University of Sweden recently put it, "Exchange has a distinct advantage over study abroad or one-way mobility because it promotes collaboration and a sense of natural relationship between home students and international students."

A different scenario that may have repercussions for the program ranging from mild to severe has to do with host country disturbances of a political or social nature that impact program functioning and participant well-being. Such possibilities are myriad, ranging from the prevalent student strikes at many host country institutions in certain locales, to such severe disturbances that entire study abroad programs have to be evacuated. The latter situation has wide-ranging logistical, academic, and personal implications.

While no hard-and-fast rule can be enunciated regarding how to deal with such situations, one of the keys to success is having a strong and solid network of knowledgeable insiders to provide up-to-date and accurate information upon which decisions can be based. Not infrequently, the media images and story do not realistically portray the on-site situation, and sometimes program directors and other local staff will need to devote significant energy to providing counterpoint perspectives to convince their U.S. colleagues of the reasons for enacting certain program decisions. In all cases, accurate dialogue and frequent updates between the home and host offices are crucial to a successful outcome of the situation.

Evaluating how to manage a situation in a locale for which a U.S. Department of State advisory is in place is extremely serious and important for ensuring program participants' safety and security. The situation is made more complex by the variety of reasons used by the U.S. Department of State to enunciate these advisory statements, which address a range of situations from serious and even dangerous ones, to ones more motivated by geo-political concerns. In some cases, the advisory may be specific to a particular area or region in the host country, which actually may be quite far from the program base (see Gobbo, Forward, and Lorenz 2005).

Whatever the actual host country situation and the reason for the travel advisory, the situation must be handled especially carefully. The reasons for the travel advisory must be carefully researched, an informed analysis (including insurance and liability assessment) of any risks must be made, and program participants and families, as well as sending institutions, must be accurately and promptly informed and updated. In some cases, involving not only the home office but also others involved with international education back in the United States, and particularly, consulting with other program providers that may be facing the same situation, can be very helpful. Whatever the situation on site, students from the United States are well advised to follow U.S. Department of State advisory guidelines regarding appropriate behavior abroad (www.travel.state.gov); they should maintain a low profile and pay attention to clothing, speech, behavior, and locations frequented by members of the host community.

PLANNING FOR EMERGENCIES

In all situations, whether medical, psychiatric, or geo-political in nature, one of the most important of the program director's hats is dealing with potential and real crises at the program site. Successful resolution of any situation depends in large part on the program leader and staff being able to steer a steady course during the emergency, whatever its nature may be; this demands steely nerves and a sharp mind, as well as careful advance preparation, good local contacts, strong communication skills, sound judgment, great personal empathy, and the ability to know when to act and when to delegate. Needless to say, emergency planning and successful on-site plan execution must be carefully coordinated with what is going on back in the United States in order to be fully effective. Successful emergency planning begins long before any crisis arises; in fact, advanced planning is one of the most important aspects of emergency preparedness. Advanced planning should focus on two areas: (1) taking steps to avoid emergencies and crises to the extent possible, and (2) establishing clear plans and procedures for how to deal with emergencies and crises should they occur.

There are several ways to reduce the chances of experiencing a program emergency. One is to inform participants and other involved individuals in advance of the possible risks involved at certain program sites and of what they can do to minimize those risks. Program participants and staff can be informed of the potential risks in various ways, such as by sending information to the home institutions via the internet, or through material that the study abroad program itself generates, such as a safety audit. Once at the program site, important information about safety and security and ways to minimize risks and prevent emergencies of various types should be made available to students soon after arrival. This information should be reiterated throughout the program's duration and updated as host country conditions warrant.

A complementary way to help reduce certain risks is to make the program participants accountable for their own behavior. Each student should be familiarized with the program's policies and procedures regarding personal safety, behavior standards and codes of conduct, and drugs and alcohol. Additionally, students should understand the reasons for the policies and procedures. As important as avoiding emergencies is establishing clear plans and procedures in the case of an emergency. Such crisis planning involves three complementary aspects: (1) information acquisition; (2) risk-management analysis, and (3) crisis team management.

Information Acquisition

All study abroad centers must have accurate and updated information for their emergency contacts in the host country. The extent of this information depends partly on the nature of the program, but at a minimum it should include reliable hospitals, doctors of different specialties, psychiatrists and psychologists, a lawyer or legal adviser, the police, ambulance companies, insurance contacts, the U.S. embassy or nearest consulate, and reliable transportation providers and travel agents (in the event that a rapid evacuation needs to be carried out).

Risk Management

All program sites should carry out their own risk-management analysis prior to program initiation and update it as the situation warrants. Risk-management analysis is a systematic form of advanced emergency planning, the end result of which is the generation of clear emergency plans and procedures. The benefits of establishing a risk-management plan include helping make the program staff and other involved individuals prepared to respond rapidly and appropriately to a crisis, demonstrating the serious commitment of the program to meeting student needs, and avoiding or lessening, in some cases, the severity of a potentially serious situation. Additionally, risk management can be a defense against lawsuits in some situations.

Part IV: Overseas Program Direction

Once the plans have been developed, they should be written down and made readily accessible to all on-site program staff. (For more on Risk Management issues, see Part III, Chapter 7, Maximizing Safety and Security and Minimizing Risk in Education Abroad Programs.)

Crisis Team Management

Establishing a Crisis Management Team

All program sites should have a designated crisis management team willing to be called on in the event of an emergency or crisis, and able to perform the following functions: provide a coordinated and comprehensive response to the crisis; determine which staff will play what roles; notify the proper authorities; coordinate travel and make medical arrangements if needed; set up a communications network for students and other concerned individuals; and evaluate and assess the response strategies. Inclusion in the crisis management team is usually based on either an individual's expertise and knowledge of an arena crucial for managing the crisis or the individual's affiliation with the program.

While members of the crisis management team do not need to physically meet, it is preferable to contact the designated individuals in advance and discuss with them the plans and procedures for crises. In some situations, the nature of the crisis may necessitate the need to incorporate a new person into the crisis management team; if this should occur, the new individual should be made familiar with the overall composition of the team as well as the program procedures. An additional consideration is that many U.S.-based sending institutions and organizations have their own crisis teams, which can prove to be invaluable resources during emergencies in certain circumstances.

Responding to Crises

Despite planning to reduce the potential for an emergency, sooner or later, an individual or group crisis will occur at nearly all study abroad programs at some point. To prepare for such a moment is wise and prudent. Depending on the location, type, and sponsorship of the program, crisis management planning usually needs to be coordinated with other institutions, both at the program locale and in the United States. Although the crisis may occur on site, it has more than one "home."

Even with the best-laid plans and procedures, emergencies can and do occur. In the event of a potential crisis, a crucial first step is to assess the situation, evaluating how serious it seems to be and whether it appears to be a real emergency or only a perceived one. What is important to point out here is that sometimes, what may seem to be a real emergency for the stateside folks might not be one for on-site staff, or vice versa. In such cases, clear and careful discussion and information sharing must occur to reach an accurate picture of the situation.

If it is decided that the event is only a perceived emergency, appropriate steps still need to be taken. Even if real risk is not an issue, perceived emergencies should not be downplayed. In some cases, a perceived emergency may indicate an event that resident staff should continue to monitor. In addition, the perception of the emergency should be dealt with, especially if sending institution staff or the students' families are concerned.

If it is decided that the event is a real emergency, the nature of the crisis will determine, to some extent, what procedures should be followed. In general, whatever the situation, it is crucial to begin to maintain a written log as soon as possible, to record all interactions related to the events as they unfold and simultaneously network with members of the crisis management team, the main U.S. office, and other relevant individuals and groups to gather and disseminate crucial information.

Knowing how and when to inform program participants of an emergency is another key component of successful crisis management. The time and manner by which participants are notified should be evaluated on a case-by-case basis. A general rule of thumb is that it is best to keep participants in the loop of what is happening, to dispel potential rumors and allay understandable fears, but to not share unnecessary details of the situation with them. What often happens during emergencies at programs with multiple staff is that one or two staff members handle the emergency while other staff focus on the participants.

An additional consideration is the program's policies regarding dealing with the media; some home offices permit local communication with the media, whereas others require that all media inquiries go through them. Whatever the official policy, it is usually a good idea for the local staff to avoid talking with the media because such communication can sometimes result in misrepresentation of the situation, adding to the already complicated on-site issues that the program director has to deal with during times of crisis.

Once a course of action has been decided on and executed, and the crisis seems to be subsiding, there is still much that needs to be done from the program staff perspective. Possible crisis follow-up steps might include debriefing the crisis management team; monitoring the situation of program participants and ascertaining if any participants need special support; maintaining regular communication with affected family members; maintaining regular communication with the sending institution; maintaining communication with the nearest U.S. embassy or consulate (if relevant); evaluating commercial insurance coverage, and more. It is crucial during this postcrisis period that program staff and participants feel there is a closure of the situation. Additionally, program directors may feel emotionally and physically drained after dealing with the crisis, and may need to take care of their own well-being. These efforts should be supported by the home office to the extent possible.

Summary

Program directors and other overseas staff are truly the frontline point people for all overseas program problems and issues that arise, whatever their nature may be. Careful planning, solid networking, strong contacts with host nationals, good communication with the home office and sending institutions, and informed and updated knowledge of a variety of realities in the host country can help overseas program staff successfully navigate through perceived and real problems on site. At their deepest core, though, emergency or crisis situations demand great personal resources and reserves of time, energy, and empathy from program staff. Such situations can be, and often are, frustrating, challenging, and extremely demanding, yet they also can be tremendously rewarding as well, providing the grist for much personal and intercultural learning and professional growth.

Contributors

EDITORS

Joseph L. Brockington, Ph.D., is associate provost for International Programs and director of the Center for International Programs at Kalamazoo College. He also holds an appointment as associate professor of German language and literature at Kalamazoo College and has been a visiting professor of German in the Department of Literary Studies at the University of Hamburg. Brockington serves on the executive committee of the Association of International Education Administrators (AIEA) and is the AIEA Representative to the Inter-associational Advisory Committee on Health and Safety (formerly known as the Interorganizational Task Force on Safety and Responsibility in Study Abroad; comprised of AIEA, NAFSA, Council on International Educational Exchange, National Association of Student Personnel Administrators, other professional organizations, and a number of study abroad providers). He is a past Chair of NAFSA's Section on U.S. Students Abroad (SECUSSA). He has served as a member of the founding board of the Forum on Education Abroad and was a member of the board of the International Wolfgang Borchert Society. He has presented numerous papers at international, national, and regional, and consortial conferences on German literature, study abroad orientation and reentry, and international programs administration; and has published on education abroad, campus internationalization, and modern German literature. He has contributed to the *Journal of Studies in International Education* and *IIE Networker*, and is slated to be the guest editor of a special issue of *Frontiers: the Interdisciplinary Journal of Study Abroad* devoted to the budgetary and financial issues of education abroad.

Patricia C. Martin is the senior overseas program manager for the Office of International Programs at the University of Pennsylvania. She has served as chair of SECUSSA, as program coordinator for the 2003 NAFSA annual conference, and as chair and dean of the annual conference workshop on Safety and Responsibility in Education Abroad. She is a member of the Advisory Council and the Assessment for International Education Committee for the Forum on International Education and serves as the chair of the Interassociational Advisory Committee on Health and Safety (formerly known as the Interorganizational Task Force on Safety and Responsibility in Study Abroad; comprised of AIEA, NAFSA, Council on International Educational Exchange, National Association of Student Personnel Administrators, other professional organizations, and a number of study abroad providers).

Contributors

William W. Hoffa is a writer, editor, consultant, teacher, adviser, and mentor. He has academic degrees from Michigan, Harvard, and Wisconsin, with teaching experience at Vanderbilt University and Hamilton College; Senior Fulbright Lecturer, University of Jyvaskyla, Finland; National Endowment for the Humanities fellow, University of New Mexico. Formerly, he has served as the executive director of Scandinavian Seminar Inc.; field director of Academic Programs, CIEE; and international education editor of *Transitions Abroad* magazine. Hoffa has been active in NAFSA for more than two decades. He served as chair of SECUSSA and has been author or editor of numerous NAFSA publications: essays, interviews, book reviews, and reports, including co-editor of the first, second, and third editions of *NAFSA'S Guide to Education Abroad for Advisers and Administrators* and *Crisis Management in a Cross-Cultural Setting*. He is the author of *Study Abroad: A Parent's Guide*. Currently, he is study abroad adviser, Amherst College; adjunct faculty, School for International Training, and principal consultant, Academic Consultants International and is at work on a volume on the history of American study abroad.

CONTRIBUTORS

Lynn C. Anderson is the associate director and director of curriculum integration in the Learning Abroad Center (LAC) at University of Minnesota, Twin Cities (UMTC), has master's degrees in German and ESL and 19 years experience in academic advising at UMTC. Anderson was the faculty adviser for students conducting research in Germany in 1981, 1988, and 2003. She has presented at numerous international, national, and regional conferences.

Mel Bolen is currently the interim director of International Programs at Brown University. She has 16 years of experience in international education, with special interests in financial management, program development, and developing international education research studies. Bolen has a master's degree in international education from Lesley College and is nearing completion of a Ph.D. in American civilization at Brown University.

Susan Holme Brick is director of International Programs at Whitman College. She has directed the study abroad programs at Whitman since 1994 and administers two Whitman programs in China. She holds a master's degree in Asian studies from the University of California at Berkeley and a bachelor's degree in history from Colgate University.

Rosa Marina de Brito Meyer is a native Carioca (born in Rio de Janeiro). She holds bachelor's, master's, and doctoral degrees in Portuguese language, including a doctoral degree in linguistics from the University of Alberta. She directs the Brown University Program at Pontificia Universidade Católica in Rio de Janeiro, where she is currently associate vice president for Academic Affairs in charge of international programs.

Jim Buschman is senior associate director of the division of international programs abroad at Syracuse University. He holds a doctoral degree and a certificate of Latin American studies from the University of Florida and has lived in Nigeria, Mexico, Brazil, and Germany. Formerly, Buschman worked in study abroad with the School for International Training, Kalamazoo College, and Alma College. He is chair of NAFSA's SECUSSA Whole World Committee. He has organized and presented at NAFSA workshops on whole world education.

Shannon Cates is currently on leave from her position as associate director for international training at Rice University.

Lisa Chieffo taught German and Italian at the University of Delaware before becoming study abroad coordinator there in 1993. As a student she studied in Vienna and in Tübingen and Bayreuth, Germany. She has served as associate director of Delaware's Center for International Studies since 2001.

Bill Cressey has been a vice president and the chief academic officer at Council on International Educational Exchange (CIEE) since 1996. Prior to joining the Council staff, he was professor of Spanish linguistics at Georgetown University, where he also served as chair of the Spanish department and director of the office of international programs.

Lisa D. Donatelli, director of the office of international education, Bucknell University. Donatelli is currently completing her doctoral degree at the Graduate School of Education and Human Development at the George

Washington University. Prior to her tenure at Bucknell, she served as director of overseas studies at Georgetown University. She is an active NAFSA presenter, and has served a three-year term as chair of the SECUSSA Telecommunications and Technology Committee.

Sara Dumont completed a doctoral degree in music history from the University of Oxford in 1985. Dumont has been director of the American University AU Abroad program since December 2003. Sara began her career in international education as an assistant director of undergraduate admissions at Yale University, where her duties included the admission of international students. From 1992 to 1997, she was assistant and then associate director of the office of foreign academic programs at Duke University, and subsequently she was director of study abroad at Towson University, from 1997 to 2003.

Jane Edwards is director of international programs at Harvard University. Coauthor with Humphrey Tonkin of *The World in the Curriculum*, she has been active in the field of international education for more than twenty years. Edwards' bachelor's degree is from Cambridge University, and her doctoral degree is from the University of Pennsylvania.

Jim Ellis, Ph.D. is director of international education at Auburn University. Ellis received his doctoral degree in curriculum and instruction with an emphasis in learning in informal settings from the University of Florida. He holds a master's degree in Latin American studies and a bachelor's degree of arts in zoology. Currently, he is vice president of the Alabama Council for International Programs and a member of the Association of International Education Administrators executive committee. During his tenure in the field, Ellis has served leading roles in technology such as regional Tech SIG and Micro SIG representative, regional Web master, and NCSA listserv manager.

Stephen Ferst is the director of the study abroad programs at Rutgers University. He has been working professionally in international education since 1989 as an adviser, recruiter, resident director, and program director. He has studied abroad in Israel and has lived and worked abroad in the United Kingdom. He earned a doctoral degree in educational administration from Rutgers University and has primary research interests in university governance and department chair responsibilities.

Mary Lou Forward, director of African studies for the School for International Training (SIT), has worked extensively in international exchange and study abroad program management at both the high school and university levels. A former overseas director for SIT Study Abroad programs in Madagascar, she also served as technical adviser for several village development projects. Forward has presented and conducted training on issues of sustainable development, environmental conser-vation, cultural adaptation, and international exchange at universities, organizations, and professional meetings. Prior to joining SIT in 1992, she worked at a variety of institutions as an administrator in higher education.

Charles Gliozzo is a professor of history and assistant to the dean, international studies and programs. Formerly, he served as director of study abroad (1973–1993) at Michigan State University. He holds a bachelor's degree (cum laude) from St. John's College, New York, and a doctoral degree in history, from the State University of New York at Buffalo. Gliozzo has been the recipient of two Fulbright grants and the SECUSSA leadership award. He served as chair of SECUSSA, NAFSA Region V, NAFSA Financial Aid Committee, NAFSA Advocacy Committee, among others.

Joan Elias Gore, Ph.D., is director of institutional relations for Denmark's International Study Program. She served formerly as a faculty member and study abroad adviser at the University of Virginia (1972–1987). From 1987 to 1997 she served with U.S. and British international exchange agencies. Her publications include *Cost-Effective Techniques for Internationalizing the Campus and Curriculum*, numerous articles, and contributions to book chapters. She has contributed to panels, workshops, and professional training programs for international education and academic associations.

Judith A. Green is senior director for member relations & leadership services at NAFSA. She is the author of two publications in NAFSA's *To Your Health* series and has received two co-op grants for international student health-related projects. She and Joan Gore previously collaborated on *HealthCheck for Study, Work, and Travel Abroad*, published jointly by NAFSA and the Council on International Educational Exchange.

Contributors

Amy Bass Henry is associate director of the office of international education, Georgia Institute of Technology. She has worked at Georgia Tech since 1995 and is a member of NAFSA Trainer Corps, IAESTE Advisory Committee, and the NAFSA Financial Aid and Resources for Study Abroad Committee.

Jennifer Hirsch is associate director of study abroad at Northwestern University. She has a bachelor's degree in American culture from Northwestern and a doctoral degree in cultural anthropology from Duke University. At Northwestern, she teaches courses on research abroad to outbound students and returnees. She also serves as a member of the editorial board of *Abroad View* magazine.

Joe Hoff is a doctoral candidate in the comparative and international development education program at the University of Minnesota. He is a graduate assistant for the Center for Advanced Research on Language Acquisition and the university's Learning Abroad Center. Hoff has more than 13 years of experience in study abroad administration. He has studied intercultural communication at the School for International Training and the Summer Institute for Intercultural Communication.

Pamela Houston is public relations coordinator for the National Clearinghouse on Disability and Exchange. Houston served two years each with the Peace Corps in Kiribati, and Food for the Hungry in Peru. As a person with cerebral palsy, she has spoken about her challenges and successes abroad at numerous conferences.

Rebecca Hovey is dean of SIT Study Abroad. She holds a doctoral degree from Cornell University, where she studied international development and social theory, with a focus on Latin America. Her current research interests are in globalization and higher education.

William P. Hoye is associate vice president and deputy general counsel to the University of Notre Dame and a concurrent associate professor of law at Notre Dame Law School. Since 1995, Hoye has served as chair of Notre Dame's risk assessment committee, a campus-wide body dedicated to preventative law and the identification and management of risk on campus. Since 1994, he has also served as co-faculty editor of *The Journal of College and University Law*. He received his bachelor's degree from St. John's University, his doctor of laws degree from Drake University Law School, and his master of laws degree from Notre Dame Law School.

Marilyn J. Jackson has more than 10 years of professional experience in the field of student/scholar exchange and study abroad. She is the coordinator for international grants and protocol at San Francisco State University. Jackson holds a bachelor's degree from Vassar College and a master's degree from Tufts University, both in German studies. During the course of her undergraduate and graduate education, she spent two years at the Karls-Eberhard University. She is currently a doctoral candidate in international and multicultural education at the University of San Francisco.

Martha Johnson has worked in education abroad since 1991 in a variety of positions, including marketing and program representation, on-site advising, program management, and university office management. She is currently a program director in the Learning Abroad Center at the University of Minnesota, where she manages a variety of study, work, and internship programs.

Stephen Johnson is director of study abroad at Old Dominion University. A NAFSA member for more than 25 years, he began his international education career at the University of Minnesota after serving in the Peace Corps in the Dominican Republic. One of the founders of the SECUSSA Whole World Committee and a former member of the SECUSSA national team, he recently received an international education administrator Fulbright award to Korea.

Margit Johnson has been employed at Carleton College since 1994 as adviser, associate director, and acting director of off-campus studies. She has a master's degree in intercultural relations from the University of the Pacific, focusing on intercultural transitions. Johnson recently coauthored a video and companion book, *Coming and Going: Intercultural Transitions for College Students*, funded by the Mellon Foundation's Global Partners Project.

Nancy Kanach is the director of the study abroad program and associate dean of the college at Princeton University. A member of NAFSA, she serves on a number of advisory boards for study abroad programs and has written and presented on issues in international education. She has taught Russian and comparative literature at Cornell University and Princeton University.

Barbara Kappler Mikk is assistant director of international student and scholar services at the University of Minnesota, is responsible for intercultural training and programs. She has a doctoral degree and 15 years of experience teaching intercultural communication and in facilitating intercultural learning. Mikk is a coauthor of the *Maximizing Study Abroad* guidebooks from the University of Minnesota's Center for Advanced Research on Language Acquisition.

Gurudharm Singh Khalsa received a doctoral degree in comparative religion from the Graduate Theological Union in Berkeley, and taught world religions for a decade. As an international educator, he has worked with study abroad programs at St. Lawrence University, School for International Training and The School for Field Studies.

Kim Kreutzer is associate director for study abroad at the University of Colorado at Boulder and is the current chair of the SECUSSA Data Collection Committee. Other NAFSA roles include co-chair for special events at the 1999 NAFSA annual conference, Micro SIG representative for Region II (1994–1997), and presenter at numerous sessions and workshops. Kreutzer earned bachelor degrees in anthropology and East Asian studies and a master's degree in anthropology from the University of Arizona.

Maryelise S. Lamet is the director of academic affairs at the Centers for Academic Programs Abroad. She retired as the director of education abroad at the University of Massachusetts Amherst in 2002. She has served twice on the SECUSSA national team, most recently as the education and training representative and has served as the SECUSSA chair of Region XI. Lamet was a member of the CIEE Academic Consortium Board and a founding board member of the Forum on Education Abroad. She holds a doctoral degree from the University of Massachusetts Amherst and has published in the fields of history and international education. She is the editor of NAFSA's *Abroad by Design* (2000).

Brad Lauman is the associate dean for academic affairs (international education) and director of the Kobe-Regent's Center for Global Education at Rockford College. He has served as a national co-chair of SECUSSA's Financial Aid Resources for Study Abroad committee, the SECUSSA representative to Region V, and is currently chair-elect of the Illinois State NAFSA organization. His fifteen years in the international education field cover education abroad and international student enrollment both at the secondary and higher education levels. Lauman holds a master's degree in international policy studies from the Monterey Institute of International Studies and a bachelor's degree in business management from Indiana University, Bloomington.

Carol J. Lebold is associate director of education abroad, University of Massachusetts Amherst. Carol has more than fifteen years of experience in international education. She is a member of NAFSA Trainer Corps and past chair for the SECUSSA Committee on Underrepresentation in Education Abroad.

Elizabeth M. Lee is the assistant director of financial services for study abroad at Northwestern University, working in both the financial aid and study abroad offices. She has also served as the chair of the Financial Aid and Resources for Study Abroad Committee of NAFSA. Prior to coming to Northwestern, Lee worked at her alma mater, Smith College.

Barbara Lindeman is assistant director of the international center and director of study abroad at the University of Missouri-Columbia. She serves as chair of the SECUSSA Health and Safety Committee and is a member of the Interassociational Advisory Committee on Health and Safety (formerly known as the Interorganizational Task Force on Safety and Responsibility in Study Abroad). Lindeman was a contributor to the NAFSA publication *Crisis Management in a Cross-Cultural Setting*.

Randall Martin is the director of SFU International at Simon Fraser University, where he has worked since 1988. Martin is the author of several award-winning mobility programs and is himself the recipient of several awards, including CBIE's Internationalization Service Award and NAFSA's Lily Von Klemperer award.

Linda E. Marx has been the coordinator of international programs and study abroad adviser at The University of Akron (UA) for more than 16 years. Marx earned a master's degree

Contributors

with a concentration in intercultural communication from UA. She has served in a number of NAFSA regional positions and the NAFSA Trainer Corps.

Cheryl Matherly is assistant dean of students at Rice University and has a doctoral degree. She has taught several classes on career choice, and most recently served as a consultant to the nationally distributed telecourse "Career Advantage." She coauthored the book *How to Get a Job in Europe*.

Les McCabe is the chief operating officer of the Institute for Shipboard Education, which sponsors the Semester at Sea program. He is a member of both the SECUSSA Committee on Health and Safety and the Interassociational Advisory Committee on Health and Safety (formerly known as the Interorganizational Task Force on Safety and Responsibility in Study Abroad). McCable received his doctoral degree in international and development education from the University of Pittsburgh.

Natalie A. Mello, director of global operations in the interdisciplinary and global studies division at Worcester Polytechnic Institute (WPI), oversees the administration of WPI's global perspective program. WPI was recognized by TIAA-CREF's Hesburgh Award in 2003, specifically for Mello's development of faculty training relevant to off-campus experiences.

Mona M. Miller is director, west regional office, International Studies Abroad (ISA). Prior to joining ISA in 2001, Mona served as the director of study abroad at the office of international programs at Colorado State University for seven years. She has been an active member of the NAFSA/SECUSSA data collection working group and has been very involved in the design and development of database software for education abroad.

Christina (Tina) Murray has 15 years of distinguished service in international education, training, and development. Her education abroad legacy began in 1984 with a study sojourn in Liberia. After receiving a bachelor's degree from American University and a master's degree from the School for International Training, Murray worked for the International Student Exchange Program (ISEP) as a program officer for Africa, Australia and select European countries. From there, she established the first staffed office for education abroad at Virginia Commonwealth University, serving first as assistant director and then as director from 1996 to 2003. She has been a member of NAFSA since 1992.

William Nolting is director of international opportunities, University of Michigan International Center. He served previously as coordinator of international programs, Colgate University. Nolting's SECUSSA leadership positions have included SECUSSA chair; founder, SECUSSA Committee for Work, Internships, Volunteering Abroad; representative for Education & Training, COOP, and Region X. He is a contributing editor for *Transitions Abroad*. Additionally he serves on the IAESTE National Advisory Committee and is a founding member, Forum on Education Abroad.

Anthony C. Ogden studied at the School for International Training international and intercultural management. He has worked in several countries including Japan, Vietnam, and Cameroon. For nearly six years, Ogden was the director for the Tokyo Center of the Institute for the International Education of Students, where he also taught courses in ethnography and intercultural communication. He is an intercultural training consultant for Cendant Intercultural and is currently the associate director of education abroad at The Pennsylvania State University.

Rosalind Latiner Raby is a senior lecturer at California State University, Northridge in the College of Education and received her doctoral degree in the field of comparative and international education from the University of California, Los Angeles. She also serves as the director of California Colleges for International Education, a consortium whose membership includes sixty-eight California community colleges. Raby also is the SECUSSA community college liaison. She has numerous publications to her credit that address the internationalization of the community college curriculum and college programs.

Gary Rhodes is the University of California, Los Angeles education abroad program administrative director. From 1989 to 1998, he was program coordinator for the office of overseas studies at the University of Southern California. Since 1998, he has been director of the Center for Global Education, a national research and resource center funded by Fund for the

Improvement of Postsecondary Education (FIPSE): U.S. Department of Education. Rhodes presents regularly at national and international conferences on issues related to effective study abroad program development and implementation.

Thomas M. Ricks is an adjunct associate professor of Middle East history, University of Pennsylvania, is a past director of international studies (Villanova University), and a former Peace Corps volunteer (Iran III). He has participated in NAFSA publications and conferences, is a recipient of two Fulbright grants for Middle East studies, and is associate editor of *Frontiers: the Interdisciplinary Journal of Study Abroad*. He received his doctoral degree from Indiana University.

Nana Rinehart is deputy executive director, ISEP (International Student Exchange Program). She received her doctoral degree from the University of Maryland and her master's degree from the University of Copenhagen. She served as program officer (French and German language sites) ISEP; taught English at The American University and Trinity College, Washington, D.C. She edited *Rockin' in Red Square: Critical Approaches to International Education* (with Walter Grünzweig), 2002.

Roy Robinson is the director of study abroad in the College of Agriculture, Food, and Natural Resources at the University of Missouri. He has worked at Claremont McKenna College, Michigan State University and as a program director in India. Robinson holds a master's degree in international affairs from the University of California, San Diego and was a Peace Corps volunteer in Benin.

Karen Rodriguez has been the director of the CIEE program in Guanajuato, Mexico since the fall of 2002. Previously she directed Pitzer College's study abroad program in Venezuela for ten semesters. She is an applied anthropologist with interests in critical pedagogy, international education, and Latin America.

Tom Roberts is on the board of directors of the Institute for Study Abroad (IFSA)-Butler University and is the president of the ISFA Foundation. Formerly, Roberts served as deputy director and then as director of ISFA-Butler; as deputy director of the Center for Education Abroad, Beaver College; and as vice president and director of program development for the Institute of European Studies. He contributed to both previous editions of *NAFSA's Guide to Education Abroad for Advisers and Administrators*, received SECUSSA's Education Abroad Leadership Award, and was chair of the Lily Von Klemperer award committee for 15 years.

Geremie Sawadogo is the director of international and intercultural education at the Maricopa Community College District in Phoenix, Arizona. He holds a doctoral degree in international and comparative education from the University of Iowa and a master's degree from the Universite de Ouagadougou. He has worked in international and intercultural education in several African countries and in the United States. He currently serves as a member of the executive committee for the American Council on International and Intercultural Education.

Michele Scheib has been the manager of the National Clearinghouse on Disability and Exchange since 1999. Prior to that, she completed her master's degree in comparative and international development education at the University of Minnesota while working on the Access Abroad project to enhance education abroad for students with disabilities.

Kathleen Sideli is associate dean of international programs and director of the Office of Overseas Study at Indiana University. Her active career includes contributions to previous editions of *NAFSA's Guide to Education Abroad for Advisers and Administrators*, chair of SECUSSA (1999–2000), chair of the IIE/SECUSSA Data Collection Committee (1999–2003) and current president and founding member of the Forum on Education Abroad.

Carla Slawson was vice president of marketing for International Education Service (IES) from 1997 through 2003. During her tenure, IES became one of the largest organizations in the field. Her strong interest in outcomes assessment led her to design/implement two of the largest research studies in the field. She is now a stay-at-home mother caring for her two young sons.

Melissa Smith-Simonet has worked with ACCENT International Consortium for Academic Programs Abroad since 1989, and since 1998 is the ACCENT Paris Center director. Melissa leads a multinational team of administrative

Contributors

staff and faculty and is responsible for the management and administration of more than 40 study abroad programs per year in Paris, France. Melissa is on the NAFSA workshop panel of the SECUSSA Basic Training for Overseas Directors.

Sarah E. Spencer is assistant director, international education, University of St. Thomas, Minnesota and is the coeditor of the NAFSA publication, *The Guide to Successful Short-Term Programs Abroad* (2002). Holding a bachelor's degree from St. Olaf College and a master's degree in English from St. Thomas, she has studied and worked in England, as well as traveling extensively. Sarah is the co-chair of the workshop "Developing and Administrating Quality Short-Term Education Abroad Programs," frequently presents at national and regional conferences, is a member of NAFSA's Trainer Corps, and currently serves as the education abroad representative to the NAFSA Education & Professional Development Subcommittee.

Michael Steinberg is executive vice president for academic programs at International Education Service (IES) and has oversight of IES' programs. He has had primary responsibility for developing new programs as IES, expanded from seven sites to twenty-three. He serves on the Task Force for Health and Safety and on the Advisory Council of the Forum for Education Abroad.

Skye Stephenson is currently director of Latin American and Caribbean Studies at The School for International Training Study Abroad. A former resident director for nearly a decade in Santiago, Chile, and Latin American regional director for the Council on International Educational Exchange, she has extensive experience with study abroad programming and implementation on site. Among her published works are: *The Spanish-speaking South Americans: Bridging Hemispheres* (Intercultural Press 2003); "Beyond the Lapiths and the Centaurs: Cross-cultural "deepening" through Study Abroad" in *Rockin' in Red Square: Critical Approaches to International Education in the Age of Cyberculture*; and "Study Abroad as a Transformational Experience" in *Frontiers: the Interdisciplinary Journal of Study Abroad*.

Nancy Stubbs is director of study abroad programs at Colorado University-Boulder. She has spent 25 years working in international education. Her responsibilities have included budgeting and finance of study abroad programs; administering study abroad programs; recruiting, choosing, and orienting students; and advising students on all of the above.

Stacey Woody Thebodo is the assistant director of off-campus study at Middlebury College, where she has designed and implemented a variety of predeparture and reentry programs. She has worked for the School for International Training (SIT) Study Abroad and as a study abroad adviser at the University of Vermont. Thebodo earned her master's degree in international administration from SIT. She has also written and presented at NAFSA conferences on the subjects of predeparture and reentry.

Susan M. Thompson is director, international programs at the University of Nevada, Las Vegas. Susan has held several positions with NAFSA including SECUSSA representative to Region XII, chair of the SECUSSA National Awards Committee, Trainer Corps member, SECUSSA representative to the Communications and Information Committee (COMINFO), chair of COMINFO, and member of the Strategic Task Force on Education Abroad. Thompson also serves on the editorial advisory board for *International Educator* magazine.

Kathy Tuma is the associate director of international and off-campus studies office at St. Olaf College and is the coeditor of the NAFSA publication, *The Guide to Successful Short-Term Programs Abroad* (2002). She has presented sessions and workshops at both the national NAFSA conference and the Region IV Conference since 1995. In addition, she is a member of NAFSA's Trainer Corps. Tuma has presented other professional practice workshops including Foundations of International Education: Education Abroad Advising and Administration of Education Abroad Programs.

Leo Van Cleve is the director of international programs for the California State University (CSU) System based in the office of the chancellor in Long Beach. In addition to being director of the system-wide study abroad program, he works with campuses to promote international programs and with chancellor's office staff to develop policy and implement system-wide initiatives. Prior to coming to the CSU, he was at Central College and the International Education Service (IES) study abroad consortium.

J. Scott Van Der Meid is the director of study abroad at

Brandeis University. He received his master's degree in intercultural relations from Lesley University. He serves on the SECUSSA advisory boards: Committee on Underrepresentation; the Rainbow Special Interest Group; and Data Collection.

Andrea Walgren is an adjunct professor at Lesley University where she teaches international educational exchange in the graduate program in intercultural relations. During twenty years with The School for Field Studies, she served as vice president for student affairs and institutional relations. She served for three years as the Region XI SECUSSA representative and has presented in national workshops addressing marketing study abroad and increasing participation of science students in education abroad.

JoAnn deArmas Wallace has worked in all areas of international education at-large and small institutions for 24 years. She has been a frequent presenter at professional conferences and has contributed to a variety of NAFSA publications on study abroad, safety and liability, and crisis management. Wallace has worked with faculty on international curriculum and policy; development, assessment and management of academic and experiential programs; selection and preparation of leaders and teachers for programs abroad and, in her current position as dean of international programs at Juniata College, leads annual workshops for faculty on advising for study abroad, integration of education abroad into general education and majors, and safety and liability off campus.

Margaret Wiedenhoeft is the associate director of the Center for International Programs at Kalamazoo College where she manages the Kalamazoo study abroad programs in Germany, Spain, Italy, France, Australia, East Malaysia, and Thailand in addition to developing faculty-led international study seminars. She holds a bachelor's degree from Emory University in international studies, a Master of Business Administration from Western Michigan University and is currently a doctoral candidate in the College of Education at Western Michigan University.

Michael ("My") Yarabinec has served as the coordinator of study abroad and international exchange programs at San Francisco State University since 1994. Prior to that, he was the campus relations officer for international programs at the central office (office of the Chancellor), where he was in charge of recruitment, publicity, and promotion for the California State University (CSU) study abroad programs in CSU's 23 campus system.

Katherine N. Yngve serves as study abroad coordinator at Macalester College. She has co-managed the SECUSS-L mailing list since 1996, serves as SECUSSA representative to the NAFSA subcommittee on distance education, and frequently presents on technology and education abroad.

Stacia Zukroff is the director of study abroad and exchange programs at Babson College. Zukroff has been involved in international education for 10 years and served as NAFSA Region I secretary and as a member of the Data Collection Committee. She has delivered numerous NAFSA presentations and workshops at regional and national conferences and contributed to NAFSA's *Abroad by Design* (2000).

References

PRINT REFERENCES

Aalberts, R. J., and K. D. Ostrand. 1987. "Negligence, Liability and the International Education Administrator." *Journal of the Association of International Education Administrators*, vol. 7, no. 2, pp. 153-163.

Aalberts, R. J., and R. B. Evans. 1995. "The International Education Experience: Managing the Legal Risks." *Journal of Legal Studies Education*, vol. 13, no. 1, pp. 29-44.

Aalberts, R. J., K. D. Ostrand, and K. C. Fonte. 1986. "The University, the Law, and International Study Programs." *Continuum*, 50, pp. 153-163.

Abrams, I. 1979. "The impact of Antioch education through experience abroad." *Alternative Higher Education*, 3, pp. 176-187.

Adams, Maurianne, and Lee Ann Bell. 1997. *Teaching for Diversity and Social Justice: a Sourcebook*, P. Griffin ed. New York and London: Routledge.

Advisory Council for International Educational Exchange, CIEE. 1988. *Educating for Global Competence. Report of the Advisory Council for International Educational Exchange*. New York, NY: CIEE.

Akande, Yemi and Carla Slawson. 2000. "Exploring the Long Term Impact of Study Abroad." *International Educator*, vol. IX, no. 3, pp. 12-17.

Alaska Outdoor & Experiential Education. 2000. *Lessons Learned: A Guide to Accident Prevention and Crisis Response*, Anchorage: University of Alaska.

Alliance for International Educational and Cultural Exchange. 1993. *International Exchanges: A Cornerstone of Effective U.S. Economic and Foreign Policy in the 1990's*.

Althen, Gary. 1994. *Learning Across Cultures*. Washington, DC: NAFSA: Association of International Educators.

American Association of Community and Junior Colleges, "Mission Statement." *AACJC Public Policy Agenda*. Adopted by AACJC Board of Directors (April, 1988).

American Council on International Intercultural Education. 1991. "Mission Statement." *AACJC Public Policy Agenda*. As approved by the ACIIE Executive Board (April, 1991).

American Council on Education (ACE). 2000. "Initiatives Promoting Internationalization of Undergraduate Experience," vol. 49, no. 9.

———. 1989. *What We Can't Say Can Hurt Us*, Washington, D.C.: American Council on Education.

———. 2002. *Beyond September11: A Comprehensive National Policy on International Education*. Washington, DC: American Council on Education.

American Council on Education. 2003. *Mapping Internationalization on U.S. Campuses: Final Report*, Fred M. Hayward and Laura Siaya, eds. Washington, DC: American Council on Education.

Angelo, Thomas A. 1995. "Doing Assessment As If Learning Matters Most."*AAHE Bulletin*, November 1995, p 7.

Annette, John. 2002. "Service Learning in an International Context," *Frontiers: The Interdisciplinary Journal of Study Abroad*, vol. VIII, pp. 83-93.

References

Arnold, William E., and Lynne McClure. 1996. *Communication Training and Development*, second edition. Prospect Heights: Waveland Press, Inc.

Association of International Education Administrators (AIEA). 1995. "A Research Agenda for the Internationalization of Higher Education in the United States, Recommendations and Report Based on August 10-11, 1995 AIEA Meeting." Washington, DC: AIEA.

Association of International Education Administrators Working Group, 1996. "A Research Agenda for the Internationalization of Higher Education in the United States." Barbara B. Burn, and Ralph H. Smuckler, co-chairs. Pullman, WA: AIEA.

Bacon, S. M. 2002. "Learning the Rules: Language Development and Cultural Adjustment During Study Abroad." *Foreign Language Annals*, vol. 35, no. 6, pp. 636-646.

Barr, M. J., and associates. 1988. *Student Services and the Law: A Handbook for Practitioners*. San Francisco: Jossey-Bass.

Beck, Melinda. 1997. "The Next Big Population Bulge: Generation Y Shows Its Might." *Wall Street Journal*. February, 3, 1997.

Bennett, Janet M. 1993. Cultural Marginality: Identity Issues in Intercultural Training. In *Education for the Intercultural Experience*, R. M. Paige ed. Yarmouth, ME: Intercultural Press.

———. 1998. "Transition Shock: Putting Culture Shock in Perspective." In *Basic Concepts of Intercultural Communication: Selected Readings*. M. J. Bennett ed. Yarmouth, ME: Intercultural Press.

Bennett, Janet, Milton Bennett, and Kathryn Stillings. 1997. *Description, Interpretation, and Evaluation Exercise. Intercultural Communication Workshop Facilitator's Manual*. Portland, OR: Portland State University.

Bennett, Milton J. 1986. "Developmental Approach to Training for Intercultural Sensitivity," *International Journal of Intercultural Relations*, vol. 10, pp. 179-96.

———. 1993. "Toward Ethnorelativism: A Developmental Model of Intercultural Sensitivity." In *Education for the Intercultural Experience*, R. M. Paige ed. Yarmouth, ME: Intercultural Press.

Bennett, Milton J., and Janet M. Bennett. 1997. "Multiculturalism and International Education: Domestic and International Differences." *Learning Across Cultures*, Gary Althen ed. Washington, DC: NAFSA: Association of International Educators

Berry, H. and Linda Chisholm. 2002. *Understanding the Education—and Through It the Culture—in Education Abroad*. New York: International Partnership for Service Learning.

Bickel, Robert D and Peter F. Lake. 1999. *The Rights and Responsibilities of the Modern University: Who Assumes the Risks of College Life*. Durham, NC: Carolina Academic Press.

Bikson, T.K. and S. A. Law. 1994. *Global Preparedness and Human Resources: College and Corporate Perspectives*. Santa Monica: RAND, Institute on Education and Training.

Blackstone, William. 1765. *Commentaries*. Oxford: Carendon Press. Quoted in Robert D. Bickel and Peter F. Lake, (1999). *The Rights and Responsibilities of the Modern University: Who Assumes the Risks of College Life*. Durham, NC: Carolina Academic Press.

Blair, Donna, Lisa Phinney and Kent A. Phillippe. 2001. *International Programs at Community Colleges*. Washington DC: American Association of Community Colleges.

Boggs, George R. and Judy T. Irwin. 2003. "Community Colleges: Making the world accessible." *International Educator*, vol. XII, no. 2, p. 44.

Bowman, John E. 1987. *Educating American Undergraduates Abroad: The Development of Study Abroad Programs by American Colleges and Universities*. Occasional Papers No. 24. New York, NY: CIEE.

Breiner-Sanders, Karen E., Pardee Lowe, John Miles and Elvira Swender. 2000. "ACTFL Proficiency Guidelines—Speaking, Revised 1999." *Foreign Language Annals*, vol. 33, no. 1.

Breiner-Sanders, Karen E., Elvira Swender and Robert M. Terry. 2001. *Preliminary ACTFL Proficiency Guidelines—Writing*, Revised 2001. Washington, DC: American Council on the Teaching of Foreign Languages (ACTFL).

Briggs, Asa and Barbara Burn. 1985. *Study Abroad: A European and an American Perspective*. Brussels: European Institute of Education and Social Policy.

Brislin, Richard, and Tomoko Yoshida, eds. 1994. *Improving Intercultural Interactions: Modules for Cross-Cultural Training Programs*. New Delhi: Sage Publications.

Brockington, Joseph. 2002. "Moving from International Vision to Institutional Reality: Administrative and Financial Models for Education Abroad at Liberal Arts Colleges." *Journal of Studies in International Education*, vol. 6, no. 3, pp 283-291.

Brown, A., and A. O. Kandel. 1991. *The Legal Audit: Corporate Internal Investigation*. Deerfield, IL: Clark Boardman Callahan.

Burak, Patricia A. and William W. Hoffa, eds. 2001. *Crisis Management in a Cross-Cultural Setting*. Washington, DC: NAFSA: Association of International Educators.

Burling, P. 1992. *Managing the Risks of Foreign Study Programs*. Boston: Foley, Hoag & Eliot.

Burn, Barbara B. 1982. "The Impact of the Fulbright Experience on Grantees from the United States." A paper presented at the annual meeting of the International Studies Association, March 1982, in Cincinnati, OH.

Burn, Barbara B. ed. 1991. *Integrating Study Abroad into the Undergraduate Liberal Arts Curriculum: Eight Institutional Case Studies*. Westport, CT: Greenwood Press.

Burn, Barbara B. and Jon Crawford, eds. 2002. "Globalizing Education at Liberal Arts Colleges in the United States" (special sectional theme with articles by J. Crawford, B. Burn, S. Gillespie, D. Blaney, and J. Brockington). *Journal of Studies in International Education*, vol. 6, no. 3, pp. 249-296.

Butcher, Thomas A. 1999. "Tom's Top Ten Tips for Study Abroad Administrators." *International Educator*, vol. VIII, no. 3, p. 5.

Carew, Joy Gleason. 1993. "For Minority Students, Study Abroad Can Be Inspiring and Liberating," *Chronicle of Higher Education*, (January 6, 1993).

Cargile, Aaron C., and Howard Giles. 1995. Intercultural Communication Training: Review, Critique, and a New Theoretical Framework. In *Communication Yearbook*, B. Burleson ed. Thousand Oaks, CA: Sage Publications, Inc.

Carland, Maria Pinto and Lisa A. Gihring, eds. 2003. *Careers in International Affairs*, seventh edition. Washington, DC: Georgetown University Press.

Carlson, Jerry S., Barbara B. Burn, John Useem, and David Yachimowitz. 1990. *Study Abroad: The Experience of American Undergraduates*. Westport, CT: Greenwood Press.

Carnoy, Martin, and Diana Rhoten, eds. 2002. "The Meanings of Globalization for Educational Change." *Comparative Education Review*, 46, pp. 1-9.

Carr, Judith W. and Ellen Summerfield, eds. 1994. *Forms of Travel: Essential Documents, Letters and Flyers for Study Abroad Advisers*. Washington, DC: NAFSA: Association of International Educators (out of print).

Carter, Holly M. 1991. *Minority Access to International Education*. New York: Council on International Educational Exchange (CIEE).

Cheshire, Julie Ann, ed. 2000. *Building Bridges: A Manual on Including People With Disabilities in International Exchange Programs*, second edition. Eugene, OR: Mobility International USA/National Clearinghouse on Disability and Exchange (NCDE).

Chickering, Arthur W. 1969. *Education and Identity*. San Francisco: Jossey-Bass.

Chieffo, Lisa and Lesa Griffiths. 2004. "Short-Term Study Abroad: It Makes A Difference!" *IIE Networker*, Spring 2004.

Chin, Hey-Kyung Koh ed. 2004. *Open Doors* 2004: Report on International Educational Exchange. New York, NY: Institute of International Education.

Cluett, Ronald. 2002. "From Cicero to Mohammed Atta: People, Politics, and Study Abroad," Frontiers: *The Interdisciplinary Journal of Study Abroad*, vol. VII, pp. 17-39.

Cohen, Arthur M. and Florence B. Brawer. 1982. *The American Community College*, first edition. San Francisco: Jossey-Bass.

———. 2002. *The American Community College*. California, fourth edition. San Francisco: Jossey-Bass.

College Placement Council Foundation/RAND Corporation. 1994. *Developing the Global Work Force: Insights for Colleges and Corporations*. Monterey, CA: Rand Corporation.

Collins, Joseph, Stefano DeZerega, and Zahara Heckscher. 2002. *How to Live Your Dream of Volunteering Abroad*. New York: Penguin-Putnam.

Council on International Educational Exchange (CIEE). 2005. *Our View: Standards*. Portland, ME: CIEE.

Council on International Educational Exchange. 2002. *A History of the Council on International Educational Exchange: 1947-1994*. New York, NY: CIEE.

Dahlen, Tommy. 1997. *Among the Interculturalists: An Emerging Profession and its Packaging of Knowledge*. Stockholm: Stockholm University.

Darrah, M. 1999. *Safety and Study Abroad, Video Learning Program*. Boulder, CO: Big World Inc.

de Wit, Hans. 2002. *Internationalisation of Higher Education in the United States and Europe: A Historical, Comparative, and Conceptual Analysis*. Westport, CT: Greenwood Press.

Diener, T. J. and L. Kerr. 1979. "Institutional responsibilities to foreign students." *New Directions for Community Colleges*, vol. 7, no. 2.

Dobbert, Marion L. 1998. "The Impossibility of Internationalizing Students by Adding Materials to Courses." *Reforming the Higher Education Curriculum: Internationalizing the Campus*, J. A. Mestenhauser and B. J. Ellingboe eds. Phoenix, AZ: Oryx Press.

Dowell, Michele-Marie, and Kelly P. Mirsky. 2003. *Study Abroad: How to Get the Most Out of Your Experience*. Upper Saddle, NJ: Prentice Hall, Inc.

Dubois, Demerise R. 1995. "Responding to the Needs of Our Nation: A Look at the Fulbright and NSEP Education Acts." *Frontiers: The Interdisciplinary Journal of Study Abroad*, vol. I, pp. 54-80.

Duenwald, Mary. 2004. "The Dorms May Be Great, But How's the Counseling?" *The New York Times*. October 26, 2004.

References

Edwards, Michael, and John Gaventa, eds. 2001. *Global Citizen Action*. Boulder, CO: Lynne Rienner Publishers.

Eliot, T.S. 1962. Excerpts from "Choruses from The Rock," In *The Waste Land, and Other Poems*. New York: Harcourt, Brace, Jovanovich.

Elsner, Paul A., Joyce S. Tsunoda, and Linda A. Korbel. 1994. "Building the Global Community: The Next Step." *Points of Departure for the American Council on International Intercultural Education/Stanley Foundation Leadership Retreat*, (November 28–30, 1994)

Engle, John and Lili Engel. 2002. "Neither International nor Educative: Study Abroad in the Time of Globalization." *Rockin' in Red Square: Critical Approaches to International Education in the Age of Cyberculture*, Walter Grünzweig and Nana Rinehart, eds. 2002. Munich: Lit Verlag.

Evans, R. B. 1991. "A Stranger in a Strange Land: Responsibility and Liability for Students Enrolled in Foreign Study Programs." *Journal of College and University Law*, vol.18, no. 2, pp. 299-314.

Falcetta, Frank M. 2003. "The Globalization of Community Colleges." In *Study Abroad: A 21st Century Perspective, vol. II: The Changing Landscape*, Martin Tillman, ed. New York: American Institute for Foreign Study Foundation.

Fantini, Alvino. 1995. Report by the Intercultural Communicative Competence Task Force. Brattleboro, VT: World Learning.

Feldman, Daniel C., William R. Folks and William H. Turnley. 1998. "The Socialization of Expatriate Interns." *Journal of Managerial Issues*, vol. 10, no. 4, pp. 403-418.

Fersh, Seymour and E. Fitchen, eds. 1981. *The Community College and International Education: A Report of Progress*, volume II. Coca, FL: Brevard Community College.

Freedman, Art. 1986. "A Strategy for Managing 'Cultural' Transitions: Reentry from Training." In *Cross-Cultural Reentry: A Book of Readings*, C. N. Austin, ed. Abilene: ACU Press.

Frist, William H. 2002. *When Every Moment Counts*. Lanham, MD: Rowman & Littlefield, Inc.

Fryer, T. Bruce, and James T. Day. 1993. "Foreign Language Curricular Needs of Students Preparing for an Internship Abroad." *The Modern Language Journal*, vol. 77, no. 3, pp.277-288.

Gee, J.P. 2003. *What Videogames Have to Teach Us About Learning and Literacy*. New York: Paulgrave MacMillan.

Gochenour, T. 1993. *Beyond Experience: An Experiential Approach to Cross-Cultural Education*, second edition. Yarmouth, ME: Intercultural Press, Inc.

Gonzalez, A. 1993. "Teaching Beyond the Classroom: Business Internships in Latin America—Issues in Cross-Cultural Adjustment." *Hispania*, vol. 76, no. 4, pp. 892-901.

Goodman, Ellen. 2002. "College Women: A National Crisis?" *Boston Globe* (September 3, 2002).

Goodwin, Craufurd and Michael Nacht. 1988. *Abroad and Beyond*. Cambridge: Cambridge University Press.

Gose, Ben. 2005. "Questions Loom for Applicants and Colleges," *Chronicle of Higher Education* (February 25, 2005).

Grandin, John M. 1991. "Developing Internships in Germany for International Engineering Students." *Unterrichtspraxis*, vol. 24, no. 2, pp. 209-214.

Green, Madeleine F. and Christa Olson. 2003. *Internationalizing the Campus: A User's Guide*, Washington DC: American Council on Education (ACE).

Greenfield, Richard K.1990. "Developing International Education Programs," *New Directions for Community Colleges Series*, No. 70, Summer 1990. San Francisco: Jossey-Bass Inc.

Grey, David. 2003. "Crisis and Study Abroad: Managing Study Abroad Programs in Times of Crisis," *IIENetworker*, fall 2003.

Griffith, Susan. 2003a. *Teaching English Abroad: Teach Your Way Around the World*, sixth edition. Oxford, U.K.:Vacation Work/Globe Pequot Press.

Griffith, Susan. 2003b. *Work Your Way Around the World*, eleventh edition. Oxford, U.K.: Vacation Work/Globe Pequot Press.

Gobbo, Linda Drake, Mary Lou Forward, Ryan Lorenz. 2005. "Opportunity not Threat: Dealing with Anti-Americanism Abroad." *International Educator*, vol. 14, no. 1, pp. 18-25.

Gross, Benedict H. and William C. Kirby, et. al. 2004. "A Report on the Harvard College Curricular Review." Unpublished paper. Harvard University.

Grünzweig, Walter and Nana Rinehart, eds. 2003. *Rocking in Red Square: Critical Approaches to International Education in the Age of Cyberspace*. Munich: Lit Verlag.

Gudykunst, William B., and Young Yun Kim. 2002. *Communicating with Strangers: An Approach to Intercultural Communication*. New York: McGraw Hill.

Gullahorn, J. T., and J.E. Gullahorn. 1963. "An Extension of the U-curve Hypothesis." *Journal of Social Issues*, vol. 19, pp.33-47.

Hall, Edward T. 1971. *Beyond Culture*. New York: Doubleday.

———. 1973. *The Silent Language*. New York: Anchor Books.

Hannigan, Terence P. 2001. "The Effect of Work Abroad Experiences on Career Development for U.S. Undergraduates." *Frontiers: The Interdisciplinary Journal of Study Abroad*, vol. 7, pp. 1-23.

Hardt, Ty. 2000. "The Role of the Media in Accident Response." *Lessons Learned: A Guide to Accident Prevention and Crisis Response*. Deb Ajango, ed. Boulder, CO: Association for Experiential Education.

Hayward, Fred M. and Laura M. Siaya. 2001. *Public Experience, Attitudes and Knowledge: a Report on Two National Surveys about International Education*. Washington DC: American Council on Education.

———. 2003. *Mapping Internationalization on U.S. Campuses: Final Report*. Washington, DC: American Council on Education.

Hebel, Sara. 2003. "Colleges Eye Discounts on Tuition to Change Student Choices." *Chronicle of Higher Education*. September 19, 2003

Hembroff, Larry, and Debra Rusz. 1993. *Minorities and Overseas Studies Programs: Correlates of Differential Participation*. CIEE ed. Ann Arbor: Michigan State University.

Henson, Harlan. 2003. "An Effective Consortial Model for Study Abroad: A History of the College Consortium for International Studies." *Study Abroad: A 21st Century Perspective, vol. II: The Changing Landscape*. Martin Tillman, ed. New York: American Institute for Foreign Study Foundation.

Herrin, Carl. 2004. "It's Time for Advancing Education Abroad." *International Educator*, vol. XIII, no. 1, pp. 3-4.

Hershey, Laura. 2004. *Survival Strategies for Going Abroad: A Guide for People with Disabilities*. Eugene, OR: Mobility International USA/National Clearinghouse on Disability and Exchange (NCDE).

Hess Gerhard. 1982. *Freshmen and Sophomores Abroad: Community Colleges and Overseas Academic Programs*. New York: Teachers College Press.

Hess, J. Daniel. 1994. *Whole World Guide to Culture Learning*. Yarmouth, ME: Intercultural Press.

———. 1997. *Studying Abroad/Learning Abroad: An Abridged Edition of the Whole World Guide to Culture Learning*. Yarmouth, ME: Intercultural Press.

Hicks, R. Eldridge. 2000. "The Jury's In: A Defense Lawyer's Perspective on Risk Management and Crisis Response." *Lessons Learned: A Guide to Accident Prevention and Crisis Response*. Deb Ajango, ed. Boulder, CO: Association for Experiential Education.

Hockenberry, John. 1995. *Moving Violations: War Zones, Wheelchairs and Declarations of Independence*. New York: Hyperion.

Hoffa, William W. 1996. "E-Mail and Study Abroad: The Pros and Cons of Travel and Living in Cyberspace." Transitions Abroad, vol. XIX, no. 4.

———. 1998. *Study Abroad: A Parent's Guide*. Washington, DC: NAFSA: Association of International Educators.

———. 2003. "Learning about the future world: international education and the demise of the nation state." *Rockin' in Red Square: Critical Approaches to International Education in the Age of Cyberspace*. W. Grunzweig and N. Rinehart eds. Munich: Lit Verlag.

Honigsblum, Gerald. 2002. "Internships Abroad: The View from Paris." *Frontiers: The Interdisciplinary Journal of Study Abroad*, vol. 8, pp. 95-112.

Houston, Pamela. 2003. Paper read at NAFSA: Association of International Educators National Conference, Salt Lake City.

Howe, Neil and Strauss, William. 1991. *Generations: the history of America's future, 1584-2069*. New York: Morrow, William & Co.

———. 2000. *Millennials Rising: The Next Great Generation*. New York: Vintage Books.

Hoye, W.P. & Gary Rhodes. 2000. "An Ounce of Prevention is Worth…The Life of A Student: Reducing Risk in International Programs." *The Journal of College and University Law*, vol. 27, no. 1, pp. 151-186.

Hubbs, Clayton, Susan Griffith and William Nolting, eds. 2003. *Work Abroad: The Complete Guide to Finding a Job Overseas*. Amherst, MA: Transitions Abroad Publishing.

Hudzik, John K., Edward C. Ingraham and Debra L. Peterson. 2002. *Widening Opportunity and Commitment to Study and Learning Abroad: Proceedings of the National Conference on Study and Learning Abroad*, Washington, DC. October 22-23, 2001. Ann Arbor, MI: Michigan State University.

International 50 Liberal Arts Colleges. 1991. In *the International Interest: The Contributions and Needs of America's International Liberal Arts Colleges: Report of International 50 Liberal Arts Colleges*.

Juffer, K. A. 1993. "The First Step in Cross-Cultural Education: Defining the Problem." *Education for the Intercultural Experience*, R. M. Paige, ed. Yarmouth, ME: Intercultural Press.

Kadison, Richard and Thersesa Foy DiGeronimo. 2004. *College of the Overwhelmed*. San Francisco, CA: Jossey Bass.

Kaplin, William A., and Barbara A. Lee. 1995. *The Law of Higher Education: A Comprehensive Guide to Legal Implications of Administrative Decision Making*, third edition. San Francisco: Jossey-Bass.

Kaplin, William A. and Barbara A. Lee. 1997. *A Legal Guide for Student Affairs Professionals*. San Francisco, CA: Jossey-Bass.

Kast, R. 1998. "In Loco Parentis and the 'Reasonable Person': Liability Issues in International Studies Programs." *International Educator*, vol. VII, no. 1, pp. 26-32.

References

Kauffmann, Norman L.; Martin, Judith N.; Weaver, Henry D. 1992. *Students Abroad, Strangers at Home: Education for a Global Society*. Yarmouth, ME: Intercultural Press.

King, Maxwell C. and Seymour H. Fersh. 1992. *Integrating the International/Intercultural Dimension in the Community College*. Washington DC: Association of Community College Trustees and Community Colleges for International Development, Inc.

Klahr, Sabine C. and U. Ratti. 2000. "Increasing Engineering Student Participation in Study Abroad: A Study of U.S. and European Programs." *Journal of Studies in International Education*, vol. 4, no. 1, pp. 79-102.

Knefelkamp, L. Lee. 1987. Presentation delivered at University of Minnesota.

Knight, Jane, and Hans de Wit. 1997. *Internationalisation of Higher Education in Asia Pacific Countries*. Amsterdam: European Association for International Education.

Knight, Jane. 1999. *Quality and Internationalisation in Higher Education*. Paris: Organisation for Economic Cooperation and Development.

———. 1994. "Internationalization: Elements and Checkpoints." *CBIE Research No. 7*, Canadian Bureau for International Education.

Kohls, L Robert. 1979. *The Survival Kit for Overseas Living*. Yarmouth, ME: Intercultural Press.

———. 1984. *The Values Americans Live By*. Washington, DC: The Washington International Center.

———. 1996. *Survival Kit for Overseas Living*. Yarmouth, Maine: Intercultural Press, Inc.

Kohls, L. Robert, and John M. Knight. 1994. *Developing Intercultural Awareness: A Cross-Cultural Training Handbook*. Yarmouth, ME: Intercultural Press.

Kolb, David A. 1984. *Experiential Learning: Experience as the Source of Learning and Development*. Englewood Cliffs: Prentice-Hall, Inc.

Koltai, Leslie. 1993. "Are There Challenges and Opportunities for American Community Colleges on the International Scene?" Keynote Address at the Comparative and International Education Society Western Region Conference, Los Angeles.

Krajewski-Jaime, Elvia R. et al. 1996. "Utilizing International Clinical Practice to Build Inter-Cultural Sensitivity in Social Work Students." *Journal of Multicultural Social Work*, vol. 4, no. 2, pp.15-29.

Krannich, Ronald and Caryl Krannich. 2002. *The Directory of Websites for International Jobs*. Manassas Park, VA: Impact Publications.

Kruempelmann, Elizabeth. 2002. *The Global Citizen: A Guide to Creating an International Life and Career*. Berkeley, CA: Ten Speed Press.

La Brack, Bruce. 1993. "The Missing Linkage: The Process of Integrating Orientation and Reentry." *Education for the Intercultural Experience*. R. M. Paige, ed. Yarmouth, ME: Intercultural Press.

Lambert, Richard. 1994. "Parsing the Concept of Global Competence." *Educational Exchange and Global Competence*. Richard Lambert ed. New York, NY: CIEE, pp. 11-23.

Lamet, Maryélise S. ed. 2002. *Abroad by Design*. Washington, DC: NAFSA: Association of International Educators.

Lapovsky, Lucie and Loren Loomis Hubbell. 2003. "Tuition Discounting Continues to Grow." NACUBO Business Officer. March 2003.

LaRose, R., C.A. Lin, and M. S. Eastin. 2003. "Unregulated Internet Usage: Addiction, Habit, or Deficient Self-Regulation?" *Media Psychology*, 5, pp. 225-253.

Larsen, David. 2002. "Knowing Who We Are." *International Educator*, vol. XI, no. 1, pp. 11-13, 42.

Lauber, Daniel with Kraig Rice. 2002. *International Job Finder: Where The Jobs Are Worldwide*. River Forrest, IL: Planning/Communications.

Laubscher, Michael R. 1994. *Encounters with Difference: Student Perceptions of the Role of Out-of-Class Experiences in Education Abroad*. Westport, CT: Greenwood Press.

Leemon, Drew. 2003. "Wilderness Risk Managers Committee Incident Data Project." *Proceedings of the Wilderness Risk Management Conference*, October 17-19, 2003, State College PA, Incident report.

Leemon, Drew and Scott Erickson. 2000. "How Accidents Happen." In *Alaska Outdoor & Experiential Education. Lessons Learned: A Guide to Accident Prevention and Crisis Response*. Anchorage: University of Alaska.

Leemon, Drew and Kurt Merrill. 2002. *Adventure Program Risk Management Report: Vol III: Data and Narratives from 1998-2000*. Lander, WY: Association for Experiential Education (AEE) and National Outdoor Leadership School (NOLS). Incident Report forms.

Leibensperger, R., S. Mehringer, A. Trefethen, and M. Kalos. 1997. "Electronic Communications—Education Via a Virtual Workshop." *Frontiers: The Interdisciplinary Journal of Study Abroad*, vol. III, pp. 224-232.

Levy, Julie. [no date] "Host Families as Cultural Providers: The Nicaraguan Experience," (SIT master's thesis).

References

Liaison Group for International Educational Exchange. 1998. *Exchange 2000: International Leadership for the Next Century*. Washington, DC: The Liaison Group for International Educational Exchange.

Lott, Juanita Tamayo. 1998. *Asian Americans: From Racial Category to Multiple Identities*. Walnut Creek, CA: Alta Mira Press.

Lustig, Myron W., and Jolene Koester. 1993. *Intercultural Competence: Intercultural Communication Across Cultures*. New York: Harper Collins.

Lutterman-Aguilar, Ann and Orval Gingerich. 2002. "Experiential Pedagogy for Study Abroad: Educating for Global Citizenship." *Frontiers: The Interdisciplinary Journal of Study Abroad*, vol. VIII, pp. 41-82.

Mahan, James M. and Laura Stachowski. 1990. "New Horizons: Student Teaching Abroad to Enrich Understanding of Diversity." *Action in Teacher Education,* vol.12, no. 3, pp.13-21.

Maki, Peggy L. 2002. "Developing an Assessment Plan to Learn About Student Learning," *Journal of Academic Librarianship*, January 2002.

Malone, A., and S. R. Craig. 1996. "Motivating Minority Students to Study Abroad." Paper read at NAFSA: Association of International Educators national conference in Phoenix, AR.

Marcum, John A. 2001. "What Direction for Study Abroad? Eliminate the Roadblocks." *The Chronicle Review* (May 18, 2001).

Martin, Judith N. 1989. "Predeparture Orientation: Preparing College Sojourners for Intercultural Interaction." *Communication Education*, vol. 38, no. 3, pp. 249-257.

Martin, Judith N., and Thomas K. Nakayama. 1997. *Intercultural Communication in Contexts*. Mountain View, CA: Mayfield.

Martin, Judith, Thomas Nakayama, and Lisa Flores, eds. 1998. *Readings in Cultural Contexts*. Mountain View, CA: Mayfield.

Mattai, P. Rudy, and Godwin Ohiwerei. 1989. "Some Mitigating Factors Against African-Americans in the Rural American South Opting to Study Abroad." Paper read at Council on International Educational Exchange conference at Washington, DC.

Mawila, Kalu. 2001. *Challenges Facing African American Students at MSU When Considering Study Abroad*. Michigan State University.

McLeod, Lorna, and Michele Scheib, eds. 2005. *Practice of Yes! Working with Overseas Partners to Include Students with Disabilities*. Eugene, Oregon: Mobility International USA/National Clearinghouse on Disability and Exchange.

McPherson, M. S., and M. O. Shapiro. 1991. *Keeping College Affordable: Government and Educational Opportunity*. Washington, DC: Brookings Institution.

Merkx, Gilbert. 2003. "The Two Waves of Internationalization in U.S. Higher Education." *International Educator*, vol. XII, no. 1, pp. 6-12.

Merva, Mary. 2003. "Grades as Incentives: A Quantitative Assessment with Implications for Study Abroad Programs." *Journal of Studies in International Education*, vol. 7, no. 2, pp. 149-156.

Mestenhauser, Josef A. 2002. "In Search of a Comprehensive Approach to International Education: A Systems Perspective." *Rockin' in Red Square: Critical Approaches to International Education in the Age of Cyberculture*, W. Grünsweig and N. Reinhart, eds. London: Transaction Publishers.

Michigan State University Office of International Studies and Programs published in collaboration with the MSU library in 2004, *A Student's Guide to Scholarships, Grants, and Funding Publications in International Education and Other Disciplines*.

Millington, W. G. 1979. *The Law and the College Student: Justice in Evolution*. St. Paul, MN: West Publishing Co.

Miner, Horace. 1956. "Body Ritual Among the Nacirema." *American Anthropologist*, vol. 58, pp. 503-507.

Monaghan, Peter. 1994. Study Abroad for Minority Students. *The Chronicle of Higher Education*, vol. 40, no. 41, pp. A35-A38.

Montrose, Lynne. 2002. "International Study and Experiential Learning: The Academic Context." *Frontiers: The Interdisciplinary Journal of Study Abroad*, vol. VIII, pp. 1-15.

Munir, Fasheh. 1985. "Talking About What to Cook When Our House is on Fire: The Poverty of Existing Forms of International Education." *Harvard Educational Review Journal*, vol. 55, pp. 123-126.

Myles, Wayne. 1996. "Quality of Service Through the Strategic Use of Technology." *Frontiers: The Interdisciplinary Journal of Study Abroad*, vol. II, pp. 101-110.

NAFSA: Association of International Educators. 2003. *Securing America's Future: Global Education for a Global Age*. Washington DC: NAFSA: Association of International Educators.

NAFSA/CIEE/IIE. 1990. *Getting on with the Task: A National Mandate for Education Abroad*. The Report of the Task Force on Undergraduate Education Abroad. Washington DC: NAFSA: Association of International Educators.

National Governor's Association. *America in Transition: The International Frontier* (Report of the Task Force on International Education, National Governor's Association, 1989)

O'Banion, Terry. 1997. *A Learning College for the 21st Century. American Association of Community Colleges Series*. Phoenix: Oryx Press.

References

Oberstein-Deballe, Elizabeth. 1999. *Study Abroad Programs in Three California Community Colleges*. Dissertation.

O'Neal, John C. 1995. "It's Like Wearing all the Hats." *Academe*, September/October 1995.

Opening Doors Overseas. 2004. Eugene, OR: Mobility International USA/National Clearinghouse on Disability and Exchange (NCDE) publications.

Opper, Susan; Ulrich Teichler and Jerry Carlson. 1990. "Impacts of Study Abroad Programmes on Students and Graduates." *Higher Education Policy Series 11*, volume 2. London: Jessica Kingsley Publishers.

Paige, Michael, ed. 1993. *Education for the Intercultural Experience*. Yarmouth, ME: Intercultural Press.

Paige, R. Michael, Andrew D. Cohen, Barbara Kappler, J. C. Chi, and J. P. Lassegard. 2004. *Maximizing Study Abroad: A Language Instructor's Guide to Strategies for Language and Culture Learning and Use*. Minneapolis, MN: CARLA.

Pederson, Paul B., ed. 1996. *Counseling Across Cultures*, fourth edition. Thousand Oaks: Sage Publications.

Perry Jr., William J. 1970. *Forms of Intellectual and Ethical Development in the College Years: A Scheme*. New York: Holt, Rinehard and Winston.

Pfnister, Allan.O. 1972. "Everyone overseas: Goshen College Pioneers." *International Educational and Cultural Exchange*, vol. 8, no. 2, pp. 1-12.

———. 1979. *Ten Year Evaluation of Study Service Trimester*. Goshen, IN: Goshen College Office of International Education.

Pickert, Sarah, and Barbara Turlington. 1992. *Internationalizing the Undergraduate Curriculum: A Handbook for Campus Leaders*. Washington, DC: American Council on Education.

Practical Penn Abroad. 2004. Office of International Programs, University of Pennsylvania.

Priest, Simon. 2000. "Effective Outdoor Leadership." *In Lessons Learned: A Guide to Accident Prevention and Crisis Response*, Deb Ajango, ed. Boulder, CO: Association for Experiential Education.

Priest, Simon and Michael A Gass. 1997. *Effective Leadership in Adventure Programming*. Champaign, IL: Human Kinetics

Pyle, K. Richard. 1981. "International Cross-Cultural Service/Learning: Impact on Student Development." *Journal of College Student Personnel*, vol. 22, no. 6, pp. 509-514.

Raby, Rosalind Latiner. 1996. "International, Intercultural, and Multicultural Dimensions of Community Colleges in the United States" in Raby, Rosalind Latiner and Tarrow, Norma, eds. *Dimensions of the Community College: International and Inter/Multicultural Perspectives, Garland Studies in Higher Education*, vol. 6, 1075, New York: Garland Publishing, Inc.

———. 1999. *Looking to the Future: Report on International and Global Education in California Community Colleges*. State Chancellor, California Community Colleges.

———. 2002. *CCIE Annual Report: Executive Summary*. Riverside, CA: Riverside Community College Publications, CCIE.

———. 2003. *CCIE Annual Report: Executive Summary*. Salinas: Hartnell Community College Publications, CCIE.

Raby, Rosalind Latiner and Norma Tarrow, eds. 1996. *Dimensions of the Community College: International and Inter/Multicultural Perspectives, Garland Studies in Higher Education*, vol. 6, 1075. New York: Garland Publishing, Inc.

Reagan, Timothy. 2000. *Non-Western Educational Traditions: Alternative Approaches to Educational Thought and Practice*, second edition. Mahwah, NJ: Lawrence Erlbaum Associates.

Reid, Joy M., ed. 1988. *Building the Professional Dimension of Educational Exchange*. Yarmouth, ME: Intercultural Press, Inc.

Rhodes, Gary M. 1994. "Legal Issues and Higher Education: Implications for Study Abroad: Key Issues for Institutions and Administrators." Ph.D. dissertation, University of Southern California.

Rhodes, Gary M. 1995. "The Internet and the World Wide Web: Uses for Study abroad." *Frontiers: The Interdisciplinary Journal of Study Abroad*, vol. I, pp. 108-112

Rhodes, Gary M. 1997. "Institutional Vulnerability to Liability for Student Injury and Death During Study Abroad," in *18th Annual National Conference on Law and Higher Education*, 11 (Stetson University College of Law, Feb. 13-14, 1997).

Rhodes, Gary M., and R. J. Aalberts. 1994. "Liability and Study Abroad: 'Prudent' Policies and Procedures Are the Best Insurance." *Transitions Abroad*, vol. XVII.

Rhodes, Gary M., and W. G. Millington. 1994. "Avoiding Liability in Study Abroad: Home Campus and International Campus Concerns." *NAFSA Newsletter*, vol. 45, no. 5, pp. 3, 44, 46.

Rinehart, Nana. 2002. "Utilitarian or Idealist? Frameworks for Assessing the Study Abroad Experience." *Rockin' in Red Square: Critical Approaches to International Education in the Age of Cyberculture*. Walter Grünzweig and Nana Rinehart eds. Muenster: Lit Verlag.

Roochnik, David. 2001. "What Direction for Study Abroad? First, Look Homeward" *The Chronicle Review*, May 18, 2001.

Roose, D. 2001. "White Teachers Learning about Diversity and Otherness: The Effects of Undergraduate International Education Internships on Subsequent Teaching Practices." *Equity & Excellence in Education*, vol. 34, no. 1, pp. 43-49.

Ropeik, David and George Gray. 2002. *RISK! A Practical Guide for Deciding What's Really Safe and What's Dangerous in the World Around You*. Boston New York: Houghton Mifflin.

References

Samovar, Larry A., and Richard E. Porter. 2003. "Understanding Intercultural Communication: An Introduction and Overview." *Intercultural Communication: A Reader*, tenth edition. L. A. Samovar and R. E. Porter, eds. Belmont, CA: Wadsworth/Thompson Learning.

Sanborn, Robert and Cheryl Matherly. 2003. *How to Get a Job in Europe: The Insider's Guide*, fifth edition. River Forest, IL: Planning/Communications.

Sanoff, Alvin, P. 2004. "Americans See Money for College Somewhere Over the Rainbow." *Chronicle of Higher Education*. April 30, 2004.

Scanlon, David G. 1990. "Lessons for the Past in Developing International Education in Community Colleges." *Developing International Education Programs (New Directions for Community Colleges*, No. 70). San Francisco: Jossey-Bass.

Schlossberg, Nancy K. 1989. "Marginality and mattering: Key issues in building community." In D.C. Roberts (Ed.), *Designing campus activities to foster a sense of community (New Directions for Student Services*, no. 48, pp. 5-15). San Francisco: Jossey-Bass.

Scriven, M. 1991. "Beyond Formative and Summative Evaluation" *Evaluation and Education: At Quarter Century*. Milbrey W. McLaughlin and D. C. Phillips, eds. New York. John Wiley.

Segal, Nina and Eric Kocher. 2003. *International Jobs: Where They Are and How to Get Them*, sixth edition. New York: Basic Books.

Shannon, William. 1978. "A Survey of International/Intercultural Education in Two-Year Colleges 1976." La Plata, MD: Charles County Community College.

Sideli, Kathleen. 1999a. "Everyone Counts!" *International Educator*, vol. VIII, no. 3, pp. 58-59.

———. 1999b. "In Pursuit of the Elusive Actual Number," *NAFSA Newsletter*, vol. 50, no. 3, pp. 1, 10.

———. 2000a. "Technology and Study Abroad: Lessons I Have Learned." *International Educator*, vol. IX, no. 4, pp. 41-43.

———. 2000b. "It's 2000: Do You Know Where Your Students Are?" *International Educator*, vol. IX, no. 2, pp.38-43.

———. 2002. "Security Issues and Data Collection in Education Abroad," *International Educator*, vol. XI, no. 1, pp. 41-42.

Sideli, Kathleen and Hey Kyung-Koh Chin. 2002. "Everyone Has to Count When it Comes to Security," *IIENetworker*, Fall 2002. 44-46.

Sideli, Kathleen, Michael Vande Berg and Richard Sutton. 2001. "Outcomes Assessment and Study Abroad Programs," *International Educator*, vol. X, no. 2, pp. 30-31.

Singer, Marshall R. 1987. *Intercultural Communication: A Perceptual Approach*. Englewood Cliffs, NJ: Prentice-Hall.

Spencer, Sarah and Kathy Tuma. 2002. *The Guide to Successful Short-Term Programs Abroad*. Washington, DC. NAFSA: Association of International Educators.

Steinberg, Michael. 2002. "'Involve Me and I Will Understand': Academic Quality in Experiential Programs Abroad." *Frontiers: The Interdisciplinary Journal of Study Abroad*, vol. VIII, pp. 207-229.

Stephenson, Skye. 1999. "Study Abroad as a Transformational Experience and Its Impact upon Host Nationals in Santiago, Chile." *Frontiers: The Interdisciplinary Journal of Study Abroad*, vol. V, pp. 2-38.

———. 2003. "I Am Dreaming of Study Abroad." Paper presented at the Latin American Studies Association conference March 2003.

Stewart, Edward C., Jack Danielian, and Robert J. Foster. 1998. *Cultural Assumptions and Values. In Basic Concepts of Intercultural Communication*, M. J. Bennett, ed. Yarmouth, ME: Intercultural Press.

Stewart, Edward C., and Milton J. Bennett. 1972. *American Cultural Patterns: A Cross-Cultural Perspective*. Yarmouth, ME: Intercultural Press.

Storti, Craig. 1999. *Figuring Foreigners Out: A Practical Guide*. Yarmouth, ME: Intercultural Press.

———. 2001a. *The Art of Coming Home*. Yarmouth, ME: Intercultural Press.

———. 2001b. *The Art of Crossing Cultures*, second edition. Yarmouth, ME: Intercultural Press.

Sussman, Nan M. 1986. "Re-entry Research and Training: Methods and Implications." *International Journal of Intercultural Relations*, vol. 10, pp. 235-254.

———. 2002. "Testing the Cultural Identity Model of the Cultural Transition Cycle: Sojourners Return Home." *International Journal of Intercultural Relations*, vol. 26, no. 4, pp. 391-408.

Talburt, Susan, and Melissa A. Stewart. 1999. "What's the Subject of Study Abroad? Race, Gender, and 'Living Culture.'" *The Modern Language Journal*, vol. 83, no. 2, pp. 163-175.

Theodore Gochenour, ed. 1993. *Beyond Experience: An Experiential Approach to Cross-Cultural Education*, second edition. Yarmouth, ME: Intercultural Press.

Thot, I.D. 1998. "State-sponsored study-abroad programs of France and Germany: What are the effects on United States students." Doctoral Dissertation at the Claremont Graduate University.

Tillman, Martin, ed. 2003. *Study Abroad: A 21st Century Perspective, Vol. II: The Changing Landscape*. New York: American Institute for Foreign Study Foundation.

References

Ting-Toomey, Stella. 1999. *Communicating Across Cultures*. New York: Guilford Press.

Toncar, Mark F. and Brian V. Cudmore. 2000. "The Overseas Internship Experience," *Journal of Marketing Education*, vol. 22, no. 1, 54-63.

United States General Accounting Office. 2002. "Foreign Languages; Human Capital Approach Needed to Correct Staffing and Proficiency Shortfalls." Washington, DC: United States General Accounting Office.

University of Massachusetts Project Plus 1999. 1999. Student Affairs Research, Information and Systems Office. Amherst: University of Massachusetts.

Van Der Meid, Scott. 2003. "Asian Americans: Factors Influencing the Decision to Study Abroad," *Frontiers: The Interdisciplinary Journal of Study Abroad*, vol. IX, pp. 71-110.

Van de Water, Jack. 1997. "Gaps in the Bridge to the Twenty-first Century." *International Educator*, vol. VI, no. 3, pp. 10-15.

_____. 2000. "The International Office: Taking a Closer Look." *International Educator*, vol. IX, no. 2, pp. 30-33, 37.

Vaughan, George, B, ed. 1980. "Questioning the Community College Role." *New Directions for Community Colleges*, no. 32. San Francisco: Jossey-Bass.

Wagner, Kenneth, and Tony Magistrale. 1995. *Writing Across Culture: An Introduction to Study Abroad and the Writing Process*. New York: Peter Lang Publishing, Inc.

Weaver, Gary. 1986. "Understanding and Coping with Cross-Cultural Adjustment Stress." In *Cross-Cultural Orientation, New Conceptualizations and Applications*, R. M. Paige, ed. Lanham, MD: United Press of America.

Weeks, William H., Paul B. Peterson, and Richard Brislin. 1979. *Manual of Structured Experiences for Cross-Cultural Learning*. Yarmouth, ME: Intercultural Press.

Weiss, C.B. 1998. "Adjustment of American student interns overseas: A case in Australia." A doctoral dissertation at the University of Michigan.

Williams, John H. 1993. "Clarifying Grade Expectations." *The Teaching Professor*, August/September 1993.

Young, Michael. 1988. "Training for Global Competence in the Legal Profession," in *Educational Exchange and Global Competence*, Richard Lambert, ed. New York, NY: CIEE, 103-120.

ONLINE REFERENCES

This list is also maintained on the NAFSA Web site (http://www.nafsa.org) where links to Web addresses are updated periodically.

AACRAO (American Association of College Registrars and Admissions Officers) and NAFSA: Association of International Educators. 1979. *Study Abroad Programs: An Evaluation Guide*. Washington, DC: AACRAO and NAFSA: Association of International Educators. Available from ERIC online document service, no. ED227783 at http://searcheric.org/

ACTFL oral proficiency guidelines of the American Council on the Teaching of Foreign Languages. Available from http://www.actfl.org/i4a/pages/index.cfm?pageid=3348

Adventure Incorporated "The Risk Management Process." In *Adventure*. Available from http://www.adventureincorporated.com

Ailes, Catherine P. and Susan H. Russell. 2002. "Outcome Assessment of the U.S. Fulbright Scholar Program." Office of Policy and Evaluation, Bureau of Educational and Cultural Affairs, U.S. Department of State. SRI International Project No. P10372. Available from http://exchanges.state.gov/education/evaluations

Altschuler, Glenn C. 2001. "Education Life College Prep: La Dolce Semester" *The New York Times Company*. May 5, 2001. Available from http://www.casdn.neu.edu/sap/articles/LaDolce.html

Allaway, William H. 1965. "The Many-Faceted Job of the Overseas Academic Program Director." (CIEE Occasional Paper Series #2, 1965). Available from http://www.ciee.org/research_center/occasional_papers.aspx

American Association of Community and Junior Colleges, "Community College Fast Facts Sheet." Available from http://www.aacc.nche.edu/Content/NavigationMenu/AboutCommunityColleges/Fast_Facts1/Fast_Facts.htm

American Council on Education (ACE). 2001. *A Brief Guide to U.S. Higher Education*. Washington, D.C: American Council on Education. Available from http://www.acenet.edu

Anderson, Keisha. 1996. "Expanding Your Horizons." *Black Enterprise*, June, 1996. Available from http://www.findarticles.com/p/articles/mi_m1365/is_n11_v26

Arabic Language and Middle East/North African Cultural Studies. 2004. University of Montana. Available from http://www.montana.edu/international/arabic.htm

Background Notes. 2004. U.S. Department of State. Available from http://www.state.gov/r/pa/ei/bgn/

Bequette, G, et al. 2001. *Computer Ethics for Educators*. Available from http://lrs.ed.uiuc.edu/students/kitzmllr/handel.htm

Bolen, Mell. "Basic Student Data and Outcomes Assessment in International Education" Forum on Education Abroad. Available from http://www.ForumEA.org

Bresciani, Marilee J. 2002. "Outcomes assessment in student affairs: Moving beyond satisfaction to student learning and development." *Net RESULTS E-Zine*. National Association for Student Personnel Administrators. Available from http://www.naspa.org

Burn, Barbara and R.H. Smuckler. 1995. *A research agenda for the internationalization of higher education in the United States: Recommendations and report*. Available from Available from ERIC online document service, No. ED 392 331. http://searcheric.org/

Chancellor's Office of California Community Colleges (COCCC). Available from "Reports" section of COCCC Web site.

Chao, Maureen, ed. *Research on U.S. students abroad, volume II, A bibliography with abstracts 1988–2000*. Available from http://www.lmu.edu/globaled/ro/index.html

———. "Online announcement" for Research on U.S. students abroad, volume II, A bibliography with abstracts 1988–2000. Available from http://www.secussa.nafsa.org/brochure.html

Cavallero, Leonore. 2003. *Surviving Re-entry: A Handbook for Parents of Study Abroad Students Returning Home*. School of International Training. Brattleboro, VT Available from http://www.sit.edu/studyabroad/parents/reentry.html

Center for International Rehabilitation Research Information and Exchange (CIRRIE). Available from http://cirrie.buffalo.edu/

Clery Act (Crime Awareness and Campus Security Act of 1990, 34 CFR 668.41 and 34 CFR 668.46). Available from http://www.securityoncampus.org/schools/cleryact/

Cobb, Nathan. 1998. "Meet tomorrow's teens." *Boston Globe Online*, 28 April, 1998. Available from http://www.boston.com/tools/archives/

Comp, David. *Research on underrepresented students and education abroad: An annotated bibliography*. Available from http://www.secussa.nafsa.org/underrepresentation

———. *Research on U.S. Students Study Abroad: An Update, Volume III, 2001-2003, With Updates to the 1989 and Volume II Editions 2000-2003*. Available from http://www.lmu.edu/globaled/index.html

Contexts of Postsecondary Education Summary 2003. National Center for Education Statistics. Available from http://nces.ed.gov/pubs2003/2003067_5.pdf

Craig, Starlett. *Global Study: Reflecting the norms of an international society*. Black Collegian 1998. Available from http://www.umi.com/

References

CultureGrams. Axiom Press. Available from http://www.culturegrams.com

Engle, John and Engle, Lilli, "Study Abroad Levels: Notes Towards a Classification of Program Types," NAFSA: Association of International Educators Conference Paper, Denver 1999. Available from http://www.nafsa.org

Engle, Lilli, "Study Abroad Program Elements," Available from http://www.forumea.org/sabelements.html

Excellence, Center for Teaching. 2004. *Enabling versus Empowering*. St. Edward's University. Available from http://www.stedwards.edu/cte/resources/enabling.htm

Family Educational Rights and Privacy Act (FERPA). Available from http://www.ed.gov/policy/gen/guid/fpco/ferpa/index.html

Federal Student Aid Handbook 2004-05. Available from http://www.ifap.ed.gov

Forum on Education Abroad. 2004. "Prospectus." and "Plans and Timetables for The Forum's Five Goals Committees 2003-2004." Available from http://www.forumea.org

Greisberger, John. 2004. *Intercultural Experiential Learning*. Ohio State University. Available from http://www.oie.ohio-state.edu/study_abroad/study_abroad_class.asp

Hains, A. H., E.W. Lynch, and P.J. Winton. 1997. "Cultural Competence: A Review of The Literature." Unpublished manuscript, CLAS Early Childhood Research Institute, Champaign, IL. Cited in Milagros Santos, Rosa, and Debbie Reese. 2004. *Selecting Culturally and Linguistically Appropriate Materials: Suggestions for Service Providers*. 1999. Available from http://www.ericdigests.org/2000-1/selecting.html

Haug, Guy and Jette Kirstein. V*isions of a European Future, Bologna and Beyond (2001)*. Available from http://www.eaie.org/about/speech.html

Hoffa, William. 1999. "Study abroad data collection, 1949 to the present: A brief overview." Available from http://www.secussa.nafsa.org/briefdatacollection.html

———. 2001. "What Are Participation Rates…And Why Should Anybody Care?" Available from http://www.secussa.nafsa.org/participationrates.html

———. *StudyAbroad.com Handbook*. Available from http://www.studyabroad.com/InfoCentre/

Hoffa, William and Sarah Spencer. 2004. "Duration of Study Abroad." Available from http://www.opendoors.iienetwork.org/

Huitt, Bill, Hummel, John, Kaeck, Dan. 2001. "Assessment, Measurement, Evaluation, & Research." Department of Psychology, Counseling, & Guidance, Valdosta State University. Available from http://www.valdosta.edu/whuitt/

IES (The Institute for the International Education of Students). 2003. *The IES MAP (Model Assessment Practice) for Study Abroad: Charting a Course for Quality*. Chicago: IES. Available from http://www.iesabroad.org/iesMap.do

Institute for International Education. 2005. *IIE Passport: Academic Year Abroad*. New York: IIE. Available from http://www.iiepassport.org

———. 2005. *IIE Passport: Short-Term Study Abroad*. New York: IIE. Available from http://www.iiepassport.org

———. *Open Doors 2002: Americans Studying Abroad*. Institute for International Education. Available from http://opendoors.iienetwork.org

———. *Open Doors 2003: Americans Studying Abroad*. Institute for International Education. Available from http://opendoors.iienetwork.org

———. *Open Doors 2004: Americans Studying Abroad*. Institute for International Education. Available from http://opendoors.iienetwork.org

———. *Open Doors 2005: Americans Studying Abroad*. Institute for International Education. Available from http://opendoors.iienetwork.org

Institute for International Education and SECUSSA. 1999. *Electronic Sampling Results*. Available from http://www.secussa.nafsa.org/samplingresults.html

Intercultural Activity Toolkit. 2004. NAFSA: Association of International Educators. Available from http://www.nafsa.org/practiceres/index.html

International Academic Programs. 2004. University of Wisconsin-Madison. Available from http://www.studyabroad.wisc.edu/programs/nonuw.html

International Center. 2004. International Office, Macalester College. Available from http://www.macalester.edu/internationalcenter/

International Organization for Standardization (ISO). 2002. Guide 73. *Risk Management*. Available from http://www.iso.ch

ISE: Institute for Shipboard Education (Semester at Sea). 2003. "Safety and Study Abroad." Video. Available from http://www.semesteratsea.com/advisors/safetyvideo.html

It's Your World: Student's Guide to Education Abroad. 2004. StudyAbroad.com. Available from http://www.studyabroad.com/handbook/handbook.html

Kalamazoo Project for Intercultural Communication (KPIC). 2004. Center for International Programs, Kalamazoo College. Available from http://www.kzoo.edu/cip/kpic/

Kelly, C. and J. Meyers. 1992. *Cross Cultural Adaptability Inventory*. Available from http://www.click.vi.it/sistemieculture/Meyers.html

Kennedy, Michael D. and Elaine S. Weiner. 2003. The Articulations of International Expertise in the Professions. Available from http://www.jhfc.duke.edu/ducis/globalchallenges/research_papers.html

Kizlik, Robert. 2003. "Measurement, Assessment, and Evaluation in Education." Available from http://www.adprima.com/measurement.htm

La Brack, Bruce. 2004. *Orientation Courses*. University of Southern California. Available from http://www.lmu.edu/globaled/safeti/

Learning Outcomes Research Project, Office of International Education, University System of Georgia Study Abroad. Available from http://www.usg.edu/oie/initiatives/saslorp.phtml

Martin, Patricia C. 2004. *Philadelphia Area Study Abroad Reentry Conference*. University of Pennsylvania. Available from http://www.upenn.edu/oip/sa

Mikhailova, Ludmila. 2002. "A History of CIEE: Council on International Educational Exchange 1947–1994." CIEE: New York. Available at http://www.ciee.org/about/history.aspx

Mindtools.com. 2004. "Decision Trees" Available from http://www.mindtools.com/pages/article/newTED_04.htm

NACADA Statement of Core Values of Academic Advising 2004. NACADA (National Academic Advising Association). Available from http://www.nacada.ksu.edu/Clearinghouse/AdvisingIssues/Core-Values.htm

NAFSA: Association of International Educators. 1996. "Statement of Professional Competencies for International Educators." Available from http://www.nafsa.org/content/ProfessionalandEducationalResources/Training/competencies.htm

NAFSA: Association of International Educators. 2003. "Code of Ethics." Available from http://www.nafsa.org/content/InsideNAFSA/EthicsandStandards/CodeOfEthics/CodeOfEthics.htm

O'Keefe, M. 2002. "Current teen generation acquitting themselves well as volunteers." Newhouse News Service. Available from http://www.newhouse.com/archive/story1a073102.html

Office of International Studies and Programs. Central Washington University. Available from http://www.cwu.edu/~intlprog/

Participation in Education: Undergraduate Education. National Center for Education Statistics. Available from http://nces.ed.gov/programs/coe/list/index.asp

Paul D. Coverdell World Wise Schools, Culture Matters. Peace Corps. Available from http://www.peacecorps.com/wws/culturematters/

Plaza, O. 1998. Overseas studies and technology education. Available from Available from ERIC online document service, No. ED420805. http://searcheric.org/

Religious Resource and Research Center at the University of Derby in the United Kingdom. Available from http://www.multifaithnet.org/

Rogers, John and David Larsen. 2002. *Optimizing Health Care in International Educational Exchange*. NAFSA: Association of International Educators. Available from http://www.nafsa.org/content/professionalandeducationalresources/publications/study.htm

SAFETI Adaptation of Peace Corps Resources. Peace Corps. Available from http://www.lmu.edu/globaled/safeti/

Science and Engineering Indicators 1998. 2004. National Science Foundation. Available from http://www.nsf.gov/sbe/srs/seind98

SECUSSA. 2004. *Departmental Census Form*. Available from http://www.secussa.nafsa.org/censusform.html

———. "Study abroad: Why numbers can help you…A data advocacy sheet." Available from http://www.secussa.nafsa.org/Advosheet.html

Slind, Mickey. 1997. "When a Reporter Calls." Available from http://www.secussa.nafsa.org

Sommer, John G. *Education Abroad*. 2000. Available from http://www.sit.edu/publications/index.html

Special Analysis 2002 Nontraditional Undergraduates. National Center for Education Statistics (NCES). Available from http://nces.ed.gov/programs/coe/2002/analyses/nontraditional/index.asp

Standard Rules for the Equalization of People with Disabilities. 2004. United Nations 1993. Available from http://www.un.org/ecosocdev/geninfo/dpi1647e.htm

Survey of Third Party Providers: Final Report. 2002. Monalco. Available from http://www.secussa.nafsa.org/3rdparty12.doc

The Evaluation Center. Western Michigan University, Kalamazoo, MI. Available from http://www.wmich.edu/evalctr/

Thompson, J. Walter. 2004. "An Exploration of the Demand for Study Overseas from American Students and Employers." Institute of International Education. Available from http://research1.iienetwork.org

Tillman, Martin (Ed.). 2000. Study abroad: A 21st century perspective. Vols I and II. Stamford, CT: American Institute for Foreign Study Foundation. Available from http://www.aifs.com/aifsfoundation/21century.htm

U.S. Census 2000. Available from http://censtats.census.gov/

References

University of Texas at Austin, International Office. 2005. *Statistical Report*, http://www.utexas.edu/international/statrepts.shtml

Vande Berg, Michael J., and Lynn Leonard. 2003. *A Guide to Whole World Study.* NAFSA: Association of International Educators. Available from http://www.secussa.nafsa.org/guide/default.html

Van Der Meid, J. Scott. 2002. "Study Abroad, Why Numbers Can Help You...A Data Advocacy Sheet." Available from http://www.secussa.nafsa.org/Advosheet.html

Whalen, Brian. 2002. *Study Abroad Outcomes Assessment: Longitudinal Studies.* The Forum on Education Abroad. Available from http://www.forumea.org/longitudinal_studies.html

What's up with culture? Available from http://www3.uop.edu/sis/culture/index.htm

White House Office of the Press Secretary. April 19, 2000. "Memorandum for the Heads of Executive Departments and Agencies. Subject: International Education Policy." Available from http://www.exchanges.state.gov/iew2002/statements/whstatement.htm

Index

A

AA (Alcoholics Anonymous), 271
AACRAO. *See* American Association of Collegiate Registrars and Admission Officers (AACRAO)
AAC&U (Association of American Colleges and University), 449
AAHE (American Association for Higher Education), 156, 446, 450
AAIE (Australian Association for International Education), 472
Aalberts, R. J., 515
ABET (Accreditation Board for Engineering and Technology), 218
Abraham Lincoln Study Abroad Fellowship Program, 13
Abrams, Irwin, 316
Abroad by Design (Lamet), 469, 470, 492
Abroad View (magazine), 311
Academe (journal), 87
Academic advising. *See* Advising/Advising offices
    Academic affairs office, 64, 545
    Academic calendars, 396
    Academic credit, 93–105, 405. *See also* Curriculum
    activities towards, 97–98
    agency consortia programs, 364
    community colleges, 155
    databases for tracking, 140–141
    defining, 94–95
    direct enrollment with host institution, 353
    from external programs, 46, 464
    first-generation college students' concern over, 219
    grades/grading policies, 101–105, 408
    for independent study, 357–358
    integration of education abroad with curriculum, 66–69
    internships for, 19
    Junior Year Abroad programs, 7
    orientations covering, 300–301
    in partnership consortia programs, 362
    policies on, development of, 96–97
    program directors' role towards, 95
    "school of record" concept, 98–99
    short-term programs, 376
    transcripts, 99–100
    transfer of, 408
    types of, 100–101
    United States institutions' criteria for, 94–95
    work abroad programs, 324 (*See also* Work abroad programs)
Academic departments/services, 70–71, 75. *See also* Faculty
Academic expectations, 559–560
Academic level, 51
Academic majors
    community colleges, availability to, 165–166
    diversity of abroad, 52
    underrepresented majors in study abroad programs, 209, 217–218
    work abroad programs in, 319
Academic Year Abroad (IIE), 34
    cost range of programs, 117
    external program providers, 459
    marketing survey, used for, 434
    as a resource for advisers, 182
Academy for International Education (NAFSA), 32
Access Abroad Web site, 234, 235
Accountability, 446
Accreditation, 446, 457
Accreditation Board for Engineering and Technology (ABET), 218
ACE. *See* American Council on Education (ACE)
ACHA (American College Health Association), 262, 495
ACIIE (American Council on International Intercultural Education), 155
ACPA (American College Personnel Association), 190
ACS (American Chemical Society), 218
ADA (Americans with Disabilities Act), 270, 409. *See also* Americans with Disabilities Act (ADA)
Administration of education abroad programs, 61–74
    academic credit policies, 96–97
    academic departments/services, 70–71
    administrative services for, 73–74
    authority for, 513–514
    campus security, 497
    campus-wide information networks, 144–149
    at community colleges, 159–162 (*See also* Community colleges)
    within the curriculum, 66–69
    faculty roles in, 78–85 (*See also* Faculty)
    financial services and development office, 71–72
    goals and policies, 65–66
    home-campus tuition model for education abroad programs, 401–402
    within the institution, 69–70
    mission and characteristics of home institution, 63–64, 69
    on-site issues, 573–585 (*See also* On-site issues)
    organization of home institution, 64–65
    student services, 72–73
    support of institution for program, 433
    technological resources for, 138–142
Admissions
    campus administration of education abroad programs, 73
    education abroad programs stressed during process, 419
    external program providers, assessment of, 462–463
    faculty role in, 79–80
    independent study abroad, 359
    integrated programs, 352
    international admissions office, 472
    partnership consortia programs, 362

Index

procedures for, 409–410
study centers, 348
Adult-learner techniques, 295
Advertising, 439–440. *See also* Marketing
Advising/Advising offices, 71, 173–191
    Chickering's seven vectors of development, 179–180
        community colleges, 161
        disabilities, students with, 229–230 (*See also* Disabilities, students with)
        faculty role of, 78–79
        group and peer advising, 186–187
        infrastructure for, 187
        for integrated model of program design, 355
        overseas faculty role of, 90–91
    Perry's nine-stage theory of cognitive development, 176–179
        process of, 180–186
        professioal development for advisers, 189–191
        program directors in overseas programs, 563–565
        program selection, 181–184
    Schlossberg's theory of mattering, 175–176
        student service model, development of, 187–189
        underrepresented students in education abroad programs, 223
            (*See also* Underrepresented constituencies)
        whole-world study, 245–246 (*See also* Whole-world study)
Advocacy roles, 28
    data collection supporting, 47–49, 139
    faculty, 84–85
African Americans, 221–225
Agency consortia, 364–365
AIEA (Association of International Education Administrators), 35, 480, 521
AIEJ (Association of International Education, Japan), 38, 123
AIESEC (International Association of Students in Economic and Business Management), 314, 326
AIFS (American Institute for Foreign Study), 57, 121
AIPT (Association for Practical Training), 327
Alcohol abuse, 270–271, 286, 521
Alcoholics Anonymous (AA), 271
Allaway, William H., 540
Alliance for International Educational and Cultural Exchange, 36, 240
Alliance Francaise, 121
Alsina, Nuria, 550
Altbach, Philip, 58
Alternative dispute resolution (ADR), 516
Althen, Gary, 301
Altshuler, Glenn C., 157, 164
Alumni, 124–125, 338
American Association for Higher Education (AAHE), 156, 446, 450
American Association of Collegiate Registrars and Admission Officers (AACRAO), 39, 50
    Open Doors survey, contribution to, 53
    transfer of credits, 472
American Association of Cummunity Colletes (AACC), 152, 154-156
American Chemical Society (ACS), 218
American College Health Association (ACHA), 262, 495
American College Personnel Association (ACPA), 190
American Council on Education (ACE), 12–13
    assessment of outcomes in education abroad, 475–476
    Educating Americans for a World in Flux: Ten Ground Rules for Internationalizing Higher Education, 77
    on financial aid, 118
    Health Insurance Portability and Accountability Act (HIPAA) (1996), information on, 495
    high school seniors wanting to study abroad, 476
    Mapping Internationalization on U. S. Campuses, 243
    student outcomes, developing, 449
American Council on International Intercultural Education (ACIIE), 155
American Councils for International Education, 37–38
American Cultural Patterns: A Cross-Cultural Perspective (Stewart and Bennett), 304
American Institute for Foreign Study (AIFS), 57, 121
American-Scandinavian Foundation, 327
Americans with Disabilities Act (ADA)
    admissions process, restrictions on, 409, 490–491
    education abroad programs complying with, 270
    litigation over, 522, 523

American University of Cairo, Egypt, 550, 581
Among the Interculturalists: An Emerging Profession and Its Packaging of Knowledge (Dahlen), 301
AMPEI (Asociacion Mexicana para la Educación Internacional), 37
Anderson, Dawn, 238
Anderson, Lynn C., 173
Andragogy, 295
Angelo, Thomas, 445
Anti-Drug Abuse Act (1988), 271
Antioch College, 8, 314
Anti-U. S. sentiment, 551, 580–581
Applications. *See* Admissions
Arbitration, 516
Arcadia University, 57, 540
Argentina, 549
Arizona
    Furrh v. Arizona Board of Regents (1983), 517
    Maricopa Community College District (MCCD), 156, 158 (*See also* Maricopa Community College District (MCCD), AZ)
The Art of Coming Home (Storti), 196
The Art of Crossing Cultures (Storti), 196, 569
Asia. *See also* under individual countries
    Freeman-Asia awards, 122
    University Mobility in Asia and the Pacific (UMAP), 39
Asian Americans, 210, 220
ASIE (Association for Studies in International Education), 42
ASIRT (Association for Safe International Road Travel), 255, 288, 488
Asociacion Mexicana para la Educacion Internacional (AMPEI), 37
Assessment, 411–413, 445–478
    "culture of assessment" in higher education, 445–448
    decisions about programs, 474–475
    developing models for education abroad programs, 448–451
    direct enrollment programs, 470–473
    external programs, 457–470 (*See also* Program providers)
    internal programs, 452–457
    longitudinal research as tool for, 476–478
    long-term impacts, 475–476
    ongoing, 473–474
    professional program directors, 543
    risk assessment audit, 519, 531–532
    of risk management, 489–490
Association for Practical Training (AIPT), 327
Association for Safe International Road Travel (ASIRT), 255, 288, 488
Association for Studies in International Education (ASIE), 42
Association of American Colleges and University (AAC&U), 449
Association of International Education, Japan (AIEJ), 38, 123
Association of International Education Administrators (AIEA), 35, 480, 521
Association of Teachers of Japanese, 122
Association of Universities and Colleges in Canada (AUCC), 36
Assumed duty, 520–521
Athletes, 219
AUCC (Association of Universities and Colleges in Canada), 36
Audits of programs, 530–532
Australia, 549
    Australian Association for International Education (AAIE), 472
    IDP Education Australia, 17, 38, 56
Authority, legal issues, 513–514
Axiom Press, 304–305

B

"Baby Boomers," 130
Bacon, S. M., 194–195
Bank accounts, 410
Banners, 428
BCCIE (British Columbia Centre for International Education), 36–37
Behaviors
    conduct codes, 491–492, 560
    cultural differences, 201–202
    disciplinary measures, 576–578
    ethics, 29–30
    interviews, 337
    respectful conduct, 286
    screening participants for education abroad programs, 490
Benjamin A. Gilman International Scholarship Program, 120

Index

Bennett, Janet, 197
Bennett, Milton, 21, 194, 304
Bequette, Glenda, 150
Berry, Howard, 464
Beyond Culture (Hall), 302
Beyond Experience (Gochenour), 569
Beyond September 11: A Comprehensive National Policy on International Education (American Council on Education), 12–13
Bickel, Robert D., 511, 517–518, 519
Big World, Inc., 493
Bikson, T. K., 319
Billing/Payment process, 141
Blackstone, William, 519
Blind copy function of e-mail, 422
Board of trustees of institutions, 65–66
Bolen, Mell, 61
Boren, David L., 13
Boren scholarships, 120, 251
Boston College, 124
Bradshaw v. Rawlings (1979), 521
Branch campus model, 8
Brazil, 549
Breach of duty, 520
Bresciani, Marilee J., 448, 449
Brethren Colleges Abroad, 57
Brick, Susan Holme, 389
Bridging Scholarships (Association of Teachers of Japanese), 122
Brislin, Richard W., 194, 302
British Columbia Centre for International Education (BCCIE), 36–37
British Council, 38
British Universities Transatlantic Student Exchange Association (BUTEX), 26, 37, 472
Brochures, 437
Brockington, Joseph, 343
    contributor to "Legal Issues and Education Abroad," 511
    contributor to "Maximizing Safety and Security and Minimizing Risk in Education Abroad Programs," 479
    expenses in emergencies, 506
    fee models for education abroad programs, 400
    survey of international educators, 27
Brown, A., 530
Brown University, 118
Budgeting for study abroad programs, 396–402. *See also* Funding/Fundraising
Building Bridges: A Manual on Including People With Disabilities in International Exchange Programs, 234
BUNAC work program, 328
Burak, Patricia A., 429, 499, 508
Burn, Barbara, 239
Bursars office, 71
Buschman, James L., 239
Butcher, Thomas, 520, 532
BUTEX (British Universities Transatlantic Student Exchange Association), 26, 37, 472
Butler University, 57

C

California
    California State University, 118
    community colleges in, 152, 154
    Loyola Marymount University, Los Angeles, CA, 58, 262, 479
    San Diego City College, 168
    Santa Rosa Junior College, 164
    Stanford University, 8
    University of California at Berkeley, 124
    University of California at Irvine, 326
California Colleges for International Education (CCIE), 159, 160
    case study profiles, 156
    costs of programs, 161
    duration of programs, 158
    financial aid to students, 162
    locations for programs, 165
    non-traditional academic-based programs, 164
    survey of study abroad participants, 157
Campus administration of education abroad programs, 61–74. *See also* Administration of education abroad programs
Campus internationalization, 8–10, 11, 64
Campus newspapers, 426–427
Campus outreach, 214–216. *See also* Marketing
Campus tours, 419
Canada
    Canadian Bureau for International Education (CBIE), 26, 36, 56
    Canadian International Development Agency, 120
    International Centre at Queen's University, 38–39
Cancellation of programs, 506–508
Career counseling office, 73, 337
Careers, international
    leveraging study abroad opportunities, 338–339
    nontraditional locations for study abroad, 250
    opportunities, 312
    work abroad experiences, 319, 334–337
Careers in International Affairs (Carland and Trucano), 335
Carew, Joy, 224
Carland, Maria Pinto, 335
Carnoy, Martin, 241
Carr, Judith W., 469
Carter, Holly M., 238
Castro, Fidel, 549
Catalogs for colleges, 419
Cates, Shannon, 75
CBIE (Canadian Bureau for International Education), 26, 36, 56
CCIE. *See* California Colleges for International Education (CCIE)
CCIS (College Consortium for International Studies), 154, 159
CCP (Community College of Philadelphia), 156, 165, 168
CDC. *See* Centers for Disease Control and Prevention (CDC)
CD-ROMs, 299, 436
CDS International, 314, 326
The Center for International Rehabilitation Research Information and Exchange (CIRRIE), 235
Centers for Disease Control and Prevention (CDC), 253, 255
    malaria information, 269
    Traveler's Health web site, 262
Centralized administration of short-term programs, 381–382
Central Washington University, 298
Chao, Maureen, 58, 59, 315
Chickering, Arthur, 179–180
Chieffo, Lisa, 389
Chile, 102, 549, 550
China, 38, 414
Chinese Education Association for International Exchange, 38
Chisholm, Linda, 464
"Choice of forum" clause, 515
"Choice of law" provision, 516
Chronicle of Higher Education, 488, 490
CIC (Committee on Institutional Cooperation), 56
CIEE. *See* Council on International Educational Exchange (CIEE)
CIRRIE (The Center for International Rehabilitation Research Information and Exchange), 235
CISM (Critical Incident Stress Management), 506
Citizenship, 325
Classroom activities, 97, 424
    presentations on education abroad programs, 428
Classroom space, 408–409
Clery Act (2003), 497, 527
Clinton, Bill, 12
Code of Ethics (NAFSA), 29, 30–33
    external programs assessed by, 459
    health, safety, and security issues covered by, 508
    on NAFSA website, 444
    negative opinions, voicing, 530
    standards of care issues, 521, 522, 529
Cognitive development, 176–179
Cold War, 10
Collaboration within institution, 69–73
College Consortium for International Studies (CCIS), 154, 159
College of DuPage, IL, 158, 164
    Zinta Conrad at, 168
    locations for programs, 165
College of the Overwhelmed (Kadison and DiGeronimo), 573

Index

Collins, Joseph, 332
Colonial America, 6
Columbia University, 58
Commitment within relativism, 177, 179
Committee on Institutional Cooperation (CIC), 56
Committees on campus, 66, 83–84
Communicating Across Cultures (Ting-Toomey), 203
Communicating with Strangers: An Approach to Intercultural Communication (Gudykunst and Kim), 301
Communications, 9, 10
    contact information card, 494
    emergencies, 266, 286–287
    families having contact information, 290
    within institution, 69–73
    intercultural learning, 204–205 (*See also* Intercultural learning)
    marketing, publicity, and promotion, 417–444 (*See also* Marketing)
    with media during emergencies, 502, 503, 504
    nontraditional locations, 256–257
    n partnership consortia programs, 363–364
    preparedness, 499
    of responsibilities, 494–495
    safety of students, 284, 286–287 (*See also* Safety of students)
    with students abroad, 47
Communities, 559
Community College of Philadelphia (CCP), 156, 165, 168
Community colleges, 151–168
    defining, 151–153
    duration and content of programs, 157–158
    funding/administrative support for, 159–162
    historical context for education abroad programs in, 154–157
    predeparture/reentry programs, 163–164
    student eligibility and admission requirements, 162–163
    types of programs at, 158–159
    work abroad programs, 164–165
Community service, 566
Comp, David, 58–59, 315
Comparative Education Review (journal), 39, 241
Computer-assisted language learning (CALL), 137
Computers/Computer services. *See also* Technology
    campus administration of education abroad programs, 73, 148
    campus-wide information networks, software for, 148
    data collection/management software, 56, 141–142
    replacement cycles for, 143
    skill-building in, 43
CONAHEC (Consortium for North American Higher Education Collaboration), 37, 371
Conduct, 286, 491–492, 560. *See also* Behaviors
Conferences, 442–443
Conrad, Zinta, 168
Consortia of institutions. *See also* Host institutions
    agreements between, 434
College Consortium for International Studies (CCIS), 154, 159
    community colleges, 159
    faculty involvement with, 80
    programs designed by, 361–365
Consortium for North American Higher Education Collaboration (CONAHEC), 37, 371
Consulates, 403–404. *See also* U. S. Department of State
Contact information, 494
Content and Process: Balancing Challenge (Bennett), 197
Continuing education, 381
Contract law, 513–516, 528
Controller's office, 72
Copyright, 149
Corporations. *See* Private sector
Cost-benefit analyses, 399, 423
Cost management of studying abroad, 115–116. *See also* Financial aid to students; Tuition
    cost range of programs indicated in Academic Year Abroad, 117
    exchange programs, 368–369
    independent study, 360
    individual costs, 397
    integrated models, 354
    locations affecting, 394–395
    nontraditional locations, 250–251
    partnership consortia programs, 362–363
    printed materials stating costs of programs, 514
    short-term programs, 384–387
    study centers, 349
Council on International Educational Exchange (CIEE), 9, 57
    assessment, 448
Council on Student Travel becoming, 58
    Educating for Global Competence, 11
    founding of, 314
    health issues, resources on, 262
    professional development opportunities, 35
    Responsible Study Abroad: Good Practices for Health and Safety, contributing to, 480, 521
    short-term work camps, 332
    work abroad programs, 328
Council on Student Travel, 9
Counseling Across Cultures (Pederson), 210
Counseling services, 161, 575. *See also* Advising/Advising offices
Country/Culture workshops (NAFSA), 32
Course databases, 143
Courses, academic, 407–408. *See also* Academic credit; Curriculum
Credit, academic, 93–105. *See also* Academic credit
Cressey, William, 93
Crime, 255–256, 497. *See also* Safety of students
Crises, 498. *See also* Emergencies
Crisis Management in a Cross-Cultural Setting (Burak and Hoffa), 429, 499, 508
Critical Incident Stress Management (CISM), 506
Cross-Cultural Reentry: A Book of Readings (Freedman), 302
Cross-cultural skills/understanding. *See also* Intercultural learning
    credit for, 98
    orientations covering, 301–305
    as qualification for employment, 17
    short-term programs, 376
    work abroad programs, 318
Culture/Cultural
    customs, 285
    defining, 200
    dual culture blending, 546, 547
    external programs providing opportunities for exploring, 465–466
    homogenous "global," 137
    identity, 303–304
    immersion, 318, 407
    immersion affected by technology, 131–134
    intercultural learning, 193–206 (*See also* Intercultural learning)
    power of American, 22
    preconceptions of, 136
    reentry, shock on, 305–306
    shock, 302–303, 574
    short-term programs, 377
CultureGrams, 304–305
Currency exchanges between countries, 393, 410–411
Current Issues in Comparative Education (journal), 39
Current Issues in Education (journal), 39
Curriculum, 407–408. *See also* Academic credit
    approval process for, 458
    course databases, 143
    external program providers, 464
    ideas for new programs, 391–392
    integration of education abroad programs with, 66–69, 352–353
    program directors developing, 86
    short-term programs, approval of, 382–383
    study centers abroad, 348
    technology affecting development of, 135–137
Customs (cultural), 285

D

Dahlen, Tommy, 301
Dante Alighieri Society, 121
Darrah, M., 493
Database management of student records, 138–142
Data collection/management, 45–60
    academic integrity, tracking, 45–46
    advocacy for education abroad, 47–49

Index

campus data collection, initiating and managing, 55–56
course databases, 143
data warehouse/real-time data information, 146
faculty involvement in, 83
history of, 49–50
incident reports, 483–484
institutional responsibilities/liabilities, 46–47
marketing surveys, 435
Open Doors survey, 49–51, 53–55 (*See also Open Doors* survey (Institute of International Education))
research role for international educators, 58–59
resources for, 56–58
student surveys, 447, 448, 452–454
trends, tracking, 51–52
work abroad programs, 325
workflow for data management, 139–140
David L. Boren National Security Education Act (1991), 13
David L. Boren Undergraduate Scholarships, 120, 251
Decentralized administration of short-term programs, 381
Decision trees, 502, 508
Declaration of Bologna, 15
Defamation, 529–530
Degrees, 26, 78–79. *See also* Academic credit; Curriculum
Delaware, 520
Delaware College, 6
Department of Defense (DOD) schools, 334
Description, Interpretation, and Evaluation exercise (D.I.E.), 205–206
Developing Intercultural Awareness: A Cross-Cultural Training Handbook (Kohls and Knight), 304
Development office, 71–72, 122
Dezerega, Stefano, 332
Diarrhea, 268–269
Didactic learning activities, 295
Differences, cultural, 201–202
DiGeronimo, Thersesa Foy, 574
Digital divide, 131
Direct enrollment, 183, 251
  assessment of, 470–473
  integrated model for program design, 351–356
  traditional exchange program models, 184
Directory listings, 439–440
Directory of International Internships, 327
The Directory of Websites for International Jobs (Krannich and Krannich), 335
Disabilities, students with, 162–163, 227–238
  accommodations for, 233–235
  advising, 229–230
  Americans with Disabilities Act (ADA), 522, 523 (*See also* Americans with Disabilities Act (ADA))
    disclosure of, 282
    fears of, 232–233
    finances for, 235–237
    learning disabilities/dyslexia, 230–231
    nontraditional locations, 258
    psychiatric, 231–232
    underrepresented in study abroad programs, 209
Disability Rights and Education Defense Fund, 235
Disciplinary measures, 576–578. *See also* Behaviors
Disciplines. *See* Academic majors
Discrimination in education abroad programs, 211–212
Diseases, 268–270. *See also* Health
Dismissal of students, 578
Display cases, 428
Dissemination of materials for marketing, 438–443
Diversity in institutions, 210, 559
Dobbert, Lundy, 195
Documents, travel, 287–288. *See also* Visas
Donatelli, Lisa, 129
Dowell, Michele-Marie, 298
Drug abuse, 270–271, 286
Dual culture blending, 546, 547
Dualism, 176, 177
Duke University, 12
Dumont, Sara, 93
Duration of programs, 51–52, 54

community colleges, 157–158
  internships, 327 (*See also* Internships)
  phases of programs, 568–569
  program development and, 81
  short-term programs, 373–387 (*See also* Short-term programs)
  teaching English, 333
  volunteer programs, 331
  work abroad programs, 324 (*See also* Work abroad programs)
Duty, 517. *See also* Legal issues
DVD format, 436
Dyslexia, 230–231

E

Eastern Michigan University, 523–524
Economy, globalization of, 10
Educating Americans for a World in Flux: Ten Ground Rules for Internationalizing Higher Education (American Council on Education), 77
Educating for Global Competence (CIEE), 11
Education, Department of. *See* U. S. Department of Education
Education Abroad Knowledge Community (NAFSA), 26, 34
  assessment of outcomes of education abroad, 475
  Committee on Work, Internships, and Volunteering Abroad, 57
  emergency preparedness, resources on, 498–499
  faith-practicing student needs, 238
  information on location safety, 486
  National Academic Advising Association (NACADA), ties with, 191
  online directories list, 439
  Research on U. S. Students Abroad: A Bibliography with Abstracts available on website, 58
  safety and health, committee on, 262, 479–480, 508
  safety information from, 287
  sample census form, 55
  training programs for program directors, 405
  Whole World web site, 248–249
  work abroad information, 314, 326
Education abroad (overview), 5–23
  fairs, 420–421
  globalization impacting, 10–11, 14–17
  historical precedents, 5–6
  internationalization of campuses, 8–10
  internships, 19
  national policy, 11–14
  students' personal development, 20–22
  work abroad programs, 19–20
  workplace globalization, 17–19
  between World War I and World War II, 6–7
  after World War II, 7–8
Educational Exchange and Global Competence (Lambert), 18
Education for One World (Institute of International Education), 49
Education for the Intercultural Experience (Paige), 569
EDUCAUSE, 148–149
Edufrance, 38
Edwards, Jane, 5
Egypt, 550
Eliot, T. S., 129
Ellis, Jim, 129
E-mail, 149
  in advising process, 189
  discussion lists, 115, 440 (*See also* SECUSS-L (online discussion list))
  emergencies, during, 290
  ePals, 559
  marketing education abroad programs, 421–422
  questionnaires using, 469
Embassies, 403–404. *See also* U. S. Department of State
Emergencies, 255, 263, 497–508
  canceling/suspending programs because of, 506–508
  communications with students during, 266, 286–287
  contacts in host country, 583
  crisis management, 584–585
  decision trees, 502
  definition of, 498
  documentation of, 505
  external programs, procedures, 468
  families having contact information, 284, 290

Index

funding, 506
implementation of plan, 504–506
media, inquiries, 502, 503, 504
media reporting of, 429
medical services, 287
natural phenomena, 276
planning for, 499–502
procedures for, 289, 503
resources for information on, 508–509
response team, 500–502
risk management, 583–584 (*See also* Risk management)
Emotional issues, 231–232, 272–274. *See also* Health
Critical Incident Stress Management (CISM), 506
on-site issues, dealing with, 578–580
reentry, 306–307 (*See also* Reentry)
risks, 480–481
work abroad, 320
Employment. *See* Work abroad programs
Engle, John, 347, 465
Engle, Lilli, 347, 465
English, teaching, 314, 332–333
English as a second language (ESL), 15–16, 32, 223, 332–333
Enrichment activities, 565–568
Enrollment
direct, 183 (See also Direct enrollment)
fluctuation of, 398
permission for, 434
"school of record" concept, 99
Erickson, Scott, 482, 483
Ethics, professional, 29–33
Ethnicity. *See* Race/ethnicity
Ethnocentrism, 2112
Ethnography, 206
Europe. *See also* under individual countries
education of students outside of national frameworks, 67, 552
European Association for International Education (EAIE), 37, 472
European Union, 15
"Grand Tour" in 17th and 18th centuries, 6
percentage of students going to, 14–15
student mobility in, 26
technology and social interaction, 132
The Evaluation Center, 446
Evaluation of programs. *See* Assessment
Evans, R. B., 515, 518
Examinations, credit by, 101. *See also* Academic credit
Exchange programs, 251
financial aid for, 116–117
as integrated model of program design, 354
marketing, students helping with, 423–424
program designed as, 368–371
teaching English, 333
traditional set up on direct enrollment model, 184
Exhibits at fairs/conferences, 420–421, 441–443
Experiential learning activities, 295, 567
External programs, 46
Extracurricular activities, 289, 311–312, 565–568

F

Faculty, 75–92
admissions, role in, 79–80
advising students, 78–79
advocacy roles, 84–85
in agency consortia programs, 364
committee participation, 83–84
community college programs led by, 158
direct enrollment in institutions abroad, 471–472
external programs, assessing, 460
financial matters, 403
grant writing, 83
including in administering education abroad programs, 70–71
input in assessment of program, 454–455
integrated programs, 352
networking, 443

orientation and reentry, 80
overseas roles for, 85–91
in partnership consortia programs, 362, 363
preparation for leading programs, 91
program design, 80–83
as program directors, 86–88, 541
program directors working with local, 550
recruitment, 79
short-term programs, 379, 383
spouses/partners of, 89
study centers abroad, 348, 350
teaching overseas, 88–91
tenure and involvement in education abroad, 76
U. S. versus abroad, 463–464
underrepresented student groups, reaching out to, 214–215
Fairs, 420–421, 440–442
Families, students staying with. *See* Home-stays, housing programs
Families of students
contact information for students, 284
health issues, 266–267
legal issues, 519
orientation, included in, 185
outreach to, 216, 249–250
parental input into assessment, 456–457
program information obtained by, 281
risks of programs communicated to, 499–500
short-term program participation, 384
support for education abroad among minorities, 222
Family Educational Rights and Privacy Act (FERPA), 149, 185, 495
legal issues, 522, 526–527
fastWeb (Financial Aid Search Through the Web), 120
Federal government
community college grant for education abroad, 155
disbursing financial aid, rules for, 113
financial aid used abroad, 108, 111
legal issues, 522–527 (See also Legal issues)
scholarships, 120
volunteer programs, 331–332
Federal Student Aid Handbook, 434
Feedback, 468–469. *See also* Assessment
Fees for programs, 365, 367, 368. *See also* Cost management of studying abroad; Funding/Fundraising; Tuition
FERPA. *See* Family Educational Rights and Privacy Act (FERPA)
Ferst, Steven, 445
Field seminars, 98
Fields of study, 52. *See also* Academic majors
Field trips, 566
Field work, 567
Figuring Foreigners Out (Storti), 196, 203, 569
FinAid Web site, 119
Financial aid to students, 106–127. *See also* Cost management of studying abroad
advising students, 182
availability, enhancing, 113–115
clarifying responsibilities of home institution, 434
community colleges, availability at, 162
consortium agreements for, 434
disabilities, students with, 236–237
disbursing, 113
from foreign governments, 122–123
institutional fundraising, 123–126 (*See also* Funding/Fundraising)
limitations to for studying abroad, 110–112
low-cost programs, 115–117
qualifying for, 112
scholarships, 117–122 (*See also* Scholarships)
short-term programs, 380
sources and types of, 108–109
transferable to study abroad programs, 398
underrepresented students in education abroad programs, 216–217
work abroad salaries, 323–324
Financial services for administering programs, 71–72
FIPSE (Fund for the Improvement of Post-Secondary Education), 479
First aid kits, 265
First-generation college students, 156, 218–219, 220

Index

Fixed costs, 397
Flat-fee model for education abroad programs, 400–401
Flex semesters, 78
Fliers, 419–420, 428, 438
Flores, Lisa, 203
Food, 271–272
Foreign Students and International Study 1984-1988 (Altbach), 58
Forms of Travel (Carr and Summerfield), 469
Forum, choice of as legal issue, 515
Forum on International Education, 190
The Forum on Education Abroad, 35–36, 57–58
    advising, resources on, 190
    assessment of outcomes of education abroad, 475
    outcomes assessment, 447
    roundtable discussions on outcomes assessment, 59
    standards as guiding principals for external programs, 459
    student outcomes, developing, 449
France, 14–15
    Alliance Francaise, 121
    Edufrance, 38
    grades in, 102
Franson, Laars, 550, 551, 581
Freedman, Art, 302
Freeman-Asia awards, 122, 251
Friends, 355
Friendship organizations, 121
Frist, Bill, 276
Froehlich, Marion, 168
Frontiers: The Interdisciplinary Journal of Study Abroad (journal), 16, 39
    international experiential education, 315, 316
    language skill acquisition, 301
    long-term impact of education abroad, 475
    program directors, information for, 569
    publishing in, 42
    service learning programs, 332
Fulbright, J. William, 7
Fulbright-Hays Act (1979), 116
Fulbright Program, 7–8
    assistantships, 20
    former participants assisting with orientation, 294
    fostering peace, 314
    Institute of International Education (IIE) administering student scholarships, 35
    scholarship program, 245
    teaching assignments, 334
Full-day predeparture orientations, 296–297
Fund for the Improvement of Post-Secondary Education (FIPSE), 479
Funding/Fundraising, 28–29, 396–402
    community colleges, 159–162
    cost-benefit analyses, 399
    currency exchanges between countries, 410–411
    disabilities, students with, 235–237
    emergencies, 506
    enrollment fluctuation, 398–399
    external programs, 462, 468
    fee models for, 399–402
    financial management of program, 28–29
    grants/grant writing, 83, 125–126
    locations affecting, 394–395
    marketing, 435–436
    money as motivation for new programs, 390–391
    problems with, 414
    program directors managing, 88
    student scholarships, 123–126
Furek v. University of Delaware (1991), 520
Furrh v. Arizona Board of Regents (1983), 517

G

Gay, lesbian, bisexual, and transgendered (GLBT) students, 59, 225–227
    nontraditional destinations, 258
    underrepresented in study abroad programs, 209
Gender, 209
    addressing imbalance in female to male students studying abroad, 219–220
    female students going abroad, 51
    nontraditional locations, 257
    Title IX, 523–525
    women following customs of host country, 289
Generational model theory, 130
"Generation Y," 130
Georgia, 56, 118, 121
Germany, German Academic Service, 122
GI Bill (1944), 151
Gihring, Lisa, 335
Gilman scholarships, 120, 251
Glimpse (magazine), 311
Gliozzo, Charles, 107
Global Challenges and U. S. Higher Education (conference), 12
The Global Citizen: A Guide to Creating an International Life and Career (Kruempelmann), 335
Global competence, 134–135, 137–138. *See also* Intercultural learning
Globalization
    education abroad impacted by, 14–17
    higher education, 8–10, 11, 64
    private sector financial aid, 121–122
    technology as catalyst for, 135–137
    of workplace, 17–19
GoAbroad.com, 117
Goals as part of administration of programs, 65–66. *See also* Administration of education abroad programs
Gochenour, T., 569
Goethe Clubs, 121
Good Practices. See Responsible Study Abroad: Good Practices for Health and Safety
Goodwin, Craufurd, 347
Gore, Joan Elias, 261
Goshen College, 314
Governance units of institutions, 65
Government officials, local, 548–549
Grades, 93–105, 353. *See also* Academic credit
Graduate degrees/programs, 58, 336
"Grand Tour" in Europe, 6
Grants/Grant writing, 83, 109, 125–126. *See also* Funding/Fundraising; Scholarships
Gray, George, 480, 511
Great Britain. *See* United Kingdom of Great Britain and Northern Ireland
Greater Expectations (Association of American Colleges and University), 449
Green, Judith, 261
Greisberger, John, 298
Grey, David, 500
Griffith, Susan, 330, 334
Gross, Benedict H., 317
Group advising, 186
Group dynamics in short-term programs, 377
Gudykunst, William B., 301
Gullahorn, J. E., 302
Gullahorn, J. T., 302

H

Hall, Edward T., 302
Hamilton College, 85
Handbooks for program directors, 82–83
Hardt, Ty, 502
Harvard College, 317
Hayward, Fred, 6, 476
Hazing, 520
Health, 261–277, 480
    collaboration with health care professionals, 267–268
    disclosure of concerns by students, 264
    emotional/mental problems, 272–274
    foreign medical practices, 274–275
    immunizations, 250, 255, 266, 269
    information sources for, 261–264
    insurance, 262, 275, 282–284, 492–493
    nontraditional locations, 254–255
    nutrition, 271–272
    on-site issues, dealing with, 578–580
    orientations covering, 265–266, 299–300
    predeparture medical examinations, 265

Index

preexisting conditions, 270
reentry, 274
risk assessment, 489
safety concerns, 275–277 (*See also* Safety of students)
screening applicants for program, 490–491
short-term programs, 378
substance abuse, 270–271
world health problems, 268–270
Health Insurance Portability and Accountability Act (HIPAA) (1996), 265, 495
Hecksher, Zahara, 332
Hemingway, Ernest, 231
Henry, Amy, 207
Heritage seeking in education abroad, 225
Herman, Inge, 238
Herrin, Carl, 41
HESA (Higher Education Statistics Agency), 56
Hess, J. Daniel, 298, 569
Hicks, R. Eldridge, 485
Higher Education Act (1965), 108. *See also* Title IV of Higher Education Act (1965)
Higher Education Act (1992 reauthorization), 112
Higher Education Statistics Agency (HESA), 56
HIPAA (Health Insurance Portability and Accountability Act) (1996), 265, 495
Hirsch, Jennifer, 445
Hispanics. See Latinos/Latinas
History, 5–7
community colleges' education abroad programs, 154–157
exclusion of people of color from education abroad, 222
work abroad programs, 313–314
HNIPD (Host-National Institution Program Directors), 541
Hockenberry, John, 227
Hoff, Joseph G., 193
Hoffa, William, 3
contributor to "Education Abroad at the Beginning of the Twenty-first Century," 5
Crisis Management in a Cross-Cultural Setting (Burak and Hoffa), 429, 499, 508
on cultural immersion, 138
introduction to Overseas Program Direction, 537
on *Open Doors* survey, 49
Study Abroad: A Parent's Guide, 216
Home-campus tuition model for education abroad programs, 401–402
Home institutions
administration of education abroad programs, 61–74 (*See also* Administration of education abroad programs)
diversity in, 210
exchange students, 370 (*See also* Exchange programs)
financial aid to students, 108 (*See also* Financial aid to students)
home-institution-sponsored courses, 407–408
maintaining relationships with host institutions, 413–414 (*See also* Host institutions)
mission and characteristics of, 63–64, 346, 430–431
program director working with, 544–546 (*See also* Program directors)
programs administered by external providers, 457–470 (*See also* Program providers)
technology in, 144–149 (*See also* Technology)
Homeland Security, Department of, 276
Home-stays, housing programs, 406, 467
host families, 552
potential hazards for, 482
program support for, 562
Hornig, James F., 87
Host families, 552. *See also* Home-stays, housing programs
Host institutions
administration of program, responsibilities of, 395–396
agreements/contracts with, 403, 409
campus visits to, 443
courses offered, 407–408
credit transferred from, 100–101
direct enrollment in, 183, 251, 470–473 (*See also* Direct enrollment)
foreign student affairs office, 472
maintaining relationships with, 413–414
program directors working with, 87, 404, 541, 549–550
Host-National Institution Program Directors (HNIPD), 541

Housing for students, 87, 406–407
as critical component for study abroad, 561–563
external program providers, 466–468
home-stays, 467 (*See also* Home-stays, housing programs)
independent study abroad, 360
integrated programs, 353–354
in partnership consortia programs, 362
study centers, 348
Houston, Pamela, 207, 228
Hovey, Rebecca, 239
Howe, Neil, 130
How to Get a Job in Europe (Sanborn and Matherly), 330
How to Live Your Dream of Volunteering Abroad (Collins, Dezerega, and Hecksher), 314, 332
Hoye, William
contributor to "Legal Issues and Education Abroad," 511
legal audits, 530
risk assessment audits, 519, 531
Hubbell, Loren Loomis, 400
Hubbs, Clayton, 330
Huitt, Bill, 446
Human resources, 546. *See also* Staff
Hybrid model for program design, 252, 356–357
Hybrid technology system, 145–146

I

IAESTE. *See* International Association for the Exchange of Students for Technical Experience (IAESTE)
IAMAT (International Association for Medication Assistance to Travelers), 263
Iceberg metaphor, 205
Identity, 303–304
IDP Education Australia, 17, 38, 56
IEEE (Institute of Electrical and Electronic Engineers), 218
IES (Institute for the International Education of Students), 57, 315
IFPA. *See* Information for Financial Aid Professionals (IFPA)
IIE. *See* Institute of International Education (IIE)
Illinois Consortium for International Studies and Programs (ICISP), 158, 165
Immigrant students, 156
Immunizations, 250, 255
record of, 266
yellow fever, 269
Improvement, assessment for, 446. *See also* Assessment
Improving Intercultural Interactions: Modules for Cross-Cultural Training Programs (Brislin and Yoshida), 302
Incidents, 498. *See also* Emergencies
Independent living centers (ILCs), 234
Independent study, 98, 183
as part of program design, 357–361
as part of whole-world study, 252
Individual costs, 397. *See also* Cost management of studying abroad
Inflation of grades, 102–103. See also Academic credit
Information for Financial Aid Professionals (IFPA), 398
Information meetings, 420
In-house systems, 145
In loco parentis concept, 519
Institute for International Public Policy, 121
Institute for Shipboard Education, 493
Institute for the International Education of Students (IES), 57, 315
Institute of Electrical and Electronic Engineers (IEEE), 218
Institute of International Education (IIE), 6
Academic Year Abroad, 34, 117 (*See also Academic Year Abroad* (IIE))
data collection efforts, 49–50
early history of, 9
Freeman-Asia awards, 122
Fulbright scholarships, 245 (*See also* Fulbright program)
oldest program in abroad guides, 313–314
Open Doors survey, 49–51, 53–55 (*See also Open Doors* survey (Institute of International Education))
professional development opportunities, 34–35
Short-Term Study Abroad, 117, 182, 434 (*See also* Short-Term Study Abroad (IIE))
student characteristics in study abroad programs in 1988, 14
volunteering abroad, 332
Insurance, 282–284

companies as resource for overseas travel medical issues, 262
health coverage for students, 275, 492–493
for repatriation, 282–283
Integrated model for program design, 351–356
Integrated study, 183
Inter-Associational Data Collection Committee, 50
Intercultural Activity Toolkit (NAFSA), 295
Intercultural learning, 193–206. *See also* Culture/Cultural; Whole-world study
adjustment support for, 574–576
concepts, teaching and learning, 195–196
credit for, 98
cultural differences, teaching, 200–202
learning styles, 198–200
orientations for, 202–205, 301–305
overseas program cycles, as part of, 568–570
as qualification for employment, 17
resistance to from students, 197–198
resources for teaching, 196
short-term programs, 376
strategies for teaching, 205–206
technology enhancing global competence, 134–135, 137–138
work abroad programs, 318
Intercultural Press, 295
International Association for Medication Assistance to Travelers (IAMAT), 263
International Association for the Exchange of Students for Technical Experience (IAESTE), 314, 326, 329
International Association of Students in Economic and Business Management (AIESEC), 314, 326
International Centre at Queen's University, 38–39
International Critical Incident Stress Foundation, 506
"International Education Week," 420
International Educator (magazine), 34, 42, 569
International educators, 25–44. *See also* Professional development
International friendship organizations, 121
Internationalization of higher education, 8–10, 11, 64. *See also* Globalization
Internationalizing the Campus (NAFSA), 239
Internationalizing the Undergraduate Curriculum: A Handbook for Campus Leaders (Pickert and Turlington), 239
International Job Finder Where the Jobs are Worldwide (Lauber and Rice), 335
International Jobs: Where They Are and How to Get Them (Segal and Kocher), 335
International Journal of Intercultural Relations, 306
International Monetary Fund, 120
International Organization for Standardization (ISO), 480
International Partnership for Service Learning, 314
International Student Exchange Program (ISEP), 116, 371
International Student Identification Card (ISIC), 185, 275, 283
International students at U. S. colleges, 9, 72, 423–424
International Studies Abroad (ISA), 57
International Volunteer Programs Association (IVPA), 314, 315
Internet, 133, 149. *See also* Web sites/resources
Internships, 19, 326–327
academic credit for, 98, 324
comparison between U. S. and international, 317
external program providers, 465
for international educators, 43
Interorganizational Task Force on Safety and Responsibility in Study Abroad, 278
Interviews, international experiences discussed in, 337
Iraqi war, 580, 581
The Ireland Funds, 124
Irish American Partnership, 124
ISA (International Studies Abroad), 57
ISEP (International Student Exchange Program), 116, 371
ISIC (International Student Identification Card), 185, 275, 283
Island programs, 252, 347, 549
ISO (International Organization for Standardization), 480
It's Your World: Student's Guide to Education Abroad (studyabroad.com), 303
IVPA (International Volunteer Programs Association), 314, 315

J

Jackson, Marilyn, 207, 222
JAFSA (Japanese Association for Foreign Student Affairs), 472
Japan
Association of International Education, Japan (AIEJ), 38, 123
Association of Teachers of Japanese, 122
communication styles, 204–205
Japanese Association for Foreign Student Affairs (JAFSA), 472
Japan Exchange and Teaching Programme (JET), 320, 333
technology and social interaction in, 132, 136
Jeanne Clery Disclosure of Campus Security Policy and Campus Crime Statistics Act (2003), 497, 527
JET (Japan Exchange and Teaching Programme), 320, 333
Jet lag, 272, 274, 560
Johnson, Margit, 479
Johnson, Martha, 313, 326
Johnson, Stephen, 345
Journaling, 206
Journal of Studies in International Education, 15, 35, 39, 42, 239
Juffer, K. A., 194
Junior colleges. *See* Community colleges
Junior Year Abroad (JYA) programs, 6–7
Jurisdiction, 516

K

Kadison, Richard, 574
KAFSA (Korean Association for Foreign Student Affairs), 472
Kalamazoo College, MI, 298, 310
Kanach, Nancy, 5
Kandel, A. O., 530
Kansas State University, 519
Kaplin, W. A., 483, 485, 513
alcohol usage, 521
Americans with Disabilities Act, 523
duty in tort law, 517, 518
Family Educational Rights and Privacy Act (FERPA), 526
litigation frequency, 522
in loco parentis concept, 519
personal liability of administrators, 528
standard of care, 520
tort law, 516, 517
Kappler, Barbara, 193
Kast, R., 519
Kennedy, Michael D., 240–241
Khalsa, Gurudharm Singh, 239
Kim, Young Yun, 301
King v. Board of Control of Eastern Michigan University (2002), 523–524
Kirby, William C., 317
Kizlik, Robert, 446
Knefelkamp, L. Lee, 190
Knight, Jane, 11
Knight, John M., 304
Kocher, Eric, 335
Koester, Jolene, 196
Kohls, L. Robert
American values affecting study abroad advising, 210–211
on cultural background of participants, 194
Developing Intercultural Awareness: A Cross-Cultural Training Handbook (Kohls and Knight), 304
Survival Kit for Overseas Living, 203
Kolb, David A., 198
Korean Association for Foreign Student Affairs (KAFSA), 472
Krannich, Caryl, 335
Krannich, Ronald, 335
Kreutzer, Kim, 45
Krueger, Roberta L., 87
Kruempelmann, Elizabeth, 335

L

Laboratory work, 97
La Brack, Bruce, 194, 298, 310
Lake, Peter F., 511, 517–518, 519
Lambert, Richard, 18, 137
Lamet, Maryélise S.
Abroad by Design, 469, 470, 492
contributor to "Education Abroad in the Campus Context," 61
Language skills

Index

assessment of program, 453
computer-assisted language learning (CALL), 137
English in non-Anglophone countries, 15–16
    exchange programs, 566
    globalization of workforce, 17–18
    home-stays reinforcing, 406
    integrated study requiring fluency, 183–184
    nontraditional destinations, 258
    orientation addressing, 301, 560
    participation in host institutions academic courses, 357
    as part of admissions criteria, 409
    as prerequisite for international careers, 336
    students learning English as a second language, 223
    work abroad programs, 318, 324–325
    workforce need for, 13
Language studies departments, 75, 76, 101
Lapovsky, Lucie, 400
Larsen, David, 262
Latin America, 369. See also under individual countries
Latinos/Latinas, 208, 221–225
Lauber, Daniel, 335
Laubscher, Michael R., 194
Lauman, Brad, 107
Law, S. A., 319
Laws. See Legal issues
League of United Latin American Citizens, 121
Learning Across Cultures (Althen), 301
Learning disabilities, 230–231
Lebold, Carol J., 207
Lee, B. A., 483, 485, 513
    alcohol usage, 521
    Americans with Disabilities Act, 523
    duty in tort law, 517, 518
    Family Educational Rights and Privacy Act (FERPA), 526
    litigation frequency, 522
    in loco parentis concept, 519
    personal liability of administrators, 528
    standard of care, 520
    tort law, 516, 517
Lee, Elizabeth, 107
Leemon, Drew, 482, 483, 484
Legal issues, 402–404, 511–533
    audits, 530–532
    community colleges, 163
    contract law, 513–516
    emergencies, 532–533
    federal laws and regulations, 522–527
    financial aid transferable to study abroad, 398
    host country laws, 285
    international education as adviser on, 29
    liability issues, 527–530 (See also Liability issues)
    professional program directors, 542
    program status, 543–544
    short-term programs, 379
    technology, 149–150
    tort law, 516–522
    torts of negligence, 517–521
Leonard, Lynn, 248
Lesley University, 26
Liability issues, 46–47
    expectations for faculty, 91
    personal liability for administrators, 527–530
    short-term programs, 378–379
    waivers, 281
Libel, 529–530
Liberal arts institutions, 9, 10
Lifestyle adjustments, 307
Lincoln, Abraham, 231
Lindeman, Barbara, 479
Litigation, 512. See also Legal issues
Living arrangements, 257. See also Housing for students
The Lizzie McGuire Movie (film), 223
Loans, student, 109, 113
Local communities, 559

Local government officials, 548–549
Locations
    assessment of program providers, 463
    community college choices of, 165–166
    disabled students selecting, 234–235
    diversity of choices, 52
    interactions with, 415–416
    internships, 327
    as risk factor in program, 486–487
    selection of, 393–396
    teaching English, 333
    volunteer programs, 331
    work abroad programs, 320, 323
Longitudinal research, 476–478
Low-cost programs for studying abroad, 115–117
Loyola Marymount University, Los Angeles, CA, 58, 262, 479
Lustig, Myron, 196

M

Macalester College, 298
Magistrale, Tony, 298
Mailing lists, 438–439
Majors (Academic programs). *See* Academic majors
Majors underrepresented in study abroad programs, 209, 217–218
Maki, Peggy L., 446, 450
Malaria, 269
Mapping Internationalization on U. S. Campuses (American Council on Education), 243
Marcum, John A., 157
Maricopa Community College District (MCCD), AZ, 156, 158, 160
    administration of, 162
    locations for programs, 165
    non-traditional academic-based programs, 164
    predeparture program, 163
Marketing, 417–444
    budgeting, 435–436
    dissemination of materials for, 438–443
    electronically, 421–423
    media, campus, 426–428
    media, community, 429–430
    off-campus promotion, 433–443
    on-campus promotion, 417–418
    plans, 434–435
    print materials for, 436–438
    program providers and, 430–433
    short-term programs, 387
    specific programs, 425–426
    students and, 423–424
    tools for, 418–421
    underrepresented students in education abroad programs, 214–216
Martin, Judith, 194, 203
Martin, Patricia C., 171, 278
Martin, Randall, 25
Marx, Linda E., 293
Massachusetts
Massachusetts Institute of Technology (MIT), 124
Middlesex Community College, 158, 162
    reentry program, 309
University of Massachusetts, 213
Matching gifts, 123
Matherly, Cheryl, 313, 330
Mattai, P. Rudy, 221
Mattering, Schlossberg's theory of, 175–176
Maximizing Study Abroad: A Program Professional's Guide to Strategies for Language and Culture Learning and Use (Paige, et al), 196, 205
    intercultural learning ideas, 569
    language proficiency, 301
McCabe, Les, 479
McLeod, Lorna, 234
Media
    community, 429–430
    images of students in, 223
    inquiries by in emergencies, 502, 503
    marketing in on-campus, 426–428

Index

Mediation, 516
Medical concerns, 270–275, 579. *See also* Health
Medical examinations, 265. *See also* Health
Mello, Natalie, 479
Memorandum of understanding (MOU), 352, 354, 403
Mental health, 231–232, 272–274. *See also* Emotional issues
Mentors, 222–223
Merkx, Gilbert, 9
Merrill, Kurt, 484
Mestenhauser, Josef A., 241, 242
Mexico, 37
Meyer, Rosa Marina de Brito, 239
Michigan, 523–524
   Kalamazoo College, 298, 310
   University of Michigan, 326, 334
   Michigan State University (MSU), 12
      funding of study abroad program, 123, 124
      minority students, 221
      travel experience of students, 223
Mid-Career Education Abroad Professionals (NAFSA), 33
Middlesex Community College, MA, 158, 162
Migniuolo, Will, 540
"Millenial" generation, 207
Miller, Mona, 129
Minnesota, 56, 58. *See also* University of Minnesota
Minority International Research Training Grant, 121
Mirsky, Kelly P., 298
Mission statements, 346, 430–431
Mobility International USA (MIUSA), 229, 234, 236, 270
Monahan, Michael D., 239
Monitors for emergencies, 501, 502
Montana State University, 298
Montrose, Lynne, 315
Morill Law (1862), 151
Motivations for new programs, 390–391
Motor vehicle accidents, 255, 288, 488
Moving Violations (Hockenberry), 227
Multiplicity, 176, 177–178
Murray, Christina S., 173
Murray, Tina, 373

N

NACADA. *See* National Academic Advising Association (NACADA)
Nacht, Michael, 347
NACUBO (National Association of College and University Business Offices), 400
NAFSA: Association of International Educators, 9
   Code of Ethics, 30–33 (*See also* Code of Ethics (NAFSA))
   college polices on studying abroad, 242
   Committee on Underrepresentation in Education Abroad, 209
   Cooperative Grant Program, 259
   Country/Culture workshops, 32
   Crisis Management in a Cross-Cultural Setting (Burak and Hoffa), 429, 499
   Education Abroad Knowledge Community (NAFSA), 26, 34 (*See also* Education Abroad Knowledge Community (NAFSA))
   Intercultural Activity Toolkit, 295
   Internationalizing the Campus, 239
   Mid-Career Education Abroad Professionals, 33
   national policy on international education, 12
   professional development programs, 31–34, 191
   Rainbow special interest group, 226
   Section on U. S. Students Abroad (SECUSSA), 26 (*See also* Section on U. S. Students Abroad (SECUSSA))
   Securing America's Future: Global Education for a Global Age, 13, 41, 77
   Strategic Task Force on Education Abroad, 41, 207, 240
   student questionnaire templates, 469
   Whole World Committee, 240, 245
   on whole-world study, 259
Nakayama, Thomas, 203
NASPA (National Association of Student Personnel Administrators), 190, 480, 521
National Academic Advising Association (NACADA), 174, 190, 191
National Association of College and University Attorneys, 495

National Association of College and University Business Offices (NACUBO), 400
National Association of Colleges and Employers, 319
National Association of Student Personnel Administrators (NASPA), 190, 480, 521
National Center for Education Statistics (NCES), 208, 523
National Clearinghouse on Disability and Exchange (NCDE), 229
   disability organizations database, 235
   information sheets on accommodations, 234
   Peer-to-Peer Network, 233
   resources for advisers, 232
National policy, 11–14
National Security Education Program (NSEP), 13, 120
National Society for Experiential Education (NSEE), 315
Natural phenomena, 276
NCDE. *See* National Clearinghouse on Disability and Exchange (NCDE)
NCDE (Peer-to-Peer Network), 233
NCES (National Center for Education Statistics), 208, 523
Negligence, 517–521
Nero v. Kansas State University, 519
The Netherlands Organization for International Cooperation in Higher Education (NUFFIC), 39
Networking
   faculty, 443
   as part of marketing plan, 436, 440–441 (*See also* Marketing)
   underrepresented students in education abroad programs, 214–216
Newspapers, campus, 426–427
New student orientation for campus, 419
New York
   State University of New York (SUNY), 56, 58, 154
   University of Rochester, 298
Nolting, William, 330
   contributor to "Work Abroad and International Careers," 313
   work abroad programs, students in, 19, 314
Nomenclature for education abroad, 347, 428
Non-credit activities, 20
Nondegree students, 384
Nongovernmental organizations (NGOs), 327, 330, 486
Nonsectarian volunteer organizations, 332
Nontraditional locations, 16, 240–243. *See also* Whole-world study
Nontraditional students, 208, 209, 218–219
Nonverbal communication, 205
Norm establishment, 576–577. *See also* Behaviors
North America, 15. *See also* Canada; Mexico
North Carolina, 152
Northern Ireland, 124
Norway, 136
NSEP. *See* National Security Education Program (NSEP)
NUFFIC (The Netherlands Organization for International Cooperation in Higher Education), 39
Nutrition, 271–272

O

Oberstein-Deballe, Elizabeth, 156
Office space, 408–409
Off-the-shelf systems, 145
Ohio State University, 298
Ohiwerei, Godwin, 221
Olsen, Mary-Kate and Ashley, 223
O'Neal, John C., 85, 87, 540
Online discussion lists
   announcements of programs, 440
   SECUSS-L, 115 (*See also* SECUSS-L (online discussion list))
Online resources. *See* Web sites/resources
On-site issues, 573–585
   administration, 85–91
   directors, 404 (*See also* Program directors)
   disciplinary measures, 576–578
   emergency planning, 582–585 (*See also* Emergencies)
   geo-political issues, 580–582
   intercultural adjustment support, 574–575
   medical/psychiatric issues, 578–580 (*See also* Emotional issues; Health)
   orientations, 89–90, 558 (*See also* Orientation)

Index

overseas program cycles, 553–571 (*See also* Overseas program cycles)
    staff as advisers and emergency responders, 573–574 (*See also* Staff)
Open Doors survey (Institute of International Education), 49–51, 53–55
    business and management majors in education abroad programs, 217
    community colleges in, 157
    diversity of students, 166
    duration of study abroad programs, 208
    enrollment in education abroad programs, 374
    foreign students in U. S. work study programs, 315
    institutions submitting data for, 146
    short-term programs, 373
    work abroad programs, 314
Operation Crossroads Africa, 314
Optimizing Health Care in International Educational Exchange (Rogers and Larsen), 262
Organizations supporting education abroad, 26, 31–40. *See also under individual organizations*
    direct enrollment, 472
    review processes for programs, 412
Orientation, 293–305, 410
    academic course on, 298
    academic information covered by, 300–301
    advising process, as part of, 185
    at community colleges, 163
    cross-cultural information covered by, 301–305
    evening session, example of, 296
    faculty role in, 80
    full-day session, example of, 296–297
    goals/objectives, 293–294
    health issues covered in, 265–266
    housing discussed in, 562
    intercultural learning fostered at, 202–205
    nontraditional locations, 253–258
    as ongoing process, 560–561
    on-site, 89–90
    overseas program cycles, as part of, 554–555, 558–561
    practical concerns covered, 299–300
    procedures for arrival at host country, 288
    program design, 294–295
    program providers, assessment of, 462–463
    reentry discussed at, 307–308
    risk management covered in, 493–494
    safety issues conveyed at, 280–281
    short-term programs, 377–378
    technology's role in host nation included in, 136
    web-based, 298–299
    work abroad programs, 325
OSAC (Overseas Security Advisory Council), 487
OSEAS (Overseas Educational Advisers), 472
Outcomes assessment, 46. *See also* Assessment
    The Forum on Education Abroad roundtable discussions on, 59
    technology and global competence, 137–138
Overseas administration, 85–91. *See also* On-site issues
Overseas Educational Advisers (OSEAS), 472
Overseas program cycles, 553–571
    academic advising, 563–565
    adjustment/accommodation, 556
    follow-up activities, 557–558
    housing, 561–563 (*See also* Housing for students)
    intercultural learning as part of, 568–570
    orientation, 554–555, 558–561 (*See also* Orientation)
    preparation/planning, 553–554
    program enrichment activities, 565–568
    reentry issues, 557, 570–571
    routines, 556–557
Overseas Security Advisory Council (OSAC), 487

P

Pace of life, 257, 307
Pacific University, 196
Paige, R. Michael, 569. *See also* M*aximizing Study Abroad: A Program Professional's Guide to Strategies for Language and Culture Learning and Use* (Paige, et al)
Parents, 249–250. *See also* Families of students
Partnership consortia, 361–364

Partners of faculty, 89
Pass/Fail credits, 105
Pathways to the Profession (SECUSSA), 211
Peace Corps, 20, 287
    English as a second language (ESL) programs, 333
    experiential learning activities, 295
    former participants assisting with orientation, 294
    online orientation/reentry information, 298
    Operation Crossroads Africa inspiring, 314
    stipend for, 323, 330–331
Pearson, Richard, 277
Pedagogy, 295
Pederson, Paul, 210
Pederson, Paul B., 212
Peer advising, 186
Peer groups, 222
Peer-to-Peer Network (NCDE), 233
Pennsylvania
    Bradshaw v. Rawlings (1979), 521
    Community College of Philadelphia (CCP), 156, 165, 168
    reentry program, 309
    University of Pennsylvania, 291
Perceptions of risk, 480–481
Perkins loans, 113
Permits, work, 323
Perry, William; nine-stage theory of cognitive development, 176–179, 180
Personal digital assistants (PDAs), 496
Peterson's Guides, 117, 182, 434, 459
Phi Beta Delta, 36
Photographs, 428, 429
Pickert, Sarah, 239
Piggybacking marketing plans, 424
Ping, Charles, 17
Placement programs for working abroad, 329–330
PLUS loans, 113
Policies
    advisers' knowledge of, 182–183
    in college catalogs, 419
    communications during emergencies, 286–287
    as part of campus administration of programs, 65–66
    program providers and, 431–432
    risk management, 484
    short-term programs, 383–384
    study centers, 348
Political instability, 254, 256
    canceling/suspending programs, 507
    location selection impacted by, 396
    on-site concerns about, 582
    security concerns, 289–292
Posters, 419–420, 438
Postgraduate opportunities, 312, 319
The Practical Penn Abroad (University of Pennsylvania), 291
A Practice of Yes! Working with Overseas Partners to Include Students with Disabilities (McLeod and Scheibe), 234–235
Practicums, 97
Preconceptions of cultures, 136. *See also* Culture/Cultural
Predeparture orientation, 89, 163, 293–305. *See also* Orientation
Preexisting medical conditions, 270. *See also* Disabilities, students with
Prejsnar, David, 168
Prescription drugs, 266
Press releases, 425, 428
Priest, Simon, 482
The Princeton Review, 434
Princeton University, 124
Principles for International Educational Exchange, 29
Print materials for marketing, 418–419, 436–438, 514
Privacy protection, 149, 265, 495. See also Family Educational Rights and Privacy Act (FERPA)
Private sector, financial aid from, 121–122, 123–124. *See also* Financial aid to students
Production environments (computer systems), 146
Professional development, 25–44
    abroad, 40–41
    advisers, 189–191

associations, 315
ethics, 29–30
NAFSA programs for, 31–34, 41
organizational resources for, 34–40
professional program directors, 543
publishing opportunities, 41–42
research roles, 58–59
roles of international educators, 27–29
skills, building, 42–43
technology training, 150
Professional Practice Workshops (NAFSA), 31–32
Professional program directors, 542–543. See also Program directors
Program design, 345–371
    consortially organized programs, 361–365
    faculty involved in, 80–83 (See also Faculty)
    hybrid model, 252, 351–356
    independent study, 357–361
    integrated model, 351–356
    mission of institution/education abroad office, 345–346
    nomenclature/typology, 347
    predeparture, 294–295
    program provider models, 365–368 (See also Program providers)
    reciprocal programs, 368–371
    study center model, 347–351
Program directors, 404–405, 539–552
    academic credit determined by, 95–96
    advising responsibilities, 563–565
    faculty as, 86–88
    faculty working with, 550
    handbooks for, 82–83
    host families, 552
    host institutions, working with, 549–550
    host nationals, working with, 547–548
    input into assessment, 455–456, 457 (See also Assessment)
    legalization and liability of program, 543–544
    local government officials, working with, 548–549
    local students, 551–552
    sponsoring institutions, working with, 544–546
    staff, working with, 546–547
    types of, 541–543
Program providers, 457–470
    academic credit, 99
    academic criteria of assessment, 463–465
    administrative/financial aspects, 468
    community colleges, 158, 161
    criteria for selection and evaluation, 458–459
    identifying options, 459–460
    learning outside of classroom, opportunities for, 465–466
    location, 463
    models for program design, 365–368, 379–380 (See also Program design)
    predeparture and admissions, 462–463 (See also Admissions)
    publicity and promotions, 430–433
    referrals, 470
    site visits, 470
    student life, 466–468
Programs, 389–416
    academic credit, 405, 408 (See also Academic credit)
    adding to curriculum, approval for, 458
    admissions procedures, 409–410 (See also Admissions)
    assessment of, 411–413 (See also Assessment)
    canceling/suspending, 506–508
    course work, 407–408 (See also Curriculum)
    cycles for, 553–571 (See also Overseas program cycles)
    database of information, 140
    design of, 345–371 (See also Program design)
    directors, choosing, 404–405 (See also Program directors)
    duration of, 51–52, 54 (See also Duration of programs)
    external, 46 (See also Program providers)
    financial issues, 396–402, 410 (See also Funding/Fundraising)
    health care responsibilities, 267 (See also Health)
    host institutions, relations/agreements with, 409, 413–414 (See also Host institutions)
    housing, 406–407 (See also Housing for students)
    ideas for new, 391–392

    legal issues, 402–404 (See also Legal issues)
    locations, selecting, 393–396 (See also Locations)
    new, implementation of, 389–396
    office/classroom space, 408–409
    Open Door survey, information in, 50 (See also Open Doors survey (Institute of International Education))
    orientation, 410 (See also Orientation)
    publicity for specific, 425–426 (See also Marketing)
    resource assessment, 392–393
    risk factors in, 487–488 (See also Risk management)
    selecting, 181–184
Promotion of education abroad programs, 417–418. See also Marketing
Proximate cause, 520
Psychological issues, 231–232, 272–274. See also Emotional issues
Publicity for education abroad programs, 417–418. See also Marketing
Publishing for professional development, 41–42

Q

Quality of education abroad programs, 448–451. See also Assessment
Questionnaires, students answering, 452–454. See also Surveys

R

Raby, Rosalind Latiner, 151
Race/ethnicity, 209, 220–225
    community college participation in education abroad, 153, 166
    immigration and, 208
    Minority International Research Training Grant, 121
    profile of study abroad students, 51
Racism, 223
Raducha, Joan A., 239
RAND Corporation, 319
Readings in Cultural Contexts (Martin, Nakayama, and Flores), 203
Real-time mainframe data, 146
Reciprocal exchanges, 251–252, 368. See also Exchange programs
Records, student, 526–527
Recreation, 289
Recruitment for education abroad programs, 79
Reentry programs, 305–312
    academic course for, 310
    advising process, as part of, 185–186, 310–311
    at community colleges, 164
    faculty role in, 80
    health issues covered by, 274
    nontraditional destinations, 258–259
    opportunities for incorporating study abroad experiences, 311–312
    overseas program cycles, as part of, 570–571
    preparation for, 307–308
    short-term programs, 377–378
    as social events, 308–309
    work abroad programs, 325
    workshops, 309–310
Registrars, 95, 100, 380
Relativism/Relativity, 176–177, 178–179
Religion, 209, 223, 237–238
Religious organizations, volunteer programs, 330, 331, 332
Repatriation insurance, 282–283
Repetition in marketing, 417
Republic of Ireland, 124
Republic of South Africa, 523
Research
    data collection, 45–60 (See also Data collection/management)
    faculty collaboration for education abroad, 83
    long-term impact of education abroad, 475–477
    work abroad programs, 315–317, 319
A Research Agenda for the Internationalization of Higher Education in the the United States (Burn and Smuckler), 239
Research on U. S. Students Abroad: A Bibliography with Abstracts (Weaver), 58
Research on U. S. Students Abroad: A Bibliography with Abstracts, volume II (Chao), 58
Resident directors (RD), 95–96. See also Program directors
Resistance to learning, 197–198
Resources for programs, 392–393
Responsibilities, legal issues, 514–515. See also Legal issues

Index

Responsible Study Abroad: Good Practices for Health and Safety, 278, 480. *See also* Risk management; Safety of students
    emergency response plans, 498
    insurance recommendation, 349
    responsibilities of participants, 492
    risk assessment recommendations, 447
    safety policies and procedures, 489
    standard of care for legal questions, 521–522
    training for staff, 485
Resumes, international experience on, 337
Revenues. *See* Funding/Fundraising
Reviews of programs. *See* Assessment
Rhodes, Gary, 511
    contributor to "Legal Issues and Education Abroad," 511
    legal audits, example of, 530
    risk assessment audits, 519, 530
Rhoten, Diana, 241
Rice, Kraig, 335
Ricks, Tom, 75
Rifat, Tomadar, 550, 581
The Rights and Responsibilities of the Modern University (Bickel and Lake), 517
Riley, Richard W., 41
Rinehart, Nana, 345
RISK! A Practical Guide for Deciding What's Really Safe and What's Dangerous in the World Around You (Ropeik and Gray), 480
Risk management, 479–509, 583–584. *See also* Safety of students
    assessment of, 489–490
    auditing program for, 519, 531–532
    behavioral standards discussed with students, 79
    campus administration of education abroad programs, 73–74
    campus security, 497
    communication, 495–496
    emergency preparedness, 497–508 (*See also* Emergencies)
    expectations of students, 494–495
    hazard potential, analyzing, 481–483
    health insurance coverage, 492–493
    incident reports, collecting and tracking, 483–484
    liability of institutions, 379, 380–381 (*See also* Liability issues)
    orientations covering, 493–494
    participation agreements, 491–492
    policies/procedures, 484
    program providers and, 431
    resources for information on, 508–509
    risk, defining, 480–481
    screening applicants for program, 490–491
    waivers, 514
Road accidents, 255, 288, 488
Roberts, Tom, 389
Robinson, Roy, 75
"The Rock" (Eliot), 129
Rockland Community College (SUNY), 154
Rogers, John, 262
Ropeik, David, 480, 511
Rotary Foundation, 251
Rotary International Ambassadorial Scholarship, 122
Round Rock, Texas, 98
Rural locations, 415, 416

S

Safety Abroad First—Educational Travel Information (SAFETI) web site, 216, 262, 287
    courses by Bruce La Brack on web site, 298, 310
    electronic resources on health and safety issues, 479
    legal audits, example of, 530
    work abroad, research on, 315
Safety and Study Abroad (Darrah), 493
Safety of students, 278–292, 488–497. *See also* Risk management
    behavior, 286
    car accidents, 255, 288, 488
    community colleges, 163
    compliance with rules/laws/customs, 284–285
    disclosure in application process, 281–282
    information and research on, 281
    insurance coverage, 282–284
    location selection impacted by, 396
    natural phenomena, 276
    orientations covering, 299–300, 559
    principles for, 287–289
    program directors' responsibilities towards, 87
    responsibilities of students, 278–281
    Safety Abroad First—Educational Travel Information (SAFETI) web site, 216 (*See also* Safety Abroad First—Educational Travel Information (SAFETI) web site)
    security issues, 289–292
    short-term programs, 378
    terrorism, 276–277
Salaries
    for professional program directors, 542
    for work abroad programs, 323–324, 332–333
Sanborn, Robert, 330
San Diego City College, CA, 168
San Diego University, CA, 118
Santa Rosa Junior College, CA, 164
Satisfaction surveys, 448, 452
Sawadogo, Geremie, 151
Sawaïe, Mohammed, 87
Scheibe, Michele, 207, 235
Schlossberg, Nancy, 175–176
Scholarships, 109, 117–122
    Boren scholarships, 120, 251
    disabilities, students with, 236–237
    Fulbright Program, 7–8 (*See also* Fulbright Program)
    Gilman scholarships, 120, 251
"School of record" concept, 98–99
Science/technology majors, 217–218
SCI-IVS (Service Civil International-International Voluntary Service), 332
Section on U. S. Students Abroad - Community College (SECUSSA-CC), 167
Section on U. S. Students Abroad (SECUSSA), 26, 27. *See also* Education Abroad Knowledge Community (NAFSA)
    bibliography of funding sources, 119
    Clery Act, 527
    Committee on Underrepresentation in Education Abroad, 238
    data collection on education abroad, 53, 54–55
    fair calendar, 441–442
    fastWeb, 120
    financial aid information, 115
    in the Inter-Associational Data Collection Committee, 50
    Pathways to the Profession, 211
    research bibliography, 315
Securing America's Future: Global Education for a Global Age (NAFSA), 13, 41, 77
Security issues, 289–292, 480, 497. *See also* Safety of students
SECUSSA. *See* Section on U. S. Students Abroad (SECUSSA)
SECUSS-L (online discussion list), 115, 117, 191
    announcements of programs, 440
    defamation issues, 530
    external programs, assessment of, 470
    health and safety discussions on, 480
    health/safety issues discussed on, 262, 430
    technology and cultural immersion discussion, 132
Segal, Nina, 335
Semester hours, 94. *See also* Academic credit
September 11, 2001, 12, 41
    anti-U.S. sentiment, 551, 580
    internationalization of curriculum intensified by, 239
    survey of students abroad after, 57
Service Civil International-International Voluntary Service (SCI-IVS), 332
Service learning, 316
SEVIS (Student and Exchange Visitor Information System), 369
Sexual harassment, 289, 523–525
Sexually transmitted diseases, 269
Shipboard cruises, 6–7
Short-term programs, 81, 373–387
    administration of, 380–382
    approval process, 382–383
    community colleges, 157–158
    design issues, 376–378
    development, 375

Index

health/safety/security, 378–379
housing for, 406
marketing, 387
policies, 383–384
whole-world study, 252–253 (*See also* Whole-world study)
work abroad, 328–330, 332 (*See also* Work abroad programs)

Short-Term Study Abroad (IIE), 117, 182, 434
    external program providers, 459
Siaya, Laura, 6, 476
Sideli, Kathleen, 45
SIETAR (Society for Intercultural Education Training and Research), 190
The Silent Language (Hall), 302
Simon, Paul, 13, 41, 44
Site selection, 393–396. *See also* Locations
Site visits
    host institutions, relations with, 413–414
    as part of assessment of program, 470, 474
    program directors meeting with home institution staff, 545–546
SIT (School for International Training), 26, 57
    experiential activities through, 295
Surviving Reentry: A Handbook for Parents of Study Abroad Students Returning Home (Cavallero), 306
Skills for professional development, 42–43
Slander, 529
Slawson, Carla, 445
Slind, Mickey, 429, 503
"The SmartStudent? Guide to Financial Aid" (FinAid Website), 119
Smuckler, R. H., 239
Social identity factors, 212–213
Social Science Research Council, 121
Society for Intercultural Education Training and Research (SIETAR), 190
Software, 56, 141–142, 148
Southeastern Community College v. Davis (1997), 523
South Korea, 132, 136
Spain, 221
Spam, 422
Spencer, Sarah E., 373
Spouses of faculty, 89
SSI (Supplemental Security Income), 237
Staff, 141, 499. *See also* Program directors
    as advisers and emergency responders, 573–574
    computer training, 142, 143
    counseling, providing, 577
    emergency response team, 500–502, 584
    hiring locals for, 546–547
    input into assessment, 455–456
    marketing, 443–444
    risk factor in program, 485–486
Stafford loans, 113
Stakes, Robert, 446
Standard Rules for the Equalization of People with Disabilities (United Nations), 227
Standards of Good Practice, 447, 459
Stanford University, 8
State Department. *See* U. S. Department of State
State governments
    financial aid used abroad, 108, 117, 120–121
    Vocational Rehabilitation department, 237
Statement of Professional Competencies fo International Educators (NAFSA), 529
State University of New York (SUNY), 56, 58, 154
Steinberg, Michael, 315–316, 389
Stephenson, Skye, 575
    contributor to "The Overseas Program Cycle and Critical Components," 553
    contributor to "The Program Director and the Program," 539
    host families, 552
Stereotypes, 249
Stewart, Edward C., 304
Stewart, Melissa A., 221
Storti, Craig, 196, 203, 569
Strategic Task Force on Education Abroad (NAFSA), 207
Strauss, William, 130

Stubbs, Nancy, 107
Student affairs office, 64, 65, 472
Student and Exchange Visitor Information System (SEVIS), 369
The Student Guide (Dept. of Education), 110
Student organizations, 215
Students Abroad: Strangers at Home (Kauffmann, Martin and Weaver), 21
Student services, 405
    advising model, 187–189 (*See also* Advising/Advising offices)
    campus administration of education abroad programs, 72–73 (*See also* Administration of education abroad programs)
    disabilities, students with, 234 (*See also* Disabilities, students with)
Student/Students
    behavior (*See* Behaviors)
    characteristics of those who studied abroad in 1988, 14, 51
    at community colleges, 153, 166 (*See also* Community colleges)
    database for records, 138–140
    development theories, 174–180, 187 (*See also* Advising/Advising offices)
    disclosing health concerns, 264–265
    evaluations, 447, 448, 452–454, 473
    evaluations of external programs, 468–469
    expectations of, 494–495
    financial aid to, 106–127 (*See also* Financial aid to students)
    global competence of, 134–135 (*See also* Intercultural learning)
    input in study abroad programs, 391–392
    learning styles, 134–135, 198–200
    local, program directors working with, 551–552, 559
    marketing program, 423–424
    Open Door survey, information in, 50
    personal development, 20–22
    preferences for locations, 394
    program directors and, 87–88
    records, 526–527
    responsibilities for decisions, 285
    as risk factor in program, 484–485
    screening applicants for program, 490–491
    tracking mechanisms for, 47, 55–56
"Study, Work, and Travel Abroad: A Bibliography," 119
Study Abroad: A Parent's Guide (Hoffa), 216, 267
Study Abroad: How to Get the Most Out of Your Experience (Dowell and Mirsky), 298
Study Abroad Advisors Group of New England (SAAG), 56
Studyabroad.com, 117, 303
Study abroad offices, 61–74. *See also* Administration of education abroad programs
Study Abroad (Peterson's Guide), 117, 182
Study and Learning Abroad (conference), 12
Study center model for program design, 347–351
Studying Abroad/Learning Abroad (Hess), 196, 298
Subsidized work, 109
Substance abuse, 270–271, 286
Summerfield, Ellen, 469
Supervision for independent study, 358–359. *See also* Independent study
Supplemental Security Income (SSI), 237
Support services, 405. *See also* Student services
Supreme Court, 523
Survey of Third Party Providers: Final Report, 57
Surveys
    assessment of programs, 411
    high school seniors wanting to study abroad, 476
    international expertise on campus, 392
    longitudinal, 476–478
    for marketing purposes, 434–435
    Open Doors survey (Institute of International Education), 49–51, 53–55
    student evaluations, 447, 448, 452–454, 473
    student evaluations of external programs, 468–469
    of students and faculty for study abroad programs, 391
Survey of Third Party Providers: Final Report, 57
U. S. News and World Report, 54
Survival Kit for Overseas Living (Kohls), 203
Survival Strategies for Going Abroad: A Guide for People with Disabilities, 234
Surviving Reentry: A Handbook for Parents of Study Abroad Students Returning Home (Cavallero), 306
Suspension of programs, 506–508
Sussman, Nan, 305

Index

Sweden, 550, 581
Syracuse University, 57

T

Talburt, Susan, 221
Target audiences, 435
Teaching by students. *See also* Faculty
    English, 314, 332
    work abroad programs, 332–334
Teaching English Abroad: Talk Your Way Around the World (Griffith), 334
The Teaching Professor (Williams), 101
Technology, 10, 129–150
    cultural immersion affected by, 131–134
    curriculum development and, 135–137
    data integrity and security, 142–143
    data management, 138–142
    digital divide, 131
    expectations of students, 130–131
    global competence and, 134–135
    integration within home institution, 144–149
    legal/ethical issues, 149–150
    replacement cycles for, 143
    staff training, 143–144
    web-based orientations, 298–299
Telecommunications, 129–130. *See also* Technology
Tenure, 76
Terminology for education abroad, 347, 428
Terrorism, 507
    advising responsibilities about, 276–277
    security advisories, 290
    U. S. Department of State warnings of, 519
Test environments (computer systems), 145–146
Texas, 152
    Round Rock, 98
    University of Texas at Austin, 56, 118, 121
Thebodo, Stacey Woody, 293
Theft of belongings, 255–256, 288
Theories of student development, 174–180. *See also* Advising/Advising offices
Third-party providers, 99, 158, 161. *See also* Program providers
Thompson, Susan, 25
Ting-Toomey, Stella, 203
Tips for Students (State Department web site), 287
Title IV of Higher Education Act (1965), 108, 111
Title VI of Higher Education Act (1965), 120, 244
Title IX, 522, 523–525
Tort law, 516–522, 528–529
TRACE (Trans Regional Academic Mobility and Credential Assessment Information Network), 472
Trainer Corps (NAFSA), 31, 32, 34
Training for program directors, 405
Transcripts, 99–100
    credit transfer, 408
    from direct enrollment institutions, 471
    study abroad credits in, 104–105
Transfer credits, 100–101
Transitions Abroad (magazine), 41, 311, 327, 330
Transportation, 9, 518–519
Trans Regional Academic Mobility and Credential Assessment Information Network (TRACE), 472
Traveler's Health web site (Centers for Disease Control and Prevention), 262
Tuition. *See also* Cost management of studying abroad
    community college education abroad programs, 161
    discounting, 400
    for exchange programs, 368–369
    at home institution, 115
    for independent study programs, 360
    "in-state" savings on study abroad, 117
    for integrated programs, 354
    for partnership consortia programs, 362–363
    short-term programs, 384–387
    for study abroad students, 125
    for study centers, 349
Tuma, Kathy, 373

Turlington, Barbara, 239
Two-year colleges. *See* Community colleges

U

U. S. News and World Report, 54
Underrepresented constituencies, 207–238
    access to education abroad, 211–212
    advisers/administrators to, 210–211
    aid for, 121
    campus climate, education abroad within, 213–216
    characteristics/trends of students studying abroad, 207–210
    disabilities, students with, 227–237 (*See also* Disabilities, students with)
    gay, lesbian, bisexual, and transgendered students, 225–227 (*See also* Gay, lesbian, bisexual, and transgendered (GLBT) students)
    gender, 219–220
    heritage seeking in education abroad, 225
    majors, 217–218
    nontraditional students, 218–219
    race/ethnicity, 220–225 (*See also* Race/ethnicity)
    religion, 237–238
    social identity models, 212–213
Understanding the Education—and Through It the Culture—in Education Abroad (Chisholm and Berry), 464
United Kingdom of Great Britain and Northern Ireland British Council, 38
    British Universities Transatlantic Student Exchange Association (BUTEX), 26, 37
    grades in, 102
United Nations, 120
    internships, 327
    Standard Rules for the Equalization of People with Disabilities, 227
    Volunteer Program, 332
United States Census Bureau, 208
U. S. Agency for International Development, 120
U. S. Department of Education, 110
    assessment of outcomes in education abroad, 475–476
    audits of institutions with federal aid, 111
    Clery Act (2003), 497, 527
    consortium agreements and financial aid, 434
    Federal Student Aid Office, 115
    Fund for the Improvement of Post-Secondary Education (FIPSE), 479
    security of students abroad, 256
    study centers abroad, 350–351
    Title VI centers, 244
U. S. Department of Homeland Security, 276
U. S. Department of State, 32
    Background Notes, 305
    Consular Information Sheets, 253
    information on host countries, 281
    internships, 327
    local consulates, 403–404
    Open Doors survey funded by, 49
    Overseas Security Advisory Council (OSAC), 487
    Tips for Students web site, 287
    travel information disseminated by, 262
    travel plans registered with, 287
    warnings/advisories from, 507, 519, 582
    Worldwide Cautions, 291
U. S. Office of Education, 155
U. S. Supreme Court, 523
University Mobility in Asia and the Pacific (UMAP), 39
University of Arizona, 517
University of California at Berkeley, 124
University of California at Irvine, 326
University of Delaware, 6, 520
University of Georgia, 56, 118, 121
University of Massachusetts, 213
University of Michigan, 326, 334
University of Minnesota, 56, 58
    Center for Advanced Research on Language Acquisition, 196
    Curriculum Integration Initiative, 218
    Learning Abroad Center, 326
University of Pennsylvania, 291
University of Rochester, NY, 298

Index

University of St. Thomas, 18
University of Texas at Austin, 56, 118, 121
University of the Pacific, 58, 196, 310
University of Virginia, 277
University of Wisconsin at Madison, 298
Uppsala University of Sweden, 550, 581

V

Values, 204
American affecting advising process, 210–211
    identity and, 304
    intercultural learning, 570
Values Majority Culture Americans Live By (Kohls), 211
Van Cleve, Leo, 345, 417
Vande Berg, Michael J., 248
Van Der Meid, Scott, 207, 220
Van de Water, Jack, 17, 455
van Gogh, Vincent, 231
Variety in marketing, 417
Virginia, 277
Visas
    health issues, disclosure on applications for, 265
    securing, 287–288
    work permits, 323
Vocational Rehabilitation department, 237
Volunteer work abroad, 330–332, 566. *See also* Peace Corps
Von Klemperer, Lily, 27

W

Wagner, Kenneth, 298
Waivers/Releases of responsibility, 485, 514
Walgren, Andrea, 417
Walk-in advising, 189
Wallace, JoAnn, 75
War, declaration of, 507
Washington, 298
Water, 266
"W-Curve" model of cultural adjustment, 302
Weaver, Henry, 315
Web sites/resources
    Access Abroad, 234, 235
    advertising program on, 439–440
    American Association for Higher Education (AAHE), 450
    data collection, 54–55
    external programs, 460
    internships, 327
    Kalamazoo College orientation program, 298
    marketing education abroad programs, 422–423, 436
    NAFSA's *Code of Ethics*, 444 (*See also* Code of Ethics (NAFSA))
    NAFSA's Rainbow special interest group, 226
    orientations given through, 298–299
    recordkeeping online, 496
    Research on U. S. Students Abroad: A Bibliography with Abstracts available on Education Abroad Knowledge Community's, 58
    Safety Abroad First—Educational Travel Information (SAFETI) web site, 216, 262, 287 (*See also* Safety Abroad First—Educational Travel Information (SAFETI) web site)
    search engines for study abroad, 460
    Security on Campus, Inc., 497
    "The SmartStudent? Guide to Financial Aid" (FinAid), 119
    student questionnaires on, 453, 454
    Studyabroad.com, 117, 303
    study abroad programs by cost, 117
    Tips for Students (State Department), 287
    Traveler's Health web site (Centers for Disease Control and Prevention), 262
    U. S. Department of State, 262
    Whole World web site from Education Abroad Knowledge Community (NAFSA), 248–249
    work abroad programs, 326
WES (World Education Services), 103
Whalen, Brian, 475
What a Girl Wants (film), 223

What's Up With Culture?, 196
When Every Moment Counts (Frist), 276
Whole World Guide to Culture Learning (Hess), 196, 569
Whole-world study, 239–259. *See also* Intercultural learning
    academic context for, 240–244
    advising responsibilities, 245–246
    institutional strengths and goals, 244–245
    preparation for, 253–258
    program assessment/selection, 247–251
    reentry, 258–259
    types of programs, 251–253
Whole World web site from Education Abroad Knowledge Community (NAFSA), 248–249
Wiedenhoeft, Margaret, 445
Williams, J. H., 101
Wisconsin, 120, 298
Women, 289
Work Abroad: The Complete Guide to Finding a Job Overseas (Hubbs, Griffith, and Nolting), 330
Work abroad programs, 19–20, 109, 313–339
    advising for, 321–325
    benefits, 318–319
    challenges, 320–321
    community colleges, 164–165
    first-generation college students, 219
    history, 313–314
    institutional support, 317–318
    international careers, 334–337
    leveraging for careers, 338–339
    participation data, 314–315
    professional associations/standards, 315
    research, 315–317
    teaching, 332–334
    types of, 326–334
    work-study model from Antioch College, 8
Workflow for data management, 139–140
Work/Working
    English in workplace, 15–16
    globalization of, 12, 17–19
    permits for, 323
    work abroad programs, 313–339 (*See also* Work abroad programs)
Work Your Way Around the World (Griffith), 330
"World at a Glance" series, 420
World Bank, 120
World Education Services (WES), 103
World University, 6–7
World War I, 314
World War II, 7, 314
Worldwide Cautions (State Department), 291
World Wide Web, 422–423. *See also* Web sites/resources
Writing Across Culture: An Introduction to Study Abroad and the Writing Process (Wagner and Magistrale), 298

X

Xavier University, 118

Y

Yarabinec, My, 417
Yellow fever immunizations, 269
Yngve, Katherine, 129
Yoshida, Tomoko, 194, 302
Young, Michael, 17–18

Z

Zukroff, Stacia, 445

NAFSA's Principles for U.S. Study Abroad

One of the most effective ways to increase U.S understanding of other languages and cultures and to improve our ability to function effectively in this interdependent world is to provide individuals with opportunities to study abroad. By living and studying in another country people learn to live with and appreciate different points of view and gain a more global perspective on life's challenges and opportunities.

The institution that endorses the concept of study abroad should provide some form of basic advisory services. Many opportunities exist for American students interested in studying abroad-sponsored programs of their own institution, programs sponsored cooperatively with other institutions, and hundreds of direct opportunities which may or may not have U.S. institutional sponsorship.

ADVISORY SERVICES FOR STUDY ABROAD

These principles apply to the delivery of advisory services as well as to the direct administration of a study abroad program or co-sponsorship of a program with other institutions.

Within the context of its overall international educational objectives, an institution should have a clearly stated policy about its intentions and goals for facilitating study abroad.

Recognizing that programs and advising may be handled by various people on campus, there should be a central point of access to useful information about overseas opportunities. A library of essential study abroad information materials should be maintained.

Faculty and staff members who are responsible for advising should be identified and listed in campus reference literature. These individuals should be given opportunities to develop their abilities to provide sound, knowledgeable, and objective advice about study abroad programs. Important components of advising include the following:

- Clarifying objectives for wanting to go abroad.

NAFSA's Principles for U.S. Study Abroad

- Identifying opportunities that are educationally sound and culturally beneficial.

- Determining the quality, value, and appropriateness of a particular study abroad experience.

- Coordinating evaluation of students' educational background with admissions personnel of foreign institution.

- Understanding the implications of a particular study abroad experience on graduation requirements, transfer credit, and financial aid.

- Returning students should be asked to provide evaluations to enable study abroad advisers to determine the usefulness of the program for those students and possible future participants in that program, and to evaluate the usefulness of the advisory services they received before going abroad.

Co-sponsoring Study Abroad Programs Administered by Other Institutions

In order to encourage study abroad or broaden the options readily available to its students, a number of institutions have elected to join consortia or co-sponsor study abroad programs in which another institution handles program administration. A consortium or co-sponsorship arrangement for study abroad should provide opportunities that are consistent with the institution's overall academic objectives, requirements, and standards; the program should be administered in accordance with the principles for study abroad program administration (see below); and the home campus role in the co-sponsorship should be evaluated periodically by faculty, staff, and students to determine if the objectives are being met.

Administration of Study Abroad Programs

Institutions administer study abroad programs in order to establish direct control over the development and provision of a specific kind of overseas learning experience. Many different kinds of institutions operate programs, including U.S. colleges and universities, foreign universities and companies, and proprietary organizations. The types of programs and amounts of structure and support services vary tremendously. Despite the wide range, all should be administered according to the following principles.

1. The purposes and specific educational objectives of the program should be carefully developed and clearly stated in the program bulletin and promotional materials.

2. Accurate, honest, and complete information should be provided to prospective applicants describing the nature and scope of the program including its opportunities and limitations, how and where instruction

will be given, the relationship if any to a foreign institution, grading practices, significant differences between a home campus experience and what can be expected abroad, information about local attitudes and mores, local living conditions, and the extent of responsibility assumed by the program for housing participants.

3. Applicants should be screened to ensure that participants have the maturity, adequate language proficiency, academic background and achievement, and motivation necessary for success in the type of program and place of study.

4. The program should include an orientation, both predeparture and ongoing, which assists participants in making appropriate personal, social, and academic adjustments. Programs maintaining centers abroad should provide counseling and supervisory services at the foreign center, with special attention to the problems peculiar to the location and nature of the program.

5. The program should encourage extensive and effective use of the unique physical, human, and cultural resources of the host environment, and the academic rigor of the program should be comparable to that at the home campus. There should be clearly defined criteria and policies for judging performance and assigning credit in accordance with prevailing standards and practices at the home institution.

6. Administrative arrangements (such as housing, transportation, and finances) and support services (such as counseling and health services) made both in the U.S. and at the program location abroad should be managed effectively by carefully selected and qualified staff who have both appropriate academic and administrative experience necessary to perform the work.

7. Programs should be evaluated periodically by student participants, program administrators, and a faculty advisory committee to determine the extent to which objectives and purposes are being met. Changes should be made in light of the findings.

Revised by the Committee on Ethical Practice and approved by the NAFSA Board of Directors on May 27, 2001.

Other Titles from NAFSA Publications

The Guide to Successful Short-Term Programs Abroad
Sarah E. Spencer and Kathy Tuma, Editors

Designed as a practical guide for practitioners who direct and administer short-term programs, the book was edited by two experts with considerable experience in the field, Sarah Spencer, from the University of St. Thomas, and Kathy Tuma, from St. Olaf College. Readers can use the tools provided in the book to build successful short-term programs tailored to their own institutions. 2003.

(#990) $39 members; $52 nonmembers

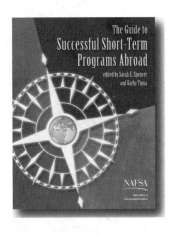

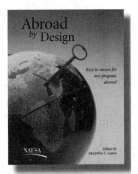

Abroad by Design
Maryélise Lamet

Discover the nuts and bolts of the study abroad program through a collection of model programs, sample budgets, health and safety guidelines, and institutional best practices representing colleges, universities, and organizations worldwide. This hefty book of study abroad program materials is compiled for use with the administration of education abroad workshops. 2000. 250 pp.

(#2052) $27 members; $36 nonmembers

Back in the USA
Dawn Kepets

Back in the USA is ideal for pre-return workshops for students overseas on year-long programs, or individually, before or after returning home. A trainer's guide enables study abroad directors to run lively reentry workshops using the manual. Checklists and case studies in the text involve students and spark discussion. 1999 revision of popular 1995 title. 34 pp.

(#1830) $12 members; $16 nonmembers
(#1830A) Bundle of 25: $79;
$106 nonmembers (includes trainer's guide

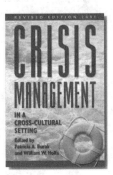

Crisis Management in a Cross-Cultural Setting
Patricia A. Burak and William W. Hoffa, Editors

An essential sourcebook, designed to prepare international educators and others to respond appropriately, expeditiously, and comprehensively to crises that befall students and scholars living and learning a long way from where they call "home." Its thesis is simple: advance planning and cross-cultural sensitivity can make all the difference. 2001. 391 pp.

(#391) $57 members; $76 nonmembers

Basic Facts on Study Abroad

This handsome brochure answers the most common student questions about study abroad concisely and authoritatively. The colorful cover will draw students' attention; the elegant text will keep them interested. A real labor-saver for the study abroad office and a great tool for promoting study abroad on campus. Revised by Dawn L. White of Portland State University. Published jointly by NAFSA, CIEE, and IIE. 2000. 28 pp.

(#300) Bundles of 50: $27 members;
$36 nonmembers

To order these or any other NAFSA publication, please call:

NAFSA Publications Center
1.866.538.1927
Or call: 1.240.646.7036